LEON TROTSKY

by the same author

The Tokolosh
Political Africa
African Profiles
Into Exile
The Crisis of India
(in USA *The Anguish of India*)
The Race War
America's Receding Future
(in USA *The Americans*)
The Struggle against History
Whose Jerusalem?
The Decline and Fall of the American Dollar

edited
Sanctions against South Africa
South West Africa: Travesty of Trust
(with Ruth First)

LEON TROTSKY

A Biography

Ronald Segal

Pantheon Books
New York

Copyright © 1979 by Ronald Segal
Maps Copyright © 1979 by Hutchinson & Co. (Publishers) Ltd.

All rights reserved under International and Pan-American Copyright Conventions. Published in the United States by Pantheon Books, a division of Random House, Inc., New York, and simultaneously in Canada by Random House of Canada Limited, Toronto. Originally published in Great Britain as *The Tragedy of Leon Trotsky* by Hutchinson & Co. (Publishers) Ltd.

Library of Congress Cataloging in Publication Data

Segal, Ronald, 1932–
  Leon Trotsky.

    1. Trotskiï, Lev, 1879–1940. 2. Statesmen — Russia — Biography. 3. Russia — Politics and govern- ment — 20th century.
DK254.T6S39   947.084′092′4 [B]   79-1901
ISBN 0-394-50704-5

Manufactured in the United States of America

FIRST AMERICAN EDITION

Contents

Illustrations

Plates

Trotsky addresses the troops from the top of an armoured train *c*. 1919
Members of the Left Opposition, 1928: Serebriakov, Radek, Trotsky, Bogslavsky, Preobrazhensky, Rakovsky, Drobus, Beloborodov, Seznovsky
Trotsky's study at Prinkipo
The Soviet paper *Krokodil* accuses Trotsky of conspiring with the Nazis to overthrow the USSR, August 1936
Zina Volkov, Prinkipo, 1931
Leon Sedov, early 1930s
Natalia and Trotsky on arrival in Mexico, 1937
Trotsky feeding his rabbits, Mexico
Sylvia Agelof after Trotsky's assassination
Mercador with police after the assassination

Maps and charts

I

Beginnings

From the reign of Ivan the Terrible in the sixteenth century, various rulers asserted the holiness of Russia by depriving Jews of any share in it. Ivan himself, acquiring Jewish subjects with his capture of Pskov, offered them a choice between adopting Christianity and being drowned in the river. Less zealous successors permitted Jews to survive and even to trade, as temporary residents. This was too much for the piety of the Tsarina Elizabeth Petrovna. In 1742, she decreed the expulsion of all Jews from her domains. She was not to be moved by representations from some of her nobles that the economy would suffer. 'From the enemies of Christ,' she declared, 'I desire no profits.' Catherine II, who was rather more enlightened and even engaged in a lively correspondence with Voltaire, proposed to permit Jewish settlement. But the opposition that she encountered discouraged her. Her manifesto of 1762 opened Russia to all foreigners 'except the Jews'.

While Jews succeeded none the less, one way or another, in slipping past the prohibition on their settlement, they did so only in insignificant numbers. It was the spread of the Russian empire that provided the Tsars with their prominent Jewish problem. Jews were permitted to remain in the territories conquered from Turkey in 1768. And multitudes of Jews were acquired with the successive annexations, from 1772 to 1815, that extended Russian rule across Lithuania and Poland, to the borders of Prussia, Austro-Hungary and Romania.

This did not mean that they acquired in turn the right to travel or reside wherever they pleased in the empire. Except for the relatively few who made their way into privileged categories, Jews were confined to what became known as the Pale of Settlement: an area of some one million square kilometres in the west, between the Black and the Baltic seas. Here, according to the census of 1897, lived around 94 per cent of the empire's total Jewish population. And here, in consequence of contemporary decrees as well as of the history that had been allowed them, they were

9

Russia before 1914

Legend:
- Russian border 1905
- Russian Siberian border
- Russian occupations
- Russia 1841
- Russian acquisitions up to 1855
- Russian acquisitions up to 1905
- Areas of most frequent Antisemitic pogroms

ARCTIC OCEAN

JAPAN
YELLOW SEA
KOREA
CHINA
Peking
Pt. Arthur
Vladivostock
Coastal Province
Amur Province 1858
1860
Manchuria 1900-1905
Chita
OUTER MONGOLIA
Tannu Tuva
Sinkiang
TIBET
INDIA
Ili Area
1895
Pamir
1876
Tashkent
Turkestan 1864
1868
1854
1873
Turkmenia 1884
AFGHANISTAN
PERSIA
Arabia

EAST SIBERIA
WEST SIBERIA
Trans-Siberian-Railway 1891-1904
RUSSIA
Simbirsk
Moscow
Samara
St Petersbg
Kronstadt
FINLAND
THE BALTIC
Minsk
Kishinev
Odessa
Vienna
AUSTRIA HUNGARY
GERMAN EMPIRE
Constantinople
OTTOMAN EMPIRE
Batum
1859

disproportionately represented in towns and occupied in crafts and in commerce.[1]*

Competition was correspondingly intense, and many Jews were driven to find what livelihood they could in wage-labour. It is scarcely surprising, therefore, that the gigantic ghetto of the Pale should have provided a marked Jewish receptiveness to Marxist ideas: the Bund (or General Jewish Workers' Union in Lithuania, Poland and Russia) was founded at Vilna in October 1897, some months before the Russian Social Democratic Labour Party. And, indeed, of the nine delegates who founded this wider party in March 1898, three represented the Bund.

But economic pressures constituted only one of the factors that promoted disaffection. Among the various discriminations to which the Jews of the empire were subject, two were especially resented. By a policy officially inaugurated in 1886, the proportion of Jewish students at any high school was limited to 10 per cent within the Pale, and 3 to 5 per cent in the rest of Russia. And, adding insult to injury, Tsarism exacted from Jews a disproportionate contribution to the defence of the regime that oppressed them. They were required to provide ten military recruits, instead of the seven required from Gentiles, for every thousand of their number.

Above all, Jews lived under the ever-present threat of pogroms. Mobs, often led by priests, would attack Jewish districts, pillaging homes before setting them aflame, raping and killing, while uniformed police took care to be beyond call or stood watching with indifference or delight. No place was safe. Odessa, a city with theatres and libraries, and even a stock exchange, was regarded by Jews in the Pale as the very Paris of southern Russia. Yet Jews had been massacred there in 1820, 1859 and 1871, and might at any time be massacred again. Throughout the Pale, pogroms were becoming ever more frequent, as the authorities sought to discourage discontent or to deflect it from themselves.

Count Vyacheslav Plehve, the Minister of the Interior, lectured a Jewish delegation from Odessa in 1903:

In Western Russia some 90 per cent of the revolutionaries are Jews, and in Russia generally – some 40 per cent. I shall not conceal from you that the revolutionary movement in Russia worries us . . . but you should know that if you do not deter your youth from the revolutionary movement, we shall make your position untenable to such an extent that you will have to leave Russia, to the very last man!

To a second delegation, he was more specific. 'Compel your men to stop the revolution, and then I shall stop the pogroms.'[2]

Whatever the actual proportion of Jews among revolutionaries in

*Notes and references follow the text, beginning on page 407.

Russia, it was certainly much larger than the proportion of Jews among Russians in general. But if being Jewish helped in reaching a revolutionary commitment, it was scarcely a prerequisite. The officially promoted persecution of Jews was simply one feature of a regime which seemed bent on behaving as though the whole Age of Reason had been a protracted moral plague. Successive Tsars considered it no less than their divine calling to protect their subjects against the infection of liberal ideas.

After an initial indulgence in cautious reform, Alexander I's reign (1801–25) closed in heresy-hunting at the universities and conspiracies among younger officers in the army. Nicholas I began his reign (1825–55) by hanging five such officers and, after a few years of toying with reform, set out to crush all intellectual dissent. The press was rigorously controlled. Many writers – among them, Dostoevsky – were arrested and exiled. The universities were purged and required to 'base all teaching on religious truth'.

Nor did Nicholas I see himself as the scourge of disaffection and disorder only within his own domains. In 1848 he sent his armies to subdue Hungarian rebellion against Habsburg rule. 'Submit yourselves, you peoples, for God is with us', proclaimed his manifesto of March in that revolutionary year. But his line to Providence was to prove faulty. In 1853 his assumption of a protectorate over all Christians in the Ottoman empire involved him in war with Britain, France and even 'thankless' Austria, as well as Turkey. The defeats suffered by Russia revealed all the weaknesses of a retarded society. Within two years, the Tsar was dead: of a broken heart, it was said by those who had been close to him.

Alexander II began his reign (1855–81) by attempting to learn the lessons of the Crimean war. Addressing the Moscow gentry, he indicated the motive of his main initiative. 'The present position cannot last, and it is better to abolish serfdom from above than to wait till it begins to be abolished from below.' In 1861 the serfs were freed and offered an opportunity to acquire land of their own. *Zemstvos*, or county councils, were introduced. There were reforms of the law courts and of the army. The press was permitted greater freedom of comment. But what had looked like the dawn was soon seen to be only the dusk, of a day that began and ended in the mind of the Tsar.

Indeed, the twenty million freed serfs were offered even less land than they had been working before and had come to regard as effectively their own. And the lands were not given to them but merely made available for purchase, at official assessments that much inflated their market value. In place of serfdom, there would now be a 'temporarily bonded' service, till the debt incurred by the purchase of allotments was redeemed.

Even had the reform been rather more generous than it was, it would hardly have reached as high as the hopes that had been raised among the peasants. The ensuing disappointment erupted into widespread rural disturbances. In Poland administrative reforms in response to gathering nationalist unrest did not prevent a popular rising. The regime, bewildered and alarmed, returned to the old certainties of repression.

In 1861 Alexander Herzen, the revolutionary publicist who was now living in London and whose writings, smuggled into Russia, so influenced the disaffected young, had exhorted the protesting students of St Petersburg: 'Go to the people!' During the years that followed, the vision of a victorious revolutionary populism took hold. There, among the peasant masses of Russia, lay the sleeping power which, once awakened, must topple the regime. There, in the villages, was the long experience of communal institutions from which socialism might grow.

In the spring of 1874, several hundred young Russians, many of them recently returned by government summons from study abroad, took themselves among the people, to teach and to learn. Their peasant dress did not allay peasant distrust. They were easily tracked down by the police, for arrest and imprisonment. This was plainly not the way. Two years later, a secret society was founded, with the name of Zemlya i Volya (Land and Liberty). But this resort to a closely disciplined band of conspirators proved no more successful in setting the countryside alight. Individual adherents of revolutionary populism sought to fire popular revolution by acts of terrorism.

In 1878, a young woman, Vera Zasulich, shot General Trepov, the police chief of St Petersburg, in retaliation for the flogging of a political prisoner. The trial was momentous. The defence produced evidence of such abuses by the police, and the defendant conducted herself with such dignity, that the jury acquitted her. The police then tried to seize her outside the court; but the intervention of the crowd, delighted at the verdict, enabled her to escape. The Tsar ordered all future trials of political offenders to be conducted by military tribunals.

In 1879, the membership of Land and Liberty split. Those committed to terrorism founded a new society named Narodnaya Volya (People's Liberty). The others, led by a certain Georgi Plekhanov, who was soon to leave for Switzerland and become the principal Russian exponent of Marxism, concentrated on agitating for an egalitarian distribution of the land.

It was a year marked by two attempts on the life of the Tsar; an attempt on the life of the general who headed the political police; and the shooting of Prince Kropotkin, Governor of Kharkov. It was also the year in which, on 26 October,[3] Lev, or Leon, Davidovich Bronstein, the future Leon Trotsky, was born.

David Leontievich Bronstein, Trotsky's father, was a farmer; his was a Jewish family which had migrated, when he was still a small boy, from a

Jewish town in the province of Poltava, to the steppes of the Ukraine. Here, within these thinly populated expanses of wheatfields and sheep, Jews had been encouraged to settle by the alleviation of the legal disabilities that elsewhere in the empire lay so heavily upon them.

Bronstein prospered, by hard work and thrift. A few months before Trotsky's birth, he moved to Yanovka, a tiny isolated village fifteen miles from the nearest post office and twenty-two miles from the railway. There he had bought 250 acres and leased a further 400 from the estate of a Colonel Yanovsky, whose own farming ventures had failed. The purchase was a timely one. Two years later, an edict prohibited Jews from buying land even in the steppes. Henceforward, Bronstein could extend his holdings only by renting tracts from his neighbours. That he managed to do so on a quite considerable scale was due as much to the decadence of the surrounding gentry as to his own vigour. The founders of the local family fortunes were by now dead, and the heirs were squandering their substance in supporting their pretensions. Their packs of white wolfhounds for hunting, their huge houses with peacocks parading on the terraces, the fashionable exertions of their leisure demanded an income which the ability to speak French and to play billiards did nothing to supply.

The Bronstein family lived in a mud house of five rooms, with a straw roof and low ceilings which leaked when the rain was heavy. It was, during Trotsky's childhood, 'the stern competence of people still rising from poverty and having no desire to stop half-way'.[4] Prosperity would in time be marked by the building of a large brick house with a tin roof, but not before Trotsky was seventeen years old. And meanwhile, David Bronstein was not one to bother about appearances.

Trotsky's mother, Anna, had been born in a city and had not at first found easy her translation to a farmhouse on the steppes. Indeed, there are suggestions in Trotsky's autobiography that her family disapproved of the match. What must have been a passion for the handsome young farmer may soon have given place to regrets. But she adapted herself firmly to her duties. If she seems to have lacked softness, she had cause. Of the eight children she bore, only four, two sons and two daughters, survived infancy. She worked a hard day, most of it in the mill, which ground the grain not just of the Bronsteins but, for a tithe, of peasants from ten to fifteen miles around. During her husband's absences, she took full charge of the farm.

In the home, her care of her husband came before everything else. Even before reaching the house on her return from work, she would shout orders for the samovar to be lit, so that he would not be kept waiting for his tea when he came in from the fields. And he, in turn, was considerate to her; calling, if he was at home first, for a chair to be brought as, white with mill-dust, she reached the door. But Trotsky himself would describe the marriage as marked by 'a strong comradeship of labour', with no display of tenderness. His father he recalled as superior in intellect and character, deeper and more reserved, 'gentler and quieter' with the children though growing 'sterner' when the demands of his business increased; his mother, as often short-tempered with the children, and taking out her tiredness and 'domestic failure' on them. He suggests a relation between husband and wife that could not disguise a mutual disappointment, and one between parents and children that failed to provide Trotsky, at least, with sufficient nourishment of his affections.

How far he suffered from this, and resented it, may only be supposed, from the muffled tone of such reminiscences. Despite accounts in his autobiography that testify to the kindness of his nurse and the warmth shown towards him by his brother and two sisters, he summed up his childhood as 'greyish'; his home as one where 'every muscle was strained, every thought set on work and savings', so that there was 'but a modest place for the children'.[5] Certainly he acquired an abiding hostility to that tight and demanding determination with which those who had left poverty behind sought to rise further in the world.

Meanwhile, he could find comfort and excitement in the machine-shop, with Ivan Vasilyevich Gryeben, who had come to work on the farm in the same year that Trotsky was born. There, he would be allowed to cut the threads of nuts and screws; tug the handle of the blower; turn the lathe. And sometimes, as Ivan Vasilyevich sat on a chest in the corner, smoking and gazing into the distance, the child would sit beside him, to play with his thick auburn moustache and examine

those unmistakable hands of the artisan. Their skin was all covered with little black spots that he had got from cutting millstones. His fingers were as tenacious as roots, but not hard. They were broad at the tips but very supple, and his thumb turned far backward, forming an arch.[6]

There is no remotely comparable physical description, of anyone from his immediate family, in Trotsky's autobiography. And no one so dominates the early pages. It is to Ivan Vasilyevich that Trotsky comes running with a bee-sting, to have his finger treated from a jar of sunflower oil in which tarantulas are floating; it is with Ivan Vasilyevich that he tries unsuccessfully to breed pigeons; it is Ivan Vasilyevich who, when Trotsky falls ill with suspected diphtheria, takes him to the doctor, because it is the Jewish Sabbath and his mother will not travel to town.

The vividness of so many memories reveals all too clearly where the child's affections found refuge. But the very welcome that they received must have made the severity of his parents the more disturbing; the preoccupation with work and the impatience with his emotional demands seem the more like withdrawal and rejection. And this in turn can only have made him the more sensitive to other signs of stress around him; other sources of puzzlement and disquiet.

The treatment of Jews in Russia must have been discussed at home, especially from 1881 onwards. For in that year Tsar Alexander II was assassinated by members of Narodnaya Volya, and the reign of his successor, Alexander III, was to be marked by a commitment to systematic persecution. Yet Trotsky's home was far removed from those protective walls of community cohesion behind which, in the poverty of the Pale, a rich culture offered its own reassurances. His parents spoke not Yiddish, the language of that culture, but a rough mixture of Russian and Ukrainian. And that mixture told, too, how removed was the home from the dominant culture of Russia itself. His mother would, in the long evenings, read Russian novels, from a lending library; but whispering the words to herself as she went, and often faltering over sentences which her children would then explain. One of Trotsky's earliest memories was of her sitting there and whispering, while he cut out the letters of the alphabet and 'stuck them fast in the frost on the window, one in each pane.'[7] And, many years later, his father would still be learning to spell out words, so as to read at least the titles of Trotsky's books.

Moreover, the mysterious Russian environment had another menacing dimension, in that underworld of want which could so suddenly surface. The Bronsteins were by no means the harshest of employers, but then the common conditions of employment were very harsh. Occasionally on the farm the labourers would protest at their diet, lying face downward in the shade of the barns and 'brandishing their bare, cracked, straw-pricked feet in the air', until Trotsky's father would given them some watermelon or dried fish, and they would return, singing, to the fields. One summer their under-nourishment produced an epidemic of night-blindness, and they moved through the twilight with their hands stretched out in front of them.

In the machine-shop and the kitchen and the backyard, when Ivan Vasilyevich and the steward, distrusted as allies of the masters, were away, the others would talk, heedless of how deeply the small boy was taking in what they said. Trotsky gives no details of what, he was to write, might well have 'laid the foundation' of his attitude towards society. The resentment that lurked behind the deference of the servant must have strikingly emerged; in all likelihood, along with glimpses of that sinister caricature that was the Jew for so many Russian peasants.

It was to a Jewish day-school that Trotsky now went, at the age of seven, to learn arithmetic and Russian and the Hebrew of the Old Testament. The school was a few miles away, in the colony of Gromokley, which was divided by a ravine into two distinct settlements. In the German one, 'the houses were neat, partly roofed with tile and partly with reeds, the horses large, the cows sleek'; in the Jewish one, 'the cabins were dilapidated, the roofs tattered, the cattle scrawny'.[8] Perhaps the contrast was not quite as sharp as Trotsky was to remember it: but the clarity of the recall suggests that it was sharp enough, for a boy so sensitive to implications.

He had no close friends at the school. The other children all spoke Yiddish. But there was ample compensation. He had been taught his letters by his elder sister and brother, who had given him his first coloured books to read. It made him the more eager to soak up whatever the school could provide, for that love of literature which was to last all of his life. At the age of eight he was printing, with a pen that he had made himself, his own little magazine. He began composing verses and was made to recite them before visitors. It was all, by his own account, painfully embarrassing; but the embarrassment doubtless diminished with successive perform- ances, and the pain must have soon given place to pleasure at the import- ance he so easily achieved.

In the summer of 1887, when Trotsky was seven years old, his mother's nephew, Moissey Filippovich Schpentzer, or Monya as he was called in the family, came from Odessa to stay for a few weeks on the farm. He was a young man much prized by his relatives for his intellect. Only some minor political offence had apparently prevented his admission to a university. He became the light of Trotsky's life: teaching him city manners and arithmetic and Russian grammar and, by his occasional comments, a more confident repugnance to the harsh treatment of the farm labourers. Then, too, Monya had brought with him a pile of books; and Trotsky, under- standing little but persevering, read as much as he could.

Monya was about to marry the principal of the State School for Jewish Girls. The Bronsteins approved of the match and they arranged that Trotsky should live with the couple in Odessa, where a school adequate to his talents was to be found. In the spring of 1888, he arrived at the Schpentzer apartment and was allotted quarters in a corner of the dining- room, behind a curtain.

The family was not in easy circumstances. Monya's own income, from translating Greek tragedies and writing children's stories, was precarious. But, augmented by his wife's, and probably by some help from the Bron- steins, it was sufficient to afford a servant and soon, as well, a wet-nurse for the baby. Certainly it supported a home unharassed and affectionate enough for Trotsky to have settled down quickly and well, despite occasional bursts of longing for the farm. He took an immediate guardian- ship of the baby and had to be kept from displaying such devotion as threatened to rock it apart in its cradle.

He seems to have adapted himself without resentment, even eagerly, to the new discipline. He was sent to bed promptly at nine; though some- times a few minutes' grace might be granted to finish the page. He was taught to keep his fingernails clean and not to eat from his knife, to treat servants with politeness and discard his Ukrainian jargon. There was an abundance of books, which he was encouraged and helped to read. There were the newspapers which he was not supposed to read but which his persistent pressure gradually gained for him. There was the talk around the table: never knowingly of politics in front of him; but the subjects of interest and concern in a cultivated and 'moderately liberal', if cautious, household. There was the city itself, with its bustle and delights. What was the magic of the machine-shop at home compared to that of the theatre? And then Monya started a small publishing concern. Trotsky was introduced to the mysteries of type-setting, lay-out, binding. He became a willing proof-reader.

The rigid restriction on the entry of Jews to state schools made it unlikely that Trotsky would get a place at a *Gymnasium*. It was decided that he should try instead for the less hotly contested admission to a *Realschule*, which ignored the classics and offered a broader course in mathematics, the natural sciences and modern languages. In the autumn he took the entrance examination to St Paul's School; but though he passed, his marks were not good enough to lift him over the limit on selection and over the bribery which in practice made the limit lower for some, only to make it all the higher for others. He was placed in the private preparatory class attached to the school, with its promise of preferential treatment at the next selection.

His first day as a city schoolboy was eventful. Proud in his uniform, complete with badge, braid, belt-buckle and eagle-decorated brass buttons, he was stopped by a young shop apprentice, who indicated his resentment at such privileged display by spitting on Trotsky's new jacket. Then, on reaching the school, he was ordered by a black-bearded monitor to remove the badge, braid, belt-buckle and eagle-decorated buttons, to which, as a member of the mere preparatory class, he was not entitled. Stripped of his glitter, he attended lessons on the second day, to a more encouraging reception. He distinguished himself in arithmetic and in copying from the blackboard, and he was praised for his clean hands.

He gave no hint of the future rebel in his conduct. Indeed, he proved to be a model pupil: never late; attentive at his desk; and always respectful when meeting his teachers in the street. In due course he passed into the school proper.

It was a new window, with views that reached into dark places. One teacher spat in the classroom, was reputed to be drinking heavily, and eventually cut his throat with a razor; another used to act strangely, went insane, and hanged himself from a window-frame.

Trotsky's studiousness and intelligence took him regularly to the top of his grade. He excelled in mathematics and also in Russian, the teacher of which would often read Trotsky's written work aloud to the class. He caused a particular stir with a magazine, called *The Drop* (in the ocean of literature) at Monya's suggestion. The teacher of Russian recited Trotsky's introductory poem with much feeling but also made clear that the first number should be the last: school magazines were strictly prohibited at the time. And then, during his stay in the second grade, Trotsky found himself in serious trouble.

The boys ragged the teacher of French in punishment for his persistent victimization of one among them. Some ten to fifteen pupils were sentenced to detention, while the others, including Trotsky, were permitted to go home. But retribution receded only to gather force. During detention, one of the boys denounced Trotsky as the ring-leader; others then hastened to volunteer accusations of further crimes. The star scholar had made enemies. On the following morning, while he stood in the corridor outside the headmaster's room, a cross-examination was conducted of his classmates. Some of the boys denied everything, and were in turn accused of being Trotsky's cronies. Fanny Schpentzer, summoned as his guardian, argued and appealed to no avail. The teachers' council met and pronounced sentence. Trotsky was to be expelled, though with the right of return to St Paul's.

The Schpentzers did what they could to belittle his offence and prepare the ground at Yanovka for forgiveness. He stayed on in Odessa till the beginning of the holidays and then spent a week or two with a friend. But the necessity of facing his parents could not be further postponed. He arrived to a snub from his mother. His father behaved for a few days as though nothing unpleasant had happened, and at last laughingly betrayed his pride that his son should have proved so daring to high officials.

Trotsky could not settle down during the summer and returned early to Odessa. He did little work for his examinations but passed them none the less and was admitted to the third grade. He was not one to forget or to forgive easily. Those boys who had denounced him, he cut with contempt. To those who had stood by him, he made plain his gratitude. He was to call the affair, in his autobiography, his 'first political test'. For he would meet, again and again in his career, those three typical groups: the 'tale-bearers and the envious'; the 'frank' and 'courageous'; and the 'neutral, vacillating mass in the middle'.[9]

There was a mysterious turbulence within him. He had a few tremulous encounters with girls and came to display a disdain that only proclaimed his uncertainty. He found at the farm a booklet, bought by his brother, on a trial for murder. The victim had been a little girl; the recorded details of the sexual crime agitated him, without opening his mind to what it all meant.

He was discovered to be short-sighted and taken to an eye specialist who prescribed glasses. Proudly he wore them, as a symbol of intellectual importance, and pleasurably he anticipated the impression that they would make at home in the holidays. But his father regarded them as mere affectation, and banned them despite protests from Trotsky that he could not even read street signs without them. Trotsky was not to be parted from his glasses, but at Yanovka wore them only in secret. Less welcome was a sort of colic which seems to have had a nervous connection, since it would worry him at times of stress for the rest of his life. In the fourth grade at school he suffered so acutely that he was unable to study. On doctor's orders he was dispatched to the country, with a tutor to keep him from slipping behind in his work. There was much muttering in Yanovka at the extra expense.

The close-fistedness of his parents increasingly irritated and embarrassed him. When his father used to accompany him to town at the end of the holidays, and the luggage was heavy with presents for the family in Odessa, he would employ a porter and then tip him so meanly as to raise a storm of indignation. Trotsky himself was always fearful of tipping too little; when travelling on his own and employing a porter, he would soon get through his pocket money in consequence. But assiduous acquisitiveness was no monopoly of Yanovka's: it was to be found at almost every turn in the town as well. Trotsky acquired a scorn for the class that seemed to see life only from behind a counter.

His visits to the farm were less and less agreeable. In the machine-shop they now addressed him, despite his protests, with the formal and respectful 'thee'. Everywhere the master–servant relationship 'stood out . . . like a spring in an old couch'.[10] He helped with the book-keeping, and often on pay-day there were barely controlled clashes between him and his father, when it seemed that the terms of employment were being interpreted too harshly. How much harsher still could be that other mastery, by the state, he was not long in discovering. One day, when Trotsky's father was away, a strutting police sergeant visited the farm to examine the passports of the workers. He found two of the passports faulty and arrested the culprits. They begged on their knees for mercy and were imperiously answered: 'I give mercy only on feast-days, and this is a weekday.' Trotsky objected but was told to mind his own business, while his sister frantically gestured at him to be silent.

Yet what was the affinity between himself and those labourers whose plight he so pitied? While they admired or merely disregarded his father's skill, they mocked his own clumsy efforts to scythe the wheat; unconcerned that he should be taking their side against his father. And they refused to be parted from their ways, even when these were demonstrably inefficient or directed to the absurd. He brought Euclid to the task of measuring the area of a field; but because his answer did not agree with that obtained by the old, time-consuming 'practical' methods, it was dismissed. Ivan

Vasilyevich insisted that he could build a perpetual-motion machine and to Trotsky's arguments against it would simply reply, 'That is all book, and this is practice.' It was the sort of outlook which infuriated Trotsky. He knew only the necessity of searching below the surface, for the laws that informed the functioning of what he saw.

Everywhere, it seemed to him, the irrational was rife. From doubting the existence of God he had passed, through indifference, to decided disbelief; and the presence of various priests at the school, to instruct in the competing certainties of the different faiths, must have promoted his repugnance to the grip of superstition. Even among his classmates who were studying science, there were those who would talk about unlucky days and betray other signs of their belief in magic. He would grow angry with them, feeling his own intelligence insulted. And he could scarcely fail to feel this intelligence insulted by the grim authoritarianism of the regime. Odessa was one of the most rigorously ruled cities in Russia; its governor, a former admiral, notorious for his arrogance and ill-temper. Trotsky saw him only once, standing in his carriage, shaking his fist and cursing, while frightened citizens peeped at him from behind the curtains of nearby windows. But Trotsky was not yet caught up in the politics of revolt.

Looking back at his early years in his autobiography, he was to describe himself then as quick-tempered, conscious of his superiority to his school-fellows and enjoying leadership among his friends but conscious that he had made enemies; and self-critical, with a striving to shine that was 'very close to vanity'.[11]

If he appeared arrogant as well, it was an arrogance that covered an uncertainty of where he belonged, and whether he had it in himself to grasp a purpose that would satisfy his needs. It was a time of particular restlessness in the minds of the young. So many yearned to make a different Russia, without knowing the way. Trotsky was to answer his time, and give a meaning beyond it; but because, first of all, in his yearning and doubt, he belonged to it.

2

Commitments

When Friedrich Engels, the co-founder of Marxism, died in 1895, and student groups in several Russian cities held meetings to his memory, Trotsky was sixteen years old. By his own account, he had, then, not yet heard of Engels. His 'dim democratic ideas' were directed to reforms that would somehow bring Russia closer to his vision of the advanced societies in the West. Having taken with ease his final examinations at St Paul's, he returned to Yanovka, intent on helping his family to understand the impulse of the age. But his father dismissed all such talk with the cry: 'This will not come to pass even in three hundred years.'

It was a sentiment shared by Tsar Nicholas II, who had succeeded to the throne in November 1894. Greeted on the occasion of his marriage, in January 1895, by delegations of respectable citizens requesting 'that the voice of the people should be heard', he described as 'senseless dreams' the object of such representations. 'I shall maintain,' he declared, 'the principle of autocracy just as firmly and unflinchingly as it was preserved by my unforgettable dead father.' On the very next day, in an open letter, prominent liberals replied: '"Senseless dreams" concerning yourself are no longer possible. . . . You first began the struggle, and the struggle will come.'

But what form was this struggle effectually to take? The liberals themselves had little more than a questionable gift of prophecy to offer. Populist terrorism had assassinated one Tsar and frightened his successor into virtual captivity on his cordoned estate. But it had not shaken the regime. Though isolated acts of terrorism would continue, the cause was unmistakably failing. Some of its disciples had been executed; others had been exiled or had fled abroad; still others had made their peace with the times and were now pursuing more conventional careers.

The current phase of Populism was dominated by the figure of Count Leo Tolstoy who, at the age of fifty-six, had abandoned the fashionable world in 1884, to dress like a peasant and work in the fields. Condemning property as the principal source of violence in society, he had renounced his own: if only, surrendering to her agitated arguments, in favour of his wife, who then encumbered his poverty with her rich solicitude. He attracted much admiration, but no real following of any consequence. His total rejection of violence left the overthrow of the social order to the day when all men had learned to love one another. Few of the disaffected were willing to wait so long.

The condition of the rural multitudes had seriously deteriorated. Efficient American agricultural methods had driven down the price of grain on the world markets, and the Russian peasant was getting for his produce close to half of what he had been paid a few years before. Those with capital or credit were the more easily enabled to augment their holdings, at the cost of augmenting as well the numbers of those engaged in scratching a precarious survival from the land or forced into becoming hired labourers. To support the massive bureaucracy and its own grandiose designs, the regime was compelled to increase the relative burden of taxation, which grew at almost double the rate that the population did.[1] The peasantry was bound to rebel sooner or later: but when, or how, who could say? Meanwhile, the revolutionary gaze moved from the fields of Russia to the factories and mines.

From the reverses of the Crimean war, the regime had come to recognize the vulnerability of a Russia in conflict with modern economies, and early in the reign of Alexander II had taken the first firm steps towards the promise of industrial deliverance. Some fifty years later, the cumulative investment of capital by the state and by foreign private enterprise had made changes that seemed momentous to those looking back across the flat expanses of Russian history. And momentous, indeed, they were. The fast-growing industrial labour force still constituted a tiny percentage of the total population, but was visibly concentrated in vast concerns and in the major cities. With the state itself owning much of the industrial infrastructure and determined to attract further foreign investment by assurances of adequate returns, the prevalent conditions of work were predictably oppressive. The infant Russian capitalism might, in Marxist terms, seem merely to be clutching at the knees of developments in Britain, France, Germany, the United States. But undivided by distinctions of responsibility and reward, unprotected by any substantial measures of social security and denied all prospect of effecting reforms through the processes of government, the industrial labour force of Russia had reached much closer to the Marxist revolutionary prediction of a monolithic, destitute and desperate proletariat. Increasingly, Russians in revolt turned from the disappointments of Populism to the hopes held out by Marx. And such hopes were sustained by a strike of 30,000 St Petersburg workers in 1896.

It was in the same year, at the age of seventeen, that Trotsky took up lodgings in the provincial town of Nikolayev, where he was to attend the seventh grade at a local school. He brought with him an air of ironic detachment and a scepticism towards the proponents of socialist panaceas. He saw himself as the intellectual who had passed beyond the common concern with simple answers to complex problems. And having once hung out his sign, he did not easily take it down. His landlady at first, therefore, found in him an ally against her children, who professed some sort of socialism, and she flourished his example before them as one that they should follow. Her confidence was distressingly misplaced. Proud of his own judgement Trotsky might be: but he cared, above all, to believe himself in the right; and once convinced that the right lay in a different direction, he would reinvest his pride in making that direction his own. After a few months of resistance, he discarded his detachment and assumed a socialist disposition, with such speed and such fervour that he frightened those friends who had been seeking to convert him.

He neglected his studies, to read voraciously but erratically: history, philosophy, aesthetics, as well as newspapers and pamphlets; searching for a system to provide him with his 'incontrovertible truths', yet rejecting the Marxism that he encountered because its very certainties seemed to confine his imagination. He was so often absent from school that an inspector called at his lodgings: if only to leave satisfied by the orderliness that he found and in ignorance of the illegal literature under the mattress.

In an orchard on the outskirts of the town lived a certain Franz Shvigovsky, a gardener of Czech origins, to whose one-room cabin came various of the disaffected, including former exiles, to read and to talk. They were generally Populists; and though Trotsky was later to claim that Populism already carried the smell of decay, it was with the Populists there that he first associated himself, in their quarrel with Marxism. Urging the Marxist cause was a young Jewish woman, Alexandra Lvovna Sokolovskaya, and Trotsky soon became her main adversary. Perhaps he was the more provoked by her patient and earnest argument: she knew so much more about the real issues than his own reading and experience afforded.[2] Perhaps, too, there was a sexual current in the conflict: within four years, they would be married. At all events, he would tease and taunt her: asking how a young girl so full of life could swallow 'that dry, narrow, impractical stuff'; that 'doctrine for shopkeepers and traders'. On the last day of 1896, the orchard subversives gathered to celebrate the coming of a hopeful new year. Trotsky announced his conversion to Marxism, and Sokolovskaya was delighted. Then, when it was his turn to choose the toast, he lifted his glass towards her and cried: 'A curse upon all Marxists, and upon those who want to bring dryness and hardness into all the relations of life!'

Sokolovskaya was furious and left the orchard, swearing that she would have no more to do with him.

Again Trotsky had hung out his sign, and again he meant it to stay against all argument and doubt. The terms in which he derided Marxism reveal what it was in the system that his imagination so resentfully resisted. The emphasis on economic laws as defining the dynamic of history seemed so intolerably to diminish the importance of the individual, the function of the artist, the scope of the independent will: it was a personal affront. He would come shortly, as he searched more deeply, to see that Marxism provided laws, of perception and method, on which his own mind might build; which, indeed, liberated rather than confined his imagination. But the source from which he drew his initial hostility would not dry up with his conversion. On the contrary: he would draw from it his efforts to liberate Marxism from the confinements of bigotry.

He must, in those early days, already have given signs of being much more than a clever young man of immodest ambition. G. A. Ziv, who was a member of the Shvigovsky group, quotes in his hostile reminiscences of Trotsky the remark of another at the time: 'From him will evolve either a great hero or a great scoundrel; either this or that, but certainly great.'[3] It was, however, the immediate prospects that agitated David Bronstein. Having discovered during a business trip to Nikolayev his son's proceedings, he forbade all further association with those trouble-makers in the orchard. Trotsky refused to obey him, and was presented with an ultimatum: 'You will either stop all this and get to work, or you will stop spending my money.'

Trotsky replied by declaring his independence. He left his lodgings and went to live with Shvigovsky, who had leased a garden with a cottage more accommodating than the cabin had been. Six of the group composed a tiny commune there. They fed themselves on stew; wore blue smocks and round straw hats; carried black canes. Trotsky was later to describe it as 'a Spartan existence', but 'Bohemian' might have been a more appropriate term. They had little money, and Trotsky began giving private lessons to earn some. But they clearly enjoyed themselves: reading and arguing excitedly, and doubtless exceedingly pleased with their reputation in the town as members of some secret organization.

They founded a society to distribute useful books. And they chose as the first beneficiaries a hired labourer and an apprentice who were working in the garden. The hired labourer was a policeman in disguise, and the apprentice was his recruit. The collection of cheap books that was to propagate the gospel went to fatten the police files instead. An attempt to organize a small university, with twenty students for mutual instruction, was at least a less costly failure. Trotsky himself was to teach sociology, but found his resources exhausted by the end of his second lecture. The elder of Sokolovskaya's brothers, whose field was the French revolution, did not get beyond the opening sentences of his first.

But there was one signal success. The board of the local public library raised the annual membership fee from five roubles to six. Trotsky and his friends, rushing to the defence of democracy, packed the register with radical members, who attended the annual meeting. The usual patrons of the library – 'officials, teachers, liberal landlords and naval officers' – saw their benevolence rewarded by a vote that restored the former fee and elected a new board of directors.

Trotsky began flourishing his pen. He composed a polemical piece against Marxism for a Populist paper in Odessa. Much to his subsequent relief, it was rejected. With the elder Sokolovsky, he set out to write a play. The two secretly acquired special lodgings and laboured to illuminate the conflicts of the times. It proved to be more difficult than they had supposed. The plot staggered under the weight of far too many long monologues. And the character of the young Marxist girl, in revolt at the dramatic design, reduced the older, love-smitten Populist hero to a whimpering condition. With the first act ready and four others in draft, the ardour of the dramatists went into a rapid decline: the secret room was abandoned, further work was indefinitely postponed, and the unfinished manuscript was later lost.

Trotsky's earlier studies stood him in good stead, and he passed his seventh grade examinations with first class honours. He decided to register at the university in Odessa for a course in pure mathematics. His father, who wanted him to be an engineer, was none the less delighted at any engagement that might take Trotsky's mind off the oppressions of the regime. But even pure mathematics proved only a temporary distraction. A distant relative, with all the patronage of a small fortune, was satisfied that Trotsky would soon return to the fold. 'We all had these ideas in our youth,' he assured him. 'Just wait ten years. I'll bet you a kopek that in ten years you will be laughing at all these ideas.' Trotsky was disgusted. 'I don't,' he replied, 'care to bring my ideas into relation with your kopeks.'

He was soon back in Shvigovsky's garden. There was a ferment of disaffection at Russian universities. Expelled students would arrive at Nikolayev and bring with them the excitement of protest demonstrations. In February 1897 a young woman student, imprisoned in the grim Peter and Paul Fortress of St Petersburg, burned herself to death in her cell. Demonstrations erupted in the university cities. It was time, Trotsky decided, to stop talking about revolution and do something to promote it.

In Nikolayev there were some 8000 workers at two large factories, and 2000 more, employed in various trades. Trotsky, assuming the political pseudonym of 'Lvov', met a young electrician, Ivan Andreyevich Mukhin, who put him in touch with disaffected workers. Mukhin was no mere go-between; he was shrewd in the ways of political agitation, and his practical advice must have been vital to the enterprise. But we have the evidence of the hostile biographer Ziv that Trotsky was himself the moving force in the founding and direction of the Southern Russian Workers' Union.

He wrote proclamations and articles: reproducing them carefully himself on the primitive copying machine. He supervised the study-groups that were the principal activity of the membership. He visited Odessa to increase his contacts with other revolutionary militants and to obtain suitable literature: taking the overnight steamer and sleeping on deck, to save working time. He acquired a suitcase of propaganda pamphlets from abroad, which were duly circulated in Nikolayev and impressed local workers with the importance of the union. Astonishingly, it was at oratory that he had his most remarkable failure. He so lost himself in the course of a speech to his colleagues that when at last he stopped, no one else took the floor, because no one else knew what the subject was. He was overcome with shame, but his colleagues seem to have appreciated him all the more for this evidence of imperfection and vulnerability.

Sokolovskaya, who had left Nikolayev shortly after the occasion of Trotsky's insult, returned as soon as she heard of the new union and was given responsibility for one of its study-groups. She was able to work so closely with Trotsky in the first place, because the union itself was composed of both Populists and Marxists, on a basic programme of exciting workers to fight for better conditions. But Trotsky was, too, moving towards Marxism, and in any event must have deeply impressed her with the force of his devotion to the revolutionary cause.

The Southern Russian Workers' Union was no such formidable organization as its name suggested. By the end of 1897 it had recruited perhaps 200 members, and it did not stretch beyond Nikolayev, let alone across the southern expanses of the empire. But its impact was none the less considerable. Its leaflets, denouncing in purple ink and in eloquent detail conditions in the local factories and workshops, were greedily snatched and circulated. The outraged employers issued counter-pronouncements, which were immediately answered in new proclamations. So bold and efficient a challenge anywhere in Russia at that time was rare, and the reputation of the union rapidly spread, to encourage further activity against the regime. The authorities needed to have done with this dangerous irritation.

Their delay in dealing with it was due to their doubt that a few youngsters in a garden cottage could really be responsible for directing such an enterprise. The police continued to hope that carelessness or chance would open a way to the secret leadership. And meanwhile they collected the reports of their spies. A certain Nesterenko, a carpenter in Sokolovskaya's study-group, was in their service. He insisted that Trotsky in person hand over to him a bundle of leaflets; and their meeting, behind the cemetery late at night, was observed.

On 28 January 1898, persuaded either that there was no secret leadership to be discovered or that further delay would prove too dangerous, the police at last swooped. Trotsky himself had gone to stay with his family for a few weeks, in an attempt to put the police off his tracks. But he had decided, in the event of any arrests, that he would not go into hiding, lest the workers should be led to believe that their leaders would desert them under fire. On the way back to Nikolayev, he was seized on the estate of a wealthy landowner where he had stopped to visit Shvigovsky, now working there as a gardener.

Trotsky himself was at first lodged, along with a young bookbinder, in a massive cell of the old prison at Nikolayev; the two would huddle together beside the tepid stove, or run from corner to corner, for warmth in the February frosts. Then, after three weeks, he was transferred to the prison at Kherson and put in a cell on his own. Little light struggled through the barred and narrow window, which was never opened. The diet was meagre stew once a day, and rye bread with a little salt for breakfast and supper. He had no soap or change of clothing, so that he was soon playing host to a multitude of appreciative lice. But worst of all for him was the loneliness, without books, pencil or paper; a loneliness which he was to recall as unequalled in his whole rich experience of prisons. To keep up his spirits he would count out one thousand one hundred and eleven steps, back and forth diagonally across the cell floor; sometimes composing in his head verses which he would describe as 'most mediocre', but which would later be transmitted and become popular. Only at the end of three months did his mother succeed at last in bribing through to him a parcel of such delicacies as sugar and oranges, fresh linen, soap and a comb.

Meanwhile, there met at Minsk, from 1 to 3 March, nine delegates of various organizations, to establish the Russian Social Democratic Labour Party. They appointed a central committee; resolved to issue a party organ; and were promptly arrested before they could proceed any further. A Marxist intellectual, Peter Struve, wrote the party manifesto, which was published shortly afterwards and which, for the first time, proclaimed the peculiar course forced upon the Russian revolution:

> The farther east one goes in Europe, the weaker, meaner and more cowardly in the political sense becomes the bourgeoisie, and the greater the cultural and political tasks which fall to the lot of the proletariat. On its strong shoulders the Russian working class must and will carry the work of conquering political liberty. This is an essential step, but only the first step, to the realization of the great historic mission of the proletariat, to the foundation of a social order in which there will be no place for the exploitation of man by man.

Marxist doctrine propounded a two-stage revolutionary process: a revolution, led by the bourgeoisie, to establish democracy; and then a revolution, led by the proletariat, to establish socialism. Now, while accepting this proposition of a two-stage process, the Struve manifesto was entrusting the proletariat with the function of ensuring both. It was a conception which would lie neglected until Trotsky made it the immediate material of revolutionary politics, and whose momentous implications he would for long be alone among the revolutionary leaders in expounding.

The nine founders of the Russian Social Democratic Labour Party were no more than the small swirl of smoke before the blaze of history. Peter Struve himself would soon abandon Marxism for liberalism. But the party would come to dominate the Russian revolutionary cause: despite the resurgence, in the year 1898 as well, of Populists with a new programme, who called themselves the Social Revolutionaries.

Shortly after receiving his parcel of delicacies, Trotsky was transferred from Kherson to the modern prison in Odessa. He must have felt as if he were surfacing at last from the dark. Though he was again in solitary confinement, he found ways of communicating with other prisoners, amongst whom were many of his former associates. To his neighbours he tapped out the verses that he had composed at Kherson, and they tapped back news. Through a window, he heard that the brief-case full of documents, hurriedly hidden on the estate where he had been seized, had recently been found and handed to the authorities. It was hardly the most welcome news, but at least it helped him to avoid the traps being set for him by his interrogators. He was even allowed visits from relatives. Prisoners were placed in special narrow wooden cages for these occasions. His father, seeing him like this and supposing such to be the way that Trotsky was kept all the time, could not speak for the shock. His mother subsequently came prepared and was less disturbed.

The prison library was in general composed of orthodox religious and historical magazines, but Trotsky could not afford to be fastidious. He devoured the attacks on such heresies as Catholicism and Darwinism; disquisitions on the kingdom of demons; and a detailed study of Paradise which ended with the admission: 'The precise location of Paradise is not known.' His sister supplied him with copies of the Bible in French, German, English and Italian, and he read the Gospels, verse by verse, using his school knowledge of French and German to move ahead in these and learn something of the other two languages. Assaults on freemasonry, in the religious magazines, stirred his interest, and he obtained books on the subject from friends and relatives in the city. He began writing down his own ideas for a treatment of freemasonry. Successive chapters, carefully edited and copied on to the pages of a notebook, were smuggled into other cells, for his friends to read and offer comments. Together with two essays, in French translation, by the Italian Marxist, Antonio Labriola, this work led him to an understanding of historical materialism which was only to be confirmed by his later reading of classic Marxist texts. He had found nothing new; but he had made his own way, with a mere sketch of theory, rather than waiting for the printed instructions to reach him. He was always in consequence to hold his work on freemasonry in particular regard and correspondingly regret the loss of the manuscript: it was, a few years afterwards, to be left with his landlady in Geneva for safe-keeping and apparently used to light fires.

Meanwhile, to prepare for his own interrogation and that of his col-leagues, he needed to exchange as much news as possible, while ensuring that any intercepted messages would not be useful to the authorities. Ziv, a prisoner as well, received from him 'an essay full of scintillating wit and satirical irony, a brilliant pamphlet',[4] which surreptitiously communicated the circumstances of Trotsky's arrest and summarized the deposition that he intended to make. Trotsky was hoping for a public trial, at which to flay the regime in the process of defending himself. But the authorities were not disposed to provide opportunities for hostile propaganda. Near the end of 1899, or almost two years after the arrests, mere 'administrative verdicts' were pronounced. While others received lighter sentences or were released, Trotsky, along with three of his colleagues, was exiled to eastern Siberia for four years. His sentence took no account of the time already spent in captivity, and would take none of the further six months that he was to spend at a 'transfer prison' in Moscow.

It was in this 'transfer prison' that, sometime in the late spring or early summer of 1900, Trotsky married Sokolovskaya. He had tried to do so during his imprisonment at Odessa, where she had also been confined, after her own arrest. But his father, blaming her for having led Trotsky astray, had resisted all pressures and even prevented any attempt to cir-cumvent his opposition, by sending a telegram to the Minister of Justice. Whether he now relented, moved by the prospect of his son's long exile alone, or simply recognized that the attainment of legal age would soon allow Trotsky to marry without parental consent, he seems to have resisted no longer. The marriage was solemnized by a Jewish chaplain, in a cell, with a wedding ring borrowed from one of the jailers. The religious ceremony was so offensive to Trotsky's beliefs that he must have swallowed hard before bowing to the necessity: but there was no other way of making the marriage legal.

Some thirty years later, in his autobiography, Trotsky was to mention the marriage as though presenting the minutes of a political transaction.

Alexandra Lvovna had one of the most important positions in the South Russian Workers' Union. Her utter loyalty to socialism and her complete lack of any personal ambition gave her an unquestioned moral authority. The work that we were doing bound us closely together, and so, to avoid being separated, we had been married in the transfer prison in Moscow.[5]

It is an account that scarcely corresponds with eyewitness reminiscences of the strong mutual attachment displayed by the couple on their journey into exile; or, indeed, with Trotsky's passionate and protracted campaign to marry her in the first place.

But then, in the Moscow transfer prison he would display a 'moving tenderness' not only to Sokolovskaya but to other women, on their visits to husbands and brothers who were his revolutionary colleagues. And, on returning from the visitors' room, he would 'spend all the excess of his tenderness on us', Ziv records, 'caressing and kissing and embracing us'.[6] He was, more than anything else, in love with the revolution; and his tenderness, his care for those whom he identified with the revolution, were expressions of that love. In this sense, therefore, what he wrote in his autobiography about his marriage mirrored the truth.

Trotsky wasted no time in the transfer prison. It was there that he first heard of Lenin, and plunged into Lenin's book, *The Development of Capitalism in Russia*. He himself wrote a pamphlet, on the movement in Nikolayev, which was smuggled out and soon afterwards published in Geneva. In this suspended community of revolutionaries from many parts of Russia, representing different social backgrounds and routes of disaffection, there was so much to approve and dispute, so much thinking and planning to do.

He remained irrepressible. When a prisoner was put in solitary confinement for having failed to take off his cap in the presence of the governor, Trotsky took the lead in mounting a demonstration of protest. The prisoners approached the guard, their hats firmly on their heads, and asked him to press the alarm signal for the governor. The guard refused. Trotsky, holding out a watch, gave him two minutes to change his mind. Then, pushing him aside, he pressed the signal himself. The governor, surrounded by armed guards, rushed into the yard and at once demanded of Trotsky, who stood defiantly in front, 'Why don't you take your hat off?' 'And you, why don't you take off yours?' Trotsky demanded in return, and was carried away, struggling, to solitary confinement.

He had gained greatly in self-confidence. He had demonstrated to others that he had the qualities of leadership. And he had demonstrated to himself that the punishments of the regime could not subdue him. He knew now that he was not afraid of death. And, indeed, he was always to face it with an easy courage: sometimes taking risks that he would have condemned as irresponsible in another revolutionary. In the transfer prison, he met for the first time an anarchist, a village school-teacher called Luzin, whose attempts to convert the other prisoners brought the two into conflict. They journeyed together into exile and Luzin, somewhat drunk, one day challenged Trotsky to cross the swollen Lena River with him in a little boat. It was a pointlessly dangerous undertaking, but Trotsky agreed. They succeeded in negotiating the loose timber, dead animals and whirl-pools; and Trotsky was given the testimonial of a 'good comrade'.

The exiles reached Irkutsk, near the Mongolian border, in late autumn. And northwards from there, by barge along the Lena River, the prisoners were put ashore, in ones and twos, at various villages. Trotsky and his wife were consigned to Ust-Kut, in one of whose hundred or so peasant huts, at the very edge of the settlement, they set up home. Gold fever had once raged across the region – there were still a few mines further north – but all that still gripped the village were memories of uproarious days and the consolations of determined drinking. It was the cockroaches that provided the most enthusiastic welcoming party. They took to the Trotskys at once, crawling over their furniture and even their faces. The only recourse was to move out of the hut altogether for a day or so and leave the door wide open for the frost to deal with the lodgers. And if the winter was cruel, the summer was not to prove much kinder. For it brought multitudes of midges so ferocious that they bit to death a cow in the nearby woods.

But Trotsky, brushing the cockroaches off the pages of Marx, bent to his work. He was not to be deflected by discomfort or the proddings of depression. All around him, indeed, he saw evidence of the danger in doing otherwise. The exile colonies were marked by little cemeteries of suicides; while among the survivors were many who had lost themselves in the local populations or in drink. For Trotsky, the lesson was clear: in exile, as in prison, only hard intellectual effort could save the mind. And he noticed that it was generally the Marxists who obeyed this rule.

The Lena River was the connecting railway of the exiles, who would gather in small groups along its banks, sometimes to talk through the night in the security of the surrounding emptiness. The increase in the number of new exiles reflected the rise in disaffection across the empire. In 1901, agrarian riots erupted in southern Russia, and there was a resurgence of terrorism. In February, the Minister of Education was assassinated, and in April, the Minister of the Interior. The Marxist exiles, after some individual hesitation, declared themselves against terrorism, as an ultim-ately ineffectual substitute for mass action. And Trotsky himself was doubtless influential in the reaching of a decision which drew a definite line between Social Democrats and Social Revolutionaries.

Soon after arriving at Ust-Kut, he began contributing occasional pieces to an Irkutsk newspaper, the *Eastern Review*: founded by Populist exiles but slipping, from time to time, under Marxist direction. He wrote about village life, its squalor and disease; about the men, whether merchants or muzhiks, who beat their wives so mercilessly; about the distracted clerks who represented the might of the empire and did not even receive their salaries regularly. Already in his little pieces there is the vivacity of detail that prefigures the achievement of his later works. He described the notables of the village: 'the justice of the peace, a college man, still young, with very slender moustaches and perfumed pocket-handkerchief', and 'the revenue officer, a small, fine-edged man of the type that is portrayed on boxes of shoe-polish'. And he dealt derisively with the 'spiritual side': the 'bustling Siberian priest who devotes much of his energy to horse-trading and other forms of commerce', with the psalm-reader who 'once summoned "the world" with the sound of the church-bell in order to raffle off his share of the clerical meadow-grass'.

He also wrote about writers, Russian and foreign, their style and ideas. In his search for a pen-name, he lighted upon the word *antidoto* in his Italian dictionary. It seemed so apt, for one concerned to counteract the poison of the regime circulating in the legitimate press. From then on, it was as 'Antid Oto' that he signed his pieces and as 'Antid Oto' that his reputation spread: through the Siberian settlements; in the luggage and memory of returning exiles, to the cities of Russia and to the émigré communities in the West. So satisfied was the *Eastern Review* with his services that it raised his payment, from only two kopecks a line to four.

Trotsky did not spend all his exile in Ust-Kut. The governor at Irkutsk at last gave permission for him to move with his family, which now included a baby daughter and was soon to include a second one, near friends some 175 miles to the east, on the River Ilim. There Trotsky took a job as a clerk to a millionaire merchant, whose inability to write his own name had proved no obstacle to the dissemination of his stores and saloons across a territory the size of Holland and Belgium put together. But the revolutionary who had not so long ago contemplated a career in pure mathematics entered a pound of red lead as a 'poud', or forty times the weight, and was dismissed as incompetent after six weeks. Not even Trotsky, it seemed, could serve two masters. The family returned to Ust-Kut for a few months and then moved again, to Verkholensk, a little to the south.

The Social Democratic movement was spreading; sending up shoots in Siberia along the tracks of the railway. Trotsky was approached and eagerly agreed to write proclamations and leaflets. It seemed to him increasingly evident that the movement could make little or no headway against the resistance of a monolithic Tsarism, while its own multitude of parts pursued independent struggles: vulnerable in their isolation, moreover, to the influence of Social Revolutionary Populism or reformist Marxism. Already the movement's revolutionary impetus was being seriously threatened by those Social Democrats, called Economists, who saw in industrial strikes for limited gains sufficient promise of change. In a pamphlet which circulated widely through the exile settlements and excited much discussion, Trotsky called for a tightly organized union of professional revolutionaries whose central committee would ensure discipline and security by excommunicating the disobedient and irresponsible.

In the summer of 1902 he received a bundle of publications from abroad and discovered the existence of the revolutionary periodical *Iskra*, which was campaigning for much the same strategy as he recommended. A copy of Lenin's *What Is to be Done?*, more exhaustively examining the problem and propounding a solution similar to Trotsky's, reached him, too. History was pealing, and the muffled sound that penetrated to Siberia summoned the exiles. There was a rash of escapes; with local peasants, affected by revolutionary sentiment, helping the 'politicals' away by boat, cart and sledge. The most devout police vigilance could not cover so vast an area, and the real risks lay rather in the terrain, where river or forest could so easily devour the fugitive.

According to Trotsky, it was Sokolovskaya who suggested that he, too, should attempt to escape, and who swept away all his hesitation at leaving her and their two young daughters behind, with the simple reply, 'You must!' There is no reason to doubt his account. For Sokolovskaya, now as ever, the cause of the revolution came before anything else. Together they prepared for his attempt. But it was his own hot temper that had already provided one prerequisite of success.

Each evening, after the children had been put to bed, Trotsky and Sokolovskaya would climb up a ladder, through a trap-door in the ceiling, to the second storey of their little house, so as to read and study. And every evening, at ten o'clock, the trap-door would open to reveal, rising from the floor, the big red-whiskered face and watery blue eyes of the police inspector: silently exploring the room, before sinking beneath the floor, as the trap-door closed. This used to infuriate Trotsky; and one evening he jumped from his chair and lunged with his foot at the intrusion. 'Don't you ever show your face above this floor again!' The inspector was suitably impressed and stopped his visitations. It would be five days before Trotsky's absence was accidentally discovered by the chief of police.

Not far short of two years after his arrival, and with the approach of autumn arguing against further delay, Trotsky set out, together with a woman revolutionary. Hidden at night by their peasant driver under hay in the fields, they were carried close to the railway, where they separated, so that each would not need to run also the risks of the other. At Irkutsk, provided with convincing luggage by friends, and with a Russian translation of the *Iliad* to read on the way, Trotsky boarded a train, while the station police looked on unregardingly. In his pocket was a passport in which he had had to write some name. He had chosen that of Trotsky.

A certain Trotsky had been the senior warder at the prison in Odessa, and a man of so strong and authoritative a personality that he had dominated staff and prisoners alike. Ziv believed Trotsky to have been so impressed by this warder as to have taken his name, and then to have retained it rather than revert to the Jewish reverberations of his own.[7] A more sympathetic biographer has suggested that this identification with a former jailer might have gratified 'a subconscious craving for safety'.[8] It is at least as likely, if he did have the imperious figure of the warder in mind, that Trotsky chose the name as a private joke. Appropriating it would have appealed to his sense of irony. And he could scarcely have supposed afterwards that the retention of a Gentile name would have enabled him to avoid any embarrassment from his Jewish origins. He seems, indeed, to have done nothing otherwise to conceal them. Doubtless, he simply stayed with the name for a while, until so many people thought of the two together that a separation would have been inconvenient.

Reading of the Trojan War in Russian hexameters, drinking cup after cup of tea and eating cheap Siberian buns, he reached Samara, where he had been told that he would find the underground headquarters in Russia of the *Iskra* organization. In charge was a certain Krzhizhanovsky, an engineer, who must have been delighted to enroll so notable a recruit, and who gave him the nickname of Pero (pen) in tribute to his success as a writer.

Far from being put on probation while his opinions and reliability were weighed, Trotsky was almost at once sent as a representative and recruiting agent to promising cities in the south. His visits disappointed him. Where the addresses supplied to him proved of any use, he encountered a parochial resistance to his intrusion. He leapt more readily, therefore, at one suggestion that he should go to London, where *Iskra* had its editorial headquarters. Lenin, who wished personally to size up someone of such apparent promise, had been pressing that he come as soon as possible, and Krzhizhanovsky supplied him with funds and contacts for the trip.

Arriving at the frontier zone in October, Trotsky found, to his surprised relief, his fabricated passport accepted without suspicion by the police. But there were other difficulties. The student who was to get him smuggled across the border into Austria was a Social Revolutionary; and, enraged by recent *Iskra* attacks on terrorism, at first refused to help him. Then, persuaded that Trotsky should not be punished for the vices of *Iskra*, he deposited him in the empty house of a commercial traveller, who returned in the middle of the night and was only just persuaded by Trotsky's protests to regard it all as a rather poor practical joke.

The next night, in a rain-storm, Trotsky was taken across the border by a Ukrainian peasant who insisted upon carrying him part of the way, so that he could keep his feet dry; charged him extra for the service; and deposited him, in wet shoes, with a warning against the disposition of Jews to charge much more than they should for the services they rendered. An old Jewish workman then took him the few kilometres to the railway station, in a light cart that overturned during the journey; spilling Trotsky into the mud, where he lost his glasses, and burying in his blanket a rooster for the rabbi's sabbath. In premature distress, the rooster began screaming for help; and it seemed that he must bring down the frontier guards on the whole bedraggled party. The two men crawled about in the dark, cursing till the rooster, at last found and released, gratefully fell silent.

At the railway station, where he took three hours to make himself presentable again, Trotsky discovered that he did not have enough money left to buy a ticket for Zurich, where Paul Axelrod was to receive him. He decided to make for Vienna instead. There, he insisted on disturbing the Sunday rest of Victor Adler, leader of the Austrian Social Democrats. But Adler, who was helpfully supplied with a Russian daughter-in-law, received him kindly, and gave him the money to continue on his way.

3
Congress and Conflicts

Trotsky was in far too much of a hurry for considerations of courtesy. At Zurich, he went straight from the railway station to Paul Axelrod's home, in the middle of the night. It was his first personal encounter with one of the founders of Russian Social Democracy.

Axelrod, too, had been born of Jewish parents in southern Russia. He, too, had kept company with Populism for a while, in the original South Russian Workers' Union, whose name Trotsky had adopted for his own movement in Nikolayev. Then, settling abroad, he had become a leading exponent of Russian Marxism and a light to the younger revolutionaries. They came to him still, on their emergence from Russia, to be questioned and fed, encouraged and instructed. He lived simply, making and selling buttermilk to meet the expenses of his household: a bearded figure who seemed to have strayed from some small Jewish town on to the highway of history and was thrusting his way, with dream-filled eyes, through the milling crowds and the convoys of power.

But time and distance were dragging at his legs, while others were pushing past him. Lenin had learned organization from him; and now, with his wife, Krupskaya, effectively directed underground communication with Russia. Axelrod had never found writing easy: but now he would apply himself month after month, often working through the night, without finishing a long-promised article. The raggedness of his nerves was revealed in a handwriting so indecipherable that it drove Lenin to distraction. Yet the splendour of his character and commitment remained undimmed: his love and generosity demanding, though never asking, a return. Trotsky and Axelrod took to each other at once. And Trotsky would visit the Axelrod home, whenever possible, during his frequent future trips to Switzerland. But immediately he was impatient for London and soon rushed off, with instructions to knock three times on the front door of the house where Lenin lived.

Arriving early in the morning, he at once approached a cab driver and pantomimed his wish to be taken to the address that he had been given on a scrap of paper. Aroused by his three sharp knocks, Krupskaya let him in, and announcing, 'The Pen has arrived', left him with Lenin, who was still in bed, while she went to pay the cab driver and prepare coffee. Trotsky plunged into talk, reporting on the state of the organization in Russia and the higher rates that the smugglers were demanding at the border for taking fugitives out and copies of *Iskra* in, while Lenin watched closely this 'real young eagle' that the letters from Samara had promised.

Vladimir Ilyich Ulyanov, who would choose the political name of Lenin, was born in 1870 at Simbirsk, on the Volga: his mother, the daughter of a doctor; his father, a senior civil servant elevated to the minor nobility. In 1887, his elder brother Alexander was hanged for participation in a conspiracy to assassinate the Tsar; and if this doubtless helped to fire his hostility to Tsarism, it might well also have fostered a distrust of terrorism as a means of achieving structural change. Already at school he had been introduced to Marxism, and he soon became a fervent disciple. His law studies were scarcely interrupted by a period of banishment for trouble-making at Kazan University, and in 1891 he was admitted to the bar. But after making little more than the gesture of starting a law practice in Samara, he devoted himself to revolutionary politics. Moving to St Petersburg, he organized study circles for workers and came to know Nadezhda Krupskaya, who was teaching at an evening school for adults. Then, in 1895, he fell ill and obtained leave from the authorities to go abroad for his health. At Geneva he met the leaders of Russian Social Democracy in exile – Plekhanov, Axelrod and Vera Zasulich, who had established the Emancipation of Labour Group.

He returned with the hollow bottom of his suitcase full of illicit literature and his head full of plans for a newspaper. But the conspirators were betrayed by one of their number and arrested just before the first issue of the *Workers' Cause* was due to appear. In prison he wrote leaflets and pamphlets invisibly in milk: making his ink-pots out of bread and swallowing them as soon as he heard a rattle at the grating of his cell. Confidently he told his sister Anna that there was no cunning in the world which still greater cunning could not outwit.[1] He was sentenced to exile in Siberia. Krupskaya, herself exiled, subsequently received permission to join him. They were married soon afterwards.

When, in February 1900, his term of exile ended, he went to live at Pskov. And there, in the summer, a secret meeting of Marxists decided that Lenin, along with Martov and Potresov, two of his colleagues, should go abroad, to publish, in collaboration with the leading Social Democratic émigrés, a paper that would be smuggled into Russia.

The ensuing negotiations between the three older revolutionaries and the three newly arrived younger ones encountered difficulties from the beginning. Plekhanov and Axelrod wanted the paper published somewhere in Switzerland, so that they could be concerned in its immediate manage-ment. But Lenin, seeking a secret centre for revolutionary organization, held out for Munich, where he had settled along with his two colleagues. And in the end he had his way, probably because the three older revolution-aries were not yet convinced that the project had much of a future. It was decided that all six would compose the editorial board, and that matters in dispute would be duly determined by a vote.

The paper was to be named *Iskra*, or the *Spark*, in allusion to the poem by Pushkin ('From the spark the flame will flare'); while a companion periodical, called *Zarya*, or *Dawn*, would deal with questions of theory. A leaflet, written by Lenin and published by the editorial board in September 1900, outlined the policy to be pursued. It urged the formation of a strong Russian Social Democratic Labour Party, with whose manifesto of 1898 it expressed itself in entire agreement. But for this, unity was needed, and unity could not be produced by simply giving orders or passing resolu-tions. A unity of ideas, fortified by a corresponding party programme and by an organization to connect all elements of the movement, had to be achieved; and to achieve it, the two papers would lend their columns to 'open polemics'.[2]

Krupskaya became editorial secretary and her husband's crucial collab-orator in constructing an organization around *Iskra*. The arrangements for smuggling the paper into Russia and distributing it there from reliable centres of support were firmly in her hands; it was she who conducted the correspondence, with messages written in invisible ink between the lines of otherwise innocent letters. Then, early in 1902, the hospitality of Munich turned cold: the printer was refusing to run any longer the risks involved, and another was not to be found. Plekhanov and Axelrod argued again for Switzerland. But Lenin, more than ever valuing the separation from them, proposed London and won support from the three other members of the editorial board. In April, he and Krupskaya, under the names of Mr and Mrs Richter, moved into two rooms at 30 Holford Square, north of the Euston Road: a convenient distance from both the Reading Room of the British Museum and the grave of Karl Marx in Highgate Cemetery.

By the time that Trotsky arrived in October, the smell of burned paper, from the correspondence that Krupskaya heated over the fire to read, was well established in the rooms. That very morning or the next, Lenin took him for a long walk, pointing out the sights with curt comments and meanwhile closely examining Trotsky on his opinions and experiences. They discussed the need for a centralized organization; Trotsky's pam-phlet on the subject; the disputes between Marxists and Populists in the exile communities of Siberia. It was agreed that Trotsky should stay abroad for a while, to familiarize himself with the work of *Iskra*, before slipping back into Russia.

Krupskaya found him lodgings a few blocks away from Holford Square, in a house where Vera Zasulich, Martov, and Blumenfeld (a compositor transformed into the publisher of *Iskra*) occupied rooms one above the other, and shared a fourth, in constant disorder, for coffee and talk.

Even Trotsky must have staggered a little in the first blast of Vera Ivanovna's personality. However he might have previously pictured to himself the romantic heroine of the Trepov shooting and subsequent trial, it could scarcely have matched this slippered, shuffling woman who smoked constantly and dropped the ash or stubs of her hand-rolled cigarettes indifferently in all directions; who had a passion for mustard and would take a pair of scissors to clip off the pieces of meat that she ate on her own; who was so lonely and looked so longingly, out of dark, deep-set eyes, for someone to cherish and protect. She must have surrounded Trotsky at once with her care, and he was to respond with an affection that survived all the differences between them.

He soon enough discovered that there were serious conflicts, of outlook and purpose and personality, within the *Iskra* board. Lenin had little time for the moral simplicities and mental confusion of Vera Ivanovna. But it was with Plekhanov that he had his most bitter disputes. Georgi Plekhanov, born in 1857 of an old noble family, enjoyed a European renown as a writer and the foremost of the Russian Marxists. He had taught many of them and was willing enough to teach more. But he now sat so high that those Russian workers who managed to surmount the difficulties of getting to see him found the air there so thin that they could scarcely breathe. They would come away much impressed by the grandeur of his mind, but with their questions unasked and their own experiences untold. He was losing touch and must have known it, but that only made him the more impatient and peevish.

And now this Lenin, who had not so long ago been a deferential pupil, was confidently pushing his own ideas of how to make a revolution in Russia. The man could not even write, Plekhanov decided, 'in the sense that the French use the term'.[3] Yet this had not stopped Lenin from putting his own stamp on the unexpectedly successful *Iskra* venture. It was in part from an indignant uncertainty that Plekhanov had taken to treating Lenin with a certain disdain, and the idea that *Iskra* was the plough of revolutionary organization, with a manifest scepticism.

'George,' Vera Ivanovna said to Lenin one day, 'is a greyhound. He shakes and shakes the adversary and lets him go. But you are a bulldog: you have a deadly bite.' Lenin took this as a tribute, repeating it with delight. This strength of his was highly strung. His disagreements with Plekhanov would so disturb him that he could not sleep at night.[4] But it was a strength that never snapped. Sometimes the dissension threatened to disrupt the whole venture. Lenin would allow himself to be pacified by

Martov, while Plekhanov was pacified by Vera Ivanovna. But it was Lenin's strength and Plekhanov's weakness that ultimately avoided the consequences of a break.

All was not well, either, between Lenin and his two editorial allies. Potresov, broad-shouldered and red-cheeked, with a neatly trimmed beard, was to prove historically the least significant of the six. Loyally he voted with Lenin in the disputes on the board. But it seems to have been a loyalty much strained. In his memoirs, he was to recall Lenin's inability to bear opinions that conflicted with his own, so that the slightest disagreement affected their personal relations: 'Frequently my editorial colleagues and I felt out of place in our own newspaper office.'[5] And, indeed, as Martov and Potresov would come to discover, Krupskaya, on Lenin's orders, no longer showed them copies of all the correspondence with Russia. For Lenin was drawing away even from Martov, who had long been his closest colleague after Krupskaya herself.

Jules Martov, whose real name was Tzederbaum, came from a family of distinguished Jewish scholars. As a St Petersburg worker, who met him in 1903, was to describe him:

His face was pale, he had sunken cheeks; his scant beard was untidy. His glasses barely remained on his nose. His suit hung on him as on a clothes hanger. Manuscripts and pamphlets protruded from all his pockets. He was stooped; one of his shoulders was higher than the other. He had a stutter. . . . But as soon as he began a fervent speech all these outer faults seemed to vanish, and what remained was his colossal knowledge, his sharp mind, and his fanatical devotion to the cause of the working class.[6]

It was Martov who had first conceived the project for an independent organization of Jewish workers that had become the Bund. But he had then discarded his own concept for that of an integrated Russian revolutionary movement. He and Lenin had got to know and to like each other in St Petersburg. Now he was the mainstay of *Iskra*'s journalism. He always had news, as though it fastened on him as he passed, and he could produce suitable copy with such speed that he seemed to have been carrying it ready in one of his pockets. He was also a tireless talker; contentedly indifferent to the glazed look in the eyes of his listeners, as he continued to switch smoothly from one subject to another. Already in Munich, Lenin had asked him to stop his interminable visits, which so interfered with work, and had arranged that Krupskaya should call on him at his own lodgings when there was anything to report or discuss.

But Martov's talkativeness was no more than an irritant. It was his weakness that drove Lenin to despair. What was to be done with someone so devoted to the cause and so selfless, but who either could not distinguish the essential or would not fight sufficiently for it? Who might so easily waver and even concede on issues of substance, for the achievement of a meaningless peace? When Trotsky reached London, Lenin and Martov were still using the familiar 'thou' in Russian to each other, but the coolness between them was unmistakable.

Trotsky had no desire to explore the complex tensions within the *Iskra* leadership. He got on well enough with Lenin. And he was moved by the affectionate regard of Vera Ivanovna and Martov, with whom he took most of his meals and shared the smoke-hugged disorder of the common room. Besides, he had much to occupy his mind. He gave a public lecture in Whitechapel and emerged triumphant from a confrontation with the doyens of the Russian émigré community, who opposed the Marxist drift of the challenge to Tsarism. He attended one Sunday, with Lenin and Krupskaya, a meeting of English Social Democrats at a church, where passages were read from the Bible, and the congregation rose to sing, 'Lord Almighty, let there be no more kings or rich men'. (Krupskaya, presumably writing of the same incident, recalled that the hymn was: 'Lead us, O Lord, from the Kingdom of Capitalism into the Kingdom of Socialism'.) Trotsky could hardly believe his ears. English socialism, he soon decided, was not interesting. He was introduced to the Reading Room of the British Museum and feasted on the books there. Above all, he involved himself in *Iskra*, studying past issues and shamefully feeling his ignorance. His first piece for the paper closed with a reference to the 'invincible hands' that the revolution was laying on Tsarism: a phrase taken from the *Iliad*. Lenin was unimpressed by the provenance of the words, and the article appeared without them.

Whether it was this contribution or a subsequent one that Lenin sent to him, Plekhanov commented: 'I don't like the pen of your "Pen".' Lenin replied: 'The style is merely a matter of acquisition, but the man is capable of learning and will be very useful.' Plekhanov was not to be misled. He did not share the enthusiasm of his colleagues for Trotsky. Vera Ivanovna spoke of the young man as a genius. But then, she was far too impressionable. And Lenin was unlikely to be backing him for any such reason. Was this not the beginning of an attempt to upset the uneasy balance of the *Iskra* board, with a seventh member who would vote with Lenin, Martov and Potresov; even perhaps draw Vera Ivanovna and Axelrod away from their proper loyalties? And to cap it all, the fellow was another Jew.

In a note of September 1900, on a discussion by the *Iskra* board, Lenin had recorded Plekhanov's 'phenomenal intolerance' on the subject of the Bund.

He said that our aim is to throw out this Bund from the party, that the Jews are all chauvinists and nationalists, that the Russian party ought to be Russian and not let itself be 'imprisoned' by the 'serpent-tribe' etc. . . . All attempts at contradicting this unfair talk was of no avail, and G.V. [Georgi Valentovich] stuck to his guns, maintaining that we simply lack the knowledge about Jewry and the vital experience of having come into contact with Jews.[7]

That Plekhanov should have spoken like that, in the presence of Axel-rod – Martov was not there – suggests the lengths to which his arrogance and insensitivity could carry him in the pronouncement of his prejudices. Perhaps Axelrod had grown accustomed to such outbursts and was willing to suffer them for the services that Plekhanov had given, and might still give, to the cause. For Plekhanov himself, Axelrod was a friend, after all, and by definition, therefore, not a Jew. The same could not be said of Martov. But Martov was becoming tolerable enough. There were always exceptions. Trotsky, now, was another matter. He was flamboyant, thrust-ing, and insidious: an unmistakable Jew.

Trotsky himself was gradually to discover the extent of this antagonism. At their very first meeting, in the common room of the house in London, he caught 'a suspicion of hidden impatience' under Plekhanov's gracious-ness and went away 'with a dissatisfied and irritated feeling'.[8] But he prob-ably put the matter from his mind with the thought that he might, after the warmth of his reception by the others, have been expecting too much. And despite Plekhanov's criticism, which Lenin probably kept to himself, Trotsky continued to write for the paper; progressing to articles and even the occasional editorial.

After the success of his public lecture in Whitechapel, he was sent to speak in Paris, where different revolutionary groups were in fervent con-flict for the allegiance of the large Russian student colony. And it was there that he met, in the house where lodging had been found for him, a Russian student of art, Natalia Sedova. Expelled from her boarding school in Kharkov for having instigated her classmates to absent themselves from prayers and to read radical literature instead of the Bible, she was now enrolled at the Sorbonne. She was much taken with the young man but reported anxiously to her diary that whenever she passed his door, he was whistling instead of working on his lecture. The apparent lack of applica-tion proved no handicap: his lecture 'exceeded all expectations'. She guided him around the art galleries. He was unimpressed. Paris, he judged, was very like Odessa, except that Odessa was better. They fell in love. Thirty-two years later, Trotsky would recall, with painful joy, their early days together:

One night we came home from the Paris Opéra to the *rue* Gassendi, 46, *au pas gymnastique*, holding hands. It was in 1903. Our combined age was 46. . . . Once, while a whole crowd of us were walking somewhere in the outskirts of Paris, we came to a bridge. A steep cement pier sloped down from a great height. Two small boys had climbed on to the pier over the parapet of the bridge and were looking down on the passers-by. Suddenly N. started climbing toward them up the steep smooth slope of the pier. I was petrified. I didn't think it was possible to climb up there. But she kept walking up with her graceful stride, on high heels, smiling to the boys. They waited for her with interest. We all stopped anxiously. N. went all the way up without looking at us, talked to the children, and came down the same way, without having made, as far as one could see, a single superfluous effort or taken a single uncertain step. . . .[9]

At some time during his stay in Paris, Trotsky's parents came abroad to see him and make their peace. If this did not involve any new understanding of his commitments, nor certainly any retreat by him from his own, it does seem to have tightened the family relationship. The Bronsteins undertook to help Sokolovskaya take care of Trotsky's children in Russia.

In March 1903, Lenin wrote to Plekhanov, proposing that Trotsky be co-opted on to the editorial board. He argued that the appointment of a seventh member was very much needed, both to end the inconvenience of even splits in the voting and to augment the resources of the paper. Trotsky was 'a man of rare abilities', with 'conviction and energy'. There were, to be sure, three possible objections: his youth; his likely departure for Russia soon; and his 'excessively florid' style.

But experience and knowledge would come with time. If Trotsky were appointed, he would not leave so soon; and, when he did, his organized connection would prove of enormous advantage. He would outgrow his defects of style and, as a member of the board, would accept correction rather more readily.

The appointment required a unanimous decision. A few days later Martov wrote to Axelrod unreservedly supporting Lenin's proposal. Vera Ivanovna, Potresov and Axelrod also agreed. But Plekhanov was adamant in his opposition. The board then voted that Trotsky should be invited to attend editorial meetings in an advisory role. Plekhanov objected to this, too. But Vera Ivanovna announced, 'I'll bring him, no matter what you say.' And bring him she did, to the next meeting, where Trotsky was greeted by Plekhanov with 'studied coldness'.

The differences within the board were becoming sharper and more frequent. Plekhanov and Axelrod again pressed that *Iskra* be shifted to Switzerland, and this time Lenin was alone in voting against the proposal. His anxieties and disappointments surfaced in a tormenting inflammation of the nerve-endings along his back and chest. Krupskaya, without the money to spare for more professional advice, consulted a medical handbook and painted him with iodine, 'which caused him agonizing pain'. When he reached Geneva in April, he suffered a breakdown that kept him in bed for a fortnight. But he could not afford the luxury of a long convalescence.

On the initiative of *Iskra*, a secret committee had been established in Russia the previous November, to prepare for the second congress of the

Russian Social Democratic Labour Party. And in the early summer, delegates from various clandestine Russian groups began arriving at Geneva, to join the leading émigrés, before the general movement to Brussels where the congress was to open on 30 July 1903. Trotsky himself was to represent the Siberian Union.

The delegates had been instructed to report in Brussels at the lodgings of a certain Koltsov. But after four Russians had appeared on her doorstep, the landlady decided that she had had enough and told the Koltsovs that they would have to go if any more such visitors arrived. Koltsov's wife was forced to stand at the corner all day, to accost likely delegates and send them on to the Belgian Social Democratic Party hotel, somewhat curiously called the Coq d'Or. There the Russians gathered in noisy groups and were soon, it seems, suitably at ease. One of them, clutching a glass of cognac, would sing operatic arias every evening with such vigour that crowds collected beneath the windows. According to Krupskaya, Lenin much enjoyed the performances and in particular the song, 'We were wedded out of church. . . .'

The opening session took place in the storeroom of a co-operative society. No sooner had the meeting been called to order than the delegates started to fidget and squirm. Without proper credentials but attracted by the proceedings none the less, a multitude of fleas had emerged from the neighbouring bales of wool, to participate in their own way. Nor were they the only ones to take an unwelcome interest. Detectives shadowed the delegates, several of whom were soon ordered to leave the country within twenty-four hours. The congress was transferred to London.

There, the delegates were unmolested by the authorities. Indeed, a policeman was placed on duty outside the trade union hall where the congress was meeting, to prevent further attacks after a juvenile gang had pelted delegates with wet paper missiles. Edwardian London was not accustomed to the sight of foreigners continuing to conduct their debates, at the tops of their voices and with passionate gesticulations, in the street.

But all this was no more than a glimmering of farce at the edge of momentous events. For the congress that had been convened to unite and quicken the party around a clear and constructive programme was to be the occasion of a split that would survive into the revolution and beyond.

Dominating the early sessions was the issue of the Bund, affiliated to the party, but more and more concerned to preserve and develop its own identity. At its third conference, in 1900, the Bund had limited its political claims to 'civil, not national, equality of rights' for Jews. Then, at its fourth, in the following year, it had switched signals: it declared that Russia would need to be reconstituted as a federation of nations, with the Jewish people as one of them, and possessed of no less autonomy than the others. In part, this was an attempt by the Bund to arrest, with a nationalist appeal of its own, the spread of support for Zionism among Jewish workers. But Jewish nationalism itself was attracting recruits from the ranks of the Bund, in response to the anti-Semitic policies of the regime, and to the apparent indifference with which even professing liberals in Russia had regarded recent pogroms.

Martov, on behalf of the *Iskra* board, initiated the assault on the Bund's attitude: he tabled a resolution which urged 'the closest unity of the Jewish proletariat with the proletariat of those races amongst whom it lives . . . in the interests of its struggle for political and economic eman-cipation and for the social democratic struggle against all chauvinism and anti-Semitism'. But it was Trotsky who rose again and again in the debate to batter the arguments of the Bund: beating down all attempts to reach a compromise and proclaiming, to the fury of delegates from the Bund, that the twelve 'Jewish comrades' who had signed Martov's resolution, 'while working in the All-Russian party, regarded and still regard themselves also as representatives of the Jewish proletariat'.

For the delegates of the Bund, Trotsky might well have seemed to be assailing the rights of Jewish nationalism with a suspicious ardour. And, to be sure, the Jewish anti-Semite was not unknown in revolutionary record. But Trotsky was never to betray that peculiar moral astigmatism that saw no justification for the nationalism of the Jew while seeing clearly enough how to defend the nationalism of the Russian, or anyone else. For him all nationalism was a denial of the revolutionary commitment to unite mankind in a socialist brotherhood.

He had, he declared at the congress, no wish to destroy the Bund. He wished only to destroy any special position for it in the party. Were Jews alone to be entitled to agitate and organize among Jewish workers? Were non-Jewish members of the party to be accordingly excluded? 'To accept such conditions would mean that we acknowledge the bankruptcy of our political morality; it would mean committing political–moral suicide. The congress will not do this.'[10] And the congress would not. There were forty-three delegates, disposing of fifty-one votes. The Bund had five deleg-ates with voting rights. Martov's resolution was carried by forty votes to five, with some abstentions.

It was a stirring salute to the overriding objective of unity before the outbreak of civil war. The commission responsible for drafting the party statute was unable to agree and presented two different texts for the article on membership. The version pressed by Lenin declared: 'A member of the party is one who accepts its programme, and supports it both materially and by personal participation in one of its organizations.' The other, pressed by Martov, proposed instead: 'A member of the Russian Social Democratic Labour Party is one who accepts its programme and supports it both materially and by regular co-operation under the leadership of one of its organizations.' The difference might, to an outsider, have appeared slight. To the delegates, it involved vitally diverging views of the relationship that should exist between a revolutionary party and the revolutionary populace. Lenin sought a small party of disciplined revolutionaries, the tried and reliable representatives of the proletarian cause. Martov, while recognizing that some such organization was needed, maintained that it could thrive only in the soil of a mass party. And moving through the thicket of the argument, sometimes as no more than a rustle, sometimes leaping suddenly into sight, was the ultimate question: how democratic could the revolutionary engagement afford to be?

Plekhanov, the chairman of the congress, was allied with Lenin in the leadership of the 'hard' line. At one session, in a speech that he was later most bitterly to regret, he defended Lenin's insistence that 'the dictatorship of the proletariat' must encompass the suppression of all social movements that directly or indirectly threatened 'the interests of the proletariat'. The success of the revolution, he proclaimed, was the supreme law. 'If the people, in a surge of revolutionary enthusiasm, should elect a good parliament, we should endeavour to make it a long parliament. If the elections miscarry, we should try to disperse it, not in two years, but in two weeks.' Some delegates hissed; others applauded.

According to Krupskaya, 'Lenin himself at that time least of all thought that Trotsky would waver.'[11] And Trotsky did, indeed, not waver: he decisively abandoned Lenin, to support Martov. Increasingly he had come to fear that Lenin sought a personal domination of the party. But how much this fear had been fed by other, personal considerations, he would doubtless have been hard put to say.

Before the congress opened, Lenin had proposed, as part of the party reorganization to be sanctioned there, that the *Iskra* editorial board and the central committee charged with directing party work inside Russia should each consist of three members only. He had apparently encountered no objections in principle.[12] But when Martov was required to face the removal of Axelrod, Potresov and Vera Ivanovna from the *Iskra* board, he could not bring himself to do so.

Trotsky also rebelled. Was this the way to treat those who had given so much to the cause of Social Democracy? Was he himself now to turn on those who had welcomed him with so much affection and trust? And for the triumph of a Plekhanov who had shown him only prejudice and scorn? True, Lenin had been kind, if never warm. But that he should now be hugging Plekhanov in sudden alliance, after the indignant lengths to which their quarrelling had gone, suggested a will to personal power that flouted all principle.

The alliance was certainly a curious one. But then each of the partners had reason to be satisfied with what it promised. As Plekhanov had come to recognize, Lenin's command of communication with the movement in Russia and his apparent ability to express their ideas as though he were reading their minds had drawn many delegates behind him. The organizational control of the party, it had been virtually decided, was to reside in a council of five; with two members nominated by the board of *Iskra*; two by the central committee; and a president chosen by the biennial congress. With Lenin's backing, Plekhanov was bound to become president; and as a member of the *Iskra* triumvirate also, would surely be in an unassailable position. Lenin had made his own political calculations. With an *Iskra* board of three, the voting deadlock would be broken; and Martov would be unlikely to support Plekhanov against him, if the present partnership failed to last. But, above all, with Plekhanov at his side, he stood far more chance of securing the centralized party that he sought.

He was not flouting principle: on the contrary, he was simply relentless in serving it. The constructing of an effective revolutionary organization allowed no room for sentiment or personal claims. He was genuinely astonished and distressed that Trotsky, of all people, should not appreciate this. At one session, he made an open personal appeal for his support. Trotsky remained hostile. Accompanied by Krasikov, another delegate, Lenin took Trotsky for a long walk. But Krasikov's abuse of the other *Iskra* editors only succeeded in strengthening Trotsky's resolve. A meeting of those delegates directly associated with *Iskra* was called, to patch up some agreement, and Trotsky was elected chairman. Tempers flared and Lenin walked out, banging the door behind him. A last attempt to win Trotsky over, made by Lenin's brother, devoured several hours of argument in the park, to no other purpose.

Plekhanov's abrasive partiality in presiding only aggravated the difficulties of reaching a compromise. On one occasion, when he had all too audibly remarked, 'Horses don't talk, but asses are unfortunately doing so now,' Trotsky proposed to Krupskaya that Lenin take the chair, 'or else Plekhanov will bring things to a split'. But Plekhanov would never have retired willingly, and given the value that he placed on their new alliance, Lenin would not consider ousting him. There was no help for it: the delegates had to decide between the two texts presented for the membership clause. Lenin's draft was defeated by twenty-eight votes to twenty-three; Martov's carried by twenty-eight to twenty-two, with one abstention. The article establishing the party council was then accepted without fuss. But this brought no more than an uneasy lull.

The delegates of the Bund had remained at the congress after their initial defeat, to press their demand for a special, effectively federal association with the party. Their demand was defeated, and they withdrew at the end of the twenty-seventh session. At the twenty-eighth, the congress voted to recognize the League of Russian Revolutionary Social Democrats Abroad, which Lenin represented, as the sole organization of émigrés inside the party; and the two delegates from the Union of Russian Social Democrats Abroad, rejected for its attachment to the heresy of Economism, lost their votes. Lenin, in consequence of the stand taken towards the Bund and towards Economism by his own opponents, now commanded a majority in the congress.

As it became evident that he intended to press his advantage, and in particular to get his way on the issue of the *Iskra* board, the delegates were seized by a passion of acrimony. They exchanged personal insults. Krupskaya was to remember one of them, being upbraided by Axelrod, silent in tears. Martov accused Lenin of wishing to introduce 'martial law within the party', on the basis of 'exceptional laws against individual groups'. Lenin replied that he was not frightened by such phrases. 'In dealing with unstable and warring elements we not only can, but are bound to, set up "martial law". . . . Against political indiscipline special, even exceptional, laws are required. . . .'

The decision to elect three members of the *Iskra* editorial board was taken by twenty-five votes to two, with seventeen abstentions.[13] The majority then elected Plekhanov, Lenin and Martov to the board; three secondary figures, all followers of the Lenin line, to the central committee; and Plekhanov to the presidency. The defeated announced that they would have nothing to do with the new order; and Martov himself refused his seat on the board. Each faction was already meeting separately, and was soon to acquire its own name: the victors called Bolsheviks (from *bolshintsvo*, the Russian word for 'majority'); the defeated, Mensheviks (from *menshintsvo*, the Russian word for 'minority').

Looking back at the congress, the principal participants could scarcely believe that they should have driven their differences so far. Lenin himself, in a letter to Potresov shortly afterwards, wrote:

And now I am asking myself: for what reason should we part to become lifelong enemies? . . . I am aware that often I acted and behaved in terrible irritation, 'madly', and I am willing to admit this my guilt to anybody – if one can call guilt something that was naturally caused by the atmosphere, the reactions, the retorts, the struggle. . . .

Yet no amount of regret in the morning, for what had been said and done in the 'madness' of the night before, was enough to produce a retreat by either side. The Mensheviks met at Geneva in September, to formulate a policy. Martov and Trotsky were agreed on the need for reconciliation; but never at the price of surrender. The delegates adopted a statement which committed them to pursue the struggle, but to avoid placing themselves outside the party or acting so as to bring discredit upon it. A 'bureau' or shadow central committee was elected: of Martov, Axelrod, Potresov, Dan and Trotsky.

But if Bolshevism and Menshevism continued to confront each other, this did not mean that even a leader remained the captive of his side. And Plekhanov, tasting his triumph, had found it sour. He was now isolated from those with whom he had worked for so long, whose infirmities he had come to regard with a certain indulgence, and whose outlook on so many matters of importance he shared. In the face of Lenin's furious protests that he had no right to flout the decisions of a party congress, he invited Axelrod, Martov, Vera Ivanovna and Potresov to rejoin the editorial board of *Iskra*. Lenin resigned, and the four Mensheviks returned, bringing along with them, much to Plekhanov's displeasure, that bumptious Trotsky.

Iskra at once became the main weapon of Menshevism in a campaign against Lenin. Plekhanov, in an article entitled 'Centralism or Bonapartism?', accused him of 'confusing the dictatorship of the proletariat with the dictatorship over the proletariat'. Vera Ivanovna wrote that Louis XIV's idea of the state was Lenin's view of the party. Trotsky assailed Lenin's character and policies in the pages of the paper. But his most powerful indictment was contained in his pamphlet, *Our Political Tasks*, which carried the dedication 'To my dear teacher Paul Borisovich Axelrod'.

Here, he belaboured Lenin mercilessly: describing him as another Robespierre, except that his 'malicious and morally repulsive suspiciousness' was 'a flat caricature of the tragic Jacobin intolerance'. Such vituperation, however, merely decorated, and came dangerously close to disguising, the structure of serious thought beneath. What Lenin sought, Trotsky argued, was an 'orthodox theocracy', with a party that did not represent but substituted itself for the proletariat. And this was not the end of the matter. 'Lenin's methods lead to this: the party organization at first substitutes itself for the party as a whole; then the central committee substitutes itself for the organization; and finally a single "dictator" substitutes himself for the central committee. . . .'

The truth was that Lenin distrusted the masses, as Robespierre had distrusted them; and that, like Robespierre, therefore, he was an essentially bourgeois politician rather than a revolutionary socialist. 'A Jacobin tribunal would have tried under the charge of moderation the whole international labour movement, and Marx's lion head would have been the first to roll under the guillotine.' Lenin and his followers pressed for a uniform party. But a revolutionary regime would be confronted by problems so complex that they could be solved only 'by way of a competition between various methods of economic and political construction, by way of long "disputes", by way of a systematic struggle . . . between many trends inside socialism'. They could not be solved 'by placing above the proletariat a few well-picked people . . . or one person invested with the power to liquidate and degrade'.

Trotsky's attacks on Lenin in the pages of *Iskra* had already gone too far for some readers in Russia, whose protests provided Plekhanov with occasion to insist that Trotsky's role on the paper be reduced. He was generally confined to supplying more or less marginal comments. But Plekhanov remained unappeased and, in the middle of March 1904, taking particular exception to an article by Trotsky on the war that had broken out between Russia and Japan, he declared that he would resign from the board if *Iskra* continued to publish Trotsky's contributions.

The other editors were unwilling to part with so valued a colleague for no other reason than that Plekhanov demanded it, and resented this attempt to make them the instruments of a personal spite. Besides, they had passed the offending article for publication themselves, so that they would be censuring their own judgement by submitting to Plekhanov's displeasure. Trotsky offered to go, suggesting that it was time he returned to underground work in Russia. They persuaded him to stay. It was an affront which Plekhanov had not expected and considered intolerable. He carried out his threat and resigned. This concentrated wonderfully the minds of the four other editors. A Plekhanov who on his own had snatched *Iskra* for Menshevism might employ his powers to snatch it back. Trotsky found himself suddenly deserted.

Nor was this by any means the only source of his estrangement from leading Mensheviks. Vera Ivanovna and Theodore Dan, whose grey temperament Trotsky found increasingly distasteful, were looking to an alliance with middle-class liberalism against the Tsarist regime. But this was an alliance that for Trotsky, then and always, could be concluded only at the grave-side of the socialist commitment. That it was being contemplated at all, by any Mensheviks of prominence, was bad enough. Far worse, it reflected a spreading disposition to accept the split in the party as permanent and concentrate on promoting the particular authority of Menshevism.

It was a disposition that Trotsky regarded as the more perverse at a time when Lenin seemed so isolated. The leading intellectual paper of German Social Democracy, *Neue Zeit*, had refused to publish Lenin's view of the split. His Russian followers were falling away, and the Bolshevik central committee itself had moved to make its peace with the Mensheviks. Trotsky urged his Menshevik colleagues to unite with those Bolsheviks ready to turn their backs on Lenin. He encountered only suspicion and hostility. What? Unite with the Bolsheviks now, when the engine-room of the party was in Menshevik possession? Risk defeat and dispossession at another congress? The young man was unreliable: he had never really accepted the principles of Menshevism. He was virtually a Bolshevik himself.

In September 1904, Trotsky announced his formal secession from the Mensheviks, in an 'Open Letter to Comrades' which he sent to *Iskra* for publication and which was rejected. It essentially accused the Mensheviks of placing their sectional preoccupations above the interests of the party. Those Mensheviks who saw some truth in the accusation were scarcely less antagonized than those who saw none. But there were few willing to welcome Trotsky's departure. Even among such as had inveighed against him most harshly for meddling with the issue of reconciliation, there was now a marked respect for the power of his pen. And others, in particular Martov, were themselves less than happy with the drift of Menshevism. A conference convened at Geneva agreed temporarily to disband the Menshevik organization abroad, and Trotsky was soon contributing a political notebook to the back pages of *Iskra*. But the marriage was beyond saving by the mere decision that each of the partners should give the other one more chance. In fact, the Menshevik organization abroad continued to function, and Trotsky to argue against it.

Meanwhile, Lenin was working against reconciliation in his own single-minded way. A long pamphlet, *One Step Forward, Two Steps Back*, assailed Menshevism as the spritual heir of that same 'aristocratic anarchism' which had produced the Russian nihilist. In August 1904, the very month in which Trotsky's own pamphlet, denouncing him and all his works, appeared, with a preface that pressed for the reconciliation of all reasonable Bolsheviks and Mensheviks, Lenin met in Geneva with twenty-two of his followers. Together they established a new Bolshevik central organization. And by the end of the year, Lenin had founded a paper, *Vperyod (Forward)*, to take the place of the *Iskra* he had lost. In April 1905, simply ignoring the old central institutions of the party, he held with his supporters a new congress in London; while the Mensheviks met on their own in Geneva. Repeatedly he made his demand to all who would listen: 'everywhere and most decisively schism, schism, schism'.[14] He wanted a united party, yes; but a party united only around his policies, with all heretics, or anyone willing to wink at heresies, excommunicated.

Meanwhile, Trotsky had found one close intellectual ally and friend in Alexander Helphand, a Russian Jew living in Germany, who enjoyed a considerable reputation as an economist and writer of the Marxist school. Helphand contributed frequently to the leading socialist periodicals of Europe; and his articles for *Iskra*, which he signed at first as Molotov and then as Parvus, were accorded a respectful prominence. He, too, like Trotsky, peered into immediate events so as to catch the glimmer of those to come; as early as 1895, he had predicted war between Russia and Japan, with revolution as the aftermath. He, too, urged reconciliation now between Bolshevik and Menshevik; though never having assailed the first or associated himself with the second as vigorously as Trotsky had done, he met with much less hostility, if no more success. It was with him that Trotsky went to stay, at Munich, in those gloomy months between April and September 1904.

Trotsky was not one to repudiate a debt because the creditor had become disreputable. And long after Helphand – or Parvus, as he came generally to be known – had betrayed the revolutionary principles and beliefs for which he had once claimed to stand, Trotsky did more than pay tribute to his 'wide vision', his 'fearless thinking', his 'virile, muscular style'. He acknowledged a service which could scarcely have been more vital. 'His early studies brought me closer to the problems of the Social Revolution, and, for me, definitely transformed the conquest of power by the proletariat from an astronomical "final" goal to a practical task for our own day.'[15]

The ideas that so influenced Trotsky were contained in a series of articles by Parvus on 'War and Revolution' published in *Iskra* from February 1904 onwards. These proclaimed that the nation-state, as a product of capitalist development, was now under sentence of death; and that the war between Russia and Japan was the first in a succession by which such states would be driven, through capitalist competition, to fight one another for survival. Russia, confronted in the west by the pressures of more developed societies, had sought in a thrust to the east both a countervailing aggrandizement and a distraction from the internal difficulties gathering around the regime. Having inevitably clashed in the process with the imperial aspirations of Japan, she was involved in a conflict which threatened not only her own position, but the precarious balance of power, everywhere. A political upheaval at home was bound to follow, which would 'shake the bourgeois world'. And by its leading role in producing this upheaval, the Russian proletariat might well prove in effect the advance guard of that victorious uprising against capitalism in the industrialized societies.

This prospect of a more or less imminent world revolution, fired by events in Russia, was one of which Trotsky's mind took immediate delivery. But it did not simply lie there, a parcel of unsorted ideas, ready for redispatch to others. Some of the ideas, Trotsky would elaborate; others, discard. In particular, he was to give the Russian proletariat an impact abroad still more momentous than that visualized by Parvus. It was to be the advance guard of the world revolution not merely by its leading role in producing a popular upheaval, but by being the first to conquer power for itself.

4

Insurrection

The Kaiser had suggested to the Tsar that Russia's historical mission lay in Asia rather than in Europe. And Nicholas II, though not quite so foolish as to suppose the advice of Wilhelm II to be altogether disinterested, was none the less encouraged to discover his sense of destiny in the east. Unhappily, however, Japan had already come to believe in a historical mission of her own, and could scarcely be expected to transplant it from Asia to Europe for the convenience of Russia. Britain at least was sufficiently aware of Japan's industrial and military muscle to have concluded, early in 1902, an alliance with her. But in the dark recesses of the Russian autocracy, where reports of the real world could only enter on their knees, the whispers of his latest favourites assured the Tsar of his invincible mission. Japanese efforts to secure an agreement with Russia over respective spheres of plunder were blocked by the war party at the palace; and Russia broke her undertaking, made in the briefly agitated wake of the Anglo-Japanese treaty, to withdraw her troops from Manchuria. In late January 1904, Japanese forces attacked the Russian fleet at Port Arthur.

V. K. von Plehve, Minister of the Interior, had fostered the war policy in the hope of fortifying the throne with a passion of patriotism, and initially he was not to be disappointed. Outside the silent multitudes of the peasantry, concerned with the war only as an increase in the requirements for military service, and the still marginal revolutionary movement, there was a general rallying to the flag. In particular, the liberals hastened to make their peace with a regime that seemed bound to emerge from victory over Japan with its prestige much enhanced. But domestic discontent was soon rekindled by a series of serious Russian reverses at the front. So convinced had been the war party that Japan would never dare to attack, that it had pursued its policy of provocation even before the main supply line of the Trans-Siberian railway was complete. Within a few months, Japan had isolated the garrison at Port Arthur and immobilized the fleet there, by destroyer patrols and mine-fields; had split the Russian land-forces and deprived those in Manchuria of adequate supplies.

In July, Plehve himself was blown to pieces by a Social Revolutionary bomb. The Tsar, persuaded that the regime now needed public as well as divine support, appointed the moderate Governor of Vilna, Prince P. D. Svyatopolk-Mirsky, to the vacant post. The new minister lifted restrictions imposed on some liberal leaders; eased censorship of the press and, outside of the continuing engagement with revolutionaries, curbed the activities of the political police. But this, with news of further reverses at the front, only promoted demands for serious reform. At St Petersburg in November, 100 members of the *zemstvos*, or provincial and county councils, formulated a petition to the Tsar for the establishment of an elected representative body to participate in the passing of laws, the drafting of the budget, and control of the administration. Academics, lawyers, journalists, engineers held special banquets which resounded with demands for change. Svyatopolk-Mirsky pressed for substantial concessions, before discontent developed beyond the capacity of the regime to contain it. But the Tsar was adamant. His December edict promised such palliatives as state insurance for factory workers and more lenient treatment of ethnic and religious minorities. It also required an end to the meetings and manifestations that had been disturbing the peace of the realm. Prince Svyatopolk-Mirsky, faced with no alternative short of resigning, agreed to order the use of force against demonstrations in the streets. It was no time for the regime to suffer a disaster at the front. But within the first few days of 1905, the capital learned that Port Arthur had fallen to the Japanese.

The news from Russia had meanwhile been stirring hope in the revolutionaries abroad. And nowhere did such hope leap higher than in the imagination of Trotsky. He wrote a pamphlet on the banqueting campaign, in which he assailed the liberals for shunning the issue of universal suffrage and associating themselves with the war. They were hoping to strike a bargain with the Tsar. But the revolution would sweep them, together with the Tsar, aside. It would emerge from a general strike, with cries to end the war and elect a constituent assembly. He offered 'by and large . . . a plan of action'.

Tear the workers away from the machines and workshops; lead them through the factory gate out into the street; direct them to neighbouring factories; proclaim a stoppage there; and carry new masses into the street. Thus, moving from factory to factory, from workshop to workshop, growing under way and sweeping away police obstacles, haranguing and attracting passers-by, absorbing groups that come from the opposite direction, filling the streets, taking possession of the first suitable buildings for public meetings, entrenching yourselves in those buildings, using them for uninterrupted revolutionary meetings with a permanently shifting and changing audience, you shall bring order into the movement of the masses, raise their confidence, explain to them the purpose and the sense of events; and thus you shall eventually transform the city into a revolutionary camp. . . .

Yet the city could not make the revolution on its own. The countryside needed immediate agitation, to release the locked-in revolutionary potential of the peasant. And the peasant in the countryside was son, brother, cousin to the peasant in the barracks. The morale of the ranks in the army was already plunging, with the inadequacy of equipment, the widespread theft and corruption in the services of supply, the persistence of defeat. The soldier who would first reveal his disaffection by firing into the air would hand over his weapon to the worker when convinced that the people knew what they wanted and were able to fight for it.

Trotsky's 'plan of action' must be accounted one of the most remarkable prophetic visions in history. For not only did Trotsky define the form that revolt in 1905 and revolution in 1917 would, in fact, take, at a time when his fellow revolutionaries scarcely even looked beyond the fact to the form. He did so with a realization of detail that he would make no more vivid when subsequently describing the event.

The Menshevik publishers to whom he submitted the pamphlet, however, had no difficulty in containing their enthusiasm. Trotsky's assault on the liberals, increasingly seen as necessary allies, was sufficient cause of disquiet; without all that impudent anticipation of history. They delayed publication and perhaps in the end decided to delay no more only because Parvus, deeply impressed when he read the galley proofs, so invested his own prestige as to contribute a preface. Indeed, it was the preface that immediately excited most dispute, with the prediction that a revolutionary provisional government in Russia would be social democratic: the regime of a workers' democracy; though not yet, to be sure, of a proletarian dictatorship.

Even Lenin rejected the possibility as a harmful illusion, on the argument that the Russian proletariat, still such a minority of the population, would not be able so seriously to affect the character of a bourgeois revolution. And in a prophecy of his own, which was, like Trotsky's on Lenin's centralism, to return one day as a rebuke, he wrote: 'Whoever wants to approach socialism by any other path than that of political democracy will inevitably arrive at absurd and reactionary conclusions both economic and political.'[1]

Early in 1904, with Plehve's personal sanction, the St Petersburg police had surreptitiously encouraged the establishment of an 'Assembly of Russian Workers', under the leadership of a certain priest, Georgi Gapon. It was an attempt to counteract the propaganda and influence of revolutionaries, by providing a rival movement to express and to contain popular grievances. For the mood, especially among workers, was increasingly menacing. As the cost of living rose, and employers actually cut the rates of pay, real industrial wages fell between one-fifth and one-quarter from October 1903 to October 1904.

By the end of the year, the Assembly had attracted almost 9000 members and a following perhaps ten times as large. But the revolutionaries had infiltrated its ranks and were there spreading the agitation for radical reforms. Gapon himself came soon enough to accept the need for such reforms, but saw them as far more likely to emerge from an appeal to the Tsar's wisdom and love for his people than from a confrontation with the regime.

On 3 January 1905, the entire labour force of 12,500 at the massive Putilov Works came out on strike, in protest at the dismissal of four workers by an unpopular foreman. Disaffection blazed through the dry grass of the Assembly, and within four days some 90,000 workers in the capital were on strike. A proposal to petition the Tsar gathered overwhelming support, and developed from numerous mass meetings into the presentation of a virtual manifesto. Though phrased with customary deference, and decorated with expressions of loyalty, the final document asked for no less than 'the election of a constituent assembly on the basis of universal, secret and equal suffrage'.

On 8 January Gapon wrote to the Tsar:

Do not believe the Ministers. They are cheating You in regard to the real state of affairs. The people believe in You. They have made up their minds to gather at the Winter Palace tomorrow at 2 p.m. to lay their needs before You. . . . Do not fear anything. Stand tomorrow before the people and accept our humblest petition. I, the representative of the working men, and my comrades, guarantee the inviolability of Your person.

Whether or not the Tsar received the letter in time and disregarded the priest's assurances as both insolent and worthless, he had no intention of receiving a rabble at its own demand. Already apprised of the plans for a march to the Winter Palace, he removed himself and his family to his estate fifteen miles from the city; leaving Prince Svyatopolk-Mirsky and his aides to deal with the challenge.

On Sunday, 9 January (or 22 January in the Western calendar), a multitude of workers and their families moved through the streets of St Petersburg; singing religious and patriotic songs; carrying icons and portraits of the Tsar. At the great square before the Winter Palace, the marchers were stopped short by a barrier of troops. All at once, without warning, a company of Cossacks charged: cutting a way through the dense crowd with their swords till they emerged at the other side, to turn and cut their way back. Then the infantry began to fire. And once the square was cleared of all but the still bodies and bloodstains on the snow, troops advanced through the city, to disperse with bullets the crowds that gathered elsewhere. An official statement admitted to some 130 killed and more than 300 wounded. A group of journalists subsequently produced a list of 4600 casualties.[2]

The Tsar himself was shocked. This was not what he had intended. He personally contributed to the fund subsequently launched for the families of the dead and wounded. He even agreed to receive a deputation of workers, provided that 'sensible men were selected'. The authorities undertook the selection. And the 'sensible' were duly presented. The Tsar delivered a short lecture and then dismissed them for food and drink in the kitchens. He might as well have saved his hospitality and his time. Gapon's own account of 'Bloody Sunday', as it came to be called, contained the comment that more and more of the Tsar's previously respectful subjects were now making.

Suddenly, in the midst of my despair, somebody took hold of my arm and dragged me rapidly away into a small side street a few paces from the scene of the massacre. It was idle for me to protest. What more could be done? 'There is no longer any Tsar for us!' I exclaimed.[3]

Strikes, soon involving a million workers, silenced railways, factories and mines. Frightened employers conceded particular economic claims. But it was essentially a political rage that had seized the country. Professors at the University of St Petersburg, a group from the Academy of Sciences and various professional societies demanded the grant of representative government. Early in February, Grand Duke Serge Alexandrovich, Governor of Moscow and uncle of the Tsar, was assassinated in broad daylight at the Kremlin. The widow, Grand Duchess Elizabeth, visited the assassin in prison and promised to plead for his life, if he would only express sorrow for what he had done. Replying that his execution would be of more use to his cause, he refused.

Returning to Geneva from a lecture tour, Trotsky read, at the *Iskra* office, the first telegraphed report of the Winter Palace massacre. He decided to leave for Russia and, with Natalia Sedova, went first to Munich, where the couple stayed with Parvus. Each day seemed to bring fresh news of the gathering revolt at home. For Trotsky, it was the revolution arrived at last; and he greeted it in an essay, later published with others under the title *After the Petersburg Insurrection*, which was like a love song.

Yes, she has come. We have awaited her. We have never doubted her. For many years she was only a deduction from our 'doctrine', at which the nonentities of every political shade mocked. . . . One day of revolution was enough, one magnificent contact between the Tsar and the people was enough for the idea of constitutional monarchy to become fantastic, doctrinaire and disgusting. . . . The real monarch has destroyed the idea of the monarch. . . . The revolution has come and she has put an end to our political childhood.

From Munich the couple went to Vienna where, at the home of Victor Adler, excited Russian émigrés were obtaining money, passports and useful addresses for their return. Trotsky himself had a hairdresser alter his appearance, so familiar to Tsarist agents abroad. Natalia Sedova went ahead to arrange for accommodation and contacts in Kiev. And there, Trotsky arrived in February.

Switching lodgings as opportunity arose, to dodge the vigilance of the police, he even stayed for a while at an ophthalmic hospital, under the protection of the doctor-in-charge; yielding in considerable embarrassment to foot-baths and eye-drops from an old nurse, and hurriedly writing as soon as he was out of her solicitous sight. Kiev was a hive of surreptitious activity, with a press that poured out rebellious literature despite all attempts by the police to discover and destroy it. Trotsky made ample use of it for his shorter proclamations and sent his more substantial writings to the better-equipped secret press that had been set up in the Caucasus. His contact with this was maintained through a young engineer, Leonid Krassin, whose trust in Trotsky proved invaluable. For Krassin gave him a number of safe addresses in St Petersburg; at one of which, that of the chief medical officer at the Konstantinovsky School of Artillery, Trotsky would find intermittent refuge in the coming months.

In St Petersburg, where he lived officially on the passport of a landowner named Vikentiev and moved among revolutionaries as Petr Petrovich, he worked with both Social Democratic factions. Krassin, a member of the Bolshevik central committee, was himself a conciliator, so that he and Trotsky collaborated closely. And under Trotsky's influence, the local Mensheviks pursued a more radical policy than that of their centre abroad. But one of their number, known as 'Nikolay of the Gold Spectacles', turned out to be a police agent. Natalia was arrested at a May Day meeting in the woods, and Trotsky himself left St Petersburg to lie low for the while in Finland. This, though nominally part of the Russian empire, had its own government; the Tsar's police in general trod more warily there; and from their effective sanctuary, revolutionaries could keep in easy touch with the mood and underground movement of St Petersburg, only twenty miles away from the frontier. Trotsky spent his time taking short walks, greedily reading the newspapers, and finally formulating his vision of Russia's revolutionary prospects.

It was the land question that he saw as the crucial one. And it followed that power would be wrested by that class or party that succeeded in leading the peasantry against the regime of the Tsar and the landlords. It was already too late for the liberals or the democratic intelligentsia to provide this leadership. For the proletariat itself had seized the revolutionary initiative. A bourgeois-democratic revolution would offer Social Democracy an opportunity to take power with the support of the peasantry; and once in power, this party of the proletariat would find itself obliged to burst the bounds of the democratic programme and institute socialist measures.

How much further it might then go would depend upon the international context, as well as upon the disposition of forces within Russia. But meanwhile socialism would have surfaced in Russia before doing so in the advanced capitalist states of the West.

In the middle of May, the Baltic Fleet, sent months before, in a mad gamble, round the world to destroy the Japanese navy in the Yellow Sea, was all but entirely lost at the Battle of Tsushima. The news of this fresh national humiliation occasioned much anger but little surprise in St Petersburg, where the autocracy was now seen as capable only of ensuring disaster at the front. And in the remainder of the Russian navy, it underlined the peculiar peril to which the ranks were so recklessly consigned, by a command as corrupt and incompetent as it was imperious.

At the beginning of June, sailors on the battleship *Potemkin*, of the Black Sea Fleet, refused to eat the rotting meat with which they were being provided, and mutinied. They threw their commander and several officers overboard, hoisted the red flag, and steamed to Odessa, where a strike was gathering force. For a moment the prospect glimmered of an alliance between workers and sailors that would set up a republic in Odessa and, by its example, fire the whole of Russia. But after shelling the town, the mutineers wavered, steamed off to Romania, and there surrendered themselves to the authorities. The Tsar had some reason at last to thank his favourite saints. The rest of the Black Sea Fleet had not joined the *Potemkin* in mutiny, and the strike in Odessa had been isolated. But the possibility that disaffection in the armed forces might make common cause with the insurgency of the workers had come close enough to encourage revolutionaries as much as it alarmed the regime.

On 6 August, the Tsar at last announced his accepted design for a Duma or parliament. The franchise was to be based on property, so that workers were effectively excluded; and the Tsar could, at will, prorogue or dissolve the institution, whose powers were in any event merely limited to preparing drafts of laws for the Tsar's appointed Council of State to consider. The opposition was thrown into immediate disarray. The Bolsheviks pressed for a boycott; the Menshevik centre abroad favoured accepting the reform; while the group in St Petersburg, influenced by Trotsky's outlook, called for a boycott as well. Many liberals, too, favoured a boycott, but the eminent historian Miliukov, their dominant spokesman, argued for co-operation with the regime on the basis of the reform. With the Tsar's manifesto, he declared, Russia was crossing the Rubicon of constitutional government.

From Finland came Trotsky's reply, in the widely circulated 'Open Letter to Professor P. N. Miliukov'. He flourished Miliukov's analogy back at him.

An historical Rubicon is truly crossed only at the moment when the material means of government pass from the hands of absolutism into those of the people. Such things, Professor, are never achieved with the signing of a parchment; they take place in the street and are achieved through struggle.

Cuttingly he reminded the historian how liberalism had elsewhere in the past believed the promises of freedom made by autocracy, and therefore backed autocracy against revolution; only to have the promises broken as soon as the autocracy no longer needed liberal help. If the 'constitutional mirage' of the Duma seemed real to Russian liberalism now, this was because of the 'dry and barren desert' through which that liberalism had been staggering for so long. And once again autocracy would show that it had no use for liberalism, when liberalism had helped it to defeat the revolution. But then, this presupposed the defeat of the revolution; and the revolution had far from spoken its last word.

Peace with Japan was concluded by the Treaty of Portsmouth on 23 August (5 September in the Western calendar), and the terms left no doubt of the extent to which Russia had been beaten. The regime had at last ended the unpopular war, but it gained no popularity for doing so. Public dispute increasingly raged around the Tsar's manifesto. The universities, especially those in St Petersburg and Kiev, became centres of argument and agitation, as revolutionaries emerged to spread their message openly in lecture halls and corridors. Count Sergei Witte, the successful Finance Minister who had been dismissed for the common sense of his representations in the spurt towards war, and then had been recalled, with much reluctance, to conclude the peace, gave the regime an appearance of readiness for reform. But this only promoted the pressures for more radical concessions.

On 19 September type-setters in Moscow went on strike for a shorter working day and a higher rate of payment for piecework. From this tiny beginning, industrial action spread throughout the city. Street demonstrators exchanged shots with troops and police. Towards the end of the month, the movement seemed to falter, and strikers returned to work. But the fire was burning low only to spread out and spring up again more fiercely than before. On 8 October railway workers in Moscow went on strike, augmenting their economic demands with political ones that included the calling of a constituent assembly to frame a democratic constitution. Within a few days, the railways of the empire, from Poland to the Pacific, were at a standstill. The railwaymen seized the telegraph system for their own use or simply cut the wires, and paralysed the power stations by damaging the cables. Postal workers joined the strike. Tram and taxi drivers, restaurant waiters, shop assistants stopped work. The factories fell silent. Schools and universities closed their doors. In some places, juries refused to sit, and lawyers to plead, so that even the courts ceased to function.

Trotsky was still in Finland, staying at an isolated inn. The proprietor had rushed off in pursuit of a Swedish writer and an English actress who had left without paying their bill; and his wife, with a failing heart, was being given champagne to keep her alive. But there was a limit to what champagne could do and she died, in the room directly above Trotsky's own. The head waiter rushed off in pursuit of her husband. Snow and silence stretched everywhere around. The post brought newspapers that carried reports of the spreading strikes in Russia. Trotsky called for his bill, ordered horses, and rushed off to catch up with the promise of revolution.

He was in St Petersburg that same evening, with a plan for an elected revolutionary organization. He found that four days before, on 10 October, the local Mensheviks had proposed just such an organization, on the basis of one deputy for every 500 workers. On the 13th, this Soviet of Workers' Deputies had met for the first time, and the few dozen delegates had issued an appeal to the proletariat of St Petersburg for a political general strike and the election of further deputies. The response was immediate and dramatic. To the second meeting, which Trotsky seems to have arrived just in time to attend, came elected representatives from the many factories on strike, from trade unions and from the revolutionary parties. The Bolshevik central committee members in the city looked askance at the new institution, as a rival for proletarian allegiance. But they could scarcely fail to be impressed by the swell of popular support for it. Unwilling to risk the consequences of their exclusion from its ranks, they agreed to participate.

The authority of the Soviet, for workers not only in the capital but beyond, soon came to be such that its decisions were effectively law for the movement of revolt. Even the strike committees in the professions – of lawyers, engineers, government officials – obeyed its command. On the Soviet executive there sat, along with various independents, three Mensheviks, three Bolsheviks and three Social Revolutionaries. The local Mensheviks, for whose distinctive radicalism he remained so largely responsible, elected Trotsky one of their representatives.

Almost immediately, he seems to have become the voice of the Soviet: drafting its numerous appeals, manifestos, resolutions; and writing editorials for its official paper, *Izvestia* (*News*), whose first issue appeared on 17 October. He did not, however, cease to believe in the need for the narrower unity, of Social Democrats, in serving the wider unity that the Soviet represented. And it was in part a reflection of the personal authority which he had come so early to possess, that the Bolshevik and Menshevik committees of the capital formed a Federal Council, to explore the possibilities of reconciliation and meanwhile co-ordinate their activities in the Soviet.

The Tsar, in a letter to his mother, recorded his astonishment at the course of events and the confusion of his councillors.

God knows what happened in the universities. Every *kind* of riffraff walked in from the streets, riot was loudly proclaimed – nobody seemed to mind. . . . It makes me sick to read the news! . . . But the Ministers, instead of acting with quick decision, only assemble in council like a lot of frightened hens and cackle about providing united ministerial action.[4]

Witte himself had become convinced that serious concessions were now imperative. He was willing to serve as president of the council only if the Tsar would sanction them.

On 17 October, after two days of discussion and much silent prayer, the Tsar signed the manifesto which Witte had prepared. It avoided the word 'constitution' altogether and explicitly left the Tsar with the title of autocrat (*samoderzhets*). But it proceeded to grant 'unshakeable foundations of civil freedom on the principles of real inviolability of person, freedom of conscience, speech, meetings and associations'. It promised an extension of the franchise and it proclaimed that no law would have force unless it carried the consent of the Duma.[5]

On the following day, an enormous crowd collected in jubilation outside the university, whose balcony, windows and spire were decorated with red banners. But when Trotsky emerged on the balcony and began to speak, the mood soon changed. He reminded the crowd that it was Nicholas II, that 'tireless hangman on the throne', who had been forced to promise them freedom. But was the promise of freedom the same as freedom itself? Had anything changed since yesterday? Were the prisoners not still in the Peter and Paul Fortress that dominated the city? Were the exiled back from Siberia? Cries of 'Amnesty! Amnesty! Amnesty!' came from the crowd. But amnesty was not all, Trotsky continued. Today the government might release hundreds of political fighters, only to arrest thousands tomorrow. Was not the order to spare no bullets hanging alongside the manifesto of the Tsar? Was not Trepov (Governor-General of St Petersburg) master of the city? 'Down with Trepov!' shouted the crowd. And was Trepov the only one? Trotsky asked. Were there not others in the bureaucracy's reserves ready to take his place? And what of the guardsmen, without whose guns no Trepov could rule? Let the troops be withdrawn from the city. Let the free citizens themselves maintain order. 'Out with the troops! All troops to leave Petersburg!' called the crowd.

'Citizens!' Trotsky cried.

Our strength is in ourselves. With sword in hand we must stand guard over our freedom. As for the Tsar's manifesto, look, it is only a scrap of paper. Here it is before you – here it is crumpled in my fist. Today they have issued it, tomorrow they will take it away, and tear it into pieces, just as I am now tearing up this paper freedom before your eyes.[6]

Doubtless the sheer audacity of the speech had taken his listeners by surprise, so that they found themselves being carried along by it before they realized where it was taking them. They had come to celebrate a victory, and he was revealing the victory as a trick, of which they were to be the victims. Suddenly they knew that this was what they had believed all along, behind their very hope that the regime had at last surrendered. For his questions had been answered with the nods of their own minds. And when he came at last to deride the design of the regime, by tearing its promises to pieces in its face, he did this for them, as their reply to the insulting assumption that they could be so easily deceived. His was the ability to express, in the flashing language of the occasion, not what his listeners might suppose that they wanted to hear, but what became, as soon as they heard it, the voice within them. And it was this ability, above all, that would make him the unrivalled orator of the revolution.

And yet he could also, in the same commotion of events, employ a style that was Augustan in its elegance of measured rhythms and contrasts; to record the still eye of the storm. Commenting on the Tsar's manifesto in *Izvestia*, he wrote:

And so we have been given a constitution. We have been given freedom of assembly, but our assemblies are encircled by troops. We have been given freedom of speech, but censorship remains inviolate. We have been given freedom of study, but the universities are occupied by troops. We have been given personal immunity, but the prisons are filled to overflowing with prisoners. We have been given Witte, but we still have Trepov. We have been given a constitution, but the autocracy remains. Everything has been given, and nothing has been given.[7]

There have been few such men of outstanding action in history who so loved words and learned so well how to use them. This was not only because he merged within himself those two so different identities: the artist for whom his medium alone allows the creative expression of his personality; and the essential man of action for whom any other medium is a screen and a delay. For Trotsky, words were themselves acts; the article and speech as much instruments of revolution as the gun and the barricade.

And certainly, for Trotsky in particular, those weeks of insurrection in 1905 were a time when act and word seemed cuts in the rock-face of the future. On 19 October the Soviet resolved that only those newspapers might be published whose editors ignored the censorship; and since the Union of Print-Workers had been associated with the Soviet from the outset, its members were quick to ensure compliance. Under this condition, and provided that they did not publish calls to violence, the reactionary newspapers in general escaped union interference. The revolutionary ones were received on the streets like food in a famine. And the excitement of those who queued and jostled for copies was more than matched by the excitement of those who produced them. The underground hectographs and hand-presses had given place to the machinery of mass circulation. Police might still raid the premises, so that the staff had to move from one print-works to another; but operations were seldom seriously interrupted. The authorities might give orders for the confiscation of particular issues; but the orders could seldom be implemented, and outlawed issues continued to be sold openly in the streets. With Parvus, drawn from Munich to the reddening sky of St Petersburg, Trotsky took over the *Russian Gazette*: and boosted its small circulation to half a million copies. With the Mensheviks, he started a paper, *Nachalo* (*Beginning*), which, from its first issue in November, reached an enormous readership across Russia.

Trotsky and Natalia,[8] who had regained her freedom after the Tsar's manifesto, rented a room, as Mr and Mrs Vikentiyev, in the St Petersburg apartment of a stock-exchange speculator, who had been driven to the indignity of lodgers by the impact of political events on the market. Their landlord, whose affairs apparently went from bad to worse, used to borrow the newspapers delivered to Trotsky and rage at what he read. On one occasion, he even pulled a gun from his pocket and threatened to shoot the author of an article that Trotsky had written. His lodgers thought of moving to less perilous premises, but decided that they did not have the time and stayed on until Trotsky's arrest.

In the Soviet, meanwhile, Trotsky was revealing his qualities of leadership. Immediately recognizing any shift of advantage to the regime, he would urge, at the risk of being charged with defeatism, a temporary retreat rather than persistence in a challenge that seemed bound to fail and, failing, bring demoralization. Even a personal triumph, however agreeable, did not blur his vision. On the very day following his speech at the University of St Petersburg, he successfully persuaded the Soviet to call off the strikes. Strikers in the provinces and in Moscow as well had begun returning to work, and those in the capital were unlikely to stay out on their own.

The Soviet then summoned a mass funeral demonstration for 23 October, to mourn the victims of police reprisals during the strikes. But it soon became clear that the police were preparing counter-demonstrations, for clashes that would invite the massive use of troops, in a trial of strength that the authorities expected to win. Trotsky, aware that popular militancy was stumbling in the dust of the Tsar's manifesto, rose in the Soviet to warn that the time for welcoming such a trial had not arrived and to plead that the funeral demonstration should be cancelled. It was a painful climb-down to accept. That the Soviet should have done so was due not just to the force of Trotsky's arguments, but also to the respect in which his judgement had come to be held.

If the Soviet had agreed to a tactical retreat on one front, however, it prepared to stand firm on another. The regime had already resorted to the traditional method of deflecting popular discontent, and its agents had been busy organizing outbursts of violence against the Jews. In Odessa alone, some 500 Jews lost their lives in a pogrom that lasted three days.

But the murder and rape and pillage that swept through a hundred Russian cities and towns did not reach the capital. The Soviet, responding to rumours and reports that a pogrom was being planned for St Petersburg, resolved on countermeasures. Plants and workshops manufactured weapons of all kinds, and militias kept watch at night. The authorities cancelled their plans.

Then, while the capital seemed to be holding its breath, mutiny broke out at the nearby naval fortress of Kronstadt. It was unorganized and distractedly led. The regime had little difficulty in crushing it and made preparations to court-martial the supposed ringleaders. At the same time, as an earnest of its intentions for the whole country, it placed Poland under martial law, on the pretext of preventing secession. Mass meetings at many factories in St Petersburg demanded action from the Soviet, to meet what increasingly looked like a major offensive by a regime that was recovering its self-confidence. And at the beginning of November, the Soviet summoned a general strike. The response of workers was immediate, and the numbers involved exceeded those in the previous protests of January and October. This time it was the regime that found it advisable to retreat. It announced that it would lift martial law from Poland and denied that it intended to court-martial the Kronstadt mutineers.

Trotsky now urged that the Soviet should not endanger the political spoils of its victory by over-reaching itself. The executive committee submitted a resolution to call off the strike. Trotsky, speaking as its rapporteur, outlined before the Soviet his strategy of struggle.

Our actions are a series of consecutive battles. Their purpose is to disorganize the enemy and to win new friends. And whose sympathy is more precious to us than the army's? Understand this: in discussing whether or not we should continue the strike, we are in substance discussing whether to retain the demonstrative nature of the strike or turn it into a decisive struggle, that is, to continue it to the point of total victory or defeat. We are not afraid of battles. . . . But for each battle we seek the most favourable conditions. The events are working for us, and there is no advantage for us in forcing their progress. I ask you: to whose advantage is it to put off the decisive clash, ours or the government's? Ours, comrades! For tomorrow we shall be stronger than we are today, and the day after tomorrow stronger than tomorrow. . . . Let us call off the strike now, let us be satisfied with its tremendous moral victory. Let us exert every effort to create and consolidate the thing that we need more than anything else: organization, organization, organization.[9]

By an overwhelming majority, the Soviet accepted the executive committee's resolution.

Trotsky had already, in his pamphlet of the previous year, pointed to the crucial role of the army. Now, in the midst of the very events that he had predicted, this role was in the forefront of his thoughts and of the strategy that he was pressing on the Soviet. The most successful general strike might paralyse the economy and the civil administration. But it could not by itself transfer power from the regime to the revolution. Only the army could do that. And the struggle in the streets was, therefore, essentially a struggle for the allegiance of the army. Such popular challenges to the regime as protest demonstrations and strikes mattered not least for the impact that they made on military morale. But they should not be pursued to the point where the soldiers were forced to choose sides before they were ready to abandon the regime for the revolution.

It was an immensely difficult undertaking, which demanded caution and daring at different moments of decision, and never more of either than was necessary. But it was being pursued, and with success. The regime had been denied its opportunity to call in confidence on the intervention of the army. And the November strike, summoned in part to prevent the threatened trial and likely execution of the Kronstadt mutineers, had stirred a response in the barracks. Political meetings were held in the St Petersburg garrison. Delegates as well as individual soldiers began appearing before the executive committee and addressing sessions of the Soviet.

Trotsky was in no doubt, however, that the source of any decisive shift in the allegiance of the army lay less in the cities than in the countryside. For it was the peasant in uniform who held the door of the barracks. And while the peasantry at large remained submissive, the disaffection caught from the urban populace would not spread much beyond those soldiers with an industrial background.

But now there were indications of spreading unrest in the countryside: as peasants captured large estates and evicted the landlords; seized livestock and crops; rallied to a strike and boycott movement for a reduction in rents and an increase in wages. In August, a clandestine peasants' congress had taken place in a large old barn near Moscow, and resolved to establish an All-Russian Peasants' Union. In the weeks that followed, local peasant congresses had been held in various parts of the country. And on 6 November there opened in Moscow, without any attempt at secrecy this time, the second national congress, attended by almost 200 delegates, from twenty-seven provinces. This congress called for the transfer of all land to communal ownership, and the convening of a constituent assembly, 'on the basis of the purest democratic principles', to formulate a just agrarian system. Furthermore, the delegates threatened strike action to achieve their aims and pledged themselves to work closely with unions of municipal, factory, and railway workers, as with 'all other organizations defending the interests of working people'. Eight days before the opening session, several rural districts had been put under martial law; eight days afterwards, police arrested the Moscow officers of the Peasants' Union.

Trotsky was well aware that the fires in the countryside remained small and scattered; they were not yet the blaze that would devour the beaters in its way. The signs were promising. But they were still only signs. And the need to see them as no more than that, in judging the mood of the army, was about to be demonstrated in the very contrast presented by the navy, with its larger proportion of those from a proletarian background. Of the sailors who had mutinied on the *Potemkin* and then surrendered, four had been shot; two hanged; and several dozen sentenced to hard labour. But the vengeance exacted by the regime promoted revolt rather than submission.

Already in October, the industrial strikes had lit a fuse among the sailors in Sevastopol. Joint mass meetings of sailors and workers grew in size, frequency and challenge. The authorities banned them. On 11 November, mutiny broke out, to the accompaniment of a strike that paralysed the port. Sevastopol was placed under martial law, and troops were sent to occupy the streets. The sailors, who had met with some support for their cause from among the soldiers of the local garrison, counted on the refusal of the troops to fire. But the soldiers, most of whom had been brought in from other towns, because the authorities were unwilling to rely on the local regiments, obeyed their officers. Artillery induced the mutinous ships to surrender. And in the face of fierce resistance, troops took the naval barracks in the early morning of the fourteenth.

The regime had at least as much cause for alarm as for relief. The revolt in Sevastopol had, indeed, been crushed. But unlike the recent mutiny in Kronstadt, this one had been seriously organized. There had been close co-operation between the mutineers and revolutionary workers, who had together maintained order in the town. And from the local garrison, the sappers, who were among the most skilled and educated of the soldiers, had actually joined the rising. True, such technically trained units were mainly recruited from the urban industrial population. Yet how much longer would the illiterate peasant ranks remain loyal?

The mounting uncertainty had begun to affect even army officers. During the strikes of early November, Trotsky was invited to the sumptuous St Petersburg home of a certain Baroness Uexküll von Hildebrandt, to represent the views of the rebellious workers. Received by the doorman, who relieved him of his overcoat, and the footman who requested his visiting card and was offered his invitation instead, he was eventually conducted from the hallway by the baroness herself, into a large room where thirty or forty officers sat on one side of the aisle, and ladies on the other. In front of the glittering rows, various speakers were gathered: among them the former Marxist Peter Struve, who now pleaded that the army should defend the Tsar's October manifesto against attack from right and left alike.

'The speeches,' Trotsky recorded, 'became more and more resolute, the atmosphere more heated, the applause more energetic.'[10] When Trotsky's turn arrived, he declared that the people, like liberty itself, were unarmed; that the officers held the keys to the nation's arsenals; and that at the decisive moment, these keys should be handed over to the people, to whom they rightfully belonged. He was not to record how energetically his own speech had been applauded. But then the most energetic applause could not have persuaded him that the regime would be toppled by these officers and their ladies.

Indeed, he saw all too clearly how, while Count Witte fidgeted, the strong-men of the regime were preparing their counter-offensive, to cries of encouragement and assurances of support from the now cohesively frightened class of capital. Near the end of October, workers at a number of factories in St Petersburg had refused to work more than eight hours a day. The Soviet had then not merely sanctioned the campaign, but formally adopted it. At first many employers had vacillated: some of them accepting the fact, but reducing wages accordingly; others conceding a cut to nine paid hours a day. With the November strikes, however, they rallied. The government led the way by shutting state plants, and private industry followed. Increasingly, meetings of workers were dispersed by force. The Soviet sought to rescue the campaign by limiting it only to sectors where success seemed likely. But this confused and divided the movement. At last, on 12 November, in what Trotsky was later to describe as the most dramatic of its sessions, the Soviet considered a proposal from its executive committee to abandon the campaign.

The resolution, which bore the unmistakable imprint of Trotsky, declared that the unity of private capital and the government had made the issue of the eight-hour day into one of state power; that the victory of the campaign could not be achieved without a victory by the workers over the system itself; and that the campaign should, therefore, be suspended. But deputies from two huge metal-working plants and from several textile, glass and tobacco factories, insisted on continuing the struggle. It took four hours of argument before the executive committee wrested agreement. And Trotsky's own contribution to the debate must have been vital. Speaking as the executive committee's rapporteur, he did not attempt to disguise the retreat, but also set out what had been captured in the campaign. 'We may not have won the eight-hour day for the masses, but we have certainly won the masses for the eight-hour day. Henceforth the war-cry: *Eight hours and a gun!* shall live in the heart of every Petersburg worker.' There was much truth in this. The simple eight-hour demand, with the resistance to it by employers and government combined, roused the most backward workers to a political awareness that years of insistent propaganda for revolution would not have produced.

The Soviet was at the height of its popular influence and prestige. Petitioners and plaintiffs of all kinds crowded its doors. Travellers fright-ened of being suspended somewhere by a railway strike would apply to the Soviet for information and advice. Individual citizens would readily dis-regard the law, to do the Soviet some service. An engraver's workshop agreed at once to make a seal for the illegal Postal and Telegraph Union, on receipt of written Soviet sanction. Appeals arrived from remote parts of the country. One letter carrying only the address, 'The Workers' Government, St Petersburg', was promptly delivered by the post. The continued survival of the Soviet was a challenge which the regime needed quickly to crush, if it was not to lose what remained of its authority.

On 26 November, Georgi Nosar, a young lawyer who, under the name of Khrustalyov, presided over the Soviet, was arrested. The executive committee was in no doubt that a direct assault on the Soviet itself would soon follow, but rejected any thought of avoiding the confrontation by deserting its commitments. It proposed the election of a temporary presid-ium and the pursuit of preparations for armed uprising. A general meeting of the Soviet, attended by some 300 deputies, adopted the proposal and elected Trotsky, with two others, to the Presidium. Meanwhile, respond-ing to an initiative from the Peasants' Union, it resolved to call for a financial boycott of the regime.

On 2 December, the manifesto on the boycott, drafted by Parvus and signed by the Soviet of Workers' Deputies, the All-Russian Peasants' Union, the Russian Social Democratic Labour Party, the Party of Social Revolutionaries and the Polish Socialist Party, was published. It asked that no payments of any kind be made to the Russian treasury; that in all trans-actions, including the settlement of wages and salaries, gold (or, where sums of less than five roubles were involved, coinage) should be demanded in place of paper money; that deposits should be withdrawn from the state and savings banks, with payment exacted in gold. Government reserves were drained of almost 100 million roubles in the month of December alone. But the immediate future of the regime was to be determined in the streets and not at the counters of the financial system. The real impact of the manifesto was to be much delayed. In a final paragraph, the signatories had warned that they would repudiate the repayment of any loans con-tracted by a Russian government 'waging war against the entire people'. In February 1918, the Soviet of People's Commissaries would repudiate

Tsarist debts: with immense losses to creditors in several Western countries, especially France.

Trotsky's dominance of the Soviet was now evident to all. Lunacharsky, who was to become Bolshevik Russia's Commissar of Education, told Lenin: 'The star of Khrustalyov is setting. Today the strong man in the Soviet is Trotsky.' And Lenin's face seemed momentarily to darken, before he replied, 'Well, Trotsky has won this by his tireless and striking work.' Indeed, with Khrustalyov shortly afterwards removed, Trotsky became leader in form as well as fact and presided at sessions of the Soviet. Furthermore, he could scarcely fail to gain in stature from the marked success with which his efforts to unite the party were meeting. His own pressures from within their ranks, publicly promoted in the pages of *Nachalo*, ensured that the Mensheviks in Russia would continue moving towards reconciliation. And the central committee of the Bolsheviks, with Lenin present, unanimously declared that the conditions of foreign exile had been responsible for the split, and that the course of the revolution made unreasonable any further factional conflict.[11]

Who, indeed, was there to rival him for pre-eminence in the popular struggle? Plekhanov stayed away from Russia in 1905, and Martov arrived so late that he was barely in time to leave. Axelrod got no further than Finland, where he met the refugees from the revolutionary reverses in December. Lenin reached St Petersburg in the second week of November but kept so far in the shadows that Krupskaya could not even remember his ever having spoken at the Soviet.[12] So far did Trotsky emerge as the central figure of the whole movement that Miliukov, the liberal leader, would refer, in the following year, to 'the revolutionary illusions of Trotskyism': the first coinage of the term.

To account for this, more must be adduced than his powers, notable as they were, of vision, judgement and expression. There was also a particular fitness for command, in the midst of so much uncertainty and confusion, that no one would identify more tellingly than Trotsky himself.

I was confident in the face of events. I understood their inner mechanism, or at least so I believed. I visualized their effect on the minds of the workers, and envisaged, in its main features, the next day to come. . . . Decisions had to be made under fire. I can't help noting here that these decisions came to me quite obviously. I did not turn back to see what others might say, and I very seldom had opportunity to consult anybody; everything had to be done in such a hurry.[13]

This self-possession was about to be singularly tested. On the evening of 3 December, troops surrounded the premises of the Soviet, blocking all escape. From a balcony Trotsky shouted down to the deputies in the hall below: 'No resistance must be made, no arms must be surrendered!' The deputies began smashing their revolvers. A police officer marched into the room where the executive committee was meeting, and set out to read the warrant of arrest. He did not get far.

'Please do not interfere with the speaker,' Trotsky interrupted. 'If you wish to take the floor, you must give your name, and I shall ask the meeting whether it wishes to hear you.' The officer, astonished, waited for the speaker to finish and was then invited by Trotsky to read the warrant, 'for the sake of information'. No sooner was he done, than Trotsky proposed that the executive committee acknowledge it, and pass to the next item on the agenda. The officer attempted to speak but was silenced by Trotsky. 'Please do not interfere. You have had the floor; you have made your statement; we have acknowledged it. Does the meeting wish to have further dealings with the policeman?' The other members of the executive, who must, at the outset, have been scarcely less astonished than the policeman himself by Trotsky's attitude, cried 'No!' Trotsky turned to the officer: 'Then, please, leave the hall.' And the officer left. But he was soon back, with soldiers. The comedy was over: though not before it had secured some dignity from a submission that only political madness would have denied. The members of the executive committee refused to give their names and were allotted numbers; their descriptions were noted; and they were taken away, to the Kresty prison.

The protest strike in St Petersburg was little more than a gesture. It started on 8 December and was already staggering by the 12th. The workers were aware that only an armed uprising stood any chance of stopping the autocracy now and that neither their resources nor the mood of the reinforced local garrison allowed this any likelihood of success. But in Moscow the Bolsheviks had, under Lenin's remote control, been particularly active in preparations for such an uprising. And there, nourishing revolutionary hopes, the garrison was showing signs of disaffection. A Soviet of Soldiers' Deputies had even been formed and was sending representatives to the local Workers' Soviet. On the 7th, a strike broke out which swept through the city and the factories scattered around. The military detachments sent against demonstrating crowds refused to fire. But on the third day of the strike, with unreliable regiments confined to barracks, soldiers and demonstrators clashed.

A rash of proclamations spread across the walls of the city, with advice on the use of guerilla tactics. Insurgents were to act in tiny groups of three or four men; attacking and disappearing quickly. Against the Cossack units being sent to deal with crowds, one or two marksmen should find appropriate buildings from which to shoot without warning and immediately withdraw. The military replied by bringing in artillery and clearing, with indiscriminate bombardment, one street after another. But for five days, a few hundred guerillas, Social Democrats from both factions of the party and Social Revolutionaries, sniped at the morale of the soldiers, many of whom began refusing to fight an invisible enemy, which might well be as numerous as some rumours suggested. The military snatched fresh troops from nearby towns and meanwhile summoned regiments from as far away as Warsaw. By the 15th, the guerillas were exhausted, and worker confidence was slumping fast. Shops, banks, offices, the stock exchange reopened. On the 19th the strike, on orders from the local Soviet, came to a formal end.

Lenin would not agree with criticism that the resort to an uprising had been a disastrous mistake. 'On the contrary', he declared,

[the leaders] should have taken up arms with greater determination, more energetically, and more aggressively; they should have explained to the masses the impossibility of having only a peaceful strike and the need for fearless and merciless armed struggle.... To conceal from the masses the need for a desperate, bloody and annihilating war as the immediate task of the future would be to deceive both ourselves and the people.

He was deceiving himself. What he saw as a pause in the flow was the beginning of the ebb.

Trotsky estimated the casualties of the uprising at about 1000 dead and a similar number injured. But this was to prove no more than a prelude. The Tsar had written in the margin of a report and repeated in a letter to his mother:'Terror must be met by terror.'[14]And the Tsar commented with particular satisfaction: 'Since the events in Moscow, Witte has completely changed. Now he wants to hang and shoot everybody. I never saw such a chameleon or a man who changed his views the way he does.'[15] In the first few months of 1906, the regime went on a rampage of retribution that claimed more than 30,000 dead and injured, with over twice that number arrested, imprisoned, exiled. By March, the Tsar was pleased to assure a deputation from the devoted Union of Russian People that the autocracy would continue to assert its traditional prerogatives.

Some Mensheviks were in favour of contesting elections to the Duma, as a form of propaganda. But in the end the Social Democrats, still hoping for a resurgence of popular revolt to compel the convocation of a Constituent Assembly, united in determining upon a boycott. The Constitutional Democrats or 'Cadets', as they came to be popularly called,[16] were the party of the liberals, established at the time of the Tsar's October manifesto, and they collected not far short of half the seats. In alliance with peasant representatives, they commanded a clear majority.

The Tsar was displeased. This was not at all the result that his principal minister had promised him. He waited long enough for Witte to conclude successfully the negotiations for a large loan from France and then dismissed him, to appoint I. L. Goremykin, an elderly and sycophantic bureaucrat, as the new president of the council. Just before the Duma was due to meet, in late April 1906, further 'fundamental laws', to diminish its powers, were proclaimed. But this failed to produce the required tractability. The 'Address to the Throne' proposed a programme of reforms. Goremykin declared the programme 'inadmissible'. The Duma voted to censure the government. The government ignored the vote and the Duma. The Cadets introduced a project for the partial expropriation of the great landed estates. And the Tsar, deciding that he had had enough, dissolved the Duma. The members, arriving on 9 July 1906 at the Tauride Palace, where they had been holding their sessions, found it surrounded by troops.

Trotsky spent some fifteen months in prison: first at Kresty; then, at the Peter and Paul Fortress; and, finally, at the House of Preliminary Detention. The trial of the Soviet leaders was postponed again and again: as the more and the less intransigent factions within the government manoeuvred to secure a form of prosecution that would lay the blame for the events of 1905 on the other. Meanwhile, the treatment that Trotsky received, as the prize captive to be put on display in the dock, was a far cry from his initiation at Nikolayev and at Kherson eight years before. In the Peter and Paul Fortress, he was placed in solitary confinement but provided with virtually all the books that he wanted, and was permitted to study late into the night. Sverchkov, a fellow prisoner, was to recall him as saying: 'I feel splendid. I sit and work and feel perfectly sure that I can't be arrested. You will agree that under the conditions in Tsarist Russia, this is rather an unusual sensation.' He would relax by reading the classics of European literature. And he made his way with mounting delight through the major French novels in their own language. It was the start of a love affair that never staled. Even during the civil war, he would snatch time to read in his railway car the latest French fiction.

Lawyers smuggled out his writings in their brief-cases. His *Peter Struve in Politics*, an assault on liberalism and a defence of revolution, was published as a pamphlet which sold many thousands of copies within a few weeks. A 'big work on rent' was begun in prison but left unfinished and later lost.[17] He edited a *History of the Soviet*, written by his colleagues, to which he also contributed a chapter. And in a long essay entitled *Results and Prospects (Itogi i Perspektivi)*, he expounded and elaborated the ideas that he had formulated in Finland. With the closest argument that culminated in a passionate call, this propounded a theory of permanent revolution: the essential doctrine of what would become known as Trotskyism.

Marxism taught that proletarian revolution would emerge from the very development of capitalism. Orthodox Marxists accordingly believed that proletarian revolution in Russia would have to wait upon the exercise of bourgeois rule which would come from a bourgeois revolution. Trotsky, for whom Marxism was, in his own words, a method of analysing social relations and not texts, examined the peculiarities of Russian society to draw different conclusions about its revolutionary prospects.

In contrast to what had occurred in the countries of advanced economic development, modern industry in Russia had brought into being a considerable proletariat without a considerable middle class. The absolutist state had exacted so much of the social product for its own purposes that it had, simply, deprived such a class of the nourishment to expand in numbers and power. Industry had been financed instead by foreign capital, which demanded liberal policies to promote its interests at home, but in Russia backed an autocracy that promised to protect its investments. In consequence, the cause of a Russian bourgeois liberalism was stillborn. Only the proletariat had the strength and the will to make a revolution; and once having done so, would not present control of the state to a bourgeoisie so weak and so frightened of the workers that it had abandoned direction of the struggle against the regime. Thus it was that in a country as economically backward as Russia, the proletariat could take command earlier than in countries of advanced capitalism. The peasants, though constituting the vast majority of the Russian people, were unable to make the revolution themselves. Social function and not numbers counted in a modern revolutionary context, where a relatively few railwaymen on strike could make a greater impact than could many times more peasants in their scattered villages. But Trotsky had not forgotten the crucial role of the army, and of the peasant within it. The proletariat would need the support of the peasants to hold the power it had grasped. This support it would receive, by such measures as sanctioning their seizure of land, and so appearing as their liberator. The support would not, however, last. For the peasantry would soon enough come into conflict with two essential thrusts of proletarian policy, collectivism and internationalism, and at the very time when the revolution was faced by the organized hostility of the bourgeois West.

Left to its own resources, the working class of Russia will inevitably be crushed by the counter-revolution the moment the peasantry turns its back on it. It will have no alternative but to link the fate of its political rule, and, hence, the fate of the whole Russian revolution, with the fate of the socialist revolution in Europe. That colossal state-political power given it by a temporary conjuncture of circumstances in the Russian bourgeois revolution, it will cast into the scales of the class struggle of the entire capitalist world. With state power in its hands, with counter-revolution behind it and European reaction in front of it, it will send forth to its comrades the world over the old rallying cry, which this time will be a call for the last attack: *Workers of all countries, unite!*[18]

Lenin would long continue to maintain that socialist revolution in the West was a prerequisite for the transition from bourgeois democracy in Russia. And, convinced that the Russian proletariat was too plainly a minority to make a revolution on its own, he looked to an alliance of worker and peasant, which would produce a 'revolutionary-democratic dictatorship of the proletariat and peasantry': a formula which Trotsky dismissed, in his essay, as 'unrealizable'.

The immediate impact of *Results and Prospects* was slight. Nearly all copies of the book by Trotsky, *Our Revolution*, in which it appeared as the final chapter, were confiscated by the police. Lenin himself, though attacking it meanwhile on the basis of reports and quotations, would read the actual text only in 1919. Furthermore, the book was published in St Petersburg at the time that the Soviet leaders went on trial; and attention was so far engaged by the conduct of the central figure as to neglect his writings.

When noticed at all, the ideas in the essay were to meet with general rebuff. Most Mensheviks were in no mood to rally round predictions of proletarian power in Russia as the first leap of world revolution. Unlike Trotsky himself, they had been intimidated rather than fired by the experience of the Soviet. In the succeeding years, they would come increasingly to believe that socialists were not yet capable of controlling a country like Russia and needed a period of bourgeois democracy for preparation of both the country and themselves. On the other hand, Bolsheviks, with the factional conflict resumed, were scarcely drawn to the views of a man whom they considered a Menshevik, and all the more dangerous for being unorthodoxly so: even if Lenin had not taken occasion to reject such views as incompatible with his own.

Trotsky left the Peter and Paul Fortress 'with a tinge of regret; it was so quiet there, so eventless, so perfect for intellectual work'.[19] In the House of Preliminary Detention, the cells were not locked during the day and the prisoners could take their walks together or play leap-frog for hours on end. Natalia was allowed to visit him twice a week, and the officials on duty pretended not to notice when letters were exchanged or manuscripts transferred. Indeed, one such official, who made himself especially agreeable, requested a book of Trotsky's and an inscribed photograph; winking suggestively as he whispered that his daughters were all college students. The climate was congenial to thoughts of escape. A few of Trotsky's colleagues, including Parvus, began plotting an attempt. They pressed Trotsky to join them. But he refused. He looked to the coming trial as an opportunity to proclaim and promote the revolutionary cause. They decided to go ahead without him but drew in too many others, and the preparations were soon discovered.

Trotsky's belief that the trial should be used to make a political impact, and not to seek acquittal on some technical point, brought him into conflict with the Menshevik leadership. Writing on behalf of the central committee, Martov proposed that the defence reject all charges of armed insurrection and argue the compatibility of Soviet policy and conduct with the terms of the Tsar's October manifesto. But Trotsky, who had publicly torn that manifesto into shreds, had no intention of running to it now for cover. Angrily he wrote back that the Soviet had never based its programme on the manifesto and should not deny having prepared politically for an insurrection. The Bolshevik central committee was taking much the same view. But even the intrusion of factional difference had no effect on the unity of the defendants. All of them endorsed Trotsky's letter and were agreed that he himself should tackle the crucial issue of armed insurrection.

On 19 September 1906 the trial at last started. Troops were stationed in the adjoining streets as well as at the gates and in the courtyard of the court building. Inside, gendarmes with drawn sabres lined the underground corridor to the prison, stood guard in all the rooms and faced the backs of the defendants. But the edge of this formidable display was blunted by flowers. Flowers stared from the dock and, all around, stood in buttonholes, sat in hands and on laps, lay along benches. The president of the court apparently decided not to risk the consequences of ordering their removal, and soon officers and officials were duly handing them to the defendants.

Between thirty and forty lawyers moved in their frock-coats among the blue uniforms of the guards; while between 100 and 120 members of the public had been admitted. Many of the witnesses were workers; and when the door to the witness room was opened, gusts of revolutionary song would reach the president's chair. Entering in groups of twenty or thirty, to take the oath, most of them were in working clothes and carried their caps in their hands. They would glance at the judges and then bow in the direction of the defendants, to call out 'Good-day, comrades!' An old priest with a portable altar had been provided to administer the oath. But nearly all of them refused his services and simply undertook to tell the truth. When the names of only fifty-one defendants were read out, questions from one of the defence lawyers drew from the president of the court the admission that the fifty-second had been executed. Defendants, witnesses, lawyers for the defence, members of the public rose in a silent demonstration of tribute to the memory of the dead man. The seated police and gendarme officers proceeded in confusion to stand as well.

Trotsky's parents attended the trial and were impressed by their son's manifest importance. His mother cried a good deal during his speech and the congratulations that followed. She was sure that he was going to be acquitted and even rewarded in some way. When Trotsky tried to persuade her that he would probably be sentenced to hard labour, he only succeeded in bewildering rather than preparing her. His father was 'pale, silent, happy and distressed, all in one'.[20]

Trotsky's speech, delivered on 4 October, was a masterly one. He quickly came to the argument that the Tsar's October manifesto afforded a legal basis for the activities of the Soviet, since the Soviet had merely put into effect the freedoms that the manifesto had promised. But, he immediately admitted, the Soviet had based its behaviour on the belief that the manifesto had, in fact, changed nothing at all. And in challenging the court to declare whether or not the Soviet had been wrong, he publicly placed it in a dilemma. For, if the Tsar's manifesto had not been a deceit, then where was the prosecution's case? And if it had, then what price the honour of the Tsar?

The court must say whether we Social Democrats were right when we argued that the constitutional manifesto was merely a list of promises which would never be voluntarily fulfilled; whether we were right in our revolutionary criticism of these paper guarantees; whether we were right when we called upon the people to engage in open struggle for true and complete freedom. Were we right, or were we not?

Of course, he continued, if the movement of popular forces, under the leadership of the Soviet, had been permitted by the old state to develop in complete freedom, a new Russia would have been born, without any bloodshed. But it was absolutism that had acted 'to keep such power as it still possessed in its hands and even to regain what it had solemnly relinquished. That is why insurrection, armed insurrection, gentlemen of the court, was inevitable from our point of view.'

Yes, their activities in the Soviet had been revolutionary. And yes, they had been preparing for armed insurrection. But they had not, as the prosecution was maintaining, prepared one.

An insurrection of the masses, gentlemen of the bench, is not made: it accomplishes itself. It is the result of social relations, not the product of a plan. It cannot be created; it can be foreseen. . . . To prepare for it meant, for us, doing everything possible to minimize the casualties of this inevitable conflict.

How, then, had they thought that such an insurrection would succeed? By winning the army over to their side. That was why the barricade, so often associated with insurrection, should be seen as playing, above all, a *moral* role. For it was not just a physical obstacle. By being a temporary barrier to the movement of troops, it brought them into close contact with the people; and, as a consequence of this contact, military discipline disintegrated and disappeared.

This, and only this, ensures the victory of a popular rising. And this is why, in our opinion, a popular rising has been 'prepared', not when the people have been armed with rifles and guns – for in that case it would never be prepared – but when it is armed with readiness to die in open street battle.

78

Finally, flourishing the indictment, he turned and flung it in the face of the regime.

The prosecution invites us to admit that the Soviet armed the workers for the struggle against the existing 'form of government'. If I am categorically asked whether this was so, I shall answer: Yes! Yes, I am willing to accept this accusation, but on one condition only. . . . What we have is not a national government but an automaton for mass murder. I can find no other name for the government machine which is tearing into parts the living body of our country. If you tell me that the pogroms, the murders, the burnings, the rapes . . . are the form of government of the Russian Empire – then I will agree with the prosecution that in October and November last we were arming ourselves, directly and immediately, against the form of government of the Russian Empire.[21]

There was clear evidence for Trotsky's charges. A certain Lopukhin, former director of the police department, had written to Stolypin, then Minister of the Interior and now Goremykin's successor as president of the council, reporting the results of investigations that he had conducted on the orders of Count Witte. His letter, of which the defence possessed a certified copy, stated that proclamations inciting pogroms had been printed on the presses of the secret police and distributed across Russia by police agents; that General Trepov, in his capacity as palace commandant, had personally reported to the Tsar on such activities and been given immense state funds for the express purpose of organizing pogroms; that there were close connections between the police department and the Black Hundreds.[22] The defence demanded that the court take cognizance of the letter and call Lopukhin himself, who seems to have been eager to appear, as a witness. The judges, shuddering at the implications, refused. The defendants, in response, insisted on withdrawing from the courtroom; and, when they were removed, their lawyers also withdrew. In their absence, on 2 November, the court delivered its verdict. The defendants were found not guilty on the principal count of having organized an insurrection. But fifteen of them, including Trotsky, were none the less sentenced to loss of all civil rights and exile in Siberia for life.[23] They were not disappointed. They had expected hard labour as well.

On 3 January 1907 Trotsky and his colleagues were taken to the transit prison and made to change into the grey trousers, jackets and caps of the convict uniform. But they were allowed to keep their own underwear, and even their boots: a concession which Trotsky must have greeted with considerable relief, since the sole of one boot concealed an excellent passport, and the high heels, gold coins. Then, on the 10th, at six in the morning, they were taken, along with those wives and children who were accompanying them into exile, to the station and put on a train.

Their escort had been summoned from Moscow, since the authorities feared that soldiers from St Petersburg might be unreliable. But soldiers from Moscow, it emerged, had not been kept reliable by distance. Most of them had read reports of the trial and admired their prisoners. Certainly they disobeyed the strict instructions against allowing letters to be written during the journey, and even seem to have helped such letters on their way. Trotsky's own letters to Natalia provided an immediate record of impressions and events, and he was subsequently to publish extensive extracts from them: first in a booklet, *There and Back*, and then in his history of the period.

The train discharged its cargo at Tyumen, across the Urals and well into Siberia. And from there the prisoners, under close guard, set out, slowly by sleigh, for an undisclosed destination in the north. It was very cold, with temperatures that hovered at thirty degrees below zero; but the air was clean, and Trotsky took pleasure in breathing it after so long a time in the stale cells. A short distance from Tyumen, in a peasant's hut packed with the prisoners, lots were drawn for possession of a wide bench, and Trotsky won. 'I'm always lucky in life,' he commented in a letter.[24]

He occasionally complained. He disliked the constant presence of others, with the pressures to be companionable: he had learned to enjoy being alone and found himself hankering after the isolated silence of the cell. He cared about cleanliness and considered the standards that the prisoners were reduced to observing as perhaps the most disagreeable feature of the journey. Once or twice, as his spirit stumbled, there came a cry of distress. 'I clench my teeth and yearn for electric street-lamps, the noise of trams and the best thing in the world – the smell of fresh newsprint.'[25] Yet there is no sullenness in the letters, no sighing of self-pity: and the rare flashes of irritation or of pain make only the more remarkable the gaiety; the delight in describing some person or incident or scene; the sense of adventure; the celebration of hope.

They do not read like the letters of someone going into Siberian exile for life. But then Trotsky was already thinking of how to escape. And, above all, he was noting, among the peasants whom he met as well as among the soldiers, a political awareness that fed his own exhilaration. The shape of the future had been there shimmering just beyond reach. Surely soon it would come close enough to grasp. It was this that made him so conscious of his luck, in merely being alive.

At Tobolsk he discovered that the convoy was bound for Obdorsk, a tiny settlement on the Arctic Circle almost 1000 miles from the nearest railway. Immediately his mind leapt to what the possibilities of escape from there would be, and then to how, in any event, his exile might be cut short.

Just keep sending books and newspapers, newspapers and books. . . . Perhaps the year we shall be obliged to spend in Obdorsk will be the last revolutionary breathing-space history will ever grant us to fill the gaps in our knowledge and sharpen our weapons still more.[26]

Day after day the long convoy, with the front sleighs for the luggage, then the prisoners in pairs, and the soldiers behind, sped north: through an area where typhus was raging and where many of the local exiles occupied themselves, like the native Ostyaks, in collecting and cleaning cedar cones, catching fish, gathering berries, hunting. At Berezov, on 12 February, Trotsky wrote the last letter of his journey. For he had decided to attempt his escape from there, rather than continue to Obdorsk and so add more than 300 desolate miles to his return. Among the prisoners was an old Social Revolutionary, Dr Feit, who taught him how to simulate sciatica; Trotsky proved so persuasive that he was left behind in the hospital, to follow as soon as he had sufficiently recovered.

There were three feasible routes for him to take. The one by which the convoy had come was the easiest but also the most risky, since it was dotted with police posts, and a telegraphed report of his escape would bring instant pursuit. A second lay directly westwards, across the Urals to the port of Archangel and a ship; but he knew nothing of conditions in Archangel and had no means of informing himself. The third, recommended by the local land-surveyor, Roshkovsky, would take him south-westwards, to a mining settlement in the Urals, from which he might travel by railway to Perm and on to St Petersburg. It was a daunting route, with few settlements of any kind; frequent epidemics of typhus in those that there were; and the ever-present chance, in a month of blizzards, that he would simply be swallowed up by the snow. But then there was neither telegraph nor police post to be feared, and a good start would leave his pursuers too far behind.

Roshkovsky sought the advice of a local peasant, nicknamed 'The Goat's Foot', who offered to organize the escape and found a red-haired Zyryan to act as guide. The Zyryan spoke not only fluent Russian but two distinct Ostyak dialects, and he was reported to be a 'real old fox'. He was also an incorrigible drunk.

The escape was set for midnight on 18 February. That evening there was an amateur production of two short plays at the barracks, and Trotsky was in the audience, to advertise his presence in the town and seize occasion to tell the local chief of police that he intended leaving soon for Obdorsk. Then, with the church bells ringing twelve, he hurried to the yard of 'The Goat's Foot', where a sleigh was waiting. He was covered with frozen hay, that gradually thawed to drip cold water on his face, and driven a short distance from the town.

The Zyryan was at the appointed meeting place and unmistakably drunk. He set off briskly enough, boasting about his reindeer, but soon became silent and limp: falling asleep again and again, almost as soon as Trotsky had prodded him awake, with the reindeer adjusting their pace accordingly. The prospect of a good start was receding fast. At last, losing his temper,

Trotsky pulled the hood from the Zyryan's head and threatened to push him off the sleigh if he did no better at his job. The icy air and the threat seemed to have an effect, for the Zyryan woke up sufficiently to reach some huts and restore his energy from a bottle there.

Meanwhile, Roshkovsky, supposing that any pursuers would look for tracks to follow, had arranged for someone to take a slaughtered calf down the road to Tobolsk, the way by which the convoy had come. And when, after two days, the police got round to suspecting that Trotsky had escaped, they wasted two days more in chasing the calf.

Trotsky's journey across the wilderness of snow took a week; with stops now and then at Ostyak huts, for such rest and refreshment and warmth as these would offer. He had brought along liquor as some return for hospitality, and with vigilance prevented most of it from disappearing down the Zyryan's throat. He slept very little, to ensure that the Zyryan did not sleep too much, and kept himself awake by pencilling his impressions in an exercise book. They were to provide a vivid account of Ostyak life in a vast expanse of Russian territory, where swear-words comprised the only Russian ever spoken and seemed, along with the vodka produced by the state monopoly, to constitute the major achievement of Russian culture.

At times he wondered whether his luck might not desert him: so that he would toss in fever, without help, like the young merchant from Berezov who had died among the Ostyaks a month before; or, the sleigh meeting with some accident in the snow, would know that each minute was burying him alive. Their leading reindeer began dragging his left hind leg and responded poorly to the Zyryan's method of treatment, which consisted of blood-letting and digging obstinately with a knife above the animal's hoof. But the Zyryan did reveal one virtue in an emergency: he seemed able to find the nearest Ostyak encampment by following such signs, imperceptible to Trotsky, as the faint smell of smoke.

New reindeer were obtained, and the journey resumed: though with twenty-four hours perilously lost. Suddenly that night, in a half-sleep, Trotsky thought of how vulnerable he was: a supposedly rich merchant with possessions that must seem well worth a murder to the noiseless Ostyak, who had been recruited to drive his own sleigh, with the luggage, in front. There was no one else for miles around, except the Zyryan. And Trotsky had no cause to suppose him a loyal or competent protector. He decided to get the revolver from his luggage at the first opportunity. But in the morning, the Ostyak looked sleepy rather than murderous. And the revolver, Trotsky remembered having been warned when buying it, was unreliable. It stayed in the luggage.

As they approached the Urals at last and encountered other travellers, Trotsky adopted the identity of an engineer and member of a celebrated polar expedition. He might have chosen more prudently. He met a clerk who had worked on the particular expedition, knew its members, and proceeded to ply him with questions. Luckily, the clerk had been drinking, and soon drowned his interest in a bottle of rum that Trotsky had been keeping for an emergency. Satisfied of the need for a less prominent guise, Trotsky posed as an official, and posed so well that he travelled much of the remaining way, without exciting any suspicion, in the company of a real official, who was on a tour of the government liquor shops.

At Rudniki he boarded the train, under the indifferent gaze of the secret police. His uneasiness was not yet at an end. For, on the local Ural railway, any stranger was conspicuous, and a police search ordered by telegraph would quickly have discovered him. After twenty-four hours of agonizingly slow progress, he reached the junction with the Perm railway; then, travelling through the very same stations that he had passed some six weeks before, he felt himself, for the first time, free. Standing alone on the front platform in the wind, he let out a loud cry of rejoicing. His escape had taken eleven days.

In his euphoria, he discarded all caution and, from one of the early stops made by the train, sent off a telegram to Natalia; asking her to meet him at a particular station where their respective trains would both call. Staying with their baby son in a Finnish village near St Petersburg, she soon had the telegram in her hands and excitedly set off without knowing the name of the station, which had somehow been dropped from the text. Already on her way, she found out that it could only be Samino; and there she ran into Trotsky on the platform. He was so indignant when he heard of the mutilated telegram that only with difficulty did she dissuade him from complaining at once to the appropriate officials. She was amazed at the 'freedom and ease' with which he laughed and chatted aloud at the station and on the train that they took to St Petersburg. 'I wanted to keep him invisible, to hide him away, because of that threat of hard labour hanging over him for his escape. But he was in full view and said that it was his best protection.'[27]

In St Petersburg, on 2 March, he received a startled welcome from his friends at the School of Artillery but was soon persuaded that it would be madness for him to stay in a city where his face was so widely known. The trains leaving St Petersburg for Finland were subject to especial scrutiny by the secret police. But Trotsky and Natalia decided to take their chance, and though several police went through the carriage, Trotsky was not recognized. In Finland he visited Martov and Lenin, who lived in neighbouring villages; and through friends of Lenin's, found a home with a family in a village near Helsingfors (Helsinki). There he wrote the account of his journey to Siberia and back; and the money that he received for it was enough to get him safely abroad. While Natalia returned with the child to Russia, he crossed the frontier into Sweden and from Stockholm took a ship: for an exile that he expected to be short but that was to last until May 1917, a decade away.

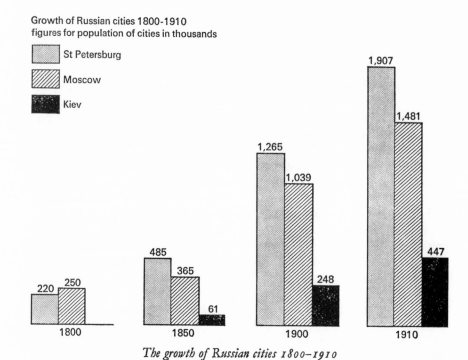

The growth of Russian cities 1800–1910

5
Recession

Soon after the first Duma was dissolved, some 200 of its members met at Vyborg in Finland and called for a campaign of passive resistance. There was scarcely a rustle of response from the Russian people, and the celebrants of autocracy gave thanks for this apparent return of divine favour. To be sure, the very defeat of the insurrection had excited a revival of revolutionary terrorism. But that, after all, only made it look the more like old times; and special tribunals were soon at work delivering death sentences, without the nuisance of juries to decide that the accused were guilty. In August 1906, a bomb at Stolypin's home narrowly failed to kill him but crippled his daughter for life. The Tsar, while proclaiming a state of emergency, was persuaded that Stolypin should have his chance to fortify the regime with reforms.

These were essentially directed towards establishing a strong encampment of support among the peasantry: without resort to the expropriation of the great estates, which would never have fitted into the Tsar's stud-box of reasonable measures. Stolypin's rural programme, inaugurated by emergency decrees, concentrated instead on the dispersal of communal lands. And this did, indeed, promote the growth of a gratefully prosperous class within the peasantry. Nature itself seemed to have entered into partnership with the regime. A succession of good harvests richly rewarded those whose resources had allowed them to invest in more efficient equipment; and this in turn provided them with incentive and resources to augment their holdings. But the relatively few could only take from the relatively many, whose capacity to resist was squeezed between the tax exactions of the state and the sheer momentum of their poverty. Reduced to shreds of land that barely yielded subsistence in the best of seasons, or driven for survival into hired labour, a multitude gathered in misery and humiliation, for their day of rage.

Politically, too, the face of the Stolypin era bore a flush that suggested health but belonged in fact to a consumptive condition. The second Duma was convoked for March 1907; and the election campaign was fierce. The Cadets, already handicapped by the exclusion of the Vyborg signatories from candidature, were still regarded, by the guardians of order, as the main immediate threat. Their meetings were disrupted by police; their spokesman assailed; and two of their leading figures murdered by licensed hooliganism. They emerged with their representation much diminished. But there was meagre comfort for the regime in that. The Social Democrats, their boycott abandoned, had carried off dozens of seats; the Social Revolutionaries had done scarcely less well; and with the peasant-based, radical Labour Group retaining its one hundred or so deputies, the left had come alarmingly close to domination of the Duma.

With the right notably weaker and much of it, moreover, unreliable, Stolypin looked to the centre for support. But the Cadets were not disposed, after their experience of the campaign and the popular verdict, to associate their fortunes with his. And the representatives of such national minorities as the Poles had reasons enough to exploit the difficulties of the regime. Stolypin wanted a pretext to disembarrass himself. The police provided one, by the framed involvement of Social Democratic deputies in an appeal for mutiny in the army. The Duma, suspicious of the evidence, did not immediately comply with Stolypin's demand that the deputies be expelled, and was dissolved on 3 June. A new electoral law reduced the representation of national minorities, especially the Poles, and increased the voting power of the gentry at the expense of workers and peasants.

The third Duma was, in consequence, so agreeable that it was permitted to run its full course, from 1907 to 1912. The only serious opposition to Stolypin's pursuit of reform came from resolute reactionaries; and the Tsar had a niche in his heart to accommodate such dissent. It was a counter-revolution whose success would determine events even after it had failed. The Stolypin era was fostering the very factors which Trotsky had identified as likely to produce a proletarian conquest of power: the land hunger of the peasant multitude; and the impotence of bourgeois liberalism.

It was fostering as well a third, that would sweep the way open for these two. In *Results and Prospects*, Trotsky had predicted that no fear of a proletarian uprising could remove the rivalries of the European powers, with the armed conflict that must ensue: and 'European war inevitably means European revolution'. Stolypin himself was loyal to the cause of Great Russian nationalism. Indeed, it was because of this loyalty that he was so determined on reform. For it was clear to him that the Russian empire would stand little chance against the assault of its enemies if its only defences were the ramparts of the past.

Yet, while there was agreement enough that the walls should be strengthened, his own attempts to do so were frustrated again and again. His colleagues in the Council of Ministers defeated his early proposal to establish effective freedom of religious belief; and when he eventually won their consent at least to some lightening of the civic restrictions on Jews, the Tsar would not hear of it. He recognized the need to reach an understanding with the Cadets, for the active allegiance of the middle class and in particular the professions; but behind his back, the Ministry of the Interior and the police department sabotaged the possibility, in the election campaign for the second Duma. And so, seeking to serve the empire as a servant of its regime, he helplessly helped both towards war and revolution. The Great Russian nationalism that would feed only on oppression and, in feeding, hunger all the more, was soon prowling for prey in the Balkans.

Stolypin was shot, in September 1911, at a gala performance of the opera in Kiev. The Tsar reported, in a letter to his mother:

Women were shrieking and, directly in front of me in the stalls, Stolypin was standing; he slowly turned his face towards us and with his left hand made the sign of the cross in the air. . . . People were trying to lynch the assassin. I am sorry to say the police rescued him from the crowd and took him to an isolated room for his first examination . . .

It was well that this last remark reached no further. For there was subsequently much whispering that the secret police had devised the assassination. Stolypin himself had felt sure that he would be assassinated by a police agent, and had told a colleague so.[1] The assassin, a certain Dmitri Bogrov, had worked for the police as an informer and been placed by them in the opera house, allegedly to keep a look-out for likely terrorists. And suspicions were only confirmed by the haste with which he was hanged, before a proper investigation could be conducted.

It is certain that Stolypin was regarded, by many supporters of the regime, as having outlived any usefulness that he might once have had. Within the Council of Ministers, there was mounting resistance to his tiresome preoccupation with reform, and the protection afforded by the Tsar was increasingly reluctant. The Tsarina herself now hated him for having banished her miracle-worker from St Petersburg.

At the beginning of November 1905, soon after signing his constitutional manifesto, the Tsar had noted in his diary: 'We have got to know a man of God – Grigory – from the Tobolsk province.' To the Tsarina herself, this Grigory Rasputin became in time scarcely distinguishable from God. For her only son had haemophilia, and Rasputin alone seemed able, almost certainly by using hypnosis, to stop the bleeding and the agony that the slightest accident would produce. Such apparently miraculous powers were, however, accompanied by such depravity as was soon a public scandal. The saviour was almost constantly drunk and given to brawling; traded favours for bribes like a wholesaler in corruption; and served a voracious sexual appetite by seduction or assault between his visits to brothels. There are entries in the dossier of the secret police that read as though they were pages from Dostoevsky:

9 September. When Rasputin went to see his brother Nicolai, who had at the time several other visitors in the house, their father made his appearance. The old man abused his son Grigory with the vilest expressions. Rasputin, in a savage fury, jumped up from the table where he was sitting, pushed his father into the yard, knocked him down and belaboured him with his fists, while the old man yelled: 'How dare you, miscreant!' They were separated with difficulty. Examination proved that the father had received a large purple bruise which completely closed his eye. Having recovered, the indomitable old man again attacked his son, abusing him worse than before; he threatened to tell everybody that Grigory was an ignorant old fool, who only knew 'how to fondle Dounia's [the maid's] soft parts'. This time Rasputin had to be held down with force to prevent him from assaulting his father again. They were both exceedingly drunk.[2]

But the Tsarina saw in every protest and complaint that reached her only the persecution that sanctity was bound to attract. And the Tsar, whose own cramped imagination could not encompass the possibility of so much vice, was persuaded that Rasputin, so contemptuous of politicians and so loyal to the autocracy, represented the simple wisdom of peasant Russia. Moreover, in the increasing isolation which was his refuge from the incomprehensibility of events, he grew less concerned or able to resist the ferocious devotions of his wife. Stolypin's departure from office would doubtless not have been much longer delayed. The bullet merely made this immediate. And if its purpose was the protection of the regime from any further experiments with reform, it signally succeeded. Rasputin was restored to the side of the Tsarina, where he came both to promote and to symbolize the political debauchery of the regime.

Meanwhile, however, with or without Stolypin, the Tsar sat on his throne. And for Russian revolutionaries abroad, the surface of Russian society looked defiantly firm. They knew, of course, that sooner or later the ground would crack and heave, as the stresses beneath grew at last too great for containment. But as year succeeded year, without any sign of a revolutionary revival in Russia, many Russian revolutionaries wondered whether the efforts made by the regime to strengthen the crust would not ensure the containment of the stresses for a long time to come. Lenin himself, writing about Stolypin's rural reforms, suggested that these might force revolutionaries 'to renounce any agrarian programme at all'. And he continued: 'It would be empty and stupid phrase-mongering to say that the success of such a policy in Russia is "impossible". It is possible.'[3]

Protracted exile, for political militants waiting to return home, is a little like living in a lift whose doors are always opening at the wrong floor. The longer that the passengers remain, the more the lift becomes for them their world; and their argument over why the controls are not working and what must be done to make them work, an end in itself.

Two men in particular, for different reasons, did not succumb to the disorientations of exile. For Lenin, the very disorientations served a determined, an imperative purpose. He wanted a party tightly united in obedience to his design for revolution; and the more acrimonious the argument became, the further there receded the prospect of a loose reunification around a divided, if not perverse, design. For Trotsky, the argument was a debilitating distraction; and when he took part, it was generally to say so, and to berate those whom he regarded as mainly responsible. Bolsheviks and Mensheviks had moved closer together in 1905 because they believed that the revolution was moving close. What, then, was their disunity now, but a faltering of faith that the revolution was coming ever closer?

Stolypin's rural reforms, or any similar efforts of the regime, must succeed only in promoting the very upheaval that they were directed to prevent. For that was the irony through which the iron logic of the historical process so often manifested itself. How, then, could the faith of a true revolutionary falter? Even Lenin was occasionally gripped by a kind of despair: that though the revolution would come, must come, he might not live to see it. Trotsky would as much have been gripped by a kind of despair that his heart might suddenly stop. He simply took it for granted that he would live to see the revolution, as he took it for granted that his heart would go on beating. Indeed, since the revolution was bound to come, each moment that passed was one moment less to wait.

The worst of exile is the homelessness: the drifting between memories and dreams that rots the spirit. Lenin, for all his commitment to the cosmopolitanism of revolution, was in spirit a Russian and so, when away from Russia, in spirit an exile. But unlike many other Russian exiles, he avoided drifting, by his hold on the hard demands of revolutionary organization. His records, his correspondence, his 'fighting campaigns' were the home that, snail-like, he carried along with him, from one foreign city to another. Trotsky, on the other hand, was not merely committed to the cosmopolitanism of revolution; he was himself a cosmopolitan revolutionary. To be sure, Russia was the country of his closest associations and political development; where he had done his most important revolutionary work, and believed that he had his most important revolutionary work still to do. Yet this belief was not due to his being Russian; it was the counterpart of his belief that Russia was the place where the fulfilment of history's socialist promise would begin. For him, home was the revolution, and the revolution belonged everywhere. He was not, therefore, ever in spirit an exile at all.

The 'third'[4] party congress, held at London in April 1905, had been boy-cotted by the Mensheviks; but Lenin had failed to persuade the partici-pants to accept his proposals for pressing ahead with a purely Bolshevik party. One year later, with the insurrection in Russia crushed, but with hopes of a resurgence running high and the pressures for party unity correspondingly strong, Bolsheviks and Mensheviks met together at Stockholm, for the fourth congress. Lenin confided to Lunacharsky his programme for the times. 'If we have a majority in the central committee, we will demand the strictest discipline. We will insist that the Mensheviks submit to party unity. . . .' Lunacharsky was troubled. 'But what if we remain in the minority? Shall we be forced to submit to them?' he asked. Lenin smiled. 'We won't permit the idea of unity to tie a noose around our necks, and we shall in no circumstances permit the Mensheviks to lead us by the rope.'[5]

The Mensheviks certainly seized one end of the rope: they were in the majority and elected seven of their number to the ten-member central com-mittee. But any subsequent tug would only reveal that the other end of the rope was loose. Lenin pocketed such victories as he had secured, including acceptance of his old formula for party membership, and turned his back on the defeats. Some Bolsheviks in Russia had taken to armed robbery, for resources with which to pursue the revolutionary cause. The congress had condemned these 'expropriations', against Lenin's own proposal that they be conducted 'under the party's supervision'. Far from discouraging any further raids in consequence, Lenin came increasingly to rely on them for funds to sustain his Bolshevik organization.

The fifth party congress, held at London in April/May 1907, drew more than 300 delegates: including representatives of the Bund, and of the Polish, the Latvian and the Lithuanian Social Democratic parties. Trotsky, fresh from his escape, attended. And there, too, was Rosa Luxemburg, the Polish socialist of Jewish family; so little and so frail, with large and beautiful eyes. She, of all his contemporaries, was most like Trotsky him-self, in her revolutionary passion and the power to express it; her creative love of ideas; her faith in the genius of the insurgent proletariat and her scorn for a leadership that distrusted and denied it. She, too, had castigated Lenin's view of what the party should be as an 'ultra-centralism' whose 'chief aim is to control the activity of the party rather than to fructify it, to limit rather than to develop it, to dragoon the movement rather than to educate it'.[6] And she, too, had warned, as though seeing far into the future: 'Mistakes made by a really revolutionary working-class movement are historically incomparably more fruitful and valuable than the infallibility of the best Central Committee that ever existed.'[7] She would become, with Karl Liebknecht, the leading figure of German revolutionary socialism; would condemn, before her murder in January 1919, the authoritarian course of revolutionary rule in Russia; and in 1932 be posthumously denounced by the Russian regime as a 'Trotskyist'. Yet she and Trotsky were never to become close friends. Their meetings, he would later maintain, were 'too brief and too infrequent'. And, he would also admit, he did not then appreciate her qualities sufficiently.[8] Both of them had little time for those who were driven to look for reassurance in the reflection of someone else's eyes. It may be that their very resemblance made each of them wary of reaching out to the other.

Maxim Gorky, then close to the Bolsheviks, attended the congress; and, when they met, he and Trotsky announced a mutual admiration. Kamenev and Zinoviev, whose blind but powerful gropings would one day help to topple Trotsky, were there. And there, too, scarcely noticed by anyone but Lenin, and by Trotsky not at all, was a certain delegate from the Caucasus, Vissarion Djugashvili, called 'Ivanovich', who was associated with the Bolshevik expropriation squads and would soon assume the name of Stalin.

The delegates held their sessions at the Brotherhood Church in the East End of London. Lenin had greeted Gorky's arrival with the promise of 'a fine free-for-all here'. And there was to be, indeed, all too evident an absence of brotherhood. When Lenin himself came to speak from the pulpit, Gorky would recall, 'he was interrupted by shouts of hatred', while one tall, bearded delegate 'kept jumping up from his seat and stuttering: "Little p-plots . . . p-playing at little p-plots!". . . .'[9] Trotsky attacked Mensheviks and Bolsheviks alike for their factional fury. 'If you think that a schism is unavoidable,' he argued, 'wait at least until events, and not merely resolutions, separate you.' But schism was, to many of the delegates, an event in itself; and one that the very lack of any other made the more desirable.

Trotsky expounded his theory of permanent revolution at the congress, and Rosa Luxemburg endorsed his views. Lenin, eager for a reconciliation with him, went out of his way to declare his support for Trotsky's advocacy of an alliance between workers and peasants. But Trotsky continued to look on Lenin as the leading 'splitter' and kept his political distance. Maintaining an independent position, he voted now with the Bolsheviks, now with the Mensheviks; inevitably angering both by his presumptuousness in judging between them. With the Mensheviks, and a majority of delegates, he voted for a party ban on 'expropriations'.

The elections to the central committee gave Lenin control; though one that was dependent upon the support of the Polish and Lett members. Even without this, however, he would have brushed aside the ban on 'expropriations'. Only a few weeks later, a Bolshevik squad, responsible to Stalin as Lenin's representative in the Caucasus, seized several hundred thousand roubles on their way to the state bank in Tiflis. And Lenin was also involved in a plan to counterfeit Russian banknotes: disclosed when the Prussian police discovered the watermarked paper in a Berlin store-house and arrested several Bolsheviks. The Mensheviks clamoured against this latest example of Leninist morality. 'If the affair is true,' Axelrod wrote to Martov, 'how can we remain in the same party as the Bolsheviks?' But there were Bolsheviks, too, who protested. Lenin wondered at the uproar. 'When I see Social Democrats announcing with pride and self-satisfaction that "we are no anarchists, no thieves, no brigands, we are above that, we reject the partisan struggle", then I ask myself – do these people understand what they are saying?'[10] He persuaded the central committee to entrust the party's foreign bureau with the investigation, and there a Bolshevik majority smothered the evidence.

While the factions confronted each other, the self-appointed conciliator could only consider bitterly how far apart he was from both. Increasingly the leading Mensheviks behaved as though 1905 had been a total defeat, rather than the near-miss that was the promise of victory at the next attempt; increasingly envisaged a mountain-side of transition that effectively left capitalism in command of the climb. Yet the leading Bolsheviks behaved as though no laws existed except those that they made for their own benefit; as though history itself could be centralized into submission. In Rosa Luxemburg's Polish socialist paper, Trotsky wrote, shortly after the congress: 'while the anti-revolutionary aspects of Menshevism are already revealing themselves fully, the anti-revolutionary features of Bolshevism strongly threaten to come to light only in the case of a revolutionary victory'. And what a scorpion-tail, indeed, this indictment would one day reveal.

From London, Trotsky went to Berlin, where he was reunited with Natalia. Parvus, who had himself been sentenced to exile in Siberia and had also succeeded in escaping, arranged for the German publication of *There and Back*. Trotsky agreed to write a special preface, and out of this there grew his subsequent book on 1905, *The Russian Revolution*. Together with Parvus, Trotsky and Natalia spent some part of the summer tramping in Switzerland, nourishing themselves on milk and mountain air, before settling for a few weeks at a village in Bohemia. When money ran short, Trotsky or Parvus would simply write an article for one of the various Social Democratic papers.

Trotsky, in particular, found such papers wide open to his contributions. The desirability of revolution in Russia, by virtually any means, was a matter on which all socialists, and even many liberals, regardless of their differences over the means of change in their own countries, were agreed.[11] He, more than anyone else, symbolized the revolt of 1905; and few could have failed to be impressed by the reports of his conduct at the trial of the Soviet leaders. To be sure, the continuing factional conflicts of the Russian revolutionaries fretted the patience of editors and readers alike. Clarifications of their cause from representatives of either faction were in general obscure and only excited demands for space to carry no less obscure clarifications from the representatives of the other. But this made Trotsky's own comments all the more welcome. He apparently stood beyond and above the factions. He knew the signposts of European culture. He had a lively and luminous style.

While Natalia went to fetch their son Leon, or Lyova as they called him, from Russia, Trotsky travelled to Stuttgart for the congress of the Second International. The major figures of European socialism were there, and they made much of him. Yet his own part in the proceedings seems to have been unremarkable. It was Rosa Luxemburg and Lenin who led the demand for a deeper commitment than a mere denunciation of militarism and agreement to oppose the outbreak of war. Due largely to their efforts, a statement was adopted which declared that if war did break out, socialists should intervene to stop it and simultaneously use the resulting 'economic and political crisis ... to rouse the peoples and thereby hasten the abolition of a capitalist rule'. It was a stirring expression of revolutionary brotherhood: which, in the event, would stir few of those who had subscribed to it.

Trotsky himself was filled with foreboding. Quelch, an English delegate, was expelled by the state government, in response to pressure from Berlin, for his insulting reference to a diplomatic conference as a meeting of robbers. There was no protest demonstration from either the German party or the congress. And Trotsky saw, behind the numerical power of German Social Democracy, 'the shadow of impotence'.[12] The conduct of the German party did not surprise him. It only confirmed the doubts that he had already felt and expressed. During his stay in the Bohemian village, he had written on German Social Democracy for a Bolshevik publishing outlet in St Petersburg and warned that it might, at a critical moment, come to the rescue of capitalism.

Even before, in *Results and Prospects*, he had glanced at the danger of such a betrayal: declaring that it was impossible to predict just what route from Russia the revolution would take, and that the movement might well be eastwards first, into Asia. But such remained for him a fall-back position. And he continued to hope that German Social Democracy, 'for us Russians ... mother, teacher, and living example',[13] would defy all doubt: by the revolt of the rank-and-file, if the leaders themselves should prove treacherous.

It was inevitably to Berlin, therefore, that he was drawn. But the police there refused him residence. And he settled instead, reluctantly, in Vienna. The Trotskys – a second son, Sergei, was born in 1908 – inhabited three rooms in a working-class suburb. One visitor, an American socialist of Russian origin, found the furniture insufficient for comfort, and Trotsky himself in clothes too cheap for the proprieties of the Viennese middle class. But then Trotsky cared nothing for such proprieties and, indeed, lived altogether more modestly than his means might have allowed. He had his earnings from books and articles, while his parents seem to have supplied him with occasional funds. It was simply that he believed the revolutionary cause to have first call on his resources, for all but the provision of necessities. And Natalia believed so, too. For they were as united in outlook as in love. He shared the housework, so that she might continue her studies in art; and with her guidance, he continued his own. He would visit the local public collections, and on his travels the foreign ones. He even began contributing reviews of Viennese exhibitions, under his old pen-name of Antid Oto, to the important Russian paper, *Kievskaya Mysl* (*Kievan Thought*).

Vienna in those days was a city of some two million people; or appreciably more than it was to have a quarter-century later. Its palaces and monuments proclaimed the grandeurs of empire; its academies and presses, and the cafés where its intellectuals met, its cultural distinction; its opera and concert halls, its special place in the history of music; the traffic of its streets, the variety and vigour of a multi-national metropolis. Yet it was at the same time a grate around whose dying fire the shadows gathered the more menacingly.

Behind the frieze of the court, the two structures of Austria and Hungary were pulling apart, while each was itself being pulled apart by the disaffection of its subjugated nationalities. In this bursting imperial parcel of fifty million people, Czechs, Poles, Ruthenes, Romanians, Serbs and Croats outnumbered the separately dominant Germans and Magyars together. And the dual monarchy of the aged Franz Joseph was little more than a blob of sealing-wax on the string of a martial aristocracy so thin and so frayed that the question was when rather than whether it would snap. It was the fear of what was likely to follow that increasingly seemed the principal binding force. But then this was a fear that was certain, sooner or later, to fulfil itself, in its very search for reassurance.

Nor was Austrian Social Democracy in a condition to offer a credible alternative. For it was doubly afflicted. Like other Social Democratic parties, it was split between revolutionaries and reformists; a split which its recent success in wresting general adult male suffrage had only widened. And, more serious still, it had the imperial disease. There were, in both the party and the trade unions, deep nationalist divisions; and these were scarcely counteracted by a very gavotte of socialist etiquette. Academic Marxists addressed one another as 'Herr Doktor', and were addressed in turn by workers as 'Genosse (Comrade) Herr Doktor', with sensuous ceremony. It was Victor Adler, the father figure of the party, who alone seemed able to maintain some semblance of unity. And he did so, to Trotsky's affectionate but hostile admiration, by the skilful exercise of a scepticism which allowed him to tolerate almost everything and adapt himself accordingly.

Trotsky joined the party; attended its meetings and demonstrations; even gave occasional short speeches in German from its platform. But he was bound to collide with the smug intellectuals in its leadership, and he did so the sooner for losing no time in seeking the views of Balkan socialists. From the Serbs in particular came indignant complaints of the Austro-German chauvinism in the Social Democratic *Arbeiter Zeitung*. He wrote what he considered to be a cautious and tempered criticism of the paper's outlook on foreign affairs, and it was published in *Neue Zeit*, the German socialist monthly of Karl Kautsky. The mandarins of the Austrian party were most displeased. Otto Bauer, one of the most eminent, who would one day be Foreign Minister, personally took him to task for exaggerating the significance of the *Arbeiter Zeitung* line. 'Foreign policy does not exist for Austria–Hungary. No worker ever reads about it. It has not the slightest importance.' Trotsky found it difficult to trust his ears.

In an article of January 1909 that he wrote for *Kievan Thought*, he called the Balkans the 'Pandora's box' of Europe; and declared that only a democratic federation of all the Balkan nationalities, on the pattern of Switzerland or the United States, could provide peace and the proper conditions for productive development in the area. Alarmed but not surprised, he watched Tsarist foreign policy, with the support of leading Russian liberals, take the lever of Pan-Slavism to the lid; and repeatedly warned Balkan socialists against an imperialism masquerading as emancipation.

For all his commitment to the social struggle everywhere, however, the course of that struggle in Russia remained his primary concern. He toured the Russian communities of exiles and students, to expound his theory of permanent revolution and feed the embers of the socialist cause. In October 1908 he accepted the editorship of an exile paper, *Pravda* (*Truth*), that was barely breathing. By the end of the year, the small group of Ukrainian Mensheviks that had invited him existed no longer; and the paper, under Trotsky's sole control was, if somewhat unsteadily, on its feet.

When there was enough money, from Trotsky's own writings for less impoverished papers or from well-wishers, *Pravda* appeared, as intended, every fortnight. But the cash box was too often empty. Issues were postponed, and there were anguished appeals from the editor for help to pay the printers, or the postage on letters to Russia, or the costs of smuggling copies across the frontier. Trotsky was forced to sell his books, and Natalia from time to time took belongings to the pawnshop. Recourse to the central committee of the Russian party encountered Lenin's demand that Trotsky accept a representative as co-editor. Trotsky refused. Lenin turned the screw by insisting that the Bolshevik printshop in Geneva charge *Pravda* commercial rates. Trotsky would not yield. And the paper survived. Indeed, it acquired a notable following in Russia. Its campaign for party unity found far more favour there than among the cantankerous exiles. Its deliberately popular style added nothing to Trotsky's reputation as a writer, but attracted readers. And if Trotsky lacked a factional organization, he did have contacts with individual revolutionary groups, such as the clandestine union of Black Sea sailors, whose own paper he had a hand in producing.

His parents brought his elder daughter to visit him in Vienna. Then, in 1910, they came abroad again, to Berlin. His mother was seriously ill and had one of her kidneys removed there. The operation seemed to have restored her marvellously to health; but within a few months of her return to Yanovka, she was dead. Her dogged courage had won Trotsky's respect. And if the depth of his feeling for her was not such as to make him grieve greatly, he could at least be glad that she had lived to take some pride in his achievements.[14]

For all the continuing conflicts in the Russian party, the frustrations of Social Democratic politics in Austria, and the difficulties of supporting his family while *Pravda* devoured his resources, he was happy enough. He was advancing the revolutionary cause, in his own way. Natalia was a source of beauty whose abundance he could never drain. As their minds developed, his two sons gave increasing delight to the teacher in him. He had few friends, but they were firm ones. In particular, the old Russian émigré Semyon Lvovich Klyachko and his family afforded affection, kindness, and often help: with the pleasure of informed political talk, cultural interests that moved easily through four European languages, and good music.

One of the most rewarding friendships of his life came to Trotsky through the door of *Pravda* itself. Among the assistants he acquired was a young intellectual, Adolphe Joffe, whose nervous breakdowns had brought him to Adler for psychoanalysis. Trotsky was excited by the new science, and would, after the revolution, warn Russian scholars against closing their minds to what was valuable in its discoveries. His own cure for Joffe, however, consisted in patiently encouraging his talent, promoting his self-confidence, and, above all, giving him a sense of purpose in serving the revolution. Joffe recovered so far as to visit Russia on a mission for the paper; and, though arrested in Odessa, to suffer long imprisonment and later exile, would emerge in February 1917 ready to play a distinguished part in events, as Trotsky's loyal and loving disciple.

Lenin was, meanwhile, beset by troubles. As though the quarrel between Bolshevism and Menshevism was not enough, Bolsheviks had begun to quarrel amongst themselves. Some of Lenin's principal lieutenants, led by Alexander Bogdanov, had succumbed to the idealism of the Austrian physicist and philosopher Ernst Mach, and were attempting to unite it with Marxism in a socialist religion. Society was, in all its manifestations, Bogdanov maintained, 'consciously psychic life'. Men looked to God as the perfection of their own attributes and the apotheosis of their goals. Through socialism, this God would become the ideal of their collectivist strivings. Lenin considered all this obeisance to the primacy of the mind and this babbling about God as outrageous. He called it intellectual necrophilia. And in May 1909, he published a long book against it.[15] But this was not the only challenge that he faced. These same 'God-builders' were at the centre of an agitation for a boycott of the Duma, with a recall of the party deputies. That he himself had once believed in the necessity of such a boycott did not matter: he believed quite otherwise now. Finally, and most formidably, the pressure for party reunification was mounting: especially in Russia, where the underground workings had suffered serious subsidence from the activities of police spies and the demoralization of many revolutionaries.

From 15 January to 5 February 1910, the leaders of the factions, with Trotsky representing his own group of conciliators, met in Paris, for a plenary session of the central committee. Lenin was an anguished participant. In a letter to Gorky, of 11 April, he would describe the meeting as 'Three weeks of suffering, every nerve is overstrained, a hundred thousand devils!'[16] He was dragged by his colleagues into an agreement that he knew would not last; if only because he intended to break it himself. Mensheviks and Bolsheviks resolved to expel their respective extremists; disband their separate organizations and suspend their separate publications; even unite their financial resources in a fund under the trusteeship of three eminent German socialists – Clara Zetkin, Franz Mehring and Karl Kautsky. It was widely regarded as a personal triumph for Trotsky. The central committee paid formal tribute to his campaign in *Pravda*; agreed to provide the paper with a regular subsidy; and appointed as intermediary Lev Borisovich Kamenev, who was the husband of Trotsky's sister Olga and himself a leading Bolshevik conciliator.

In the event, Lenin did not need to work against the settlement. The Mensheviks wrecked it for him, and within a few weeks. For they refused to expel their own extremists. These, the so-called 'liquidators', who were agitating for an end to clandestine revolutionary activities and a concentration on constitutional pressures instead, were simply too numerous. Their departure from the party would have left the Bolsheviks in indisputable control. Lenin, who had already excommunicated the 'God-builders' and boycotters from his own faction, could convincingly claim that the Bolsheviks alone had kept to the terms of the bargain.

Trotsky himself publicly laid the blame for the breakdown of unity on the Mensheviks. But he resisted Kamenev's demands to come out still more vigorously: regarding these as an encroachment on his editorial independence and an attempt to capture *Pravda* for Bolshevism. To be sure, the 'liquidators' were detestable. No one recognized more clearly than he did the crucial revolutionary role of the underground. Yet, as Martov and others among the more congenial Mensheviks lost no occasion to remind him, Lenin would consider his success at ironing out the crease of the 'liquidators' as only a beginning. To that dictator, any opinions but his own were intolerable. Trotsky asked the central committee to withdraw Kamenev as intermediary and appoint someone else. The central committee replied by withdrawing its subsidy.

Trotsky was angry with both factions and took them to task in the German Social Democratic press: declaring in one article that the exile leaders did not really represent the revolutionary movement in Russia, which desired unity and saw no sense in their squabbles. When he arrived at Copenhagen in October 1910 for a congress of the International, he found Plekhanov and Lenin heading an attempt to have the article formally condemned by the Russian delegation. Suspecting that most delegates had been fed with distorted reports, Trotsky insisted that his article be read out in full before any further discussion. Presented with the text, the delegates overwhelmingly rejected the proposal to censure him. The German Social Democratic press was, after all, in the family. The general impatience of the movement in Russia at the squabbling in exile was no secret. And Trotsky had only written about the leaderships of both factions what each had been trumpeting about the other. Indeed, a new source of embitterment was emerging, as each sought to wrest the funds deposited with the three German trustees, and impugned the other's qualifications in the process. Since much of this money had originally come from 'expropriations', there was a certain comic irony in the self-righteousness with which both, but especially the Mensheviks, pressed their claims.

Lenin now decided on a course of action that amounted to the kidnapping of the party. To Russia he dispatched representatives for an organizing commission that would select delegates to a 'general party conference'. The initiative met with little enthusiasm from local Bolshevik committees. But the secret police, apprised of the plans, and practised in promoting revolutionary division, took an uninvited hand. They arrested known Bolshevik conciliators and left the field free for such professing hard-line Leninists as included their own agents. At Prague, in January 1912, there accordingly assembled fourteen voting delegates – of whom at least two were police spies – claiming to constitute 'the supreme organ of the party'.[17] And assuming the powers of a party congress, the conference appointed a new central committee which included one of the spies, a certain Roman Malinovsky. In *Pravda*, Trotsky raged at this shameless attempt to snatch the party. But Lenin was not to be pushed from his purpose by the outcry of the outmanoeuvred. He and his supporters would henceforward continue to assert that they were no longer a faction, but the party itself.

The social unrest in Russia that the revolutionaries had expected to surface from the depths of reaction seemed instead to have drowned there. Trotsky, seeking for a theory that would fit the facts, concluded that economic difficulties tended to depress a working class exhausted from unsuccessful struggle, and that only an industrial revival would provide Russian workers with sufficient self-confidence to undertake the struggle again. Party economists declared that such a revival could not occur in a period of reaction. Trotsky maintained that it could and inevitably would.

In large measure due to considerable foreign investment, an economic quickening began in 1910, and expressions of labour discontent did not lag far behind. On 4 April 1912, troops fired on striking miners at the Lena goldfields of northern Siberia, causing some 500 casualties. When the news reached western Russia, a week or so later, spontaneous strikes of protest swept the major industrial cities. It was not yet the morning of the revolution. But, for the more wakeful of the revolutionaries, it was the first blur of light in the sky.

The government sought to release some of the pressure by easing the restrictions on political activity. And on 22 April there appeared in St Petersburg the first issue of the Bolshevik daily, *Pravda*, under Stalin's immediate command. It was premeditated plagiarism: an attempt to appropriate the popularity of Trotsky's paper. And Trotsky was furious. He railed at this 'theft' in the pages of his own *Pravda* and even threatened 'further steps'. Lenin, who was at the very least an accessary before the fact, advised Stalin to ignore alike the fury and the threats.

Trotsky had never ceased to hope that the party would reunite, if only driven to do so by events: and now, with the new mood in Russia, he believed that it was time to try again. At Vienna, in August, there gathered a group of Russian revolutionaries in response to his initiatives. But the purpose of the meeting was undermined from the start. Lenin and his supporters had simply declined to attend. Moreover, though the participants were certainly far more representative of the party at large than Lenin's Prague conference had been, they were less determined or unscrupulous. Indeed, they did not claim to be constituting a party conference at all, but only a conference of party organizations; and they called their organizing committee no more than that. In consequence, they effectively left the illegitimate assumption of party leadership by the Leninists uncontested. Nor could the coherence of this 'August Bloc', as it came to be known, survive on the husks of opposition to Lenin. There was far too much that divided its assortment of Mensheviks, dissident Bolsheviks, Bundists and Trotskyists. Trotsky himself was quick to see that the attempt had failed. And feeling the need to escape for a time from the pre-occupations of Russian exile politics, he accepted in September the offer from *Kievan Thought* to go as its military correspondent to the Balkans, where the outbreak of war seemed imminent.

The Young Turks, who had snatched command of the Ottoman empire from its palsied Sultanate, had disclosed no disposition to liberate its subject peoples, but also no such strength as suggested that they had a right to such rule. In July 1911, Italy, driven beyond endurance by the injustice of having, in a world of empires, no empire of its own, declared war on Turkey, so as to acquire Libya; and with much of the Turkish army locked away there, several Balkan states moved in concert to take on Turkey themselves, for the extensive remains of its empire in their midst.

In a campaign of some six weeks, during October and November 1912, Montenegro, Serbia, Bulgaria and Greece together pushed the Turks back virtually to the gates of Constantinople. The campaign was to start a good deal more than it finished. Vienna saw in dismay Serbia emerge with territories and prestige much enlarged, and turned to Bulgaria among the victors as a countervailing force. Within a year of the first Balkan war, the second would break out: as Bulgaria, dissatisfied with its share of the spoils and encouraged by Vienna, sought to show itself the lion of the Balkans. But the Serbs and the Greeks were prepared for it to pounce; and with the Romanians leaping in from the north, compelled Bulgarian submission to a humiliating peace. If there was a lion of the Balkans, it was Serbia now; and Vienna grew increasingly concerned to tame it, before it should rend, by subversive example or attack, the Austro-Hungarian empire apart. The 'Pandora's box' of Europe had been well and truly opened.

When Trotsky reached Belgrade in October 1912, he watched, marching off to the frontier,

the eighteenth infantry regiment, in uniforms of protective colouring and bark sandals, and wearing a sprig of green in their caps. The sandals on their feet and the little sprig of green in their caps, in combination with the full fighting outfit, gave the soldiers the look of men doomed for sacrifice. At that moment, nothing so deeply burned the madness of war into my consciousness as those sprigs and bark sandals.[18]

He was an outstanding correspondent. He knew that the purpose of detail was not to provide a reflection of events, as though the eye was merely a mirror, but to reveal their meaning. He did not pretend to be telling the disinterested truth: so often the practice of those who are merely indifferent to any distinction between the truth and the lie; or of those who seek to conceal that partisanship alone distinguishes for them the one from the other. Virtually whatever he wrote declared his own interest. It was the assertion of human dignity against the degradations of war. And to this interest he remained loyal: wherever it took him.

He set out with a sympathy for the oppressed of the Ottoman empire and support for the endeavours of the Balkan states to liberate them. But he soon grew disgusted at the supposed liberators themselves, whose rich and powerful clamoured for freedom and justice while exploiting the poor and the weak; at the debaucheries of propaganda; and the violence of nationalisms blind to all humanity outside. He denounced Bulgarian atrocities against wounded and captured Turks. The Bulgarian censors, led by a radical poet who had two years before addressed with him a socialist rally in Sofia, confiscated his reports and barred him from visiting the front. Trotsky replied in an 'Open Letter to the Censor', which denounced the motives and function of military censorship. The controversy over atrocities reached Russia, where the Bulgarians were being presented as crusaders. Miliukov, the liberal historian, questioned the accuracy of Trotsky's accusations, to a chorale of Slav solidarity. Trotsky offered the confirmation of reputable English and German correspondents. As the argument raged, government papers hinted that 'Antid Oto' was not only a notorious exile but also an agent of the Austro-Hungarian empire. Then, with the outbreak of the second Balkan war, the Serbs became the crusaders and the Bulgarians the infidels for both the government and much liberal opinion in Russia. Trotsky, so recently their scourge, now turned to defend the Bulgarians, against the violence of the victorious.

He was, from the outset, far more than a military correspondent. While he eagerly grasped opportunities to visit the front, where he doubtless lodged in his mind his first lessons in warfare, he was concerned as well to get behind the fighting and explore the structures of the societies involved. And it was in pursuit of this purpose that he came to consider, during a visit to Romania in August 1913, the 'Jewish question'.

Austrian law required all children at school to receive religious instruction in the faith of their parents. Trotsky and Natalia, both confirmed atheists and with no religion listed in their documents, chose to comply by registering their children as Lutherans. One writer has suggested that Trotsky might have wished to protect his sons from the distresses to which Jews were subject; might unconsciously have been seeking to identify himself with Marx, who had been born to a long line of distinguished rabbis but had been reared as a Lutheran; might have taken this step as one more away from the ghetto, towards an association with those clean, tidy and industrious German Lutherans who had so impressed him as a child.[19] Yet the two Trotsky boys were, in fact, not Jews at all; since in Jewish law, children are born into the condition of their mother, and Natalia was by origin an unquestionable Greek Orthodox Gentile. There is no reason to doubt the explanation given by Natalia herself: that

Lutheranism had been chosen 'because it was a religion which seemed easier on the children's shoulders as well as their souls'.[20]

Certainly, as with his earlier assumption of a permanent new name, there is not the slightest evidence that Trotsky was attempting to disengage himself from his Jewish origins. Such an attempt would have demanded the camouflage of indifference to any peculiarly Jewish suffering. And where even Rosa Luxemburg's compassion seemed at times to find only the special plight of Jews a little tiresome, Trotsky saw this plight for the special one that it was. This did not mean that he saw any special answer to the Jewish question. For him, there was only one answer to all such questions; in the classless unity of mankind. But his consciousness, his acknowledgement of the special question itself can scarcely be dismissed as unimportant, when so many of his revolutionary colleagues with Jewish origins chose rather to avoid or deny it. His own values were, simply, more consistent and rational.

He went further, in his series of articles for *Kievan Thought*, than establishing the existence of a Jewish question in Romania. He maintained that 'Romania as a whole manifests itself through its Jewish question'. In an impassioned account, he described how the 300,000 Jews in the country had the obligations but not the rights of citizenship: were subject to taxation and military service, but were forbidden to reside in villages or take government jobs; to practise many of the professions; to acquire normal schooling for more than a tiny quota of their number. And the reasons for all this, Trotsky delineated in the person of Purishkevich, a leading conservative deputy and anti-Semite.

Romania is ruled by Purishkevich. . . . Purishkevich 'hates' Jews. But this hate is a special one: without Jews Purishkevich cannot manage, and this he knows full well himself. He is in need of Jews, but which ones? – those without rights. . . . Such a Jew has to serve as middleman between Purishkevich's landowner and peasant, between Purishkevich's politician and his clientele – in the capacity of leaseholder, money-lender, middleman, hired journalist. He has to carry out Purishkevich's dirtiest assignments – and Purishkevich has none but such. Moreover, while doing service for exploiting feudalism, the Jew, deprived of his rights, has to serve at the same time as lightning rod for the indignation of the exploited. While robbing the peasantry of everything, ravaging the treasury . . . [Purishkevich] then fulfils his highest mission when from the speaker's platform, or through the columns of his press, indignantly denouncing the Jewish leaseholders, the Jewish usurers. . . . This is the servile base of Romanian anti-Semitism.[21]

What was there in Romania, however, to compare with what was taking place in Russia itself? In 1840, some Jews in Damascus had been charged with having murdered an elderly monk so as to drink his blood for ritual purposes. *'Chacun à son goût'* ('Everyone to his taste') had commented Heinrich Heine, the great German poet and himself a Jew converted to Christianity for convenience's sake: mocking the madness of this attempt to resuscitate the monsters of Christian medievalism. Even in the latter-day darkness of the Ottoman empire, the trial had ended in acquittals. Yet now, well over a decade into the twentieth century, and in a major city of European Russia, the attempt was being made again.

On 12 March 1911, a thirteen-year-old boy, Andrei Yushchinsky, living in a suburb of Kiev, went off to school and disappeared. Eight days later, his dead body, with multiple stab wounds, was discovered. And at his funeral, mimeographed leaflets were distributed, blaming the Jews for his ritual murder and calling for a pogrom of revenge. In the months that followed, investigations leading directly to the evident guilt of several known criminals were suppressed; the investigators themselves were victimized; and more tractable substitutes were put in charge of the case. The resolve to ensure a ritual murder trial stretched from fanatics in the local Union of the Russian People, through various officials of the Kiev administration and reactionary deputies in the Duma, to the Minister of Justice, Shcheglovitov, and the Tsar himself.[22]

On 22 July 1911, a thirty-nine-year-old Jew, Mendel Beiliss, who worked as a dispatch clerk at a local Jewish-owned brickworks, and whose most remarkable characteristic appeared to be his very unremarkableness, was arrested. He was kept in prison for the remaining months of that year, for all the months of the next, and for month after month of still another, while the authorities sought to scrape together a case. When his trial at last opened, on 25 September 1913, the indictment, based on assertions that Jews were required to use the blood of Christians for a whole variety of ritual purposes, met with overwhelming incredulity in the civilized Christian world outside. Derisively, *The Times* of London wondered how 'the huge supply of such a demand has escaped general attention hitherto'. And there was little comfort to be drawn by the authorities from the response within Russia itself, where disgust and shame at the proceedings reached far beyond the encampments of revolutionary and liberal opinion. Leading monarchist and anti-Semite V. V. Shulgin, whose daily *Kievlyanin (Kievan)* was the reactionary rival of *Kievan Thought*, denounced the intimidation of honest officials that lay behind the bringing of such a case, and called the indictment mere 'claptrap'. For the first time in the life of the paper, copies were seized and confiscated by the censor.

In the event, despite the diligent prejudice of the presiding judge, and the care with which the jury was chosen, Beiliss was acquitted, on 23 October. Still, the authorities were not too displeased, and the Minister of Justice attended a 'victory banquet' in St Petersburg. For the questions directed to the jury had been so phrased that acquittal implied no rejection of the general charge that Jews engaged in ritual murder. Indeed, the jury found it proved that the boy Andrei Yushchinsky had been attacked 'in one of the buildings of the Jewish surgical hospital . . . when he had lost five glasses [*sic*] of blood'. The presiding judge was rewarded with promotion to chief justice of the Kiev appellate court and the present of a gold watch from the Tsar.

There can be no doubt of Trotsky's ardent interest in the affair. He followed the course of the trial closely, through the extensive reports carried by the Russian press; and his long essay on the case, published by *Neue Zeit* in November, has a dramatic quality that he could scarcely have made more distinct and immediate had he been sitting, day after day, in the courtroom himself.

A suburban shoemaker, a Jewish capitalist, a peasant drayman, a police detective, street arabs, liberal journalists, thieves, a Greek Orthodox monk (a Jewish convert), a convict, spinsters of light conduct, a priest, an officer of the gendarmerie, a cashier of a bankrupt loan bank in the role of a leading patriot, a former revolutionary in the role of a voluntary investigator, a lawyer-witness, a medical professor, a Catholic priest, a professor of a spiritual academy and a Jewish rabbi – thieves and 'reputable' people, learned specialists and fanatics, refuse of pogromist reaction and revolutionary splinters – all these passed before the amazed eyes of twelve obscure people, chiefly peasants, deliberately placed there by the Ministry of Justice for the greatest convenience of the medieval trial court.[23]

Trotsky cited the Dreyfus case, but only to stress the differences between the two. For there was little likeness between such cynical and erudite figures of French republican government as Poincaré, who believed in neither God nor the Devil, and a Tsar who was still convinced that witches went riding at night on their broomsticks. There was little likeness between an accusation of military treason, however 'stunning was the deliberate falsity of it', and the plight of an ordinary Jewish worker, suddenly torn away from his family to be told that he had drained the blood of a living child, with the object of drinking it to the joy of his Jehovah. Indeed, 'one need only visualize for a moment the state of this wretch during twenty-six months of isolated imprisonment to cause one's hair to stand on end'.

And having captured something of the horror, he captured, too, something of the gruesome farce.

For three days the swindlers of the prosecution joined hands with the swindlers of the experts in a study which lasted hours long in order to define the meaning of 'Se'ir' in the Talmud – a word completely unknown to Beiliss. And thus it emerged, in the circumstances of the case, that if 'Se'ir' meant merely 'goat', Beiliss stood a chance, perhaps, of returning to his family, but if, according to certain texts of the third century, 'Se'ir' also meant 'Roman', then Beiliss would not escape imprisonment for life with hard labour.

Moreover, he had so mastered the details of the whole affair that he was able convincingly to establish the connection with the Crown and the course of the conspiracy against the proper processes of justice. The era of reaction, he concluded, had so exhausted its internal resources that it was searching for sustenance in external excitements. Yet such exploits would only prove self-defeating. And, indeed, what had the government achieved? It had counted on pogroms, so that it might flourish its authority by subduing them. The Black Hundreds had promised pogroms, especially in the event of an acquittal. There had been an acquittal. But there had been no pogroms. For the government did not have such popular forces at its disposal as could be left to provide spontaneous outbursts of anti-Semitism. The Beiliss affair presaged a new era, informed by a profound revolutionary mood, in Russia.

There was rather less occasion for encouragement in the conduct of the Russian revolutionary exiles. The August Bloc was now little more than Menshevism by another name, and a Menshevism scarcely less set on schism than were the Leninists. Trotsky's own resistance to this development encountered mounting impatience from the Menshevik leaders: Martov, writing to Axelrod, maintained that the time had come to show Trotsky their 'teeth'. And, from the other encampment, Lenin assailed him with a new bitterness: accusing him of 'resounding but hollow phrases' and 'incredible bombast'; of having no opinions on any point of substance; of always 'creeping through the crack of this or that controversy and running from one side to the other'.[24] Trotsky did not publicly reply to these attacks with corresponding invective. But he did write, in a private letter to the Menshevik, Chkheidze: 'the whole foundation of Leninism at the present time is built on lying and falsification and carries within itself the poisoned element of its own disintegration'. The letter was intercepted by the censorship and placed in the archives, where it would be discovered after the revolution. And Stalin would have it published, in the campaign against Trotsky that followed Lenin's death and transfiguration.

It is all too probable that Stalin required no prodding from Lenin to regard Trotsky with antipathy even in these early years. For he could scarcely fail to resent someone possessed of so many qualities, as thinker and writer and orator, that he himself lacked; who was so close to him in age and so far away in achievement; who had not even noticed him when they had both attended the congress of 1907. They were now to meet for the first time.

One day in early 1913, while back in Vienna between the two Balkan wars, Trotsky was visiting Skobelev, a Menshevik who had been his principal assistant in the production of *Pravda*. As they talked, the door was opened, without warning, by a man of middle height, with a dark and pock-marked face. Perhaps taken aback at seeing Trotsky, he paused;

growled what might have been meant as a greeting; went over to the samovar, where he filled the empty glass in his hand; then turned and left the room, without saying a word. Skobelev reported that the stranger was a certain Djugashvili, a Bolshevik from the Caucasus who was now a member of Lenin's central committee. In the very last year of his life, Trotsky would recall that meeting; and the 'glint of animosity' in Stalin's 'yellow' eyes.[25]

6

War and Revolution

While Bolshevik and Menshevik leaders were brawling in exile, their followers in Russia were generally responsive to the pressures for reconciliation from among the mass of reawakened workers. For the elections to the fourth Duma, in September 1912, the candidates of the two factions collaborated closely and pledged themselves to work for a united functioning of the Social Democratic contingent. In the event, six Bolsheviks, including Roman Malinovsky, and seven Mensheviks were elected. The new deputies did, indeed, begin by acting as members of the same party. They even took a decision, against the vote of Malinovsky, that they should write for both the Bolshevik *Pravda* and the Menshevik *Luch* (*Ray*), in an approach to the issue of a single Social Democratic daily.

Lenin had no intention of indulging such defiance from his faction. And by October 1913, with Malinovsky as their commander in the preparatory campaign, the Bolshevik deputies had formally broken with their Menshevik colleagues. Soon rumours started circulating that Malinovsky was a police spy. But Lenin refused to believe it; and resisted demands, led by the Mensheviks, for a full investigation. (Only when, with the revolution, police records became available were the rumours confirmed. Malinovsky, who had been conducting Bolshevik propaganda among Russian prisoners in German camps, voluntarily returned to Russia. He might well have believed that Lenin would protect him. He was tried and shot, with some dispatch, in November 1918.)

The shock waves produced by the Bolshevik repudiation of Social Democratic unity in the Duma looked likely for a while to shatter Leninism. The circulation of *Pravda* fell to almost half of what it had been; dissension disrupted much of the clandestine organization; and there was soon little left in the Bolshevik purse but its lining. In response to widespread insistence that it intervene, the Bureau of the Socialist International convened at Brussels, in the middle of July 1914, a conference of all groups associated with the Russian party. Lenin did not attend. But three delegates, furnished with detailed instructions, arrived to represent the Bolshevik central committee. They found themselves virtually isolated. Plekhanov went so far in his attack on Lenin that the chairman put a stop to it. A resolution, accepted by all but the Bolshevik and Lett delegates, called for unity; and Lenin was left in no doubt that the next congress of the International, due to be held at Vienna in August, would deal decisively with any further recalcitrance from him.[1]

In 1913, Lenin had written to Maxim Gorky: 'War between Austria and Russia would be very useful to the cause of the revolution in western Europe. But it is hard to believe that Franz Josef and Nicholas will grant us this pleasure.'[2] It was not quite the word that Trotsky would have chosen to use. But certainly help, to the revolution in Russia, and to the Bolshevik cause, was soon to be given by the two emperors.

On 28 June, at Sarajevo, a Bosnian nationalist assassinated the heir to the Habsburg throne. Within a few weeks, most of Europe was at war. The Austro-Hungarian government, with German support assured against any intervention, was determined to stamp out the Serbian mischief. The government of the Tsar, confident in its alliance with France and Britain, dedicated itself, in a war manifesto, to succour Serbia, 'a kindred land', and 'safeguard the honour and dignity of Russia as a great Power. . . .'

The prevailing mood of sullen confusion in Russia seemed translated overnight into one of patriotic ecstasy. To be sure, the Social Democratic deputies, with sudden unity of purpose, refused to vote for war credits and even issued a public declaration repudiating the war. But their example was not followed in the streets, which resounded with demonstrations of loyalty. And the rest of the Duma, recently so agitated by questioning and criticism, joined in obeisance to the regime, as representing now the cause of Russia itself.

At a solemn service in the Winter Palace, the Tsar, avoiding the risks of originality, repeated the oath sworn by Alexander I at the time of Napoleon's invasion, 'not to make peace so long as there is a single enemy on Russia's soil'. The implicit analogy did not bear serious examination: but who was then disposed to undertake any? When the Tsar and Tsarina appeared on the balcony, the multitudes gathered below, in the square which had been the site of 'Bloody Sunday' nine years before, sank to their knees and sang the national anthem. At a subsequent ceremony in Moscow, the Tsar kissed the more sacred and supposedly more efficacious of the icons, in the Cathedral of the Assumption. Afterwards, walking along a narrow platform above a kneeling multitude of his subjects, 'some of whom even kissed the ground as he passed', he was 'acclaimed with one never-ending cheer'. The British ambassador was much moved. But he remained sensible enough to wonder how long all the rapture would last, and 'what would be the feeling of the people for their "Little Father" were the war to be unduly prolonged'.[3]

In Vienna, the cry of the streets was 'Death to the Serbs!' and Trotsky's six-year-old son, Sergei, disputing the sentiment with other young boys, came home with a black eye. Trotsky himself, moving through the centre of the city, watched the workers from the suburbs mingle with their masters in common excitement. He saw how war was immediately strengthening the power of the state, as the one certainty among so much that was uncertain. But he saw, too, how the feeling of the poor and oppressed, that they were now on an equal footing with the rich and the powerful, might make revolution out of war. The new social unity, he wrote, was no more than a sort of political moratorium. 'The notes have been extended to a new date, but they will have to be paid.'

On the morning of 3 August, he sought advice on whether the Russian revolutionaries in Austria should prepare to leave. At the headquarters of the Austrian party, he found Victor Adler's son listlessly busy with the material for the imminent congress of the International, which no one now believed would be able to meet. He was taken by Victor Adler himself to see the chief of the political police, who warned him to leave the country at once. By the evening, he and his family were on the train to Zurich.

All was in turmoil. Jaurès, the French socialist leader, who had sought so zealously to prevent the outbreak of war, had been assassinated on the eve of mobilization, by a deranged patriot. It seemed to symbolize the madness raging across Europe. Yet surely, and despite their dismal record of confusion and retreat, avowed socialists in the advanced industrial states would recognize this madness for what it was, and resist it; would repudiate the call to mutual slaughter in the service of the rival regimes that held them captive. Were they not committed to do so by the Stuttgart congress of the International? Had not the Russian Social Democratic deputies, and their Serbian counterparts as well, not taken the first steps? But there was to be no such challenge from any other socialist party among the belligerents. On 4 August, the representatives of German Social Democracy, with only two exceptions, voted in the Reichstag for war credits. Lenin at first simply refused to believe it possible. The copy of *Vorwaerts*, which carried the report, he pronounced a forgery. Then, finally convinced otherwise, he exclaimed, 'The Second International is dead!' Trotsky himself was to write years afterwards that the news had shocked him 'even more than the declaration of war', and that the vote 'remained one of the tragic experiences of my life'.[4]

It was no time for silent sorrow. In *The War and the International*, a pamphlet primarily directed at German Social Democrats, he denounced the excuse that in fighting the Russia of the Tsar, the Germany of the

Kaiser was performing a progressive historical function. The objective of all socialists must be a democratic peace, produced by a rising of peoples against their rulers in the belligerent countries, for 'the creation of a new, more powerful and stable fatherland, the republican United States of Europe, as the foundation for the United States of the World'. The illicit circulation of the pamphlet in Germany led to Trotsky's indictment before the courts there; and he was sentenced in his absence to a term of imprisonment. It was to prove of some use: providing him with a ready reply to Russian accusations that he was an agent of the Central Powers.

Neutral Switzerland did not escape the passions of belligerency. In parliament there sat two socialist deputies of one name: Jean Sigg from Geneva, fervent for a French victory; and Johann Sigg from Zurich, fervent for a German one. But such Social Democratic distraction was generally confined to the top floor, and there was a warm welcome lower down for the Russian who took sides only with revolution. The labour union, Eintracht, which was internationalist in membership and outlook, made much of him. It adopted the manifesto that he drafted, repudiating the war and those socialists who had fallen into patriotism. It promoted his influence within the Swiss party, to whose national convention he was elected a delegate. But Trotsky found Switzerland stifling. A shortage of potatoes and a surplus of cheese seemed to be the main public preoccupations. He accepted with eagerness an invitation from *Kievan Thought* to be one of its war correspondents. On 19 November, he left Switzerland for France.

There he found his former colleagues in the International devoted, above all else, to the defeat of Germany, and summoning sacrifices for the altar of the bourgeois state. But then he was not one to despair of socialism, in France or anywhere else, because it had been betrayed by those who claimed to represent it. In place of the many deluded or demoralized by the war, he now sought out others, to speak in France for a movement of revolutionary purpose. And, indeed, from among those stirred by his efforts, were to come the founders of the French Communist Party: itself in its early years remarkable for its particular attachment to him, among all of the Soviet leaders.

But it was the condition of the Russian revolutionary movement that continued to concern him most closely. And here, there appeared at first to be much that was promising. To be sure, Plekhanov had decided that the Germany of the Kaiser represented a greater threat to progress than did the Russia of the Tsar. Yet those in the party who had chosen to follow him into the lap of the motherland, or the Defencists as they came to be called, were relatively few.

And with the killing well under way, there was a quickening of revolutionary commitment, which looked beyond the quarrels of the past. Martov, for instance, had been squandering his energies in café debate; but now his passion rang out from the pages of *Golos* (*Voice*), a Russian daily published in Paris under his editorship, to uphold the internationalist cause. Even Lenin, though doubtful that Martov 'would long remain in the position he had taken', publicly praised *Golos* as 'the best socialist paper in Europe'.[5] And Trotsky, glad to put behind him his former differences with Martov, soon became a leading contributor.

He called, in *Golos*, for a final break with those who had betrayed their socialist principles; and, like Lenin, he proposed the establishment of a Third International. But Martov, after taking a few firm paces towards this prospect, readjusted his glasses and turned away. It was not that he was wavering in his opposition to the war. He was simply not willing to regard as lost for ever those who had strayed into supporting it. To abandon the Second International was to abandon all hope that the established socialist parties would yet find their way home. Moreover, most of the Defencists were Mensheviks; and others in the faction, still undecided, might well declare for Defencism, if forced to choose. The break that Trotsky was demanding threatened to spell the end of Menshevism as a force of any significance.

Golos, starved of funds and savaged by the censorship, succumbed in the middle of January 1915. But before the end of the month, it had been succeeded by another Russian daily, *Nashe Slovo (Our Word)*. The paper's initial impulse came mainly from a Menshevik, Antonov-Ovseenko, who had been an officer in the army of the Tsar; had rebelled in 1905; had been sentenced to death, but had escaped. He proposed that Trotsky be invited to become joint editor with Martov; and the invitation was extended, despite the fears expressed by one colleague that 'such a strong personality might take over the newspaper altogether'.[6] Trotsky, suspecting that the paper was being planned to promote Menshevism, at first refused. But then, solicited with reassurances, he agreed.

He lost little time in effectively testing his new colleagues. When the paper was barely two weeks old, he published a statement that disclosed the course of his conflict with the Mensheviks. He was not disappointed in the value of the reassurances he had received, but his relations with Martov were further disturbed. Meetings of the editorial board came increasingly to be dominated by the disagreement between the two editors. Martov avoided 'with astounding mental agility . . . a direct answer to the question whether he would break with the Defencists', and Trotsky, at times with extreme anger, attacked him.[7] By July, Trotsky was praising the Bolsheviks for their faithful internationalism, and had even taken to suggesting that this might have had something to do with the pre-war divisions in the party. Martov threatened to resign from the editorial board rather than continue to bear responsibility for such opinions. Yet if

Trotsky was now openly closing the gap between himself and the Bolsheviks, he was doing so with due regard to the distance that remained. In the very process of paying his tribute to them, he took them to task: for rejecting all progress to unity that was not on their terms. And he successfully resisted those former Bolsheviks on the board who, moving rapidly towards Lenin again in reaction to the war, pressed for a corresponding movement in the paper's policy.

As though editorial strains and the blades of the censors were not enough, *Nashe Slovo* had to contend with a continual shortage of funds. Often it seemed impossible that the paper should see the start of another week. But then the printers would agree to wait for payment, and the compositors would go hungry themselves, while money was collected, most of it in small coins, from the local Russian community. And the paper did not merely survive. It came to exercise a considerable influence, far beyond its immediate Russian readership and the rebellious French socialists nearby. It reached into Italy; the Balkans; and even Germany, where extracts were quoted in the press, for the very different purposes of the government, but to nourish the cause of internationalist dissent none the less. And for this Trotsky himself was largely responsible. His own articles, on ideological issues or the condition of European culture, on the conduct of a military campaign or the plight of a single soldier, blazed a way through the fog of contemporary journalism. By his example and encouragement, he drew numerous contributions of intellectual distinction from Russian revolutionaries in various parts of Europe. Above all, by the very force of his 'strong personality', he secured sufficient unity and firmness of purpose to keep the venture from falling in on itself.

His family joined him in May 1915, to live at Sèvres, near Paris, in a house lent by a friend. It was, he would recall, a spring whose 'greenness seemed especially caressing'. But there were already many women in mourning – more and more of them each day – as the slaughter at the front splashed its living shadows across France. In Paris itself, to which the family moved after a few months, the streets were increasingly deserted, and the clocks which had once presided over their bustle stopped, one by one.

Trotsky, of course, was not satisfied to follow the fighting and write of its effects from the reports reaching Paris through the road-blocks of the censorship. He paid frequent visits behind the lines: to hospitals, for talks with the wounded; to towns where he might find, in the cafés and markets, soldiers and refugees to tell him of their experiences. And his imagination transformed this material into vivid dispatches, which captured for his readers the monotonous horror of the trenches and the plight of individual civilians hurled from their homes by events.

Virtually from the first, in defiance of patriotic belief, he had predicted the emergence of the stalemate which it would take so much blood to maintain. Now, behind the cries for movement, more movement, over the unburied bodies of yesterday's dead, he listened for the murmur of rebellion. Carefully choosing his words so as to dodge the censors, he wrote in *Nashe Slovo* of the 'terrible madness' that was the Battle of Verdun. 'However great the military significance . . . may be, the political significance is infinitely greater. In Berlin and other places they have been wanting "movement" – and they will have it. Hark! under Verdun there is being forged *our* tomorrow.'[8]

From 5 to 8 September 1915, there met at Zimmerwald, in Switzerland, socialists ready to speak for internationalism against the war. There were thirty-eight delegates from eleven countries. And as they were being conveyed to the little village, high in the mountains, a few miles from Berne, they joked amongst themselves over how, a half century since the founding of the First International,[9] four coaches were sufficient to carry all the internationalists. The reality was harsh enough. The Swiss and Italian participants represented substantial parties; while the German ones brought greetings from Karl Liebknecht, whose imprisonment for opposition to the war had provided the internationalist cause with a worthy hero. But there were others, such as those from France, whose voices were hardly more than their own. And the Russians had arrived to speak, as ever, in various voices. Lenin and Zinoviev were there for the Bolsheviks; Axelrod and Martov for the internationalist Mensheviks; Chernov and Bobrov for the internationalist Social Revolutionaries; while Trotsky himself, who was accorded full voting rights only over the vigorous protests of Lenin, represented the revolutionaries responsible for *Nashe Slovo*.

Lenin pressed for a declaration which would call the peoples of the belligerent states to civil war and initiate the establishment of a Third International. The majority, though differing over how far to go, had no doubt that this was going too far. Trotsky was drawn towards supporting Lenin's position. It was, after all, essentially his own. But his overriding concern was to prevent the conference from disintegrating, with the delegates leaving behind only a record of mutual denunciation. Entrusted with the task of drafting a generally acceptable formula, he produced one which condemned the regimes of capitalism for the outbreak of war, and the treacherous socialist parties for its continuation; which urged all workers to end the butchery for a 'peace without indemnities and without annexations', based upon 'the self-determination of peoples'. The statement was duly adopted – though Lenin and his supporters insisted on recording their reservations – to take its place in history as the Zimmerwald Manifesto. It contained no call for the creation of a new International. But before dispersing, the delegates did elect an international committee, which was to prove the precursor.

The conference was a considerable event: its declaration, paradoxically, the more impressive for the very loneliness of the defiance it proclaimed. And this loneliness in turn illuminated the personal courage displayed by many of the delegates. They had met with citizens of enemy countries to denounce their own governments: and not as a prelude to finding sanctuary somewhere, but as part of a struggle which they were going home to promote. There was every likelihood that they would be punished; none at all, that popular opinion would be moved to rescue them. And some of them were, indeed, to be imprisoned or sent to the trenches. Even Trotsky, returning to a belligerent country that was not his own, ran at least the risk that France would refuse him further refuge. The conference had kept its proceedings secret, to protect as far as possible the identity of the participants until they got safely back home. When Trotsky arrived at the frontier, his case containing the Zimmerwald documents was opened for inspection. The top sheet of paper bore the slogan, *Vive le Tsar!*, which Trotsky had derisively doodled during one of the sessions. The official was satisfied.

When reports of the Zimmerwald conference were in due course released, censorship proceeded to suppress them. But the character of the meeting and the content of its manifesto were made the more widely known by the very attacks on them, from within both belligerent camps. In an article much mutilated by the censors, Trotsky asked why, if the conference had been as 'impotent and insignificant' as its adversaries claimed, the authorities were so concerned to smother any mention of it. And why, all the same, was the conference being discussed? It would continue to be discussed. 'No force will delete it from the political life of Europe.'

'The French press,' he declared, 'has written more than once that Karl Liebknecht has saved Germany's honour. The Zimmerwald conference has saved the honour of Europe.'[10] The honour of Europe? What was rather more to the point, it had saved the honour of socialism; from those socialists whose dishonour now belonged only to themselves. It was a dishonour that Trotsky felt the more keenly when it took from him old colleagues and friends. The sharpest cut had come, soon after the outbreak of war, from the betrayal of Parvus, who had profitably placed his services at the disposal of the German government. Trotsky, proclaiming the extent of the intellectual debt that he owed, mourned the passing of Parvus for him, in an article that he entitled, 'An Obituary on a Living Friend'.[11] Chkheidze, leader of the Menshevik deputies, addressed the Duma on the Zimmerwald conference in such equivocal terms as to leave his listeners wondering whether he had defended or denounced it. And even while Trotsky offered excuses for this performance from an associate to whom he had written so bitterly about his differences with Lenin, he prepared himself for the snapping of the association. Potresov and Vera Ivanovna, with whom he had stood against Lenin at the very birth of the party split, were won over to the war. If he recalled especially the kindness that Vera Ivanovna had shown to him in London, and the affection that he had come to feel for her, this was only to make the imperative break the more painful.

Surely, then, Lenin had been right in his refusal to concede unity with those whose fitness had been found so wanting at the first real test of principle. Yet this did not mean that Lenin had been right about everything: that he had been right in his despotic concept of centralism; right in his unscrupulous attempts to seize possession of the party; right in believing that the future belonged only to him and those who bowed to his leadership. He was not right now, in proclaiming his latest dogma: that Russia's military defeat would promote the revolution. For this risked encouraging revolutionaries to suppose that a Russian defeat in the war would do their work for them. Should they not, rather, be encouraged to concentrate on working for the revolution, regardless of the military consequences? And would not socialism itself, after all, best be served if the war came to an end without victors and vanquished?

It was not easy, either, for Trotsky to ignore the nudges of resentment. That latest of Lenin's attacks, on his credentials at Zimmerwald, had smacked more of personal malice than any issue of principle. But to raise resentment to the level of revolutionary politics only lowered revolutionary politics to the level of resentment. He and Lenin were at one over most of what mattered. He steered the editorial policy of *Nashe Slovo* towards an accommodation with the Bolsheviks. Martov argued and threatened, but to little effect. In April 1916 he resigned.

Later in the same month, the Zimmerwaldists met again, in the Swiss town of Kienthal: without Trotsky, who had been refused permission by the French authorities to cross the frontier. This time, Lenin and his followers, while failing still to get all that they wanted, succeeded in securing a substantially more militant declaration. This urged workers to use 'every means at your disposal . . . to end quickly this slaughter'. And it proclaimed: 'There is but one effective means of preventing future wars: the seizure of political power and the abolition of capitalist property by the working class.' Trotsky at once announced, in *Nashe Slovo*, his support.

The French Ministry of Foreign Affairs, in response to pressures from the Russian embassy, had long seen to it that the censorship paid meticulous attention to the paper. But the Russian government was unimpressed by the results. The French censors were apparently incapable of recognizing the most subversive remarks. That the paper should be published at all was an outrage. The French government, however, was reluctant to move against the paper on no firmer ground than that of affronted Russian feelings. Partnership in war had not altogether dispelled the disrepute of

Tsarism. A pretext was required. And a pretext was duly provided, by the Russian political police. One of their agents busied himself among Russian soldiers in Marseilles, who mutinied and stoned to death an officer in the courtyard of their barracks. When the mutineers were seized, they were found to have in their possession copies of *Nashe Slovo*, which the agent had distributed during the disturbances.

On 15 September 1916, the French authorities banned the paper. And on the following day, they ordered Trotsky to leave France, for any country that he chose. But their generosity in disposing of him was not matched by the gratitude of others. Italy would not have him. He could get to Holland or Scandinavia only through Britain, and Britain would not give him passage. Switzerland would neither accept nor reject him, while it waited for events to save it from the embarrassment of doing either.

For six weeks, Trotsky stayed on in Paris: dodging the detectives detailed to follow him, by leaping in and out of métro trains at the last moment, or by diving suddenly into the darkness of a cinema. It was, he recognized, no more than a game; but one at which his skill provided some distraction from his predicament. The authorities were not bemused. Trotsky was summoned by the prefect of police and told that he would be conducted by two inspectors, 'in plain clothes' as a mark of consideration, to the Spanish frontier.

His guardians were garrulously attentive on the train and took their leave at the frontier with the earnest advice that he do his best to look like a tourist, so as to avoid arousing the suspicions of the Spanish police. Reaching Madrid, where he knew no one and felt a Saharan loneliness, he went to the Prado. The interest in art, which Natalia Sedova had first awakened, rescued him now. He spent hours gazing at pictures and communicating his comments to his notebook. He still hoped for good news from Switzerland, where his friends, he knew, continued active on his behalf. Then, on 9 November, he was arrested by the police, who told him that he was to leave Spain as soon as possible, and meanwhile be subjected to certain limitations. The Spanish police had caught up with him on information from Paris. His solicitous French guardians had returned, to telegraph that a dangerous anarchist had crossed the frontier, with the intention of settling in Madrid.

The certain limitations included imprisonment: though in a cell of the first class, at a charge of one and a half pesetas a day. He appreciated the logic in this blurred reflection of the social inequalities outside, and laughed at the whole absurd turn of events. He did not laugh when asked for his fingerprints. Force was, if politely, employed. He was invited to take off his boots. He refused. And less accustomed, perhaps, to the problem of refractory feet, the officials gave way in confusion. It was a small enough victory to celebrate; but then these were not victorious times. News of his arrest had meanwhile begun to stir protests from the opposition press. After three days, he was put on a train to Cadiz, at the expense of the Crown since he declined to pay for his ticket. His police companions clearly took much pride in the distinction of their charge: who was, they hastened to inform the other passengers, no mere counterfeiter of money but a *caballero* possessed, unfortunately, of unsuitable views.

At Cadiz, Trotsky was told that a boat would be leaving for Havana on the following morning and that he must be on board. He rushed to the telegraph office and dispatched urgent appeals to government ministers, republican deputies, liberal newspapers. He rushed back to the prefecture which telegraphed his insistence on remaining, in prison if necessary, till a boat could take him to New York. It was, he would recall, an exciting day. It was also a productive one. Orders came from Madrid that he should be allowed to stay until a boat for New York arrived.

Trotsky was never one to waste time. In the local library, which no one else seemed to visit, he studied Spanish history and verbs, and prepared himself for the United States by adding what he could to his English vocabulary. The detective assigned to watch him proved unusually agreeable: leaving him to his own devices at the hotel, on the understanding that they would meet there at a particular time; steering him away from pot-holes in the pavements and protecting him against the tricks of local traders. The next boat for New York left from Barcelona, and Trotsky wrested permission to join his family there. On Christmas Day, the *Monserrat*, carrying four Trotskys and a 'multicoloured' company of other passengers, in flight from military conscription or in search of fortune, began its journey.

It arrived at three o'clock on the cold, wet, windy Sunday morning of 13 January 1917. Trotsky was much impressed by New York, that city of 'prose and fantasy', with its streets 'a triumph of cubism'.[12] He was soon at work in one of the public libraries, studying the economic history of the United States. And only ten days after his arrival, he was publicly considering, at a meeting to welcome him, the implications of the current boom in American exports. With the economic life of Europe bleeding away, would the world's centre of gravity not shift to the United States? As a European, by all the attachments of experience, he could scarcely fail to feel some regret at this prospect. But such regret was quickly left behind by his excitement as a cosmopolitan of revolution, exploring the complexities of progress.

The Trotskys rented an apartment in the Bronx. And for their eighteen dollars a month, they assumed unaccustomed command of such conveniences as electric light, a telephone, a fitted bath, a gas range, a garbage chute, an automatic lift. Trotsky would recall that his children were captivated by all this. And so, doubtless, given his own abiding delight in the wonderland of human inventiveness, was their father. Two days after the family moved in, the janitor absconded with the rent: but not, it emerged, without exercising an admirable discrimination. He took the rent of only those tenants to whom he had issued receipts, so that no one but the landlord would be robbed. The Trotskys, whose payment of three months' rent in advance could not be entered in the receipt-book, because the landlord had meanwhile removed this to do his accounts, found their money wrapped and hidden amongst their crockery.

The memoir industry would subsequently manufacture legends out of Trotsky's short stay in the United States. Need, it would be variously recorded, drove him to work as a dishwasher, a tailor, and even as a film extra at the Brooklyn studios. In fact, he managed to make an adequate living by giving lectures, in German as well as Russian, and by writing for various papers. From the first, he was drawn to the group of Russian revolutionaries who were publishing a daily, called *Novy Mir* (*New World*), from offices on the Lower East Side. They were committed Bolsheviks: led by Alexandra Kollontai, a woman of aristocratic lineage and extensive culture, who had written for *Nashe Slovo* before becoming one of Lenin's most ardent disciples; and Nikolai Bukharin, a young intellectual of erratic brilliance, whose temperament needed a hero to twine itself round and now found one in Trotsky. Despite his refusal to identify himself as a Bolshevik, and the reverberations of Lenin's attacks on him, Trotsky very soon came to dominate the editorial board.

But the Russian political community was too small a basin for the abundance of his interests and energy. The smell of the sea was still clinging to his clothes when he set out to rescue American socialism from its leaders. Their pretensions of superiority to their European colleagues infuriated him, as did their smugly distant acquaintance with ideas. Their private motor cars, marking their material prosperity, seemed their principal qualification for appointment to the important committees of the party. Only Eugene Debs, among the eminences, although 'a romantic and a preacher', he considered 'a sincere revolutionary'.[13] And Debs in turn, disregarding the hostility of his associates towards Trotsky, would clasp and kiss him, whenever the two men met. Trotsky and his friends decided to establish a militant Marxist weekly, which would seek to rouse the rank-and-file of the socialist party and the unrecruited workers beyond. Preparations were well advanced when they were interrupted. The first confused reports had arrived of revolution in Russia.

Russia had entered the war with hopes of a quick victory and accompanying conquests which would sweep away any contemplation of the costs. But success against the Austro-Hungarian armies was not repeated against the might of Germany. For the first ten months of the war, the Russian war office admitted to losses, in killed, wounded and captured, of 3,800,000.[14] The hopes were left lying on the battlefields, while the costs went on rising, to submerge the contemplation of conquest and eventually the regime itself. For this was a war of the industrial age: and mere multitudes of men were no more than meat for its machines.

Russian industry could not produce such devastating new weapons as the heavy guns of the German forces. Indeed, it could not produce nearly enough conventional equipment. As early as the middle of December 1914, the French and British ambassadors were stunned to learn 'that, though Russia had in her depots men enough and to spare to make good her colossal losses in the war, she had no rifles wherewith to arm them and that her reserves of artillery ammunition were exhausted'.[15] Attempts were made, amidst much public excitement, to expand the military output of industry. But the successes, when serious, were not sustained. Civilian officials attacked one another's policies, even countermanded one another's orders, in pursuing their own ambitions; though collaborating to much effect in decisions which revealed their jealousy and distrust of their military counterparts. The problems of economic backwardness, augmented by such mismanagement, were reflected in a railway system so unequal to the demands upon it that horses had to be used for the transport of war material, while men were made to march their way to the front.

Discrepancies in the quality and quantity of armaments were not, however, everything. It also mattered what men did with the armaments they had. And here again, the immense mobilizations of Russia masked weaknesses which all too rapidly emerged. The army reforms that had followed the humiliations of the war with Japan had done little more than fuss with the fringes. The mass of the ranks remained peasants in uniform; not just technically untrained but culturally unprepared for their thrust into the world of modern battle. This infirmity proved grave enough when the fighting began. It became fatal with the failure to treat it. But then how could it be treated, while the same social order was there which had produced it in the first place?

A mutely dogged obedience was all that was expected of the soldiers; and exacted rather than encouraged by the severity with which lapses were punished. Yet a mutely dogged obedience seemed to bring only slaughter and defeat. Defeat after defeat drained away any belief in a decisive victory which would end the slaughter. And the fear of slaughter came to overwhelm the intimidations on which discipline depended. Increasingly the ranks refused to fight. Disregarding the orders that exploded over their heads, they retreated, or surrendered, or fled.

And the regime was coughing away its life as incurably in the market-place as on the battlefield. From Count Witte's currency reform of 1897 until the outbreak of the great war, the Russian rouble had maintained its value. By 1916, the budget deficit had been expanded to meet more than three-quarters of state expenditure, and the authorities were making frantic use of the printing presses. In 1914, the notes in circulation totalled some 1600 million roubles, all but entirely backed by the gold reserves. By the eve of the revolution, there were close on 10,000 million roubles of issued notes, backed by scarcely more than the value of pulp.[16] Inflation promoted speculation and hoarding; speculation and hoarding increased the shortage of commodities; the increasing shortage of commodities promoted inflation. In the cities, workers found their wages falling ever further behind the rises in prices and took to protest strikes which cut the industrial product, already fast contracting from the scarcities of fuel and raw materials. In the countryside, stripped of some ten million men and two million horses for the front, output was accordingly reduced; and where the demands of subsistence did not divert supplies from the market, the distrust of paper money, with the lack of consumer goods for immediate purchase, did so instead.

Deprivation might have been more tolerable had it been supported by a sense that the whole society was suffering, in the service of a just and necessary war. But it existed alongside a lavish consumption by those whose means seemed only to have fattened on the want around them, and whose hostility to any talk of peace fortified suspicions that the war was being fought for their benefit alone. It was, indeed, as if the rich of Russia had a presentiment of calamity, and sought to cram what advantage and pleasure they could in the time that was left. The workshop of the court jeweller, Fabergé, was busy as never before. Audiences at the opera and ballet displayed the latest in resplendent dress. The night-clubs were crowded, almost as though such celebration, by sympathetic magic, might translate to sudden victory the carnage at the front.

Those within the middle classes who could afford, from the profits of their peculiar undertakings, admission to this delirium, were few. Many, sinking into the anonymous misery of Russia's multitudes, found corresponding cause to look for a rising against the regime. Most held on grimly to their status and values: indignant at the price they were having to pay, and fearful that they might have to pay a much higher price yet. Increasingly, they came to see that the only real prospect of preventing revolution lay in serious reform, but were at a loss to know just how they might secure the second without precipitating the first. Their representative spokesmen turned, in a very fury of frustration, on those figures of the regime whose retirement might yet regenerate it.

The Tsar had been responsible for sufficient mischief, when ruling Russia from behind the screen of his court. Yet if he seemed to select his ministers for their conspicuous mediocrity, lest anything like talent should belittle him by comparison, this reflected the stubbornness with which he resisted the wild appointments urged on him by his wife. Then, in early September 1916, against all advice from his ministers, but armed with prayers distributed among several icons, he left for the front to assume the high command himself. There he revealed as marked an ineptitude in military, as he had ever done in civilian, leadership. And worse, he took to sanctioning most of the various proposals for fortifying the autocracy at home with which the Tsarina bombarded him by letter.

So besotted by Rasputin that she saw in all hostility to him merely the confirmation of his messianic credentials, she gave him the government of Russia to enjoy. And enjoy it, he did. One by one, those ministers with the slightest competence or reputation for honesty to recommend them were plucked from office, for successors of such manifest unsuitability that their very disrepute appeared to have directed their appointment. At less elevated levels, official careers were subjected to more definite criteria. The husbands of those women who accepted Rasputin's invitations to bed were rewarded by the state; while the husbands of those who refused were informed that the state had no further need of their services.

By the middle of November 1916, the rage of deputies in the fourth Duma was bursting all conventional bounds. Miliukov, leader of the liberal Cadets, attacked the Tsarina, Rasputin, and the whole conduct of government; punctuating his remarks with the defiant refrain, 'Is this folly or treason?' Maklakov, a right-wing liberal, declared that the confidence of the country was enough to overthrow a minister, as its hatred confirmed him in office. Then, quoting Pushkin, he cried: 'Woe to that country where only the slave and the liar are close to the throne!' Even from the benches of the far right, a certain Vladimir Purishkevich rose passionately to denounce Rasputin and all his works. Indeed, leading members of the nobility were now so alarmed that they seriously considered the possibilities of compelling the Tsar's abdication, with one of the grand dukes acting as regent till the Tsarevitch came of age, but were dissuaded by doubts that the monarchy, and with it their own prerogatives, would survive. Instead, from among them, and with the participation of Purishkevich, came a conspiracy aimed at saving the Crown from itself, by the murder of Rasputin.

What followed had elements of both Grand Guignol and farce. Invited to the home of Prince Felix Yusupov, husband of the Tsar's niece, on the night of 19 December, Rasputin was ushered into a cellar especially furnished for the occasion. The other conspirators, who included the Grand Duke Dmitry Pavlovich, cousin of the Tsar, remained in a room above; playing a record of 'Yankee Doodle' repeatedly on the gramophone. Yusupov himself entertained his guest with poisoned cakes and poisoned wine. Cyanide, however, only excited in Rasputin a desire to hear Yusupov play the guitar. And so Yusupov played the guitar; glancing again and again at his guest for the promised convulsions, and suppressing with more and more difficulty his superstitious fear as they failed to arrive. He rushed upstairs to confer with his colleagues and returned, holding the Grand Duke Dmitry's revolver hidden behind his back. Rasputin was beginning to show some signs of wear, but rapidly revived with another glass of wine and suggested that they visit a gipsy establishment 'with God in thought but with mankind in the flesh'. Yusupov fired at his heart, and Rasputin fell backwards, with a roar, on to the bearskin rug.

The other conspirators rushed down into the cellar, where one of them brushed against the electric light switch and plunged them all into darkness. With light restored, their confusion and fright subsided; they examined Rasputin and, satisfied that he was dead, retreated to the room above for further conference. But then Yusupov decided to revisit the cellar and shook the corpse to reassure himself. The corpse twitched an eye; rose from the floor; clambered after the fleeing Yusupov upstairs; and burst through the locked door leading into the snow-covered courtyard. Purishkevich fired four times, and Rasputin fell. Purishkevich kicked him in the head. Yusupov battered him with a steel press. The body was wrapped in a blue curtain and dropped from a bridge into the icy waters of the Neva. It was recovered a few days later, with its lungs full of water. In the end, it seems, Rasputin had drowned.

The Tsarina was grief-stricken and went day after day to pray at Rasputin's graveside. But if there were those who hoped that the murder would make her quite unquestionably mad, they were to be disappointed. And besides, the Tsar himself, who had hurried back from the front to comfort her, now seemed no less bent than she was on challenging history to do its worst. The British ambassador was much disturbed. He considered the murder, for all its 'patriotic motives', a 'fatal mistake'. It 'set a dangerous example; for it prompted people to translate their thoughts into action'.[17] And he obtained an audience to press upon the Tsar the paramount need of concessions. 'Your Majesty, if I may be permitted to say so, has but one safe course open to you,' he declared: 'namely, to break down the barrier that separates you from your people and to regain their confidence.' The Tsar, looking hard at the ambassador, asked: 'Do you mean that *I* am to regain the confidence of my people or that they are to regain *my* confidence?'[18] The case was hopeless.

It was a more than usually severe winter; and with the frozen railway system unable to move even such scant supplies as were available, the cities and the front were fast running out of food and fuel. Perhaps the outstanding chronicler of the coming upheaval was working as an economist, under his real name of Nikolai Nikolayevich Himmer, in the Ministry of Agriculture, while contributing to Gorky's paper *Letopis*, under the pen-name of Sukhanov. Sitting in his office on Tuesday, 21 February 1917, he overheard two typists discussing the difficulties of getting food, the quarrels that shook the shopping queues, the gathering unrest among women. 'D'you know,' one of the girls suddenly said, 'if you ask me, it's the beginning of the revolution!'[19] Sukhanov had given long revolutionary service. As far back as 1904 he had been imprisoned for his association with a clandestine Social Revolutionary print-shop and, recently, had been one of the very few writers who had managed to declare, in the legal Russian press, a Zimmerwaldist opposition to the war. Moreover, that high-sloping forehead, dropping down to the ledge of his nose, with long backward-sloping ears so that his face suggested nothing so much as an arrested landslide, covered one of the most sensitive of intellects. A revolution, he commented to himself, was highly improbable. 'Those philistine girls whose tongues and typewriters were rattling away behind the partition didn't know what a revolution was.'[20]

On Thursday the 23rd, 'Women's Day' in the socialist calendar, there poured into the streets, from the factories and working-class districts of the capital, a commotion of women, crying out for bread. And a simultaneous lock-out at the massive Putilov metal plant, in response to a wage dispute, released some 20,000 of the most turbulent workers in Petrograd[21] for participation in the clamour. On Friday the 24th, 200,000 were on strike; demonstrating against the autocracy and against the war, in mass meetings and marches. Yet the mounted Cossacks, authority's traditional flail, now seemed reluctant to move against the crowds and themselves showed distinct signs of hostility towards the police. Sukhanov was now persuaded that those typists had, after all, been right, and that this was the revolution at last. But his political friends remained sceptical.

On Saturday, the strike was general, with a marked growth in the size and self-assurance of demonstrations. The Tsar demanded the suppression of all disorders; and the Petrograd military command, which had been avoiding the use of guns, issued instructions that troops were to fire on any crowd refusing to disperse after due warning. On Sunday the 26th, many thousands of demonstrators set out to reach the centre of the city. They were checked by troops at the bridges and began crossing the frozen surface of the Neva. They encountered gun-fire; they scattered; they coalesced; they continued on their way. In the streets and squares, there was more shooting. Then, towards evening, a momentous incident emerged from the very confusion. A small detachment of mounted police, with orders to disperse a crowd along the Catherine Canal, started firing from the bank opposite. A contingent of the Pavlovsky regiment, passing along the bank occupied by the crowd, saw unarmed citizens falling, and fired back. The revolt of the army had begun.

For a few hours it wavered. The mutineers were attacked at their barracks by loyal troops and forced to surrender. But that night, soldiers of the Volinsky regiment, the same soldiers who had been firing on crowds and had caused most of the casualties, discussed the events of the day and resolved that they would obey their orders no longer. On the morning of Monday 27th February, they greeted the arrival of their captain with shouts of 'We will not shoot!' and rushed off to rouse the regiments quartered nearby. A mass of mutinous soldiers, sweeping aside any resistance offered by their officers, and swelling with new recruits by the minute, moved to the Vyborg district, where they joined up with workers to hunt down police; break open arsenals and seize weapons; burst into prisons and release the prisoners.

The Duma, meeting in the Tauride Palace, learned that it had been dissolved by decree of the Tsar and that mutiny was spreading through the Petrograd garrison. It formally accepted the decree but authorized the establishment of a provisional committee, to restore order in the capital. Within hours, the overriding objective of most deputies had become, instead, to contain the revolution by recognizing and attempting to direct it. 'If we don't take power,' argued one leading conservative, V. V. Shulgin, 'others will take it, those who have already elected some scoundrels in the factories.'[22] In the evening, the committee committed itself to 'the creation of a government corresponding to the desires of the population and capable of enjoying its confidence.'

Though their own agitation had fuelled the rising and their own adherents had been in the forefront of its thrust, the revolutionary parties were left gasping by the rush of events. It was 1905 that came to their rescue, with the vital memory of the Soviet. Indeed, as Shulgin's fears reflected, workers had already been electing deputies to a Soviet that did not yet exist. By the close of the 27th, it unquestionably did. Meeting in another part of the Tauride Palace, socialist members of the Duma and prominent trade-unionists established a Provisional Executive Committee, which summoned workers to elect deputies immediately, for an inaugural session of the Soviet the following night.

To his diary, on Tuesday the 28th, Louis de Robien, a young French diplomat, confided his hope for a 'drastic repression', as alone able to save the cause of the war and the Allies.

Police stations are being burned down and looted. I walk past the one in Mokhovaya Street at the moment when they hurl a grand piano out of the window, and it lands on the pavement with a crash, with all its strings vibrating. In the snow nearby they are making a bonfire of bursting files out of which fall cascades of paper.... Half-blackened pages blow away and scatter on the snow.[23]

From Gorky's apartment, Sukhanov watched in the afternoon motor cars, decked with red flags and filled with armed workers and soidiers together, speeding through the streets; while smoke from the burning district court across the river drifted over the city. When he reached the palace, he saw Miliukov, mandarin of the middle-class reform movement and central figure of the Duma committee, walking alone and giving the appearance of not in the least knowing what to do. Information was being exchanged excitedly, as acquaintances met for a moment, before hurrying onwards. There were wide-eyed reports: troops loyal to the regime were advancing on the capital; soldiers led by police were looting and destroying.

At nine o'clock precisely, the Soviet was called to order. As soon as the Presidium had been elected, the soldiers present clamoured for permission to make their reports; and with enthusiastic support from the worker deputies, this was formally granted.

Standing on stools, their rifles in their hands, agitated and stuttering, straining all their powers to give a connected account of the messages entrusted to them ... in simple, rugged language that infinitely strengthened the effect of the absence of emphasis – one after another the soldiers' delegates told of what had been happening in their companies.[24]

And to roars of applause, it was proposed and approved that the Soviet of Workers should forthwith become the Soviet of Workers' and Soldiers' Deputies.

The threat of a counter-attack to rescue the regime, or of such disorder and want that the populace might turn to the restoration of the regime for rescue, demanded a display of decisiveness and certain instant measures. The Soviet elected a supply commission, to undertake the provision of food; ordered the establishment of a workers' militia for urgent police duties; and, by determining after much debate that all newspapers might again be published, on the responsibility of their respective editors, asserted the ultimate control over the press that it possessed through the allegiance of the print-workers.

Of the three main revolutionary groups in the Soviet, the Bolsheviks were, in numbers and in influence, conspicuously the weakest. Their major leaders were in enforced or voluntary exile, and their organization had suffered the most severely from the activities of the political police. The Mensheviks, on the other hand, had a number of their own leaders prominently at work in the capital; had developed, overall, the strongest connections with trade unions; and seemed, accordingly, to occupy the heights of the Social Democratic cause. The Social Revolutionaries, with their attachment to the Russian visionary tradition of a village socialism, far outstripped the others in recruitment, as the peasant soldiers of the garrison were drawn to join one or other of the revolutionary parties. But they were the most loosely organized; had ideals rather than policies; and felt largely like lodgers in the metropolitan home of immediate revolutionary politics. Virtually from the outset, they looked to the Mensheviks for guidance. And the Mensheviks, whatever their differences over the war, were generally agreed that, in the backward economic condition of Russia, only a bourgeois revolution could be sustained. Any attempt to advance, at once or foreseeably soon, to the second, socialist revolution, was not merely bound to fail, but would, in the process, invite the defeat of the first.

When, therefore, the provisional committee of the Duma gave hurried birth to a Provisional Government, with Prince Lvov, a liberal noble, as the figurehead, and Miliukov, the effective leader, as Minister for Foreign Affairs, it seemed that history was taking its predicted and proper course. But the very peril in which the revolution stood, and the prevailing mood of the Soviet deputies, ruled out any surrender of the powers so recently assumed. On 2 March, the same day that the Tsar agreed to abdicate, and Soviet negotiators reached an understanding with Miliukov on the policies to be pursued by the Provisional Government, the Soviet issued its celebrated Order Number One. This abolished the traditional forms of subservient address in the armed forces; called for the election of military committees by the ranks; entrusted such committees with complete control of weapons, which were to be kept at all costs from falling into the hands of officers; and placed all military units under the ultimate authority of the Soviet. The Provisional Government maintained that the very existence of this order made nonsense of its own authority. And, indeed, a more crucial challenge to the prerogatives of any government, especially in time of war, could scarcely be conceived.

Yet what else was a socialist leadership, caught between dogmatic dependence on a liberal regime and empiric distrust of the liberal disposition, to do? A bourgeois revolution, according to the chimes of the Marxist grandfather clock, this must be. But it was a bourgeois revolution, then, which the bourgeoisie had not made and plainly, in the immediate predicament, could not sustain; while the workers and soldiers, who had made and were capable of sustaining it, would reject it as no real revolution at all, without such far-reaching reforms as the bourgeoisie, left with the decision, would never concede. A 'dual power' appeared to be the only answer. The Provisional Government, in overall command of the state and its massive administration, would promote bourgeois and, in particular, bureaucratic support for the revolution; while the Soviet, exercising its own brand of sovereignty, would protect the revolution and promote appropriate reforms. Distinct but together, they would secure a democratic republic. The separation of functions argued for a formal separation of responsibility; and the Soviet Executive Committee declined, by a large majority, the offer of official representation in the Provisional Government. Alexander Kerensky, a Social Revolutionary member of both the Duma and the Soviet Executive committees, determined to accept, in his personal capacity, the portfolio of Justice.

In the months to come, he would seem like nothing so much as an ageing juvenile lead, who had strayed from the stage into the centre of historical upheaval, and behaved there as though cast for the star part in a melodrama. Thirty-five years old, thin and of middle height, he had a waxen complexion, half-closed eyes which darted with sharp uneasiness, and thick brushed-back hair which always looked on the point of leaping out of bed. But if his presence was somewhat less than commanding, his voice, by all accounts, was a very repertoire of special effects. It could drop to a clutching whisper; rise to a roar; throb with distress. And this voice now served an instant intuition.

'During those critical days in the destiny of Russia', he was to record many years later,

considerations of dogma or party simply did not exist for me. It seemed to me that in any case no party programme was any longer applicable. All one could do was to build the new order with such human material as was at hand. For myself, I was by this time inseparably connected with the destinies of the revolution. Everyone round me seemed to treat me in a manner subtly changed, different, as though some special power was in my hands, some peculiar influence over the stormy masses. No doubt my position was an historical accident, but there it was![25]

Posturing as the very personification of Providence, he set out to resolve all contradictions himself. Beyond party or programme or class, he would unite the country and save the democratic republic.

If the Bolsheviks were, in the event, to be the wave of the future, they seemed meanwhile no more than a ripple from the past. Near the close of the second week in March, Stalin and Kamenev returned from their Siberian exile, to take control of the *Pravda* editorial board. A short article by Stalin, on 14 March, reflected virtual submission to Menshevik policies. An article by Kamenev, on the following day, flew straight in the face of Lenin's attitude to the war. 'When army faces army, it would be the most inane policy to suggest to one of these armies to lay down its arms and go home.' In the Tauride Palace, there was open delight at this Bolshevik display of moderation and patriotism. But in the factories, Bolshevik workers protested angrily. The editors of *Pravda* issued no further such calls to stand firm at the front. They continued, however, to refrain from any fundamental attack on the Provisional Government and its evident determination to prosecute the war.

At the All-Russian Conference of Bolsheviks, which opened in Petrograd on 28 March, Stalin presented the chief political report. 'It is not to our advantage to force the course of events now,' he declared; 'accelerating the secession of the bourgeois layers. . . . We have to gain time . . . for the struggle against the Provisional Government.' And, at a subsequent session, he argued that unification was possible with those Mensheviks of internationalist commitment. To criticism of this view, he replied: 'We ought not to run ahead and anticipate disagreements. Party life is impossible without disagreements.' It was, given his later career as perhaps the most ferocious Grand Inquisitor in history, a statement of terrible irony. But then, the supreme irony was that few, if any, inside or outside Bolshevism, suspected for a moment that he had it in him to be historically remarkable at all. Sukhanov confessed himself perplexed that such a man should have risen so high in the Bolshevik hierarchy.

The Bolshevik Party, in spite of the low level of its 'officers' corps', had a whole series of most massive figures and able leaders among its 'generals'. Stalin, however, during his modest activity in the [Soviet] Executive Committee produced – and not only on me – the impression of a grey blur, looming up now and then dimly and not leaving any trace. There is really nothing more to be said about him.[26]

Which, if any, of these Bolshevik 'generals' might, in Lenin's continued absence, have raised a substantial revolt against the prevailing policy of accommodation with the Provisional Government, it would be idle to speculate. Trotsky himself would subsequently maintain that a struggle within the Bolshevik party was inevitable; but that 'a disoriented and split party might have let slip the revolutionary opportunity for many years'.[27] What is certain is that Lenin's return vitally affected the course of events, and virtually at once.

The successful uprising in Russia had taken him, too, by surprise. Indeed, as late as January 1917, in his Zurich exile, while trumpeting to a young audience his faith in the eventual triumph of socialism, he had sadly concluded: 'We of the older generation may not live to see the decisive battles of this coming revolution.'[28] When, so soon afterwards, someone burst in upon him with the news – 'There is a revolution in Russia' – he could scarcely believe it. With Krupskaya, he rushed down to the lakeside, where copies of all the newspapers were brought straight from the presses, to be hung up rather like laundry. Again and again, they read the abrupt telegraphed reports. And then Lenin's mind began frantically to grope for a way of getting back to Russia. Sleepless at night, he had thoughts of chartering an aeroplane; only to dismiss them in the morning, as mad. More seriously, he proposed posing as a neutral Swede. But he knew no Swedish. Perhaps as a Swedish mute, then? But Krupskaya mocked him out of the plan. He would, she said, fall asleep; see Mensheviks in his dreams; and swear aloud at them in unmistakable Russian.

At last, after racking delays, he and other Russian revolutionary exiles in Switzerland, acting on a suggestion made by Martov, and with the assistance of Parvus, arrived at an agreement with the German government. They would be permitted to pass by train, unmolested, through German territory, and on reaching Russia would press the authorities to repatriate an equal number of Austro-German prisoners. The German government was, of course, far less interested in the fate of a few Austro-German prisoners than in the prospect that the returning revolutionaries might, by the infection of their views, promote the withdrawal of Russia from the war. And for Lenin, any mud that might be flung by his political opponents, on the evidence of his dealings with an enemy government, seemed a small enough price to pay for going home and taking immediate charge of his errant party.

On 3 April, he arrived at Petrograd. His followers had set out to provide an impressive reception; and no one needed to teach them how to organize. The whole square in front of the Finland Station was filled with welcomers; while others, mainly soldiers, lined the platform, which was decorated with banners and triumphal arches in red and gold. In the Tsar's waiting-room sat Chkheidze, somewhat dejectedly, with Sukhanov and with Skobelev, Trotsky's one-time disciple who was now a Menshevik member of the Duma and of the Soviet Executive Committee. When Lenin finally made his way there, 'running to the middle of the room, he stopped in front of Chkheidze as though colliding with a completely unexpected obstacle'.[29] Chkheidze, as chairman of the Soviet, glumly welcomed Lenin in its name, and then continued:

But – we think that the principal task of the revolutionary democracy is now the defence of the revolution from any encroachments either from within or from without. We consider that what this goal requires is not disunion, but the closing of the democratic ranks. We hope you will pursue these goals together with us.

Lenin looked 'as though nothing taking place had the slightest connection with him'. Turning away from the delegates of the Executive Committee altogether, he replied by greeting his 'dear comrades', the soldiers, sailors and workers, as 'the vanguard of the worldwide proletarian army', and events in Russia as the dawn of the worldwide socialist revolution. 'It was,' commented Sukhanov, 'very interesting!'[30] And scarcely less interesting was Lenin's considered reply, delivered on the following day at the Tauride Palace to a meeting of Bolsheviks, Mensheviks and independent Social Democrats, called together by those who believed that this might be an occasion to promote the cause of party unity.

They could not have been more mistaken. Lenin seized the occasion to present what were to become celebrated as his 'April theses'. The current phase in Russia, these declared, was one of transition: from the first stage of the revolution, in which the bourgeoisie had taken power, to the second, which should give power to the proletariat and the poorest of the peasantry. It was absurd to demand of the Provisional Government, 'a government of capitalists', that it renounce territorial annexation as a war aim. The war was an imperialist one, and would remain so, until turned into a civil war for the attainment of worldwide socialism. It was the Soviets that offered 'the one possible form of revolutionary government'. But for that, they needed to be released from their subjection to the influence of the bourgeoisie. And once this had happened, they might proceed to take control of social production.[31]

The speech was accompanied by mounting uproar. It rejected virtually everything for which the Soviets stood: the priority of protecting the bourgeois revolution, by a partnership with the Provisional Government; the objective of a parliamentary republic for the realistic future; the prosecution of the war as translated into a democratic commitment. Not least it denied any prospect of party unity.

That evening, Skobelev, Sukhanov and Miliukov discussed the speech. For Skobelev, it was an autopsy on Lenin's leadership. By his 'lunatic ideas', he had placed himself outside the movement of Social Democracy and was no longer a threat of any kind. Sukhanov and Miliukov took a different view. When Lenin had acclimatized himself and under the pressure of his colleagues abandoned his 'ravings', he would come to occupy a place of leadership again. Menshevik, independent Social Democrat, Cadet: they were all three to be proved wrong.

The pressures of Lenin's colleagues were soon public. On 8 April, the day after the theses appeared in *Pravda*, the paper carried an editorial note, signed by Kamenev, which repudiated them on the grounds that they assumed the end of the bourgeois democratic revolution. And on the same day, the Petrograd committee of the Bolsheviks rejected the theses by thirteen votes to two. But Lenin was not to be acclimatized or isolated. Bolshevik groups in one workers' district after another declared their support for his theses. At the conference of Petrograd Bolsheviks on 14 April, Lenin proposed that the party work for a transfer of all power to the Soviets. Kamenev's amendment, which sought only an exercise of 'the most watchful control' by the Soviets over the Provisional Government, was decisively defeated. Four days later, the note from Miliukov to the Allies, pledging loyalty to the war undertakings of the Tsarist regime, was published. And Lenin's denunciations of the Provisional Government seemed crushingly confirmed. At the All-Russian Conference of Bolsheviks, on 24 April, Stalin's desertion of Kamenev was a last-minute leap from a fast-crumbling ledge. The main resolutions sponsored by Lenin were passed by overwhelming majorities. And, in particular, the party adopted the slogan, 'All power to the Soviets!'

The Soviets were not democratic institutions in any accepted sense. But the very limitation of their electoral base, in individual factories and regiments, made them uniquely representative of revolutionary forces; especially since the deputies were elected for no specific period and could be recalled at will. With every further decline in the economy, every further reverse at the front, opinion in the factories and barracks, Lenin believed, must move against the Provisional Government and the commitment of the moderate socialists to sustain it. The Soviet system would enable this movement of opinion to be translated immediately into new deputies of Bolshevik persuasion. And the assertion of supreme sovereignty by the Soviets might, in consequence, lift the Bolsheviks to command of the revolution and the state. Meanwhile, moreover, the slogan served other purposes. It assailed the claims of the Provisional Government to a revolutionary role of any kind; and by associating the Bolshevik Party with the exclusive cause of the Soviets, effectively declared that the moderate socialists, in their opposition to this cause, were promoting the claims of the Provisional Government, against those of the Soviets and the revolution itself.

Miliukov's note to the Allies produced a clamour of popular protest. And instant major repairs became imperative, if the 'dual power' alliance was to be kept from collapsing. It was not enough to force Miliukov himself from office. A ministry that represented the bourgeoisie alone had to go. After much argument, the Soviet Executive Committee decided, by forty-one votes to eighteen, with the Bolsheviks joined in opposition by a few internationalist Mensheviks, to support a coalition ministry. And early in May, the extent of the renovation was revealed.

Prince Lvov remained premier. As the new Minister of Foreign Affairs, there emerged a certain Tereschenko. The young French diplomat, De Robien, expressed his astonishment:

... and to think that, three months before the fall of the old regime, he was refused the post of attaché in a small legation. The only public position he has ever occupied is that of attaché to the Imperial theatres; and it was to him that one telephoned through the *chasseur* when one wanted a box for the ballet.[32]

Of much more moment, six moderate socialists were now included as official Soviet representatives. Kerensky himself was transported to responsibility for War and Marine. As Miliukov was subsequently to comment, 'the moderate socialists took under their protection the principle of bourgeois democracy which the bourgeoisie had let fall from its hands'.[33] They took under their protection, also, the pursuit of a ruinous war.

With the earliest reports of the upheaval in Russia, Trotsky in New York made eager preparations to return. His family now saw him only 'in abrupt flashes'. He rushed from meeting to meeting; with audiences patiently sitting through hour after hour of delay, for their turn to hear him. He wrote numerous articles. He gave numerous interviews. And whatever the occasion, his essential message was the same. After the ministries of the Miliukovs and the Kerenskys, 'we,' he promised, 'shall be the next'. Well before Lenin presented the April theses, Trotsky was assailing the Provisional Government; greeting the emergent Soviets as a rival power bound to assert itself; and proclaiming the second stage of the revolution, which must produce the victory of the proletariat. With particular foresight, he held that an agrarian insurgency would soon confront the politics of patriotism pursued by the Mensheviks and Social Revolutionaries in place of proper reform. The call to take Constantinople would not deflect the peasant masses from their intention to take instead the land of the landlords.

Above all, he reaffirmed the faith that he had been the first of the revolutionary leaders to formulate. The Russian revolution was the start of the world revolution. Indeed, it had only now to discard its patriotic mask and reveal its 'true proletarian face' for the German proletariat to respond. But what, he asked himself, if the German proletariat failed to rise? That was altogether improbable.

The war has transformed the whole of Europe into a powder magazine of social revolution. The Russian proletariat is now throwing a flaming torch into that powder magazine. To suppose that this will cause no explosion is to think against the laws of historical logic and psychology.

But still: what if the altogether improbable were to happen? Well, then, he answered, the Russian working class would, arms in hand, defend the revolution and 'carry it to other countries'.[34]

On 27 March in the Western calendar, Trotsky and his family began, on a Norwegian boat, their journey back to Russia. He had been provided with the necessary Russian papers by the consul-general, and been assured at the British consulate in New York that the British government would place no obstacles in his way. But when the boat reached Halifax on 3 April, it was boarded by a British naval force, with orders that Trotsky, his family and five other passengers accompany the party ashore. They refused. Several sailors seized Trotsky; and his eleven-year-old son Leon, in a reaction that foreshadowed much of his own future, struck one of the officers, shouting, 'Shall I hit him again, papa?' The passengers were carried from the boat and taken by naval cutter to Halifax, where Natalia and the children were left under surveillance, and the rest conveyed to a camp for German prisoners at Amherst.

There, Trotsky was stripped and searched in the presence of a dozen men. In his memoirs he would call it a 'shameful humiliation' and contrast it with his previous treatment in the Tsar's fortress, where the police had at least conducted the exercise 'in privacy'.[35] There was rather more to his response than the outrage which he felt at this affront to his own, and to the revolution's, dignity. He was, for all the public commitment of his life, a deeply private person.

At all events, the incident did little to convince him that he should reconsider his hostility to the vaunted value of the British system. Nor was he converted by the camp commander, a British colonel who had earned his promotion to such responsibilities by suitable service in the British colonies, and whose fond memories of the different disciplines there led him to wish aloud that he might have had Trotsky to deal with 'on the South African coast'. Pressed by the Russian prisoners to explain why they were being held, the colonel announced that they were dangerous to the Russian government. When they protested that the Russian government had provided them with passports and might properly be left, after all, to take care of itself, he curtly informed them that they were dangerous to the Allies in general. Both were assertions whose substance Trotsky would not have wanted to deny. Indeed, keeping him in the camp could limit, but it could not eliminate, the danger he had set himself to be. He led group discussions and gave lectures on the causes and meaning of the war and of the Russian revolution. He became so popular with the mass of German prisoners that he had difficulty in persuading them to let him stand in line for his food or do his share of compulsory work. The German officers, increasingly alarmed, at last complained to the British colonel about these attempts to subvert the loyalties of their men. And Trotsky was ordered to make no more public speeches. A written protest against this order was signed by some three-quarters of the German sailors and workers interned at the camp.

News of Trotsky's arrest and detention excited an outcry from the Russian revolutionary press. The British embassy in Petrograd, driven to provide some face-saving explanation, declared that the arrested Russians had been making their way back, with resources supplied by the Germans, to overthrow the Provisional Government. *Pravda* derided the claim that a tried revolutionary of Trotsky's calibre, the leader of the Soviet in 1905, had 'anything to do with a scheme subsidized by the German government'. The campaign for his release gathered force, with public meetings of protest. The Soviet Executive denounced the internment as an intolerable intervention in Russia's domestic affairs and an insult to the Russian revolution. The British decided to return the embarrassment to sender. It was Miliukov who had secretly asked that they continue to hold the Russians captive. But Miliukov was understandably disinclined to accept public responsibility.[36] On 29 April, Trotsky and his fellow Russians were told that they would be taken to board a Danish boat. Prisoners eager to shake their hands lined the route of their departure from the camp, while an improvised band played the *Internationale*.

On the train journey across Finland, Trotsky found himself lodged in the same compartment with two prominent Belgian socialists, Vandervelde and De Man, bound for Russia to drum up enthusiasm for the war. The conversation, Trotsky would recall, was brief. 'Do you recognize us?' De Man asked. 'I do,' Trotsky replied, 'although people change a lot in time of war.' At the Russian frontier on 4 May (or the 17th in the Western calendar), Trotsky was met by a delegation of internationalists from Petrograd, which included Uritsky, an old friend from his first Siberian exile, and an official, if minor, representative of the Bolshevik central committee. The Mensheviks had sent no one to greet him. His return was unlikely to prove of such value to their cause that they wished to celebrate it in advance.

At the Finland Station in Petrograd, to the excited crowd gathered to welcome him, he issued his call for a second, socialist revolution. He was seized and lifted shoulder-high, while his sons, distrustful after their recent experiences, looked on, pale and anxious. He was soon at the Smolny Institute, where the Soviet Executive Committee was meeting. But if he expected a warm reception, he was to be disappointed. Chkheidze greeted him dryly from the chair. The Bolsheviks formally proposed that the leader of the Soviet in 1905 be immediately invited to join the committee. A scurry of whispering betrayed the discomposure of the Social Revolutionaries and most of the Mensheviks. They flinched from affording him a place in the leadership. But they could scarcely question his credentials. He was given his membership card and a glass of tea with black bread.

On 5 May, the Petrograd Soviet met to consider the inclusion of socialist ministers in the Provisional Government. Trotsky's presence was assiduously ignored by Chkheidze but soon enough noticed by others. Cries of 'Trotsky! We want Comrade Trotsky!' rang through the hall. He was addressed by Skobelev, once his disciple in Vienna and now the newly appointed Minister of Labour, as 'dear and beloved teacher'. And he was invited to speak. He was uncertain of his audience, so many of whose members seemed to have been supporting policies that he was determined to assail; and he was worried by a refractory cuff, which 'kept constantly shooting out of his sleeve and threatening to fall on the heads of his nearest listeners'.[37] But it would have needed much more than this to hobble the supreme orator of the revolution.

He began by directing the gaze of the Soviet beyond the squat difficulties of the present to the elevations of the future. The Russian revolution, he proclaimed, had aroused the hopes of people everywhere; had opened a new era, in which the struggle of nation against nation was giving place to the struggle of the oppressed against their rulers. He did not go further, to denounce the war commitment of the moderate socialists, for there was no need to do so: by implication, he was consigning that commitment to the delusions of the past. His immediate attack was on the coalition government. 'I cannot conceal,' he announced, 'that I disagree with much that is going on here.' The formal association of socialist and bourgeois representatives, he argued, did not eliminate the division of power, but merely shifted it to within the ministry. Only a single sovereignty could save the Russian revolution.

Tseretelli, the dominant figure of Menshevism now, who had been translated in little more than two months from convict to Minister of Posts and Telegraphs; Chernov, leader of the Social Revolutionaries and now Minister of Agriculture; Skobelev himself; rose to defend their policy of sharing power. And the Soviet voted overwhelmingly to support them. Trotsky's intervention had succeeded in swaying few, if any, of his listeners. But few, if any, of his listeners were likely to have been left unaware that a new and formidable challenge to the current command and course of the revolution had arrived.

7
The Thrust to Power

'Now that the great revolution has come,' Uritsky said to friends during the spring of 1917, 'one feels that however intelligent Lenin may be, he begins to fade beside the genius of Trotsky.'[1] And, indeed, while Lenin, after the roar of his arrival, seemed to have become merely a murmur, Trotsky's voice was soon resounding through the city. But Lenin's strengths were not those that necessarily lent themselves to display or lost anything by being wrapped for the while in the shadows. He had brought his party to accept the righteousness of his views; and he was now devoted to making it the effective instrument of such righteousness, by intensive organization. In January 1917, Bolshevik membership had sunk to below 24,000; by the last week of April, it had risen to almost 80,000; and in August it would reach 200,000.[2] These were not, of course, figures to stand comparison with the Social Revolutionary multitudes, in the arithmetic of democracy. But the arithmetic of revolution, as Lenin knew and Chernov did not, was an altogether different matter. The Bolshevik numbers were not only by far the more cohesive and disciplined. They were drawn disproportionately from those sectors where the real revolutionary power lay: the proletariat and the urban military garrisons so susceptible to its influence. Already by the end of May, a campaign master-minded by Lenin had produced a sweeping Bolshevik majority at a conference of Petrograd factory committees.

Trotsky was not deceived by public acclaim into supposing that he might accordingly come to lead the revolution for socialism. The very nature of that revolution narrowly confined the role that anyone, however resourceful and resolute, could play without a mobilized mass party behind him. And what was he but a leader without such a party to lead? He was, to be sure, the dominant figure in a group of 'united social democrats', called the Mezhrayontsy, which had been formed in 1913 and included revolutionaries, such as Uritsky and Lunacharsky, of undoubted distinction. But this had a minor following, in only a few working-class districts of the capital, and stood no chance of seriously challenging Bolshevism for command of popular resistance to the regime of compromise. It was essentially an association of those who had finally abandoned hope of reuniting the Social Democratic party; who were persuaded that Menshevism had set its face against the future; but who were still held back, by the differences of the past, from joining the Bolsheviks.

On 10 May, Lenin and Trotsky met, for the first time since their encounter at Zimmerwald, to discuss the possibilities of a merger between the Bolsheviks and the Mezhrayontsy. Lenin made no effort to conceal his eagerness. Trotsky's adherence to Bolshevism now would dramatically demonstrate how right he himself had been, all along, in his view of how the party of revolution should be shaped. And he was not so captivated by the qualities of his own close colleagues as to believe that Bolshevism could well do without Trotsky and his companions. He was prepared to be generous. He proposed that the Mezhrayontsy join the Bolshevik party at once; and that Trotsky and his principal associates take posts on its major committees and serve on the editorial board of *Pravda*. He made it clear that they now saw the future in the same way. The bourgeois revolution in Russia, unable to fulfil its undertakings and effect sufficient reform, must soon become a proletarian one, to pioneer the insurgency of socialism throughout the world. It was what he had been saying, and had succeeded in getting the party to say, since his return. And it was a tacit admission that Bolshevism had seen the Trotskyist light. But on one point Lenin would not budge. The Bolshevik Party, with all its organizational power and proletarian support, was of his making. He would not concede the disappearance of its identity. To Trotsky's insistence that a joint congress be held, to establish a new party, with a new name, he replied with a categorical no.

The meeting, therefore, ended without agreement. And Lenin was sure where the blame belonged. When asked, shortly afterwards, what still separated Trotsky from the Bolsheviks, he curtly replied: 'Now don't you know? Ambition, ambition, ambition.'[3] It was, Lunacharsky would write several years later, usual to say of Trotsky that he was ambitious. But this, Lunacharsky maintained, was 'utter nonsense'. He recalled the remark that Trotsky had made on Chernov's acceptance of office in the Provisional Government: 'What despicable ambition – to abandon one's place in history in exchange for the untimely offer of a ministerial post.' And Lunacharsky commented: 'In that, I think, lay all of Trotsky. There is not a drop of vanity in him, he is totally indifferent to any title or to the trappings of power; he is, however, boundlessly jealous of his own role in history and in that sense he is ambitious.'[4]

It was not the sense in which Lenin was likely to have used the word. But then Lenin was far from infallible in his judgement of character. And, in fact, had ambition, as commonly understood, been Trotsky's preoccupation, he would have snatched the opportunity presented by Lenin's proposals. For there was always the risk that the terms might become less generous, as Bolshevism thrived without him; and there were prominent Bolsheviks, he knew all too well, who would make of his refusal an argument against associating with him at all. But to accept Lenin's terms was to pass a balance-sheet in which much of his own long struggle against Bolshevism emerged as misguided and mischievous. Was he not being asked, in effect, to short-change his historical role? If it had become possible now for him to work with the Bolsheviks, was this not precisely because they had abandoned Bolshevism, partly in response to that role? Or was the refusal to abandon the party and its name not a sign that Lenin himself still clutched at the hem of Bolshevism? 'I cannot describe myself as a Bolshevik,' Trotsky said, according to Lenin's own notes of their meeting. 'It is undesirable to stick to old labels.'

Around him, in the Mezhrayontsy, were those still concerned at the excessive centralism in the Bolshevik Party. Yet what was the alternative? Certainly, there was none for him in an association with the moderate socialists, who were captive to the conduct of a cruel and senseless war; whose response to the call for a socialist revolution was to cling more closely to the alliance with the bourgeoisie and counsel patience, as though the people of Russia were children demanding to be treated as adults before their time. They were digging a ditch in the sand to hold the flow of history; but history was bound to sweep over them and drown them in its depths. The only real alternative lay not there, but in accepting the confinement of a virtually independent revolutionary.

And, for a while, he played with it. On 25 May, he visited the offices of *Novaya Zhizn (New Life)*, Maxim Gorky's paper, of which Sukhanov was editor, to test the possibilities of developing some association with it. But the meeting with the editorial staff went badly. Trotsky found, by his own account, only a 'circle of literary wiseacres, for whom revolution reduced itself to the problem of the leading editorial'.[5] And he concluded the discussion with the comment: 'it remains for me and Lenin to make our own newspaper'.[6] Yet he still resisted Lenin's beckoning. He launched a weekly called *Vperyod (Forward)*. It had neither the financial resources nor the mass organization behind it to make much of a mark. His experience with it can only have fed the belief that continued separation from Bolshevism must relegate him to the footnotes of the coming revolution.

It was an alternative: if one that would necessarily have had its own tragic consequences. But it was not an alternative for Trotsky. Indeed, the paradox of the tragic dilemma is that the rejected alternative is there only to be rejected. What Trotsky chose, he chose inevitably. To choose otherwise would have been to turn and walk away from himself. His decision was, in the end, an essential declaration of faith. The exploited of mankind, having shaken off at last the mastery of capital, would never allow a new mastery to shackle them. Who, within the socialist emancipation, would dare even attempt to impose one? And now, what true revolutionary could doubt that the moment of emancipation was near?

The Bolshevik cries for land, bread and peace proclaimed and promoted the three major challenges to the policies of moderate socialism and the purposes of coalition government. Already from the end of March, peasants impatient at the delay in agrarian reform had begun seizing church lands and large private estates. The Social Revolutionary leadership, committed to sustaining a bourgeois power that encompassed crucial land interests, through direct ownership or the mortgage and loan involvements of the banks, condemned the seizures. The party's rank-and-file, concerned to retain peasant support, condoned and even, more or less covertly, encouraged them. Direct action spread and intensified. The coalition government thundered against it, while conspicuously unable to undertake effectual countermeasures. To disillusionment with a revolutionary regime that seemed embarrassed by revolution was added scorn of its authority. This did not mean that disaffection in the countryside was accordingly reflected in adherence to Bolshevism or to the emergent identity of Left Social Revolutionaries. The peasant multitudes conducted their particular assault without pausing to consider which of the party standards they should carry along. It did mean that a regime which had lost not just their trust but their respect would find few, if any, among them to answer a call for rescue from an insurrection by industrial workers and allied elements of the army. And it meant, too, meanwhile, that large numbers of peasant soldiers, whether watching the rural upheaval from local garrisons or hearing of it by rumour and report at the front, responded the more readily to the promptings of revolt.

Industrial production had long been contracting because of the decrepitude of equipment and the deficiencies of fuel and raw materials. As workers demonstrated by strikes their discontent with deteriorating economic conditions, and employers by lock-outs a determination to impose their own remedies, it contracted the more perilously. Only the production of banknotes continued to expand. By the middle of the year, Alexei Peshekhonov, Minister of Supply, was helplessly wringing his hands.

We cannot take grain by force, the peasants don't want to take money, they must be supplied with those city products which they need. But there isn't enough of these products; there is no iron, no leather. Productivity of labour must be raised.[7]

Yet how was it to be raised, when the shortage of food enfeebled the physical capacity of workers, while fortifying their resolve to wrest relief by the pressures of industrial action?

The central issue was, of course, the war. It was the war that so insatiably devoured the men and the material resources of Russia, with defeat after defeat as the only reward. It was the war that had, more than any other single factor, incited the uprising against the regime of the Tsars. And it was not least to end the war, without seeking annexations or indemnities, that a Soviet majority had agreed to back a coalition government. Yet the war did not end. And increasingly the spokesmen of moderate socialism seemed determined to continue it, while denouncing its imperialist nature. Russian soldiers needed only to read or hear the texts of Soviet resolutions on the war to conclude that they were being asked to risk their lives in a disreputable enterprise. And since the collapse of the old Tsarist military discipline had not been succeeded by the establishment of a credible revolutionary one, they felt themselves safely entitled to disregard orders that they should risk their lives none the less. General Brussilov, who had been foremost among the army commanders in urging abdication on the Tsar, was plainly perplexed by the policies of moderate socialism.

The position of the Bolsheviki I understood, because they preached: 'Down with the War and immediate peace at any price,' but I couldn't understand at all the tactics of the Socialist Revolutionaries and the Mensheviki, who first broke up the army, as if to avoid counter-revolution, and at the same time desired the continuation of the War to a victorious end.[8]

The new rulers of Russia were no less allured than the old had been by the promise of a sudden breakthrough at the front that would defeat all doubt and discontent. The old had looked for conquest as the prize. The new, at least for the record, sought only a resurgence of Russian power and prestige to press successfully for a general peace. They ordered preparations for a massive offensive, in mesmerized disregard of the warnings against it from army commanders, whose desire for movement by the Russian forces had given way to fears that the most likely form of any such movement now would be precipitate flight. Trotsky, calling as witnesses the collapsing economy, the demoralization of the troops, and the increasing discredit of the regime, maintained that failure was inevitable. Kerensky, Tseretelli and Plekhanov greeted, with martial matins, the end of the night.

The signs of disaffection in the armed forces surfaced first in the navy – as Trotsky, in writing of 1905, had suggested they would – and close to the turbulence of the capital, at Kronstadt. In the middle of May, the sailors there arrested their officers; invested the local Soviet with 'sole power in the city'; and, brushing aside the Provisional Government, announced that the Kronstadt Soviet would deal directly with the Petrograd one 'in all matters of state order'. To the clamour of outrage from the moderate socialists at this challenge to their policies, Trotsky rose in the Petrograd Soviet to predict that the time would arrive 'when a counter-revolutionary general tries to throw a noose around the neck of the revolution . . . and the Kronstadt sailors will come to fight and die with us'. The moderate socialists were unimpressed. They were not disposed to picture themselves on their knees. Trotsky went to address the Kronstadt Soviet and won unanimous agreement to a tactical retreat. The sailors would hold to the principle of their decisions, but release their arrested officers to the custody of the Provisional Government.

On 3 June, there opened in Petrograd the First Congress of Soviets. Of the 822 delegates with the right to vote, 777 made known their respective party affiliations. And of these, 285 were Social Revolutionaries; 248, Mensheviks; 105, Bolsheviks; and 10, including Trotsky himself, from the Mezhrayontsy.[9] The moderate socialist leadership accordingly secured a support for its policies that was, on paper, politically crushing. But then it was the fatal failing of that leadership to confuse paper votes with revolutionary power. Lenin was very far from feeling crushed. The mass of acquiescent delegates had been drawn from the provinces and from the army. But was acquiescence really the mood of the provinces, where peasant rage was sweeping landlords from their estates; or of the army, where the murmuring against the government mounted with every breath of the war? The capital, with its proletariat of mobilized awareness, was more and more looking to the Bolsheviks. And where the capital led, surely the rest of the country would follow. Were Moscow and several other cities not doing so already? The Bolsheviks needed only to encourage the conviction that they alone had the will, as well as the policies, to take command of events. Tseretelli, on the second day of the congress, proclaimed, 'There is no political party in Russia which at the present time would say, "Give us power".' Lenin called out from his seat, 'Yes, there is.' And when his own turn came to speak, he made it clear that this had been no mere retort which he now regretted. 'The Bolshevik party is ready at any moment to assume full power. , . . The war can only be ended by further development of the revolution.'

Indeed, though moderate socialism was safe enough at the congress, it was scarcely able to walk the streets outside without fear of attack and lack of any adequate protection. A Declaration of Soldiers' Rights, promulgated by the coalition government, had subsequently been modified by Kerensky, as Minister of War, so that commanders might employ armed force against insubordination and appoint or remove officers without consulting the military committees. Soldiers of the garrison, angered and alarmed by this retreat into the disciplines of the old regime, listened the more readily to Bolshevik agitators; and if few regiments as yet had been captured by the party, the allegiance of many was wavering. On 8 June, at a special conference, the Bolsheviks decided to call for popular demonstrations two days later: in protest at the war; at the presence of 'ten capitalist ministers' in the government; and at Kerensky's changes to the Declaration of Soldiers' Rights. But the protests were to be no more than a backdrop to the demand for the immediate assumption of all power by the Soviets.

Pressed by its patently perturbed leadership, the congress voted, on the 9th, to ban all public demonstrations for the next three days. It was a dangerously high-handed proceeding. The freedom to demonstrate was the most commonly celebrated of the revolution's conquests. And certainly, if there was any supposed threat of disorder in the city, it was the business of the local Soviet, not of the congress, to take action. Nevertheless, now the Bolsheviks could persist with their plan only by defying the very same Soviets whose assumption of total sovereignty the demonstrators would be demanding. At a meeting of the party's leaders late that night, Lenin hesitated, until he received the assurance that there was still time to snatch the call from the next issue of *Pravda*. The demonstration was cancelled. And emissaries were soon hastening through the city to convey and explain the decision. They experienced some difficulty in lowering a level of excitement that the party itself had done so much to raise. But at least they were not received as enemies. Delegates of the congress, visiting different parts of the city to undertake dissuasion of their own,

were met everywhere with extreme unfriendliness and allowed to pass only after lengthy disputes. . . . 'Demonstrating' was extremely popular amongst the workers, and held out the only real hopes for a change. Among the regiments the Congress was proclaimed a gang of landlords and capitalists, or their hirelings; the liquidation of the Coalition Government was considered urgent. Only the Bolsheviks were trusted, and whether the demonstration took place or not depended solely on the Bolshevik Central Committee.[10]

In the event, a display of Bolshevik strength was delayed for only eight days. The moderate socialist leadership, persuaded that demonstrations were inevitable, decided that the congress should summon them itself, in other cities as well as Petrograd, for 18 June: the date set for the start of the massive new offensive at the front. These official demonstrations, it was publicly hoped, would reveal to the world outside, 'the unity and strength of the democracy'. These, it was hoped privately, would restore the authority of moderate socialism at home. The hopes were to prove all too hollow. In the capital, where well over 300,000 marched through the streets, the cautious calls recommended by the congress, for the democratic republic and a general peace, were submerged by the seemingly endless waves of Bolshevik banners. And in other cities, the difference was merely one of scale.

Trotsky himself was meanwhile playing an unremarkable part in the proceedings of the congress. For there had developed, in effect, if not by design, a division of labour between the two leading figures of the revolutionary thrust. Lenin spoke to the multitudes indirectly through congress speeches reported in the press or through the voices of innumerable agitators. And he spoke as the commander of a great party. Trotsky spoke, to similar purpose, directly. And he spoke with little more at his command than his own voice. But it was a voice to which the very city seemed drawn. There were meetings everywhere: in factories, in schools, in theatres, in streets and in squares: as the populace of Petrograd pressed to be shown the promise in the turbulence of the times. From early morning until after midnight, on occasions for more than two hours at a stretch, Trotsky addressed crowds silent with excitement, while delegations waited patiently to capture him for some meeting elsewhere. At the huge Modern Circus, which soon came to be regarded as his personal stronghold, he attracted such numbers that he would have to be carried over the heads of his audience to reach the platform.

Lunacharsky, who claimed to have heard not just all the great orators of socialism, but many of the most celebrated amongst its opponents besides, considered Trotsky the supreme orator of the age.

His impressive appearance, his handsome, sweeping gestures, the powerful rhythm of his speech, his loud but never fatiguing voice, the remarkable coherence and literary skill of his phrasing, the richness of imagery, scalding irony, his soaring pathos, his rigid logic, clear as polished steel – those are Trotsky's virtues as a speaker.[11]

Yet in all this there is missing the interaction between orator and audience; and without that interaction, Trotsky's oratory is recalled only as a photograph; with the features frozen into flat shapes on the page. For the dimension of depth and glimpses of the movement within it, we must go to Trotsky himself who, in his memoirs, caught so much of the peculiar drama that is the process of oratory.

At times it seemed as if I felt, with my lips, the stern inquisitiveness of this crowd that had become merged into a single whole. Then all the arguments and words thought out in advance would break and recede under the imperative pressure of sympathy, and other words, other arguments, utterly unexpected by the orator but needed by these people, would emerge in full array from my subconsciousness. On such occasions I felt as if I were listening to the speaker from the outside, trying to keep pace with his ideas, afraid that, like a somnambulist, he might fall off the edge of the roof at the sound of my conscious reasoning.[12]

Trotsky's powers and popularity were soon to face a formidable test. Unrest continued to mount in the capital. Strikes multiplied, with demands for control of production by the workers themselves; and in several regiments, threatened with dispatch to the front, there were stirrings of mutiny. On 2 July, four Cadet members of the coalition ministry resigned, ostensibly in protest at concessions made by their moderate socialist colleagues to the movement for autonomy in the Ukraine. To the discontented of the capital, this seemed the obvious occasion for a final break with the bourgeoisie. On 3 July there were demonstrations, led by a machine-gun regiment of the garrison and attracting tumultuous support from among workers, for the seizure of all power by the Soviets at once. The Bolshevik leadership, caught off guard, at first sought an end to the demonstrations; and then, having conspicuously failed to calm the soldiers, who shouted down two of the most popular party agitators, summoned a 'peaceful organized demonstration' for the following day.

On 4 July, some 20,000 armed sailors arrived from Kronstadt and marched to Bolshevik headquarters at the Palace of Kshesinskaya, where Lenin greeted them with a short speech that recommended restraint. But as they proceeded through the main streets of Petrograd, there were shots. Suspecting that they were the targets of snipers, the sailors broke into nearby houses and executed summary sentence on the occupants. By the late afternoon when, along with a large number of workers they stood before the Tauride Palace, they were in an ugly mood. Chernov, the Social Revolutionary Minister of Agriculture, attempted to address them, but was seized and pushed into a motor car. Trotsky was inside the palace, at a meeting of the Central Executive Committee.[13] Hearing that Chernov was in danger of being lynched, he rushed out to rescue him. According to Sukhanov's recital of events, Trotsky failed for some time to quieten the sailors and came close to becoming a victim of their fury himself. Midshipman Raskolnikov, the most prominent of the Kronstadt Bolsheviks, would recall that the crowd obeyed at once when Trotsky, 'with an energetic wave of his hand, like a man who was tired of waiting, gave the signal for silence'. But whatever their initial reactions may have been, Trotsky did succeed in dominating the demonstrators. At last, he asked all those who were in favour of violence to raise their hands; and when no one did so, he took Chernov, scarcely conscious, from the motor car and supported him up the steps into the palace.

The demonstrators had the government of Russia at their mercy. Those regiments of the garrison on whose loyalty some reliance had been placed were understandably reluctant to confront the considerable armed forces in the streets and rejected, with declarations of neutrality, appeals to intervene. 'Take power, you son of a bitch, when they give it to you,' a worker, shaking his fist, shouted at Chernov that day. But if those sons of bitches in the Central Executive Committee of the Soviets shrank in confusion and fright from the power being thrust at them, what were the demonstrators to do? The very leaders to whom they looked for guidance were urging only restraint. And yet, what else were such leaders to urge; when they saw so clearly that the capture of the capital would, by provoking a civil war which they were in no condition to win, postpone indefinitely their conquest of the country? Discouraged, the demonstrators dispersed. The mass of sailors returned to Kronstadt. And the city seemed suddenly to have lost its voice in the night.

It was the tide standing still before the turn. Reassured by the dispersal of the demonstrators, and stirred by reports that the government had proof of Lenin's paid employment by the German general staff, soldiers from loyal regiments, singing the *Marseillaise*, arrived at the Tauride Palace. The moderate socialist members of the Central Executive Committee leapt to their feet and, holding hands, joined triumphantly in the singing. 'A classic scene of the beginning of a counter-revolution,' Martov snapped. And certainly the signs were ominous. The offices of *Pravda* were invaded, on orders from the Minister of Justice, by soldiers who confiscated papers and arrested everyone there. When the soldiers had left, a mob arrived and sacked the premises. On the morning of the 5th, the allegations of Lenin's complicity with the Germans appeared in the press. 'Now,' Lenin predicted to Trotsky, 'they will shoot us down, one by one. This is the right time for them.'

The offensive at the front was proving to have been a calamitous gamble. After some celebrated successes, against the scarcely less demoralized and heavily outnumbered Austrian troops, the Russian armies had encountered German forces and were soon in disorderly retreat. Such was the disintegration of discipline that during a single night, on the outskirts of a single town, 12,000 deserters were detained by special detachments. As reports of the developing rout reached the capital, those whose earlier promises of deliverance rang so alarmingly now in their own ears hastened to lay the blame on the Bolsheviks, for having undermined military morale in pursuit of Lenin's commitment to the enemy. On 6 July, writs were issued for the arrest of Lenin, Zinoviev and Kamenev. Lenin and Zinoviev had already gone into hiding. Kamenev, believing it necessary to stand trial and disprove the charges in court, surrendered himself.

The moderate socialists, though in general treating the allegations against Lenin with scant private respect, publicly made much of his refusal to face his accusers; while most in the internationalist opposition censured him by their silence. Sukhanov himself would subsequently describe Lenin's conduct as 'incomprehensible'. Lenin was in no real danger. He risked, at worst, imprisonment; and in the summer of 1917, this would have restricted his freedom of political action no more than his furtive existence effectively did. Those of his colleagues who stayed to defend themselves and were forced to spend a few weeks in prison found no difficulty in publishing their views; served, by their temporary martyrdom, to fuel agitation against the government; and emerged not only unharmed, but with their reputations enhanced. And, meanwhile, how was Lenin's own behaviour to be taken, but as a betrayal of those who had trusted him?

The masses mobilized by Lenin, after all, were bearing the whole burden of responsibility for the July Days. They had no means of ridding themselves of this burden. Some remained in their factories or in their districts – isolated, slandered, in sick depression and unspeakable confusion of mind. Others were under arrest and awaiting retribution for having done their political duty according to their feeble lights. And the 'real author' abandoned his army and his comrades, and sought personal salvation in flight![14]

Lenin and Zinoviev explained their decision, in the Kronstadt Bolshevik paper, on the 15th: declaring that there was no guarantee of justice in Russia; and that their surrender to the authorities would place them 'in the hands of infuriated counter-revolutionists for whom the whole accusation against us is a mere episode in a civil war'. Trotsky, long afterwards, would defend Lenin's decision in much the same terms.[15]

Yet he himself behaved otherwise at the time. To be sure, he was not in Lenin's particular predicament. But if this had, indeed, proved to be a counter-revolutionary convulsion, he would have been, as he knew, a scarcely less obvious victim. At first, he did take certain precautions. He stayed away from the Soviet and slept away from home. These were not, however, measures that would have done much to prevent arrest or assassination; and whatever the reasoning behind their adoption may have been, he abandoned them after only two or three days. At their invitation, he addressed the demoralized Bolshevik members of the Central Executive Committee, and heartened them with his confidence that their cause would emerge twice as strong from its current trial. 'Lenin is away,' commented Muralov, an old Bolshevik, 'and of the others only Trotsky has kept his head.'

On 10 July, in an 'Open Letter to the Provisional Government', Trotsky pronounced those differences, which had separated him for so long from the Bolsheviks, outdated and meaningless; and he challenged the authorities to arrest him.

You can have no grounds for exempting me from the action of the decree by virtue of which Lenin, Zinoviev and Kamenev are subject to arrest; you can have no grounds for doubting that I am as irreconcilably opposed to the general policy of the Provisional Government as my above-mentioned comrades.

He then took his campaign into the Petrograd Soviet and the Central Executive Committee: warning the moderate socialists that a victorious counter-revolution would overwhelm them as well; and denouncing those who could suggest that a revolutionary of Lenin's long devotion, or of his own, might be a German mercenary.

He was not yet, in fact, accused of having conspired with German militarism; but he was clearly eager to have himself identified with Lenin as the subject of such charges none the less. He doubtless supposed that he might best assist Lenin in this way: since if the two of them were to be bracketed together, Lenin would benefit from the incredulity with which these charges against himself were bound to be greeted. And he can only have derived considerable satisfaction from showing that now, when he was on the point of formally joining the Bolsheviks, he came not as a suppliant to the strong, but as a protector to the persecuted. Perhaps it was for just such an opportunity, to give rather than to receive, that he had been waiting.

On 23 July he was arrested and consigned to the same Kresty prison where in 1905 a Tsarist government had placed him. But, as usual, his spirits rose to the occasion. The charges against him were based on the manifest nonsense that he had for some time been a member of the Bolshevik central committee and had travelled with Lenin through Germany in a sealed train. He must have enjoyed writing the articles and open letters in which he derided them. For a few weeks, too, he allowed himself to be interrogated; but then, losing patience with the whole protracted travesty, refused to take any further part in the processes of investigation. Meanwhile the Mezhrayontsy had at last officially joined the Bolsheviks, and Trotsky had been elected to the party's central committee. His claim to a prominent place in the leadership could not seriously be disputed. But lingering resentment at his criticism of the party in the past and almost certainly, too, the fear of his potential for dominance in the future promoted a rearguard movement of resistance. A proposal that, on his release from prison, he should join the chief editorial board of the Bolshevik press, was defeated by eleven votes to ten.

The Provisional Government emerged from the July Days with a new coat of paint. Kerensky took the place of Prince Lvov as premier; and there was a preponderance of moderate socialists in the ministry. But this did not reflect any decline in the influence of the bourgeois representatives. On the contrary: it was they who more than ever now dictated the conditions of the democratic compromise. There was to be no separate peace, since this would betray the Allies; and no acquiescence in the seizure of private estates by the peasants, since this would betray the rights of property. Yet what choice did the moderate socialists have? Beyond the ledge of their alliance with the bourgeoisie, they faced only the dark drop into that second revolution which Bolshevism had, moreover, made its own. And Bolshevism was still very much alive. Some of its leaders might be in prison or in hiding, while others had withdrawn into a circumspect lassitude; but its many rank-and-file agitators were hard at work in the factories and barracks, confirming and augmenting allegiance to the party.

The rot could not be stopped by covering it with a layer of colour. The democratic compromise had regained control of the streets, but it had not won them over to its cause. The turbulence in the countryside continued to mount. And, in the trenches, discipline continued to disintegrate. The British government sent help: supplying a propaganda mission, one of whose functions was

to coax the Russians into fighting by showing them war films of the fighting on the Western front. The effect of these war pictures on the mind of the now undisciplined Russian army can be imagined. Not unnaturally, they served merely to increase the number of deserters.[16]

Within a few weeks, the rot was more evident than ever. And a bourgeoisie persuaded that the democratic compromise was bankrupt began turning to the alternative of a military dictatorship.

Aware that his authority was crumbling, Kerensky called, for the middle of August, a state conference to advise the government. Representation was so arranged as to magnify the appearance of support for his conduct of affairs; and Moscow rather than Petrograd was selected as the site. It proved an unprofitable exercise. The Cadet delegates used the occasion to acclaim General Kornilov, a former monarchist recently appointed commander-in-chief of the armies. The hysterical rhetoric of Kerensky abashed rather than rallied the ranks of moderate socialism. And the Moscow trade unions, under Bolshevik command, called a general strike which virtually paralysed the city during the conference. The local Bolshevik paper, the *Proletarian*, tartly asked: 'From Petrograd you went to Moscow – where will you go from there?'

General Kornilov had given his own answer in a speech to the state conference, when he warned that the fall of the city of Riga might necessitate rapid and decisive action to save the army from collapse and the country from ruin. On 21 August, the Germans took Riga, to little resistance from the Russian forces. Kerensky himself was now contemplating dictatorial measures to deliver Russia from disorder. But his contemplation did not include a rival for the role of deliverer. His request to Kornilov for cavalry, to support a projected state of martial law in Petrograd, was succeeded by his discovery that Kornilov intended to dispatch troops there for a dispensation of his own. In the early hours of the 27th, the cabinet met, at Kerensky's summons, to hear his account of Kornilov's intentions and grant him the unlimited powers that he demanded to deal with the threat. The ministers duly offered their resignations. For the Cadets among them, however, this proved to be no mere formality. Drawn to the cause that they were being called upon to confront, they confirmed their departure by staying away from their offices; while their cabinet colleagues, in accordance with Kerensky's request, continued to perform their administrative functions. Kerensky ordered Kornilov to surrender his command and proceed to Petrograd immediately. Kornilov ignored the orders. It was his troops which, instead, proceeded towards Petrograd.

Despite repeated Soviet representations and a storm of demands from mass meetings, Kerensky refused to release Trotsky and other captives of the July reaction. But he did, as Trotsky had predicted, appeal to Kronstadt for help. A delegation of sailors visited Trotsky in his cell. Should the garrison protect Kerensky from Kornilov? Or set out to pull down both of them together? Trotsky advised the sailors to concern themselves with Kornilov first. Kerensky's fall, he assured them, would follow fast enough.

The moderate socialists were now more intent on securing their own survival than on clinging to an alliance with the bourgeoisie which the bourgeoisie seemed impatient to abandon. And, in the process, they were rediscovering the distinctive virtues of the Soviets, with an eagerness which brushed past recent denunciations of the Bolsheviks. The Provisional Government continued to issue orders for the defence of the regime. But that was a costume piece acted to rows of empty seats. It was a special Committee for Struggle against Counter-Revolution, acting with the authority of the Soviets and encompassing members from all three major socialist parties, that proceeded to mobilize and co-ordinate popular resistance. Railwaymen tore up or barricaded tracks; shifted rebel forces in divergent directions; shunted rebel artillery into sidings. Telegraph clerks held up messages from Kornilov's headquarters, while transmitting copies to the committee. Party agitators, local workers and soldiers waited at stations to meet the troops in their bewildered progress and won them over with ease. The Kornilov rebellion collapsed, without the firing of a solitary shot.

The impact was none the less shattering. The Cadets were indelibly stained with the attempt at counter-revolution, whether or not they had been guilty of anything more than a surreptitious sympathy with it. And since they constituted the only conceivable bourgeois partner in the democratic compromise, the democratic compromise itself came to seem like so much refuse ready for collection. Kerensky's own credit sank unsalvageably, as distrust of his essential motives was confirmed by disclosures of his dealings with Kornilov just before the rebellion. The leading moderate socialists withdrew to an eloquent distance from him. But they gained nothing from this belated retreat. Their policies had succeeded in bringing Russia to the brink of counter-revolution. And, indeed, had not Bolshevism warned that this would be so?

At the beginning of September, the Petrograd Soviet passed a Bolshevik resolution that demanded immediate peace negotiations, confiscation of the large estates, and worker control of industry. The Presidium, dominated still by the moderate socialists, maintained that the vote, taken in the early hours of the morning when many deputies had gone home, did not represent the real disposition of the Soviet. It summoned a special session for the 9th, to vote again. Trotsky, released at last on the 4th in response to a political pressure that had become irresistible, attended the special session; and his very appearance divided the excited assembly into rival demonstrations of silence and applause. The Bolsheviks, attempting to deflect defeat by a compromise, proposed that the Presidium be elected on a proportional basis. But Tseretelli would have none of this. The Presidium, he declared, wanted to know whether the Soviet was determined to change direction.

Trotsky then made what was undoubtedly a decisive intervention. He, in turn, wanted to know whether Kerensky was still a member of the Presidium. The Presidium hesitated, but saw no escape from admitting the fact and so binding itself to Kerensky's disrepute. It was decided to conduct the vote by having those withdraw who had no confidence in the Presidium. Deputies kept drifting through the door; till the Bolsheviks, gathered in the lobbies, dared to hope for defeat by only a narrow margin. The result was announced. The Presidium had been rejected by 519 votes to 414, with 67 abstentions.

The moderate socialist leaders lifted their eyes to the Democratic Conference. It had been initiated to counteract the challenge from the right, during the Kornilov rebellion. Now, they hoped, it would counteract the challenge from the left. With delegates drawn from the municipal and district councils and from the co-operatives, as well as from the Soviets and the trade unions, the Bolsheviks were bound to be heavily outnumbered. Yet, for all the efforts of the promoters, the production, which opened at the Alexandrinsky Theatre in Petrograd on 14 September, was an expensive flop. Kerensky, appearing as head of the government, gave a performance of startling ineptitude. Setting out to explain why he bore no responsibility for the Kornilov rebellion, he found himself opening shutters which he wished to keep closed, and stopped: to leave his audience more suspicious than ever of his conduct and intentions. Interrupted by a question on the death penalty, which he had restored for the armed forces, he lost his footing altogether. 'Wait a little,' he cried. 'When one single death penalty has been signed by me, the supreme commander-in-chief, then I will permit you to curse me.' Trotsky's reply was scathing.

If the death penalty was necessary, then how does he, Kerensky, dare say that he will not make use of it? And if he considers it possible to give his promise to the democracy not to apply the death penalty, then . . . its restoration becomes an act of light-mindedness transcending the limits of criminality.

Trotsky himself spoke as head of his party contingent. And his main object was to lay out for burial the corpse of the democratic compromise which the moderate socialist leadership was now desperately attempting to revive. He derided those who sought to excuse a new coalition with the

Cadets, on the grounds that it would be wrong to blacken the whole Cadet party with the Kornilov rebellion. In the July Days they had shown themselves a great deal less devoted to discriminating between different Bolsheviks. Moreover, then it had been 'not a question of inviting them into the ministry, but of inviting them into the jails'. Cheers and laughter greeted his next sally. 'We say now too: If you want to drag the Cadets to prison for the Kornilov movement, don't do this wholesale, but inspect each individual Cadet from all sides.' The question, however, was whether the Cadets should be invited to join a new ministry. And here what mattered was not that one or other of them had been in contact with Kornilov behind the scenes, but that the whole bourgeois press had either openly welcomed the rebellion or waited in cautious silence for a Kornilov victory. 'That is why I tell you that you have no partners for a coalition!'

The conference, in manifest confusion, could only agree. By 766 votes to 688, it supported the coalition principle. By 595 to 493, it voted to exclude the Cadets from any coalition. Then, recognizing that a coalition without the Cadets would be nonsense, it rejected this, by 813 to 133 votes.[17]

On 23 September, Trotsky was installed, to tumultuous applause, as chairman of the Petrograd Soviet. Some moderate socialist deputies had withdrawn, while others had been recalled for Bolshevik replacements, and the Bolsheviks were now in a decisive majority. But it was a majority that chose, much to Lenin's disgust, leadership rather than domination. All the parties in the Soviet were represented on the new Presidium in accordance with their strength; and even Gorky's group, so small that to give it proportional representation would have meant making the Presidium too large, was allocated seats. Trotsky, in his inaugural speech, proclaimed: 'We are all party people, and we shall have to cross swords more than once. But we shall guide the work of the Soviet in a spirit of justice and complete independence for all fractions. The hand of the Presidium will never oppress the minority.' Three years later, Sukhanov would remind him of these words. And Trotsky would dreamily reply: 'What a happy time!'[18]

For that was a time, indeed, when events seemed for Trotsky to be unrolling like a carpet at the feet of the future. Socialism would soon take possession of Russia and, from there, sweep through the world, to bring an end to the war and a beginning of that collective investment in individual freedom which the despotism of capital denied. To be sure, for a while, until the development of the classless society, a dictatorship would be required. But this would be a dictatorship by the liberated, over those who would otherwise contrive to restore their dominion; a dictatorship by liberty itself. It was a time for happiness. And it was a time that was especially his own.

Shortly after the issue of the writ for his arrest, Lenin, his beard and moustache exchanged for a wig, had been smuggled to refuge in Finland. He was living there still. And no number of newspapers, letters, and secret meetings with trusted colleagues could supply corrective glasses for the distortions of distance. As early as 15 September, the Bolshevik central committee was considering, aghast, letters in which he demanded immediate armed insurrection. The Bolshevik delegates, he insisted, were to be withdrawn from the Democratic Conference, for work in the factories and barracks.

> In order to treat insurrection in a Marxist way, i.e. as an art, we must, without losing a single moment, organize a general staff of the insurrectionary detachments; we must distribute our forces; we must move the loyal regiments to the most important strategic points; we must surround the Alexandrinsky Theatre; we must occupy the Fortress of St Peter and St Paul; we must arrest the general staff and the government. . . .[19]

The project was preposterously premature. Lenin was summoning to insurgency Bolshevik delegates who would reject, by seventy votes to fifty, even a boycott of the Pre-Parliament, or Council of the Republic, that the Democratic Conference, in its very despair, had decided to convoke. The central committee turned down Lenin's demand unanimously. Some members were opposed to the insurrection altogether. Others, in favour of an insurrection at the right moment, 'thought that the moment of the conference was the least advantageous of all'.[20]

Lenin was undeterred by this resistance. He pressed Smilga, who headed the regional committee of Soviets in Finland, to launch an assault on the Kerensky government with Russian troops stationed there, and with backing from the Baltic Fleet. The project never got off the ground. And if it ever had, it would, almost certainly, have crashed, to bury any other Bolshevik challenge in the wreckage. Then, in a letter of 30 September to the central committee, Lenin again demanded immediate insurrection. He suggested that it might well be mounted first in Moscow, 'so as to catch the enemy unawares': though, when the insurrection did occur, Petrograd would fall as if all it had needed was a nudge, while days of ferocious fighting would be needed to take Moscow. This time, he reinforced his demand for immediate action by tendering his resignation from the central committee and reserving 'the freedom to agitate among the rank and file' of the party. 'For it is my profound conviction that if we "wait" for the Congress of Soviets and let the moment pass now, we shall *ruin* the Revolution.'[21]

The First Congress of Soviets, which had ended on 24 June, had called for the next one to meet within three months; and the Second Congress was, therefore, overdue. Lenin believed that the Central Executive Committee, still dominated by the moderate socialists, intended to go on delaying the opening date, until it had ceased to matter any longer whether the

congress met at all. He saw only that the Kerensky government was
preparing a counter-revolution, whose success would crush the Bolsheviks, perhaps for years. Trotsky was not blind to the danger. He, too,
believed that an armed seizure of power was imperative; both to save the
revolution and to advance it. But, from the prow of politics in the capital,
an attempt at counter-revolution looked much less imminent; and its
success, moreover, much less likely, unless the Bolsheviks themselves, by
a precipitate move to prevent it, promoted it instead.

He saw how time itself was working for them. With every lengthening
line along the pavements for a reduced ration of bread; every factory shut
by strikes, lock-outs, or lack of supplies; every rumour that soldiers of the
local garrison would be sent to fill the gaps in the trenches, the cities
moved closer to support for an uprising. From the trenches, letters and
messengers arrived, to report the swelling clamour there for someone,
somehow, to stop the war. The regiments might not march from the front
to overthrow the government. But they seemed less and less likely to
rescue it from an uprising that proclaimed the commitment to an immediate peace. Peasant fury at the persistent failure of the regime to provide
land from the private estates was blazing through the countryside. To be
sure, if it admitted a particular leadership, this belonged to the Left Social
Revolutionaries. But then the Left Social Revolutionaries were increasingly
looking for leadership to the Bolshevik Party, in the struggle of the revolution against the regime. And, here again, it was not so much what the
countryside might give to an armed uprising as what it would deny to the
government when the uprising took place.

The Bolsheviks were, day by day, winning control of more and more
Soviets. And it was Trotsky's own conviction that the seizure of power
should, as far as the conditions of conspiracy allowed, involve the Soviets
directly. Their popular appeal was significantly wider than the party's; and
Trotsky, at the instrument panel of the principal Soviet, saw to what
decisive organizational advantage that appeal might be turned. But also,
the more evident the involvement of the Soviets, the more the seizure of
power would be invested with the proper authority: in particular for the
proletariat abroad, on whose response everything would then inevitably
depend.

The right moment for the insurrection looked like being just before the
Second Congress of Soviets, with its now certain Bolshevik predominance,
met: so that the power, which the delegates themselves could scarcely
seize, might be duly handed over to them. The Central Executive Committee, he felt sure, would not dare delay the opening date much longer:
lest the congress, through enough of the Soviets acting in its name, should
ignore the committee altogether and summon itself. No more than a few
weeks, in all probability, remained. They were weeks which would enable

the design for an armed uprising to develop the required organization and assurance of support, while a frightened and feckless government was sucked down still further into failure by its very endeavours to escape. In the 'art' of insurrection, Trotsky was to prove the master.

Despite the majority vote at the Democratic Conference against another coalition with the Cadets, Kerensky proceeded to form one. The Allied ambassadors were not impressed by this mere shuffle of cards for another game of patience. On 26 September, they called on Kerensky in the Winter Palace: and Sir George Buchanan, the British ambassador, conveyed their anxieties. Kerensky was offended and stalked from the room, with the exclamation: 'You forget that Russia is a great power!' And De Robien noted in his diary: 'The Tsar also refused to listen to Sir George in similar circumstances: a few weeks later he lost the crown!'[22]

Soon afterwards, German naval operations in the Gulf of Finland seemed to be battering at the gates to Petrograd. The government proposed moving the capital to Moscow. It was, in the political climate of the time, a momentous mistake. Bolsheviks raised the cry that the real source of the proposal lay less in the difficulties of defending the city than in the readiness to abandon it for the Germans to purge.

The temper of the Petrograd garrison, so essential to the success of the contemplated insurrection, hardened against the regime. And on 6 October, the soldiers' section of the Soviet, which had long been a moderating counterweight to the militancy of the workers, carried with acclaim the resolution introduced by Trotsky: 'If the Provisional Government is incapable of defending Petrograd, it must either make peace or give place to another government.' Dismayed by the force of the outcry it had provoked, the government repudiated its proposal. But, like Kerensky's recent assurance to the Democratic Conference – that he never intended to implement the death penalty he had restored – this in turn only increased the disrepute of the regime.

On 7 October, amid the magnificence of the Mariinsky Palace, the Pre-Parliament met. Little more than a fortnight before, Trotsky had failed to secure a majority of Bolshevik delegates for a boycott. Now he succeeded. At the end of the opening session, he rose to make an emergency statement.

He denounced the measure of representation that had been granted to the propertied classes. Elections across the country indicated no such entitlement. And what was the purpose of this new body? The Constituent Assembly, to which the government would have to answer, was supposedly due to meet in a month and a half. There was clearly a determination that the Constituent Assembly would not meet at all. The plan to abandon Petrograd was part of the plot to achieve a counter-revolution.

A mounting uproar accompanied these remarks. There were shouts of 'Lies!' 'Berlin!' 'German gold!' and spittings of personal abuse. Sukhanov was to write that never, throughout the revolution, had Soviet sessions been marked by such behaviour; and that it needed 'the company of polished lawyers, professors, financiers, landowners, and generals, for the tavern atmosphere of the bourgeois state Duma to revive immediately'.[23] Trotsky raised his voice above the hubbub.

> We have nothing in common with that murderous intrigue against the people which is being conducted behind the official scenes. We refuse to shield it either directly or indirectly for a single day. In withdrawing from the provisional council we summon the workers, soldiers and peasants of all Russia to be on their guard, and to be courageous. Petrograd is in danger! The revolution is in danger! The people are in danger! . . . We appeal to the people: Long live an immediate, honourable democratic peace, all power to the Soviets, all land to the people, long live the Constituent Assembly![24]

And he leapt from the platform, to lead the Bolshevik delegates out of the hall.

Three days later, on 10 October, the Bolshevik central committee held what was to become the most celebrated of its meetings. Twelve of the twenty-one members gathered in the apartment of an unknowing Suk-hanov, who would sometimes spend the night near his office rather than travel the several miles home, and whose Bolshevik wife had ensured his absence on this occasion by her 'friendly, disinterested advice – not to inconvenience myself by a further journey after work'.[25] Lenin, who had returned secretly to Petrograd three days before, attended without his beard and wearing spectacles and a wig. Tea, bread and sausage were provided for reinforcement through some ten hours of discussion, deep into the night. And the proposal to mount an armed insurrection, hurriedly written by Lenin 'with the gnawed end of a pencil on a sheet of paper from a child's notebook ruled in squares', was passed by ten votes to two.[26] The committee did not decide upon any practical preparations. Although by Trotsky's account, it set the date at 15 October, five days away and five days before the Congress of Soviets had at last been summoned to meet, this was 'merely for purposes of orientation'.[27]

A political bureau of seven, which included Trotsky, Lenin, Stalin, Zinoviev and Kamenev, was elected to undertake appropriate measures. But Lenin himself returned to his refuge in Finland; Stalin was preoccupied with his editorial responsibilities; and Zinoviev and Kamenev, the two who had opposed the decision, appealed against it at once to the ranks of the party. 'Before history, before the international proletariat, before the Russian revolution and the Russian working class, we have no right to stake the whole future at the present moment upon the card of armed insurrection.' In the Moscow committee, as well as many provincial ones, there was strong support for their view. And even within the party's military organization, most of the leaders were either hesitant or hostile to the central committee's decision. The October politburo, far from performing the function assigned to it, never even met.

In fact, Trotsky had, before the central committee vote, already begun to shape the crucial instrument of the insurrection. The Kerensky government, sleep-walking its way along the roof of events, decided that it was time to remove from the capital the most disaffected of the regiments, and made known its intention to draft troops from the garrison for service at the front. The soldiers were not alone in their alarm and anger. Was Petrograd to be deprived of defenders, with the German threat so close? On 9 October, the Mensheviks proposed that a special committee of revolutionary defence be formed, to organize workers for the protection of the city, and to establish whether there was any basis for Bolshevik claims that the intended withdrawal of troops had a political purpose. Trotsky snatched the proposal and had it substantially amended by the Bolshevik majority in the Soviet. The ensuing resolution instructed the Executive Committee of the Soviet, in conjunction with the soldiers' section, to create a committee that 'would concentrate in its own hands all data relevant to the defence of Petrograd'.

When, three days later, the project for a Military Revolutionary Committee emerged, it presented a very different formation from that which the Mensheviks had envisaged. The membership was to comprise the Presidium of the full Soviet and of the soldiers' section, together with delegates from the central committee of the Fleet; the trade unions; the factory committees; and the various party-organized worker militias, which essentially meant the Bolshevik Red Guards. Furthermore, the scope of the committee's functions was so defined as effectively to seize responsibility for defence from the agencies of the government, and to assume, in subservience to the Executive Committee of the Soviet, the disposal of all military power.

On the 16th, a meeting of the Petrograd Soviet, attended by 1000 deputies, discussed the project. A Menshevik spokesman protested that the proposed committee was 'nothing but a revolutionary staff for the seizure of power', and he challenged the Bolsheviks to 'answer the straight question whether or not they are preparing a coup'. Trotsky was not discomposed. 'The Menshevik representative is preoccupied with whether the Bolsheviks are preparing an armed demonstration. In whose name has he asked this question: in the name of Kerensky, the counter-intelligence, the secret police, or some other body?'[28] It was not an answer. But it buried the question in cheers. And the project itself was overwhelmingly approved.

The Left Social Revolutionaries agreed to join the committee. The Right Social Revolutionaries and the Mensheviks refused; relieving Trotsky of the problems that their representatives, by scrutiny and argument, might have produced. The garrison regiments, in what amounted to a border crossing between allegiance and rebellion, declared that they would defy any command from the Kerensky government to leave the city. And the door to the government arsenals, which Trotsky supposed bolted against him, he found suddenly opening at his knock. Workers reported to him that they had approached a particular munitions factory for arms and had been told that they would need to bring an order from the Soviet. Trotsky signed an order for 5000 rifles, and 5000 rifles were delivered the same day. It was as though history had written the script in an invisible ink which required only the closeness of the commitment, for one line after the other to leap into life.

The first tentative date for the insurrection had come and gone. On the 16th, while Trotsky presided over the debate in the Soviet on the Military Revolutionary Committee, an emergency Bolshevik conference was being held, at Lenin's summons. The participants were either members of the central committee or prominent in the Petrograd organization of the party; and they confirmed the commitment to an armed uprising, with the 20th set as the date. But the mood was very far from that general passion of purpose for which Lenin must have hoped. Zinoviev's proposal, to reject as 'inadmissible' any such initiative 'before a conference with the Bolshevik section of the Congress of Soviets', received six votes to fifteen against, with three abstentions. More than one-third of the party leaders present were prepared to place on record their misgivings.

On the following day, the Central Executive Committee announced that the opening of the Soviet Congress was being postponed, until the 25th. It was engaged in a final, frantic attempt to get more delegates of the beleaguered moderate socialist persuasion elected. Trotsky saw nothing to fear from the attempt, which merely betrayed the weakness of those who were making it. And the five extra days looked like proving invaluable to the development of his design. But it was a design, he was now to be reminded, in constant danger from someone letting in the light. Doubtless encouraged by the vote on Zinoviev's proposal at the Bolshevik conference, Kamenev gave, with Zinoviev's agreement, a public statement to Gorky's newspaper, *Novaya Zhizn*:

Not only Zinoviev and I, but also a number of practical comrades, think that to take the initiative in an armed insurrection at the present moment, with the given correlation of social forces, independently of and several days before the Congress of Soviets, is an inadmissible step ruinous to the proletariat and the revolution. . . .

In the Petrograd Soviet, on the 18th, moderate socialism rose with a gleam in its eyes. What had Trotsky to say about the reports of an imminent insurrection? Why had he signed a Soviet order for 5000 rifles to arm the

Red Guards? Adroitly, he made his way between a denial that the insurrection was imminent, which would have disconcerted his own forces, and an admission, which could scarcely have failed to arouse the government from its stupor. The Soviet, he replied, was an elected revolutionary parliament, whose decisions could not be concealed. It had not decided on any armed action (as, indeed, it had not: the Bolshevik central committee had taken the decision). But should events compel it to such a course, the workers and soldiers would respond as one man to its call. Yes, he had, in the name of the Soviet, ordered the delivery of rifles to Red Guards. And the Soviet would continue to organize and to arm the workers. 'We must be ready. We have entered a period of more acute struggle. We must be constantly prepared for attack by the counter-revolution.'

Kamenev, sitting beside him, leapt to his feet and announced that he signed his name to Trotsky's every word. The moderate socialists, mindful of Kamenev's proclaimed opposition to an uprising, stirred with reassurance. But it was not to reassure them that Kamenev had spoken. It was to kidnap Trotsky for a defensive formula with which to campaign against the central committee decision. Trotsky was furious. On the same day, in a speech to the All-Russian Conference of Factory and Shop Committees, whose delegates, he knew, would be quick to catch the implication of his remarks, he declared: 'A civil war is inevitable. We have only to organize it as painlessly as possible. We can achieve this not by wavering and vacillation, but only by a stubborn and courageous struggle for power.'

Neither Kamenev nor Zinoviev attended the next Bolshevik central committee meeting, on 20 October. But it proved acrimonious enough without them. The party paper had, that very day, published a letter in which, adopting Kamenev's device, Zinoviev had subscribed to Trotsky's statement in the Soviet. And an accompanying editorial note had commented:

> We in our turn express the hope that with the declaration made by Zinoviev (and also the declaration of Kamenev in the Soviet) the question may be considered settled. The sharpness of tone of Lenin's article does not alter the fact that in fundamentals we remain of one opinion.[29]

Lenin was also absent from the meeting. But the committee was furnished with a fiery letter from him, which denounced 'Kamenev's trick at the session of the Petrograd Soviet'; described Kamenev and Zinoviev as strike-breakers for their public statement in *Novaya Zhizn*; and demanded their expulsion from the party forthwith, as an exemplary punishment.

Kamenev himself had already tendered his resignation from the central committee, as the prelude to his campaign among the rank and file. Trotsky, who was opposed to expelling either culprit, spoke in favour of accepting Kamenev's resignation. But he also widened the dispute: protesting against the editorial note in the party paper, which he called 'inadmissible'. Sokolnikov, one of the two editors, hastened to make it clear that he had not been consulted and that, moreover, he considered the note a mistake. Stalin, it accordingly emerged, bore the sole responsibility. And it was Stalin now who argued that Kamenev and Zinoviev should be permitted to remain members of the central committee, in the interests of unity, and because 'our whole position is contradictory'.

It was decided that Kamenev's resignation should be accepted; and, again with Stalin opposed, that Kamenev and Zinoviev should be expressly forbidden to campaign against the policy of the central committee. Stalin immediately announced that he was resigning from the editorial board. But his colleagues were not moved to gather round him, for some expression of their confidence. The minutes suggest rather a mere impatience. The matter was left for the editorial board to discuss, and the committee meanwhile 'decided to pass on to next business without discussing comrade Stalin's statement or accepting his resignation'.[30]

So jealous and so mistrustful, Stalin might well have seen this as a treacherous siding with Trotsky against him. He had served the party long and loyally; while Trotsky had been heaping anathemas upon it and all its works. Yet here was that same Trotsky, with the sprinklings of his Bolshevik conversion hardly dry on his head, laying down canons of conduct for his comrades to follow; and the central committee, instead of rising up to put him in his place, bent in obedience before him. If anything deserved to be called 'inadmissible', this did. But then, Stalin had learned how to wait. That Jewish peacock was so taken with the spread of his tail that he would strut one day straight into the fencing around him and catch his head in the wire.

For the last few months, the Soviet had had its home at the Smolny Institute, in Tsarist times a convent school for the daughters of the nobility. Plenary sessions were held on the second floor, in the former commencement hall, where chandeliers sparkled among white columns, and the dais was decorated by a large gold frame from which the portrait of royalty had been cut, so that it must have looked a little like a mouth wide open in wonder at such unprecedented proceedings. In many of the more than 100 rooms which the rest of the building contained, various organizations associated with the Soviet pursued their particular activities: the enamelled plaques on the doors, which had once so politely identified 'Ladies' Classroom Number 4' or the 'Teachers' Bureau', covered by rudely written signs that proclaimed an occupation by the 'Union of Socialist Soldiers' or the 'Central Committee of the All-Russian Trade Unions'. And busiest of all, in one of them, Trotsky met with his revolutionary staff. Yet, the very last to suppose that revolution might be made in a room, he would somehow manage to deliver a speech at a factory here, a barracks there, till his opponents found themselves blinking away the belief that he could actually be in several places at once.

Those opponents were busy, as well: but to what real purpose, their busyness was directed precisely to keep them from considering. Delegates to the Soviet Congress had begun arriving in Petrograd and visiting the Smolny to register. The credentials committee, dominated by moderate socialists, challenged many of them, with the claim that they had not been legally elected: rather as a hospital patient, terminally ill, might seek to delay his death by altering the entries on the chart at the bottom of his bed. And in the Winter Palace, Kerensky fussed with state papers while he waited for his call. To the prods of the British ambassador, that the rumours of imminent insurrection demanded resolute action against the Bolsheviks, he responded, more than once: 'I only wish that they would come out, and I will then put them down.'[31]

The insurrectionist hold on the military forces in the capital had meanwhile been tightened by the establishment of a garrison conference, which comprised the regimental committees. For this provided a passage to control of the various units both more certain and more direct than any that the soldiers' section of the Soviet, with its distinctive political character, could afford. On Saturday, 21 October, the garrison conference overwhelmingly adopted resolutions proposed by Trotsky, which promised full support for any steps undertaken by the Military Revolutionary Committee, and summoned the Soviet Congress to assume power, so as to secure peace and land and bread for the people. In the Winter Palace, however, they continued sitting with their backs to the windows. The one member of the government who had turned round far enough to catch some sight of what was happening outside was a member of the government no longer. Verkhovski, the Minister of War, had declared, on the night of the 19th, that Russia must make peace immediately, with or without the consent of the Allies. His colleagues had insisted that he retract his declaration, and he had, instead, resigned. The British ambassador wrote in his diary that Verkhovski seemed 'to have completely lost his head'.[32]

Sunday, the 22nd had been designated the 'Day of the Petrograd Soviet', on which mass meetings were to take place throughout the capital. Trotsky hoped that the populace would see, in this unarmed muster, the strength and determination of its numbers, with the isolation and impotence of its opponents. He was not to be disappointed. While the propertied classes stayed anxiously indoors, there gushed from the attics and basements, the slums and the barracks, multitudes with caps or shawls on their heads and mud on their shoes, to flood, again and again, the halls at which meetings had been called. At the huge House of the People, Sukhanov noted, the ovation for Trotsky was shorter than usual, as though cut by impatience to hear what he had to say. He began by depicting, 'with extraordinary power', the suffering in the trenches. A Soviet regime, he went on, would end that suffering. It would bring peace. And it would end also the suffering at home in the cities and villages. It would bring bread to the hungry and land to the landless. 'All round me,' Sukhanov would recall, 'was a mood bordering on ecstasy. It seemed as though the crowd, spontaneously and of its own accord, would break into some religious hymn.' And when Trotsky asked the thousands there to join him in declaring that they would defend the cause of the worker and the peasant 'to the last drop of our blood', they answered him as one, with arm raised and with burning eyes.[33]

On Monday the 23rd, while a debate on foreign policy was droning on, to desultory heckling, in the Pre-Parliament, the Military Revolutionary Committee confronted a stretch of fog across its strategy. Meetings of the garrison conference had indicated an island of doubt, in the Fortress of St Peter and St Paul. An island elsewhere, in such an expanse of commitment, might be securely contained, until the success of the insurrection submerged it. But this was one from whose cliffs the surrounding city could be raked by fire. Antonov-Ovseenko, the former Tsarist army officer turned rebel, who had invited Trotsky to edit *Nashe Slovo* in those beleaguered Paris days, and who was now secretary of the committee, offered to lead reliable troops in an attempt to take the fortress at once. Trotsky was against so drastic a measure. It would provide the officers at the fortress with occasion to encourage bloodshed, which might blind many soldiers to the purpose of the attempt. And, since the government was bound to react, the trigger of the insurrection would have to be prematurely pulled. He suggested instead that he go himself and see if he could capture the fortress from within. The undertaking carried obvious risks. But Trotsky discounted them. He refused to believe that the ranks were as reluctant as their representatives; and, even if they were, that he would be unsafe in their hands.

Arriving with a single colleague, he found a meeting of soldiers already in progress. He was given the floor. And the floor gave him the fortress. His intuition had not failed him. The soldiers agreed with enthusiasm to obey only the orders of the Military Revolutionary Committee. And their capture brought with it the unexpected prize of 100,000 rifles in the armoury. At the Soviet session that evening, there was tumultuous delight at the news. The moderate socialists exclaimed that this had been one further move in the Bolshevik conspiracy, and that it would all inevitably end in disaster. Trotsky, satisfied that the time for disguise had passed, replied: 'Yes, an insurrection is going on, and the Bolsheviks, in the form of the Congress majority, will take the power into their own hands. The steps taken by the Military Revolutionary Committee are steps for the seizure of power.'

On a leather couch in his room at the Smolny that night, Trotsky, without troubling to undress, snatched what sleep he could, between the ringing of the telephone and the knocking of urgent messengers at the door. Cold winds from the sea whipped along the quays and through the streets of the capital, as the morning of Tuesday the 24th greyed from the edges. Trotsky wandered through the half-dark corridors: checking that all was in order and dispensing reassurance to anyone who seemed uneasy. On the staircase, he bumped into two breathless workers, running to report that government agents, accompanied by military cadets, had sealed the Bolshevik presses. For a moment, Trotsky hesitated: held, he was later to write, by the power that 'legal formality' exercised over the mind.[34] And then one of the workers asked: 'Couldn't we break the seals?' He instantly answered: 'Break them: and to make it safe for you, we will give you a dependable escort.' By eleven o'clock the same morning, Bolshevik newspapers were once again in the streets.

A similar fate attended other government initiatives. An order that the cruiser *Aurora*, at anchor in the Neva, put to sea, was immediately countermanded by the Military Revolutionary Committee. The cruiser did not move. Detachments of military cadets were dispatched to raise the bridges, so as to prevent crowds of workers from reaching the centre of the city. Confronted by forces of Red Guards and soldiers, they generally offered little resistance and withdrew. Sailors from the *Aurora* helped to expel the cadets posted at the Nikolaevsky Bridge.

In the Pre-Parliament that afternoon, Kerensky, white-faced and almost vibrating with nervous excitement, declared that a state of insurrection existed, and explained at length why the government was blameless. He promised decisive measures. And he received an ovation from all but a few internationalist Mensheviks. 'Do not think,' he had said, a few weeks before, at the Democratic Conference, 'that when the Bolsheviks bait me, the forces of democracy are not there to support me. Do not think that I am hanging in the air.' He returned to the Winter Palace now, satisfied that his feet were, indeed, on the firm floor of his Pre-Parliament. But, even there, he had only been standing on a trapdoor. And, by the evening, this had been pulled. Speaking for the internationalist Mensheviks, Martov agreed that the Bolsheviks should be condemned for their endeavour to seize power. But it was the government which had, by its policies, prepared the ground for the uprising. Civil war was to be prevented only by immediate measures for the distribution of land and the attainment of peace. And not the government, but a Committee of Public Safety, drawn in the main from the organizations of the revolutionary democracy, should have the task of dealing with the Bolshevik threat. To widespread astonishment, Martov's formula, composed in conformity with these remarks, was passed by 113 votes to 102, with 26 abstentions.[35] Kerensky, informed of the vote, maintained that he was left with no choice but to surrender his mandate. Leading moderate socialists hastily assured him that their members had voted for the formula only so as to snatch the trumpet from Bolshevik lips, and argued that a government crisis now would be 'untimely'. Kerensky agreed to stay, in the interests of Russia.

That night, soldiers, sailors and armed workers stood, in iron knots, around the Smolny, and lined the corridors and stairways inside. Whatever opportunity the government might have had, a day or two before, to mount a surprise assault on the building and arrest the insurrectionist leadership, was now gone. A meeting of welcome to the congress delegates by the Central Executive Committee had been called, and the commencement hall was crowded with newcomers: their faces seeming to lour the more menacingly at the platform because the lighting had, for some reason, been dimmed. It was midnight when Dan, for the moderate socialist leadership of the Executive, rose to give a report. At first he was received in silence. But when he began denouncing Bolshevik intentions and warned of the consequences, there was uproar. 'The Central Executive Committee will defend the revolution with its body!' he cried. 'It was a dead body long ago!' came the retort. The chairman rang his bell. 'Silence, or I'll have you put out!' To cheers and whistling, someone shouted, 'Try it!' Pushing forward against the noise, Dan announced that the Pre-Parliament had earlier decided to demand the distribution of land and immediate negotiations for peace. But this was only greeted by laughter and cries of 'Too late!'

When Trotsky rose to reply, the applause was thunderous. Cuttingly he recalled how moderate socialism had resisted the very policies that it was now, frightened by its popular isolation, proclaiming. Dan had told them that they had no right to make an insurrection. 'Insurrection is the right of all revolutionists! When the down-trodden masses revolt, it is their right. . . .' Nor were they to be deflected by threats of civil war. 'If you do not weaken, there will be no civil war, for the enemy is already capitulating, and you can assume the place of master of the Russian land which of right belongs to you.'[36]

At two o'clock in the morning of Wednesday the 25th, while this meeting of welcome was still tumultuously proceeding, insurrectionist detachments began moving through the capital. They occupied the railway stations, the power plant and waterworks, food and munition stores, the central telephone exchange, the post and telegraph offices. Nowhere did they encounter resistance. At Kresty, a commissar presented the soldiers on guard with a list of Bolshevik prisoners whose immediate release the Soviet required. The prisoners were immediately released. Trotsky, from his small corner room on the third floor of the Smolny, followed events and issued instructions by telephone. And keeping him company was Kamenev who, recognizing at last that the insurrection was not to be stopped, had come to identify himself with it. At some stage, satisfied that all was going well, Trotsky sat on the couch to rest for a moment and asked Kamenev for a cigarette. Then, after taking a puff or two, he fainted. His first sight was of Kamenev's frightened face looming over him. 'Shall I get some medicine?' Kamenev asked. 'It would be better,' Trotsky answered, after a little thought, 'if you got something to eat.' He tried to remember when last he had eaten, but couldn't.[37]

Kerensky's night was no less agitated; but to no more effect than a display of his own isolation. Representatives of the three Cossack regiments assured him of support, if he would promise them to be relentless in victory. The promise was given. But it soon became clear that the representatives had lost their constituencies. The ranks of the regiments, while not ready to associate themselves with the uprising, were also not minded to risk their lives for a regime that could hardly provide them with bread; and that might, once its authority was restored, send them to die in the trenches. They began saddling their horses to go home. Kerensky had long been treating his own party as merely the bent back on which he had stood, to mount his mission of national leadership. In his sudden need, he called to it for help. But none was forthcoming. In all likelihood, the Social Revolutionary Right could not have supplied, so late, a sufficient armed force to make the slightest real difference. It was not, however, willing even to try, for the sake of someone whose posturing imperiousness lacked the excuse of success, and whose grasp now might drag the party down to disaster with him. Kerensky's conferences with his ministers in the Winter Palace, and with officers of the district military headquarters on the opposite side of the square, fed his dismay. At last, around ten o'clock in the morning, he decided that his only chance lay in making his way to the front and returning at the head of loyal troops. Cloaked by an American embassy car with its admonishing flag, he sped through the many Red Guard patrols and out of the city.

Even while he was determining to leave, the Military Revolutionary Committee issued a proclamation to the citizens of Russia: announcing that the Provisional Government had been overthrown and that state power had passed to the committee as an instrument of the Petrograd Soviet. It was less a report than a prediction. The provinces had not spoken. The front might yet prove refractory. In the capital itself, the Pre-Parliament was still sitting, and at the Winter Palace the residue of the cabinet remained a symbol of sovereignty. But the committee had cause enough for confidence. The regime was falling in on itself, with an inaudible sigh, like a soufflé at the plunge of a spoon. It was difficult to believe that anything of much moment had happened. When John Reed, an American journalist, went walking down the Nevsky Prospect at noon, he saw the streetcars running as usual, with men, women and boys hanging from every projection. The shops were open. But the state bank was not. At its gates, he found soldiers standing with fixed bayonets. 'What side do you belong to?' he asked. 'The Government?' And one of them replied with a grin: 'No more Government! Glory to God!'[38]

So smoothly had it all gone, indeed, that Lenin was apparently unaware it had got going at all. When, wearing his wig, and with a handkerchief bandaging part of his face to disguise himself further, he arrived at Smolny in the middle of the day, he was still distrustful of the strategy that had been chosen. He had wanted the party on its own, in close conspiracy, to gather itself for a quick armed pounce on power; and he had, repeatedly, warned that the slow and exposed Soviet course might merely provoke the government to strike first. As late as the evening of the 24th, in a final peal of alarm, he had sought to mobilize workers and soldiers for pressure on the insurrectionist leadership to act at once. And now, new suspicions had been raised in him by press reports that negotiations between the Military Revolutionary Committee and the government's district military headquarters were proceeding favourably. The moment he met Trotsky, he asked, 'Are you agreeing to a compromise?' and gave him a piercing look. Trotsky assured him that the reports had been no more than a manoeuvre. And Lenin began to pace up and down; rubbing his hands in excitement. 'Well, that is g-o-o-d. That is v-e-r-y good!' As he learnt how much of the city the insurrectionists controlled, his delight exploded in exclamations and laughter.[39] Then, falling silent, he thought for a while, and at last announced: 'Well, well – it can be done that way too. Just take the power.'[40]

In the early afternoon, detachments of soldiers and sailors occupied the entrance hall and staircase of the Mariinsky Palace. Fewer than half the members of the Pre-Parliament had assembled; and to precisely what pertinent purpose they had done so, they would doubtless have found it difficult to decide. In the event, however, the detachment commanders promptly relieved them of the problem, by demanding that the premises be cleared. After the briefest debate, the members determined, by fifty-six votes to forty-eight, with two abstentions, that they would yield to force and go home. As they filed downstairs, and again at the exits, their cards were carefully examined. But even leading Cadets, like Miliukov, who had hastily begun dressing their minds for arrest, were instead waved away. Instructions had only been given to seize members of the Provisional Government. Suddenly, a prize was discovered: Dubois, a prominent Menshevik, had been identified by his card as Assistant Minister of Labour. But the soldiers were besieged by protests. Dubois was, after all, a socialist. He had been in prison. During the Kornilov days, he had personally arrested one of the chief conspirators at the front. And, in the end, Dubois too, was allowed to leave.

Soon afterwards, an emergency session of the Petrograd Soviet opened to a report from Trotsky. The Pre-Parliament, he declared, had been dissolved; and he specified the major installations that had been occupied. The Winter Palace, he added, had not yet been taken; but its fate would be decided in the next few minutes. 'They told us that an insurrection would drown the revolution in torrents of blood. . . . We don't know of a single casualty.' There was continual applause; but it was, Trotsky himself would recall, 'rather thoughtful'. For if the capture of power now lay behind, ahead loomed the struggle to keep it. And then, to greet Lenin, there came a tumultuous ovation, that was a shared sense of the victory achieved.[41]

Lenin offered a vision of the new Soviet regime which held the future of all humanity in its frame.

The oppressed masses themselves will form a government. The old state apparatus will be destroyed root and branch, and a new administrative apparatus will be created in the form of the Soviet organizations. . . . One of our routine tasks is to end the war at once. But in order to end this war, closely bound up with the present capitalist order, it is clear to everyone that our capitalism itself must be conquered. In this task we shall be helped by the worldwide working-class movement which has already begun to develop in Italy, Germany, and England. . . . We shall win the peasants' trust with a single decree which will annihilate landed property. We shall institute a genuine workers' control of industry. We have the strength of a mass organization that will triumph over everything and bring the proletariat to the world revolution.[42]

The fate of the Winter Palace would not be decided in the next few minutes; or even, indeed, the same day. There was a far from formidable jumble of defenders inside: a women's battalion, cadets from various military training schools, a contingent of veteran Cossacks. And the Cossacks, along with some of the cadets, were possessed of such fragile morale that they would slip away before the fighting began. But the insurrectionist command, uncertain of the resistance to be encountered, rejected a quick attack, which might collect too many casualties, for a tentative, tightening pressure. More and more detachments of armed men arrived, to encircle the palace completely. It was already dark when John Reed passed by a group of soldiers, staring up at the brightly lit building, and heard one of them declare: 'No, comrades. How can we shoot at them? The Women's Battalion is in there – they will say we have fired on Russian women.'[43] Suddenly, as by a stroke from some great brush, the building, too, was dark. The insurrectionists had cut off the electricity. Then, at ten o'clock, the women's battalion, swept by rumours that an eminent general was being besieged in the district military headquarters opposite, rushed out to rescue him and immediately fell into the hands of the encircling force.

An hour or so later, the guns at the Fortress of St Peter and St Paul began firing at the palace. The shots either missed altogether or merely shattered the windows. But each new clap of the bombardment must have struck at the nerves of those sealed in the flickering dark. In the city Duma, the moderate socialist members resolved to attempt a rescue of the ministers or, if need be, accompany them in death. With a few dim lanterns to provide a bobbing passage through the night, they marched in procession, singing the *Marseillaise*, down the Nevsky Prospect. But they were soon brought to a stop by a party of sailors blocking the road. An exchange of challenges followed. And then, left in no doubt that the sailors would fire if it advanced, the procession retired, in silence, the way it had come.

At the palace, where the Provisional Government had withdrawn to an inner room, spirits had risen at this promise of rescue and now fell all the further at the news of the retreat. One of the Cadet ministers, and a close friend of Kerensky's, Dr Kishkin, had been invested with the particular responsibility for restoring order in Petrograd. He telephoned a Cadet colleague to beg for reinforcements, but was informed that none were available. 'What kind of a party is it,' he cried in despair, 'that cannot send us at least three hundred armed men?'[44] And there returned, from the vast hollow of Russian liberalism, only the fading echo of the question.

By one o'clock in the morning of 26 October, a substantial number of the besiegers had filtered into the building, through one or other of its many entrances. Gradually they overcame resistance along the tortuous corridors by fervent appeals or, when these failed, by disarming the defenders in scuffles. Maliantovich, counsel for the defence in the trial of the Soviet leaders eleven years before, and now Minister of Justice, was vividly to record the last moments of the Provisional Government. 'Suddenly a noise arose somewhere and began to grow, spread and roll ever nearer. And in its multitude of sounds, fused into a single powerful wave, we immediately sensed something special, unlike the previous noises – something final and decisive.' A military cadet ran in, drew himself up, saluted, and asked for orders. Should it be resistance to the last man? 'No, it is not necessary! It is useless! The picture is clear! We want no bloodshed! We must surrender,' clamoured the ministers. The door burst open, and 'a little man flew into the room, pushed in by the onrushing crowd which poured in after him and, like water, at once spilled into every corner. . . .'

The little man was Antonov-Ovseenko. And, with his long reddish hair, small red beard and moustache, his loose open coat and wide felt hat, he must have looked to the ministers like the very demon of the wind which was about to sweep them away. Instead, he was to save their lives. For the discovery that Kerensky himself had escaped infuriated the crowd. There were shouts of 'These will run off too! Kill them, finish them off!' A sailor, stamping the floor with his rifle, and looking around, called out: 'Run them through, the sons of bitches! Why waste time with them?' And there were cries of assent. But Antonov-Ovseenko interrupted sharply: 'Comrades, keep calm! All members of the Provisional Government are arrested. They will be imprisoned in the Fortress of St Peter and St Paul. I'll permit no violence. Conduct yourselves calmly. Maintain order! Power is now in your hands. You must maintain order!' And the immediate threat, which would have broken through any irresolution, shrank back into itself and was gone.

It was soon to be succeeded by another. With each of them guarded by two men, the ministers were taken on foot towards the fortress, through a mob which looked for Kerensky and, failing to find him, grew the more menacing with every moment. Then, as the convoy reached the middle of the bridge, and it seemed that the guards must be simply sucked aside by the surrounding hatred, machine-guns opened fire from the fortress. Amidst cries of 'Comrades! Comrades! Stop it! You're firing on your own!' part of the mob fled, while those who remained, together with the ministers and their guards, flung themselves to the ground. As abruptly as it had begun, the shooting stopped; and picking itself up, the convoy continued, in safety now, to the gates of the prison.[45] In the taking of the Winter Palace, five sailors and one soldier had been killed among the assailants. Among the defenders, not a single life had been lost.

A little before eleven o'clock on the night of the 25th, bells rang in the Smolny to announce the opening session of the Second Soviet Congress. The huge commencement hall was so packed that there were delegates perched on the window-sills, and a thickening cloud of bluish cigarette smoke hung in the heavy air. Delegates, guests and guards continued to press through the doors, despite all warnings from the platform that the floor might give way under the weight. Repeated appeals to all comrades please to stop smoking were greeted by choruses of approval, in which the smokers eagerly joined and then smoked even more than before. Philips Price, an English journalist, noted how young most of the delegates were. Sailors from the Baltic Fleet and soldiers from the trenches sat alongside the skilled artisans, in collarless black shirts and fur caps, from the cities, and, as peasant representatives from the villages, the army deserters who were leading the rural revolt. Conspicuous by their relative rarity were the traditional peasants with long beards and the middle-aged intellectuals with decades of socialist struggle behind them.[46] The political complexion of the congress, too, was very different from that of its predecessor. In June, the moderate socialists had amounted to some 600 of the 832 voting delegates. Now, they were reduced to less than a quarter of the 650 initially entitled to vote. As many as 390, or 60 per cent of the total, were Bolsheviks. And the Left Social Revolutionaries outnumbered, roughly in the proportion of three to two, their remote colleagues from the Right of the party.

Dan, in the crumpled uniform of an army doctor, formally opened the congress, on behalf of a Central Executive Committee that was presiding over its own burial service. And he produced an immediate uproar with his plaintive reference to the plight of his party comrades in the Winter Palace. The session then proceeded to the election of a presidium. And the Bolsheviks proposed that this be done on the basis of proportional representation: with fourteen Bolsheviks, seven Social Revolutionaries, three Mensheviks and one internationalist. The Social Revolutionary Right and the mainstream Mensheviks announced that they would have no part of the new presidium; Martov's internationalists, that they were deferring a decision until satisfied on several issues. The congress majority frowned and then rose to acclaim the election of fourteen Bolsheviks and seven Left Social Revolutionaries. Kamenev, installed in the president's chair, proclaimed that the order of the day would be the organization of a government, the issue of war and peace, and the calling of the Constituent Assembly.

Suddenly there came, reverberating through the hall, the first rumble of the guns from the Fortress of St Peter and St Paul. Martov demanded the floor on a point of order. Civil war, he cried, in his cough-roughened voice, was beginning; and it was vital that a united democratic government be established at once, to obtain a peaceful solution. Many Bolsheviks joined in the ensuing applause; and, on behalf of all the Bolshevik delegates, Lunacharsky offered support. The proposal was put to the vote, and there was not a single hand raised against it. Now, if the moderate socialist groups withdrew from the congress, in the face of this conciliatory move, they would be jumping into the grave of the regime. Yet this is precisely what they proceeded to do. A prominent Menshevik rose to declare that the only solution lay in opening negotiations with the Provisional Government, for the formation of a power that would be based on all components of the democracy. And when the tumult at this had abated, at least so far that he could once again be heard, he announced that he and his colleagues were leaving the congress. A spokesman for the Social Revolutionary Right made a similar statement; as did a spokesman for the Bund. Through a commotion of foot-stamping, catcalls, curses and jeers, some seventy moderate socialists struggled out of the hall.

In this multitude, any gaps caused by their going were instantly closed. Almost half of the moderate socialist delegates decided to remain; transferring their allegiance to other groups, mainly the Left Social Revolutionaries. But the impact of the withdrawal was more than a matter of numbers. The whole mood of the congress had changed. And when Martov again spoke, to deal in detail with his proposal, and suggest that a delegation be elected to negotiate with all socialist parties, he was received with irritation and impatience. Trotsky's answer was sharp.

What has happened is an insurrection, and not a conspiracy. We hardened the revolutionary energy of the Petrograd workers and soldiers. We openly forged the will of the masses for an insurrection, and not a conspiracy. The masses of the people followed our banner, and our insurrection was victorious. And now we are told: renounce your victory, make concessions, compromise. With whom? I ask: with whom ought we to compromise? With those wretched groups who have left us or who are making this proposal? But after all we have had a full view of them. No one in Russia is with them any longer. A compromise is supposed to be made, as between two equal sides, by the millions of workers and peasants represented in this Congress, whom they are ready, not for the first time or the last, to barter away as the bourgeoisie sees fit. No, here no compromise is possible. To those who have left and to those who tell us to do this, we must say: you are miserable bankrupts, your role is played out; go where you ought to be: into the dustbin of history!

'Then we'll leave!' shouted Martov, into the storm of applause that broke over Trotsky's remarks. Speech succeeded passionate speech, around a resolution moved by Trotsky to condemn the conduct of the moderate socialists. And the meeting rapidly became so overwrought that a collapse into collective hysteria seemed certain, without some respite. A half-hour's recess was announced. Just inside the door, a bitterly quarrelling group of internationalist Mensheviks gathered. Sukhanov argued that the group should stay at the congress; Martov, that it should withdraw; and by fourteen votes to twelve, Martov won. When the session resumed, Kamenev reported the fall of the Winter Palace and read out the names of the arrested ministers, to bursts of cheering. A Left Social Revolutionary rose to protest at the arrest of socialist ministers. Trotsky replied that political arrest was not a matter of vengeance, but was dictated 'by considerations of expediency'. And, besides, there was no reason to stand on ceremony with those who had imprisoned so many of their Bolshevik opponents. But this dispute was pushed out of the way by the arrival of a commissar, breathless and spattered with mud, from the nearby garrison of Tsarskoye Syelo, who mounted the platform with a delegate from the Third Bicycle Battalion.

Their news probed like a torch the emptiness of the shadows cast over the congress by the moderate socialist predictions of impending disaster. The Third Battalion, selected as especially reliable by the government's military staff, had been ordered from the south-western front 'to the defence of Petrograd'. And the Soviet of the garrison at Tsarskoye Syelo, informed of the battalion's approach, had hurriedly prepared to resist. But the bicycle men, recognizing the purpose of their orders, resolved that they would take no part in propping up a regime led by the bourgeoisie and the landlords. Now, together with the garrison, they were ready to stand guard at the gates of revolutionary Petrograd.

It was in the midst of the jubilation at this reassurance that a spokesman for the internationalist Mensheviks rose to announce their withdrawal from the congress. There were cries of 'What! Are you still here?' And, to a chorus of scornful good-byes, the group trickled out of the hall. For Sukhanov, it was more than the suicide of internationalist Menshevism. 'By quitting the Congress and leaving the Bolsheviks with only the Left SR youngsters and the feeble little *Novaya Zhizn* group, we gave the Bolsheviks with our own hands a monopoly of the Soviet, of the masses, and of the revolution.'[47] He would account his failure to break with his colleagues and stay at the congress, his own greatest mistake. And Martov himself, in walking from the hall, was to walk out of history.

A proclamation to the workers, soldiers and peasants of Russia had been composed for the congress urgently to issue. But its presentation was repeatedly delayed by particular pronouncements. And then, so tired that he was hardly in control of his legs, Krylenko, who had been the leading Bolshevik agitator at the front, struggled to the tribune with a telegram in his hand. The Twelfth Army sent greetings to the congress and announced the formation of a military revolutionary committee which had assumed custody of the northern front. The front's commander-in-chief, General Cheremissov, had submitted to the committee. Voitinsky, the commissar of the Provisional Government, had resigned. The delegates cheered and wept and hugged one another. The northern front was the closest to the capital.

At last Lunacharsky was called, to read out the proclamation. The Second All-Russian Congress, representing the vast majority of the Soviets, was assuming power. The Provisional Government was deposed. The Soviet authority would 'at once propose an immediate democratic peace to all nations, and an immediate truce on all fronts'. It would assure the free transfer of landlord, crown and monastery lands to the land committees; enforce a complete democratization of the army; establish workers' control over production; and 'ensure the convocation of the Constituent Assembly at the proper date'. It would 'take means to supply bread to the cities and articles of first necessity to the villages'. It would 'secure to all nationalities living in Russia a real right to independent existence'. All local power was transferred to the Soviets, which were to maintain revolutionary order. Soldiers, railwaymen and other workers were to resist any counter-attack by Kerensky and his followers.

This proclamation, manifesto and appeal combined, was adopted with no more than two votes recorded against it, and with twelve abstentions. It was six o'clock in the morning of Thursday, 26 October, when the delegates streamed from the hall, to disperse through the cold dark of an autumn dawn.

8

The Revolution Transformed

In the light of morning, as the tramcars brought their customary clatter back to the streets, and the shops emerged again from behind their shutters, knowledgeable Petrograd began shrugging off its fears. To be sure, the stock market plunged, and the Cadet paper *Rech* appeared capable only of wringing its hands in despair at Russia's fate. But these were precipitate reactions. Considered opinion gave the Bolsheviks two or three days. Already, it was believed, Kerensky was marching on the city with loyal troops from the front. In government offices, employees held meetings and determined on a boycott of the new regime. The central executive committee of the Railway Workers' Union demanded an immediate socialist coalition. A Committee for Salvation of Country and Revolution – drawn from the city Duma, the executive committee of the Peasants' Soviets, the disbanded Council of the Republic and the moderate socialist delegates who had left the congress – proclaimed itself, in posters and leaflets, sole legal heir to the Provisional Government, and called on all citizens to defy the power of violence.

Natalia Sedova found Trotsky, with Lenin and a crowd of others, in a room at the Smolny. Their faces were greenish-grey with lack of sleep, their eyes inflamed, their collars soiled. And the air was thick with smoke. It seemed to her that she was seeing them in a dream, and that the revolution was in danger of being lost if they did not get some sleep and put on clean collars. Lenin himself, awkwardly shy, confided to Trotsky: 'You know, from persecution and a life underground, to come so suddenly into power. . . .' And he paused, in search of the word he wanted. '*Es schwindelt*' – 'It makes one giddy' – he said at last in German; circling his head with his hand. The two men looked at each other and laughed. But there was time for only a little laughter. Together with a few other members of the party's central committee, they were soon in a corner of the room, for an impromptu session to discuss the formation of a government. 'What shall we call them?' Lenin asked. He would not have 'ministers'. It was a vile and hackneyed word. Trotsky suggested 'commissars', but then added that there were too many commissars already. Perhaps 'supreme commissars'? But he did not like the sound of 'supreme'. What about 'people's commissars'? Lenin allowed that this might do. But what of the government as a whole? 'A Soviet, of course, . . .' Trotsky replied, 'the Soviet of the People's Commissars, eh?' And Lenin, trying out the phrase, was delighted. 'That's splendid; smells terribly of revolution!'[1]

When the central committee came to consider the list of particular appointments for submission to the congress that night, it did not need to risk setting foot outside the party enclosure. The Left Social Revolutionaries had declined the offer of posts, in the belief that this would make it easier for them to mediate between the Bolsheviks and the moderate socialist opposition. But this did not mean that the responsibilities were all smoothly assigned. Lenin proposed that Trotsky be elected the chairman. And Trotsky immediately jumped to his feet in protest. 'Why not?' Lenin persisted. 'You were at the head of the Petrograd Soviet that seized the power.' Trotsky moved that the proposal be dismissed without further discussion, and the motion was carried.

Lunacharsky, the following day, would tell a congress delegate, in Sukhanov's presence, that Lenin had wanted to stay out of the government, for work within the party's central committee. 'But we said no, we wouldn't agree. We made him take first-hand responsibility; otherwise, everyone likes just criticizing.'[2] Yet there is nothing in Lenin's life, before or since, to suggest that he might seriously have considered giving up direct command of the revolutionary government. He had far too fervent a faith in the necessity of his leadership to risk the consequences of having anyone else assume its functions, especially at so perilous a time. Still less was he likely to have contemplated excluding himself from the government altogether. Recent events had demonstrated that even the closest of his colleagues – for who had been closer than Zinoviev? – were not to be trusted out of his sight. And was he, all the same, now intent on confining himself to the basement of decision; leaving them to mislead one another as soon as they had closed the doors behind them, in the room above his head? Finally, so supreme a political strategist could scarcely have failed to recognize how damaging would be the implications of the course that he proposed. The government would surface as so subservient to the party that he who commanded the second had disdained to bother with the first. It would support what the moderate socialists had been saying: that the Bolsheviks were simply using the institution of the Soviets to establish their exclusive dictatorship over the state.

Almost certainly, therefore, Lenin's proposal was based on his conviction that it stood not the slightest chance of being agreed. What, then, might its purpose have been? Perhaps this was his way of paying tribute to Trotsky's insurrectionary leadership. And perhaps, too, this was his way of making it clear that despite Trotsky's insurrectionary leadership, he himself remained, indispensably, the leader of the revolution. Did Trotsky see in the proposal, 'so unexpected and inappropriate', a manoeuvre aimed at putting him in his place, by offering him one that the party would never have permitted? Or was it only that Lenin had pre-empted, by his knowingly unacceptable proposal, Trotsky's own attempt to stay out of the government? There is, in Trotsky's account, a sour note so rare in his references to Lenin after the revolution that it sounds the more sharply the remembrance of a particular resentment.

I felt like a surgeon who has finished a difficult and dangerous operation – I must wash my hands, take off my apron, and rest. Lenin was in a different position. He had just arrived from his refuge, after spending three and a half months cut off from real, practical direction. One thing coincided with the other, and this only added to my desire to retire behind the scenes for a while.[3]

Certainly, he had cause enough for feeling that he had been stretched too far and had earned a right to some rest. And yet, over and over again in his life, his mere recognition of the need always enabled him somehow to stretch himself further, without a backward glance at any such rights as he might have earned by his exertions already. His own account refers to other factors. And all the more because these references flicker – rather as though, in composing his recollections, he could not make up his mind what to leave in the dark – they draw the eyes to seeking out just what such factors might have been.

The conquest of power brought up the question of my government work. Strangely enough, I had never even given a thought to it; in spite of the experience of 1905, there was never an occasion when I connected the question of my future with that of power. From my youth on, or, to be more precise, from my childhood on, I had dreamed of being a writer. Later, I subordinated my literary work, as I did everything else, to the revolution. The question of the party's conquest of power was always before me. Times without number, I wrote and spoke about the programme of the revolutionary government, but the question of my personal work after the conquest never entered my mind. And so it caught me unawares.[4]

Of Trotsky's passion for literature, his various critical writings provided more than sufficient proof. Of his urge, and his ability, to produce creative writing of his own, there were more than sufficient signs in his journalism and in his account of the 1905 insurrection. But they were, as he would have been the first to acknowledge, still only signs. Art, he knew, was not to be made out of scraps of devotion. 26 October 1917 was his thirty-eighth birthday. The occasion might well have nudged him into an awareness of how late it was becoming to begin the work of realizing a childhood dream. Yet to turn aside from the revolution now, just when it seemed to be hovering between defeat in Russia and the advance of its victory throughout the world: that was impossible. And, indeed, he proposed that he undertake the direction of the press: a responsibility which scarcely promised to prove any less burdensome than that of a post in the cabinet. Clearly, therefore, it was a cabinet post itself from which he flinched. And the flinching reflected a feature of his personality which was to have the most momentous consequences.

No one has written more joyously of the creative universal culture that socialism would bring, or of history's rational process that promised the attainment of socialism. No one has written more bitterly of the violence done to the imagination and to reason by the subservience to property and the confinements of nationalism. And no one has written throughout with more manifest a moral passion. For there, in the liberation of the mind, lay the source of Trotsky's morality. It was, in its flow, a morality of revolution. But it was for him, necessarily, as well, a morality of the revolutionary. For who were most likely to infuse others with their faith and ensure that the struggle did not stray, but those who approached most closely in the dignity of their conduct, the dignity of the cause that they served? And how could the new world of the mind be made by those whose own minds were mildewed with the treacheries and vanities of the old?

Disloyalty, deviousness, and a devotion to personal power had seemed to him Lenin's contribution to the split in the party. And he had predicted that Lenin's way must lead in the end only to the degradations of despotism. His break with Lenin had been so imperatively right. And yet it was Lenin's way that alone in the end had led towards the socialist revolution: while Menshevism had strayed, like Vera Ivanovna herself, into the perversity of patriotism and an apology for war; or, with Martov, into indecisiveness and sterility. This had opened up a gap, between what he recognized as right for the revolution and what he believed to be right for the revolutionary, which he would never manage to close. And what appeared to others as moral inconsistency in his conduct was no more than the choices which he made – which he could not, in his tragic predicament, escape making – between conflicting moral demands.

He might have come now to acknowledge the achievements of Lenin's leadership. He might even have come to acknowledge that for Lenin, personal power was somehow impersonally conceived, as the very will of the revolution. But this had not converted him to the sort of methods that Lenin employed. Still less had it reconciled him to those who were ready enough to employ Lenin's methods, without the excuse of being Lenins themselves. As he looked round the table at that central committee meeting to choose the members of the new government, he would have known that there were those who waited hopefully for him to make a false move. They might have been prepared to forgive him his past quarrels with

Bolshevism. But what they would not forgive him was the success of his insurrectionary leadership or their own failure to recognize the necessity of the insurrection. And Lenin would have done little to reduce their resentment by proposing that Trotsky should head the government. How was Trotsky to defend himself against the intrigues of those who saw him primarily as a rival, without his becoming like those whom he despised? How was he to work trustingly with those whose very commitment to the revolution he distrusted?

When the revolution reached at last that permanent noon of the classless society, the light would allow little or no shadow to be cast. But meanwhile, in its rise, there fell the shadow of bureaucracy from leadership itself: the enjoyment of power over others; the fear of any further change as a threat to established positions; the retreat from the questioning of the streets to the reassurances of routine. If the revolution was to be saved from such betrayal, by those who pursued the prerogatives of rule in the requirements of administration, was resistance not most effectively to be conducted from outside the government, among the untitled revolutionaries of the party, and by the criticism of the revolutionary press? Was it not the duty, the right, of the true revolutionary to serve the revolution as best he knew how, in his own way?

Yet if thoughts such as these were likely to have passed through Trotsky's mind, they would have done so as flashes of landscape, seen through the window of a fast-moving train. For what chance was there to leap safely from his carriage and run alongside the train to jump into another of his choice? His fellow passengers would not allow him to use the communicating doors. To refuse, against all expectation and pressure, an appointment to the government would be regarded as an act of intolerable indiscipline: with those who secretly longed for his exclusion, quickest to denounce him for deserting his duty to the revolution. And, indeed, was it not right that the central committee, as the collective leadership of the party, should impose on each of its members the conditions of revolutionary service? For if the central committee could not do so, and each member was left to decide the conditions for himself, all collective leadership, and with it the revolution, must succumb to anarchy. That Trotsky hesitated, then, is no more certain than that his hesitation was the frame of his inevitable acceptance.

Lenin seems simply to have ignored Trotsky's offer to take charge of the press and proposed his appointment as Commissar for the Interior, since the most important task now was to ensure the defeat of any attempt at counter-revolution. But the prospect of assuming responsibility for the spies and police of the revolutionary regime was one from which Trotsky recoiled. He raised various objections; and principally that to place someone of Jewish origin in such a post would play into the hands of the enemy.

Lenin could hardly command his temper. 'We are having a great international revolution. Of what importance are such trifles?' Trotsky replied good-humouredly that the revolution was undoubtedly great, but that there were still many fools about. 'Why create additional complications at the outset?' Sverdlov, the effective organizing secretary of the party, whose manifestly selfless service and soundness of judgement had earned him general respect, and who was himself of Jewish origin, supported Trotsky and swung a majority behind him. Lenin accepted defeat with a sigh and a reproachful shake of his head. But Sverdlov also opposed releasing Trotsky for the press: a job, he argued, that was best given to Bukharin. 'Lev Davidovich should be set up against the rest of Europe. Let him take charge of foreign affairs.' Lenin was unconvinced. 'What foreign affairs will we have now?' But at last he agreed; as, with no less reluctance, did Trotsky. At least, Trotsky consoled himself, his job would not involve much departmental work. He was, soon afterwards, to assure a comrade: 'I will issue a few revolutionary proclamations to the peoples of the world, and then shut up shop.'

The department of the interior was assigned to Rykov, a cautious Bolshevik who glowed with bureaucratic promise; while Stalin himself became Commissar for Nationalities. Trotsky was, in the event, the only Bolshevik of Jewish origin in the new government. Sverdlov was to continue concentrating on the organization of the party; Kamenev was to head the Central Executive Committee of the Soviets; and Zinoviev was to edit the official newspaper of the Soviets, *Izvestia*.

When the Soviet Congress met again, shortly before nine o'clock that evening, Lenin entered with members of the Presidium to an explosion of cheers. He was dressed in shabby clothes, John Reed noted; with trousers too long for him. And his chin was smudged with the resurgence of his well-known beard. Kamenev, from the chair, reported various decisions of the Military Revolutionary Committee. The death penalty, which Kerensky had restored for insubordination in the army, was abolished. All food supplies in private storehouses were to be confiscated. Freedom of propaganda was proclaimed. But by then the regime had already indicated that it did not intend to include in any such freedom the propaganda of those whom it regarded as enemies of the revolution. Earlier that day, detachments of sailors had visited the distribution centres of the two principal Cadet papers; piled all available copies in the streets; and there set fire to them, before enormous crowds. Orders, with military escorts to ensure compliance, had subsequently locked up the entire bourgeois press. And though no move whatsoever had been made against any of their own newspapers, the moderate socialists hastened to denounce the evident Bolshevik contempt for elementary democratic principles.

Kamenev's report was received with excited approval from the mass of delegates, and with predictions of imminent doom from one or two of the few moderate socialists who had not yet withdrawn from the congress. Then Lenin came to the lectern; gripping its edge and gazing at the crowd which for several minutes roared a welcome to him. At last there was an expectant hush. And he began: 'We shall now proceed to construct the socialist order!'[5] When once again he was able to make himself heard, he read, without any accompanying gestures or attempt to modulate his voice, as though reciting the terms of the revolution's contract with history, a proclamation to the peoples and governments of all the belligerent nations. This proposed an immediate peace, without annexations or indemnities. The revolutionary government itself was abandoning all secret diplomacy; would forthwith publish in full the secret treaties confirmed or concluded by its predecessor in the previous eight months; and now announced its repudiation of such clauses as aimed at procuring advantages for Russian imperialism. In making its offer of peace, it appealed in particular to the 'conscious workers . . . of the three most important nations among those taking part in the present war – England, France and Germany'. Their long and splendid service in the struggle for socialism was a guarantee that they would understand the duty imposed upon them: to help revolutionary Russia, by their own decisive action, achieve peace and advance the cause of the exploited everywhere.

During the discussion that followed, one delegate pointed to a problem merely brushed aside by the statement. 'First you offer peace without annexations and indemnities, and then you say you will consider all peace offers. To consider means to accept. . . .' But Lenin was already ahead of him. 'We want a just peace,' he interrupted,

but we are not afraid of a revolutionary war. . . . Probably the imperialist governments will not answer our appeal – but we shall not issue an ultimatum to which it will be easy to say no. . . . If the German proletariat realizes that we are ready to consider all offers of peace, that perhaps will be the last drop which overflows the bowl – revolution will break out in Germany. . . . We consent to examine all conditions of peace, but that doesn't mean that we shall accept them. . . . For some of our terms we shall fight to the end – possibly for others will find it impossible to continue the war. . . .[6]

Here glinted the issue that was soon to cut through the Bolshevik leadership, down to the very bone of what revolutionary Russia's commitment ought to be. But it was lost in the sheet lightning of so many hopes. When the proclamation was put to the vote, the single delegate raising a hand in dissent dropped it again at the uproar that broke out around him. The congress thundered to its feet and sang the *Internationale*. An old soldier sobbed like a child, while a young worker cried in rapture, 'The war is ended! The war is ended!'

Lenin then began to read the proposed Land Decree. But it had been so badly written that he faltered in confusion and finally gave up in despair, passing the piece of paper to someone else on the platform, who could make his way through the scrawl. Private property in land was abolished at once, without compensation. But ordinary peasants – and the Cossacks – would be permitted to keep the land that they held. Until definitive determinations by the Constituent Assembly, the course of rural reform would conform to the model decree, published by the Central Executive Committee of the Peasants' Soviets, which had taken all land into national ownership; outlawed hired labour; and invested all citizens with the right to use of the land, provided that they worked it themselves. What was this, voices rang out, but the programme of the Social Revolutionaries? Lenin was unperturbed.

Very well. Isn't it all the same who composed it? As a democratic government we could not get round a decision of the rank-and-file, even if we disagreed with it. Life is the best teacher, and it will show who is right. Let the peasants starting from one end and ourselves from the other settle this question. Life will force us to come together in the common stream of revolutionary creativity. We must follow life, and leave the masses of the people complete freedom of creation. . . .[7]

This trumpet call drowned, as intended, the sound of long-proclaimed principles in hasty retreat. The revolution was sanctioning the seizure of land by individual peasants and effectively the establishment of a petty-bourgeois proprietorship as the basis of the rural order. What had this to do with Marxist prescriptions for developing the productive forces of agriculture by large-scale, socially owned and collectively worked units, integrated with industry? What sort of advance was this towards the attainment of a classless society? Rosa Luxemburg, in her book on the Russian revolution, would recognize the formidable difficulties which confronted the regime in the traditional outlook of the peasantry. But she maintained that the regime should at least have moved in the direction of a socialist agriculture, by devoting the great estates to collectivist development. And she predicted that those peasants whose snatched proprietorship the regime had sanctioned in order to secure their support would not only resist the more strongly any subsequent socialist measures, but refuse to defend the revolution against the onslaught of its enemies. In this last critical particular, however, she was to be proved wrong. 'The point is for the peasantry to be firmly persuaded that there are no more landlords in the country,' Lenin had declared, in advocating the Land Decree. The new class of peasant proprietors did rally to the revolution under attack: and less out of any real allegiance to the regime than out of a fear that a defeat would be succeeded by the restoration of the landlords.

When the Land Decree had been jubilantly adopted, Kamenev proceeded to read the short Constitution of Power, which set up the Soviet of People's Commissars: with control over its activities, and specifically the right to dismiss it, vested in the Congress of Soviets and its Central Executive Committee. To bursts of applause which were especially loud and long at the mention of Lenin and of Trotsky, he announced the list of commissars. And then Boris Avilov, a former Bolshevik who was now on the staff of Gorky's paper, stood up to speak: his frock-coat in flamboyant contrast to the shapeless and shabby clothing of other delegates. At first he was greeted by cries of contradiction and hisses. But gradually, as his reasoned argument made itself heard, these died away into a troubled silence. The previous government had been toppled so easily, he stated, because it had been unable to give the people peace and bread. How was a victorious Bolshevism to bring bread, when grain was so scarce? How was it to win over a majority of the peasants, when it could not provide them with the machinery that they needed? And it would find the bringing of peace even more difficult. For its government would be recognized neither in London and Paris nor in Berlin. The proletariat in the Allied countries was far from revolutionary struggle. And even representatives of the extreme left in Germany were reported to believe that revolution there was impossible during the war.

The isolation of Russia will fatally result either in the defeat of the Russian Army by the Germans, and the patching up of a peace between the Austro-German coalition and the Franco-British coalition at the expense of Russia – or in a separate peace with Germany. I have just learned that the Allied ambassadors are preparing to leave, and that Committees for Salvation of Country and Revolution are forming in all the cities of Russia. . . . No one party can conquer these enormous difficulties. The majority of the people, supporting a government of socialist coalition, can alone accomplish the revolution.

It was a challenge made immediately much more serious by the speech of a young and influential Left Social Revolutionary, who announced that his party had rejected the offer of representation in the Soviet of People's Commissars, because it did not wish to separate itself forever from that part of the revolutionary army repudiating the congress. 'We cannot sustain any government except a government of socialist coalition.' Doubt, like a dust track, billowed behind him. But Trotsky replied with a force that swept it away and lifted the delegates to a vision of themselves as the advancing front line of freedom for all mankind. There was nothing new, he declared, in this talk of their dangerous isolation. On the eve of their insurrection, their defeat had been confidently predicted. Yet the Provisional Government had been overturned almost without bloodshed. It was the most striking proof that not they but the Provisional Government had been isolated: as now the democratic parties marching against them were isolated and forever cut off from the proletariat.

The Provisional Government had, indeed, provided little bread. But would a coalition with those democratic parties provide any more? 'The problem of bread is the problem of a programme of action. The struggle with economic collapse demands a definite system from below, and not political groupings on top.' And how would such a coalition contribute to the attainment of peace?

> Avilov tries to frighten us by the threat of a peace at our expense. And I answer that in any case, if Europe continues to be ruled by the imperialist bourgeoisie, revolutionary Russia will inevitably be lost. . . . Either the Russian revolution will raise the whirlwind of struggle in the west, or the capitalists of all countries will crush our revolution.

This did not mean, of course, that a peace treaty would have to wait for the insurrection of the European workers. It was also possible that the bourgeoisie, frightened by the very approach of such insurrection, would hasten to make peace.

> The dates are not set. The concrete forms cannot be foretold. It is important and it is necessary to define the method of struggle, a method identical in principle both in foreign and domestic politics. A union of the oppressed here and everywhere – that is our road.[8]

The Constitution of Power was adopted by an enormous majority. And this was followed by the election of a new Central Executive Committee: with 70 Bolsheviks among the 108 members, and Left Social Revolutionaries composing nearly all the remainder. There would be places, Trotsky announced, for representatives of the peasantry; and for those of the factions which had seceded, should they choose to return, as well. It was after five o'clock in the morning of 27 October when the Second All-Russian Congress of Soviets came to a close, and the exhausted delegates crowded into the waiting streetcars. There was no lingering in Petrograd. Most of the delegates were soon on their journey home, to carry across Russia their reports of a revolutionary leadership that seemed to know the way into the future.

Even De Robien, an aristocrat fallen among bourgeois republicans at the French embassy, was impressed.

> I cannot deny having a certain sympathy for these men who at least have an ideal. . . . What seems to me the most hateful is the hybrid rule of bourgeois republics with imperial policies. If autocracy has had its day, if the aristocracy must disappear because it did not know how to fulfil its mission, then let it be in favour of a universal democracy in which all peoples are brothers and in which property will be fairly divided. . . . [The Bolsheviks] are perhaps dreamers, but I prefer their dreams to the gross realism of the 'get-out-and-let-me-in' people of the first revolution.[9]

Trotsky, for all the firmness of his own faith in the future, did not need an Avilov to point out the perils of the present. He had identified too clearly the factors that had prepared the defeat of the Provisional Government. The success of the insurrection would not itself stop the armies from disintegrating as fast as the feet of desertion allowed; the economy from staggering as though each step that it took would be its last; starvation from moving on the cities like a storm whose first flashes were already catching at faces in the streets. It was going to be a race against the past: a race between the Bolshevik programme of action and the very processes of disintegration which had provided that programme with its opportunity; between the capabilities of a liberated people and the hold that the corruptions of their long captivity still had on their lives. And it was, much to his disappointment, though not for a moment to his dismay, the power of the past that looked like setting the pace at the start.

Those who had dulled with drink the experience of oppression, now celebrated the achievement of their release with a monumental spree. Soldiers broke into wine cellars and pillaged wine shops. The Preobrazhensky regiment, detailed to guard the Winter Palace, began draining the vast stores of the Tsars. The Pavlovsky regiment, regarded as the most reliable in Petrograd, was dispatched to display its overriding revolutionary devotion, and rapidly succumbed. The mixed detachments sent instead fared no better. Members of the regimental committees, the revolutionary leadership of the garrison, were then assigned to stand guard and were soon scarcely able to stand. Men of the armoured brigades, ordered to disperse the crowds collecting before the palace, decided to fortify themselves first. The entrances to the palace were sealed. But the crowd simply seeped through the windows. The fire brigade was called, to flood the cellars with water. The fire brigade got drunk. Finally sailors from Helsingfors, bound by a solemn oath, seized sober command of the cellars. But there were so many other sources of supply in the city. The government appointed a special commissar, with emergency powers and a strong escort, to stop the flow. The special commissar proved unreliable. The contents of all known wine cellars had to be consigned to the Neva before the situation was brought under control. And by then the spree had spread to the provinces, where it persisted for several weeks.

Had Kerensky been able to find a few thousand resolute troops to follow him, the course of history might have been different. But who believed in Kerensky any longer? Reaching Pskov, the headquarters of the northern front, he was coldly received by the commanding general, who had made his own examination and concluded that the Provisional Government was dead. Only General Krasnov, commander of the Third Cavalry Corps, for all his evident distrust and dislike of Kerensky himself, was willing to answer his call, in hopes that a blow at the Bolsheviks would further the monarchist cause. With 700 of his Cossacks, the most that he could muster on the spot, he proceeded by train to Gatchina, less than twenty miles south-west of Petrograd and, meeting no resistance, took the town on the morning of 27 October. In Petrograd, where rumour magnified the advancing force to many times its size, Trotsky and his Military Revolutionary Committee were in charge of defensive preparations. Two army officers, Walden and Muraviev, whose knowledge of Marx hardly extended beyond a recognition that his side seemed to be winning, and whose knowledge of Kerensky was extensive enough to convince them that he at least could be counted upon to lose, offered their services. Trotsky, all too aware that successful leadership of an uprising was no substitute for experience of command in conventional battle, accepted the offer. It was a decision that stirred much disquiet and some indignant dissent in the Petrograd Soviet, among Bolsheviks and Left Social Revolutionaries alike. But Trotsky was undeterred. Almost all the army officers were hostile. The revolution could not afford to reject the professional skills of the few who volunteered to help secure it, if only out of concern for their own careers.

On the 28th, Krasnov approached Tsarskoye Syelo and put to flight the small force of Red Guards in his way. The 16,000 soldiers of the local garrison appeared morosely indifferent. And mounted on a white horse, Kerensky entered the town, to a jangle of church bells. On Sunday the 29th, the military cadets in Petrograd, encouraged by Krasnov's advance and impatient for victory, rose in revolt. There was a fury to the fighting that foreshadowed the conflict to come. At one of the schools, cadets shot down two of the Soviet delegates proceeding under the protection of a white flag to demand their surrender; and when the school was captured, at the cost of many casualties, some of the now helpless cadets were beaten or stabbed to death. By the afternoon, the revolt was effectively over. But the news from Moscow soured this success. In the fierce dispute for power there, military cadets and Cossacks controlled the centre of the city.

For a while it seemed that the fate of Petrograd, too, would have to be decided in the streets. Preparations to bar Krasnov's way had to contend with the almost total disorder of the garrison and problems of supply made all the more formidable by the hostility of the technical personnel. Arms and ammunition were scattered and concealed: rifles were found in one place, cartridges in another, guns without their carriages or shells in a third. But rapidly, under Trotsky's command, a force was mobilized and equipped. Thousands of workers streamed from the city to dig trenches on the Pulkovo heights. Those employed in the gun factories assembled the artillery and placed it in position. On the 30th, Trotsky reported to the Petrograd Soviet that the battle at Pulkovo had begun. 'Why aren't you out there with the Red Guards?' someone shouted. 'I'm going now!' Trotsky replied and rushed out to his waiting car. It was the last time that anyone thought it necessary to ask why he wasn't already at the front.

Krasnov's Cossacks were in poor heart. They had been promised infantry support, attracted to their cause and their success, but none had materialized. They were battered by the Bolshevik artillery and confronted by lines of sailors and Red Guards who were evidently determined to fight until they fell. The garrison at Tsarkoye Syelo, antagonized by Kerensky's demand for its submission, was threatening to attack from the rear if the Cossacks continued fighting. Krasnov ordered a retreat while he still had troops to obey him. From the retaken radio station at Tsarkoe Syelo, in the early hours of 31 October, Trotsky dispatched a jubilant message of victory. Two days later, at Gatsina, Krasnov and his Cossacks surrendered. Kerensky had contemplated suicide; and then snatched at an offer from secret sympathizers to help him escape. Disguised as a sailor, he slipped past the various guards and patrols; went into hiding; and was eventually smuggled out of Russia, to reach in exile an old age ripe with early reminiscences. Krasnov was arrested and taken to the Smolny. But these were still, for the revolution, magnanimous times. He was soon released and he withdrew to the Don, where he would lead a Cossack movement against the revolution a few months later.

On the same day that Krasnov surrendered, Bolshevik forces in Moscow captured the Kremlin, and resistance collapsed. The fighting had gone on for a week, despite the Bolshevik superiority in numbers and possession of all the heavy guns.[10] The insurrectionary command had delayed too long and adopted measures, undertaken in Petrograd days before, only when the news of the insurrection there reached Moscow: while the forces of defiance, accordingly forearmed, were also efficiently led and bitterly determined. But nowhere else in central and northern Russia did the Bolsheviks encounter such serious and sustained opposition. In factory towns, the seizure of power was quick and bloodless. And where workers were not a dominant part of the population, soldiers of the local garrison often joined them in overcoming any resistance. In other parts of Russia, the situation was more confused. But whether without or only after armed clashes, the vast majority of towns came under Bolshevik control. The most menacing exception was the emergence to command of Kiev and the western Ukraine by the Rada, as the institutional representative of Ukrainian nationalism. Despite a strong Bolshevik challenge from the more industrialized areas in the east, by 20 November the Rada felt itself sufficiently entrenched to proclaim the Ukraine an independent people's republic. It was a development which Germany would not be slow to exploit.

Meanwhile, however, the rapid spread of Bolshevik power was remarkable, especially since it occurred alongside a rift within the party leadership. For, even as Trotsky was preparing to prevent Krasnov from entering Petrograd, several members of the central committee and of the government began looking for rescue in a reconciliation with the moderate socialists. They recoiled from the prospect of a protracted civil war, which they believed that Bolshevism on its own would be bound to lose; and were immediately alarmed by a threat from the executive of the Railway Workers' Union to stop the trains if a coalition government was not formed. In the absence of both Lenin and Trotsky, the central committee decided to initiate negotiations with the moderate socialist parties. But the moderate socialist leaders seemed disposed to negotiate less over the conditions for compromise than over the terms of a Bolshevik surrender. A coalition government, they demanded, must be responsible not to the Soviets, but to 'the broad circles of revolutionary democracy'; must exclude Lenin and Trotsky; and must disarm the Bolshevik Red Guards.

Trotsky hurried back from the victory at Pulkovo to take part in the discussions on this reply. He was totally opposed to any coalition that entailed the loss of Bolshevik control over the government. Precisely to achieve such control, so as to pursue socialist policies, had been the whole purpose of the uprising. And now the moderate socialists were essentially demanding a return to their own control, so as to place it once more at the service of a bourgeois dominion. He had hoped that they would come to accept the will of the congress and play the part of a loyal revolutionary opposition. Instead, they had shown themselves determined to defy that will, and to deny the supremacy of the very Soviets they had helped to establish. They were self-proclaimed counter-revolutionaries. And the revolution had either to fight back or invite its inevitable defeat. Lenin, with Trotsky's support, proposed that all negotiations be broken off at once, in response to such intolerable terms. The more fearful in the central committee seemed already prepared to concede the exclusion of Lenin and Trotsky from the government, in the cause of compromise. Between defiance and fear, most members took refuge in delay. They voted to continue the negotiations: though on a basis that, rejecting any retreat from the supremacy of the Soviets, ruled out any chance of agreement.

Trotsky and the leaders of the moderate socialist parties might agree that reconciliation was impossible between two incompatible concepts of constitutional power, representing two incompatible revolutionary commitments. The Bolshevik conciliators, however, were not daunted. If no crack had appeared through which compromise might come, they would make one themselves. In the Central Executive Committee of the Soviets, Kamenev proposed, from the chair, the dismissal of the Bolshevik government, for a coalition successor; and in the ensuing vote, the conciliators ranged themselves with opponents of the party against the vast majority of its representatives. Lenin was enraged. And at a meeting of the central committee, he secured a majority for his demand that such open indiscipline should not be permitted to continue. If it did, an emergency congress of the party would be called to endorse the policy of the conciliators or expel them. On the following day, 4 November, the loyal Bolshevik majority in the Central Executive Committee of the Soviets secured a decree which gave the government control over all newsprint and wide powers to act directly against the dissident press. To this and to Lenin's ultimatum, the Bolshevik conciliators replied with a challenge of their own. The five who were members of the central committee – Kamenev, Zinoviev, Rykov, Miliutin and Nogin – resigned: declaring that its policy was fatal and that they would take their campaign for a coalition of socialists to the masses of workers and soldiers. Rykov (the Interior), Miliutin (Agriculture), Nogin (Commerce and Industry), Shliapnikov (Labour) and Teodorovich (Supplies) resigned from the Soviet of People's Commissars. In a joint manifesto, reminiscent of the warning once sounded by Trotsky himself, they predicted that a purely Bolshevik government could only be preserved 'by means of political terror'; would produce an 'irresponsible regime' and 'eliminate the mass organizations of the proletariat from leadership in political life'.

A dispute within the leadership over so fundamental an issue, and taken so far that almost half the members of the Bolshevik government had chosen to abandon it, might well have been expected to rend the Bolshevik ranks. The command of the party wasted no time in regret. Kamenev was immediately dismissed as chairman of the Central Executive Committee, and Sverdlov elected in his place. Lenin, in a manifesto issued by the central committee, denounced as deserters those who had resigned. They were men of little faith who, unlike the millions of workers and soldiers still unwaveringly behind the party, had 'let themselves be frightened by the bourgeoisie'. But the mass of Bolshevik militants paid little mind to the fuss. They saw no need to rise in rejection of the challenge. They simply refused to recognize that it had the slightest relevance for them. They had work to do in extending the authority of the Soviets across the country. Lenin and Trotsky, the two men principally associated with the new revolution, remained reassuringly at one over the policy that the party should pursue. And since the conciliators had nowhere to lead, why should anyone follow them? With both the party and its moderate socialist opponents striding away from negotiations, the whole campaign for compromise became an exercise in soliloquy. Zinoviev quickly recanted and was readmitted to the central committee. The others were not far behind and in due course were also restored to positions of leadership.

The conciliators had feared that the failure to form an all-socialist government would leave the Bolsheviks to confront on their own a much augmented reaction. But, in the event, it fed the development of a close alliance between Bolsheviks and the Left Social Revolutionaries, who themselves now despaired of compromise and blamed the moderate socialists for having made such immoderate demands. It was an alliance that would prove of immense value to the regime in the crisis produced by the elections for the Constituent Assembly.

The Provisional Government had, shortly before its fall, at last set a date for these: 12 November. It was far too soon for Bolshevism to reach out from the towns and grasp the peasant multitudes with the promise of the new revolution. Lenin was convinced that the elections should be postponed. Trotsky did not support him. And Sverdlov, who was believed to know more than any other leading Bolshevik about peasant Russia, was the most strongly opposed. The party had clamoured too long for elections; had too indignantly claimed that the Provisional Government intended to postpone them indefinitely, in fear of the results. For a Bolshevism now in power to turn round and postpone them must be seen as an admission of fear and an attempt to do without a Constituent Assembly altogether. The party was too weak in the countryside, and this would make it even weaker. Lenin, isolated, accepted defeat. But he shook his head with foreboding. 'It is a mistake, an open mistake, that may cost us very dear! If it only does not cost the revolution its head. . . .'[11]

The combined vote for the several conservative and liberal parties was a mere 13 per cent: a poor showing for which the closure of their newspapers and the harassment of their leaders could not adequately account. Beyond the urban enclaves of the middle class, there was, simply, little allegiance left to a cause that had proved so irrelevant. But the Bolsheviks themselves had no reason to rejoice. They had received only 25 per cent of the vote, while other claimants to the prompt-box of socialism had together polled 62 per cent. In a Constituent Assembly of 707 seats, the Bolsheviks were to have 175. And if the Mensheviks had been reduced to a humiliating sixteen seats, this was scant consolation for the success of the Social Revolutionaries, who had emerged with 410, or a seemingly solid majority on their own.[12]

But then, was that majority as solid as it seemed? For the massive vote recorded by the Social Revolutionaries masked an anachronism. The various party lists had been compiled some weeks before the fall of the Provisional Government; and the Social Revolutionary one had combined representatives of Left and Right sectors which had already been straining apart. Since then, events had increasingly summoned the Left Social Revolutionaries to make a choice between the new regime and the developing challenge to it from the Right of their own party. That they would choose to break with the Right looked all too likely. They wanted only sufficient encouragement from the Bolsheviks and a suitable occasion. They got both.

Even as the election results were becoming known, Lenin set out to secure an alliance, at the All-Russian Congress of Peasants' Deputies then meeting in Petrograd. The Left Social Revolutionary delegates were led by Maria Spiridonova, whose slight figure, pale complexion, spectacles, and hair drawn down flat behind her head might have suggested that she belonged at the blackboard of a village school. She had shot dead a Tsarist general, notorious for his ruthlessness in crushing peasant unrest; been raped by soldiers of his guard; and had emerged from all her trials with her fire so much fiercer than before that it seemed at times as if it must rage out of all control. She was herself eager for an agreement with the Bolsheviks. And, on 14 November, one was reached which, commanding a majority of the delegates, proceeded to recognize and reinforce the supreme sovereignty of the Soviets by electing 108 representatives of the congress to join the Central Executive Committee.[13] The new alliance was then sealed with the appointment of Left Social Revolutionaries to various government posts, including the three People's Commissars of Agriculture, Justice, Posts and Telegraphs.

The formal split of the Social Revolutionaries enabled Lenin credibly to claim that in deciding on the composition of the Constituent Assembly, the people had 'voted for a party which no longer existed'. And there could be no reasonable doubt that the Left Social Revolutionaries enjoyed a far wider measure of peasant support than their share of the candidates elected on the party list allowed. But however useful these arguments might be for purposes of propaganda, the Constituent Assembly would still be controlled by the opponents of the regime. With no more than 40 of the 410 Social Revolutionary members declaring for the Left, the Right would still command a majority on its own, while able also to count on the minor opposition parties. By its repeated calls for the popular verdict of a Constituent Assembly; its confirmation of the polling date; and then its vigorous involvement in the election campaign, Bolshevism had painted itself into a corner.

And yet, what was there to prevent it from walking away, except for the marks that it must make across so much fresh paint? It had received a majority of votes in the industrial towns; in Petrograd and Moscow, and in the army units closest to them. Its Red Guards were far and away the largest, best organized and disciplined of the party militias. The Left Social Revolutionaries, who might otherwise have posed a threat with their ability to mobilize the more militant of the peasants, indicated that they would support the forcible dismissal of a defiant Constituent Assembly. The Bolshevik leadership still hoped that this might be avoided. There was no knowing beforehand how deep the popular attachment to a Constituent

Assembly really was, or how revolutionary socialists abroad would react. But it appeared less and less probable that the moderate socialist opposition would appreciate the difference between having taken most of the votes and holding most of the rifles. All the signs pointed to its insistence on a constitutional confrontation: at the very time when hostile armies were gathering, under former Tsarist generals, in southern Russia, and the government was seeking to achieve the promised peace.

On 28 November, in a burst of impatience, forty-three elected members of the Constituent Assembly, most of them Right Social Revolutionaries, marched with thousands of supporters to the Tauride Palace, their banners, bright between the blue of the sky and the white of the snow, proclaiming 'Long Life to the Constituent Assembly, the Master of Russia'. They found the gates closed and guarded by soldiers. Sorokin, a Right Social Revolutionary writer and himself one of the elected members, climbed the iron fence and addressed the crowd. Others clambered over into the court-yard and managed to unlock the gates. The crowd flooded through them. The soldiers hesitated. Sorokin proceeded to thank them 'for their welcome to the highest authority in Russia and their apparent willingness to guard its liberties'. In evident confusion, the soldiers stood by, as the doors of the building were forced open. The elected members stalked inside, followed by part of the crowd. 'In the passage,' Sorokin would recall,

Uritsky, an exceedingly repulsive Jew, demanded that we go to his office to register, but contemptuously we pushed him aside, saying that the Constitutional Assembly stood in no need of his services. In the Hall of the Palace we held our meeting and called upon the Russian nation to defend its Constitutional Assembly. A resolution was passed that the Assembly, in spite of every obstacle, should open on January 5th.[14]

Three days later, in a speech to the Central Executive Committee of the Soviets, Lenin warned that the Constituent Assembly had been conceived for use against the people and that no such use of it would be allowed. But a rather more considered treatment of this theme was needed. It came in a set of *Theses on the Constituent Assembly*, written by Lenin, and published anonymously in *Pravda* on 13 December. These began by conceding that in a bourgeois republic, the constituent assembly was 'the highest form of the democratic principle'. That, indeed, was why its appearance as an objective in past Bolshevik programmes had been legitimate. But a republic of soviets was itself 'a higher form of the democratic principle than the customary bourgeois republic with its constituent assembly'; was, in fact, 'the only form capable of assuring the least painful transition to socialism'. The spread of revolutionary ideas through the army and the peasantry, alongside the developing counter-revolutionary challenge, had removed all possibility of resolving 'the most acute questions in a formally democratic way', and produced an inevitable clash between the Constituent Assembly and the socialist revolution begun on 25 October. The Constituent Assembly would have unconditionally to declare its acceptance of Soviet power and of the Soviet revolution; or the 'crisis' created by its refusal would have to be 'solved . . . by revolutionary means'.

On 20 December, the Soviet of People's Commissars issued a decree, convoking the Constituent Assembly on 5 January 1918. And on 22 December, the Central Executive Committee resolved to convoke, for an opening session on 8 January, the Third Congress of Soviets. Zinoviev left no doubt of the design behind this chronology. 'We see in the rivalry of the Constituent Assembly and the Soviets the historical dispute between two revolutions, the bourgeois revolution and the socialist revolution.'[15] Both sides were now preparing for the clash that they had come to see as inescapable. But they were preparing rather differently.

Lenin ordered the transfer to Petrograd of an all but entirely working-class Lett regiment. 'The peasant may hesitate in this case,' he explained to his colleagues. 'Proletarian decision is necessary here.' And, at his insistence, Bolshevik deputies to the Constituent Assembly, arriving in Petrograd from various parts of Russia, were forthwith assigned, under Sverdlov's direction, to mobilize support in factories and barracks. The Right Social Revolutionaries made tentative efforts to recruit armed groups of workers and to win over some of the soldiers, especially in the two former regiments of the Imperial Guards that were showing symptoms of disaffection. But among the minority of workers opposed to the regime, there were very few who could be stirred by the stammer of irresolution that reached them; while any chance of rousing the soldiers disappeared when the central committee of the Social Revolutionary Party rejected proposals for an armed demonstration. How far the countryside was likely to answer a call for organized defence of the Constituent Assembly remained only a momentous question. For no such call was issued. The Right Social Revolutionaries were essentially relying on a spontaneous insurgency of popular opinion that would gather instantly to meet and overwhelm any assault from the government on the democratic symbol of the Constituent Assembly. Meanwhile, however, their elected representatives from the provinces, recovering from the shock of the hostility that they encountered in the capital, proceeded to equip themselves for the coming confrontation. 'They brought candles with them,' Trotsky was derisively to write, 'in case the Bolsheviki cut off the electric light, and a vast number of sandwiches in case their food be taken from them. Thus democracy entered upon the struggle with dictatorship heavily armed with sandwiches and candles.'[16]

But then, it might no less derisively have been said of the revolution that, entering upon the struggle with German militarism for an acceptable peace, it was inadequately provided even with sandwiches and candles. The bread ration in Petrograd had been cut to one-eighth of a pound a day; and the sugar ration to half a pound a month. The advancement of workers' control seemed only to be accelerating the approach of industrial collapse. Individual factory committees were bartering machinery for raw materials and requisitioning railway trucks for their own needs. The banks were engaged in a campaign to paralyse the regime by limiting withdrawals of cash and denying credit. And, at the front itself, what was left of the Russian armies all too conspicuously lacked the will or the weapons to fight.

The Bolsheviks had promised to abandon secret diplomacy. And early in November 1917, they set out to keep their word. There was, however, a little delay. When Trotsky arrived to take charge of his domain, he found it deserted. The permanent head of the ministry was soon tracked down and told to secure the attendance of his officials or accept the responsibility for their disobedience. They were hastily assembled. Trotsky demanded the keys to the safes. He might just as well have been knocking on the doors of the safes themselves. The principal officers were conducted to the Smolny and there placed under arrest. Two days laters, the permanent head, a count whose family had long supplied Russia with diplomats and whose distress at his peculiar plight may easily be imagined, accompanied Trotsky on a tour of the ministry, to open the safes and surrender their contents. Disclosed at last were the terms of those secret treaties whose very existence had been so indignantly denied. Victory was to give Russia, as her share of the plunder, Constantinople, Galicia, and domination of the Balkans. As the treaties began appearing in public print, it might have seemed as though the flag of the revolution was fluttering from the faces of the Allies. But the German government was not encouraged to enjoy the spectacle. Trotsky was quick to proclaim his confidence that when German socialists opened the safes in their own foreign ministry, the world would see that the Allies were equalled in 'cynicism and banditry' by German imperialism.

The continued refusal of the Allied governments to recognize the Soviet regime aroused De Robien to private protest. 'It is America who is being the most intransigent, and who is the most obstinately refusing to have any relations with "the revolutionaries of Smolny". . . . These sewing-machine and canned pork merchants really do go a bit far and they are rather too ready to forget in what way free America was founded.' But he had scarcely more patience with the campaign in the French newspapers against the 'so-called Bolshevik atrocities . . . which provoke the righteous indignation of well-meaning people . . . those same people who, nevertheless, coolly remark that "the last offensive did not cost very much".'[17]

On 7 November, General Dukhonin, commander-in-chief of the Russian armies, was ordered to offer the enemy an armistice; and Trotsky dispatched to the Allies a proposal for the early commencement of general peace talks. The Allied governments ignored the proposer and proposal alike; and proceeded to deal directly with Dukhonin, as the only power in Russia they were disposed to recognize. They warned him that any separate peace negotiations with Germany would entail 'the gravest consequences' and hinted that Japan might be provoked to invade Siberia. Dukhonin proved compliant enough but regrettably incapable of wielding the power with which they had credited him. On his refusal to obey the order from Petrograd, he was dismissed from his post; soon afterwards to be killed by soldiers enraged by reports that he had planned to continue the war. Krylenko, appointed commander-in-chief in his place, communicated his government's offer to the German high command, which agreed on 27 November (the 14th in the Russian calendar) to negotiate an armistice.

Trotsky again turned to the Allies. Russia had requested, he wrote, a delay of a few days in the opening of talks with the Germans, so that the Allied governments might have time to define their attitude. The Soviet of People's Commissars was asking these governments, 'in the face of their own peoples, in the face of the whole world', whether they would join in the talks. 'We appeal to the allied peoples and above all to their working masses: do they agree to drag on this senseless and purposeless slaughter and to rush blindly towards the doom of European civilization?' The answer should be given now. The Russian army and the Russian people could not and would not wait. 'If the allied peoples do not send their representatives, we alone shall negotiate with the Germans.' And he ended: 'We appeal to the soldiers of the allied countries to act and not to lose a single hour: Down with the winter campaign! Down with the war!'

The Allied governments did not deign to reply. Indeed, they must have rubbed their eyes at first in disbelief. The appeal to their peoples in a formal communication to themselves was outrageous enough. The appeal to their soldiers was incitement to mutiny. And the implication that all the sacrifice of men and money, to protect mankind from the menace of German militarism, had been meaningless, added insult to injury. But then, happily, as all the experts on Russia were agreed, the Bolshevik regime would soon be overthrown; and the country, saved for the cause of freedom by some efficient military dictatorship, would return to the trenches for the achievement of that victory which only its departure now postponed. Meanwhile, of course, there could be no question of recognizing a regime so devoted to infecting the rest of the world with its own revolutionary mischief.

In London, Litvinoff, newly appointed Russian ambassador, had a hard time of it. One day, at a lunch in a restaurant of the Lyons chain, he was delighted to see '*pouding diplomate*' on the menu and asked the waitress to bring him a portion. She returned to tell him that there was none of it left. Shrugging his shoulders, Litvinoff acknowledged the message: 'Not recognized even by Lyons!'[18]

At Brest-Litovsk, a Polish town whose old citadel was all that had survived the fury of the Russian retreat, the German high command had its eastern headquarters. And there, on 2 December (19 November in the Russian calendar), the armistice talks began. Joffe, Trotsky's disciple and friend, led a Russian delegation that included two Left Social Revolutionaries and, for their symbolic value, a peasant, a worker, a soldier and a sailor. The Germans were not impressed by the symbolism: the soldiers had abandoned the trenches and the sailors the sea; the worker had difficulties with his knife and fork at official banquets; and the peasant seemed determined to enjoy rather more of the free drink provided than was evidently good for him. Nor were they comfortable with the other company they were required to keep. As though the Bolsheviks were not bad enough, there was the infamous Anastasia Bitsenko, a Social Revolutionary who had assassinated the Tsar's Minister of War. But fixing their minds on the objective of removing Russia from the war, the German delegates reserved their distaste for the abandon of their diaries.

The Russians offered an armistice to last six months: if certain islands were evacuated by the German army, and if no German troops were transferred from the eastern front for the war in the west. Trotsky, at a public meeting in Petrograd, declared that Russia would regard such a transfer as 'impermissible, because we are proposing an honest armistice and because England and France must not be crushed'. But the Allies were unmoved by this expression of concern for their welfare. And the Germans were indignant that Russia should presume so far as to lay down conditions. The Central Powers, General Hoffmann remarked with asperity, had not been beaten. They would not surrender the islands. They must remain free to do with their troops whatever they wished. And peace talks should follow the conclusion of an armistice. The negotiations stumbled alarmingly. But the Germans then put out a finger to stop the fall. Only those troops would be shifted as had received their orders before 5 December (22 November), when an initial armistice of ten days would come into force. It was not much of a concession. Orders had already been given to shift the bulk of the eastern army to the western front. The Russians agreed. Once more, Trotsky appealed to the Allies. Once more, there was no reply. On 15 December (the 2nd), the armistice was extended for a further thirty days, to encompass the opening of peace talks, on 22 December 1917.

On 22 December (the 9th in Russia itself), Trotsky addressed a joint meeting of the government, the Central Executive Committee of the

Soviets, the Petrograd Soviet, the town council of Petrograd, and trade union leaders. And his speech, in all the twists of its passion, revealed the anguish of his acknowledgement that the revolution might soon find itself faced with the most hideous of choices. The government of a Soviet Russia, he announced, would talk with the Hohenzollerns and the Habsburgs 'as with freedom's enemies'; would talk, determined 'that not a single atom of freedom should be sacrificed to imperialism'. For only then would the real meaning of Russia's revolutionary endeavours reach deep into the consciousness of the German and Austrian peoples. If those peoples failed to respond; if the German working class did not exercise a decisive influence, peace would be impossible. He had brought himself to the brink and it seemed that he was willing himself to look down.

But if it should turn out that we had been mistaken, if this dead silence were to reign in Europe much longer, if this silence were to give the Kaiser the chance to attack us and to dictate terms insulting to the revolutionary dignity of our country, then I do not know whether – with this disrupted economy and universal chaos entailed by war and internal convulsions – whether we could go on fighting.

Then he turned away with a cry. 'Yes, we could!' There was ecstatic applause. 'For our life, for our revolutionary honour, we would fight to the last drop of our blood.' Again there was applause, pressing him onwards. 'The weary and the old ones would step aside . . . and we would create a powerful army of soldiers and Red Guards.' The Bolsheviks would refuse to sign an unjust and undemocratic peace. They – and, he hoped, the Left Social Revolutionaries as well – would summon all peoples to a holy war against the militarists of all countries.

He might, elatedly enough, have left his listeners there; with that defiance pealing its promise in their ears. But there needed to be a faith beyond that: a readiness to accept the defeat of such defiance, without doubting for a moment that victory remained inevitable. 'If in view of the economic chaos,' he continued, 'we should not be able to fight, the struggle would not be at an end: it would only be postponed, as it was in 1905, when Tsardom crushed us but we lived to fight another day.'[19] And that it might, indeed, be not the men of the revolution who survived, but only their ideas, and the illumination of their lives, he had already allowed in an earlier part of his speech. Even, he had proclaimed, 'if the enemies of the people were to conquer us and we were to perish . . . our memory would still pass from generation to generation and awaken posterity to a new struggle.' It was the ultimate source of his own courage and strength: this sense of immortality; this belief that he and his fellow revolutionaries were now an essential part of that tradition which lined, like flares in a fog, the path from the past. That was why the negotiations for peace were to be approached 'without black thoughts'. At Brest-Litovsk, the revolution would be speaking not just to Hohenzollerns and Habsburgs, so as to speak beyond them, to the peoples of the earth. It would be speaking to and for history itself.

To the conference table, where Joffe again headed the Russian delegation, duly came representatives of the Quadruple Alliance: Germany, Austria–Hungary, Bulgaria and Turkey. It was less than ever an equal partnership. Bulgaria and Turkey did little more than flap their wings occasionally, as a reminder of their right to pick bits of territory out of the peace. And the Austro-Hungarian empire was in scarcely better case than Russia to contemplate a continuation of the war. Its principal delegate, the Foreign Minister, Count Czernin, was as conciliatory as he dared. But since the empire survived from day to day on German supplies, he was more often given to melancholy than to daring. The dominance of Germany was manifest. And if it was a dominance asserted in two distinct voices – that of the Foreign Minister, von Kühlmann, and that of Hoffmann, from the high command – this distinction soon proved to provide no footing for hope. Von Kühlmann was quite as determined as Hoffmann to batten on the weakness of the Russians. 'There is only one thing for them to choose now,' he reassured Czernin; 'under what sauce they are to be devoured'.[20] The politician and the general did not speak for different appetites. It was just that their eating habits were not the same.

At the start, Joffe obtained agreement that the proceedings should be public and then proclaimed several principles that his government maintained should inform the terms of the treaty. All occupied territories were to be liberated; nations that had not enjoyed political independence before the war were to have the opportunity of deciding their future by free referendum; minorities in multi-national states must have their rights protected by special laws; and no indemnities were to be imposed. On 25 December (the 12th), von Kühlmann gave his reply. The Quadruple Alliance, he declared, was ready to conclude a general peace without annexations or indemnities: though, he added, the Russian proposals could be realized only if all the belligerents bound themselves to observe the same conditions. And, on behalf of the Quadruple Alliance, he denied any intention of forcibly annexing the occupied territories.

At Joffe's request, the talks were adjourned for ten days, so that the absent belligerents might be approached to reconsider their attitude. In Petrograd, a mass demonstration celebrated the moral victory that the revolution seemed to have gained. The revolution had gained only an illusion, and one which it was almost immediately to lose. Von Kühlmann was content to let the Russians walk away with the words, if this made it any easier for them to let the Germans walk away with the territories. And besides: he saw no advantage in presenting the enemies of Germany with material for denouncing its oppressions. Painted with colourful phrases and carefully lit, conquest might be made to look very like liberation. General Hoffmann had neither aptitude nor taste for such deviousness. And he was not disposed to risk encouraging ridiculous assumptions. On the day after von Kühlmann's statement, he informed Joffe at lunch that no forcible annexation would be involved, if former parts of the Russian empire, such as Poland, Lithuania and Courland, should decide to unite with Germany or any other state. Since Poland, Lithuania and Courland were then under German military control, there was no mistaking his meaning. The Russian delegates were soon on their way home, to communicate in person their dismay.

Trotsky was reluctant to leave a revolutionary Russia for the company of imperial generals and diplomats. It was at Lenin's insistence, he would write, that he agreed to attend the resumed talks, as leader of the delegation. Lenin would hardly have succeeded in persuading him, however, had he himself not been largely persuaded already, by the very thought that the front line of the revolution was now at Brest-Litovsk. His journey there was a slow fall from a narrow ledge. No reports had prepared him for the sight of the virtually deserted trenches on the Russian side. According to the German officer who conducted him across the silence, between the remnants of one army and the other that stood there whole and waiting, able to conquer as quickly as it moved, he grew 'more and more depressed'.[21] But from the first handshake of his arrival, his adversaries would search in vain for any sign of uncertainty.

At the railway station, one of the Russian delegates stepped from the train and immediately began handing out pamphlets to the German soldiers on the platform. The officials and diplomats proceeded with the ceremony of welcome in stiff indifference. They were soon enough released to discuss the scandal and were scarcely mollified to learn that the delegate concerned was a certain Karl Radek, a Polish Jew, who was nominally a subject of the Austro-Hungarian empire, and who had acquired some repute as a pungent pamphleteer in the German Social Democratic Party. The incident had been a deliberate challenge to the citizenship of contending nationalisms from the international citizenship of revolution.

Nor did Trotsky permit any such concession to conventional courtesies as might tend to blur the image of the moral conflict. He rejected the distinction of being presented to Prince Leopold of Bavaria. And he demanded that the Russian delegates be furnished with facilities to dine on their own. Both Hoffmann and Czernin hastened to inform their diaries that Trotsky had brought a different mood with him. Von Kühlmann, however, was not to be deterred from testing his particular skill. Finding Trotsky at the coat-rack in the hall, before the first session of the resumed talks, on 9 January

1918 (27 December 1917), he introduced himself and expressed his considerable pleasure at the prospect of dealing directly with the master rather than the emissary. Trotsky recoiled in evident disgust. And von Kühlmann, nothing if not flexible in such matters, adopted a more formal tone at once.

A more formal tone was certainly more appropriate a preparation for the statement that he was to make almost as soon as the delegates met. The previous undertaking of the Quadruple Alliance to seek neither annexations nor indemnities, he declared, had applied to a general peace; and since, with the failure of Russia's allies to respond, only a separate peace was now being discussed, that undertaking was withdrawn. He could not agree to the Russian request that the conference be transferred to a neutral country. And he protested at the propaganda of the Russians, which raised serious doubts about their desire for peace. It was a protest that General Hoffmann repeated more vigorously; gesticulating towards a pile of pamphlets in front of him.

Trotsky reserved his reply for the following day, when von Kühlmann pressed him to state whether he would recognize the right of the Ukrainian Rada to separate representation at the talks. He had no intention of providing the Germans with the pleasure of a dispute between Russians and Ukrainians, so that they might then proceed to adjudicate in their own interests. Bolshevik forces were moving against Kiev, and the struggle would be decided there, not at Brest-Litovsk. He began, accordingly, by declaring that he did not object to Ukrainian participation in the conference.

He would not, he continued, apologize for the revolutionary propaganda being distributed among German soldiers. He had come to discuss peace; not to agree that his government's voice should be silenced. Soviet Russia did not object to the counter-revolutionary propaganda of the Germans. It was sufficiently confident of its case to welcome an open debate. The claim that its propaganda raised doubts of its genuine desire for peace was groundless. Indeed, there was more reason to doubt the genuine desire of a German government that so soon after undertaking to conclude a peace without annexations or indemnities, proclaimed itself no longer bound by the principle. His government must protest yet again at German insistence on holding the conference in the isolation of Brest-Litovsk. The German chancellor had offered the Reichstag the excuse that the conference would be exposed in a neutral country to Allied intrigues. But the job of protecting the Russian government from hostile intrigues belonged to the Russian government alone. The fact was that Germany had presented a simple ultimatum: talks at Brest-Litovsk, or no talks at all. And he ended with a warning and an ultimatum of his own. If the Russians agreed to stay at Brest-Litovsk, it was to leave not a single chance of peace unexplored; to learn, 'clearly and precisely', whether a peace was possible without violence to the peoples whom the revolution had promised the right of self-determination. They would not, however, submit to German pressure for private talks. The negotiations were to be conducted in public throughout, or not at all.

These were, of course, merely the preliminaries. But they were not to be considered correspondingly of little account. Leading Social Democrats on both sides of the war were scornfully maintaining that the peace negotiations were a sham, and that the Soviet government had been stirring up the ideological dust to cover the substance of the surrender which had already been agreed. It was a campaign that had immediately to be countered, if the workers of the West, whose awaited revolt was so vital, were not to succumb instead to the despair of believing that the Russian revolution had betrayed them. Every day of delay before a decision had to be taken must be a day won for the evidence that here, at Brest-Litovsk, was a real and still undecided struggle between power and principle. And no opportunity must be missed to reveal the cynicism of the one and the dignity of the other.

When von Kühlmann came to present the draft of a peace treaty, Trotsky at once objected to the phrase in the preamble that proclaimed the desire of the contracting parties to live in friendship. The seasoned diplomats could scarcely have been more disconcerted had the very chairs beneath them suddenly complained of the weight that they were carrying. He was asked for an explanation. Surely the sentiment was unexceptionable? Trotsky would have none of this cant: 'such declarations, copied from one diplomatic document into another, have never yet characterized the real relations between states'. The phrase was dropped from the draft. Von Kühlmann had no wish to make a fuss over whether Russia was prepared to protest its friendship. Such friendship was, after all, of small account.

What he did require was that Russia accept an annexation of the occupied territories under the guise of self-determination. And it was Trotsky's imperative purpose to demonstrate that Russia was being invited to connive at fraud. He insisted that only a free referendum, conducted after the withdrawal of foreign troops, would allow a proper expression of the popular will. Von Kühlmann ruled out the withdrawal of German occupation troops. And he claimed that the territories concerned had expressed their will already, through the institutions established under the regime of occupation. The Russian government, he recalled, was committed to permitting the secession of territories, should their inhabitants wish it. Trotsky replied that the Soviet government was not defending the possessions of Russia, 'but the rights of separate nationalities to free historical existence'. And it would never consent to recognize decisions taken under the control of German occupation authorities, by organizations that these authorities had themselves created or arbitrarily declared to be representative. 'We are revolutionaries, but we are also realists, and we should prefer to talk directly about annexations, rather than to substitute pseudonyms for real names.'

All this doctrinal disputation proved too much for General Hoffmann. He exclaimed that the Russian delegates were talking the language of victors. 'The facts contradict this; victorious German troops are on Russian territory.' And then, somewhat incompatibly, he proceeded to berate the Soviet government for its reliance on force. Extracting copies of Russian newspapers from his brief-case, he cited Social Revolutionary articles that denounced the Bolsheviks for suppressing freedom of speech and violating the principles of democracy. Since it had apparently not struck him that such articles themselves indicated a measure of press freedom in Russia for which many subjects of the Kaiser might reasonably sigh, Trotsky drew this to his attention. He would not deny that the Soviet government used force. But he submitted that no government so far in history had managed to dispense with it. And he continued: 'What surprises and repels the governments of other countries is that we do not arrest strikers, but capitalists who subject workers to lock-outs; that we do not shoot peasants who demand land, but arrest the landowners and officers who try to shoot the peasants.' Von Kühlmann, who derived an ill-concealed pleasure from the discomfiture of his colleague, asked whether General Hoffmann wished to speak any further on the subject. 'No, no more!' General Hoffmann barked back and stared at the window in rage.

As the argument dragged on, from day to day, there was no doubt that Trotsky was proving, in Czernin's own description, a 'clever and very dangerous adversary'. Indeed, one leading German newspaper protested that 'in Brest-Litovsk, Trotsky has created for himself a platform from which his voice is carried throughout the world', and it demanded an end to the peace talks as soon as possible.[22] But the civilian German negotiators continued to hope that he might yet be pressed into accepting a settlement that camouflaged the guns behind it. And, besides, time was needed to secure an agreement with those upstart Ukrainians, who were seeking territorial gains of their own in return for supplies of food to Germany and Austria.

In Petrograd, De Robien followed closely the reports from Brest-Litovsk. He noted that Trotsky's 'latest statements seem to have disconcerted the Germans, and one must truthfully admit that they are cool little masterpieces'. But his initial admiration of the Bolsheviks was already fast evaporating, as their dreams threatened to promote a new reality in Europe.

The contagion of Bolshevism may infect the German masses! And it also constitutes a danger for us as, if the revolution breaks out tomorrow in Germany, it will reverberate very closely to our own frontiers. . . . In order to save established society and civilization, one should never hesitate to stifle any sympathy one may feel towards certain generous ideas, because the fulfilment of these ideas can only be achieved at the cost of ruin and sorrow.[23]

Certainly in his own diary henceforth, there was to be far more concern with ruin and sorrow than with generous ideas.

Trotsky employed his enforced leisure to write a short account of the Russian revolution, meant especially for foreign workers; and this would, in due course, reach a considerable readership in many countries.[24] It is an incisive recital of events, but too declamatory to be dramatic. He would come to write a history of the revolution which compacted character, imagery and rhythm, to re-create rather than merely to relate events. But this would have to wait for the refinements of time and a very different enforcement of leisure. Count Czernin, too, found a way of filling his empty hours. He read reminiscences of the French revolution and offered his diary a hopeful comparison between the Jacobins and the Bolsheviks. 'These Bolsheviks will disappear again and – who knows? – perhaps there will yet be a Corday for Trotsky.'

On 18 January (the 5th in the Russian calendar) 1918, General Hoffmann bluntly communicated the impatience of the high command. He presented a map on which a blue line, running northwards from Brest-Litovsk to the Baltic, defined the future frontier of Russia. Territorial arrangements south of Brest-Litovsk, he explained, would depend on the issue of negotiations with the Ukrainian delegates. Trotsky asked acidly what principles guided the drawing of the line. It was dictated, Hoffmann replied, by military considerations. And, indeed, the line coincided precisely with that held by the German army. It removed from the former Russian empire, and now from the revolution's promise of self-determination, most of Poland, all of Lithuania, much of Latvia, and certain islands inhabited by Estonians. Trotsky secured an adjournment of the conference, so that he might return to Petrograd for consultations with his government. And it was while he was on the train that his government disposed of the Constituent Assembly.

The Central Executive Committee of the Soviets adopted, on 3 January, a draft Declaration of Rights of the Toiling and Exploited People, for the Constituent Assembly to accept, in an effective act of abdication. This vested all power, central and local, in the Soviets; and proclaimed the Russian Soviet Republic 'a federation of national soviet republics', based on 'a free union of free nations'. A further resolution of the Central Executive Committee, published in *Izvestia* on the following day, warned that

... any attempt on the part of any person or institution whatever to usurp this or that function of state power will be regarded as a counter-revolutionary act. Any such attempt will be crushed by all means at the disposal of the Soviet power, including the use of armed force.[25]

The Constituent Assembly was due to meet on 5 January. And in the morning, Edgar Sisson, President Wilson's special representative in Russia, went to watch the parades organized to demonstrate support for the Assembly.

The marchers might have been the middle-class citizens of any continental city or of New York or Chicago. Only their terrible soberness set them apart from their kind all over the world. ... The walks of the Nevskii were crowded with onlookers, smiling labourers out to see a show. They jeered but did not attack. ...

Suddenly he heard shots. And, as his sledge took him through the streets, he saw the debris of broken banners and the bloodstains on the snow. A count of six dead and thirty-four injured was subsequently reported. Sisson recorded in his diary that this was probably an underestimate.[26]

The hall of the Tauride Palace was decorated in red and gold. Many deputies had not yet arrived in the capital. But the quorum of 400, set by the Soviet of People's Commissars, had been reached. Uritsky had been appointed to ensure order. He arrived late. On his way, two men had set upon him in the street and stripped him of his overcoat. But ostentatious arrangements to protect the Assembly, if only from itself, had already been made. A strong force of sailors surrounded the palace; while, within, there were armed guards stationed along the corridors, in the gallery, and on the floor of the chamber. At four o'clock, after several hours' delay, the first session began. A certain Shvetzov, a Right Social Revolutionary, to whom, as the oldest member present, custom gave the honour of presiding until a chairman was elected, rose from his seat and advanced towards the platform. There was uproar from the Bolsheviks. The moderate socialists stood and applauded. Sverdlov cut in front of the old man and announced that the Central Executive Committee of the Soviets had empowered him to open the meeting. The moderate socialists dropped bewildered to their seats. Sverdlov then proceeded to read the Declaration of Rights. The Bolshevik deputies cheered every clause and, at the end, rose to sing the *Internationale*, an anthem whose summons the moderate socialists could scarcely ignore.

But the majority was not to be outmanoeuvred forever. The Right Social Revolutionaries insisted upon the election of a chairman and nominated Chernov. The Bolsheviks, offering no candidate of their own, backed Maria Spiridonova. She was defeated, by 153 votes to 244. Speaker followed speaker. Tseretelli, having emerged from two months of concealment to warn of civil war and denounce the gathering assault on civil liberties, was greeted by catcalls from the Bolshevik deputies and the raised rifles of sailors in the gallery, but at last succeeded in commanding attention. Lenin himself took no part in the debate. For most of the time, he lay stretched out, apparently asleep, on one of the benches provided for members of the Presidium. Suddenly he got up and left the hall. Feeling his overcoat in the anteroom, he found that the revolver, which he kept in an inside pocket, had gone. 'There you see,' he complained to Uritsky. 'Today your fur coat was taken from you in the middle of the street. And tonight robbers stole my revolver. Now do you understand the sort of order that exists among us?'[27]

At midnight, the Declaration of Rights was put to the vote and defeated in favour of a Right Social Revolutionary motion to discuss current issues of policy. Soon afterwards, Raskolnikov rose to announce that in view of 'the counter-revolutionary majority' confronting them, the Bolsheviks would withdraw from the assembly; and their departure was followed, an hour later, by that of the Left Social Revolutionaries. The remaining deputies addressed themselves to Right Social Revolutionary proposals for a Land Decree and an appeal to the Allies for the conclusion of a general democratic peace. At five o'clock on the morning of the 6th, acting on orders from the Bolshevik central committee which had been meeting elsewhere in the building, a sailor approached Chernov and informed him that the deputies must be dispersed, 'since the guard is tired'. The Land Decree and peace appeal were hastily adopted, together with a decree proclaiming Russia a federal democratic republic, before Chernov announced an adjournment of twelve hours. Later that morning, the Central Executive Committee of the Soviets issued a decree of its own, dissolving the Constituent Assembly. Armed guards at all the approaches to the palace ensured the compliance of the deputies. Four days afterwards, the Third Congress of Soviets met at the Tauride Palace instead and adopted the Declaration of Rights.

In the number of *Novaya Zhizn* dated 9 January, Gorky, who had long been assailing the Bolsheviks for their policies, lamented:

For almost a hundred years the finest Russians have lived by the idea of a Constituent Assembly, a political institution which would give the entire Russian democracy the opportunity freely to express its will. In the struggle for this idea, thousands of the intelligentsia and tens of thousands of workers and peasants have perished in prisons, in exile and at hard labour, on the gallows. Rivers of blood have been spilled on the sacrificial altar of this sacred idea, and now the 'People's Commissars' have given orders to shoot the democracy which demonstrated in honour of this idea.

And passionately he drew the comparison, again and again, between this and the shooting at unarmed and peaceful demonstrators by Tsarist soldiers, on 9 January 1905.[28] Yet the shots of thirteen years before had resounded across Russia and roused a popular protest that was soon threatening the very survival of the regime. The shots of January 1918 died as fast and as relatively unremarked as the Constituent Assembly itself. For the 'sacred idea' had, at the moment of its realization, lost its capacity to confer martyrdom on those who suffered in its cause.

The truth was that the Constituent Assembly, having finally got to its feet, had found virtually nothing to say. Its major measure, the Land Decree, was little more than a copy of the one which Lenin had introduced at the Second Soviet Congress. Its appeal to the Allies for support in the engagement to a general democratic peace was in substance the same as that which the Soviet government had made. Its sole offering was its proposal to co-operate in the calling of an international socialist conference. But that was a letter with no address or stamp on the envelope, and only a prayer inside.

Above all, its decree proclaiming Russia a democratic federal republic defied the Soviet formulation, without offering any real alternative of its own to the Soviet regime. And it offered no such alternative because no such alternative existed. The Constituent Assembly represented the cause of a system for which the overwhelming mass of Russians cared little or nothing, and whose most passionate adherents belonged to a middle class in moral eclipse. The very threat flourished by Tseretelli, of inevitable civil war, pointed to the plight of the democratic movement. For this civil war, it was increasingly evident, would be fought between the forces of the regime and those of a reaction whose militarist leadership had even less time for the democratic parties than did the Bolsheviks themselves.

Rosa Luxemburg, writing from her German prison cell, was critical of the treatment meted out to the Constituent Assembly. It seemed to her a dangerous display of impatience with democracy. She admitted the need for a proletarian dictatorship to restructure society. But she considered that this dictatorship should consist 'in a particular application of democracy, not in its abolition'. She agreed that the sternest measures ought to be taken against those who resisted the measures of a revolutionary socialist regime. But she would not allow that freedom of criticism, even for enemies of the Soviet regime, should be denied. And she warned darkly:

Freedom for supporters of the government only, for the members of one party only – no matter how big its membership may be – is no freedom at all. Freedom is always freedom for the man who thinks differently. This contention does not spring from a fanatical love of abstract 'justice', but from the fact that everything which is enlightening, healthy and purifying in political freedom derives from its independent character, and from the fact that freedom loses all its virtues when it becomes a privilege. . . .

The suppression of political life throughout the country must gradually cause the vitality of the Soviets themselves to decline. Without general elections, freedom of the press, freedom of assembly, and freedom of speech, life in every public institution slows down, becomes a caricature of itself, and bureaucracy rises as the only deciding factor. . . . In the last resort, cliquism develops a dictatorship, but not the dictatorship of the proletariat: the dictatorship of a handful of politicians, i.e., a dictatorship in the bourgeois sense, in the Jacobin sense. . . .[29]

Trotsky himself was unhesitatingly to defend the dissolution of the Constituent Assembly. It was not that he was any less alive than Rosa Luxemburg to the existence of such dangers as she identified. But he did not associate them with the furling of an institution which he regarded as the ragged flag of a bourgeois republic. He saw no way of achieving a compromise between the socialist regime and the democratic movement. For the democratic movement derived its surviving dynamic from its denial of the very possibility. It continued to demand the immediate abandonment of socialism as its price for collaboration. And even had the goods been a great deal less shoddy than they were, this was a price which Trotsky would not contemplate paying. Nor did his commitment to democracy require that he should. On the contrary, real democracy for him was inseparable from the freedom that only socialism allowed; and the expression of that freedom was the essential function of the Soviets. To be sure, in the singular social conditions of Russia, which had, so paradoxically, enabled it to surface there first, socialism stood in a thin layer of soil, above centuries of sand. It would need the spread of its revolutionary roots to the industrial West, for the nourishment necessary to thrive. But this made it all the more imperative to protect, meanwhile, the democracy of the Soviets; and all the more unreasonable to mourn a Constituent Assembly whose own essential function had been to confront them, before the hungry eyes of German imperialism.

On 8 January, the Bolshevik central committee met with leading Bolshevik delegates to the Third Congress of Soviets, in a special conference to consider the reply that Trotsky should take back to Brest-Litovsk. Trotsky himself was against agreeing to a peace that might seem to support accusations of Soviet duplicity and discourage a German workers' revolt. Yet he had seen the Russian trenches at the front, like so many open doors. He proposed that he refuse to sign the treaty but announce that Russia was none the less withdrawing from the war. Lenin, fearing that this refusal would detonate a German attack which the Soviet regime might not survive, or survive only at the cost of a peace on far harsher terms still, argued for acceptance of the treaty.

Bukharin led the call for an immediate rupture of negotiations, in a commitment to revolutionary war. The debate became fierce. And at one point, Radek, glaring at Lenin, cried: 'If there were five hundred courageous men in Petrograd, we would put you in prison.' Lenin replied coldly:

'Some people, indeed, may go to prison; but if you will calculate the probabilities you will see that it is much more likely that I will send you than you me.'[30] But in the event, he only mustered fifteen votes, to sixteen for Trotsky's formula, while thirty-two were cast for Bukharin's call to revolutionary war.

This vote was not binding on the party, since it came from a consultative conference. But the war group within the central committee could now confidently claim that it represented the dominant view among crucially placed Bolsheviks without. And the Left Social Revolutionaries were already pressing their own opposition to the German demands. Lenin was undeterred. When the central committee met, three days later, to decide what to do, he again urged acceptance of the peace, 'shameful' as he conceded it to be. 'Germany is still only pregnant with revolution; and a quite healthy child has been born to us – a socialist republic which we may kill if we begin war.' Stalin went further. 'There is no revolutionary movement in the West. There are no facts; there is only a possibility, and with possibilities we cannot reckon.' But this was going altogether too far for Lenin. Of course, there was a mass movement in the West. Were it probable that the German movement might develop immediately, in the event of a rupture at Brest-Litovsk, 'we should be obliged to sacrifice ourselves, because the German revolution in its force will be greater than ours'.

He was bitterly attacked by members of the war group. Dzerzhinsky accused him of timidly surrendering the whole programme of the revolution; Bukharin, of a readiness to betray the German and Austrian workers; Uritsky, of approaching the problem 'from a narrow Russian and not from an international standpoint'. It was not that they necessarily saw an imminent proletarian seizure of power in Germany or rejected Lenin's calculation of the immediate military odds. But of what worth was the revolution if it could not rouse the Russian people to defend it against the irruption of German imperialism, and if the workers of the West were to remain unmoved by the resistance of the Russian people? What faithful revolutionary would sign away his principles out of fear of defeat? Such questions tugged at Trotsky with no less insistence. And he was undoubtedly all the more drawn to a war group that included so many of those who had been his political companions well before their joint attachment to Bolshevism; so many of those whose eyes were level with his own, above the crouching opportunists behind Lenin in the agitation for peace. Yet he could not lightly dismiss Lenin's political insight or ignore arguments for which his own mind had already found room. Precisely, then, because there was something to be said for either side, a choice between them ought to be avoided, until events themselves moved decisively to reinforce one or the other. His formula provided a chance to test the strength of the

German proletariat's resistance to militarism, while depriving that militarism of any chance to offer defensive reasons for an attack.

Lenin, recognizing that his proposal was certain to be lost, abandoned
it for one that went part of the way with Trotsky. He suggested that
Trotsky be authorized to delay by all possible means the signing of the
peace. Zinoviev alone dissented. Then Trotsky submitted his own formula: 'We interrupt the war and do not sign the peace; we demobolize the
army.' And this was adopted by nine votes to seven.

Before leaving Petrograd, Trotsky had a private conference with Lenin.
They had no authority, of course, to alter a formula adopted by the central
committee. But the formula itself had stopped short of any German response. What, asked Lenin, if the Germans should answer Russia's refusal
to sign the treaty by resuming the war? That, Trotsky allowed, must
change his attitude. 'We will sign peace at the point of a bayonet. The
situation will be clear to all the world.' The two men supposed that they
were agreed at last. But each, looking into the other's mind, saw only his
own. Lenin assumed that Trotsky intended to sign the treaty in the face of
an unmistakable ultimatum; Trotsky, that Lenin would support the policy
of refusing to sign, except in the face of an actual offensive.

And now events seemed at last to be wheeling towards the revolution.
Even as Trotsky was travelling back to Brest-Litovsk, strikes spread across
Austria and Germany. Demonstrating workers demanded an immediate
peace without annexations or indemnities, and in accordance with the
principle of popular self-determination proclaimed at Brest-Litovsk by
the Soviet delegates.

On 30 January (the 17th in the Russian calendar), the peace talks
resumed at Brest-Litovsk. Trotsky announced that his delegation now
included two representatives of the Ukrainian Soviet Republic. And it was
the Ukrainian issue that would, indeed, dominate the proceedings. The
rule of the Rada was rapidly shrinking under the assault of Soviet forces.
But the Germans were not to be deflected from their design for the
Ukraine. On 1 February (19 January), Count Czernin, on behalf of the
Quadruple Alliance, formally recognized the Ukrainian People's Republic
'as a free sovereign state, fully authorized to enter into international
relations'.

Meanwhile, the strike movement in Austria and Germany was collapsing, as the authorities banned the labour press, dispatched police to break
up meetings, and drafted thousands of workers in the army reserve to
their regiments. That the danger was far from past, no one was more aware
than Germany's effective war leader, Ludendorff, who sent each army commander a secret order to keep two battalions ready for use against the
civilian population.[31] Trotsky himself could only cling to his faith, and
rejoice in the news that Soviet forces were now in control of Kiev.

On 7 February (25 January), he informed the conference that there was nothing left of the Rada government; that the Central Executive Committee of the Soviets of the Ukraine had been proclaimed the supreme power there and had 'adopted a federative connection with Russia'. Two days later, the delegates of the Quadruple Alliance signed a separate peace treaty with the representatives of the Rada. Trotsky might scathingly protest that the domains of the Ukrainian People's Republic were restricted to the rooms of its delegates at Brest-Litovsk; and General Hoffmann, confess to his diary that there was 'unfortunately ground for regarding Trotsky's statement as not unfounded'. What did it matter if the key of the Rada no longer fitted the lock? It would serve well enough for appearances, while the door to the Ukrainian granary was kicked open.

Trotsky had all but exhausted the possibilities of delay. At the most, a few more days might be gained, but only at the risk of permitting the impression to develop that Russia was blind to German designs upon the Ukraine or, worse, disposed to connive at them. On 10 February (28 January), Trotsky rose to address the conference:

We are removing our armies and our people from the war. Our peasant soldiers must return to their land to cultivate in peace the fields which the revolution has taken from the landlord and given to the peasants. Our workmen soldiers must return to the workshops and produce not for destruction but for creation. . . .

At the same time we declare that the conditions as submitted to us by the governments of Germany and Austria-Hungary are opposed in principle to the interests of all peoples. . . . We cannot place the signature of Russia under these conditions which bring with them oppression, misery and hate to millions of human beings.

Russia would not sign an annexationist treaty. Russia declared that the state of war with the members of the Quadruple Alliance was at an end. Russian troops were being ordered to demobilize along the entire front.

His adversaries sat stunned. There was no precedent, in all that they had ever learned and experienced, for such a course of conduct by a state. Indeed, it was with the single word, '*Unerhört!*' (literally, 'unheard of'), that General Hoffmann at last burst the silence. Von Kühlmann, groping for the proprieties, proposed a plenary session of the conference. But Trotsky replied that there was nothing left to discuss. The Soviet delegates withdrew and that night took the train back to Petrograd.

Recovering their composure, the diplomats were united in favouring the effective acceptance of Trotsky's formula. And in Vienna, there was rejoicing in the streets at the promised peace. But Hoffmann and the German high command were of a different mind. There would be no food from the Ukraine if they did not dispatch their armies to get it. And Ludendorff wanted the German line advanced to enclose Latvia and Estonia: so establishing, in the ethnic map of his mind, a cordon of conquest between Bolshevism and the Teutonic peoples of eastern Europe. Von Kühlmann resisted, but to no avail.

In Petrograd, the Soviet Central Executive Committee unanimously approved 'the action of its representatives at Brest-Litovsk'. Three days later, at noon on 16 February,[32] Trotsky was in Lenin's room, at a conference with Left Social Revolutionaries, when a telegram arrived from Brest-Litovsk, transmitting General Hoffmann's announcement that Germany would consider itself at war with Russia from midnight, 17/18 February. The conference was hurried to a close; and when the two men were alone, they turned to face each other over the news. Trotsky's own account records the terms of the argument, and cites some of Lenin's remarks, without conveying the mood.[33] But it would have been strange if acrimony had not accompanied exchanges which revealed how each had misunderstood the other and how far they still disagreed. All that remained, Lenin stated, was to sign the treaty as it stood, if the Germans would permit this. Trotsky insisted that Hoffmann should be left to start his offensive, so that the workers of Germany, and of the Allied countries also, would learn of it as a fact rather than just as a threat. 'No,' replied Lenin. 'We can't afford to lose a single hour now. The test has been made. . . . This beast jumps fast.'

When the central committee met on the 17th, Trotsky's attitude proved to be decisive, since the membership was, without him, evenly divided. By voting with the war group, he secured the defeat of Lenin's proposal for an immediate peace approach to Germany; and then, by voting with the peace group, the defeat of the proposal for revolutionary war. His own proposal, to delay any approach until the political and military impact of a German offensive became clear, was passed, with the backing of the war group, by a majority of one vote. In the early morning of the 18th, when the central committee met again, Trotsky reported that the offensive was a fact. Prince Leopold of Bavaria had proclaimed that it was Germany's mission to save the world from the 'moral infection' of Bolshevism. Once more, Lenin pressed his peace proposal. And once more, he was defeated, by Trotsky's vote. They must wait to see, Trotsky argued, whether the offensive would produce 'a serious explosion' in Germany.

The beast did, indeed, jump fast: snatching territory as though all that it needed to do was to follow its eyes. Hoffmann assured his diary that this was 'the most comic war' he had ever experienced. A few soldiers, with machine-guns, would be put on a train, travel to the nearest station, seize it and arrest 'the Bolsheviks', before another detachment rattled onwards, to the next station on the line. By the evening, when the central committee met to hear the latest reports, the German armies seemed to be rolling across Russia and about to invade the Ukraine. The argument was often acrid with recrimination. Lenin assailed those who were 'playing at war' and claimed that history would hold them responsible for having delivered the revolution to the enemy. 'We could have signed a peace that was not at all dangerous to the revolution.' Trotsky objected to the phrase, 'playing at war'. Had Lenin not agreed 'to feel out the Germans'? He himself was still against appealing for peace. It would be better to sound out German intentions and demands. Stalin wanted peace at once. 'I disagree with Trotsky,' he announced, and added sneeringly: 'To pose the question as he does is all right in literature.' No one spoke as though converted by events. And it seemed that Lenin's proposal would be defeated yet again. But when the vote came to be taken, Trotsky, to the surprise of all the others, abandoned his position and gave the peace group its majority.

Certainly, 'the point of a bayonet', which he had been so insistent must be seen, was now so plain that the workers of the West could hardly be confused any longer by claims of Bolshevik complicity with the German government. Yet it seems unlikely that this would altogether account for the sudden turn of his vote, after his argument for further delay. Indeed, he would not have been Trotsky, if the very challenge of German force had not urged him to meet rather than submit to it. But history was not a game of blind man's buff. It had looked, a few weeks before, that peace should be signed, on the terms provided, in the face of an offensive. And he had committed himself accordingly, at that meeting with Lenin. Well, then, let the success of Lenin's proposal establish whether those terms were still available. Here too, after all, was a way of gaining time, perhaps even of securing some pause in the offensive, while the possibility of material help from the Allies was explored. He had been seeing Bruce Lockhart, Britain's special agent in Petrograd, and assuring him of Russia's readiness for partisan warfare.[34]

On 19 February, despite the opposition of the Left Social Revolutionaries in the government, Lenin and Trotsky sent a radio message to Berlin, protesting against the German invasion, but agreeing to sign a peace treaty on the terms laid down at Brest-Litovsk, and promising prompt consideration of any further conditions. For three days, while the German armies continued to gobble up territory, there was no reply. Lockhart himself would record the open rejoicing of the Russian bourgeoisie at the prospect of its deliverance and the 'frenzied fury' with which the opposition press was 'emboldened . . . to attack the Bolsheviks'. The Soviet of People's Commissars issued an appeal for popular resistance and ordered the destruction of railways, food and munition stores in the path of the enemy. Trotsky told Lockhart that if the Allies would now send an assurance of support, he could sway the government in favour of war. And at a meeting of the central committee on the 22nd, he secured, by a majority of one vote, agreement to the policy of taking aid from the Allies, provided that no pledges, in any way infringing Soviet sovereignty or independence in foreign affairs, were required in return. Lenin had not been present but subsequently scribbled a note for the record: 'I ask to add my vote in favour of taking potatoes and arms from the bandits of Anglo-French imperialism.' Lockhart had meanwhile dispatched several telegrams to London, requesting a message that might strengthen Trotsky's hand. No message arrived.[35]

On 22 February, the German reply at last reached Petrograd. The former terms were no longer sufficient to buy peace. Now, all of Latvia and Estonia were to be ceded, while all Russian soldiers and Red Guards were to be withdrawn from Finland and the Ukraine. There was a twist of the bayonet in the requirement that the Soviet government sign a treaty with the Ukrainian Rada.

The complete demobilization of the Russian army, 'including the portions of any army newly formed by the present Government', was to be conducted without delay; and Russia should undertake to cease 'all official or officially supported agitation or propaganda' against the governments and army institutions of the Central Powers. Furthermore, there was to be neither negotiation nor any attempt at delay. The new terms must be accepted within forty-eight hours; Soviet representatives were to leave for Brest-Litovsk immediately, so that the treaty might be signed within three days; and ratification was to follow within two weeks.

When the central committee met on the 23rd, Lenin presented an ultimatum of his own. If these terms were not accepted, he would resign from the committee and from the government. Even Stalin was so shaken by the extent of German demands that he suggested an attempt to reopen negotiations. But Lenin was adamant. 'Stalin is wrong. We must sign on these conditions. If you do not accept them and sign, then you are signing the warrant for the death of the Soviet power, in three weeks' time.'[36]

The leadership of the party was now, almost certainly, Trotsky's for the taking. Within the central committee itself, he could give the war group a majority, and one that was likely to be sustained by the command posts of Bolshevism in the cities. Crucially, most members of the Petrograd committee and the entire Moscow regional bureau were in favour of revolutionary war.[37] It was not, of course, merely a matter of his vote. The essential weakness of the war group lay in its lack of a leader whose prestige among the mass of party militants, or of workers and soldiers outside, stood the slightest chance of successfully defying Lenin's own. If Trotsky would accept direction of the war group, then the split in the party might be made to represent a rupture not with the leadership of the revolution, but with a particular leader whose demand for the revolution's surrender had been rejected. 'If Lenin threatens to resign,' declared Lomov, chief of the Moscow Bolsheviks, 'that is nothing to be terrified about. We must take power without Lenin.'

Trotsky himself dismissed Lenin's claim that the Soviets were incapable of defending themselves. A unanimous leadership could organize a resistance that would survive even the loss of Petrograd and Moscow, while keeping 'the whole world in tension'. And of what value was the alternative? 'If we sign this German ultimatum today, we may be confronted by another one tomorrow. . . . We may gain peace, but we shall lose the support of the advanced elements of the proletariat.' Yet, for all this, he proceeded to announce that he would not stand in Lenin's way. 'We cannot wage revolutionary war with a split in the party. . . . I shall not take upon myself the responsibility of voting for war.'

There had been splits in the party before, at times that had been scarcely perilous: in the preparation of the October uprising and, soon afterwards, over the refusal to conciliate the moderate socialists, amidst the first trumpetings of civil war. Unity had been rapidly restored not by bending to pressure from the minority, but by resolutely pursuing the policies that the majority had adopted. But on this occasion, it would be a split with Lenin in the minority, and Lenin's influence was not limited to his membership of the central committee. He had the will and the means to take the whole issue down from the balcony into the streets of the party, and his threat to resign from the central committee was an unmistakable warning of this. It was inconceivable that in the conditions of revolutionary war, he should be permitted to do so. Yet it was inconceivable, too, that he could be prevented by constitutional procedures. Sooner or later – and the sooner, the more safely – measures of terror would have to be instituted inside the party, to silence him and all of those who continued to resist in his name. Nor would the process stop there. While comrade hunted down comrade to protect the new leadership, the border between legitimate criticism and the effectively subversive must become so blurred as to require the denial of any real democratic functioning. Some fifteen years before, Trotsky had denounced a Leninism that might lead to placing above the proletariat one person invested with the power to liquidate and degrade. Was he now, in a climax of irony, to find himself forced, by the logic of events, to play the role of the single dictator?

In the vote of the central committee, Trotsky abstained; as did his disciple Joffe, Dzerzhinsky, and one other member of the war group, Krestinsky. Lenin commanded seven votes for peace. And the four who voted against him, then resigned, in protest, from their offices in both the party and the government. Trotsky felt no less keenly than they did the shame of submission to German demands. He wished, he announced, to resign immediately as Commissar of Foreign Affairs and to withdraw from all institutions of government. But the central committee urged him to consider how dangerous this would be. And he eventually agreed to make his resignation public only after the treaty had been signed, and to attend at least those meetings of the government at which foreign affairs were not due to be discussed. Stalin suggested that the four recalcitrants of the war group, in resigning all their offices, had shown such disregard of discipline as to place themselves outside the party. But Lenin and Trotsky turned on him at once, and he hastily retreated.

The defeated might now sit back with a sour smile. For there was a conspicuous scramble among the victors to escape the honour of heading the delegation that would soon have to leave for Brest-Litovsk. The most impassioned in the pursuit of peace now shrank from putting his name indelibly on the document that would produce it. At last, Sokolnikov, after threatening to resign from the central committee rather than undertake such a commission, allowed himself to be conscripted. And, on 3 March, he duly signed the treaty: making it clear that he was doing so under duress, by merely glancing at the text and refusing to discuss the contents. As Trotsky had predicted, the acceptance of one ultimatum had merely provoked another. New terms notably included the surrender to Turkey of territory in the Caucacus. In all, the former Russian empire lost slightly more than a quarter of its population, of its railways, and of its sown area; half of its industrial plant and equipment; three-quarters of its iron and steel capacity; and no less than 90 per cent of its coal production.[38]

'If the German Emperor', crowed the *Münchener Post*, 'had demanded Moscow as his capital and a summer residence in the Ural Mountains, the Russians would have signed without winking an eyelash.' But there were those in Germany who did not exult. Already in the Reichstag, to jeers and hisses from the right, a spokesman for the left had expressed indignation and foreboding.

> We fought to defend our country from Tsarism but we are not fighting for the partition of Russia. . . . We do not wish in the circumstances to attain a dominating position which would force us to conclude a peace with the Entente on such terms as those on which Lenin and Trotsky are now concluding peace with the Quadruple Alliance.[39]

On 6 March, there opened, at the Tauride Palace, the emergency Seventh Congress of the party, which was to decide whether or not to recommend ratification of the treaty to the forthcoming Congress of Soviets. In the event, Bukharin's proposal to refuse ratification was decisively defeated. But this issue came to be almost a side-show, as argument raged over the role that Trotsky had played. In his initial speech on the need to ratify the treaty, Lenin referred to Trotsky's 'great mistake', in pressing the formula of 'neither war nor peace', on the basis of a belief that the Germans would not attack. Radek, from the war group, was soon on his feet, to defend the formula: describing it as one of 'revolutionary realism', and reproaching Trotsky himself only for having decided, after achieving so much at Brest-Litovsk, to join 'the other side'. Trotsky justified both his original policy and its abandonment to prevent a split in the party. But there must, he maintained, be a limit to surrender. The demand of the Germans that the Soviet government sign a separate peace treaty with the puppet Ukrainian Rada must be rejected, as a betrayal of the Ukrainian workers and peasants. In their headlong pursuit of peace, Lenin and his group were in danger of 'sacrificing life's only end for the sake of mere living'. Lenin replied by once more threatening to resign his offices if his freedom of action was restricted in this way. And he drew a large majority of the delegates behind him.

All the more insistently did Trotsky and those who were loyal to him seek some formal expression of approval for his Brest-Litovsk policy. There was much more to this than the issue of a compress for the inflammation of his injured pride. Lenin had imposed an initial retreat which might soon enough reveal the danger of persisting in the process. And what Trotsky sought was that the congress should recognize this, much as he himself had done in the central committee: by an abstention which effectively allowed Lenin his peace treaty, for the sake of keeping the party together, while indicating that defiance of the German ultimatum would have been the more faithful, and finally, therefore, the more creative, revolutionary way. Such an abstention would have been registered by retrospective assent to the formula of 'neither war nor peace', which had prepared the moral ground for the policy of defiance. But just such an abstention Trotsky failed to get. And it was small comfort that the congress should have expressed its continuing confidence in his value to the revolution by placing him, with Lenin, at the top of the poll in the election of a new central committee.

It has long been a platitude of historiography outside the Soviet system, and the most inviolable of dogmas inside, that Lenin rescued the revolution from virtually certain disaster by imposing his policy of peace upon the party. Trotsky was to pay his own tribute, at a joint meeting of the main government institutions, on 3 October 1918, or seven months to the day from the signing of the treaty.

I deem it my duty to say, in this authoritative assembly, that at the hour when many of us, including myself, were doubtful as to whether it was admissible for us to sign the Brest-Litovsk peace, only Comrade Lenin maintained stubbornly, with amazing foresight and against our opposition, that we had to go through with it to tide us over until the revolution of the world proletariat. And now, we must admit that we were wrong.[40]

It seemed an appropriate moment for such a tribute. On 3 October, Prince Max von Baden, the new German chancellor, appointed to put the imperial scheme into liquidation, addressed to President Wilson an appeal for an immediate armistice. It was clear that Germany was close to military collapse. And clearly, too, it was close to revolution. Indeed, revolution would break out at last, one month later, as the Allies hammered home their demand for unconditional surrender. It would not be, or become, the sort of socialist revolution that the Soviet government had been hoping for history to provide. But the Russian revolution itself had no more to fear from German arms and might look now to regaining much, if not all, of the territory that it had surrendered to force. The Treaty of Brest-Litovsk was to be annulled by Germany, in terms of the general armistice concluded on 11 November. And on 28 June 1919, Germany would sign, among the mirrors of Versailles, a Brest-Litovsk peace of its own.

Yet, what if the advocates of revolutionary war had not been wrong? What if, in February 1918, Trotsky had voted with the war group in the central committee, and the Soviet government had defied the German ultimatum? Was there anything more that Germany was likely to have done than it was doing already? It might have been provoked to take Petrograd. But the revolution was moving its capital to Moscow in any event, and a German march to Moscow would have been an altogether different matter. Napoleon had not simultaneously been waging a war in the west when he set out for Moscow; and even then, the precedent was scarcely an encouraging one. In fact, the German high command was all too aware of the risks involved in probing Russian weakness too far. As Ludendorff himself was to reveal in his memoirs, 'a deep German offensive had been out of the question', and only 'a short energetic thrust' had been planned.[41]

Nor was the German military morale anywhere as solid as would have sustained an attempt to occupy much of Russia. German divisions on the eastern front proved an easy prey to the propaganda spread, in contravention of the treaty, by leaflet or by word of mouth. As Hoffmann himself would subsequently admit to an American journalist: 'Immediately after conquering those Bolsheviks, we were conquered by them. Our victorious army on the Eastern Front became rotten with Bolshevism. We got to the point where we did not dare to transfer certain of our eastern divisions to the West.'[42] Indeed, on 8 August, or little more than five months after the ratification of the treaty, significant numbers of German troops in the west began inviting capture by offering no resistance.

In both Finland and the Ukraine, there was a considerable sector of the population behind the cause of the Soviets. Partisan warfare, supplied with trained men and with material from the vast expanses of Russia beyond the German grasp, and recruiting more and more support on the spot from the very experience of German occupation, might soon have convinced the German high command that the conquests of Brest-Litovsk were not worth their running costs. Even in its abandonment by the Russian revolution, the Ukraine was to prove difficult to digest. Stirred by German exactions and the return of the landlords, peasants took to forming guerilla bands, which cut off small parties of soldiers and raided the great estates, while Left Social Revolutionaries, resorting to their own tried methods, assassinated the German military commander and blew up powder stores at Odessa and Kiev. Had the Soviet government nourished this resistance, the Germans would have faced an evident choice of evils. To limit reprisals to the Ukraine would have left the guerilla forces free to retreat at will, for immediate safety and reinforcement, across the frontier. To extend reprisals by advancing the line of conquest would have increased the area of local insurgency and the number of troops required to sustain any semblance of control. In fact, of course, given the overriding importance of the western front, there was virtually no chance that the German high command would have chosen to extend the struggle in the east.

Furthermore, a Soviet government committed to revolutionary war would have retained the allegiance of the Left Social Revolutionaries and accordingly a broader appeal, especially in the countryside. Not least, the Allied governments, even had they still refused to provide the regime with any material aid, would have been deprived of occasion to intervene against it instead. In the event, and largely to deal with such intervention, the regime would create, and in conditions arguably far more unfavourable than those at the time of Brest-Litovsk, a Red Army that would triumph, under Trotsky's leadership, over foreign and domestic enemies alike. Might it not have done so, to similar effect, out of the need to resist the Germans? Would Lenin really have pressed his opposition to the point of attempting to divide the ranks of the party, once the decision to conduct revolutionary war had been translated into actual measures? And, if he had made the attempt, would he have mustered much of a following?

As it was, the Soviet government stood by, while the Germans crushed the revolutionary regimes in Finland and the Ukraine. And the fall of the Ukraine was to furnish, indirectly, the Allied governments with both incentive and pretext to intervene. Fighting to slow the German advance were some 30,000 Czechoslovak soldiers, who had been mobilized under the sponsorship of the Kerensky government, mainly from deserters and prisoners-of-war, to serve with the Russian armies. Driven from the Ukraine and all prospect of contributing on the eastern front to the defeat of the hated Habsburg empire, they began moving eastwards across Russia towards Vladivostok, where they hoped for Allied help in reaching France and the war in the west. Largely at first through a mutual misunderstanding of motives, they soon clashed with Soviet detachments and emerged from the ensuing conflict the virtual masters of Siberia.

It was a doorknob that the Allied governments were quick to turn. They dispatched forces of their own 'to succour', in the record of Lloyd George, 'the Czecho-Slovak troops in the Urals and Vladivostok, and enable them either to reconstitute an anti-German front in combination with the pro-Ally Cossacks and other Nationalist forces in Russia, or to withdraw safely and join the Allied forces in the West'.[43] Two thousand British troops seized Archangel on 2 August, to overthrow the local Soviet and set up a Provisional Government of the North. On the following day, British and Japanese troops landed at Vladivostok, in advance of two American regiments from the Philippines and a small French force from Indochina. The wars of intervention had begun. And the Communist Party, as Bolshevism had renamed itself in March 1918, stood alone.

Immediately after the Fourth Congress of Soviets ratified the Treaty of Brest-Litovsk, the Left Social Revolutionaries withdrew in protest from the Soviet of People's Commissars. They continued to serve in most departments of government, but in expectation less of avoiding than of preparing the occasion for a break. The *peredishka* or 'breathing space' for which Lenin had so ardently argued the necessity of signing the peace seemed more and more the gasps of a critically ill asthmatic. Hunger riots erupted in a number of towns, as the supply of food further diminished. It was not only that Russia had lost the granary of the Ukraine and that the surpluses of the Volga provinces and Siberia were now under the control of forces hostile to the regime. Peasants elsewhere, offered only bundles of paper roubles with which they could purchase nothing that they wanted, preferred to hoard their stocks or turn them into whisky. In the moral climate of a partisan war against the German invader, and with the enthusiastic backing of the Left Social Revolutionaries, the regime might have encountered a more co-operative mood in the countryside. In the existing circumstances, it was driven to rely on compulsion.

A government decree in May 1918 invested the People's Commissariat of Supply with powers to dismiss or reorganize local food authorities and 'apply armed force in the event of resistance being offered to the removal of grain or other natural products'. In June, a further decree established 'committees of poor peasants' to wrest grain surpluses from the richer proprietors. The Left Social Revolutionaries were all the more antagonized by a policy that seemed to them, as one of their spokesmen claimed, 'little short of war declared by the town on the country'.[44]

On 4 July, the Fifth Congress of Soviets opened at the Moscow Opera House. And nothing ever performed there in the times of the Tsar could have exceeded in dramatic force what was soon to occur. On the second day, Maria Spiridonova rose from her seat at one end of the long Presidium table on the stage. At first, her voice was little more than a nervous trickle. But soon it was swelling and leaping towards hysteria; her right arm moving up and down in rhythm. Turning to Lenin, she accused him of betraying the peasants; of using them only to serve ends of his own. And arriving at her climax, she cried: 'When the peasants, the Bolshevik peasants, the Left Social Revolutionary peasants, and the non-party peasants, are alike humiliated, oppressed and crushed – crushed as peasants – in my hand you will still find the same pistol, the same bomb, which once forced me to defend. . . .' The remaining words were lost in the acclaim of her followers. A Communist delegate hurled some obscenity at her. Left Social Revolutionaries jumped to their feet and shook their fists. Lenin walked slowly to the front of the stage; pausing to pat Sverdlov, who was presiding , on the shoulder, and tell him to put his bell away. Then, holding the lapels of his coat, he stood smiling at the uproar before him. When at last he managed to make himself heard, he coldly proceeded to defend the Brest-Litovsk Treaty and came so to dominate his audience that even some of the Left Social Revolutionaries cheered him at the end of his speech.

But it was to be a very short-lived armistice. Kamkov, one of the leading Left Social Revolutionary orators, rose to launch an impassioned attack on the treaty. Reaching his peroration, he strode across the stage towards the box where the German ambassador, Count Mirbach, was sitting, and thundered: 'The dictatorship of the proletariat has developed into a dictatorship of Mirbach. In spite of all our warnings the policy of Lenin remains the same, and we are become, not an independent Power, but the lackeys of the German Imperialists, who have the audacity to show their faces even in this theatre.' At once the Left Social Revolutionaries were on their feet; roaring insults and waving their fists at the box. Hastily Sverdlov rang his bell and declared the session at an end.[45]

When the delegates reassembled on the 6th, in the middle of a hot and heavy afternoon, many of the seats on the stage were empty, as was the box reserved for the German diplomats. Most of the prominent Left Social Revolutionaries, including Maria Spiridonova, were in their places. More and more of the leading Bolsheviks who had taken their own seats were seen to leave. At six o'clock, the first reports rustled through the audience that the Opera House had been surrounded by troops and that all exits were barred. British and French special agents, present as observers and alarmed at the prospect of a search, tore any compromising papers that they carried into tiny pieces, which they stuffed down the lining of the sofa cushions or, still more circumspectly, swallowed. Those delegates and visitors who had long been stirring with murmured speculation were soon to have their puzzlement relieved.

A little before three o'clock, two Left Social Revolutionaries had driven to the German embassy and, gaining admittance with forged authority from the Cheka, the political police of the regime, had assassinated Count Mirbach. It was part of a Left Social Revolutionary revolt. But so negligent had been the rest of the planning that Trotsky, who took personal charge of counter-measures, easily defeated the attempt, with the few detachments at his disposal. The Left Social Revolutionary delegates at the Opera House were arrested. They offered no protest, let alone resistance.

Maria Spiridonova would subsequently insist that the central committee of her party had never intended to overthrow the government. And when Dzerzhinsky, seeking the assassins of Mirbach, fell into the hands of the main Left Social Revolutionary force, he was told by its leaders:

> You have before you an accomplished fact; the Brest-Litovsk Treaty is torn up; war with Germany is unavoidable. We don't want power; let it be here as in the Ukraine; we will go underground. You can remain in power; but you must stop being lackeys of Mirbach. Let Germany occupy Russia up to the Volga. [46]

Forcing the revolution into war seems to have been the only clear objective; and the attempt to snatch control of the capital, a sort of back-up weapon to the assassination, rather as a terrorist might seek to provide himself with a knife in case his pistol failed to fire. For surely the murder of Mirbach would provoke Germany to reopen hostilities, or at least make such punitive demands that even the most timorous of the Communists must be drawn to defiance.

Germany, however, was not disposed to oblige. The assassination of an ambassador was certainly provoking, but it did not change the calculation of military priorities. Lenin was left in possession of his breathing space. Most of the Left Social Revolutionary leaders were imprisoned, and amnestied a few months later. But some, and in particular those who were held to have abused their trust as officials of the Cheka, were executed. For the party itself, there was no forgiveness, and it was forthwith expelled from the Soviets. Many of its members, rather than accept their isolation from the regime, joined the Communist Party. Blumkin, one of the assassins, went into hiding for a while, then offered his services to the Soviet government; was formally pardoned; and found employment with the political police.

Whether a rejection of the Brest-Litovsk treaty in the face of Lenin's threats would have necessitated the establishment of a different dictatorship cannot be known. It might, on the contrary, have summoned the development of democracy, as essential to the effective conduct of revolutionary war. What is known is what followed the signing of the peace and the resultant rupture in the revolutionary alliance. The Soviets, deprived of the Left Social Revolutionaries, lost – as Rosa Luxemburg had warned – all their vitality. They became no more than the mirror of the Communist

Party. And because the Soviets constitutionally embodied the state, the Party itself became, in the minds of its members, the state by another name. To defy the party was to defy the state. To defy the state was treason. And to discourage such treason, the regime came increasingly to rely on terror.

'If the attribute of popular government in peace is virtue,' Robespierre declared, 'the attribute of popular government in revolution is at one and the same time *virtue and terror*, virtue without which terror is fatal, terror without which virtue is impotent.'[47] And Thomas Jefferson was to defend the terror of the French revolution in his very acknowledgement that it had been often unjust.

In the struggle which was necessary many guilty persons fell without the forms of trial, and, with them, some innocent. These I deplore as much as anybody and shall deplore some of them to the day of my death. But I deplore them as I should have done had they fallen in battle. It was necessary to use the arm of the people, a machine not quite so blind as balls and bombs, but blind to a certain degree.[48]

Marx himself provided his disciples with the clearest guidance on the subject. In the autumn of 1848, denouncing 'the cannibalism of the counter-revolution,' he proclaimed that there was 'only one means to curtail, simplify and localize the bloody agony of the old society and the bloody birth-pangs of the new, only one means – the revolutionary terror.'[49]

Lenin, of course, never doubted the need for such terror. But Trotsky, too, from the earliest days of the new regime, warned that it would be 'merciless' in defending the conquests of the revolution. 'We shall not enter into the kingdom of socialism,' he advised a Congress of Peasants' Deputies, 'in white gloves on a polished floor.' When the regime outlawed the Cadets, he gave a more ominous direction to his threats.

At the time of the French revolution more honest men than the Cadets were guillotined by the Jacobins for opposing the people. We have not executed any-one and do not intend to, but there are moments when the fury of the people is hard to control.[50]

And in the middle of 1920, Trotsky would write *The Defence of Terrorism*, in reply to an attack by Karl Kautsky, the German Social Democratic leader, on the Red Terror.

The problem of revolution, as of war, consists in breaking the will of the foe, forcing him to capitulate and to accept the conditions of the conqueror. . . . The bourgeoisie itself conquered power by means of revolts, and consolidated it by the civil war. In the peaceful period, it retains power by means of a system of repression. As long as class society, founded on the most deep-rooted antagon-isms, continues to exist, repressions remain a necessary means of breaking the will of the opposing side. . . . The degree of ferocity of the struggle depends on a series of internal and international circumstances. The more ferocious and dangerous is the resistance of the class enemy who has been overthrown, the more inevitably does the system of repression take the form of a system of terror.[51]

Rosa Luxemburg took a different view. The programme of the German Communist Party, which she drafted in December 1918, proclaimed: 'The proletarian revolution needs for its purposes no terror, it hates and abominates murder.' But then the German Communist Party was not given much occasion to propagate this principle. In the following month, whatever immediate revolutionary challenge it might have represented was crushed by the Social Democratic government; and Rosa Luxemburg herself, along with Karl Liebknecht, murdered in Berlin by army officers. The murders had been repeatedly incited, and were afterwards excused, by *Vorwaerts*, the official paper of the Social Democratic Party, which announced that Liebknecht had been 'shot while attempting to escape', and that Rosa Luxemburg had been 'killed by the people'. In the developing struggle between revolution and reaction, revolutionaries could no more escape the use of terror by renouncing it than soldiers on one side in a war might avoid the effects of artillery by refusing to use it themselves. And, indeed, the White Terror was first, by far, in the ferocity of reprisal and intimidation.

On 13 January 1918, De Robien wrote in his diary:

> The Cossacks and the Bolsheviks are fighting savagely in the Caucasus and on the Don. A few days ago three sealed wagons with the inscription 'fresh meat, destination Petrograd' arrived at one of the Petrograd stations. When the wagons were opened they were found to be filled with piles of the stiffened corpses of Red Guards, covered with frozen blood, with grimacing faces, placed in obscene positions.... I certainly no longer have any sympathy for the Bolsheviks ... but I cannot find words to describe this ghoulish farce.[52]

In fact, for some months after its establishment by the Soviet of People's Commissars on 7 December 1917, the Cheka, or 'Extraordinary Commission' to combat counter-revolution and sabotage, displayed little of the blade that the rhetoric of Trotsky had threatened. It was in the summer of 1918, when substantial Allied intervention was unmistakably imminent; when the capital seethed with rumours and reports of conspiracies; and when riot and revolt in the provinces were beckoning to the armies of reaction, that the Red Terror really began. The former Tsar, his wife and children were reportedly shot, by order of the regional Soviet, at Ekaterinburg, on the night of 16/17 July, some ten days before the capture of the town by Czechoslovak forces. De Robien commented in his diary: 'The Bolsheviks have turned savage and have certainly changed during the last fortnight. I am afraid that the Russian revolution, which up to now has hardly shed any blood, has entered a period of Terror.'[53]

And here, the Left Social Revolutionary challenge was material not only because, despite its failure, it was bound to sharpen still further the alarm of the government. The ensuing purge of Left Social Revolutionaries from the Cheka eliminated those whose distinctive political outlook had in itself constituted an internal restraint on the institution's activities. And the very failure of the challenge might well have convinced certain of the Social Revolutionaries that the only effective means of opposition lay in the old commitment to terrorism. On 20 August, Uritsky, who was now chairman of the local Cheka, was assassinated in Petrograd; and Lenin himself, seriously wounded in Moscow. The Cheka struck back at once. In Petrograd alone, more than 500 hostages were summarily shot, while the victims in Moscow included 'many Tsarist ministers and a whole list of high personages'.

A revolutionary leadership that had contended with the Okhrana of the Tsars was, of course, well aware of the depravities to which a political police was professionally prone. But it hoped that those appointed to direct the Cheka would, by their integrity and discipline, secure the proper loyalties of subordinates. Dzerzhinsky, who was put in supreme charge, had, with his high forehead and burning eyes, his long bony nose and his beard, the look of some Grand Inquisitor. And there was, indeed, a sort of terrible piety in the pitilessness with which he pursued his mission. Yet if this was a fire that all too often seemed blind, it was at least one that burned within the moral bounds of a revolutionary devotion. There were few so devoted who chose to serve the revolution in the role of its spies and executioners. As the Cheka extended its operations, its recruitment included more and more of those drawn by the opportunity to satisfy some depraved appetite of their own: while others were soon corrupted by the pressure of example; by the fungus of conspiracy and suspicion which grew along their lives; by a very solidarity of violence, in response to the fear and the hatred that their profession aroused.

9

The Heel of Achilles

On 13 March 1918, it was announced that Trotsky had resigned as Commissar of Foreign Affairs to become Commissar of War and Chairman of the Supreme War Council. No one was more aware than he himself of his inadequate preparation for his new responsibilities. Apart from that short campaign against Krasnov's Cossacks, he had seen battle only from behind the lines, as a war correspondent, or waged across the pages of military books. He tried to argue. But he had no answer to the challenge flung at him by Lenin and Sverdlov: 'Whom else can we appoint? Name them!'

As Trotsky moved to take direction of defence, the capital itself was moved from Petrograd to Moscow, despite some strong opposition from a minority within the leadership. It was not so long ago that the party had denounced as treachery the Kerensky government's design to move the capital. How, then, were the workers of Petrograd to be persuaded that they were not about to be betrayed? And what confidence could the people of Russia have in a revolutionary government that withdrew from the very home of the revolution? But Lenin and Trotsky insisted that with the government there, Petrograd was as alluring as it was vulnerable; while, without the government, it would be merely another cold and hungry city, whose capture the Germans, or any other foreign enemy, were bound to consider more of a burden than a prize. There was, in the event, little resistance to the move. And by succeeding where Kerensky had failed, the revolutionary government, in admitting its weakness, revealed also its strength.

The Smolny, with its past as a school for the daughters of the nobility, had been a paradoxical place for the revolutionary command post of the future. But the Kremlin, with its medieval wall and its gilded cupolas, provided a paradox still more striking and more pertinent. For here, among the beginnings of imperial Russia, were constant reminders of the cultural backwardness which the revolution had to confront. The musical clock on the Spassky tower was reconstructed to ring out the *Internationale* instead of *God Save the Tsar* each quarter of an hour. And the double-headed gilt eagle over the tower was deprived of its crown. But the outlook of the Russian multitudes was not to be altered so easily by a few men on scaffolding high above the ground.

The Trotsky household was provided with rooms, across the corridor from Lenin and Krupskaya, in a building previously occupied by officials of the Kremlin. And the two families generally dined together, from plates decorated with the double-headed eagle, whose correct positioning was assiduously secured by an old servant flitting behind the chairs and silently turning the plates this way or that. He had waited on more than óne Tsar and became no less loyally attached to the two commissars, whose meals of vegetable soup and unpolished buckwheat were so different from those he had served. But the entire staff of attendants was soon dismissed. And the old servant was found a suitable place in a palace that had been turned into a museum. Natalia herself, joining the Commissariat of Education, was put in charge of museums and ancient monuments. And occasions for dispute between her department and the Commissariat of War were abundant. As the civil war raged, the museum officials denounced the military commissars for disregarding the claims of culture; the military commissars, the museum officials, for setting the interests of the dead above those of the living. To outsiders, Trotsky would recall in his memoirs, he seemed engaged in an endless departmental quarrel with Natalia. And their relationship became the butt of frequent jokes.

Soon after their arrival in Moscow, they were joined by an unexpected refugee. Trotsky's father, now in his seventies, had been dispossessed in the rural upheaval and left Yanovka to seek the relative safety of Odessa. He travelled the whole perilous distance on foot and was stopped along the way by different groups of partisans. Bolshevik supporters, to whom the name of Bronstein meant nothing, insulted him as a *kulak* or rich peasant. Bolshevik opponents, better informed, abused him as the father of that execrable Jew, Bronstein-Trotsky. After this, even Odessa seemed unsafe, and he made his way to Moscow.

Father and son greeted each other with warmth. But if old Bronstein was proud of his son's importance, he refused to show it. Natalia noticed 'a little mischievous flash in his eyes' as he would complain: 'we fathers slave away all our lives to put something by for our old age, and then the sons come along and make a revolution'. He was given a job on a state farm and would work productively there till his death from typhus in 1922. Natalia would recall him as 'large-boned, well-built, tall, with prominent features, a white beard and deep-set blue eyes . . . a man of great vitality and strength of character . . . having one of those simple Russian faces painters so often give to mystics and village elders'.[1]

Trotsky himself had nothing but scorn for the belief that socialism could

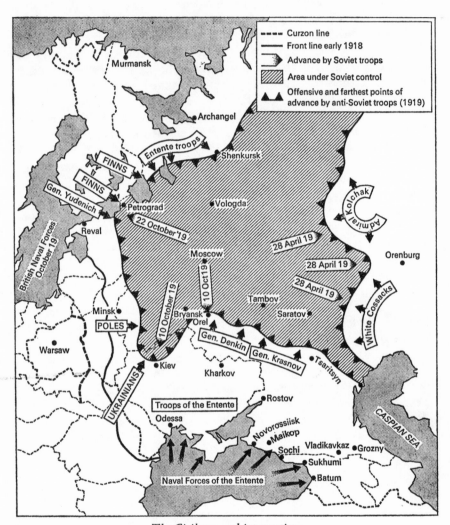

The Civil war and interventions

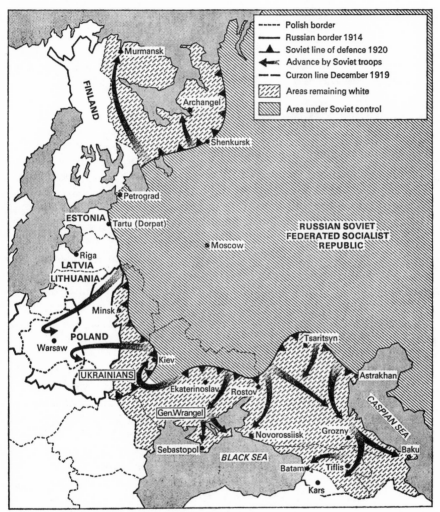

Legend:
- - - - - - Polish border
———— Russian border 1914
▲▲▲ Soviet line of defence 1920
◀——— Advance by Soviet troops
– – – – Curzon line December 1919
▨ Areas remaining white
▩ Area under Soviet control

Murmansk

FINLAND

Archangel

Shenkursk

Petrograd

ESTONIA

Tartu (Dorpat)

Riga

LATVIA

LITHUANIA

Minsk

POLAND

Warsaw

UKRAINIANS

Kiev

Moscow

RUSSIAN SOVIET
FEDERATED SOCIALIST
REPUBLIC

Tsaritsyn

Astrakhan

Ekaterinoslav

Rostov

Gen.Wrangel

Sebastopol

Novorossiisk

Grozny

CASPIAN SEA

Baku

BLACK SEA

Batam

Tiflis

Kars

The end of the Civil war 1920/21

somehow be attained in the middle of the air, by leaping from the past, as from half-way up a cliff. And what applied to the attainment of socialism applied no less to the prerequisite defence of the revolution. This did not mean attempting to preserve what remained of the old army; any more than using the industrial equipment of Tsarism meant preserving what remained of the old economic system. It did mean that the new army should readily employ the military skills of those officers who had served in the old and who now offered to serve the revolution. The value of this policy had been proved for Trotsky in the earlier battles against Krasnov's Cossacks. But this did not diminish the opposition that he once again encountered.

Against him were the so-called Left Communists like Bukharin, who had pressed for revolutionary war at the time of Brest-Litovsk and who pressed now for armies organized along the most libertarian lines. For them, the officers of the old army bore the ineradicable guilt of their association with the defence of Tsarism; were almost certain to prove treacherous; and in any event, would bring with them the fatal infection of the old disciplines. But resorting to such arguments as well were those who had pressed for the peace of Brest-Litovsk, and who resisted Trotsky's policy less from any attachment to libertarian principles than from a concern that it might confront the encampments of their own authority. Nor was Lenin himself convinced that Trotsky was right. While he gave emphatic support to the employment of civilian 'specialists' and insisted that these be treated with due respect, he reserved judgement on the employment of military ones. Trotsky, however, was not to be denied. If he was to bear the responsibility for organizing the army of the revolution, he demanded the right to determine the appropriate means.

If his opponents were not prepared to go as far as proposing that the responsibility be taken from him, they none the less assailed his policy. Lashevich, head of the party's military section, in an evident endeavour to discourage the officers from offering their services, proclaimed that the party would make use of the old generals only to 'squeeze them like lemons and then throw them away'. One such old general, who had already volunteered, protested in an open letter to Trotsky that he had not come forward in order to be treated like a lemon. Trotsky's reply went further than mere reassurance. Former generals, he declared, however conservative their outlook, who gave conscientious service to the revolution, deserved more respect from the working class than did those 'pseudo-socialists who engage in intrigue'. It was not a statement calculated to conciliate his critics. But he was not interested in massaging their minds. He wanted, rather, to ring an alarm, that men would be judged not by their pretensions or their past, but by their real and present readiness to serve as the revolution required.

His insistence on employing former officers was not the only source of dissension. There was resistance as well to the tightness of control that he sought to impose on the military command. His critics complained of his despotic disposition. But he was confronted by a very chaos of parochialism, so that in the Ukraine alone there were numerous local leaders who styled themselves commander-in-chief. 'Every county', Trotsky complained, 'almost every township, believes that the Soviet power can be best defended by concentrating on the territory of the given township as much as possible of aviation *matériel*, radio equipment, rifles, armoured cars.'[2] This was a recipe for disaster in any organization of defence. And it was in supreme contradiction to Trotsky's essential strategy. For he saw in the very encirclement of the Soviet republic by various enemies and the very contraction of its territory a corresponding advantage. With shortened lines of communication, the army could the more effectively concentrate its forces to strike at the most vital or vulnerable point along the enormous front. It was not personal temperament or political principle but military logic that informed Trotsky's insistence on a centralized structure of command.

The government provided by decree for universal conscription. But Trotsky himself decided that the Red Army should depend at the beginning on the moral commitment of volunteers. The military specialists argued that such recruitment would not lend itself to the development of the necessary discipline. Trotsky replied that the volunteers would bring along their own revolutionary discipline, to make all the easier, with their example and help, the imposition of discipline on the conscripts to come. His approach was essentially one of political osmosis, which he then applied to the processes of conscription itself. The first conscripts, enlisted in June 1918, were drawn from among the workers of Moscow and Petrograd. And only when he was satisfied that the Red Army had a sufficiently strong proletarian content did Trotsky move to conscript the poorest of the peasants.

Above all, he relied on party members; insisting that in each platoon, section and squad there should be a Communist, even if a young one – 'but devoted to the cause'. And, indeed, these Communists were to be the white corpuscles of the Red Army; moving at once to combat any infection of despair and to close any opening in the line. The cost was correspondingly great. There were some 180,000 of them in the army at the start of October 1919; some 280,000 by the end of the civil war; and, in between, no less than 50,000 lost their lives at the front.[3]

Kerensky had appointed commissars to be his shadows in the army. They had been attached only to the highest commands, and their functions had been as insubstantial as their purpose. Trotsky attached a commissar to every officer, from the level of company command to the 'top' military post, and defined their respective functions. The officer was responsible for military training and the conduct of military operations; the commissar, for the morale of the troops and the loyalty of the officer. No order was valid without the approval of both. It was an arrangement that gave rise to mutual resentment and to rivalry. But it worked. And without it, the Red Army would almost certainly have lacked either the skills or the morale to survive.

It was an arrangement whose success owed much to trust in Trotsky's personal leadership. For from the first, he showed himself concerned to promote dedication, aptitude and initiative; to repel obsequiousness; and to defend duty against intrigue. And if there were those who resented this, as an obstacle to their advancement, there were many more who valued it, as an assurance that they would be treated with justice. It is not necessary to accept the assertions of his followers. The very fear that came to be expressed by his adversaries, that he might call out the army against their command of the state, was their acknowledgement of the deep and widespread loyalty that his qualities of leadership had earned.

In August 1918, the crushing of the Soviet republic must have seemed to most observers a mere matter of time. In the north, British forces had established a Provisional Government. In the south, Krasnov had raised a Cossack army from the region of the Don. To the east, the Czechoslovaks were assailing Kazan, on the further bank of the Volga. And in the west, the Germans, who already occupied Lithuania, Latvia, White Russia and the Ukraine, were threatening to advance still further, if forces in league with the Allies looked like capturing Moscow. On 7 August, Trotsky left by special train for the Volga front and learned during the journey that Kazan had fallen. There was now little in the way of a Czechoslovak advance across the plains, to take Moscow itself.

At Sviyazhsk, the closest substantial station to Kazan, he halted the train and set out to rally troops who were slipping from demoralization into panic. He had brought with him fifty young members of the party and he flung these into the midst of the battle. They fell, one after the other, in their reckless devotion, before his eyes. The nearby Latvian regiment, badly mauled, threatened him with 'dangerous consequences' if it was not immediately relieved. He summoned the commander and the chairman of the regimental committee. With only his communications officer for support, he risked their resistance and placed them both under arrest. The commander was committed to trial by a revolutionary tribunal and was subsequently sentenced to imprisonment. The regiment remained at its post. Trotsky issued an order, which was printed on the press in his train and distributed throughout the army: if any unit retreated without orders to do so, its commissar and then its commander would be shot. His resolution was soon put to the test. A fresh regiment, on which he had been relying, suddenly abandoned its ground and seized the steamer that was being held for the headquarters staff. All eyes turned to the river. Trotsky ordered a small party of trusted men to board an improvised gunboat and arrest the deserters. A single shot might have produced a mutinous stampede. But the gamble succeeded. The deserters surrendered without resistance. Trotsky appointed a field tribunal, which sentenced the commissar, the commander and several from the ranks, to death. He explained his reasons to the rest; and the regiment, given a blood transfusion of party members, returned under new officers to the battlefield.

Gradually, with reinforcements of Communist workers rushed from the cities, and with a growing awareness that in Trotsky they had a leader at last who defied the possibility of defeat, the distracted units coalesced into an army. Trotsky scraped together an air squadron which was soon in command of the skies and making daily raids on Kazan. For the first time, his army had eyes. And he was as ready to use the water as the air. With a small force of armed steamers and torpedo boats, he set out one night to destroy the enemy ships and shore batteries. It was a mission that looked for a while like being his last. His own boat was separated from the rest and, with its steering gear broken, drifted, an apparently helpless target, in the glow from a burning oil barge. But the raid had done its work. The shore batteries were silent. And by running alternately the right and left engines of the boat, its commanders brought it to safety. Only then did they all discover that at some time during the raid, the bow had been holed by a shell. The mission did more than accomplish its immediate purpose. The enemy, driven first from the air and now deprived of their control over the river, came to believe that German forces must be fighting with the revolutionary army. The prosperous classes began fleeing from the city, while the workers' districts stirred with revolt. On 10 September, a month after Trotsky's arrival, Kazan was recaptured.

Trotsky's train was to be the mobile heart of the Red Army throughout the decisive period of the war. It contained a secretariat; a printing press and a library; radio, telegraph and electric power stations; an arsenal and a storeroom for other supplies; a barracks; a garage; and even a bathhouse. It would speed from one front to another, bringing help wherever it seemed most urgently needed: summoning appropriate reinforcements and meanwhile providing a force of experienced fighters; arms and ammunition; medicines and maps; boots and watches; tobacco and baths; news and propaganda. Moreover, it brought Trotsky to the troops and, along with him, a new incandescence of leadership and a consciousness that they were now at the very centre of the war. The arrival of the train succeeded, time and again, in stopping a gap through which the enemy threatened to flood.

One loyal Communist, who would abandon the Russia of Stalinist purges, has written a telling account of the effect produced by the train and Trotsky's presence.

Gomel was just about to fall into the enemy's hands when Trotsky arrived. Already the convoys of refugees, their miserable carts piled high with boxes, papers, and odds and ends of possessions, were dragging their way along the roads leading to Novozybkov; already the local authorities were on the move in their cars. There was nothing left at the station but the last armoured train, a sort of forlorn hope, commanded by a fanatical ex-sailor. Then everything suddenly changed, and the tide began to turn. Trotsky's arrival meant that the city would not be abandoned, and he brought with him teams of disciplined organizers, agitators and technicians, all animated by a spirit of dauntless determination. . . .

Trotsky paid a visit to the front lines. He made us a speech. We were lifted by that energy which he carried wherever a critical situation arose. The situation, catastrophic but twenty-four hours earlier, had improved since his coming as though by a miracle.[4]

It was not only the adversary without, however, that Trotsky had to confront. The cutting of the rail link with the northern Caucasus, the sole major granary still under Soviet control, threatened Moscow with starvation; and Stalin, accompanied by a large reinforcement of Red Guards, was sent south to Tsaritsyn, with a mandate to restore supplies as speedily as possible. One month later, he was asking for special military powers, in a message that could only be taken as an attack on Trotsky's policies. 'If only our war "specialists" (the shoemakers!) had not slept and been idle, the line would not have been cut; and if the line is restored, this will be so not because of the military but in spite of them.' The Tenth Army at Tsaritsyn was commanded by Klim Voroshilov, who had worked with Stalin in Baku ten years before, while 'Sergo' Ordzhonikidze, another close colleague of those earlier days, was political commissar. Encouraged by Stalin, they openly defied the authority of Sytin, the former Tsarist officer who was commander of the southern front, and then proceeded to ignore the orders that came, in response to Sytin's reports, from Trotsky himself. Trotsky replied with an order of 5 October, unifying all forces on the southern front and threatening insubordination with immediate punishment. To Lenin, he telegraphed his insistence on Stalin's recall.

Lenin had a high regard for Stalin's administrative qualities, but saw no reason to take his side against Trotsky in a conflict on the conduct of the war. He at once agreed to Stalin's recall. But concerned to soften the blow, he sent Sverdlov, now president of the republic, in a special train to bring him back with reassuring honours. Sverdlov secured a meeting of his quarrelling colleagues on Trotsky's own train. And according to Trotsky's account, Stalin assumed 'a tone of exaggerated subservience' in pleading for his protégés. 'Do you really want to dismiss all of them?' he asked.

'They're fine boys.' Trotsky's reply was sharp with impatience. 'Those fine boys will ruin the revolution.'[5]

When Stalin struck back, he did so from the shadows. But it was not long before Trotsky learned of it. A certain Menzhinsky, who had met him at Bologna in 1910, visited him at the southern front and, after finishing with his official business, began to stammer and shuffle. Then, apparently discarding his doubts, he at last spoke out: Stalin had insinuated to Lenin and others that Trotsky was gathering around himself men who were opposed to Lenin's leadership. Trotsky dismissed these confidences abruptly. 'You must be mad, Menzhinsky.' But when Menzhinsky had gone, Trotsky found himself returning to what he had heard and recalling incidents that seemed to confirm it. Soon afterwards, on a visit to Lenin in Moscow, he seized the occasion to test the truth of Menzhinsky's statement. Lenin's immediate excitement and flushed rejection of the whole matter as 'Trifles! Trifles!' revealed not only the existence of Stalin's campaign but some measure of the success that it had achieved. Trotsky's reproachful questioning of how such mischief could ever have gained any credit seemed to reassure Lenin, and the two men separated with a friendliness that had not been there when they met.

Yet if Trotsky was now convinced of Stalin's malice, his very conviction made him discount its menace. He was ready to believe that it might thrive in the tainted air of a different society. But the revolution would ensure that it ended by devouring itself. Menzhinsky did not share Trotsky's faith or innocence. He had seen how the old world was already thrusting its way back between the paving stones of the new. He had hoped to earn Trotsky's gratitude and patronage by informing him of Stalin's intrigues. He had found instead a man antagonized by the disclosure that reality did not correspond to his own ideals. Menzhinsky lost no time in applying to a more promising patron. He attached himself to Stalin and would in due course receive his appropriate reward, with an appointment to head the political police.

On 9 November 1918, German sailors raised the red flag at Kiel. Revolution spread rapidly and, two days later, Germany capitulated to the Allies. The Treaty of Brest-Litovsk belonged now only to the archives, and on 26 December a Soviet government was established in Riga. But the disappearance of the German threat was accompanied by the reinforcement of the Allied one, mainly through increased support for the indigenous White armies of counter-revolution. By the end of the year, there were some 15,000 British and American troops in the north; 70,000 Japanese holding eastern Siberia and the Pacific provinces; and, in the south, French naval forces occupying Odessa. The Czechoslovaks were a diminishing military factor, but their place was being taken by the White armies of Admiral Kolchak, strengthened by some 7000 British troops; while to the south, in the northern Caucasus, were the White armies of General Denikin, backed by Krasnov's Cossacks and supplied with Allied money, equipment and instructors.

Yet this did nothing to extinguish the dispute over Trotsky's military policies. An article, signed by a member of Voroshilov's staff and published by *Pravda* in December, did not refer to Trotsky by name but unmistakably aimed at him the allegation that 'the best comrades' in the army were being shot 'without a trial'. Trotsky appealed to the central committee, which reprimanded both the author of the article and the *Pravda* editorial board. But his opponents continued to make the claim, and Trotsky was at last driven to demand a formal investigation. A commission of inquiry found that only one commissar had been shot – during the battle for Kazan; that he had been duly given a trial; and that he had, indeed, been guilty of desertion.

But no sooner was the fire put out in one place than it was lit in another. Reports of reversals on the Ural front and of widespread demoralization in the Third Army there led Lenin to propose sending Stalin on a mission of inquiry. Trotsky wired back his willingness at the beginning of January 1919, and Stalin set off with Dzerzhinsky. The resultant report blamed the general staff and recommended changes to it, in a clear attack on Vatzetis, the commander-in-chief, who was Trotsky's trusted appointment. Lenin and the central committee, doubtless suspecting that the attack was not altogether disinterested, ignored the related recommendation. But the whole report was damaging, and not least because of Dzerzhinsky's association with it. Stalin was acquiring important allies.

And his power was now rapidly to increase. The report had recommended the establishment of a special commissariat to supervise the processes of administration. Lenin was much taken by the proposal, as a way of promoting efficiency and curbing corruption. With his enthusiastic support, a People's Commissariat of State Control, later renamed the Commissariat of Workers' and Peasants' Inspection, was established. The choice of someone to direct this machinery of bureaucratic control was crucial. But Lenin looked no further than the author of the proposal. For he had come to rely on Stalin's readiness to act as his clerical major-domo. And he did not even think it necessary that the new Commissar of State Control should resign his old post as Commissar of Nationalities; despite the apparent conflict of functions involved.

At the eighth party congress, which opened on 18 March 1919, Zinoviev, as Lenin's spokesman, proposed that the central committee should establish two subsidiary bodies: a political bureau, to decide urgent matters of policy; and an organizational bureau, subservient to the political, with the function of assigning party members to particular posts and corresponding power to remove them. There was some opposition. One delegate complained that the political bureau would reduce the domain of the central committee to one of 'general conversation'. But the proposals were passed. The new central committee elected Lenin, Trotsky, Kamenev, Krestinsky and Stalin to the political bureau, or Politburo as it came to be known; and Stalin, with four other members, to the organizational, or Orgburo. As the only member of both, Stalin was effectively the corridor between them.

The forebodings of those who opposed these developments were soon enough to prove justified. The Politburo came to decide not only urgent matters of policy but all policy that mattered; while the central committee met less to consider than to confirm the decisions taken. Above all, those who were uneasy at the growth in Stalin's power were, in due course, to find the reality far outstripping their fears. But Lenin himself had no doubts. To the objections raised against Stalin's appointment to command the People's Commissariat of Workers' and Peasants' Inspection, he replied: 'It is necessary to have at the head of it a man of authority, otherwise we shall sink in a morass, drown in petty intrigues.' There was no one but Comrade Stalin, he declared, suitable to this 'gigantic undertaking'.

The cult of Lenin's leadership, where Trotsky, too, in time, would light a candle of his own, continues still to have a blankly polished stone over the entrance to the Stalinist cellar. Yet it was an entrance that Lenin himself made by his organizational changes and by his advancement of Stalin. The further contraction of the base in determining policy was a sacrifice of creative dispute to the cause of efficiency. The advancement of Stalin was the sponsorship of an efficient functionary. Both betrayed calamitous limitations of vision. In contracting the base, Lenin saw only the problems of the present, and not of the future that his very solutions informed. In seeing Stalin as the efficient functionary, he did not see, until it was too late, the essential despot which all that efficiency cloaked. Trotsky did not see the despot either. But he saw at least enough to condemn and distrust. His own mistake was to despise as well. Of Stalin, Lenin made too much and Trotsky too little. And, in between, Stalin would climb over them both.

But then Trotsky had little mind for developments in Moscow. He returned before the opening of the congress, where he knew that his military policies were bound to come under attack. And he made certain of Lenin's support. Walking into Lenin's Kremlin office, he asked him abruptly: 'Do you know how many Tsarist officers we have in the army?' Lenin did not know and refused even to guess. 'Not less than thirty thousand!' Trotsky told him. 'Now count up the percentage of traitors and deserters among them, and you will see that it is not so great. In the meantime, we have built an army out of nothing.' Lenin appeared finally convinced and several days later praised Trotsky's policy as an exercise in building Communism 'out of the bricks gathered by the capitalists for use against us. We have no other bricks.' With Lenin's support, Trotsky had little to fear from his opponents on the issue. And receiving news of a drive by Kolchak's forces towards the Volga and Moscow, he decided to leave for the front immediately. In his absence, the congress formally ratified his policies. But its military section, meeting in secret, approved a directive that he should pay more regard to Communist opinion in the army and hold regular monthly discussions with the more important commissars. This 'warning', as Zinoviev described it, in forwarding the directive, Trotsky rejected. He would not, he replied, summon commissars from the midst of battle to monthly debates.

Trotsky succeeded in rallying the army on the eastern front and preparing a counter-offensive that soon had Kolchak's forces in disorderly retreat. Sergey Kamenev,[6] a former colonel on the imperial general staff and commander of the front, proposed to pursue them beyond the Urals. Vatzetis, as commander-in-chief, vetoed the plan. He feared that Kolchak might have extensive reserves in Siberia and might even be baiting a trap with his headlong retreat. Trotsky, now at the southern front, supported him: accepting the objections to the risk; concerned to sustain the authority of the commander-in-chief, where there was no apparent reason to discard his advice; and eager for a respite in the east which would enable him to withdraw reinforcements for the crucial engagement to stop Denikin's advance. Kamenev, however, insisted on his plan, and Trotsky deprived him of his command. The commissars of the eastern front appealed to Stalin, and Stalin persuaded Lenin to take their side. Kamenev was restored to his command and, empowered to proceed with his plan, pursued Kolchak's forces beyond the Urals without encountering serious resistance. His success was, moreover, the more marked for the failure of Trotsky himself, with his 'barefoot, naked, hungry, lice-ridden army', as he described it in a message appealing for supplies, to stop Denikin's push through the Ukraine and an initially welcoming peasantry.

Trotsky returned to Moscow at the beginning of July, ready enough to admit his mistake over the rejection of Kamenev's plan. And the decision, proposed by Stalin and supported by Lenin, to appoint Kamenev as commander-in-chief in place of Vatzetis, was one that he did not resist. But the central committee went further, to reconstitute the Revolutionary Council of War: leaving Trotsky as chairman, but dismissing three of his supporters and appointing in their place Sergey Kamenev and two of the commissars from the eastern front. Moreover, in the conflict between Sergey Kamenev and himself over how the campaign in the south should be conducted, the four other members of the Politburo voted together against him. All this was more than Trotsky could take, and he immediately resigned from the Politburo, the War Commissariat, and the Revolutionary

Council of War. It was an appropriate response to what must have seemed a total lack of confidence in his judgement.

Lenin, whose scant knowledge of military matters had not been matched by any recent reluctance to determine them, now stood at the edge of the political consequences and sounded their depths. Seizing a sheet of paper that carried the seal of the Soviet of People's Commissars, he wrote in red ink: 'Knowing the strict character of Comrade Trotsky's orders, I am so convinced, so absolutely convinced, of the correctness, expediency and necessity for the success of the cause of the order given by Comrade Trotsky that I endorse this order unreservedly.' Then, having signed it, he handed it to Trotsky with the words, 'I will give you as many forms like this as you want.' Together the Politburo and the Orgburo unanimously rejected Trotsky's resignation and undertook 'to make Comrade Trotsky's work at the Southern Front – the most difficult, the most dangerous and the most important at the present time, which Comrade Trotsky has himself chosen – as convenient as possible for him and as fruitful as possible for the Republic.'

A few months before, to Lenin's urgent request that he should allow Stalin to work with him on the southern front, Trotsky had replied: 'Compromise is, of course, necessary, but not a rotten one.' And now, reassured by this display of confidence in him, he accepted just such a rotten compromise and agreed to the plan for the war in the south that his colleagues supported. Sergey Kamenev's strategy was to drive at the Cossacks in their home provinces and so deprive Denikin's army of the aid and protection available at its back. Trotsky's was drawn from political and psychological, as well as military, maps. He saw that the Cossacks had not joined Denikin for the thrust north-westwards into the Ukraine and now northwards to Moscow. And he concluded that they were concerned only with controlling their homelands. To strike at them there, he argued, would rouse them to ferocious resistance and commit them to Denikin's cause. Instead, the Red Army should aim its main attack at taking Kharkov: so as to cut through Denikin's forces in a region that was relatively industrialized, where the mass of the local population would rally to the regime.

By October, Kamenev's strategy had brought only the disasters that Trotsky had foreseen. And even Stalin had come round to denouncing it.[7] Denikin was threatening Tula, the last large town in the way of his direct drive on Moscow and the site of the republic's major remaining munitions works. And in the west, the forces of General Yudenich, armed by the British, had advanced from Estonia almost to the gates of Petrograd. Lenin himself was shaken and ready to abandon Petrograd, so that the Red Army might concentrate its resources on the defence of Moscow. Trotsky reorganized the southern front in accordance with his own strategy and ordered an offensive for 10 October. Then, rushing to Moscow, he rallied his colleagues in the leadership. He refused to abandon Petrograd, whose fall to the counter-revolutionaries would provide them not only with men and machinery for their cause but with a symbol of immeasurable value. Lenin proved difficult. And it took twenty-four hours of passionate argument to persuade him. The Politburo adopted Trotsky's emergency measures for total mobilization and agreed to let him take personal command of the efforts to hold Petrograd.

He set off for the city on 16 October and arrived to find the army disintegrating, the party demoralized, and Zinoviev himself, at the centre, in a paralysis of depression. But then Zinoviev, he would recall, was always one for extremes. When events were going his way, he 'climbed easily to the seventh heaven'. When they confronted him, 'he usually stretched himself out on a sofa – literally, not metaphorically – and sighed. . . . It was either the seventh heaven or the sofa'.[8] And if it was the sofa this time, he had some excuse. Nothing seemed likely to stop Yudenich, whose mounted scouts were soon so close that they could see the gilded dome of the cathedral. And the people of Petrograd, expecting its imminent fall, had deserted its streets, which lay like so many arms stretched out in submission.

Trotsky transformed the mood immediately. In place of distraught officials, he put hardened and resolute fighters from his military train. He roused district committees of the party, workers in the factories, soldiers in the barracks, to a determined resistance. Trenches appeared in the suburbs; artillery, in the squares; barricades, in the streets. Posters proclaimed his pledge to hold the city, even if every house had to become a battlefield. And his personal commitment rang through his oratory. At the Tauride Palace, in the white-columned meeting place of the old imperial Duma, he addressed the Petrograd Soviet. 'The city which has suffered so much,' he cried, 'which has burned with so strong an inward flame and has braved so many dangers, the city which has never spared itself, which has inflicted on itself so much devastation, this beautiful Red Petrograd remains what it has been – the torch of revolution!'

Sweeping aside such political differences as the threat of counter-revolution had made irrelevant for him, he ordered the party to supply the anarchists with weapons. And when the danger to the city was at its height, the anarchists went loyally to defend with their lives the printing works of the hated Bolshevik press. But they had their own way of dealing with their enemies. Discovering in their midst two young White spies with hand-grenades, they disarmed them, locked them in a room, and then fell to arguing over what to do next. A proposal to shoot the two spies was rejected with horror. They would not behave like the executioners of the Cheka. At last it was agreed that Kolabushkin, the most illustrious of their number, should take the spies to the Fortress of St Peter and St Paul. It was a repugnant compromise, since there the Cheka would almost certainly shoot them at once. On the way to the fortress by motor car, Kolabushkin remembered his own youthful journey between Tsarist guards and, looking at the faces of his captives, could bear it no longer. He stopped the car and turning to the two, said, 'Hop it, you bastards!' And afterwards, both irritated and relieved, he confessed: 'I was a fool, wasn't I? But you know, all the same, I'm glad of it.'[9]

Trotsky did not have these scruples. And he would not have saved Petrograd if he had. But he refused to tolerate an unnecessary or vindictive violence. As the fighting outside of the city became increasingly ferocious, he issued an order solemnly warning 'the unworthy soldier who raises his knife over a defenceless prisoner or deserter'. And he was no less determined that the forces of the revolution, in their very fervour, should remember the principles for which they were fighting. In an order to the army and navy, marking the loss of more than 500 seamen whose torpedo boats had been sunk by English warships in the Gulf of Finland, he recalled the extent of English intervention only to insist on the need never to forget that there were two Englands. 'It is the base and dishonest England of the stock exchange manipulators that is fighting us. The England of labour and the people is with us.'

As in the early battle on the Volga, Trotsky's first purpose in the field was to arrest the sheer momentum of defeat. And shortly after his arrival in Petrograd, he did so by flinging himself into the middle of the actual fighting. When a regiment in rapid retreat reached the divisional headquarters, he leapt on the nearest available horse and chased the soldiers, one after the other, back to the lines, while his orderly, a Muscovite peasant, raced at his heels, flourishing a revolver and shouting in high excitement: 'Courage, boys, Comrade Trotsky is leading you!' The troops were soon advancing at the rate of their previous retreat, and Trotsky himself, returning to headquarters on a truck, was certain that Petrograd could be saved. Within the next few days, it was. Conscious of the clenched city behind them, Trotsky's troops stopped Yudenich at the Pulkovo heights on 21 October, and on the 22nd seized the offensive. In two weeks, the White forces were driven back to the Estonian frontier, and the Estonian government, no longer contemplating intervention, disarmed them before permitting them to cross.

On the same day that Yudenich was stopped on the Pulkovo heights, Denikin's offensive was turned at Orel, some 200 miles south of Moscow, and his army was soon in full retreat. In the middle of November, Kolchak, accepted as the supreme commander of the White armies, lost his capital at Omsk, in western Siberia, and would soon afterwards be captured, tried and shot. The triple threat of counter-revolution, so abundantly supplied from abroad with money, military equipment, advisers and even troops, effectively collapsed in a few weeks from having reached the very edge of success. Denikin himself, in his memoirs, would ascribe his failure to the corruption of his own troops, whose pillage and pogroms warped their minds and destroyed their discipline. The causes, however, went deeper. For the very purpose of the White armies set against them the population that they had supposedly come to save. Often welcomed at first, as in the Ukraine, by the peasantry, they provoked only fear and hatred by their rejection of rural reform and their reinstatement of the landlords. The revolution had given too much that the counter-revolution seemed dedicated only to retrieve.

Yet the civil war was not only lost by the White armies; it was won by the Red. And that Trotsky, more than anyone else, had been responsible for this, was now generally acknowledged and acclaimed. The Politburo decided to award him, along with the city of Petrograd, the Order of the Red Flag, which he himself had instituted for exceptional service under fire. This at least should have been an occasion free of the old conflicts. It was not. At the close of the meeting, Kamenev proposed that the Order should be awarded to Stalin as well. Kalinin, who had become president of the republic after Sverdlov's death in March, protested: 'For what? I can't understand why it should be awarded to Stalin.' But a joke or two jostled him into silence, and the proposal was adopted. As soon as the meeting was over, Bukharin took Kalinin aside and explained. 'This is Lenin's idea. Stalin can't live unless he has what someone else has. He will never forgive it.'[10]

Trotsky, so concerned in his memoirs to establish the closeness of outlook between Lenin and himself, would maintain that he had 'understood Lenin, and inwardly agreed with him'. At the time, however, he seems to have been understandably indignant. For, writing shortly after the decision on the award of the Order to Petrograd, he commented: 'When rewards are given to individuals, mistakes and accidental privileges are always possible. But when the distinction goes to Petrograd, there is no mistake and no bias.' Stalin's own absence from the ceremonial presentation of the awards, at a joint session of the major Soviet institutions, suggests that he had his doubts over how the decision to distinguish his military achievements would be received. And this offers some support to Trotsky's account that only faltering applause greeted the award to Stalin, in marked contrast to the ovations which had preceded it.[11]

In January 1920, Britain and France appeared to admit defeat by lifting their blockade and agreeing to trade negotiations. Persuaded that the danger had passed and that it was now in a position to afford reform, the Soviet government abolished the death penalty and curbed the powers of the Cheka. But the threat to the republic proved to be far from over. Marshal Pilsudski, the ruler of Poland, had designs on the Ukraine and made no response to the secret advances from Moscow for the conclusion of a peace settlement. Trotsky, satisfied that Pilsudski was preparing for war, began drafting Soviet forces to the Polish front. Strengthened by supplies of military material from France and a fifty million dollar food loan from the United States, Pilsudski struck at the Ukraine on 26 April and twelve days later captured Kiev. Simultaneously, Baron Wrangel, who had gathered the remnants of Denikin's army, launched his own offensive from the Crimea. The Soviet government annulled its recent reforms.

The main challenge was manifestly the Polish one, and Trotsky's early preparations had in large measure already mobilized the Red Army to meet it. Moreover, the invasion united behind the regime even those elements otherwise hostile to it, in a rage of Russian patriotism against a traditional enemy. The Orthodox Church gave its blessing to a war against Roman Catholic Poland, and former Tsarist officers, previously unavailable, now offered their services. Trotsky, far from encouraging these religious and nationalist passions, denounced them in the name of the revolution. He closed down the periodical of the general staff, for insults to 'the national dignity of the Polish people'. And once again he issued a special military order against the killing of prisoners, the disarmed and the wounded. By the middle of June, the Red Army had recaptured Kiev, and the Polish forces were soon in headlong flight.

The British government now offered to mediate. Trotsky pressed his colleagues to accept the offer and call a halt to the Red Army advance at the so-called 'Curzon line'. Britain had proposed this as the frontier between Russia and Poland when a White victory in the civil war seemed likely, and it was therefore based on the principles of national demarcation rather than on any Polish aggrandizement. But Lenin was transported by the prospect of carrying the revolution across Poland to the borders of Germany, whose workers might then at last be excited to rise and seize power. Trotsky disagreed. The Red Army was exhausted and living now on its nerves. More than a century of Tsarist rule over the greater part of Poland had implanted there a deep distrust of Russian designs. And the invasion of Polish territory by Russian soldiers yet again, however conspicuously the red flag fluttered above them, would be likely to fire a popular patriotism, unless the Soviet government could show that the continuation of the war was Pilsudski's entire responsibility. The Soviet government should make an immediate and public offer of peace, that excluded any abridgement of Polish independence or any acquisition of Polish territory. Lenin was unmoved. He saw the Red Army welcomed by Polish workers and peasants as their liberators. And he carried all but Trotsky in the Politburo along with his vision.

Trotsky's forebodings were soon enough confirmed. The Polish workers and peasants stubbornly refused to recognize that Russian soldiers had come only to liberate them. In a war between the over-stretched Red Army and a fervently united Polish people, Pilsudski would almost certainly have triumphed in the end. Special factors only speeded up the process. The French government, as alarmed as Lenin was allured by the prospect of a Bolshevik presence at the German border, sent General Weygand, with a detachment of experts, to Warsaw; and Weygand helped to restore the disrupted services of supply. Far more importantly, the Red Army offensive fell apart in a clash between the commands of its two sectors. By 11 August the northern forces had already reached the outskirts of Warsaw, while the southern were moving on Lvov. The general staff ordered the southern command to switch direction and drive towards Warsaw, so as to attack the flank of the Polish armies in between. But Stalin, sent as political commissar to the southern front, had set his heart on taking Lvov. For several days, he refused to countenance a change of course. And when at last he bowed to the necessity, it was too late. On 16 August, the Polish army struck back on the northern front, and sent the Red Army reeling towards the frontier.

On 12 October an armistice was signed. Now the Red Army was free to deal decisively with Wrangel. It began its offensive only three days later, and within a month had cleared the last of the White armies from Soviet territory. The Politburo was now in favour of renewing the war with Poland. But Trotsky would have none of this. He argued that the army was incapable of raising itself to a victorious advance along a road scattered with its own fragments, and declared that rather than submit again to a policy he regarded as disastrous, he would appeal against the leadership to the ranks of the party. It was the sort of threat that Lenin himself had used often enough, and he recognized the force that Trotsky could give it. He proposed a postponement of any decision until Trotsky had visited the western front and reported on conditions there. Only the formalities remained. Trotsky found at the front little enthusiasm and still less readiness for a second war with Poland. He reported accordingly, and the Politburo submitted. On 18 March 1921 a peace treaty was signed that gave Poland significantly more than a frontier drawn at the 'Curzon line' would have done.

Meanwhile, a postscript to the civil war was being written in Stalin's own hand. The Soviet republic had, during the war with Poland, signed a treaty with the Menshevik government of Georgia which solemnly undertook to respect Georgian independence. On 11 February 1921 Red Army forces, acting on orders from the Revolutionary War Council of the Caucasus, whose chief commissar was Stalin's friend, Ordzhonikidze, invaded Georgia. Trotsky, who was visiting the Urals, had not been consulted. Nor had the Politburo. But assured by Stalin and Ordzhonikidze that a popular Bolshevik uprising had broken out in Georgia, and that the

Red Army had intervened to advance the inevitable outcome, the Politburo, in Trotsky's absence, accorded its approval. Both Stalin and
Ordzhonikidze were Georgians, and their representations were regarded
as authoritative. Events, however, were to provide a different version.
The Red Army met with widespread popular resistance and only after a
fortnight of fighting captured Tiflis, the capital. The Politburo, satisfied
with the results, was not now disposed to make too much of the means.
Lenin effectively limited himself to warning that the people of Georgia
should be treated with especial consideration; and their autonomous institutions with especial respect. Trotsky had intended to raise the whole
issue at a plenary session of the central committee. But he found on his
return to Moscow a refusal by his colleagues to recognize that the issue
existed. And he was unwilling to threaten them again with a campaign in
the party, so soon after getting his way over peace with Poland. He
denounced the concept of revolution by armies of conquest. And he
acquiesced. It was to be no more than the beginning of the momentous
Georgian affair.

The Bolshevik regime had survived all military attempts, foreign and
indigenous, to destroy it. It had not succeeded in rolling its revolution
across Europe. But with few exceptions, such as Stalin, who regarded the
world beyond Russia with consistent distrust, the Russian leaders continued to believe that a proletarian rising in the West could not be much
longer delayed. To proclaim and disseminate their faith, they invited to
Moscow, for a meeting in March 1919, representatives of various foreign
revolutionary groups. And this became the founding congress of the
Third, or Communist, International.

Within a month it seemed that history had, indeed, merely been catching
its breath. Revolution had established Soviet republics in Hungary and
Bavaria. From the eastern front, where he received the news, Trotsky
wrote of the happiness that it was to live and to fight in such times. Surely,
the second congress of the Communist International would be held in
Berlin, or Paris, or London.

Soviet Bavaria was quickly crushed by troops under the command of
the same General Hoffmann whom Trotsky had confronted at Brest-
Litovsk. Soviet Hungary lasted little more than four months, before collapsing at the beginning of August, as Romanian troops advanced on
Budapest and a counter-revolutionary movement swept the countryside.
Trotsky, in a secret memorandum to the central committee, suggested that
if the front way to Paris and London was so securely barricaded against
world revolution, the back way, through Asia, might prove the easier to
take. And he proposed that a revolutionary centre should be established in
Turkestan or the Ural region, to train political and military specialists for
colonial insurgency. His colleagues seem to have given scarcely a glance to

these ideas. And when the second congress of the Communist International was held a year later, it was in Moscow once more.

Alfred Rosmer, who was to become a close friend in the days of Trotsky's exile, arrived as a delegate from France. He found the hotel reserved for the participants suitably functional and simply furnished. In the prevailing disorder of the times, he was pleasantly surprised. It was Trotsky, he was told, who was in charge of the operation. Rosmer was even more surprised. 'But how did that happen? It's got nothing to do with his commissariat!' And he was answered at once, 'Of course not, but if you want to get something done, properly and on time, it's always Trotsky you go to.'[12]

A French writer, who knew Moscow well, guided Rosmer through the traffic of the leadership. Lenin was 'the left'. Bukharin was the 'the real left'. Zinoviev and Kamenev were 'the right'. And Trotsky was 'unclassifiable'.[13] It was a problem for all those who felt safe only with classifications. Once again, eyes were turned in hope towards the West. For these were the triumphant weeks of the Polish war, and the Red Army was moving on Warsaw. Lenin, pointing to the appropriate places on a large military map, provided exultant daily reports on the Red Army's progress. Trotsky himself, in the manifesto that he presented, made no mention of these victories. He saw how soon they were likely to become defeats.

His face too, was turned towards the West – had only for a moment turned aside, to find another way of reaching it – but to a West that would be liberated from capitalism by its own workers and not by the bayonets of the Red Army. His faith, therefore, was not to be affected by the outcome of the Polish war. But for many of the Soviet leaders, seeing a darkness all the deeper for the radiance that it had displaced, the retreat from Warsaw came to mark in their minds the end of one era and the start of another, in which they faced only the walls of their isolation. And certainly, within their hard-won survival, the economic and social challenges remained at least as formidable as the military ones that had been beaten back on the battlefield.

In February and March 1919, an English writer, Arthur Ransome, had visited Russia and reported on conditions in the cities during the civil war. The pigeons of Moscow, once confident in the security provided by their supposed religious connections, were gone from the streets; and starving crows forced their way through the small ventilators of hotel windows, to pick up any scraps that human hunger had left. Everyone was cold. In the Kremlin, the Keeper of the Archives, sitting in an old sheepskin coat and felt boots, rose repeatedly to beat life into his freezing hands; and in the lecture rooms at the universities, science professors got frostbite touching their instruments. But there was, too, a resolve, even among socialist opponents, to support the regime against the armies of counter-revolution and foreign intervention. Sukhanov might abuse the Bolsheviks and refer direly to the disappearance of all metal spoons from Moscow, but at the same time he accepted the regime as the only answer for the while. Ransome travelled back to the frontier in the company of Bill Shatov, the commandant of Petrograd, and an anarchist who had done much to promote the distribution of Kropotkin's writings in Russia. The moment that other people stopped attacking them, Shatov confided, 'he would be the first to pull down the Bolsheviks'. Asked how long he thought that the Soviet government could hold out, he replied: 'We can afford to starve another year for the sake of the Revolution.'[14]

Now, one year later, the armed challenge of the revolution's enemies was virtually at an end, and the cities were more stricken than ever. The peasants were still refusing to sell their grain to the state at fixed prices in a rapidly depreciating currency, when there were no consumer goods available to buy. The regime had resorted to requisitioning surplus stocks and had sent special commissars, with extraordinary powers, into the countryside. The requisitioning detachments encountered furious resistance, and food commissars would be found by the roadside, their bellies slit open and packed with grain. But pitchforks were a poor defence against guns, and the peasants soon took instead to cultivating no more than they needed for their own subsistence. By 1920, the area sown had shrunk by almost 30 per cent and the yield per acre by 40 per cent, so that the total harvest was little more than two-fifths of what it had been in the years before the First World War.[15] With food supplies to the cities drastically reduced, many workers took themselves and their families to refuge among relatives in the countryside: cutting still further in consequence not only industrial output but, by what they consumed there, the agricultural surplus for requisition. By the autumn of 1920, the population of forty provincial capitals had fallen by almost one-third from the figure in 1917; of Moscow, by 44.5 per cent; and of Petrograd, by no less than 57.5 per cent.[16] It was rather as though the film of economic history, after a few jumping frames, was being run backwards.

The policies pursued by the regime came collectively to be known as 'war communism'. For orthodox Marxism, this was an implied contradiction in terms. Communism had always constituted the ultimate stage of development, when the economic abundance produced by a socialist world order would be able to support the functioning of a classless society. But the revolution in Russia could not continue helplessly to wait for the proletarian capture of the advanced capitalist states. And in the recognition that ideology was its one abundant resource, the regime set out to make a virtue of necessity. Since the possibility of constructing communism on the roof of economic development remained for the while beyond reach, the possibility of constructing a makeshift in the ruins would give Soviet society the strength of a moral mission. The general repudiation of the currency had led to an increasing reliance on payment in kind, and by 1920 workers were receiving some 90 per cent of their wages in direct rations or in orders on the co-operative stores. It was proclaimed as heralding an end to the dominion of money. There was no paper or coloured ink available for the printing of stamps, and a decree abolished postal charges, as 'a new step in the realization of socialism'. The reality was all too grim: as one account of life in Petrograd, from the recollections of an ardent revolutionary, reveals.

The rations issued by the State co-operatives were minute: black bread (or sometimes a few cupfuls of oats instead); a few herrings each month, a very small quantity of sugar for people in the 'first category' (workers and soldiers), and none at all for the third category (non-workers). . . . In the dead factories, workers spent their time making pen-knives out of bits of machinery, or shoe-soles out of the conveyor-belts, to barter them on the underground market. . . .

Winter was a torture . . . for the townspeople: no heating, no lighting, and the ravages of famine. Children and feeble old folk died in their thousands. Typhus was carried everywhere by lice, and took its frightful toll. . . . Inside Petrograd's grand apartments, now abandoned, people were crowded in one room, living on top of one another around a little stove of brick or cast-iron which would be standing on the floor, its flue belching smoke through an opening in the window. Fuel for it would come from the floor-boards of rooms nearby, from the last stick of furniture available, or else from books. Entire libraries disappeared in this way.[17]

If total economic collapse was to be avoided, the leadership agreed, labour would have urgently to be mobilized for the restoration of industry. And the military successes of the regime now opened up the prospect of transferring soldiers from the front for a primary effort in forestry and mining. The Commissariat of War was made responsible for the conduct of this new policy, and in the middle of January 1920 a decree established the first 'revolutionary army of labour' in the Urals. Trotsky's design was simple. The army would discover the particular productive skill of each soldier, mark his service-book accordingly, and direct him to the place of work where he was likely to be of most value.

On 8 February Trotsky set out with his staff on a tour of inspection. His train was derailed in a snowstorm, and there it lay, just beyond sight of a small station but undisturbed among the drifts, for the rest of the night and throughout the following day. Railway officials had ceased to signal even the passage of a train that carried the war leader of the revolution. Trotsky was enraged. But as he continued on his journey, his rage gave way to a deep and questioning disquiet. A very paralysis seemed to be creeping through the country. And the rain of edicts from the revolutionary regime ran off the mood of sullen listlessness everywhere, as though meeting only an impermeable film of despair.

Trotsky returned to Moscow convinced that the commitment to war communism had immediately to be modified by some recourse to personal incentives. In a statement to the central committee, he declared that no amount of improvement in the methods of requisitioning would create supplies of food that were not there. The government should abandon such methods and extract its supplies as a percentage of production; to institute a form of progressive income tax in kind, which would provide some measure of profit for all increases in the area ploughed or for more intensive agriculture. And this profit the peasant should then be enabled to exchange for industrial goods, on an individual rather than on a collective basis.

More than a year later, when the pursuit of war communism had wrought still further economic damage, Lenin would present his New Economic Policy, in terms scarcely distinguishable from this earlier initiative, and come in consequence to be acclaimed for his imaginative and courageous leadership. But now he resolutely resisted Trotsky's proposal. And it was rejected in the central committee by eleven votes to four. Others who questioned the wisdom of persisting with the policies of war communism suffered more than an adverse vote. Rozhkov, a Marxist historian who wrote to warn Lenin that only an immediate change in economic relations with the countryside could prevent catastrophe, was sent to contemplate his ideological shortcomings at Pskov, near the Estonian border. Lenin, in a personal letter, replied that he had no intention of surrendering to rural counter-revolution.

Trotsky himself, smarting under accusations that he was pressing for an essentially Menshevik policy of free trade, submitted to the decision of the central committee. But he insisted that if war communism was to remain the party's prescription, then it must be applied with system and without shirking the implications. His colleagues readily agreed and appointed him their principal spokesman on economic policy to the ninth party congress in March. And there he appeared, accordingly, as the proponent not of reform but of a still harder line than any that the leadership had previously drawn. The need now, he declared, was to 'militarize' labour, with measures whose severity 'must correspond to the tragic character of our economic situation'. And addressing himself in particular to the trade unions, he denied them the right to any independent role.

Militarization is unthinkable without the militarization of the trade unions as such, without the establishment of a regime in which every worker feels himself a soldier of labour, who cannot dispose of himself freely. If the order is given to transfer him, he must carry it out; if he does not carry it out, he will be a deserter who is punished. Who looks after this? The trade union. It creates the new regime. This is the militarization of the working class.

There was no open dissent. Shliapnikov, who had attacked the commitment to subjugate the trade unions, did not attend the congress. He had been sent on an official trade union mission abroad.[18]

At Lenin's special request, Trotsky was already engaged in restoring a railway system so close to collapse that engineers had taken to predicting the precise date on which the last of the trains would run. Now, with the authority of the congress behind him, he placed the railway workshops under martial law. His measures achieved a rapid rehabilitation of the rolling stock but brought him into open conflict with the leadership of the railwaymen's union. At a meeting of the central committee on 28 August, he proposed the dismissal of the union leadership and the appointment of a new executive authority in its place. Lenin and even Stalin supported him, against the protests of Tomsky, the principal spokesman for the trade unions. And the railwaymen's leadership was duly removed. But this was the last flourish of a majority in support of Trotsky's policies. The start of peace talks with Poland promoted a disposition to retreat from emergency measures. And at the end of September, the central committee condemned 'all petty tutelage and petty interference' in trade union affairs. Indeed, noting the decisive improvement in the transport system, it recommended that the special administrative units, established to secure the political backing of transport workers for Trotsky's efforts, should be transformed into trade union instruments.

The very success which most of his colleagues saw as a reason for relaxing the control of the trade unions by the state, Trotsky considered an argument for tightening and extending it. And at the beginning of November, at a meeting of party delegates to a trade union conference, Trotsky proclaimed the need to 'shake up' the other trade unions, as the government had shaken up the union of railwaymen. A few days later, the central committee returned acrimoniously to the issue. Trotsky's draft resolution was defeated by eight votes to seven; a margin narrow enough to encourage him in maintaining his attitude. And Lenin's successful resolution, which distinguished between 'healthy forms' of militarization and forms liable to degenerate into bureaucracy, settled little. The issue was effectively left to be decided by the next party congress in the spring of 1921.

In the months that followed, the dispute raged ever more furiously at party meetings and in the party press. Stalin's public contribution was a polemic against Trotsky in the pages of *Pravda*. But the extent and nature of his activity behind the scenes would be indicated by the taunts of a delegate to the party congress, who sarcastically referred to 'that war strategist and arch-democrat, comrade Stalin', so busy in Moscow drafting 'reports that such and such victories had been won on this or that front, that so many had voted for Lenin's point of view, and only six for Trotsky's....'[19] Zinoviev, whose command of the party in Petrograd was marked by a ruthless authoritarianism, attacked Trotsky's dictatorship and predicted that a democratic dawn would follow its defeat. Indeed, he was so transported by the prospect of triumphing over Trotsky, whose qualities of intellect and character he saw as a rebuke to his own, that he took the conflict even to the sailors of Kronstadt, and fed there a discontent whose depth he did not suspect.[20]

In the last week of February 1921, Petrograd was swept by strikes and demonstrations. Food supplies were rushed to the city; and with the further aid of mass arrests, order was restored. Then, on the 28th, in nearby Kronstadt, sailors on the battleship *Petropavlovsk* passed a resolution that amounted to a manifesto of revolt. They demanded the immediate re-election of the Soviets by free and secret ballot. They demanded freedom of speech and the press for all political parties of peasants and workers. They demanded an end to the special position of the Communists, since no one party should 'enjoy privileges for the propaganda of its ideas and receive money from the state for this purpose'. They demanded that peasants be permitted to do what they wished with their land, provided that this did not involve any hiring of labour. On the following day, a mass meeting in the main square of Kronstadt enthusiastically adopted these demands. And on 2 March, representatives of the fleet and the garrison established a Provisional Revolutionary Committee, whose members were all ratings of peasant or proletarian origin. From Moscow came an order that the committee surrender at once. The committee refused.

Kronstadt had, a few years before, belonged to Trotsky as to no other revolutionary leader. Its sailors had acclaimed him, sought his advice, followed him. And many of them had subsequently given their lives in the civil war. Their successors were disillusioned with a leadership that had promised so much freedom but provided so little. In their newspaper, the Kronstadt *Izvestia*, they denounced 'the new bureaucracy of the communist commissars and civil servants'. And they protested: 'From a slave of the capitalist, the worker has become the slave of the state-owned enterprises. . . . Every expression of free thought, every just criticism of the actions of the criminal rulers has become a crime, punished by imprisonment and often even by the firing squad.' They came to proclaim: 'Here in Kronstadt we have laid down the first stone of the third revolution . . . and have opened up a new, wide road of socialist creation.'[21]

Trotsky himself had, a few years before, called Kronstadt 'the pride and the glory of the revolution'. Now he was in no doubt that a Kronstadt in revolt had to be subdued. And here he was at one with all his colleagues in the leadership. The Kronstadt cry for freely elected Soviets was already being popularly translated into a demand for 'Soviets without Communists'. In European Russia alone, there were more than fifty centres of peasant insurgency. And, to the south of Moscow, a large peasant army had gathered under the command of a Right Social Revolutionary, committed to the elimination of the Soviet system and the return of the Constituent Assembly.[22] Submission to the demands of the Kronstadt rebels seemed certain to produce not a reinvigorated Soviet democracy but an interval of chaos which would end in counter-revolution.

The leadership could not afford to delay. At any time, a thaw might divide Kronstadt from the mainland and make the mutinous garrison, with its protective navy, impregnable. On 7 March, the Red Army began its assault. Lines of infantry, with white sheets over their uniforms, advanced across the ice, to fall before the fire from the fortress and the fleet, or disappear into the black water as the crust gave way beneath them. Again and again, the attacks were beaten back. And then, on the 18th, the anniversary of the day on which the Paris Commune had succumbed, the last and most ferocious of the assaults burst its way into Kronstadt. Some of the rebels fled to Finland. Others fought on to the end; driven from street to street within the citadel and dying with cries of their own revolutionary faith. Still others chose to surrender and were taken prisoner. Trotsky had not led the assault. He was not even in Petrograd. But his had been the strategy and his the responsibility for its success. At the victory parade on 3 April, he went out of his way to distinguish the rebels as comrades; though comrades blinded to the consequences of what they were doing. He could not have failed to recognize, in their demands, much that he had promised them the revolution would bring. The agents of the Cheka were less discriminating. Over the next few months, they would shoot, in successive small batches, the comrades who had been taken prisoner.

While Kronstadt was still defying the attempts to subdue it, the tenth party congress opened on 8 March, with the main immediate purpose of determining the trade union dispute. At one apparent extreme there stood the Workers' Opposition, led by Shliapnikov and Alexandra Kollontai. This assailed the state as the seed-bed of bureaucratic privilege and argued that its control of industrial production should be surrendered to the trade unions, as the institutions directly representative of the workers. Furthermore, it demanded more democracy in the party and, in particular, facilities for the dissemination of dissident opinion. But its libertarianism had distinct limitations. It was the most vigorously opposed to such concessions as might conciliate the peasant majority. And it was so far from associating itself with the wider democratic demands of the Kronstadt rebels that its spokesmen were foremost in offering their services to crush the rebellion.

At the other apparent extreme, Trotsky, supported most prominently by Bukharin, pressed for a trade union policy consistent with the principle that Soviet Russia was a workers' state. An independent role for the trade

unions could logically rest only on the assumption that the regime represented more than one class, and that the trade unions were there to represent the distinctive interests of the workers. But on that assumption, where
was the dictatorship of the proletariat? And without the dictatorship of
the proletariat, what was the party's domination of the state but the very
despotism that its enemies denounced it for being? Indeed, on that
assumption, the upheaval of October 1917 had marked not a second revolution for the attainment of socialism but a mere seizure of power, within the
limits laid down by the bourgeois revolution of the previous February,
and the coinage of party rule was ideological counterfeit.

The leadership had already discussed Lenin's proposals for a New
Economic Policy. And in the face of the Kronstadt rebellion, the delegates
to the tenth congress would vote, almost without debate, to abolish the
requisitioning of foodstuffs from the peasantry; to introduce a graduated
income tax in kind; and even to allow some measure of private trade at the
local level. These liberal concessions made Trotsky's trade union policy
seem all the more authoritarian by contrast: especially since there were so
few who knew that the economic reforms had been his own defeated
recommendation, a year before. But Trotsky saw only that it was all the
more imperative to confirm and clarify the strategy of a workers' state,
when the regime was having to engage in a tactical retreat.

Lenin was not troubled by logical inconsistencies. In warding off
attacks on his New Economic Policy from those who described themselves
as 'representatives of the proletariat', he would even come in due course
to argue that there was no real proletariat in Russia.[23] Now, at the tenth
party congress, he sought to resolve the trade union dispute by a determined ambiguity, which recognized both the autonomy of the unions and
their subservience to the state. It was a policy whose very evasiveness was
its virtue, and it attracted 336 votes, to 50 for Trotsky's programme and
only 18 for that of the Workers' Opposition.

Trotsky predicted that it would not survive until the eleventh party
congress. And he was to be proved right. In developing the New Economic Policy, the government formally conceded independence to the trade
unions. But the individual unions were controlled by their All-Russian
Central Council, and this was in turn tightly controlled by the party. The
subservience of the trade unions, proposed by Trotsky as an essential
constituent of the workers' state, had been rejected in principle only to be
achieved in practice, by a form of institutional ventriloquism.

Trotsky was the victim of his own intellectual integrity. In the congress
elections to the twenty-five posts on the enlarged new central committee,
he came only tenth, and several places behind Stalin. To be sure, there was
little correlation between the vote that an established leader received and
his relative authority. Zinoviev, who came eighteenth, exercised far more

authority than Radek, who came second. But Trotsky's association with Lenin in pre-eminence had usually been reflected in such polls. And his slide revealed how far the denunciations of his dictatorial tendencies had damaged his prestige.

They were denunciations that had come with hardly less vigour from proponents of the victorious compromise than from the Workers' Opposition. Yet it was Lenin himself who introduced measures at the tenth congress that were to prove crucial to the destruction of the party's own democratic functioning. Clearly alarmed at the fissures produced by the trade union issue, he referred in his opening remarks to a 'luxury of discussions and disputes' that was 'truly astounding' in a party surrounded by the enmity of the capitalist world. And he asked: 'Has this luxury in your view been fully consistent with our material and moral resources?'

He gave his own answer on the last day of the congress, with two sudden resolutions. The first, 'On Party Unity', established the new crime of 'fractionalism', which was defined as 'the appearance of groups with special platforms and with the ambition to form in some degree a unit and to establish their own group discipline'. And those found guilty faced summary expulsion from the party. A secret rider empowered the central committee, meeting jointly with the Central Control Commission,[24] to inflict, by a two-thirds majority vote, this punishment even upon one of its own members. The second resolution, 'On the Syndicalist and Anarchist Deviation', condemned the attitude of the Workers' Opposition to trade unions as 'incompatible with membership of the Russian Communist Party'. Lenin carefully defined this new political error for which the proscriptions of Marxism had so far not found room. 'A deviation is not a fully formed movement. . . . People have strayed a little from the path or are beginning to stray, but it is still possible to correct it.' Frightened by the spreading peasant revolt and the signs of disaffection among workers in the cities, the delegates overwhelmingly approved the measures to promote their own cohesion. What the measures came to promote instead was the ascendancy of a single leader, who would use the ban on fractionalism to excommunicate opponents and the concept of deviation to treat as heresy all dissent from his revealed opinion. The tenth party congress was seminally Stalin's own. And it was Lenin who, more than anyone else, was responsible for making it so.

This responsibility extended beyond his two emergency resolutions. The delegates effectively advanced the functional dominance of the Politburo, by increasing its membership to seven and reducing the required meetings of the central committee from once a fortnight to once only every two months. It simplified for Lenin the operations of leadership. It simplified as well the means by which Stalin would come to command the party. A second development served Stalin's more immediate purposes. The mounting importance of the party Secretariat had been mirrored in the growth of its staff, from a mere thirty at the time of its inauguration, less than two years before, to more than 600 now. The three presiding secretaries had supported Trotsky in the trade union dispute. They now lost not only their posts but their membership of the central committee. And of the three new secretaries, all elected to the central committee, two were Stalin's adherents. Of Lenin's decisive weight in such organizational appointments, there can be little doubt. And that he could significantly affect even elections to the central committee, he demonstrated at the same congress. Shliapnikov of the Workers' Opposition seemed certain to lose his place. Lenin, probably judging that Shliapnikov would be more easily controlled from within the leadership, insisted on his re-election and secured it.

The New Economic Policy recorded rapid successes. The harvest of 1922 was the largest since the revolution and some three-quarters of the normal crop before the First World War. Small-scale industry, rural and artisan, recovered in 1922 to produce 54 per cent of its 1912 output, from scarcely more than a quarter two years before. Private trade, emerging from among huddled figures on the outskirts of the cities, flourished in markets and streets. Restaurants opened, and there were even edible pastries to excite a wide-eyed wonder. But there was a darker side. Credit was made available to state enterprises on the basis of its profitable employment; and the enterprises, concerned to cut labour costs, swelled the mass of urban unemployed. Those who were quick to see how the concessions of the regime might be exploited, acquired personal fortunes, often corruptly as agents of the state enterprises. And a market to satisfy their appetites followed closely behind.

Dan, the Menshevik leader, released from prison in January 1922, found a Moscow in which speculators seemed to be everywhere; shops stocked luxuries beyond the reach of any but the rich; and prostitutes were once more plying their trade. Already by the autumn of 1921, Lenin was admitting, to a conference of Communists from the province of Moscow, the defeat of his central purpose.

It was intended throughout the state to exchange the products of industry in a more or less socialist manner for the products of agriculture and, through this exchange of goods, to restore large-scale industry as the only possible basis of a socialist organization. What was the result? . . . Nothing came of the exchange of goods; the private market turned out stronger than we; and instead of exchange of goods we have got ordinary buying and selling, ordinary trade.

But far from proposing that the regime should change direction, he declared that a further retreat had become necessary. The state would have to accept the private market and attempt to regulate it through the control of money. And he advised the delegates: 'Be so good as to adapt yourself to it, otherwise the element of buying and selling, of monetary circulation, will overwhelm you.' The regime began moving towards a balanced budget and the re-establishment of a stable currency, based on a gold-backed rouble. In *Pravda* Lenin promised that after the victory of revolution throughout the world, gold would be made the material of public lavatories. It was small comfort to those for whom the restoration of confidence in money defined only their own poverty and need.

The confusion and discontent produced by these developments were voiced in protests against not only the course of the New Economic Policy but the dictatorship exercised by the party bureaucracy. Shliapnikov had not been silenced by his re-election to the central committee. Lenin moved to have him expelled from the party. But he failed by one vote to secure the required two-thirds majority, at a special joint meeting of the central committee and the Central Control Commission. Less prominent critics were more easily punished. Party 'discussion clubs' had been authorized by the tenth congress. The one in Moscow was soon a centre of criticism and protest. It was summarily closed.

Twenty-two leading critics, seeing no other way open to them, took the unprecedented but constitutionally permissible step of appealing against the Russian party to the Communist International. Trotsky himself defended the party to the executive of the International, which decided that the Russian leadership was well aware of the dangers cited in the appeal and that the twenty-two were endangering party unity by 'knocking at an open door'. At the eleventh party congress, in March 1922, there was more agitated knocking, and not only by those associated with the former Workers' Opposition. Riazanov, Trotsky's old friend who had contributed to his *Pravda* in the Vienna days, denounced the arbitrary rule of the Politburo. Antonov-Ovseenko, who had led the assault on the Winter Palace, protested that the party was surrendering to the rich peasant and the foreign capitalist. Skrypnik, from the Ukraine, attacked the government's excessive centralism that recalled the conduct of Tsarist Russia. But whatever echoes of disquiet the knocking produced, the door itself was closed. And again it was Trotsky, on behalf of the central committee, who defended the policies of the leadership. He did not associate himself with those who were outraged by the appeal to the Communist International. The twenty-two, he conceded, had acted within their rights. But he indicted them for expressing their opposition in such a way that they seemed to be separating themselves from the party, as though they already had another 'in reserve'.

Lenin was in no mood for leniency. In his principal report, he compared the party's economic retreat to that of an army, when a few voices might produce a general panic.

Then the danger is immense. When such a retreat is being carried out with a real army, machine-guns are brought out and, when the orderly retreat becomes disorderly, the command is given: 'Fire.' And quite right. . . . At such a moment it is indispensable to punish strictly, severely, unsparingly the slightest breach of the discipline.

Communicating the command in this case was a special commission, composed of Stalin, Zinoviev and Dzerzhinsky, which convicted the twenty-two of having broken the ban on fractionalism and recommended expulsion from the party for the five held principally responsible. The congress approved the punishment for only two. The other three, including Shliapnikov and Alexandra Kollontai, were reprieved. The mass of delegates were not yet creatures of the machine, and enough of them still flinched from excommunicating those whose revolutionary service and very prominence in the party engaged respect. But almost in guilt at their own tolerance, they instructed the central committee to take the firmest measures against 'cliques and groupings'. And they pressed for a continuing purge of the party membership.

The previous congress had sanctioned such a purge, and almost a quarter of the more than 650,000 members had already been expelled. The sweep had been directed mainly at the mass of manifest careerists, who had joined the party when its predominance had seemed assured, and whose conduct had become an abundant source of scandal. But now that these had supposedly been removed, a continuation of the purge was the more likely to be directed at crushing criticism and dissent. A month before, the Cheka had been abolished and its place taken by the GPU[25] in the Commissariat of the Interior. It was effectively to mark the changing function of the political police from one limited to hunting down opponents outside of the party to one that encompassed the hunt within, for opponents of the leadership. Almost at once, the GPU and the control commissions of the party engaged in a collaboration of mutual advantage.

The multiple power of which Stalin already disposed was about to be momentously augmented. And perhaps because the possibility of this had reached his ears, Preobrazhensky, himself a former secretary to the central committee, rose at the congress to ask whether it was 'thinkable that one man should be able to answer for the work of two commissariats as well as for work in the Politburo, the Orgburo and a dozen party committees'.[26] But if this was a warning against any expansion of Stalin's domain, its failure was soon all too plain. On 4 April, two days after the congress had dispersed, *Pravda* announced the names of the three secretaries elected by the new central committee; and next to the name of Stalin was the designation 'General Secretary'. It was an appointment that Lenin himself had sponsored. And though there is no evidence that Trotsky had resisted it, he would scarcely have accorded it a conspicuous welcome.

One week later, at a meeting of the Politburo, Lenin proposed Trotsky's appointment as deputy chairman of the Soviet of People's Commissars. Perhaps he had begun at long last to have misgivings over the extent of Stalin's power in the party and sought a counterbalance by extending Trotsky's power in the state. Perhaps he saw, in the very collaboration that such an appointment would bring, a means of closing the distance that now stretched between him and Trotsky. But whatever the reasons for the proposal, Trotsky himself curtly rejected it. The Soviet of People's Commissars already had two deputy chairmen: Rykov, who headed the Supreme Council of the National Economy; and Tsurupa, who was Commissar of Supplies. And both were treated by Lenin essentially as executive assistants, whose readiness to pursue his policies rather than their own had recommended their promotion. The proposal that Trotsky should become yet another one of these might well have seemed an attempt to diminish him; and all the more significantly such, for coming so soon after Stalin's latest elevation. At all events, the manner as much as the fact of his refusal clearly damaged still further his relations with Lenin. And how damaged these already were may be inferred from the absence of any preparatory private meeting between the two, at which Lenin might have explained the purposes of his proposal and explored Trotsky's response.

The trade union dispute had divided them far more deeply than Trotsky was in his memoirs to admit. And its conclusion had only provided the more room for other conflicts of policy to develop. During the last gasps of 'war communism' and largely at Trotsky's insistence, the Soviet of People's Commissars had agreed to establish an authority for general economic planning, that came to be known as the Gosplan.[27] Lenin had shown little enthusiasm for the project: to the very man appointed to head it, he derided the idea of a comprehensive plan, in the pauperdom of Soviet Russia, as 'bureaucratic Utopia'. He showed still less interest as the New Economic Policy gathered force. And influenced by his attitude, as by its own uncertainty of purpose, the Gosplan concentrated on minor administrative matters.

For Trotsky, however, the very development of the New Economic Policy made economic planning more rather than less imperative. The progress made, with the profitable engagement of private enterprise, by certain consumer industries, could not continue without supplies of new machinery; and new machinery was needed, too, for a sound agricultural advance. Yet in the crucial metallurgical industry, output was less than one-tenth of what it had been in 1912.[28] Nor were the socialist objectives of Soviet society to be served by encouraging private enterprise to thrive, while the state sector of the economy was left to languish in confusion and neglect. Lenin himself seemed to recognize this in what seemed a veritable passion for a programme of electrical development. But how was such a programme to be pursued without a restructuring of industry to provide the necessary equipment? Again and again, Trotsky urged that the Gosplan should be given adequate powers and personnel to produce a design for the growth of the economy. Lenin remained stolidly unconvinced.

Not least, the two leaders had clashed over the Workers' and Peasants' Inspectorate. Trotsky had failed to see how the mere establishment of a special department to keep watch over the functioning of others could ensure that it escaped the mistakes it existed to correct. And the appointment of Stalin to direct it had not contributed to dispelling his doubts. Indeed, as Stalin increasingly used the Inspectorate to further his own purposes, Trotsky complained of its meddling and described it as a refuge for misfits. By late September 1921, Lenin himself had become critical of it and had even written to Stalin accordingly.[29] But to Trotsky, he appeared only as its protector. And the appointment of Stalin as general secretary of the party must have seemed the most telling indication of Lenin's confidence in the way that the Inspectorate had functioned.

However irritated, even angered, by Trotsky's reaction Lenin might have been, he was not to be deflected from his objective of securing Trotsky's appointment as deputy chairman. But any campaign of persuasion and pressure which he might have been contemplating was arrested by an event that apparently he alone within the leadership had expected. His colleagues had come to think of him as somehow indestructible and had either failed to notice or merely dismissed the signs of a faltering vitality. On occasions, Lenin would clasp his head and remain quite still for several minutes. Then, from the beginning of 1922, he had spells of dizziness, so that he would catch hold of the nearest firm object to prevent himself from falling. His doctor found his heart strong and ascribed his symptoms to overwork. But he was not reassured. 'Remember my words,' he said to some of his friends, 'I will end in paralysis.'[30] And on 25 May 1922, a month after a successful operation to remove one of the two bullets remaining from the attempt on his life in 1918, he had a stroke. He lost his speech and all movement in his right arm and leg.

Trotsky was in bed, nursing an injured foot. And it was another two days before the news was brought to him by an agitated Bukharin, who explained: 'We did not want to disturb you and were waiting to see how his illness would develop.' By his own account, Trotsky at the time found nothing suspicious in this delay. It was only much later that he came to see in it the design of some among his colleagues to keep him in the dark, while they consulted together and prepared for the possibility that Lenin's stroke would prove fatal; though he would acquit Bukharin himself of anything more than merely repeating what the 'grown-ups' had persuaded him to believe.[31]

And, indeed, it was almost certainly now, as the alarm bell of Lenin's mortality rang in their ears, that Stalin, Zinoviev and Kamenev initiated the conspiracy of what would come to be known as the triumvirate.[32] The three were drawn together by a single fear: that Trotsky would assume the supreme command of the revolution. For, in any apparent hiatus produced by the loss of Lenin, the party might well turn to follow the only one left among its leaders whose popular authority was comparable; whose picture hung, alongside Lenin's, in so many homes, and whose hold on the army reached beyond the command of the commissars.

It was an eventuality that threatened Stalin and Zinoviev with their political eclipse. How far either of them saw from the first, in the formation of a front against Trotsky, the means of promoting his own ascendancy instead, must remain the merest conjecture. But it may safely be supposed that each would have considered the possible pretensions of the other only to dismiss them. As president of the Communist International, Zinoviev held the highest party office of all; and as head of the Petrograd Soviet, one of the highest offices in the state. Moreover, his personal loyalty during ten bitter years of exile had earned him, despite his desertions in the decisive weeks of 1917, a reputation as Lenin's closest disciple. But Stalin would soon have taken the measure of Zinoviev's weaknesses: his inattention to detail, his evident vanity, his ultimate cowardice. And Zinoviev would have failed to take the measure of Stalin's strengths: the patient cunning which could dress in deference his vanity, the relentlessness of his ambition, the very camouflage that his shortcomings supplied. Zinoviev doubtless saw what Lenin, too, had seen: the supreme functionary whose usefulness lay, by definition, in his aptitude for service. For what but a functionary, however elevated, should Stalin expect to be? Audiences shifted in their seats during his speeches; and in an ideological movement, he wore ideas as though they had been made to fit somebody else.

That Kamenev himself was no candidate for the succession, both Stalin and Zinoviev would have had cause enough to rest assured. His inclination was to conciliate rather than to command; and the very qualities that had made him one of Lenin's most valued negotiators were those, as he would have been the first to declare, least suitable to the demands of dominance. If ambition was not a factor in his attachment to the conspiracy, nor was fear of his own political eclipse. He had no reason to suppose that Trotsky disliked or distrusted him. He had not embittered, with personal disparagement, the policy differences between them. He recognized Trotsky's extraordinary abilities without resentment or even reluctance. But they were abilities which, in their very contrast to his own, he thought likely to prove disruptive, if elevated to a position of command. With Lenin's departure, the danger that the party might disintegrate in dissension would greatly increase. It was not a danger to be dispelled by dispensing with Trotsky's abilities. But it did require their subjection to the discipline of a

Trotsky's mother,
Anna Bronstein

Trotsky's father,
Davyd Bronstein

L. D. Bronstein (Trotsky), aged nine

Right: Nicholas II and the Tsarina in royal robes at a fancy dress ball at the Winter Palace, 1903

Below: Nicolayev, 1897 — Alexandra Lyovna Sokolovskaya with her brother Ilya on her right, L. D. Bronstein on her left, and Dr. G. A. Ziv, a fellow conspirator, at her feet

Lenin (Vladimir
Ilyich)

Krupskaya
(Nadezhda
Konstantinovna)

Plekhanov

Martov

Vera Ivanovna Zasulich

Natalia Sedova as a young woman in Paris

The procession to
the Winter Palace
dispersed with
bullets, January 1905

Left: Witte
Right: Stolypin, 1906

Below: Rasputin with a group of admirers, *c.* 1914

The Russian army — the Tsar blesses his troops, 1914

Kerensky

Sukhanov

Stalin, 1917

An incident in the street fighting in Petrograd, the July Days, 1917

Right (top to bottom):
Kamenev, *c.* 1920
Zinoviev, *c.* 1922
Bukharin, *c.* 1922

Trotsky addresses the troops from the top of an armoured train, called *Guard of the Revolution, c.* 1919

Below: Members of the Left Opposition, 1928
Seated, left to right:
Serebriakov, Radek, Trotsky, Bogslavsky, Preobrazhensky
Standing, left to right:
Rakovsky, Drobus, Beloborodov, Seznovsky

Trotsky's study at Buyule Ada
in Prinkipo

The Soviet paper *Krokodil* accuses
Trotsky of conspiring with the
Nazis to overthrow the USSR,
August 1936

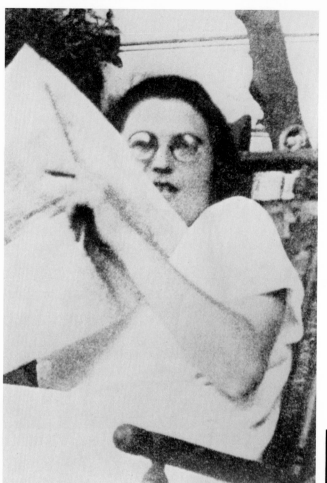

Zina Volkov,
Prinkipo, 1931

Facing page:
Natalia and Trotsky on
arrival in Mexico, 1937

Trotsky feeding his
rabbits, Mexico

Leon Sedov, early
1930s

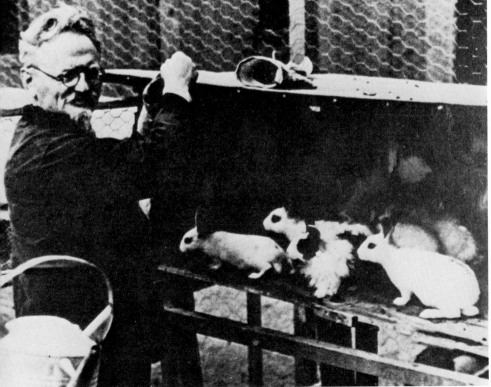

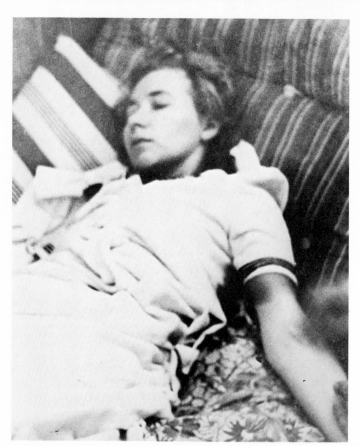

Sylvia Agelof, stricken
with grief after
Trotsky's assassination
by her lover

Mercador with
police after the
assassination

collective leadership. This, almost certainly, is what Kamenev saw to be the purpose of the conspiracy. And if Zinoviev or Stalin saw it somewhat differently, the difference was not one which either would have allowed Kamenev to suspect.

Lenin, learning with Krupskaya's help how to write with his left hand and to speak again, made a slow recovery. And his doctors, encouraged by his progress, pressed him the more insistently not to risk a relapse by abandoning his regimen of rest. He waved away their warnings with impatience. His illness had interrupted the pursuit of a particular objective, and he returned to this now with all the more determination. From his retreat at Gorki, near Moscow, he telephoned Stalin on 11 September to ask that the Politburo discuss as a matter of urgency the appointment of Trotsky as deputy chairman. Again there had been no prior consultation with Trotsky. And again, Trotsky rejected the post. In all probability at Lenin's prompting, the Politburo then passed a resolution, proposed by Stalin, that effectively censured Trotsky for his attitude. Trotsky's adversaries might well have felt uneasy at the purpose of Lenin's new concern with the appointment. They had every reason to be delighted at the outcome. But the rift between Lenin and Trotsky was soon to be closed, in response to the conduct of their colleagues.

For all the concessions of the New Economic Policy, the Soviet government had maintained its monopoly on trade with the outside world, as a necessary measure of what Trotsky had called 'socialist protectionism'. Without such a monopoly, Lenin himself had argued, foreigners would 'buy up and take home with them everything of any value', while the peasantry, enticed by conditions in the international market, would rise against a regime that seemed determined to 'deprive it of its own interest'. Indeed, he had found it necessary to marshal his arguments again and again, to prevent the monopoly from erosion by those in the leadership who considered it damagingly incompatible with the New Economic Policy. But these opponents had been no more than temporarily stopped. During his illness, they organized their forces and at last, on 6 October, they succeeded in securing the central committee's approval for a relaxation of the monopoly.

Lenin had returned to Moscow four days before but had felt himself unequal to taking part in the central committee meeting. Its decision deeply disturbed him, and he proceeded at once to mobilize support for a review at the next plenary session. He bombarded his colleagues with letters and, on the thirteenth, wrote formally to the Politburo demanding a reversal of the decision. Stalin remarked that Lenin's letter had not made him change his mind on the issue, but that in view of Lenin's insistence, he would vote to postpone any execution of the new policy, so that it might be discussed, with Lenin present to participate, at the next full meeting of the central committee.[33] And so it was decided. Throughout the next few weeks, Lenin continued to prepare for the decisive meeting. But as his health deteriorated, he became convinced that he would be unable to attend it. He turned for help to Trotsky. 'I will fight at the Plenum for the monopoly,' he wrote. 'And you?'[34] It was a question to which he already knew the answer. And Trotsky wrote back to give it; while seizing the occasion to press once more the case for a state planning commission of enhanced responsibilities and powers.

In a letter of 13 December, Lenin suggested a willingness to reconsider his attitude on this and meanwhile 'earnestly' asked that Trotsky take upon himself the task of presenting their 'common opinion of the unconditional necessity of preserving and reinforcing the monopoly of foreign trade'. It was a question on which he considered it 'impossible to yield'. And in the event of their defeat in the central committee, they should declare their continuing dissent to the party caucus at the coming congress of Soviets and carry their case to the next party congress. Here was fractionalism, by his own definition, with a vengeance. But then he had never supposed that the ban would be applicable to him. By the 15th, he had reached full agreement with Trotsky and announced this in a letter to Stalin and other members of the central committee. Three days later, at its plenary meeting, the central committee reversed its decision.

To Krupskaya, on 21 December, Lenin dictated a jubilant letter to Trotsky.

It seems we captured the position without firing a shot by mere movements of manoeuvre. I propose that we should not stop but continue the attack, and to that effect introduce a resolution to raise the question at the party congress of reinforcing the monopoly of foreign trade and of measures looking to its better enactment.

Stalin in particular was becoming much alarmed by the signs of Lenin's increasing closeness to Trotsky. And he must have felt keenly the humiliation of the surrender which such closeness had secured. For now, apparently enraged beyond his customary cunning, he made a dangerous mistake. Duly informed by his spies that Krupskaya had written to Trotsky at Lenin's dictation, he telephoned her on the 22nd and – as she subsequently described it – subjected her to a storm of the coarsest abuse. He even threatened to have her prosecuted by the party's Central Control Commission for disobeying the orders of Lenin's doctors: though she had, in fact, obtained the presiding doctor's consent to take Lenin's dictation. For the while, she said nothing of the telephone call to Lenin. And that night, Lenin had a second stroke, which again lost him the use of his right arm and leg. But his speech was unaffected, and he insisted on being permitted to dictate for a few minutes each day. His latest attack had clearly placed in the forefront of his mind his concern with what would follow his permanent incapacity or death. For already on the 24th he began dictating the notes that were to become known as his Testament.

The 'basic factor in the problem of stability' he associated with Stalin and Trotsky, whose conflict constituted 'a good half of the danger of a split'. And seeking at last to broaden rather than narrow the base of leadership, he recommended, as one means of meeting the danger, an enlargement of the central committee to 50 or 100 members. 'Having become General Secretary, Comrade Stalin,' he continued,

has acquired immense power in his hands, and I am not certain he will always know how to use this power with sufficient caution. On the other hand, Comrade Trotsky, as his struggle against the Central Committee over the question of the Commissariat of Railways has already shown, is distinguished not only by his remarkable abilities. Personally he is, no doubt, the most able person in the present Central Committee, but he also has excessive self-confidence and is overly attracted by the purely administrative aspect of affairs.

Lenin then turned to Zinoviev and Kamenev, with a comment whose very brevity belittled them. Their attitude in October 1917, he declared, had been, 'of course', no accident. But, he added, 'it should no more be held against them personally than his non-Bolshevism against Trotsky'. Finally he dealt with Bukharin and Piatakov, whom he described as the most able of the younger leaders; and though he cited their differing faults, he explained that he did so on the assumption that in time they would correct them.

At the beginning of December, or a fortnight before the formation of their front to defend the trade monopoly, Lenin had met Trotsky to discuss with him in private at last the necessity of his accepting an appointment as deputy chairman. Trotsky had used the occasion to attack the interrelated bureaucracies of party and state. And Lenin had replied by offering him 'a bloc against bureaucracy in general and against the Organizational Bureau in particular', with a special commission, of which they would both be members, to serve this objective. Years later, in his memoirs, Trotsky would maintain:

This commission was essentially to be the lever for breaking up the Stalin faction as the backbone of the bureaucracy, and for creating such conditions in the party as would allow me to become Lenin's deputy, and, as he intended, his successor to the post of chairman of the Soviet of People's Commissaries.[35]

If he believed this at the time, then the subsequent closeness of his collaboration with Lenin over the trade monopoly issue would have confirmed his belief, just as it would have fed Stalin's fears. But the content of Lenin's late December notes suggests that Trotsky and Stalin were alike misled.

For in spite of his express misgivings, Lenin was effectively promoting Stalin's authority. To have included Stalin among the only four senior leaders whom he regarded as deserving of remark was probably as far as Stalin's hopes would have reached. That he should, further, have dealt with Zinoviev and Kamenev so as to place them firmly on a lower level, conferred a distinction on Stalin that few in the party, not to mention the demoted themselves, might have expected. Even this, however, paled beside his elevation of Stalin to equal pre-eminence with Trotsky. He not only considered them together, but went on to describe them as 'the two most prominent leaders of the present Central Committee'. Nor was this the limit of the damage to the cause of Trotsky's ascendancy. The criticism of his 'excessive self-confidence', combined with the reference to his 'struggle against the Central Committee' – a reference which only Lenin would have found it unembarrassing to make, so soon after his own recent 'struggle' – was bound to provide support for those who complained of Trotsky's rebellious individualism. And the particular reference, moreover, could scarcely fail to recall Trotsky's former commitment to the militarization of labour. There was still another damaging reminder. To be sure, Lenin declared that Trotsky's pre-Bolshevik past was not to be held against him. But it would have served Trotsky better to have foregone the appeal to forgiveness along with the exhumation of the offence. Accompanied by all this, the tribute to Trotsky's supreme abilities would not have struck Stalin himself as unduly distressing.

It seems clear that at this stage of his thinking, therefore, Lenin intended no one to succeed him, except in the most nominal sense. He was seeking a collective leadership to prevent precisely such a personal ascendancy as he had enjoyed. And since he believed Trotsky to be the only one capable of achieving this ascendancy, it was Trotsky's claims which he had set out to confront. He had signally failed, for all his recent misgivings, to take the measure of the threat posed by Stalin's character; or for all his celebrated political insight, to have recognized the full force of the movement to the concentration of power which he himself had done so much to promote. But at all events, he was, almost immediately, to experience a very upheaval of second thoughts. For, on 4 January 1923, he dictated a postscript to his notes on the leadership:

Stalin is too rude, and this fault, quite tolerable in our midst or in relations among communists, becomes intolerable in one who holds the office of General Secretary. Therefore I propose to the comrades that they consider a means of removing Stalin from that post and appointing to it another person who in all other respects differs from Stalin in one advantage alone, namely, that he is more patient, more loyal, more polite, and more considerate to comrades, less capricious, and so forth. This circumstance may seem to be an insignificant trifle. But I think that from the point of view of the relations between Stalin and Trotsky which I discussed above, this is not a trifle, or it is a trifle that may acquire decisive significance.

The specific fault cited and the repeated references to a 'trifle' strongly suggest that Krupskaya, either because she was unable to contain herself any longer, or because Lenin suspected from her behaviour that something was wrong and worried it out of her, had told him of Stalin's telephone call. But Lenin was also now profoundly disturbed by what he saw in the unfolding of the dispute with the Georgian Communists and had begun a repentant reconsideration of the whole issue. The report of Stalin's telephone call in all likelihood only advanced the timing and affected the tone of Lenin's codicil.

The leading Georgian Communists had welcomed the Red Army conquest of 1921, but soon showed how far they shared the popular nationalism which the experience of independence under a Menshevik government had fed. While committed to close ties with Moscow, they resisted any attempt to reabsorb Georgia into a greater Russia. And in particular they opposed, as part of such an attempt, the Caucasian federation of Georgia with Armenia and Azerbaijan, for which the government in Moscow was pressing. Stalin's friend Ordzhonikidze had, ever since the conquest, commanded the Caucasian bureau of the party with all the democratic susceptibilities of a colonial governor. He impatiently dismissed the representations from the Georgian central committee and in March 1922 announced plans to establish a federal government for the three Caucasian republics. Georgian resistance only increased.

During the months of Lenin's absence from office, Stalin instigated moves to deal with the wider problem of the constitutional relationship between the existing Russian federation and the five formally independent republics: the three in the Caucasus, Byelorussia and the Ukraine. Given the record of Tsarist Russian domination and the revolution's claim to have abandoned the imperial priorities of the past, it was an undertaking that required the most considerate and sensitive treatment. The special commission, appointed by the Orgburo on 11 August, had Stalin himself as chairman and mainly his own nominees, including Ordzhonikidze, among its members. Before the middle of September, the commission had resolved to recommend the inclusion of the five republics in the Russian federation, whose own governing institutions would constitute the government of the new entity. Indeed, half-way during the commission's deliberations, on 29 August, Stalin had informed Mdivani, the Georgian Communist leader, that decisions taken by the supreme governing bodies of the Russian federation were binding on all the republics.[36]

The reaction from Armenia and Azerbaijan was predictable: both republics were governed by docile nominees of Ordzhonikidze's Caucasian bureau. But the central committees in Byelorussia and the Ukraine expressed cautious dissent; and the central committee in Georgia, total opposition. Stalin was unmoved. The Caucasian bureau ordered the

Georgian central committee to comply and to refrain from making its differences with Moscow public. To the Politburo, Stalin indicted the Georgian protesters as 'national deviationists'. Trotsky was suspicious. The whole affair had an imperial flavour. But most members of the Politburo were persuaded that the authority of Stalin, as Commissar for the Nationalities and himself a Georgian by origin, should be respected. It was an attitude taken towards the Georgian issue by Lenin as well. But he did have certain criticisms of Stalin's scheme and suggested instead a linkage of the Russian federation with the five borderlands in a Union of Soviet Republics, whose overall Soviet of People's Commissars would include under its jurisdiction the Russian government itself.

Stalin was so agitated by this sudden intervention that in communicating to the Politburo the text of Lenin's proposals, he attached a letter of comment which accused Lenin of 'national liberalism' and of encouraging the separatists. But almost immediately, he thought better of it and adjusted his scheme to accommodate Lenin's suggestions. Lenin's recovery was such as to promise his early return to work, and his recorded criticisms were already enough to ensure the defeat of Stalin's unamended scheme in the central committee. Besides, as Stalin doubtless reassured himself, the letter counted for considerably less than the spirit which had the interpretation of it.

On 9 October 1922, the central committee duly adopted the amended scheme. It was one which the Georgians appeared ready to accept, but only on condition that Georgia was admitted to the Union as an independent republic and not as submerged in a Caucasian federation. For Stalin and Ordzhonikidze, such a concession was unthinkable. The defeat of their Georgian opponents had become a virtual obsession. Stalin informed them that their objections to the Caucasian federation had been dismissed, while Ordzhonikidze, with the backing of the Secretariat, ordered some of the recalcitrants to leave the republic at once and place themselves at the disposal of the central committee in Moscow. Two of the leading Georgian Communists wrote privately to Kamenev and Bukharin, protesting in particular at the imperious conduct of Ordzhonikidze. They received in reply a demand that they submit to party discipline. And when Lenin was informed by Bukharin of the protests, he responded, on 21 October, with a telegram of impatient rebuke. The central committee had, he declared, dealt thoroughly with all 'divergences' in its recent resolutions. 'Consequently, I firmly condemn the invectives addressed to Ordzhonikidze and insist that your conflict, conducted in a more seemly and loyal tone, should be settled by the Secretariat of the Central Committee of the Russian Communist Party.'

Advised that their only hope of redress lay in appealing against Stalin to Stalin, the members of the Georgian central committee took the unprecedented step of collectively resigning. Ordzhonikidze's Caucasian bureau immediately appointed a new central committee from among those qualified by their subservience, and the Moscow Secretariat hastened to record its approval. But all this only strengthened the resolve of Georgian Communists to preserve a national identity, and measures to promote the Caucasian federation met with mounting resistance. Lenin himself received a letter from a leading Georgian Communist which accused Ordzhonikidze of having threatened party members; and whether this excited his disquiet or merely confirmed such doubts as other information had raised, he now showed increasing concern over the Georgian issue.

The Secretariat appointed a special commission, headed by Dzerzhinsky, to investigate the conflict in the Georgian party and recommend appropriate measures. When, on 24 November, Lenin came to vote on the list of members submitted for approval to the Politburo, he abstained. By the time that Dzerzhinsky returned from Georgia, on 12 December, Lenin had had the private meeting with Trotsky at which the two men had discussed the need for a bloc against bureaucracy. Dzerzhinsky, in his report to Lenin, absolved Ordzhonikidze of all blame and placed responsibility for the Georgian party conflict on the national deviationists. But, in the process, he also disclosed that the commission had ordered to Moscow the leaders of the former Georgian central committee; and that, in the course of a meeting with his opponents in the party, Ordzhonikidze had lost his temper and struck one of them. The report, with its whitewash all the more apparent from the patches of black it revealed, disturbed Lenin profoundly. And it doubtless contributed to the series of attacks which Lenin suffered from 13 December and which culminated in his second stroke on the 23rd.

One week later, he began dictating his notes on the Georgian affair. He blamed himself 'for not having intervened energetically and decisively enough' in the 'notorious' national question. But he had been ill; and it was only with the revelations in Dzerzhinsky's report that he had realized 'in what sort of a mess we have got ourselves'. All that had happened in Georgia and elsewhere had been excused by the argument that 'we needed a single apparatus'. Yet this apparatus was no more than the old imperial one 'anointed with a little Soviet holy oil'. The small nations were being subjected to the ravages of 'the Great Russian chauvinist, in substance a rascal and a tyrant, such as the typical Russian bureaucrat is'. He had supposed, indeed, that it was from among former members of the old oppressive bureaucracy that the guilty were alone to be found. He had been mistaken. They might be found even among the most highly placed of party leaders.

Ordzhonikidze and Stalin had behaved like bullies and flouted the principles of proletarian internationalism. Dzerzhinsky had displayed a truly Russian state of mind – but then Russified aliens were always much more Russian than the Russians themselves – and so unpardonable a partiality that the work of his commission must be regarded as useless. Ordzhonikidze should be given an 'exemplary punishment' for his part in the affair, while Stalin and Dzerzhinsky, as bearing the political responsibility, were to be officially condemned. The whole project for union with the border republics, Lenin admitted, had probably been premature and essentially unjust. And though he agreed that it should continue to be pursued, he did so only on the understanding that the process of integration might, if necessary, be reversed, and that meanwhile the independence of the republican governments would be restored in all spheres but those of foreign policy and defence.

Lenin was not yet ready to show his hand. It is clear that his notes constituted for him no more than a preliminary indictment, which required corroboration. And on 24 January 1923 he asked his private secretary Fotieva to procure for him at once the papers of the Dzerzhinsky commission. She was unable to do so. But on 3 February she let him know, as though 'by clumsiness', that the Politburo had approved the commission report; had upheld the policies pursued by Ordzhonikidze and Stalin; had condemned the dissident Georgian Communists and sanctioned the effective deportation of their leaders to Moscow. Lenin became the more insistent on being furnished with the papers of the commission. Stalin replied that he could not release them without the permission of the Politburo and threateningly suggested to Fotieva that she might be letting Lenin know too much, in view of the decision that he was not to be troubled by day-to-day matters. Lenin, informed of the remark, scathingly commented: 'So the national affair is a day-to-day matter, is it?' But in any event, Stalin no longer considered it safe to continue denying Lenin the papers, without the approval of the Politburo; and the Politburo agreed to release them.

Stalin might well have felt that the ground had begun moving beneath him. For early in February, Lenin sent to the Politburo for publication an article that called for bureaucratic reform and that indicted in particular the commissariat which Stalin had headed and staffed with his followers.

Let us say frankly that the People's Commissariat of the Workers' and Peasants' Inspection does not at present enjoy the slightest authority. Everybody knows that no other institutions are worse organized than those of our Workers' and Peasants' Inspection, and that under present conditions nothing can be expected from this People's Commissariat.

Indeed, he saw no purpose in still one more reorganization of 'this hopeless affair', and he recommended the establishment of a new and much smaller agency. The Politburo was opposed to publication. But how was suppression of the article to be kept from Lenin? Kuibyshev, a candidate member, suggested that a single copy of *Pravda*, carrying the article, should be printed, for Lenin alone. Trotsky would have none of this and insisted that the article should be published. Defeated in the Politburo, he addressed a letter to members of the central committee; disclosing the decision of his colleagues to suppress the article and threatening to take the issue 'before the entire party'. His opponents in the Politburo submitted. And on 4 March *Pravda* at last published Lenin's article under the title of 'Better Few, But Better'.

Lenin had meanwhile appointed from among his secretaries a private commission of inquiry into the Georgian affair. And his success in gaining possession of the Dzerzhinsky material was the more marked as evidence of a hasty cover-up emerged. Fotieva learned to her astonishment that the declaration from the victim of Ordzhonikidze's attack had simply disappeared from the records of the Central Control Commission. Indeed, the report of the private commission, delivered to Lenin on 3 March, was itself in due course to disappear. But there can be little doubt that it confirmed Lenin's worst suspicions. For on 5 March, deciding to delay no longer, Lenin dictated a secret letter for immediate dispatch.

Esteemed Comrade Trotsky:
I earnestly ask you to undertake the defense of the Georgian affair at the Central Committee of the party. That affair is now under 'prosecution' at the hands of Stalin and Dzerzhinsky and I cannot rely on their impartiality. Indeed, quite the contrary! If you would agree to undertake its defense, I could be at rest. If for some reason you do not agree, send me back all the papers. I will consider that a sign of your disagreement.
With the very best comradely greetings,
Lenin.[37]

Trotsky himself was confined to bed, with back trouble, in another apartment of the Kremlin; and there Fotieva brought him the letter, along with the notes that Lenin had dictated at the end of December and other papers on the Georgian affair. On the 6th, there was much scurrying between the two apartments. Informed that Kamenev was about to leave for the Caucasus, Trotsky suggested that the documents should be shown to him as well, so that he might initiate corrective measures when he reached Georgia. Fotieva returned with a categorical veto from Lenin: 'It is entirely out of the question. Vladimir Ilyich says that Kamenev would show the letter to Stalin, and Stalin would make a rotten compromise in order to deceive.' But she was soon back again. Lenin had decided to give Kamenev a copy of the letter that he had dictated for dispatch to the party dissidents in Georgia.

Esteemed comrades:
I follow your affair with all my heart. I am outraged at the rudeness of Ordzhonikidze and the connivance of Stalin and Dzerzhinsky. I am preparing for you notes and a speech.

Trotsky expressed surprise at his sudden change of mind. But Fotieva explained that Lenin's condition was getting worse hour by hour. He had said to her: 'Before it is too late . . . I am obliged to come out openly before the proper time!'[38] Trotsky suggested that Fotieva ask Kamenev to come and see him. And an hour or so later, Kamenev arrived in an agitated state. He scarcely needed to be shown the papers from Lenin that Trotsky now held. He had just been to see Krupskaya, who had told him that Lenin had dictated a letter to Stalin, in terms which convinced her of his intention 'to crush Stalin politically'.

Very respectable Comrade Stalin,
    You allowed yourself to be so ill-mannered as to call my wife on the telephone and to abuse her. She has agreed to forget what was said. Nevertheless, she has told Zinoviev and Kamenev about the incident. I have no intention of forgetting what has been done against me, and it goes without saying that what was done against my wife I also consider to have been directed against myself. Consequently, I must ask you to consider whether you would be inclined to withdraw what you said and to apologize, or whether you prefer to break off relations between us.[39]

Trotsky proceeded to reassure Kamenev. He made it clear that he could not speak for Lenin; and that if Lenin recovered in time for the twelfth party congress, there would have to be further discussions on the issue. But he himself wanted no fight at the congress over organizational changes. 'I am against removing Stalin, and expelling Ordzhonikidze, and displacing Dzerzhinsky from the commissariat of transport.' He did, however, agree with the substance of Lenin's criticisms. And he insisted on corresponding changes in policy. There was to be a radically different approach to the 'national question', with an end to the hounding of Stalin's Georgian opponents. Stalin himself was to alter the statement he had prepared for the party congress and reassure the non-Russian nationalities that their rights would be respected. There was to be a firmer commitment to industrialization. And there was to be no more 'administrative oppression of the party'. The intrigues would have to stop and give place to 'honest co-operation'. Stalin in particular was to revise his behaviour and make a start by apologizing at once to Krupskaya for his rudeness.[40]

Kamenev was manifestly relieved and agreed to all of Trotsky's conditions. That night, he returned to report that he had been to see Stalin in the country and that Stalin too, had agreed. Trotsky found him more confident than before and only later, looking back, recognized the reason. Lenin's condition had meanwhile markedly worsened. On 9 March he suffered his third stroke. And this time, there seemed little likelihood of recovery.

In the event, he was to survive for another ten months. In the middle of May, he was taken again to Gorki. And there, in July, he began to struggle out of the strait-jacket of his illness. He practised writing with his left hand and managed to walk short distances with a stick or supported on Krupskaya's arm. But his speech, for all his strenuous efforts, never reached beyond a few repeated syllables. He read or listened attentively; sometimes asking questions by gestures. And all the while his brain continued falling in on itself. The German specialist who attended Lenin's autopsy found that the brain had shrunk 'in its material composition' to about 'one quarter' the normal size of the cerebral mass. And Professor Rozanov, after measuring the extent of the sclerosis, wondered less at how Lenin had retained his 'thinking power' than at how he could have lived at all 'so long with such a brain'.[41]

Politically, Lenin's life was over by 8 March, and the rest was a protracted postscript. Yet, for the following few decisive weeks, Stalin was ultimately no less vulnerable. Trotsky was still in possession of Lenin's papers on the Georgian affair and could use them to speak at the congress on Lenin's as well as on his own behalf. Against the attack from such an alliance, there could be no effective defence. And Stalin knew it. His apparent self-abasement was complete. And Trotsky agreed to let the Politburo decide whether Lenin's notes should be communicated to the congress. The decision was to acquaint only a few chosen delegates, and only in the strictest confidence, with the contents.

But Stalin would not permit himself a premature triumph. When the Politburo came to consider which of its members was to take Lenin's customary place and deliver the principal political report on behalf of the central committee, he proposed Trotsky. And Trotsky, concerned that his assumption of such a role would be interpreted as a grasp at the succession while Lenin was still alive, refused. Instead, he suggested: 'The report should be made in keeping with his office, by the General Secretary. That will eliminate all grounds for idle speculations.' It was a remark whose implicit disparagement must have scratched Stalin's pride; and all the more so for having been made with no such purpose in mind. Trotsky was not dismissing Stalin's claim to the succession; it simply did not occur to him as a possibility. But if Stalin had cause for offence, he did not show it. He rejected the appointment, as one which the party would not understand. 'The report,' he insisted, 'must be made by the most popular member of the Central Committee.'[42]

Zinoviev was not so studiously modest; and, unlike Trotsky, was eager to be seen as the immediate claimant to Lenin's place. He was duly chosen to deliver the political report. But it did him little good. When the twelfth congress opened on 17 April, it was to Trotsky that the delegates looked, in their alarm at the reported gravity of Lenin's illness. They echoed in their applause the frequent tributes paid to him in greetings from party groups across the country. There was scarcely any mention of Stalin in the messages, and little enough of Kamenev or Zinoviev. Moreover, when Zinoviev rose to deliver the political report, there was none of the customary applause. Nor did his speech succeed in prompting any. The extravagance of his references to Lenin produced embarrassment rather than enthusiasm. His denunciation of dissent provoked restlessness and resentment. For the thrust of his remarks was less an appeal for loyalty than a demand for subservience. He castigated 'every criticism of the party line' as objectively a 'Menshevik criticism'. And given the connotations of Menshevism, with the treatment meted out to its adherents, this implied that any such criticism would be regarded as counter-revolutionary. There were protests at this assumption of 'papal infallibility' by the leadership, even from among prominent old Bolsheviks who were not associated with the Workers' Opposition. Trotsky alone might have led a successful revolt. But committed by his previous assurances to preserve the solidarity of the leadership, he crushed by his silence the very criticisms he approved.

Perhaps he had reached the limit of his self-restraint. For when the debate on the national question began, he left the hall, ostensibly to prepare his report on economic policy. The Georgian dissidents had been led by Lenin to expect some decisive expression of his support for them against Stalin. They heard instead Stalin himself, the chief of the Great Russian bullies, condemn Great Russian bullying. To confront this mockery, they demanded that Lenin's notes on the issue should be read. The demand was dismissed. The mood among the mass of delegates was as hostile as the disposition of the platform. When Rakovsky, head of the Ukrainian government, and Bukharin, in a last notable spasm as spokesman of the left within the leadership, intervened to denounce the policies that Stalin had pursued, they met with an impenetrable silence. It was the attacks from the floor on Ukrainian and Georgian nationalism which brought rolls of applause. From a debate that had threatened him with political oblivion, Stalin emerged with his reputation and authority much enhanced.

He had judged that the delegates were looking, at such a time, above all else for reassurance. And he had provided it. With supreme hypocrisy, he had ended his address:

Comrades, I must say that I have not for a long time seen a congress so united, so imbued with one idea. I regret that Comrade Lenin is not here. If he were here, he would be able to say: 'For twenty-five years I have been forging a party, and now here it is, complete, great and strong'.

Trotsky was not given to supplying sedatives. And certainly there was none in his own speech to the congress. After two years of the New Economic Policy, he declared, the growth in industrial production was still lagging far behind the recovery in agriculture. The resultant 'scissors', opened between the high price of industrial products and the low price of agricultural ones, threatened to cut the economic and political ties between city and countryside. The peasants would stop hoarding much of their surplus and sell it instead only if the 'scissors' were closed. And this was to be done not by raising agricultural prices but by lowering industrial ones, through the planned modernization, concentration and expansion of industry. Such was the socialist way. It did not mean the immediate abandonment of the New Economic Policy. It did mean a working from within that policy towards socialist objectives, till planning eventually reached through the entire economy, to absorb and to abolish the market. He made no attempt to suggest that this would be a painless process. The commitment to industrialization would involve widespread sacrifices. There was simply no escape, he warned the delegates, in a society as backward as theirs, from the need for the 'primitive accumulation' of capital. And the workers must help to provide this, by work for whose value they would be paid only in part.

He was heard with respect, but with mounting bewilderment and disquiet. The mass of delegates had come to think of the New Economic Policy as a permanent panacea and refused to recognize the signs of a dying revival. Trotsky seemed to be sounding the alarm with no force even in sight of assaulting the gates. The recourse to the market-place had gone far towards conciliating the peasants and reinvigorating agriculture. Would a retreat not once again produce rural revolt? And how loyal would the workers remain, if they were offered only the prospect of further sacrifice? The very phrase 'primitive accumulation' set flickering in many minds the images of the capitalist experience, and the film did not change because the word 'socialist' was added and the necessity of planning emphasized. Trotsky was being honest with the delegates. But paradoxically they were provoked by this honesty to wonder whether he was being honest enough. Was he not attempting to manoeuvre them back to the policy of war communism and the experiment with labour armies? Did his declaration that the market economy was to be gradually eaten away from within not conceal a commitment to dispose of the New Economic Policy, as soon as possible, in a single gulp?

Trotsky carried the congress with little difficulty. He stood higher in the party than ever before, now that Lenin was widely believed to be dying. And besides, he spoke on behalf of the leadership. His adversaries in the Politburo, keeping to their side of the bargain, had not given a glint, during the debate, of their opposition to his views. But the bewilderment and the disquiet remained in the minds of the delegates. And this made it all the easier for his adversaries subsequently to ensure that the relevant resolution never reached beyond the recording of the vote. Among them, Stalin moved, within a few days, from being the most vulnerable to a new ascendancy. Lenin had been pressing for an enlargment of the central committee. Stalin secured its enlargement from twenty-seven members to forty; and the additions, overwhelmingly the candidates of his apparatus, transferred control from Zinoviev's following to his own. The seven full members of the Politburo – Lenin, Trotsky, Rykov, Tomsky, Zinoviev, Kamenev and Stalin himself – were reappointed. With Lenin ill and with Tomsky still suspicious from the earlier trade union dispute, the votes of the triumvirate were enough to deal with Trotsky. The Central Control Commission was enlarged from only seven members to fifty; provision was made for its members to participate in plenary meetings of the central committee; and its functions were so redefined as to invest it with the powers of a supreme political police against any opposition in the party.[43]

Trotsky was, some seven years later, to confess: 'I have no doubt that if I had come forward on the eve of the twelfth congress in the spirit of a "*bloc* of Lenin and Trotsky" against the Stalin bureaucracy, I should have been victorious even if Lenin had taken no direct part in the struggle.' And he provided his own explanation for his failure to do so.

Independent action on my part would have been interpreted, or, to be more exact, represented, as my personal fight for Lenin's place in the party and the state. The very thought of this made me shudder. I considered that it would have brought such a demoralization in our ranks that we would have had to pay too painful a price for it even in case of victory.[44]

There can be little doubt that one element in Trotsky's decision was, indeed, this horror of even appearing to be concerned primarily with his personal advancement. It was a horror fed through the years, and being fed still, by the charge of his various adversaries that ambition was his governing principle. And his consciousness that the charge was not only unjust, but generally applicable to those from whom it came, did not make it any less damaging or any easier to ignore. To that degree, his decision would have been directed by pride: that classic pride whose sin consists in dislocation, whether by reaching too far or by refusing to reach far enough. But there is also every reason to accept the strength of his revulsion from the wider impact that his appearance of self-seeking might have had. He had always considered personal example to be among the supreme obligations of leadership. And he had never disguised his particular contempt for those of his colleagues who engaged in the duplicities of intrigue for their own advancement, as though their behaviour was irrelevant to the cause that they proclaimed and would not inevitably affect the outlook of others. That his own motives in confronting the bureaucracy would be misrepresented would do nothing to alter the impact of the misrepresentation. Instead of helping to remove the corruptions of careerism, he might be helplessly promoting the very mood in which they thrived.

That these were by no means the only factors, however, may safely be inferred from his increasing preoccupation with economic policy and the tenor of his remarks to Kamenev on 6 March. His reassurance was emphatic: 'Remember, and tell others, that the last thing I want is to start a fight at the congress for any changes in organization. I am for preserving the status quo.' And he proceeded to give the more specific reassurance: 'I am against removing Stalin. . . .'[45] One explanation is that 'Trotsky's revenge was to display magnanimity and forgiveness.'[46] But it is more likely that his concession was neither so gratuitous nor so self-indulgent. The driving of Stalin from office would, it is certain, have involved not only a prerequisite 'fight at the congress', but an accompanying organizational upheaval: and at a time when the party was not only deprived of the stability that Lenin's leadership had provided, but confronted by an economic challenge which it had so far failed even to recognize. To keep the party united for a commitment to meet this challenge might well have seemed to Trotsky the overriding obligation of the ascendancy that he could now exercise.

The central mystery remains: of how he could so decisively have misjudged Stalin's nature and the danger involved in leaving him to control the organization of the party. He was never, indeed, to understand Stalin, even at the end. Looking into Stalin's mind for its ideas, he found only the trivial and the vain. History might have shown him the paradox by which triviality of thought has informed an immensity of violence, and vanity has manifested itself in the fullness of evil. But staring at history, he lost sight of the personal shadows among the flames of ideas. It was the limitation of one who looked only for the light. And it is this that reveals the most vital reason of all. He believed not only in the irresistible power of liberating ideas. He believed in the imminence of liberation: the coming rush of mankind through the prison gates that the Russian revolution had burst open. What, then, were the intrigues and the pretensions of a Stalin but the cardboard boxes of the past that would be kicked out of the way? The heel of this Achilles was not his pride. It was the innocence and the integrity of his faith.

10

The Fall

The twelfth congress of April 1923 was invited to recognize the over-riding need for unity and discipline at a time when Lenin was stricken and unable to guide the party. Trotsky, rising to speak in support of the resolution, declared that he would not be the last to defend it, to put it into effect, and to fight ruthlessly against all who might try to infringe it. His own solidarity with the Politburo and with the central committee was, he proclaimed, 'unshaken'. Was he hoping, by this display of support for his associates in the leadership, to win them away from their suspicions and their jealousy of him? Was this his public renunciation of any attempt to impose his individual will, as Lenin had so often sought to do? But if these elements were present, so also was the call of the leader for obedience; for the abandonment of doubt and dissension in reliance on authority. Other revolutionaries, once mounted on their horses, had become Cossacks. Trotsky was to remain a revolutionary all his life. But he had sat on a horse too long. People had come to look different from above. And he would have to be thrown from his mount before he could see them as once he had, his eyes level with their own.

The new central committee, elected by the congress, contained only three of Trotsky's political allies: Piatakov, Radek and Rakovsky. And Stalin was duly reappointed general secretary. His fellow triumvirs, not yet aware of how far his own ambition reached, worked smoothly with him in removing Trotsky's allies from strategic positions. The more notable were provided with high diplomatic posts, which ensured that they would exercise their revolutionary virtues at a safe enough distance. But while Kamenev and Zinoviev were rubbing their hands at their success, Stalin was using his own to much greater effect. Regional and local secretaries whose loyalty was doubtful were removed from office, and Stalin's nominees appointed in their place. Within a few months, Stalin had turned most of the party organization into an instrument of his personal will.

Meetings of the Politburo became a mockery of the understanding that

Trotsky had allowed himself to believe he had reached with his colleagues. Decisions were taken without him or, when he was present, effectively as though his remarks were irrelevant. In vain did Trotsky press, again and again, for action on the economic policy adopted by the twelfth congress. The votes were stacked against him. Only the news from Germany lifted his spirits. For the regime there looked like choking to death on the terms of the Versailles Treaty.

Shortly after Germany had failed to meet its reparation commitments, the French government, in January 1923, dispatched troops to occupy the Ruhr. Workers there immediately began a general strike, accompanied by acts of sabotage and attacks on French soldiers. The occupation forces responded with arrests, deportations and executions. The Ruhr continued to resist. And meanwhile the fall in the value of the mark accelerated. From 75 to the dollar in 1921, the rate had reached 18,000 with the occupation of the Ruhr. By the beginning of July, it was 160,000, and by the beginning of August, one million. The rate would come to be quoted in millions of millions. But already, for most people, it had ceased to matter how far the process would go. The savings of a lifetime could not buy a single potato.

Victor Serge, in Germany for the Communist International, noted working-class women with those grey complexions that he had seen in the famished towns of Russia years before. Mobs collected in the streets and broke into shops. Each day brought another rash of strikes; each night, revolver shots.[1] But in the Politburo, Trotsky failed to carry his colleagues with him in giving the German party decisive encouragement and help. They were more concerned with the risks than with the rewards. Besides, they had other matters on their minds. Industrial unrest was spreading around them, with spontaneous strikes of protest at the level of wages. And Trotsky remained too dangerously dominant in the military domain. Some way must be found to bind his hands.

In the Politburo, Zinoviev moved that Stalin should be made a member of the Military Revolutionary Council. The meaning of this latest manoeuvre was unmistakable. Trotsky announced at once that he was resigning as Commissar of War and president of the Military Revolutionary Council, as well as from the Politburo and from the central committee. With the agreement of the Politburo, he would go to Germany and help the party there in its revolutionary attempt.[2]

This was not at all to the taste of his opponents. What if he should go and prove successful? He would, in a single stride, have far outstripped them. He would be unassailable. Yet, what if he failed and fell in the fighting? History would raise him high over their heads, while they sought meanwhile to survive the blame of having sent him deliberately to his death. Zinoviev's reply was inspired. He was president of the Communist

International and he would go instead. Nothing more was needed to make the whole discussion unreal. Stalin remarked that the Politburo could not afford to release from their responsibilities either of its most eminent members. And he would gladly remain excluded from the Military Revolutionary Council, to keep the peace. The Politburo voted to accept this compromise. And Trotsky, in helpless anger, stormed out of the meeting.

On 8 October, he wrote to members of the central committee. The industrial unrest, he declared, was a result of the failure to produce an appropriate and planned economic policy. The evident discontent in the party was due to an unprecedented 'bureaucratization of the party apparatus'. The system of appointment from above made secretaries the masters of their local organization, in a hierarchy which 'created' party opinion, discouraged any expression of independent views, and addressed the rank and file only in terms of command. It was scarcely surprising that dissent, denied all opportunity of influencing decisions, accumulated to emerge in unrest. The regime was much further now from any workers' democracy than it had been in 'the fiercest period of war communism'. And it was time that the high pressure of civil war discipline was relieved, to produce 'a livelier and broader party responsibility'.

One week later, forty-six eminent members of the party issued their own statement of complaint. Amongst the signatories were close associates of Trotsky's: Piatakov, the distinguished economist and industrial administrator; Preobrazhensky, who had written with Bukharin the celebrated *ABC of Communism*; Ivan Smirnov, who had organized the victory over Kolchak in the civil war; and Antonov-Ovseenko, who was now chief political commissar of the Red Army. Others, far from being identifiable as followers of Trotsky, had clashed with him in the past over their protests at the party's dictatorial leadership. The need for immediate changes had brought them together, in a declaration that largely resembled the terms of Trotsky's letter.

The forty-six formally requested the central committee to acquaint the party at large with the contents of their statement. The request, in defiance of custom, was refused; and the signatories were warned that they would face disciplinary measures if they circulated the statement themselves. At a special session of the central committee, the triumvirate assailed Trotsky for this further evidence of his overweening ambition. The central committee resolved to reprimand him for his attitude and the forty-six for having broken the party ban on 'fractionalism'.

Under Zinoviev's command, the executive of the Communist International, revealing rather more skill in manipulating the calendar than in promoting the downfall of capitalism, had fixed the date of the German revolution, to commemorate the Bolshevik seizure of power in Russia, for 25 October.[3] Whether or not the attempt would in any event have failed, dithering and delay ensured a fiasco. As though having caught the infection from Moscow, the central committee of the German Communist Party busied itself in deciding which posts its members should be allotted in the future revolutionary government. And meanwhile, Victor Serge noted, the unemployed were passing from insurgent enthusiasm into weary resignation.[4] The executive of the Communist International was not disposed to accept any blame for the outcome. It condemned the 'opportunism' of the German party leaders.

That Trotsky should, in this turbulent and dismal period of Soviet politics, have completed a work of literary criticism, was altogether in character. Revolution and art were alike for him aspects of human creativity, and a book on *Literature and Revolution* was a book on the two seminal loves of his life. Nor was the mounting conflict within the Soviet leadership a reason to put the work, which he had begun in the summer of the previous year, aside. On the contrary: it made all the more necessary a different and deeper struggle, for the mind of the revolution. When he returned to Moscow from his summer holiday in 1923, he brought the completed manuscript with him. He would dedicate it to his close associate from the Balkan days: 'Christian Georgievich Rakovsky – Warrior, Man and Friend'.

Trotsky accepts that without individuality, there can be no artist. But such individuality is not a unique element. For if it were, there would be no communication possible to it. It is, rather, a unique combination of elements, each of them common to the recipient, in whom they are differently but no less uniquely combined, for being artistically unexpressed. And it is the function of the critic, therefore, to identify the common elements which are struts in the bridge of art between one individuality and another.

Only through the common can the unique come to be known. And the common is determined in man by the deepest and most persistent conditions which make up his 'soul'; by the social conditions of education, of existence, of work and of associations. The social conditions in historic human society are, first of all, the conditions of class affiliation.[5]

This thesis flows direct from its Marxist source. And whole regions of criticism have been washed from this flow, to produce only stretches of sand. Trotsky's first achievement was to apply a tillage of formal criticism so creative that the writers and writings he denounces come alive on the page no less than those he admires. And in the process he reaches beyond criticism into art. His thesis becomes a dramatic theme; and the relationship to it of each character that he depicts on his stage, a further development of the revelation that is the experience of the spectator in the dark.

It is the artistic lifelessness of those who have fled from Russia and the revolution which he begins by bringing alive.

It will take a long time before the horses will be got ready for Moscow, and the passengers express their emotions in the meantime. . . . They are ironical, they reminisce, they pretend to yawn somewhat; but, out of politeness, suppress the yawn. They quote in various tongues, make skeptical predictions and immediately deny them. At first this appears amusing, then boring and in the end disgusting.[6]

Then there are the internal émigrés, who have fled the revolution, sometimes for God and sometimes for the asylum of pure style.

The lyric circle of Akhmatova, Tsvetaeva, Radlova, and the other real and near-poetesses, is very small. It embraces the poetess herself, an unknown one in a derby or in spurs, and inevitably God, without any special marks. He is a very convenient and portable third person, quite domestic, a friend of the family who fulfils from time to time the duties of a doctor of female ailments. How this individual, no longer young, and burdened with the personal and too often bothersome errands of Akhmatova, Tsvetaeva and others, can manage in his spare time to direct the destinies of the universe is simply incomprehensible.[7]

It is a lost individualism, cast by the revolutionary upheaval on to an island, where it paces up and down as a distracted and sterile preoccupation with self. And the prime example is Andrey Biely, whose stagnant thinking, 'essentially medieval', is betrayed, in his very attempt to disguise it, by mere tricks of style. His rhythmic prose is related not to any movement of the image, but to the imposition of a metre. And the 'premonition' that yet another sentence will end rhythmically produces only irritation, just as when one waits for the shutter to squeak again when one is sleepless. Alongside this, there goes his 'fetish of the word', as though the mere juggling of sounds might in itself provide the substance that the sense does not afford:

Biely seeks in the word, just as the Pythagoreans in numbers, a second, special and hidden meaning. And that is why he finds himself so often in a blind alley of words. If you cross your middle finger over your index finger and touch an object, you will feel two objects, and if you repeat this experiment it will make you feel queer; instead of the correct use of your sense of touch, you are abusing it to deceive yourself. Biely's artistic methods give exactly this impression.[8]

Such writers have turned away from the transforming social fact of their time and are deprived of its vivifying force. Others have accepted it, but only in part. And they are the 'fellow-travellers' who, like their class and their culture, go no more than some of the way. It is they who most notably speak for a liberated peasantry rather than a liberating proletariat. And so there is something that is ultimately enclosed and immobile in their work. Thus in the work of Nicolai Kliuev there is a clutter of imagery that impedes action and makes one 'move about cautiously not to break and destroy'.

. . . his Revolution is without political dynamics and without historic per-
spective. To Kliuev it is like a market or a sumptuous wedding where people
come together from various places, get drunk with wine and song, with embraces
and dances, and then return to their own houses: their own earth under their
feet and their own sun above their heads. . . . He promises paradise through the
Revolution, but this paradise is only an exaggerated and embellished peasant
kingdom, a wheat and honey paradise: a singing bird on the carved wing of the
house and a sun shining in jasper and diamonds. Not without hesitation does
Kliuev admit into his peasant paradise the radio and magnetism and electricity;
and here it appears that electricity is a giant bull out of a peasant epic and that
between his horns is a laden table.[9]

Yessinin too, the leading poet of the Imagist group, has his roots in the
village. They do not go down as deep, for he is younger and he became a
poet when the village was being shaken up by the revolution. But they
still feed a poetry slow of movement, 'like a beast of burden'. An abundance of imagery is not necessarily evidence of creative power; it may
arise instead from

the technical immaturity of a poet who is caught unawares by events and
feelings which are artistically too much for him. The poet almost chokes with
images and the reader feels as nervously impatient to get on as fast as possible to
the end as when one listens to a stuttering speaker.[10]

Boris Pilnyak is a restless realist. He strives to see and to depict the
revolution. Yet he does so only in snatches, because he cannot grasp it
intellectually, as a whole. His revolution is a small town one. And that
can be an organic approach. But if you can approach the revolution through
the small town, you must not have a small town vision of it.

A district council of the Soviets – a sled road – 'Comrades, help me in' – bast
shoes – sheepskins – the waiting line to the Soviet house for bread, for sausages,
for tobacco – Comrades, you are the sole masters of the Revolutionary Council
and township – oh, sweetheart, you give little, so little! [this reference to
sausages] – it is the last decisive battle – the International – the Entente – international capitalism. . . .
   In such bits of discussion, of life, of speeches, of sausages and of anthems,
there is something of the Revolution; a vital part of it grasped with a keen eye,
but as if in a hurry, as if rushing past. But something is lacking there that would
tie these bits together from within. The idea which underlies our epoch is
lacking.[11]

In short, the 'fellow-travellers' lack the consistent realism, the power of
thought, the 'lucidity and solidity of line' that belongs to the revolution
and that comes not from the village or the small town, but from the city,
from industry. And that is why their art seems to squat or to stumble, out
of breath with the times.

What, then, of the Futurists, whose landscape is the city, and who associate their own violent break from tradition with the revolutionary reach? But theirs is essentially a Bohemian revolt, whose uniform yellow blouse is a 'grand-niece' of that 'sensational red vest' which a leading French romanticist put on 'for the ultimate shaming of the bourgeoisie'.[12] They are not revolutionaries, for revolutionaries live in traditions. They want to jump out of history and they end, instead, by falling into whatever political upheaval against bourgeois values prevails. In Italy, they have merged with Fascism. In Russia, they have sought to merge with the revolution. But their art betrays their romantic ancestry. And even Mayakovsky, the greatest of them all, is most an artist at precisely the point where he is least a Communist.

'Just as the ancient Greek was an anthropomorphist and naively thought of the forces of nature as resembling himself, so our poet is a Mayakomorphist and fills the squares, the streets and fields of the Revolution with his own personality.' It is an arrogance that denies him a necessary sense of measure, so that it becomes impossible to establish the difference between the little and the big. He speaks of the most intimate feeling, like love, as though he were speaking about 'the migration of peoples'. And so he cannot find different words when he comes to speak of the revolution. 'Mayakovsky shouts too often, where he should merely speak; that is why his shouting, in those places where he ought to shout, seems insufficient.'[13] His very excess of violent imagery results in quiescence.

A work of art must show the gradual growth of an image, of a mood, of a plot, or of an intrigue to its climax, and must not throw the reader about from one end to another end, no matter if it is done by the most skilful boxing blows of Imagery. Each phrase, each expression, each image of Mayakovsky's works tries to be the climax. That is why the whole 'piece' has no climax. The spectator has a feeling that he has to spend himself in parts, and the whole eludes him. To climb a mountain is difficult, but worthwhile, but a walk across plowed-up country is no less fatiguing and gives much less joy.[14]

Such is the paradox of Futurism. It is entirely founded on action; and action is, indeed, what it artistically lacks.

Is there, then, a specifically proletarian art, to be encouraged and acclaimed? Trotsky denies the very possibility of such a phenomenon. For it would require a correspondingly developed culture. And the dominion of the proletariat is no more than a transitional phase; the prelude to the establishment of a classless society, with its own culture and art. There exists neither the time nor the stability for the development of a proletarian equivalent to the culture of the feudal or of the bourgeois age. 'We are, as before, merely soldiers in a campaign. We are bivouacking for a day. Our shirt has to be washed, our hair has to be cut and combed, and, most important of all, the rifle has to be cleaned and oiled.'[15] This is not an epoch of new culture. It is only the entrance to one.

To deny the possibility of an organic proletarian art, however, is not to deny the possibility of a new art, created by proletarians, during the transitional phase. Such an art cannot fail to place the struggle of the proletariat in the centre of its attention. 'But the plow of the new art is not limited to numbered strips. On the contrary, it must plow the entire field in all directions. Personal lyrics of the very smallest scope have an absolute right to exist within the art.'[16] And certainly Marxism has nothing to do with any desire to dominate art by decrees. 'Art must make its own way and by its own means. The Marxian methods are not the same as the artistic. . . . The domain of art is not one in which the Party is called upon to command.'[17]

This does not, to be sure, imply a renunciation of all control. A revolution that has the right to destroy irreplaceable monuments, where required by the needs of its defence, can scarcely stop at counteracting any endeavour in art that 'threatens to disintegrate the revolutionary environment'. But for this very reason, the limits of censorship must be clearly defined, to allow 'a broad and flexible policy . . . free from petty partisan maliciousness'.[18] And just how 'broad and flexible' Trotsky believed that such a policy should be is evident from his remarks on the need for a Soviet comedy, of laughter and of indignation.

How much woe there is from being too wise, or from pretending to be too wise, and how good it would be if a stage Inspector General would walk across our Soviet life. . . . Of course, if your comedy will try to say: 'See what we have been brought to; let us go back to the nice old nobleman's nest' – then, of course, the censorship will sit on your comedy, and will do so with propriety. But if your comedy will say: 'We are building a new life now, and yet how much piggishness, vulgarity and knavery of the old and of the new are about us; let us make a clean sweep of them', then, of course, the censorship will not interfere, and if it will interfere somewhere it will do so foolishly, and all of us will fight such a censorship.[19]

All this composes a mounting dramatic movement. The life of bourgeois art has been re-created, in the differing strengths and weaknesses of significant literary figures, and then left behind. Proletarian art has been laid out for burial, along with the pretensions of the existing Proletcult, the Organization for Proletarian Culture. The climax is reached in a long lyric description of the future communist society. It is a society that emerges not as some monolithic building of social discipline, with special quarters for art, but rather as a soaring of human creativity, from its long encagement, with science as the beating of its wings, and art as its song.[20]

Yet how soon the very revolution that Trotsky saw as the bursting of the cage was to become the occasion and the excuse for the ultimate confinement. A human creativity that had struck against the sides of bourgeois culture was to be enclosed within the pupils of one man's eyes. Yessinin and Mayakovsky were to commit suicide; Kliuev, the poet of the peasant paradise, was to be imprisoned and to die soon after his release; Pilnyak and several others, whose work is variously evaluated in the pages of *Literature and Revolution*, were to vanish in one or other of Stalin's purges. Marietta Shaginyan, whom Trotsky had described as 'anti-revolutionary in her very essence',[21] was, exceptionally, to survive and even achieve the distinction of a Stalin Prize.

One weekend in October 1923, shortly after he had hit back at the triumvirate with his letter to the central committee, Trotsky went on a hunting trip to the marshlands of the River Dubna outside Moscow. Watching the skies for flying wild duck and geese, in a silence broken only by the warning whispers of his friend and guide from a nearby village, had long been his favourite way of resting his mind and replenishing his energies. But this time, the respite ended badly. Trotsky brought back with him a mysterious fever which stayed for months and would leave him only to return, again and again.

It was now, when Trotsky was contained by his apartment in the Kremlin, that the triumvirs, seeking to reduce the pressure of discontent, or perhaps only to take the measure of its strength, opened the press and the party organization in Moscow to democratic debate. They were all but swept off their feet by the blast. At meetings of party militants and in factories, they were received with scorn, while one or other representative of the opposition was heard with acclaim. The central committee of the Communist Youth, with the overwhelming majority of student cells, supported the demands of the forty-six. And most alarmingly, Antonov-Ovseenko was winning over the party organizations of the garrison. But Antonov-Ovseenko was not discreet. He claimed that the military sectors of the party were united, 'as one man', behind Trotsky.

The triumvirs were quick to strike back. Distorting this statement into a virtual threat of military revolt, they had Antonov-Ovseenko dismissed from his post as the Red Army's chief political commissar. The party's General Secretariat, in defiance of the relevant statutes, dismissed the central committee of the Communist Youth and appointed a new one instead. Pretexts were found to demote or transfer influential supporters of the opposition. But reprisals were only part of the counter-attack. The triumvirs had used timely lip service before, in outmanoeuvring Trotsky. They now submitted a resolution that denounced the party's bureaucratic regime and proclaimed a commitment to freedom of criticism and debate.

Trotsky was not to be caught again in the trap of trading his silence for empty promises. Yet he knew that any refusal to endorse the resolution would be used by his enemies to claim that it was he who feared and resisted democratic reform. He proposed particular amendments, to tighten the commitment. All were accepted. On 5 December, the Politburo recorded a unanimous vote in favour of the resolution. But already on the day before, *Pravda* had published the first of a few short articles, which he wrote to keep the issues from being buried beneath a mere stone effigy of reform.

He assailed the dependence of officialdom, in his own department of the armed forces 'and elsewhere', on custom and cant; the fear of any criticism or initiative; the promotion of a sterile sycophancy from subordinates. For all the skill of the thrusts, however, the point was buttoned. Then Trotsky heard that the triumvirate, seeking to deprive the forty-six of their claim to his support, was denying his own discontent and declaring his devotion to discipline. This was beyond bearing; and on 8 December, Trotsky addressed an 'Open Letter' to party meetings.[22]

Within the leadership, he warned, there were already signs of an intention to back away from the commitment to reform. But the party could secure the New Course if its rank and file would rely on themselves, their own understanding and courage. The young should cease to regard the authority of the Old Guard as absolute; and do so for the sake of the Old Guard itself, which could be saved from bureaucratic degeneration and preserved as a revolutionary factor only by a vigorous democracy within the party. It was time for the party to free itself from the tyranny of its machine; to replace the 'mummified bureaucrats' with fresh elements; and, most importantly of all, to remove from leading posts those who, at the first word of criticism or protest, wielded their whips. It was imperative for the New Course to begin 'by making everyone feel that from now on nobody will dare terrorize the party'.

This was drawing blood, indeed. And his adversaries leapt at him. To vote with the other members of the Politburo for the New Course and then rouse suspicion of their sincerity was both inconsistent and disloyal. To incite the young against the Old Guard, and the ranks of the party against those who served it with so much diligence and devotion, was as irresponsible as it was dangerous. The truth was that all his talk of bureaucratic repressiveness and of the need for more democracy came from his resentment at the refusal of his colleagues to support his dictatorial ambitions. It revealed how much of a Menshevik, for all his supposed conversion to Leninism, he remained.

There were many members of the party for whom Trotsky's letter sounded like the turn of the key at last in a long-locked door. But others were uneasy and confused. They had been assured so often, without a word from Trotsky in denial, that theirs was a leadership whose collective insight had brought them safely through innumerable perils. They wavered and waited to see who was likely to win. Still others were angered and afraid. For at whom was Trotsky's letter directed, if not at them? And it was they, of course, who operated the party machine. Local newspapers and bulletins gave much greater prominence to the attacks on Trotsky's letter than to its terms, and crowded their correspondence columns with hostile comment. Branch meetings were arranged, and the discussions conducted, to secure a formal condemnation of Trotsky's criticism. And when a meeting misfired to produce some resolution of support for such criticism, another was soon enough organized to adjust the record, or the resolution itself simply suppressed. Above all, the functionaries applied their aptitudes to the selection processes for delegates to the thirteenth party conference, which would determine the issue.

The opposition maintained that at the primary level of party cells, in Moscow and other major cities, the vast majority of members had rallied behind it. But from level to level of the indirect election process, its representation was reduced. And when the conference met in January 1924, there were no more than three delegates who would cast their votes against a resolution that condemned Trotsky and his forty-six associates for a 'petit bourgeois deviation from Leninism'. That this made the Politburo's own commitment to freedom of criticism and dispute a heap of discarded peels scarcely troubled Trotsky's adversaries. It had served its purpose, and the scraps could be dropped in the bin of another Politburo resolution, at some suitable time. Meanwhile, the party had been shown how hopeless, even with the help of all Trotsky's personal prestige, the course of opposition to the will of the leadership was.

Trotsky himself would claim that the triumvirate could never have succeeded in defeating him, without the double accident of a fatally stricken Lenin and his own illness.[23] And it is relevant that even in the midst of the campaign against him, most of his adversaries were so persuaded of his residual power that they recoiled from the consequence of an ultimate break. Zinoviev, translated to his seventh heaven for the moment, was pressing for Trotsky's expulsion from the party and even for his arrest. Rumours began circulating in Moscow that Trotsky was about to be dismissed from every office that he held. Stalin himself took the lead in denouncing these as 'malicious slander', and on 18 December *Pravda* proclaimed: 'Nobody can conceive of the work of the Politburo, the Central Committee or the State without the active participation of Comrade Trotsky.' It remains, however, difficult to see how Trotsky, in the very best of health, might have altered the outcome of a conflict within the perimeter of the party. His presence at meetings, with the force of his oratory, might have brought the membership in Moscow, and such other centres as he visited, cheering to its feet. But this would not have affected the disposition of the apparatus or in consequence the character of the decisive conference. Since the twelfth congress in April, Stalin had done his work far too well for Trotsky to undo it within a few weeks; even in the unlikely event that the triumvirate would have waived its mastery of the machine and afforded him an adequate opportunity to try.

Was there another way? Some of his adherents were later to maintain that Trotsky might have won in 1923 by holding his base in the army and personally appealing to the workers in the cities.[24] But this, given the triumvirate's control over the party's governing institutions, would effectively have involved an appeal to the proletariat against its own party. It is almost certain that such a course never occurred to Trotsky at the time; and certain that if, at someone else's nudging, it had, he would have rejected it with horror at once, as opening an ideological chasm that must swallow up the revolution. Nor would his base in the army have meant anything, without his readiness to use it. His adversaries, indeed, might well have been wondering whether he would. The speed with which they had pounced on Antonov-Ovseenko's indiscretion revealed as much of their anxieties as of their astuteness. But such a threat was only a reflection of themselves, standing in Trotsky's clothes before the mirror of their minds. A Trotsky who would not have considered calling on the proletariat against the party would still less have considered calling on the army against it. The accident of Trotsky's illness weakened hands which were already tied. It was not that which decided the issue for his adversaries: it was their control of the party, which he had given away months before, and which he essentially refused to challenge on any terms but those that they were able to dictate.

He fought all the more ardently at the meetings of the Politburo in his apartment. And Natalia, who sat in the adjoining bedroom, listened.

He spoke with his whole being; it seemed as if with every such speech he lost some of his strength – he spoke with so much 'blood'. And in reply, I heard cold, indifferent answers. Everything, of course, had been decided in advance, so what was the need of getting excited? After each of these meetings, [his] temperature mounted; he came out of his study soaked through, and undressed and went to bed. His linen and clothes had to be dried as if he had been drenched in a rain-storm.[25]

At night, in Natalia's dreams, the faded old carpet on the study floor would come alive, in the form of a panther.

It was a more than usually hard winter. Trotsky's doctors, certain only that his illness was not responding to their treatment, urged him to leave Moscow for the southern warmth of the Black Sea coast. Heavy with the recognition of his inevitable defeat, he readily agreed. And without waiting for the formal decision of the special conference, he set off on 18 January 1924. Three days later, while his train was at the Tiflis station, his assistant

Syermuks brought him a decoded telegram from Stalin. The young man's face, beneath his reddish hair, was leaden, and he handed the message to Trotsky without looking at him. Lenin was dead.

Trotsky's first thought was to return at once, and he wired the Kremlin. But he was advised by Stalin that he would never be able to get back in time for the funeral and that no purpose would be served by his risking his health. Trotsky decided to continue with his journey. Only when it was too late did he learn that Stalin had lied. The funeral would, in fact, take place on the 27th; in more than enough time for Trotsky to have returned and attended. But then it was too late for so much more. While Lenin lived, there had always been a chance that he might recover and snatch back the victory from the triumvirs, even as they were celebrating it. But now, even that flicker had gone.

In the dining-room of the rest-house at Sukhum, there were two portraits on the wall; one, draped in black, of Lenin; and the other of Trotsky himself. Trotsky and Natalia talked of taking the second one down, but decided that this would seem 'too demonstrative'.[26] The January sun was warm, and the surroundings bright with camellias and with mimosa in flower. Trotsky lay on the balcony and gazed, over the heads of the huge palms in between, at the glittering sea. And through his mind, vividly as in a dream, there progressed his memories of Lenin; from that earliest encounter in London, through the many years of conflict, to their reconciliation and their final fellowship. The future was cold enough in that sunshine, to call for the lighting of a fire from the past.

As he lay, on the day of Lenin's funeral, listening to the tribute of the artillery from the seashore below, he thought of sending Krupskaya, so alone now, some message of comfort. But all the words that he found fell short of what he wanted to say. And it was Krupskaya, sensing his own need of comfort, who wrote instead, a letter that arrived a few days afterwards. She told him that Lenin, a month or so before his death, had been looking through one of Trotsky's books and stopped at the passage comparing him with Marx. He had asked her to read it; had listened attentively; and then looked at it again. 'And here is something else I want to tell you. The attitude of Vladimir Ilyich toward you at the time when you came to us in London from Siberia did not change until his death. I wish you, Lev Davidovich, strength and health, and I embrace you warmly.'

The way she had felt for him deeply moved Trotsky. And it was for her, in turn, that he immediately felt, when he heard of the Politburo's decision to embalm Lenin's body and place it on display in a specially built mausoleum, beside the Kremlin wall in Red Square. 'How Nadezhda Konstantinovna must be suffering,' he said. 'She knows better than anyone else what Lenin would have thought of such goings-on.'[27] It was too late for his own protests to matter. And Krupskaya herself kept silent in her distress.

From Moscow, came the newspapers, with their long obituaries, articles, and reports of memorial speeches. And there came, too, a letter from Trotsky's elder son Lyova, who had been waiting so impatiently for his parents to return. Natalia was to recall its 'bewilderment and diffident reproach'. At the elaborate ceremonies, with the members of the Politburo in place beside the body, like so many mourning successors to the estate, no empty space was needed to mark the absence of Trotsky. The enormous crowds, as his own son, looked for him and wondered why he, of all Lenin's closest colleagues, was not there.

His adversaries lost no time in further undermining his position and reinforcing their own. Skylansky, his loyal second-in-command at the war department, was put in charge of the Moscow textile industry; and his place taken by Frunze, an adherent of Zinoviev's. A delegation from the central committee visited Sukhum to consult with Trotsky: but the decision had already been taken, and the visit was no more than a nod to the proprieties.

Militant students were expelled from the party and from the universities; dissident workers dismissed as redundant; and prominent opponents posted to remote areas. And at the same time, as a proclaimed mark of tribute to the memory of Lenin, some 240,000 workers were recruited within a few months, to increase the membership of the party by well over half. But this 'Lenin levy' was less a surrender to the opposition demand for more democracy than an outflanking manoeuvre. It was in the main Stalin's secretaries who supervised the enlistment, and it was not with any purpose of promoting democracy that they accepted or rejected particular recruits.

In the spring, with his illness subsiding, Trotsky returned to Moscow. And he found it the capital of a cult, closer to the medieval than to any Marxist disposition. The mummy of Lenin was preserved like the remains of a saint; his writings were cited as though they were sacred texts; and Trotsky's adversaries were assuming the authority of high priests in interpreting what was Leninism and what was not. It was all the more momentous, therefore, when Krupskaya produced, a few days before the opening of the thirteenth party congress on 23 May, Lenin's Testament, with the communication of his 'definite wish' that it would be read to the next party congress after his death. The Politburo decided instead that it should be presented to a joint meeting of the central committee and of delegation heads, on the 22nd.

If the references to Kamenev and Zinoviev were effectively belittling asides, those to Stalin in the codicil were crushing. And there could no longer be any doubt that it was Trotsky whom Lenin would have wanted to see leading the party. Radek, sitting beside him, leaned towards Trotsky and said: 'Now they won't dare go against you.' But Trotsky had come to know his adversaries better. No, he replied; they would 'have to go the limit', and as quickly as possible.[28] When Kamenev and Zinoviev argued that Stalin should be allowed to remain as general secretary, Trotsky was silent. When the central committee voted, over the protests of Krupskaya, to suppress the Testament, Trotsky was silent. Only the movements of his face and shoulders, like so many helpless twitches, told of the disgust that he was unable to contain. It would, he knew, make no difference to the outcome, if he complained. Indeed, in this company, his complaint would only be taken as a last frantic play for personal power. He would only degrade himself by engaging in the degradation of the proceedings.

Max Eastman, his English translator and a friend, was in Moscow for the congress, and entreated him to read the Testament from the platform. Trotsky refused. He must have felt that this would merely mean a repeat performance of the arguments and outcome at the meeting on the 22nd, but on a far more significant occasion. He owed it not merely to his own dignity, but to the memory of Lenin and, even more, the repute of the revolution, to avoid the disgrace that a similar decision, from a full party congress, must entail.

He expected the congress to condemn him, as the special conference in January had done. He was not prepared for the call from Zinoviev publicly to recant. But Zinoviev had misjudged the mood among even these carefully selected delegates. When Krupskaya protested at this 'psychologically impossible demand', there were few who did not acclaim her rebuke. And Trotsky was accorded a generally respectful hearing when he rose at last to defend himself. Wryly he remarked that no great moral heroism was needed to admit, before one's own party, one's mistakes. Nothing, indeed, would be easier than to say that all those criticisms and declarations, warnings and protests, had been wrong, from beginning to end.

I cannot say so, however, because, comrades, I do not think so. I know that one ought not to be right against the party. One can be right only with the party and through the party because history has not created any other way for the realization of one's rightness. The English have the saying, 'My country, right or wrong'. With much greater justification we can say: My party, right or wrong – wrong on certain partial, specific issues or at certain moments. . . .

Preobrazhensky, speaking for the 'forty-six', was bolder, or less oblique. And the delegates relieved their feelings with abuse.

One month later, the fifth congress of the Communist International met in Moscow. The central committees of the French and Polish parties, which had shown an intolerable independence the year before in protesting at the campaign against Trotsky, had been suitably purged. The leadership of the German party, required to take the blame not only for its own mistakes but for those of the Soviet Politburo, in the miscarriage of the German revolution, had been changed. In the deepening dusk of their own revolutionary promise, the foreign parties were the more easily converted from their original status as colleagues to mere clients of the leadership in Moscow. Stalin had never attended a congress of the International before. Now, without taking part in any of the debates, he advertised his presence: 'he was wearing military uniform, although the civil war had finished four years earlier, and he had boots on, even though it was July'.[29] Under Zinoviev's direction, delegates denounced Trotsky and even demanded that he appear before them to recant. He ignored both the denunciations and the demand. In the elections for a new executive, he lost his place to Stalin.

It was for Trotsky a summer of silence; and for the triumvirate itself, one of increasing strains. Trotsky's succession to Lenin's predominance had been prevented; but Kamenev and Zinoviev had not intended in the process to promote the ascendancy of Stalin instead. They had come to his rescue in May, since the publication of Lenin's Testament would have rid them of Stalin only at the cost of reviving Trotsky's claims. They had expected Stalin to be grateful. But gratitude was not a quality of Stalin's. During a speech in June, he criticized both Kamenev and Zinoviev, for having erred in matters of doctrine. And a few weeks afterwards, he posted Zelenskii, the secretary of the Moscow party organization and an adherent of Kamenev's, to Central Asia.[30]

Events, however, relieved the strains for a while. Driven beyond endurance by the repressive policies of Moscow, the Georgians rebelled in late August. The uprising was rapidly crushed by the Red Army. But the emergence of rebellion anywhere concentrated the minds of the triumvirs on the dangers of division. And scarcely less effective was the way that Trotsky now chose to break at last his silence. The state publishers were still producing instalments of Trotsky's *Works*, in accordance with a central committee decision that had not yet been revoked. The forthcoming volume was to contain his speeches and writings of 1917, and he proceeded to provide a preface for it, called 'The Lessons of October'.

Drawn from both the successful insurrection of 1917 in Russia and the unsuccessful one of 1923 in Germany, they were the lessons of leadership. No Communist Party could, at will, create revolutionary opportunities: for these resulted from the decay of a social order. But it could, under determined leaders, seize the occasion as it came; or, under timid and indecisive ones, miss the flood-tide, to flounder for many years in the shallows. A Bolshevik, indeed, was to be judged not by how he behaved in the ebb of events, as in the partly 'irrelevant manoeuvres of émigré politics', but in the flow, as in 1917.

Trotsky brought history to bear witness on his behalf. And the witness exploded the pretensions of Trotsky's assailants to the infallible judgement of the Bolshevik Old Guard. Kamenev and Zinoviev were once more revealed as the 'strike-breakers of revolution'; Rykov, Kalinin and others, as opponents of Lenin's policy in 1917.[31] Nor was there much comfort for Stalin in Trotsky's failure to deal with him at all. Nothing, in the circumstances, could so tellingly have drawn attention to the insignificance of his role in 1917 as did this careful neglect.

As soon as the book left the presses in the autumn, Trotsky's adversaries moved against it. The edition was virtually suppressed; so that only a few copies escaped, for mainly surreptitious circulation. But any Soviet circulation was bound to be dangerous. And besides, reading habits abroad were not susceptible to the same control. A more effective reply was required. Trotsky had relied on history to speak for him. But history was a witness that could be suborned. Stalin, ignoring his own anniversary article for *Pravda* in 1918, which had acknowledged Trotsky's crucial role in the October insurrection, now disclosed that this role had been grossly exaggerated. The real leadership had been exercised by a special committee of five members, to which Stalin himself but not Trotsky had belonged. It would have been difficult to explain why so momentous a matter should have been kept concealed for seven years. But questions were not encouraged. And doubt was soon distracted by still other adjustments to the record.

Nor was this more, for the moment, than a minor part of a massive denigration campaign. The main battleground was that of doctrine. For it was not enough to belittle Trotsky's achievements. The revolution would never have been made without ideas, and ideas remained the principal sustenance of the international Communist movement. It was of Trotsky's mind that his enemies were the most frightened. But they saw, too, how its very qualities of originality and consistency might be made to serve their own purposes. Ideology was, to be sure, not a domain in which they had generally so far distinguished themselves. But this made them, and among them Stalin especially, all the more eager to try.

What began in the autumn of 1924, accordingly, was a campaign less against Trotsky than against Trotskyism: the identification of a heresy, which must subject its founder and all who would follow him to the rage of the one true faith. Much of Trotsky's ideological renown rested on the doctrine of permanent revolution, which he had enunciated eighteen years before. And his enemies could scarcely avoid dealing with it. Yet the ground floor of this doctrine, that a bourgeois revolution in Russia would necessarily give way almost at once to a regime of the proletariat, which would go beyond bourgeois objectives, had the policies of Lenin in 1917, and the subsequent career of the Bolshevik government, to support it. Trotsky in 'The Lessons of October' had gone back to 1917. His enemies were forced to go back very much further. Had Lenin himself, at the time that the doctrine appeared, not denounced its 'semi-anarchist' views, and proposed 'a revolutionary democratic dictatorship of the proletariat and peasantry'? If Trotsky had been right, then Lenin had been wrong. And could Lenin have been wrong?

Trotsky had argued that the peasantry was bourgeois in its aspirations and would therefore always have to be led by the proletariat. And Lenin had certainly pursued political policies, from 1917 onwards, which reflected this formulation. But again, it was a formulation that he had fiercely attacked at the time. And there was an abundance of holy writ available to brandish. Furthermore, the triumvirate could turn for immediate confirmation to the dispute over economic policy. If Trotsky had been guilty of 'underestimating the peasants' as far back as 1906, what else was he now, with his calls for a programme of rapid industrialization?

The challenging paradox, however, was that Trotsky remained most dangerous where he was most orthodox; in his consistent belief that socialism was impossible on a national basis, and that the Russian revolution itself could not long survive without the support of revolution in the advanced capitalist states. It was here that he might most effectively attack his opponents, for sacrificing the cause of world revolution to that of their own misplaced security, and rouse the mass of Communist Party members abroad against the subservience of their leaderships to a conservative dispensation in Moscow. It was here, therefore, that his opponents would have to meet and overcome him. And Stalin set out, with one of the boldest strokes of his entire career, to do so.

An excavation of Lenin's writings brought to light an article dating from 1915, which recognized the possibility that in consequence of the capitalist system's unequal development, revolution might occur in merely a few countries or even in one. Trotsky himself, of course, had said as much; long before, and with particular reference to Russia. But this had as little to be regarded as the rest of the relevant article, which might bewilderingly reveal that Lenin had not been referring to Russia at the time and had, moreover, argued that any such event must be accompanied by immediate attempts to spread the revolution elsewhere. The statement of Lenin's remained. And if it was not so wide as a church door, still it would serve. In December 1924, Stalin delivered himself of the new orthodoxy. Even if the proletariat elsewhere had to be considered the ultimate guarantee against a restoration of the bourgeois order, socialism could be developed in a single country.

Stalin's very lack of intellectual distinction now combined with a show of careful civility to still the disquiet of the younger Communists at the campaign against Trotsky.

We were impressed at first by the fact that now when Stalin did write or speak, in his bare first-reader style, there did not seem to be a trace of rancour in his attitude. While other leaders freely engaged in personalities, Stalin appeared to be the cool, devoted Leninist, patiently searching out the 'theoretical' errors of his colleagues and presenting them in a dispassionate spirit. It was precisely his lack of brilliance, his plainness, which inclined us to believe what he said. We did not know that he was directing and egging on these more personal polemics.[32]

And his doctrine itself thrived on the tiredness and disappointment of the times. It dangled before the Soviet people a chance of release at last from their many trials, for progress towards that prosperity which socialism promised. And it promoted a mood of mingled impatience and distrust towards those who seemed, by contrast, only concerned to demand yet further trials, for the sake of others. Not least, to Communists abroad, confused and discouraged by the receding revolutionary prospects in their own countries, the doctrine offered reassurance in submission to the will of Moscow. If socialism could be victorious within the Soviet Union, it must, by its strength and its example, advance the victory of socialism everywhere; so that to serve Soviet interests was to serve the interests of socialism. Stalin was eventually to achieve what neither the Tsars nor Marx could ever have imagined: the effective subjection of a world-wide revolutionary movement to the power and the purposes of the Russian state.

The start of the campaign against Trotskyism in the autumn coincided with a return of Trotsky's mysterious illness. And, indeed, whatever the physical genesis of his fever, successive recurrences would increasingly indicate a close connection with mental stress. At first, he followed the course of the torrent in the press. But soon, when the morning newspapers were brought to him in bed, he would only glance at them and then throw them aside. To read them, he commented, was 'like pushing a funnel brush down one's own throat'. He did produce a reasoned reply – the manuscript resides in his archives – but it went unpublished. He might, in disgust and depression, simply never have submitted it. Friends called to see him, more often at night than during the day. And at the Commissariat of Education where she was still employed, Natalia had to be satisfied with looks of silent sympathy from most of her colleagues.

The campaign was conducted with no less fury abroad, and those Communists who resisted it with protest and argument were summarily expelled. In their official publications, the Communist International and its obedient parties were developing a special jargon, to praise the Soviet leadership and condemn its opponents. Dissidents called it 'Agitprop Pidgin' and wondered why no more than 'one hundred per cent approval for the correct line of the Executive' was constantly being sought. Now in Vienna, Victor Serge would meet, discreetly in some outlying district, with others of his disposition, to read and discuss the recent writings of Trotsky. A friend joked about the fortieth congress of the International in

Moscow, where a ninety-year-old Zinoviev would be seen 'propped up by nurses and waving his Presidential bell'.[33] But Zinoviev's tenure of authority, as Kamenev's too, was coming to an end.

On 17 January 1925, a plenary session of the central committee met in Trotsky's absence to deal with him. Kamenev and Zinoviev wanted his expulsion from the party, but Stalin was satisfied with his dismissal as Commissar of War. Trotsky was allowed to remain a member of the central committee and of the Politburo, but was warned that expulsion must follow his engagement in any new controversy. The central committee did not impose similar restraint on the party's propaganda departments, which were duly instructed to reveal the 'anti-Bolshevik character of Trotskyism' since 1903. Stalin's resistance to the pressure from his fellow triumvirs for greater severity was not due to some sudden flare of compassion. His power had passed beyond the need for a triumvirate at all, and he was planning to dispense with it. Cunning and caution suggested that he should appear more moderate in his attitude to Trotsky. It confirmed Trotsky in his belief that Zinoviev was the most virulent and dangerous of his adversaries. And it left the back door unlocked, for Stalin to seek an agreement with Trotsky, if events should advise this.

Trotsky himself lay low and spent the spring in writing a book, *Where is Britain Going?* In November 1924, a delegation from the British Trade Union Congress had visited Moscow and revealed a readiness for closer ties with the Soviet regime. A revolutionary alliance with militant labour in Britain glimmered before the Soviet leadership: promising a nearer and more credible prospect than the tiny Communist Party there could provide, of storming capitalism in its historical citadel. Trotsky was less concerned with the handshakes between functionaries of the Soviet party and those of the British labour movement than with persuading the British workers themselves that their only hope of escape, from poverty and unemployment, lay in revolution. And he set out to do so in part with a witty and withering exposure of the hypocrisy and humbug that was such a feature of British parliamentary politics at the time.

Stanley Baldwin had declared that the Conservative commitment to 'gradualness' was in closer accord with the character and conditions of the British people than were any traditions or principles of violent change. But the seizure of India and of Egypt, or the history of Ireland, seemed curious proofs of this. It would appear that the principle of evolutionary gradualness, commended as some universal first cause, suspended its operations beyond the confines of Britain itself. And it was possible to conclude that the more successful Britain was in applying force to other peoples, the greater was the degree of gradualness realized within its own borders. Indeed, before the era of imperial expansion, gradual and peaceful development was by no means so governing a feature of Britain's internal history as Conservative philosophers pretended. The character of the British people, like the traditions of the Conservative Party, had been welded by the hammer of the revolution in the seventeenth century. Conservative old ladies might lie awake and shudder at nights to recall the execution of Charles I. But it was the consequences of this fatal blow to the power of kings which the adherents of parliamentary gradualism still enjoyed.

To hear this praise of peaceful evolution from the mouths of Conservative leaders was bad enough. To hear it from the mouths of their Labour counterparts was as much as Trotsky's scorn could contain. The opinions expressed by Ramsay MacDonald he likened to the 'ideological shop of an old furniture-dealer, where the stifling scent of naphthalene does not interfere with the successful work of the moths'.[34] The Fabian pretension to socialism was, in MacDonald's own words, about a religion of service to the people; about the Christianizing of government; about compassion for the poor; even about poetry. For socialists were accused of being poets, and poets they were. 'The policy of Sidney Webb as an artistic creation!' Trotsky commented. 'The Ministry of Thomas as colonial poetry! And finally, the budget of Mr Snowden as the song of triumphant love of the City of London!'[35] MacDonald was much taken with drawing analogies from the natural world, and cited the intelligent transformation of the caterpillar into a chrysalis and the movement of the worthy tortoise, as models for the process of social change. Trotsky was not convinced that either the caterpillar or the tortoise provided lessons in how to break through the confines of the capitalist state. But he found this preoccupation with analogy suggestive.

British pigeon fanciers, by means of an artificial selection, achieve special varieties, with a continually shortening beak. But there comes a moment when the beak of a new stock is so short that the poor creature is unequal to breaking the egg-shell, and the young pigeon perishes, a sacrifice to compulsory restraint from revolutionary activites, and a stop is put to the further progress of varieties of short-bills.[36]

Mr Lansbury declared that he did not believe in force. Yet if a thief were to break into his home, he would, it must be supposed, use force to secure the thief's departure, or summon the nearest policeman for that purpose. And even if he mercifully permitted the thief to depart in peace, this would be only on the condition that the thief agreed to do so immediately. Moreover, he might allow himself the luxury of such a Christian gesture only because his home was protected by the British laws of property and 'their innumerable Arguses', so that nightly visits from thieves were the exception rather than the rule. Of course, Mr Lansbury might claim that breaking into a private Christian house was itself force and necessitated resistance. But then he should be told that resistance was necessitated, too, by the daily invasion of capitalism into the life and labour of the proletariat.

The truth was that he renounced the use of revolutionary force to liberate the proletariat, but lived in excellent harmony with the force that sustained the framework of bourgeois society.

Mr Lansbury is in favour of retail force and against wholesale force. He is like a vegetarian who could reconcile himself with equanimity to the flesh of ducks and rabbits, but who recoils with holy indignation from the slaughter of larger animals.[37]

Against the prevalent reformism of the Labour leadership, Trotsky placed the Puritan revolution of the seventeenth century. Cromwell himself, whose dictatorship had produced the triumph of the bourgeoisie over absolute monarchy, aristocratic privilege and a church adapted to the needs of both, Trotsky saw as one of the giants of history. And he suggested that Lenin might be called, with some truth, the proletarian Cromwell of the twentieth century.[38] In the Chartist movement, Trotsky saw the second, and the truly proletarian, revolutionary tradition in British history. It had failed because it had come too early; as the revolution of 1905 in Russia had failed for the same reason, before the triumph of its own tradition twelve years later. Chartism, with its rapid progress from petition to armed insurgency, prefigured for Trotsky a proletarian struggle that would discard its assorted reformists for revolutionary change.

Trotsky was to prove, on the time-scale of half a century, wrong in this, as in other predictions of where Britain was going. The conflict between capital and labour was certainly to intensify, and sooner than even Trotsky had supposed likely. But it would culminate in a general strike whose failure dampened rather than fired mass militancy in the labour movement. A financial crisis would subsequently persuade the leadership of the Labour Party to join a Conservative-dominated national government; and MacDonald in particular was to be denounced by his former followers with more violence and less wit than Trotsky had employed against him. But the place of one reformist leadership was in due course taken by another, without loosening the hold of the Labour Party on the mass of British workers. Fifty years afterwards, the British Communist Party, in whose flourishing Trotsky invested so much hope, would be an even more feeble political plant than it was at the time of his book.

Above all, Trotsky misjudged the leadership of British capitalism, which was to prove both less nationalist and more intelligently flexible than he depicted it. Far from resisting, to the point of war, the growth in American economic dominance, it would contentedly accept a dependence which provided political protection along with ample opportunities for profit. And far from resisting, to the point of revolt, a Labour government programme of nationalization, it would soon enough come to recognize how its own interests might be served by state control and support of such essential but unprofitable sectors of the economy as coal mining and the railways. By its very readiness to accommodate reform, therefore, it would help to shorten that revolutionary beak of the proletarian pigeon. But the shortness of the beak would be due as well to another factor: a sufficiently popular revulsion in Britain from the results of the pecking by the longer-beaked Russian variety.

When the Politburo came to discuss a new appointment for Trotsky, Zinoviev proposed a minor post in the management of the leather industry. Again Stalin argued against an unnecessary humiliation and carried the majority of his colleagues with him. Zinoviev seized the occasion to complain in Leningrad that Stalin and other members of the Politburo were leaning towards Trotsky and might even be considered 'semi-Trotskyists' themselves. Nothing further was needed to persuade Trotsky that any differences among his adversaries were concerned not with matters of principle but merely with the manoeuvrings of power. He the more eagerly accepted his appointment in May to the Supreme Council of the National Economy; ignoring the measured belittlement in making him serve under Dzerzhinsky, and flinging himself into work that demanded a creative intellect rather than a capacity for intrigue.

He became chairman of the Concessions Committee, which dealt with the involvement of foreign firms in the economy; of the Electro-technical Development Board; and of the Industrial-Technological Commission. The last gave him especial satisfaction, since it took him into laboratories where he might watch experiments and listen to explanations from the foremost scientists in the country. He experienced again the excitement of science, which had once made him plan on studying physics and mathematics at university; and now, in his spare time, he read textbooks, as on his train in the civil war he had read French novels. His work for the Board of Electro-technical Development sent him travelling through the country to consider likely sites for the construction of power plants; and on his return from one such trip, he brought before the Politburo a proposal to harness the rapids of the Dnieper river. Stalin remarked that the project would be about as much use to Russia as a gramophone to a peasant without a cow, and the proposal was defeated. But he was, characteristically, to change his mind as soon as it suited him, and to declare his peasant's gramophone an essential instrument of socialism. Trotsky's rejected power station would become a primary industrial undertaking of the thirties and, on its completion, be proclaimed a triumph of Stalin's personal foresight.

The Politburo had hoped that Trotsky would be kept busy, at his administrative desk, dealing with mere matters of detail. But Trotsky knew how to make of just such matters connecting steps to issues of policy. It had become inveterate practice to derive the latest measure of

Soviet industrial production from a comparison with the depths sounded in the civil war or with the Tsarist level of 1913. As its chairman, Trotsky maintained that the Concessions Committee could not properly perform its functions without investigating the international context of the Soviet economy and relating productive forces in the Soviet Union to those in the countries of advanced capitalism. The studies that he undertook, with the help of those who had been his secretaries on the military train in the civil war, disclosed the full extent of Soviet backwardness in industrial equipment and a measure of productivity so low that it was no more than one-tenth of that in the United States. He was not disturbed by the predictable cry that such findings only served to demoralize the workers. His own comments reflected his belief that the workers would climb the more readily and rapidly, if they looked ahead of them instead of behind. But besides, the findings reinforced Trotsky's case for an urgent programme of planned industrialization. And not least, by rolling up the blinds and letting in the light from the world outside, they revealed the doctrine of socialism in a single country as a flimsy contraption whose parts were of painted paper.

While Trotsky was involved in such activity, the old alliance that had defeated him disintegrated into open conflict. Of the former triumvirs, Kamenev was by far the weakest and little more now than a Politburo vote. He was still chairman of the Moscow Soviet, but the local party apparatus was completely under Stalin's control. Zinoviev was an altogether different matter. As president of the International, he was nominally the world's leading Communist. But this was now no more than a matter of prestige. The Soviet party gave, and the Soviet party might, as easily, take away. It was his place in this party that counted. For if Stalin controlled the organization in the rest of the country, Zinoviev had made all his own, by similar methods, the organization in the city and district of Leningrad.[39] And Leningrad was not to be treated by the General Secretariat as though it were just another provincial town. The mass of its party members, still militantly mindful of the predominant role that their city had played in the early history of the revolution, might be aroused by Zinoviev's functionaries against the appearance of unwarranted dictation from Moscow.

But no one knew better than Stalin where to prowl and how to lie warily in wait. He moved first through the undergrowth of the Communist International, stirring doubts of Zinoviev's real authority. Then the Leningrad Communist Youth Organization strayed within reach of party discipline by attempting to assert its independence from Moscow, and Stalin leapt at once, to secure the dismissal of Zinoviev's adherent from its leadership. Zinoviev, increasingly alarmed, looked for an issue around which to mobilize more general support for his position and found this in the policies pursued towards the peasantry.

The gap between the price of manufactured goods and the payment for agricultural produce was as wide as ever, so that the well-to-do peasants, with stocks to spare, continued to hoard them rather than supply the market. Kamenev and Zinoviev had helped to dispose of Trotsky's solution through industrial development. Now, under Stalin's leadership, a majority in the Politburo turned to the alternative of concessions to the countryside. Bukharin, a full member since the year before, had become a passionate proponent of more scope for private enterprise. And in April 1925, he issued his rousing appeal to the peasantry, or at least to that sector with the prerequisite land and equipment: 'Enrich yourselves, develop your farms, do not fear that you will be subjected to restrictions.'[40] Two weeks later, the fourteenth party conference voted to reduce taxes on the peasants by a quarter and to lift restrictions on the leasing of land and the hire of agricultural labour. Zinoviev, careful to avoid the charge of fostering a 'fraction', publicly praised these decisions as a compromise between differing views in the party. But covertly he encouraged his adherents to assail in the Leningrad press the deviation to the right by certain members of the party leadership.

The new measures whetted rather than satisfied the appetite of the dominant peasants for reform. During the summer, deliveries of grain unexpectedly fell, and the price of bread rose in the towns. Bukharin and his disciples pressed for further concessions to the farmers. And Peter Zalutsky, secretary of the Leningrad organization, drew an historical analogy which Trotsky was soon to make his own. The movement within the leadership away from the ideal of equality threatened a Soviet Thermidor.[41] Stalin succeeded in securing Zalutsky's dismissal for such subversive remarks but failed to have his own nominee appointed instead. The lid was off the struggle. In the summer, Zinoviev's book, *Leninism*, appeared with a direct challenge to Stalin's doctrinal authority. The promise of socialism in a single country, Zinoviev dismissed as impossible of fulfilment. And in an essay on 'The Philosophy of the Epoch', which *Pravda* published as two articles in September, he proclaimed the principle of equality as the original, overriding purpose of the October revolution.

Shortly before, Max Eastman had published in the United States his book, *Since Lenin Died*, which contained an accurate account, obtained from Trotsky himself, of the contest over the succession and the contents of Lenin's Testament. Trotsky's colleagues in the Politburo abandoned their differences for the moment to unite in insisting that he deny the disclosures and in threatening him with drastic disciplinary measures if he did not. At the beginning of September, the *Bolshevik* published a statement, signed by Trotsky but essentially dictated by the Politburo, that all talk of such a Testament, 'allegedly suppressed or violated, is a malicious invention and is directed wholly against Lenin's real will and the interests of the party of which he was the founder'. The statement was immediately republished in the foreign Communist press and then deposited by Stalin to his account, for withdrawal as occasion required.

Trotsky himself was later to claim that his closest associates had pressed him to issue the denial. And it doubtless seemed to them neither the time nor the right issue for defiance. But the decision was, of course, finally his own. And it was an unworthy one: a bearing of false witness not only against a loyal supporter and friend but against himself. The obvious explanation, that he was aware of the conflict among his adversaries and did not care to become the cause of their reconciliation, is contradicted by his own diary notes of the period. Indeed, he seems not only to have been altogether unaware of any such conflict when he agreed to issue his statement, but to have remained so for the next few agitated months. Having withdrawn in disgust from the unprincipled intrigues of his colleagues in the leadership, he was wrapped away in his own work and sought only to be left for the while in peace. It was this peace that was threatened by the reaction of the Politburo to Eastman's disclosures. And the repugnance to abandoning this peace for subjection again to a campaign of abuse and misrepresentation might well have proved a decisive factor. At all events, it was one of the very rare occasions when Trotsky deserted his dignity.

The conflict within the leadership now intensified. At a plenary meeting of the central committee in October, called to prepare for the long overdue fourteenth congress, Zinoviev and Kamenev were joined by Krupskaya and by Sokolnikov, Commissar of Finance, in a demand for free debate within the party, on the agricultural issue dividing the leadership. The demand was refused. Each side proceeded to mobilize its forces. Zinoviev's functionaries ensured that only his adherents were elected as congress delegates from the Leningrad area. From Moscow came an open attack on the Leningrad organization. The Leningrad press fired back, to be answered by a barrage from the press under Stalin's command. Seeing the approach of certain defeat, Zinoviev offered Stalin a last-minute deal. In return for a guarantee that there would be no subsequent attempt to wrest his control of the Leningrad organization from him, he would abandon his intended challenge at the congress. Stalin was unimpressed. He knew as well as Zinoviev how to count votes.

The congress opened on 18 December to an immediate storm. Jeers and catcalls greeted Zinoviev's presentation of a minority report. And Mikoyan, one of Stalin's minions, was quick to deride Zinoviev's sudden conversion to the virtues of democracy. 'When Zinoviev is in a majority, he is for iron discipline . . . when he is in the minority . . . he is against it.' Even Krupskaya was treated with scant respect. Arguing that the majority was not always and inevitably right, she reminded delegates that at the Stockholm congress of 1906, it was the Bolsheviks who had been in the minority. And this produced such an uproar that only her withdrawal of these remarks enabled her to continue. Far more furious still was the reception accorded to Kamenev's attack on Stalin and the 'doctrine of one-man rule'. A virtual riot of protest broke out, which Stalin's managers then brought to an end in a staged ovation for him.

Only one subject seemed to unite the contenders in tribute, as it had previously united them in abuse. Lashevich, political commissar of the Leningrad garrison and one of Zinoviev's principal lieutenants, announced that Trotsky had not been altogether wrong in 1923. Various Stalinists praised Trotsky for the exemplary observance of party discipline which he had displayed in defeat. Spokesmen of each side disclosed and denounced the shabby way in which Trotsky had been treated by the other. And all the while Trotsky sat silent. By his own subsequent account,[42] he was amazed and confused. The open breach in the triumvirate was 'absolutely unexpected'. And he needed now to stand back and consider what it meant.

What Stalin's triumph meant for his former allies was made immediately clear. At the first meeting of the new central committee, enlarged to accommodate still more of his adherents, Stalin proposed measures to deal with the rebellious Leningraders. Trotsky at last intervened, to oppose reprisals. But the tributes paid to him so shortly before by leading Stalinists were no longer regarded as relevant. Early in January 1926, a special commission arrived in Leningrad and proceeded to purge the party organization. Sergei Kirov, Stalin's nominee, slipped neatly into Zinoviev's place as chairman of the Leningrad Soviet. There was no popular protest. Zinoviev had bullied the workers of Leningrad too long for them to think of stirring in his defence. Meanwhile, Kamenev had lost most of his posts, including the chairmanship of the Moscow Soviet, and was demoted from full to a mere candidate member of the Politburo.

Stalin was now less concerned to keep open the possibility of some compact with Trotsky. And he might well have wondered whether the deference shown to Trotsky at the fourteenth congress had not been dangerously overdone. At all events, his functionaries began campaigning against Trotskyism again; and with his consent, if not at his express command, alluded to the coincidence that the leaders of both opposition groupings were Jews. Certainly the allusions were clear and widespread enough for Trotsky to hear of them and take them seriously. That any Communists, let alone those in responsible positions, should descend to using that most disreputable instrument of Tsarist reaction shocked him profoundly. Was it possible, he asked in a personal letter to Bukharin on 4 March, that anti-Semitic agitation should be conducted with impunity in their party? Two weeks later, he brought the matter before the Politburo, but was met only with denials or a silent embarrassment. He must have had little doubt that Stalin was ultimately to blame. And this would have made him the more willing to consider an accord with Kamenev and Zinoviev, to confront the menace of such leadership.

Early in April 1926, Trotsky met in private with the two men who had done so much to put Stalin where he was and who now fluctuated between fear and euphoria. They were full of revelations about Stalin's malice and confessed that both of them had written letters, consigned to a reliable place, which would identify Stalin as responsible, in the event of their sudden and unaccountable deaths. Kamenev advised Trotsky to do the same. 'You can expect anything from that Asiatic.'[43] Yet somewhat inconsistently, they seemed almost ready to celebrate their imminent victory over him. 'It is enough for you and Zinoviev to appear on the same platform,' Kamenev cried, 'and the party will find its true Central Committee.'[44] Trotsky attempted to moderate their excitement, and did not spare them in pointing out how far their collaboration with Stalin had corrupted the party. They would have, he insisted, to prepare 'for a long and serious struggle'. They nodded their heads, but not their minds. The new alliance could not be taken much further. Trotsky left almost at once for medical treatment in Germany.

His Moscow doctors, unable to explain, let alone cure, his recurrent fever, had long been pressing him to seek expert opinion abroad, and the Politburo had at last reluctantly agreed that he should be left to take the final decision himself. With Natalia and a bodyguard that included a representative of the GPU, he set off for Berlin; travelling beardless under the name of Kuzmyenko, whose provenance was the commissariat of education in the Ukraine. On his arrival, he was placed in a private clinic and there presented to various specialists for their mystification. Eventually it was decided to remove his tonsils; a proceeding as unpleasant as it soon proved ineffective, for his fever returned. But meanwhile he made what use he could of his time. Each day he read through the political range of German newspapers. He attended a wine festival outside the city and noted the grey doggedness behind the merry-making. On May Day, he visited various parts of Berlin to see the processions and listen to the speeches and mingle with the crowds. He found it refreshing to move about namelessly and unnoticed. In one place his photographs were being sold. But he was satisfied that he looked different enough to be safe.

Then, a week before his intended date of departure, the clinic was suddenly invaded by police, with the claim that they had learnt of a plot by Russian White Guards to assassinate him. Trotsky was later to suspect that the secret of his stay might have leaked through some loose diplomatic washer; and that the police, offended by the failure to confide in them, were providing evidence of their indispensability. In response to their undesirable attentions, Trotsky moved to the Soviet embassy.

He had more than the possibility of a plot against his life to occupy his mind. During his stay in Berlin, the British general strike broke out; quickly to confirm his warnings against the alliance between the Soviet regime and the reformist leadership of the British labour movement. The general council of the Trades Union Congress hastened to reject the offer of help from Soviet trade unions and to wind up the strike before it should assume a revolutionary character; while the British Communist Party, prevented by the alliance from confronting the general council, achieved no more than a share in the discredit. In Poland, at much the same time, Marshal Pilsudski seized power with the help of the Communist Party, whose leader, a client of Stalin's, seemed persuaded that he was promoting a democratic dictatorship of the proletariat and peasantry. It was to be a dictatorship, right enough, but one which Pilsudski soon made clear was only his own.

Back in Moscow, Trotsky met with his new allies again, to discuss the merging of their followers in what soon came to be known as the Joint Opposition. Not all of Trotsky's associates were in favour of the project. Antonov-Ovseenko and Radek would have preferred an alliance with Stalin to one with Zinoviev. Mrachkovsky, who had been among the most brilliant commanders in the civil war and who had become one of Trotsky's closest friends, warned him against either alliance: 'Stalin will deceive us and Zinoviev will sneak away.' When reports of the decision to merge reached the Trotskyists in Leningrad, they could barely hold down the thought that they would have to sit at the same table with bureaucrats who had hunted and abused them. How, moreover, were they to reveal all their names to those who might so easily turn from their present praise of Trotsky to making their peace with power and persecuting his followers again? No one was more loyal to Trotsky's leadership than Alexandra Lvovna Bronstein, his first wife, plump now and white-haired, who was affectionately known as Babushka, or 'Grandmother', by the Leningrad group of Trotskyists. But she, too, was troubled. Victor Serge, who had returned from abroad in disgust at the activities of the International, belonged to the group and visited Moscow to inform Trotsky of its objections and fears.

He found Trotsky shivering and violet-lipped with fever, yet with his intelligence and determination as alive as ever in his face. It was essential, Trotsky argued, to unite the opposition forces in the two proletarian capitals, if the struggle to save the revolution was to be won. It would be a hard task, but he had high hopes of success. In the waiting-room of the Concessions Committee, there were two bearded peasants in sheepskin and plaited-bark clogs. They pressed to see Trotsky, so that he might settle some legal dispute with the local authorities in their district. 'Now that Lenin is dead, there is only Comrade Trotsky to give us justice,' they kept saying. Syermuks, Trotsky's personal secretary, assured them that Comrade

Trotsky would see them but could do nothing now, since he was no longer a member of the government. They only shook their heads in disbelief. Trotsky's secretaries knew better. One of them advised Serge to put his handkerchief in front of his face, as though blowing his nose, when he left. There were agents of the GPU with cameras in the building opposite.[45]

During the summer of 1926, the Joint Opposition set out to muster its forces. Cautiously it called small private meetings of likely supporters; mainly at the homes of trusted workers, where the tiny rooms available were quickly crammed with those known to hold dissident views. But the local party committees were not idle and, on instructions from Stalin's Secretariat, organized special brigades for strong-arm disruption. The Opposition moved to garages, to woods and to cemeteries. The local committees sent their spies and their brigades in pursuit. In the middle of July, Trotsky proclaimed the existence and the purposes of the Opposition to a meeting of the central committee. He called for a rise in the wages of workers to promote productivity, and for a programme of rapid industrialization; for a shift from indirect taxes, that fell most heavily on the poor, to far higher rates of direct taxation on profits. The single agricultural tax, which treated poor and rich peasants as though they were the same, should give place to a progressive system that exempted the really poor altogether and made the rich pay in proportion to their means. Neither he nor his colleagues could accept the doctrine of socialism in a single country, which reflected an abandonment of hope in the international revolution and which had already led its proponents into subservient alliances with reformists abroad. Above all, the Opposition would work to free the party from the tyranny of its apparatus and to restore its internal democracy.

The subsequent proceedings were marked by a macabre incident. After delivering a two-hour tirade against the Opposition, Dzerzhinsky collapsed with a heart attack and died. In his strange tormented life he had moved from being a poet of revolution to becoming its principal policeman. The functionaries who now composed Stalin's majority had far less complex characters. And they determined the issues before them without strain. One after the other, Trotsky's calls and criticisms were rejected. But Stalin was not to be satisfied with this. He accused his opponents of violating the Leninist ban on fractions. Lashevich had addressed a surreptitious meeting in the woods outside of Moscow. He was expelled from the central committee and dismissed from his post in the commissariat of war. Zinoviev had abused his position as president of the Communist International, by providing the Opposition with facilities at his headquarters. He was deprived of his seat in the Politburo. Trotsky was allowed to retain his own. And the knowledge that he did so only at

Stalin's pleasure was as much his humiliation as it might have been the twist of Stalin's triumph.

The leaders of the Opposition now carried their case direct to the factories and party cells. But the agents of the Secretariat went before them, to prepare not a reply but a clamour to drown all dissent and doubt. Even Trotsky, whose powers of oratory were part of revolutionary legend, found himself for the first time unable to get a hearing. The experience of Victor Serge in Leningrad goes a long way towards explaining the source of the Opposition's defeat. He belonged to the party cell of the evening newspaper, *Krassnaya Gazeta*, which had some 400 members. Of these, only three were Old Bolsheviks, and they clung to their managerial posts. Ten had fought in the civil war, and half of these were members of the Opposition. The remaining 387 had all joined the party in the 'Lenin levy' of 1924. Each fortnight a general meeting was held and inaugurated by a long address from some official spokesman, declaring that socialism in a single country was possible and denouncing the Opposition for its lack of faith. Then came the avowed activists: elderly workers chosen by the cell committee to proclaim their loyalty, and young careerists carefully making their way. All was so far orderly. But when an adherent of the Opposition rose to speak, he was greeted at once by heckling and cries of 'Traitors! Mensheviks! Tools of the bourgeoisie!' There were no more than twenty who produced this barrage. But the others would make no effort to stop them and would sit watching in silence.

Stalin now threatened to deal with any continuing resistance from the defeated dissidents by having them expelled from the party. There were those, and among them some of Trotsky's own followers, who had already begun to talk of the need for the Opposition to break away altogether, denounce the party as the instrument of a bureaucratic counter-revolution, and present itself as the true party of the proletariat instead. Trotsky would not accept this. The party might have wandered from its way under leaders whose only concern was to stay in front and who were always looking backwards to make sure that no one should be trying to overtake them. But it was still the historical party of the proletariat. Sooner or later the mass of its members would recognize that they were lost and turn from those who had misled them. And precisely for this reason, the Opposition needed to remain within the party, provided only that it was able to do so without abandoning its purpose. Yet Zinoviev and Kamenev were themselves now moving towards just such an abandonment. Their spirits falling the further for having risen so high before, they wanted only to make their peace with the central committee.

To keep the leadership of the Opposition united behind at least the principles of its commitment, Trotsky was prepared to concede much. And eventually the terms of a truce with Stalin were agreed. The Opposition leaders restated their criticisms of party policy, but declared the decisions of the central committee to be binding; promised to stop all fractional activities; dissociated themselves from those who were calling for the creation of a new party; and disavowed those Communists abroad who, in consequence of declaring their support for the Soviet Opposition, had been expelled from their own parties. Never again was Trotsky to bend his head so low. And he bent it now, moreover, to no purpose. One week afterwards, Stalin broke the truce. He had doubtless intended to do so soon, in any event. But he was provided with an occasion, if not one that was to his liking, almost at once.

From one source or another, the full text of Lenin's Testament had been supplied to dissident Communists abroad. And on 18 October 1926, the very day after the Opposition statement had appeared in *Pravda*, the Testament was published by the *New York Times*.[46] Five days later, on the 23rd, the central committee met to discuss the agenda for the imminent fifteenth party conference and decided that Stalin should deliver there a special report on the Opposition. Trotsky's protests at this rupture of the truce were of no avail. On the 25th, the day before the opening of the conference, Stalin presented the outlines of his proposed report at a meeting of the Politburo, attended as well by many members of the central committee. He denounced the Opposition as a 'social democratic deviation' and demanded that its leaders publicly repudiate their views.

Trotsky again protested at this rupture of the truce and warned that such a course of conflict as Stalin proposed must end in the destruction of the party. Then, pointing at Stalin, he cried: 'The First Secretary poses his candidature to the post of Grave-Digger of the Revolution!' Stalin leapt to his feet, controlling himself with difficulty, and then rushed from the room, slamming the door behind him. The meeting broke up in turmoil.

At Trotsky's apartment in the Kremlin, meanwhile, a few of his friends were waiting with Natalia for him to return. Piatakov arrived first, looking very pale and shaken. He gulped down a glass of water and said: 'I have been under fire, but this – this was worse than anything I have ever seen! Why, oh why, did Leon Davidovich say that? Stalin will never forgive him or his children for generations to come!' When Trotsky himself arrived, Piatakov rushed up to him. 'Why, *why* did you say that?' he cried. But Trotsky brushed the question aside. And Natalia noted that he was exhausted but calm.[47] On the following day, before the conference opened, the central committee voted to deprive Trotsky of his seat in the Politburo and Zinoviev of the right to represent the party on the executive of the Communist International.

In a long speech to the conference, Stalin resurrected Trotsky's early conflict with Lenin; recalled Trotsky's denunciations of Zinoviev and Kamenev, along with theirs of him; and attacked all three for a policy of headlong industrialization which would condemn millions of workers and peasants to misery. He demanded a resolute struggle, without respite, until the Opposition at last repudiated its false views. Trotsky, in his reply, measured the dimensions of the economic crisis not with rhetoric but with a ruler; for 'arithmetic knows neither pessimism nor optimism'. And he ridiculed Stalin's assault on the Opposition as Social Democratic deviationism: repeating each one of the Opposition's criticisms, to ask whether that was Social Democratic. But the main thrust of his assault was on the doctrine of socialism in a single country. Bukharin had written that they could complete the construction of socialism, if they left aside international affairs. 'You can go for a walk naked in the streets of Moscow in the month of January, if you leave aside the weather and the militia. But I am afraid, neither the weather nor the militia will leave you aside. . . .' The West was unlikely to stagnate, while the Soviet Union devoted decades to the building of socialism. If capitalism flourished, it would have the means to crush the Soviet Union. If it declined, the workers would overthrow it. Either way, the doctrine of socialism in a single country was a mirage. He was expected to accept a 'black and groundless pessimism' about the European proletariat, alongside an uncritical optimism about the building of socialism by the isolated forces of the Soviet Union. It was in no sense his duty as a Communist to do so. And he ended by warning that Stalin's disloyal and unscrupulous methods might produce an ultimate split and lead to a struggle between two parties.

It was a performance so masterly that the delegates extended, again and again, the time assigned to him. But their allegiance to the party leadership was unshakable. And they showed their feelings when Zinoviev rose to speak. He was persistently interrupted, and they rejected with contempt his appeal for a mere ten-minute extension of his time. The conference duly sanctioned the various measures taken against the leaders of the Opposition and warned them of further reprisals if they reopened the dispute. Stalin himself triumphantly announced that Krupskaya had decided to dissociate herself from the Opposition. It was rumoured in Moscow that Stalin had threatened to expose certain covered areas of Lenin's life: doubtless Lenin's relations with Inessa Armand.[48] 'I shall appoint someone else to be Lenin's widow,' he was supposed to have told Krupskaya. But if any such threat was made and did affect her decision, there were more certain factors involved. She had been subjected to continual harassment for several years. And, according to her own subsequent explanation, published in a letter to *Pravda*, she had come to fear that the extent of Opposition criticism might lead the masses to doubt whether the party and the Soviet government any longer represented their interests.

For a few months, the leaders of the Opposition lay low. Kamenev and Zinoviev were all but totally demoralized. And Trotsky himself was waiting for the appropriate moment to renew the struggle. It came in the spring of 1927, with events in neighbouring China. Early in 1926, the Communist International had admitted the Kuomintang as an associate party and elected Chiang Kai-shek as an honorary member of the executive. It was a reflection of the belief, firmly held by Stalin in particular, that the revolutionary future in China, for as far as could be foreseen, lay not with the Chinese Communist Party but with the nationalist coalition of the Kuomintang. Trotsky's gaze was far more frequently fixed on the workers of the West than on the sunken multitudes of Asia. But from the beginning of 1924, he had, from time to time, expressed his misgivings of a Soviet policy that ignored the existence of conflicting classes in China and insisted that the Chinese Communist Party subordinate itself to the priorities of nationalism. Indeed, he protested to the Politburo at the decision of the Communist International to admit the Kuomintang and described as a bad joke Chiang Kai-shek's honorary membership of the executive.

By March 1926, Chiang Kai-shek was taking measures against Communists in the Kuomintang; and the Communists, convinced that he was preparing to crush them, sought Soviet assistance to equip armed forces of their own. The Soviet representatives in China ordered the abandonment of any such project, and the Politburo dispatched a special emissary to see that its own policy was pursued. The Soviet leaders also cautiously advised Chiang Kai-shek against his planned expedition to deal with the northern warlords, but here they were in no position to impose their will. And as his forces swept northwards, Communist organizers stirred the peasants and the workers to social revolt. Stalin, thoroughly alarmed, fired off a telegram to the Chinese Communists in October; urging them to restrain the peasant movement.[49] But the Chinese Communists were no longer so ready to listen.

In the early spring of 1927, the armies of Chiang Kai-shek approached Shanghai, the richest and most important of the cities; the stronghold of Western interests, but the home as well of China's largest and most militant proletariat. It was this proletariat that, under Communist leadership, now rose and wrested the Chinese-governed sectors of the city from the local warlord. How was Chiang Kai-shek likely to react? If Kuomintang and Communist forces combined, military intervention, in particular by Britain, to protect Western interests, would almost certainly follow; and effective resistance would necessitate the arming of the peasantry. The influence of the indigenous rich over the nationalist movement would be swept away; and the cause of freedom from the foreigner merge into that of social revolution.

Trotsky had kept silent, wondering whether any initiative of his would not do more harm than good, since the central committee might then treat the issue primarily as one between itself and the Opposition. But as reports of what was happening in China filtered through to him, he could keep silent no longer. At the end of March, in a letter to the Politburo, he pressed the party to recognize the strength and significance of the Chinese proletarian movement. Moscow should promote the revolutionary momentum: by encouraging the Chinese workers in the main industrial cities to elect Soviets; and by calling for the closest collaboration in insurgency between workers and peasants. Otherwise, he warned, there would be nothing to stand in the way of a military engagement to crush the revolution. Again and again in the days that followed, he protested at the Soviet policy of support for the Kuomintang and declared that Chiang Kai-shek was preparing to establish a military dictatorship. Stalin was not to be moved, and Moscow exhorted the Communists in Shanghai to bury their arms and surrender rather than defy the forces of Chiang Kai-shek. In a speech to party functionaries at the Bolshoi Theatre, Stalin referred to Trotsky's warnings only to dismiss them. 'We are told that Chiang Kai-shek is making ready to turn against us ... but it is he that will be crushed. We shall squeeze him like a lemon and then be rid of him.' The speech, suitably expurgated, was being processed by *Pravda*, when publication was cancelled. On 12 April, Chiang Kai-shek's troops turned their machine-guns on the workers of Shanghai.

The resurgent Opposition assailed the whole range of official policy, domestic and foreign, in a statement which carried the signatures of 84 – subsequently increased to 300 – prominent members of the party. And on 24 May 1927, Trotsky exercised his right of appeal to the Communist International; appearing before the executive and delivering his indictment, in particular of the policy towards China. Stalin was not one to go on wearing his own clothes when these had grown shabby. But if he was to put on those of the Opposition, he needed first to dispose of the Opposition itself. And the British government now gave him a helping hand. For even as the executive of the Communist International was considering Trotsky's indictment, Britain broke off diplomatic relations with the Soviet Union.[50] 'There is no need,' Stalin told the executive, 'to prove that what is intended is a wholesale crusade against Communists. The crusade has already started. Some threaten the party with war and intervention; others with a split. There comes into being something like a united front from Chamberlain[51] to Trotsky. . . .'

Trotsky's protests at this attempt to smear the Opposition were useless. Stalinist propaganda proclaimed alike the danger of war and the disloyalty of the Opposition in challenging the leadership at such a time. It promoted the appropriate mood for measured reprisals. Some of the more prominent dissidents were demoted; others effectively silenced by appointment to embassies abroad or administrative posts in parts of the Soviet Union where few but themselves would pay any attention to the sound of their voices. Those on the lower slopes were more ruthlessly treated: expelled from the party; deprived of their work permits; even arrested. One of these last belonged to the party cell of the Leningrad evening newspaper. And when Victor Serge rose at a meeting to protest, he was met with bursts of rhythmic chanting: 'Slanderers! Traitors!'

In the middle of June, Smilga, who had led the Baltic Fleet in the October Revolution, was ordered to an administrative posting on the border with Manchuria. At the Moscow railway station, on the day of his departure, a large crowd of dissidents gathered to demonstrate their protest, and Trotsky addressed them in terms that carefully avoided any direct reference to the party dispute. Stalin seized the occasion for further reprisals. Those rank-and-file members known to have attended the demonstration were driven from their party cells. And Stalin initiated proceedings to expel Trotsky and Zinoviev from the central committee, on the grounds that both had appealed, against their own party, to the Communist International, and both had made speeches to the demonstrators at the railway station.

When Trotsky appeared before the Presidium of the party's Central Control Commission, in late July, he answered the specific charges against him with contemptuous brevity. Since the party acknowledged the ultimate authority of the Communist International, this court was as little entitled to sit in judgment on him for his speech to the executive, as a district commission would be in trying him for a speech that he had given to the central committee. He was accused, too, of having engaged in a collective demonstration against the central committee by participating in the collective farewell to Smilga. But since the leadership was claiming that Smilga's assignment had been no more than a matter of administrative routine, how should the farewell be construed as a demonstration? And if the assignment had, indeed, been a disguised form of banishment, then the claim of the leadership was the merest duplicity. The charges were, however, only pretexts for persecuting opponents and preparing for their physical annihilation. He drew, at length, an analogy with the Thermidorian close of the French Revolution. 'The Jacobin Clubs, the crucibles of revolution, became the nurseries of Napoleon's future bureaucracy. We should learn from the French Revolution. But is it really necessary to repeat it?' And he concluded with a solemn warning to his judges: 'Beware, lest you should find yourselves saying later: we parted company with those whom we should have preserved and we preserved those from whom we should have parted.'

Stalin was unable to wrest the verdict he expected. And he proved no more successful in early August, with a new indictment that seized on certain remarks of Trotsky's to charge that the Opposition would not be loyal in the event of war.[52] Trotsky again demolished the case against him;

and the party tribunal went no further than censuring the two leaders of the Opposition. Trotsky and his colleagues now prepared, for presentation to the long-delayed fifteenth congress of the party, a statement of policy. This pressed for a new leadership and, in particular, for the election of a central committee 'closely related to the masses' and 'independent of the apparatus'.

The statement was then submitted to the central committee along with a formal request that it should be published and circulated to congress delegates. The central committee refused and, further, forbade the Opposition to publish and circulate the statement. The Opposition decided to disobey by reproducing the statement for signature by its adherents. And now Stalin used the weapon with which he would cut his way from dominance to despotism. He called in the secret police. On the night of 12 September, the GPU raided the room, in a working-class district of Moscow, where a few young supporters of the Opposition were typing and duplicating the statement. The Soviet and foreign Communist press announced the discovery of a secret printing works, operated by members of the Opposition with the help of a former officer in Baron Wrangel's White Guards. The former officer, it subsequently emerged, had been employed by the GPU. But by then, several Opposition leaders had been expelled from the party; and one of them, Mrachkovsky, imprisoned.

On 27 September, Trotsky faced the executive of the Communist International, convoked to consider his expulsion from its ranks. Before the ceremony began, J. T. Murphy, the British party representative, who had been selected to propose the relevant resolution, found him in the corridor, standing at the fully occupied coat rack. 'Can I help you, Comrade Trotsky?' Murphy's secretary asked. 'I am afraid not,' Trotsky flashed back. 'I am looking for two things – a good Communist and somewhere to hang my coat. They are not to be found here.' And it was with similar contempt that he answered the executive. His judges had no minds of their own, he told them, but were only carrying out Stalin's orders. They did not even have the dignity to save appearances. They were ready to sit in judgment on a Russian revolutionary, while Chiang Kai-shek was still nominally one of their number. They had not dared to call a congress for four years; had not once discussed Stalin's policy, despite its evident wreckage; had trampled on their own statutes and now charged the Russian Opposition with breaches of discipline. The Opposition was guilty, he confessed, with what must have been a heavy heart; but only of having been 'too amenable' to the calamitous schemes of the Stalinist Secretariat. He 'marched out of the room,' Murphy would recall, 'with head erect'.

In the middle of October, the leaders of the Opposition were in Leningrad for a meeting of the Soviet Central Executive Committee, called to sanction and celebrate Stalin's largesse: the introduction of a seven-hour working day and a five-day working week, without any cut in wages. Trotsky protested that the Opposition call for a moderate rise in wages had been repeatedly denied on the grounds that the economy could not afford it. What was this much more costly measure, then, but a massive deception?[53] Outside the Tauride Palace, a parade past the party leadership had been organized. It was a day of grey drizzle, brightened by the red calico that decorated the stands. The marchers paid their required tribute to the officials on the platform and then, as they drew level with the leaders of the Opposition standing some distance away, lingered, stretched out their hands, waved handkerchiefs or caps. Trotsky and Zinoviev were elated. 'The masses are with us!' they sang that night. But as Victor Serge noted, there was submissiveness as well as courage in that 'dumb acclamation'.[54]

Trotsky and Zinoviev, protected by their membership of the central committee, addressed meetings of militants, crowded into the little rooms of rickety apartments. Entering the street after one such meeting, Trotsky raised his overcoat collar and lowered the peak of his cap, to escape any unwelcome attention. To Serge, who was accompanying him, he 'looked like an old intellectual in the underground of long ago, true as ever after twenty years of grind and a few dazzling victories'. Together they approached a cabman, and since they were short of money, Serge proceeded to bargain for the fare. But the cabman, a bearded peasant, leant down: 'For you the fare is nothing. Get inside, comrade. You are Trotsky, surely?' And Trotsky smiled. 'Don't tell anyone that this has happened. Everybody knows that cabmen belong to the petty bourgeoisie, whose favour can only discredit us. . . .'[55]

Such incidents were heartening. But in the end, they were no more than tacks scattered in the way of the Stalinist steam-roller. Back in Moscow, Trotsky faced again the party tribunal. And this time his judges, their minds adjusted to Stalin's will, were in no mood to listen. They whistled. They shouted: 'Menshevik! Traitor! Scoundrel! Renegade! Scum!' They threw inkpots and books at Trotsky's head. 'Your books are unreadable nowadays, but they are still useful for knocking people down. . . ,' he answered. And raising his voice above the uproar, he warned of the purges to come, which would eliminate not only members of the Opposition but those who were so blindly following Stalin now. His judges only tried the more furiously to silence him. Skrypnik, among the loudest, would blow out his brains in 1933; Unschlicht would be shot in 1937; Chubar, whose loyalty was, in due course, to be rewarded with full membership of the Politburo, would then be arrested, tortured, and sometime after 1938 secretly shot. And these were but a few of those who bayed at Trotsky that day, to be butchered on another.

The leaders of the Opposition, still elated by the demonstration in

Leningrad, prepared an 'appeal to the masses' on the tenth anniversary of the revolution. But Stalin, apprised of the plans, issued immediate commands that unofficial demonstrations were to be suppressed, with whatever force might prove necessary. In Leningrad, where Zinoviev arrived in confident mood to lead them, the Opposition demonstrators were allowed to march past the official stands beneath the windows of the Winter Palace and then, in side streets, dispersed by detachments of mounted militia. In Moscow, police and party activists were less restrained. Groups of Opposition demonstrators were attacked before they could reach Red Square and, their banners torn from their hands, were pushed into the official procession. Only the Chinese students of the city's Sun Yat-sen University succeeded in their purpose: by forming a long sinuous dragon and, in the middle of the square, throwing Trotsky's proclamations up in the air. Outside the square, Opposition demonstrators were plucked from the procession, beaten up, and driven off or arrested. Some Oppositionists had placed, at windows or on balconies, banners and portraits of Trotsky. Gangs broke into their homes; destroyed banners, portraits, and often much else besides. Trotsky himself tried to address a column of workers marching towards the Lenin Mausoleum. There were shouts of 'Down with Trotsky, the Jew, the traitor!' Shots were fired. The windscreen of his motor car was shattered. And the column, having watched in silence, continued its march. Frightened or bewildered or apathetic, 'the masses' were not to be moved by the Opposition appeal.

One week later, meeting in extraordinary session, the central committee and the Central Control Commission expelled all the Opposition leaders from their ranks. Trotsky and Zinoviev, found guilty of having incited counter-revolutionary demonstrations, were expelled from the party. On 16 November, Trotsky's close friend Joffe shot himself. He left a long letter for Trotsky, which the GPU seized. But Trotsky had already been told by telephone of its existence. Soon foreign correspondents were reporting its fate. And since further suppression seemed likely to do more damage than disclosure of the contents, a photocopy was at last released to Rakovsky.

Joffe's letter began with an explanation of his suicide. He felt that he could no longer be useful to the cause he had served.[56] But his death might yet prove more valuable than his life. For his suicide was 'a gesture of protest' against those who had reduced the party to such a condition that it could acquiesce in the disgrace of Trotsky's expulsion. He should be happy to think that the two events – the 'great one' of the expulsion and 'the little' of his suicide – would reawaken the party and halt it on its path to Thermidor. He doubted it, but not that the awakening would eventually come. Meanwhile, he called on decades of their work together and of personal friendship to point out, in parting, where Trotsky had been wrong.

Politically you were always right, beginning with 1905.... But you have often abandoned your rightness for the sake of an overvalued agreement, or compromise. This is a mistake. I repeat: politically you have always been right, and now more right than ever. Some day the party will realize it, and history will not fail to accord recognition. So don't lose your courage if someone leaves you now, or if not as many come to you, and not as soon, as we all would like. You are right, but the guarantee of the victory of your rightness lies in nothing but the extreme unwillingness to yield, the strictest straightforwardness, the absolute rejection of all compromise; in this very thing lay the secret of Lenin's victories. Many a time I have wanted to tell you this, but only now have I brought myself to do so, as a last farewell.

And he concluded by entrusting his wife and child to Trotsky's care.

This last was to be a commission beyond Trotsky's powers. Joffe's widow, Maria Mikhailovna, would spend many years in prison and in exile, before finding a refuge in Israel. Joffe's son would die in Central Asia. But the words of Joffe's last farewell were not wasted. The deviations of compromise were now behind Trotsky forever.

The funeral took place on 19 November. And the central committee, concerned to avoid an embarrassing demonstration, had fixed two o'clock in the afternoon, when workers would find it difficult to attend, as the time for the departure of the procession. Joffe's friends delayed the removal of the body for as long as possible. And it was four o'clock when a crowd, already numbering several thousand, set out singing, with red flags, slowly through the snow. At the gateway to the Novo-Devichy cemetery, on the outskirts of Moscow, police attempted to stop the procession, on orders from the central committee that only twenty or so mourners were to be permitted inside. The crowd resisted; and to prevent the scandal of a full-scale battle on such an occasion, representatives of the central committee intervened. The whole procession was allowed to gather round the open grave. The coffin floated for a moment above the multitude and was then lowered. Some official declaimed the condolences of the central committee but was met with impatient murmurs. At last, Trotsky spoke, his voice carrying far through the frosty air:

Joffe left us not because he did not wish to fight, but because he lacked the physical strength for fighting. He feared to become a burden on those engaged in the struggle. His life, not his suicide, should serve as a model to those who are left behind. The struggle goes on. Everyone remains at his post. Let nobody leave.

But Zinoviev and Kamenev were already preparing to do so. When the fifteenth congress opened on 2 December, the more than 1600 delegates included not a single member of the Opposition. Unanimously they declared that adherence to the Opposition programme was incompatible with membership of the party. Meeting at the same time, the leaders of the Opposition disputed on their own attitude. Zinoviev passed a slip of paper to Trotsky: 'Lev Davidovich, the hour has come when we should have the courage to capitulate.' And Trotsky wrote back: 'If that kind of courage were enough, the revolution would have been won all over the world by now.' But all such argument was useless. Zinoviev, Kamenev and others of the Leningrad group claimed that expulsion from the party must mean political death. On 10 December they announced that they would submit to all decisions of the congress and carry them out, however hard this might be. Kamenev went before the congress to beg that, in turn, they should not be required to renounce their views. The party leadership refused. Eight days later, Zinoviev and Kamenev capitulated completely. They condemned their former opinions as 'wrong and anti-Leninist'. The party leadership had a further humiliation in store. Despite their agreement to recant, Zinoviev and Kamenev were not readmitted to the party but placed on probation for six months.

The congress that expelled the Opposition was also one that moved, at Stalin's command, towards some of the measures that the Opposition had been urging. There was to be a moderate programme of rural collectivization and a five-year industrial plan. Stalin had even prepared for a revolutionary triumph in China, by dispatching emissaries to promote a proletarian uprising in Canton. But the tide had already turned and, isolated, workers fell uselessly in their thousands to the bullets of the Kuomintang.

For the remaining members of the Opposition, there now came the first reprisals. Mere followers were collected by the GPU and deported. The leaders were offered minor administrative posts in remote areas. They refused to assist in disguising their own deportation. On 12 January 1928, the GPU informed Trotsky that in consequence of his counter-revolutionary activities, he would be deported to Alma-Ata in Turkestan, close to the border with China. And the date of his departure was fixed for the 16th, a mere four days away. Since the night of 7 November, when he had moved from his apartment in the Kremlin rather than wait for his inevitable eviction, he had been living at the home of Beloborodov, until lately Commissar of the Interior, in the House of the Soviets. It was there that Victor Serge came, to say good-bye.

The Old Man received me in a little room, facing the yard, in which there was only a camp-bed and a table loaded with maps of all the countries of the world. He had on an indoor jacket that had seen much wear. Vigilant, majestic, his hair standing nearly white on his head, his complexion sickly, he exhaled a fierce, caged energy. In the next room the messages he had just dictated were being copied out; the dining-room was used to receive the comrades who kept arriving from all corners of the country, with whom he held hasty conversations between calls to the telephone. At any moment it was possible that we would all be arrested.[57]

On the morning of 16 January, Natalia was giddy with fever. Visitors brought flowers, books, sweets, warm clothing; embraced Trotsky, shook his hand, expressed their sympathy. The luggage went off to the station. And the family waited. At ten o'clock, when the train was due to leave, the telephone rang. It was the GPU, to say that Trotsky's departure had been postponed for a further two days. Half an hour later, excited followers and friends began arriving. A crowd of thousands had gathered at the station; demonstrators had moved on to the tracks and stopped the train from moving; there had been clashes with police and arrests. Trotsky and Natalia slept until eleven the next morning and had just finished breakfast when the doorbell rang and the apartment suddenly filled with agents of the GPU. Trotsky was arrested and told that he was to leave under escort for Alma-Ata at once.

The official Tass News Agency had denied all reports of reprisals against Opposition leaders: who were, it had maintained, moving voluntarily to take up posts in other parts of the country. Trotsky was, accordingly, all the more determined to show that his own removal was nothing of the sort. With Natalia, their two sons, and two visitors who had arrived just before the police, he locked himself in one of the rooms. On the other side of the door, the GPU agents consulted authority by telephone and then announced that they were ordered to use force. A hammer shattered the glass panel in the door; and thrusting his arm inside, Kishkin, a former Red Army officer who had been one of Trotsky's bodyguards on the train in the civil war, shouted: 'Shoot me, Comrade Trotsky, shoot me!' Trotsky soothed him: 'Don't talk nonsense, Kishkin. No one is going to shoot you. Get on with your job.' The agitated agents opened the door; found Trotsky's shoes, fur coat and cap, and put them on him; then lifted him in their arms and carried him down the stairs.

Following behind, Lyova rang all the doorbells and cried: 'They're carrying Comrade Trotsky away!' But the frightened faces at the doors were quickly withdrawn. Through the freezing streets of Moscow, the motor car sped; not to the central railway station but to a small one at Faustovo. There were only a few railway workers to watch as Trotsky was carried from the car; and watch is all they did, when Lyova shouted at them: 'Comrades, see how they are carrying Comrade Trotsky away!' Sergei, Trotsky's younger son, struck one of the GPU agents in the face. An engine with a solitary carriage was waiting, to take the party some fifty kilometres from Moscow, where the carriage would be attached to the main train for Tashkent, at a desolate station. And there Sergei, who wished to continue his studies, parted from his parents and brother. Lyova, who had been working fervently for the Opposition, was going to Alma-Ata as well, to help his father with whatever work was possible. There had been no time to bid his wife good-bye.

As the train rattled along the rails, Trotsky relaxed and became almost merry. All the luggage had been left behind, including the cases of books and writing materials. There was nothing to do but rest. Lying stretched out on his bench, Trotsky said to Natalia: 'I didn't want to die in a bed in the Kremlin. . . .' His guards grew the more considerate, the greater the distance from Moscow, and shopped along the way to provide him and Natalia with such luxuries as soap and tooth powder. The meals all came from station restaurants, and Trotsky, who had been following the strictest of diets, ate everything with glee, while Natalia watched him with astonishment and anxiety. Then, at Arys, not far from Tashkent, there was occasion for much rejoicing. Lyova found Trotsky's loyal secretaries, Syermuks and Poznansky, playing chess in the station restaurant. Trotsky decided that Poznansky should stay in Tashkent, until he received other instructions, while Syermuks was to make for Alma-Ata on his own.

At Frunze,[58] the train journey came to an end, and the party proceeded by bus, through whipping winds and snow drifts, across the Kurday mountain range, to Alma-Ata. There, at a hotel in Gogol Street, the family was given two rooms, while those adjoining were taken by the guards of the GPU. Syermuks arrived four days later and moved into the hotel. But he was to have only one short whispered talk with Trotsky and Natalia in their room. On the second night of his stay, he was arrested; as was Poznansky, about the same time, in Tashkent. Trotsky was never to see them again. Both were to spend the rest of their lives in prison or banishment. The third of Trotsky's secretaries, Georgy Butov, had been arrested before Trotsky's departure and would die in October 1928, after a hunger strike that lasted fifty days.

Two hundred and fifty kilometres from the railway line and 4000 from Moscow, Alma-Ata was a little world of its own. The snow, seldom marked by traffic, lay clean and dry all round throughout the winter; in the spring, the steppes were covered with red poppies, while the orchards were bright with blossom; and in the summer, the straw mats under the trees were carpets of apples and pears. But the town had no lights or paved roads; malaria raged through the region, and there were visitations of plague; in the bazaar, the shopkeepers sat sunning themselves and searching their bodies for lice, while mad dogs ran through the streets.

Protests to Moscow yielded some results. Three weeks after his arrival, Trotsky was granted a four-roomed apartment in the town. He was given permission to go on hunting trips. But these were never more than a necessary respite. For he was soon at work, with Lyova as his all-purpose secretariat. Lyova even found a young girl able and willing to type for them. But since she was not molested by the GPU, it seemed certain that she had agreed to report on her work. For the GPU was quick to pounce.

A local official established secret communication with Trotsky. He was arrested. A comrade from Moscow arrived, to set up business as a carter, and used to meet Trotsky in the public baths. He disappeared.

There was so much work to do. Almost at once, Trotsky began to write a long statement of the Opposition case, for presentation to the congress of the Communist International that had been promised for that summer. In the spring, he started on the memoirs that were to become *My Life*. Neither project supplemented his meagre allowance, and his savings were diminishing fast. Riazanov, an old friend, who was director of the Marx–Engels Institute in Moscow, came to Trotsky's rescue. He employed him to translate one of the volumes, and then edit the translations and read the proofs of the others, in a complete Russian edition of writings by Marx and Engels. It was with his income from this that Trotsky met the costs not only of his new home but of his main work. For Alma-Ata became the operational headquarters of the banished Opposition. From April to October 1928, Trotsky dispatched some 800 political letters, many of considerable length, and some 550 telegrams; while receiving, after the hefty subtractions of censorship, some 700 telegrams and 1000 political letters, most of them from organized groups of adherents.

There was more than the exchange of information and the sustenance of morale in this massive correspondence. There was increasing debate over how the Opposition should respond to developments in Moscow. Trotsky had not misjudged the dimensions of the agricultural crisis. The peasants were still refusing to sell their crops, since the money that they would have received could not buy the goods that they wanted. Bukharin and his allies wanted to woo the countryside with further concessions. Stalin took the opposite course. Emergency measures subjected the richer peasants to forced loans, while party detachments moved through the countryside, confiscating stocks and even stripping the crops from the fields. Was Stalin, some of the deported now asked, not adopting the Opposition policy and confronting at last the growth of capitalism in the countryside? Was this not, then, an opportunity to make peace, without sacrificing principles? Was it not, indeed, a duty to help Stalin against Bukharin and others, who looked to the *kulak* or rich peasant for salvation?

Trotsky agreed that the Opposition should support Stalin's present economic policy. But he insisted that such support should be accompanied by all the more resolute a resistance to Stalin's political oppression. Piatakov, who had capitulated, along with Antonov-Ovseenko, soon after the fifteenth congress, described Trotsky's attitude as self-contradictory. 'But all contradictions,' Trotsky replied, 'disappear in a man who makes a suicide jump into a river.' As turbulence in the countryside increased, with peasants setting fire to stocks of confiscated grain and the GPU employed to suppress virtual revolts, the breach between Stalin and Bukharin widened. And each of them looked towards the banished Opposition.

It was a very different Bukharin now from the man who had exulted at the capitulation of Zinoviev and Kamenev: 'The iron curtain of history was falling, and you got out of its way in the nick of time.' He visited Kamenev in the summer; pale and trembling; so frightened that he talked only in whispers and kept turning his head to see that no one was watching. 'He is the new Genghis Khan,' he said of Stalin. 'He will strangle us.' Stalin intended to crush the peasantry, and anyone who stood in his way, whatever the cost. It was no longer a question of this policy or that, but of preserving the party and the state from Stalin's 'lust for power'.

The surreptitious reports of Bukharin's new attitude that reached Trotsky roused a response that dismayed many in the banished Opposition. He restated his differences with the policies of Bukharin, but was prepared for an agreement limited to the purpose of restoring democracy in the party. And more guardedly, he made a similar response to the tentative approaches from Stalin. He would do no deal over policy that preserved the 'bureaucratic combinations'. He and his followers would return only to a party that provided full freedom of criticism and elected its leadership by secret ballot of all its members.

At last, too late, he had come to recognize that the general issue of democracy took precedence over particular issues of policy. Only for this would he have any truck with Stalin. Yet only on this, he must have realized, was any truck with Stalin impossible. His apparent readiness to compromise was in reality a refusal to compromise at all. And any agreement with Bukharin proved no more attainable. Perhaps, for all his shudderings of horror, Bukharin still placed particular issues of policy above the general issue of democracy. Perhaps he was by now too frightened of Stalin for anything but obeisance. At all events, by the autumn, Bukharin and his allies were effectively on their knees.

They were to be followed, sooner or later, by almost all of Trotsky's prominent adherents, whose repentance marked their passage to a moral desolation. One of them would tell Anton Ciliga, the Yugoslav Communist: 'Let's not forget that Russia is an Asiatic country; the way of Genghis Khan and Stalin suits it better than the European civilization of Leon Davidovitch.' And another would declare: 'A workers' democracy is out of the question in Russia. Here the working class is so feeble and demoralized that to give it liberty would be to ruin the revolution once and for all.'[59] Their subsequent confessions to fictitious and extravagant crimes at Stalin's show trials would be the final echo of a self-abasement that they had already sounded.

Trotsky had never belittled the consequences of his defiance for himself. And he was ready from the first to pay with his own life. Much harder to bear was the death and the suffering of those for whom he felt a special love and responsibility. The husband of his younger daughter, Nina, had been arrested and deported; and Nina, already consumptive, living in acute poverty, and continuing to work for the Opposition, finally collapsed. When, in the spring, Trotsky was informed, he telegraphed immediately his concern and a request for news to Zina, his elder daughter, who was herself ill with consumption but nursing her sister. He got no reply to this, or to the ever more urgent inquiries that followed. On 9 June, Nina died, and he received the news a few days later. She had written a letter from the hospital in Moscow. It took seventy-three days to reach him and arrived after her death. Zina, whose husband had also been deported, promised to visit Alma-Ata. But her own condition was now so poor that Guetier, Trotsky's doctor and friend in Moscow, insisted on having her placed in a sanatorium.

Trotsky's own health began to give way. He had attacks of fever, which brought him blinding headaches; gout and colitis. As reports of his illness reached them, the colonies of the deported protested to Moscow. And some even proposed a hunger strike. When he heard of this, Trotsky sent immediate messages to dissuade them. His illness, he assured them, was not so serious: he was still able to work. The authorities in Moscow went further. Responding to evidence of some unease within the party, Uglanov, secretary of the Moscow committee, announced that Trotsky's illness was 'fictitious'. Natalia sent off an indignant telegram, which accused him of deliberately deceiving the party.

It would be understandable if you had said that L.D.'s health did not interest you at all. In that case you would be consistent with that dangerous consistency which, if it is not stopped, will lead to the grave not only the best revolutionaries but possibly the party and the revolution itself. . . . The fact that you are now obliged to answer inquiries from the masses and to try to wriggle out in such an unseemly manner, proves that the working class does not believe the political slander of Trotsky. Neither will it believe your lies about L.D.'s state of health.

But what the workers were thinking, behind their boarded-up faces, Trotsky in banishment could not know. And neither, for all the spying of his secret police, could Stalin. Now, in the autumn, he was preparing to pursue the policies of the Opposition, with a concentrated violence that seemed fired by a virtual paranoia. The extent of the resistance he would encounter, he had no means of measuring. But of Trotsky's powerful appeal, as a promise of alternative leadership which might promote popular discontent, he was sufficiently persuaded.

In October, the snowdrifts of the censorship surrounded Trotsky with silence. No letters or telegrams reached him; and on the anniversary of the revolution, none of the expected messages from friends and followers arrived. November brought a harsh frost, and Natalia wrote that the cold in their rooms was agony. On 16 December, Volynsky, arriving from Moscow as a special represensative of the GPU, presented an oral ultimatum: either Trotsky must pledge himself to stop directing the Opposition, or steps would be taken to isolate him from political life. In a long letter to the central committee of the party and the Presidium of the Communist International, he replied with an indictment of official policy and a declaration of defiance. 'To abstain from political activity would mean to abstain from getting ready for tomorrow. . . . We know our duty and we will do it to the end.'

II

The Freezing Sea

On 20 January 1929 Volynsky presented himself at Trotsky's house with armed agents of the GPU who proceeded to stand guard at all the exits. He handed Trotsky an extract of GPU minutes, dated two days before. It read:

Considered: the case of citizen Trotsky, Lev Davidovich, under article 58/10 of the Criminal Code, on a charge of counter-revolutionary activity expressing itself in the organization of an illegal anti-Soviet party, whose activity has lately been directed toward provoking anti-Soviet actions and preparing for an armed struggle against the Soviet power.

Resolved: Citizen Trotsky, Lev Davidovich, to be deported from the territory of the USSR.

Asked to sign a slip confirming that he had acquainted himself with the decision, Trotsky wrote: 'The decision of the GPU, criminal in substance and illegal in form, has been announced to me on January 20, 1929.' And he signed his name. Natalia and Lyova were determined to go with him. But where? What country would admit them? And what traps were being laid for them? Volynsky seemed concerned at their plight but could not tell them anything more. He only knew that they were to be met somewhere in European Russia by another representative of the GPU, who would inform them of where they were going.

The family packed frantically throughout the next day, and at dawn on the 22nd set off with an escort to cross the Kurday mountains. At the summit, the winds were whipping the snow into enormous drifts, and the tractor towing the cars was covered up to its neck. The party transferred to sleighs, then back to a car ,and finally, at Frunze, to a railway carriage. When the train was on its way, Bulanov, the new emissary, revealed the determined destination. It was to be Constantinople.

Trotsky insisted on seeing his son Sergei and his daughter-in-law, Anya,

Lyova's wife. They were brought from Moscow to join the train. Bulanov recited the advantages of life in Constantinople. But Trotsky was unimpressed. He refused to leave the Soviet Union voluntarily. It was a reaction that had not been foreseen and that might cause the Turkish authorities to reconsider their compliance. Bulanov communicated with Moscow over the wires. The train, diverted on to a side-track, stopped near a small desolate station and there stayed, as though suspended between two stretches of forest, for twelve days and nights. The cold was intense, and the engine rolled back and forth to keep from freezing to the rails. In Trotsky's carriage, they gave one another flu; reread books and played chess; discussed the various arrests reported in the newspapers that arrived with their midday meals.

At last, on 8 February, Bulanov announced that the German government would not offer asylum and that Trotsky would be taken to Constantinople. The train now sped resolutely towards the south, and on the night of the 10th reached Odessa. Through the carriage window, Trotsky caught flashes of the familiar, from the years that he had spent as a schoolboy in the city. Troops and agents of the GPU provided the only reception on the otherwise deserted pier. Anya and Sergei said their good-byes. Aware of the risks that they were running, they had decided to stay behind in Russia. Then, along with their escort, Trotsky, Natalia and Lyova boarded the waiting cargo ship *Ilyich*, empty of all but its crew. It left at once; towed by an ice-breaker for sixty miles through the freezing sea.

On 12 February, it entered the Bosphorus. And one of his GPU escorts handed Trotsky a grant of 1500 dollars from the Soviet government, 'to enable him to settle abroad'. Trotsky recognized Stalin's sinister sense of humour and took the money. To the Turkish police who boarded the ship, he handed a letter, addressed to Kemal Pasha, president of the Republic. It declared that he had not chosen to arrive at the Turkish frontier and would cross it only in submission to force. The president communicated obliquely, through the governor of Constantinople, a few days later. Trotsky was assured that he might stay as long, or leave as soon, as he pleased; and that while he stayed, the Turkish government would extend to him every hospitality and ensure his safety. It was not meant to be a reply.

From the docks, Trotsky, Natalia and Lyova were driven to the Soviet consulate and welcomed there with every mark of respect. A wing of the building was placed at their disposal. It was a reception that did not reassure them. They feared that the GPU agents on the staff would examine, steal, or simply confiscate papers from the archives which Trotsky had brought with him. But the danger of moving to a hotel, in a city where so many White Russian émigrés had chosen to settle, was more serious. The hospitality of the consulate would, for the while, have to serve.

It was a hand that did not remain open for long. Trotsky wrote a series of articles, reporting on the struggle within the party and denouncing Stalin, which appeared in such newspapers as the *New York Times* and the *Daily Express* of London. The Soviet press replied with accusations that Trotsky had sold himself to the world bourgeoisie, and with cartoons that depicted him clutching a bag of dollars. The GPU in Constantinople informed him that his safety would no longer be guaranteed and that he was to be evicted from the consulate. Helped by a Russian airman who was working for the GPU but who remained mindful of the kindness that Trotsky had shown him in the past, Natalia found a somewhat dilapidated house, the possession of a bankrupt *pasha*, to rent. It was on the Prinkipo Islands, in the Sea of Marmara, where the Byzantine emperors had exiled those royal rivals spared a more decisive dispatch. An hour and a half's journey by steamer from Constantinople, the islands were now a summer resort of the rich and otherwise inhabited only by a few fishermen and shepherds.

Trotsky moved there with the intention of staying only until he could find a more likely refuge. The president of the German Reichstag, to the applause of most deputies, had already referred in a speech to the possibility of granting him the democratic right of asylum. Trotsky applied to the German consulate for a visa. An unofficial reply from Berlin required to know what restrictions he was ready to accept. He undertook to live isolated outside Berlin; to refrain from speaking at any public meetings; and to confine himself to literary work within the bounds of the German laws. This proved insufficient. He was asked whether he would agree to visit Germany only for purposes of medical treatment. He offered to submit himself to examination by a medical commission and leave Germany 'at the close of the health-resort season'. The German government reflected and then replied that his application had been refused.

The Norwegian government proved no more accommodating. The Minister of Justice explained to the Storthing that the costs of protecting Trotsky would be too great for the national budget. The French government replied simply that the order for Trotsky's expulsion from France had never been rescinded. Early in May, Beatrice and Sidney Webb visited Prinkipo. It looked as though a Labour government might soon be formed in Britain, and Trotsky declared that in this event, he would apply for a visa. Sidney Webb demurred. A Labour government might be too dependent upon the good will of the Liberals. Soon afterwards, the Labour Party took power. Trotsky's application for a visa was denied. The Liberals protested, but to no avail. The Labour Home Secretary advised the House of Commons that the right of asylum did not mean the right of an exile to demand asylum, but only the right of the state to refuse it.

Holland, Czechoslovakia, Austria slammed shut their doors at Trotsky's approach. His friends even explored the possibility of finding asylum for him in the Duchy of Luxemburg. They were told it was out of the question. The government of the United States was saved the formality of a refusal. Trotsky, persuaded that he stood not the slightest chance of gaining admission, did not trouble to apply. For the foreseeable future, he recognized wryly, it was a 'planet without a visa'.[1] And soon the island house was turned into a makeshift home. The dirt was swept away, and the walls were painted white. A secretariat, with Lyova in charge, was established on the ground floor; a small square room nearby set aside for meals; and Trotsky provided with a study on the floor above. Secretaries, bodyguards and guests were accommodated in rooms that usually boasted no more than a bed and a chair, while the garden was left to the weeds. It was an austerity that derided the pretensions of the *pasha*, noted by a correspondent of the *Manchester Guardian* in 'the dingy marbles, sad bronze peacock and humiliated gilt'.

The refuge had its consolations. Trotsky relaxed by fishing in the sunlit sea and would return from a successful expedition with his energies straining for release. He would dictate for hours on end and say afterwards: 'It is as if the brain were working all by itself. The brain has its own momentum and all I have to do is to follow it.'[2] Usually he was accompanied by two island fishermen, who came to be accepted as members of the household. But sometimes he went off on his own and would stay away so long that his family and friends grew anxious. One of his followers asked him whether he was not afraid that the GPU might seek to deal with him at such a time. If the GPU decided to deal with him, Trotsky replied, he would be helpless against it. There was no point in making himself his own jailer meanwhile. He knew that among those who came to serve him as his secretaries or bodyguards, there might be an agent of the GPU. And, indeed, it was subsequently discovered that at least two such agents, posing as his followers, had joined his household; one of them, a Latvian, to stay for as long as five months.

But he had little time for thoughts of his own safety. His correspondence was enormous. Questions from disquieted or dissident Communists arrived by every post. The task of rallying his followers abroad and attempting to settle the differences among them demanded unending attention. From the 10,000 dollars that he had received for his various newspaper articles, he had set aside more than half for a special publication fund, mainly to produce the *Bulletin Oppozitsii* or *Opposition Bulletin*. With all the difficulties and delays involved in finding suitable printers and then communicating with them in Paris, it was no small feat to have had the first issue ready by July. And all this was being done at the edges of his time. For he was principally occupied in the writing of his autobiography.

He had already begun it at Alma-Ata; but only to draft the opening chapters, on his childhood and youth. By the early autumn, the last of the manuscript was in the hands of the German, French and English translators, and sections were already appearing in newspapers. Yet *My Life*, for all the interruptions, distractions and anxieties that jostled its still so rapid composition, must be numbered among the rare examples of autobiography as art.

Like Dickens, Trotsky enables the reader to see once again as a child.

We often found ourselves alone in the house on winter days, especially during my father's absences, when all the work of the place fell on my mother. In the dusk, my little sister and I used to sit side by side on the sofa, pressed close together, wide-eyed and afraid to move.

A giant would come out of the cold outside into the dark dining-room, shuffling his huge boots, and wrapped in an enormous great-coat with a huge collar, and wearing a huge hat. His hands were encased in huge mittens. Large icicles hung from his beard and moustache, and his great voice would boom out in the darkness: 'Good evening!' Squeezed together in a corner of the sofa, we would be afraid to answer him. Then the monster would light a match and see us in our corner. The giant would turn out to be one of our neighbours. . . .[3]

It is a capacity for dramatic recall that does not stop with the eyes.

One day, Ivan Vasilyevich and I went together to get some pigeons for breeding purposes from Kasimir Antonovich. In a corner room of the great empty house, Kasimir Antonovich gave us tea, butter, honey, and curds on large plates that smelled damp. I sat drinking tea out of my saucer and listening to the lagging conversation. . . . At last we climbed up into the loft over the barn, carrying a lantern. 'Look out now!' cried Kasimir Antonovich to me. The loft was long and dark, with rafters in all directions. It had a strong smell of mice, bees, cobwebs, and birds. Someone put out the lantern. 'There they are! Grab them!' Kasimir Antonovich whispered. An infernal uproar broke loose; the loft was filled with a whirlwind of wings. It seemed to me for a moment that the end of the world had come, and that we were all lost.[4]

And re-created, through a few sharp strokes of detail, is not only the opening mind of a child, but the life of a class in decline. The assertive and self-assured founders of the gentry are gone, and poverty is closing in on their decadent heirs. There is Ghertopanov, whose family had once owned a whole county and whose younger son is now an apprentice in the Bronstein machine-shop.

Ghertopanov lived by writing petitions, complaints and letters for the peasants. When he came to see us he used to hide tobacco and lumps of sugar up his sleeve, and his wife did the same. With drivelling lips she would tell us stories of her youth, with its serfs, its grand pianos, its silks and its perfumery.[5]

And there is Moisey Kharitonovich, who had visited in a phaeton and whose garden had been proud with peacocks, but who soon came to visiting in a wagon drawn by farm horses, while his garden fence fell to pieces, and cattle trampled the fruit trees and the flowers. How vividly he is summoned from the past.

He spoke French fluently, played the piano, and knew something about literature. His left hand was weak, but his right hand was fit, he said, to play in a concert. His neglected finger-nails, striking the keys of our old spinet, made a noise like castanets. . . . He would often stop in the midst of his playing and get up and go to the mirror. Then, if no one was by, he would singe his beard on all sides with his burning cigarette, with the idea of keeping it tidy. He smoked incessantly, and sighed as he did so, as if he disliked it.[6]

With the same controlled luminosity of recall, he can be lyric as well as comic. Here he is recounting his escape from Siberian exile in 1906.

The sleigh glides smoothly and in silence, like a boat on a crystal-clear lake. In the darkening twilight the woods seem even more gigantic. I cannot see the road; the movement of the sleigh is hardly perceptible. The enchanted trees rush toward us, the bushes run away on the sides, slim birches and old stumps covered with snow fly past us. Everything is filled with mystery. *Chu-chu-chu-chu* resounds the even breathing of the deer in the wooded silence of the night.[7]

The imagery and rhythm can resound with the heartbeats of history. Here he describes a mass meeting at the Modern Circus, in the autumn of 1917.

I made my way to the platform through a narrow human trench, sometimes I was borne overhead. The air, intense with breathing and waiting, fairly exploded with shouts and with the passionate yells peculiar to the Modern Circus. Above and around me was a press of elbows, chests, and heads. I spoke from out of a warm cavern of human bodies; whenever I stretched out my hands I would touch someone, and a grateful movement in response would give me to understand that I was not to worry about it, not to break off my speech, but keep on. No speaker, no matter how exhausted, could resist the electric tension of that impassioned human throng.[8]

And, finally, there is the wit, which leaves a character spread out and impaled on the paper.

Bukharin's nature is such that he must always attach himself to someone. He becomes, in such circumstances, nothing more than a medium for someone else's actions and speeches. You must always keep your eyes on him, or else he will succumb quite imperceptibly to the influence of someone directly opposed to you, as other people fall under an automobile. . . . I never took Bukharin too seriously, and I left him to himself, which really means, to others. After the death of Lenin, he became Zinoviev's medium, and then Stalin's. At the very moment that these lines are being written, Bukharin is passing through still another crisis, and other fluids, as yet not known to me, are filtering through him.[9]

My Life is unmistakably the work of an artist. But it is a work like a gallery of windows, of which only some are of clear glass, while others are clouded; still others, pasted over with posters; and others again, bricked up altogether. And the reason is that Trotsky interfered with the flow of his own creative faculty in the cause of his continuing struggle with his enemies. Sometimes it is a matter of what is said; as when he answers the attacks upon him or submits testimonials to the value of his revolutionary role. The richly implicit prose seems to screech to a stop, as though the lights had suddenly changed, to let through a rush of special pleading. And sometimes it is a matter of what demands to be said but is not; so that the interruption becomes, rather, a rush of silence.

Indeed, the scenes that concern the course of Trotsky's relations with Lenin are like the successive issues of a newspaper subjected to the scissors of the censor and appearing with spaces more eloquent than the columns of print. And just as, in such successive issues, it is the surrounding print that lends to the spaces their eloquence, so, in the book, it is the surrounding artistry, and not any extrinsic knowledge, that makes eloquent the silences in these scenes.

It was not a deception directed at deceiving others. Trotsky's honesty would allow him to deceive only himself. But to self-deception he increasingly succumbed. By diminishing the scope and the scale of his differences with Lenin, he not only confronted the accusation of his enemies, that his career had been essentially a series of assaults on Lenin's leadership. He simultaneously promoted his claim to being regarded as Lenin's sole legitimate heir. And by transforming Lenin himself into a figure of virtually infallible political genius, he not only proclaimed the extent of his loyalty. He buried his own mistakes in his association with that infallibility. Yet art is not mocked. And if he opened wide the front door of his mind to this self-deception, the door far behind, to the workshop of the imagination, remained closed.

We cannot, accordingly, connect what we experience of Trotsky's consciousness with the character of Lenin we are given. We never, in consequence, really understand why Trotsky broke with Lenin in the first place; and why, once the break had occurred, it should have lasted no less than fourteen years. Nor, presented with statements of the mutual trust and respect that then informed the relations between the two reconciled leaders, can we understand how Lenin should later have lent so ready an ear to Stalin's misrepresentations of Trotsky's conduct and motives. Above all, we cannot understand how, given the extent of his authority, Lenin should have used it not to edge Stalin out of the leadership but, instead, so disastrously to advance him.

That Trotsky himself should always have underestimated Stalin does not conflict with the dramatic development of the book. Indeed, the sort of personal consciousness that we come to share is one which had to regard Stalin with contempt. But this only makes it all the more inexplicable that such a man as Stalin should have reached a position from which to seize, so easily, command of the party and the state. And, in the end, we must not only doubt the infallibility of Lenin's political genius, but question the nature of a revolution which Stalin could come to command. Paradoxically, therefore, the same commitment to propaganda which confronts the artistry of the book for a political purpose, confronts the political purpose as well. Denied any real understanding of how the revolution went wrong, we are denied any real association with Trotksy's continuing struggle to put it right.

Yet even as Trotsky was correcting the French and German translations of *My Life*, he was preparing to start on a book which would transform a political purpose into a consummate work of art. In November 1929, he provided Alexandra Ramm, his German translator, with a synopsis of his *History of the Russian Revolution*. And according to Natalia, he wrote the 'four long volumes' of the work – published as three, with a total of some half a million words, in the English version – 'during the next year'.[10] He did so, furthermore, while continuing to deal with his enormous daily correspondence; to edit the *Opposition Bulletin*; and to receive numerous visitors seeking his advice. The work, however, shows no defects of haste or distraction. On the contrary; it has all the precision of style and tightness of control that suggest the slow, sustained, concentrated effort of years. And the reason may be that just such an effort had already been made, within his imagination, so that the process of putting it all on paper now was almost a form of automatic writing.

Certainly it was his imagination that was, throughout, in command. There was no interference from the need to explain himself. His role in the revolution needed no explanation. He was satisfied that it was bound to emerge irreproachably from the re-enactment of events. Indeed, it is an aspect of the work's essential achievement that Trotsky the author and Trotsky the actor acquire different identities in the reader's mind. It is not merely that Trotsky the author writes of himself as 'Trotsky' instead of as 'I'. The device is necessary, but on its own would have done little. It is the drama itself that defines all the actors, by their parts. And the drama is that of history, with revolution as its theme.

There are innumerable histories informed by the Marxist doctrine of class struggle. Trotsky's *History of the Russian Revolution* towers over them all. What distinguishes it from all the others, therefore, is not the doctrine but the translation of the doctrine into art. And it is a translation evident from the first, in the very exposition of theory that introduces the ensuing drama. A few measured sentences lay the basis for an understanding of Russia's historically slow development.

The population of this gigantic and austere plain, open to Eastern winds and Asiatic migrations, was condemned by nature itself to a long backwardness. The struggle with nomads lasted almost up to the end of the seventeenth century; the struggle with winds, bringing winter cold and summer drought, continues still. Agriculture, the basis of the whole development, advanced by extensive methods. In the north they cut down and burned up the forests, in the south they ravished the virgin steppes. The conquest of nature went wide and not deep.[11]

And then, with a single image, Trotsky illumines what he calls 'the law of *combined development*', which enabled Russia to skip certain intermediate stages. 'Savages throw away their bows and arrows for rifles all at once, without travelling the road which lay between those two weapons, in the past.'[12]

The features of this development in Russia are incisively described: an industry dominated by giant enterprises, with 'no hierarchy of transitional layers' between populace and the leadership of capital, alongside a system of land cultivation, virtually stuck in its seventeenth-century tracks, whose surplus labour supplied the new needs of industry. And so,

in Russia the proletariat did not arise gradually through the ages, carrying with itself the burden of the past as in England, but in leaps involving sharp changes of environment, ties, relations, and a sharp break with the past. It is just this fact – combined with the concentrated oppressions of czarism – that made the Russian workers hospitable to the boldest conclusions of revolutionary thought – just as the backward industries were hospitable to the last word in capitalist organization.[13]

It is a masterly piece of historical analysis, contained within a mere dozen pages. And by style and substance both, it is not outside of what follows, like so many programme notes, but a part of the structure; a prologue that is the door to the drama. For the drama is not that of the revolution. The revolution is the protagonist. The drama is that of history itself. And the theme of the drama is the inevitability of the protagonist's triumph.

Inevitability, of course, is no barrier to the achievement of dramatic tension. Indeed, taking their material from popular myth, where the outcome of every issue was known beforehand, the ancient Greek tragedians involved their audiences in the very tension between the protagonist's reach and the inevitability of his downfall. And it was this same tension which informed one of the most effective of their dramatic devices: that of irony.

Trotsky turns this tension, between reach and inevitability, inside out. For just as the inevitability is that of the revolution's triumph, so the reach is that of those who would oppose the revolution. And the irony which this tension informs relates correspondingly not to the revolution but to the revolution's opponents. It is not, in consequence, tragic irony. For irony can only be tragic when it relates to the protagonist's downfall. But it is irony the more abundant, the richer and the finer even, in the precisions of its variety, for that. Indeed, it becomes, from the start of the action, no mere occasional contrivance, but the primary expression of the theme.

Russia engages in war against the industrial might of Germany, without enough weapons or even shoes for the troops, and with commanders whose incompetence is matched only by their readiness to sacrifice the lives of their men.

> The one thing the Russian generals did with a flourish was to drag human meat out of the country. Beef and pork are handled with incomparably more economy. Grey staff nonentities ... would stop up all cracks with new mobilizations and comfort themselves and the Allies with columns of figures when columns of fighters were wanted.[14]

If the mood of this irony is one of revulsion, it is also one of satire and scorn for a Tsarism that confronts the culture of modern man with the relics of medievalism.

> The more isolated the dynasty became, and the more unsheltered the autocrat felt, the more he needed some help from the other world. Certain savages, in order to bring good weather, wave in the air a shingle on a string. The czar and czarina used shingles for the greatest variety of purposes. In the czar's train there was a whole chapel full of large and small images, and all sorts of fetishes, which were brought to bear, first against the Japanese, then against the German artillery.[15]

Yet irony is most dramatic when it is made internal, to emerge from within the mind of the relevant character. And this is done with particular success in Trotsky's treatment of the Tsar himself. Gone is the Grand Guignol monster of *1905*: 'the royal blood in his veins poisoned by all the vices of many generations', who 'combines filthy sensuality with apathetic cruelty'.[16] Instead, we are introduced to a man who is, above all, unequal to the challenge of his place and his time.

> Nicholas II inherited from his ancestors not only a giant empire, but also a revolution. And they did not bequeath him one quality which would have made him capable of governing an empire or even a province or a county. To that historic flood which was rolling its billows each one closer to the gates of his

palace, the last Romanov opposed only a dumb indifference. It seemed as though between his consciousness and his epoch there stood some transparent but absolutely impenetrable medium.[17]

Through quotations from his diary, we are provided with evidence of his essentially mediocre mind. And then we are led to see how such mediocrity required the contemptible to feed its vanity.

He selected his ministers on a principle of continual deterioration. Men of brain and character he summoned only in extreme situations when there was no other way out, just as we call in a surgeon to save our lives. It was so with Witte, and afterwards with Stolypin. The czar treated both with ill-concealed hostility. As soon as the crisis had passed, he hastened to part with these counsellors who were too tall for him.[18]

We come to understand his dependence on superstition, his deceit, and even that cruelty which applauds and promotes the pogroms. It is the cruelty of the coward frightened at his fate. Yet just as the drama demands the development of his individuality, so the drama, paradoxically, then demands its denial. Louis XVI and Nicholas II, Marie-Antoinette and Alexandra, behaved, for all their differences, in much the same way.

Similar (of course, far from identical) irritations in similar conditions call out similar reflexes; the more powerful the irritation, the sooner it overcomes personal peculiarities. To a tickle, people react differently, but to a red-hot iron, alike. As a steam-hammer converts a sphere and a cube alike into sheet metal, so under the blow of too great and inexorable events resistances are smashed and the boundaries of 'individuality' lost.[19]

This illustrates another feature of Trotsky's art: his masterly use of images. Even when they are conventional, they are made vivid, by the addition of detail and appropriate rhythm: as with 'that historic flood which was rolling its billows each one closer to the gates of the palace'. But they are, indeed, seldom conventional. And their dramatic impact often goes beyond the immediate illumination of character or idea, to the essential theme. The image of the steam-hammer which converts a sphere and a cube alike into sheet metal, is drawn from the world of science, to which history itself, with its 'law' of class struggle, belongs.

More directly dramatic is Trotsky's narrative prose.

In spite of the auspicious rumours about the Cossacks, perhaps slightly exaggerated, the crowd's attitude toward the mounted men remains cautious. A horseman sits high above the crowd; his soul is separated from the soul of the demonstrator by the four legs of his beast. A figure at which one must gaze from below always seems more significant, more threatening. The infantry are beside one on the pavement – closer, more accessible. The masses try to get near them, look into their eyes, surround them with their hot breath. A great role is played by women workers in the relation between workers and soldiers. They go up to the cordons more boldly than men, take hold of the rifles, beseech, almost command: 'Put down your bayonets – join us.' The soldiers are excited, ashamed, exchange anxious glances, waver; someone makes up his mind first, and the bayonets rise guiltily above the shoulders of the advancing crowd. The barrier is opened, a joyous and grateful 'Hurrah!' shakes the air. The soldiers are surrounded. Everywhere arguments, reproaches, appeals – the revolution makes another forward step.[20]

The reader is transported into the street and placed among the demonstrators, to look up at the horsemen and then into the eyes of the infantry. He sees the hesitation of the soldiers; the first bayonet lifted; the abandonment of resistance. He shares the relief, the rejoicing and the tumult. He is part of the revolutionary consciousness. But the consciousness itself is that of the people on the pavements: not of the liberals in the Duma; of the moderate socialist leaders; or even of the laggard Bolsheviks, so lost until the arrival of Lenin from exile in Switzerland. And this is essential to the subsequent drama. For it is within this developing popular consciousness that Lenin confronts and overcomes the caution and confusion in his own party; within this developing popular consciousness that the irrelevance of the bourgeois revolutionary regime is realized.

Again, it is irony that principally expresses the theme.

The portfolio of Finance was given to a young man named Tereshchenko. 'Where did they get him?' everybody was inquiring with bewilderment in the Tauride Palace. The well-informed explained that this was an owner of sugar factories, estates, forests, and other innumerable properties, worth some eighty million roubles in gold, president of the Military-Industrial Committee of Kiev, possessed of a good French pronunciation, and on top of it all a connoisseur of the ballet. And they added – more importantly – that . . . Tereshchenko had almost taken part in the great conspiracy which was to have overthrown Nicholas II.[21]

Miliukov, leader of the Cadets and distinguished historian, would afterwards reveal in his writings a remarkable insight into why the liberal forces failed and the Bolsheviks succeeded. But meanwhile he is the captive of his own anachronism.

His strength lay, and his weakness too, in this: he expressed more fully and elegantly than others in the language of politics the fate of the Russian bourgeoisie – the fact that it was caught historically in a blind alley. The Mensheviks wept because Miliukov ruined liberalism, but it would be truer to say that liberalism ruined Miliukov.[22]

Yet it is precisely to the dominion of liberalism that Bolshevism's Marxist rivals, the Mensheviks, too, are committed. For they see in Russia's backwardness support only for a bourgeois revolution, which the wild men of Bolshevism would sacrifice by leaping across history into socialism. And so they promote only their own defeat; with the victory of the very rivals whose undertaking they reject as unreal. Seeking to save the revolution by restraining it, they are swept away by those who seek, in risking the revolution, to advance it. They have their representative leader in Tseretelli who, of them all, 'revealed in the events of the revolution the widest horizon and the desire to pursue a consistent policy. For this reason he, more than any other, helped on with the destruction of the February regime'.[23]

But the ultimate irony is that of the Social Revolutionaries, who enjoy by far the largest following of any party and would set themselves in place of the class struggle, at the centre of history.

The power of this party seemed unlimited. In reality it was a political aberration. A party for whom everybody votes except that minority who know what they are voting for, is no more a party, than the tongue in which babies of all countries babble is a national language. . . .[24]

The leader to whom such a party inevitably turns is Kerensky, who makes no secret of his contempt for all parties and his view of himself as the directly chosen of the nation.

This idea of a master of destiny rising above all classes, is nothing but Bonapartism. If you stick two forks into a cork symmetrically, it will, under very great oscillations from side to side, keep its balance even on a pin point: that is the mechanical model of the Bonapartist superarbiter. The degree of solidity of such a power, setting aside international conditions, is determined by the stability of equilibrium of the two antagonistic classes within the country.[25]

There is no such stability, of course. And Kerensky is as doomed in the role he has chosen to play as the last of the Tsars was in his. Indeed, the parallel with Nicholas II, shaking his shingle in the face of history, has already emerged, in a flash of dramatic imagery; as in June 1917, the Provisional Government undertakes a calamitous new offensive at the front. 'All was left to the will of Providence. Only the icons of the czarina were lacking. They tried to replace them with the icons of democracy. Kerensky travelled everywhere, appealing and pronouncing benedictions.'[26]

Taking his own party contemptuously for granted, he concentrates on conciliating the Cadets. But the Cadets take him contemptuously for granted in turn; using him and the coalition that he crowns, like the 'cross' on a 'church steeple',[27] to prepare their own thrust for power. At the state conference in August, which Kerensky calls to confirm his authority, it is Kornilov whom the Cadets acclaim and encourage, while Kerensky's hysterical oration stupefies the moderate socialists helplessly committed to sustain him. By the Democratic Conference in the middle

of September, he is commander-in-chief as well as head of the government; but he has added only the hollowness of his authority at the front
to the hollowness of his authority at home. The Bolshevik insurrection
finds him virtually isolated in the Winter Palace. 'Remembering that he
was the member of a party – as others remember only on their death beds
about the church – Kerensky called up the Social Revolutionaries on the
telephone and demanded that they send fighting companies immediately.'[28]
But who is ready to die in order to save him? Having set his place above
all classes and parties, he can fill it only with himself.

And what fighting companies are there left for the Social Revolutionaries to send? Their own nemesis is as just and as complete.

In July, when the government was coming down on the villages with
measures of repression, the peasants in hot haste ran for defence to those same
Social Revolutionaries. From Pontius the young they appealed for protection to
Pilate the old. . . . Hiding behind Social Revolutionaries from the blows of a
Social Revolutionary government, the peasants steadily lost confidence both in
the government and the party. Thus the swelling out of the Social Revolutionary
organizations in the villages became fatal to this universal party, which was
rebelling at the bottom but restoring order at the top.[29]

Yet none of this conveys the supreme dramatic control with which
Trotsky mingles character, comment, mood and event. And no passage
snatched from the design can ever suffice, since the only sufficient measure
is the composition intact. To cite any single passage is to shine a torch
in a dark room on the painting of a hand or merely a sleeve from a
portrait.

This is not history in that tradition of liberal scholarship which pretends
to let the facts speak for themselves: as though the very selection of facts
does not always reverberate with the voice of the scholar's own liberal
prejudice. Nor is it the 'proof of scientific objectivism' that Trotsky
claimed might be found 'in the inner logic of the narrative itself'.[30]
Whatever else may be held against the Stalinist school of counterfeiters,
it is not a lack of inner logic in the historical narrative they produced.
But theirs is the inner logic of propaganda. The inner logic of Trotsky's
history is that of art. Indeed, by the standards of science, Trotsky's work
must be accounted a colossal failure. For whereas history as art ends
only with itself, history as science – in so far as it may properly be considered a science at all – is subject to constant revaluation, as the future
becomes the past and provides different evidence. And in this latter case,
the history of the Russian revolution ends not with the triumph of the
Bolsheviks in October 1917, but continues, through Trotsky's downfall
and Stalin's despotism, down to the bureaucracy of today. It would be
unlikely to contradict Trotsky's own emphasis on irony. But the direction
of the irony would, surely, not be the same.

Thomas Hobbes, the seventeenth-century English philosopher, in introducing his translation of *The Peloponnesian War*, referred to Thucydides as 'the most Politick Historiographer that ever writ'. And, indeed, it is to Thucydides, of all the great classical historians, that Trotsky comes closest. Both men wrote of events in which they had themselves played important parts. Thucydides fought on the side of Athens, as one of its generals. For both of them, such events had a moral meaning; and it was to illuminate this meaning that they wrote their histories. Above all, they were, in pursuing their purposes, masters of the dramatic form. What Hobbes remarked of Thucydides is no less true of Trotsky. 'He filleth his Narrations with that choice of matter, and ordereth them with that Judgement, and with such perspicuity and efficacy expresseth himself that (as Plutarch saith) he maketh his Auditor a Spectator. For he setteth his Reader in the Assemblies of the People, and in the Senates, at their debating; in the Streets, at their Seditions; and in the Field at their Battels.'

There is, too, a tragic parallel between the two men. Thucydides had written after the defeat of the Athenian democracy. He had seen and recorded the moral darkening of a Greek world at war with itself. Trotsky was writing his *History of the Russian Revolution* to record a triumph. And across the paper fell the light of his own faith, while the dark, not only in Russia but across Europe, deepened around him.

Stalin dealt with the economic difficulties, which his own policies had promoted, by adopting the Opposition commitment to socialist measures; but with a blind and relentless fury that transformed it beyond all recognition. Trotsky had sought to counteract the growth of a capitalist class in agriculture. Stalin directed his course to nothing less than the total and immediate collectivization of the countryside. And what ensued was a virtual war between the regime and the peasantry. While *Pravda* and foreign guests reported on the enthusiasm with which the campaign was being popularly received, the peasants attacked party agents in the villages and, rather than surrender their property to the state, set fire to their grain and slaughtered their animals. Between 1928 and 1934, the Soviet Union lost more than half its livestock population, and starvation reached from the cities into the most remote of the villages.

Stalin did not take kindly to resistance. Between 1929 and 1933, vast numbers of peasants were forcibly removed from their homes: subsequent estimates by Western economists would put the total figure as high as 5,000,000 families, or some 25,000,000 people.[31] Indeed, so predatory did the terror in the countryside become that Stalin himself grew alarmed. He signed a secret circular, dated May 1933 and directed to party, secret police and judicial functionaries, in which he condemned the 'saturnalia of arrests'; ordered that, in future, arrests should be made only in cases of 'active struggle' or 'organized resistance'; and laid down maximum deportation quotas for certain regions.

Trotsky had repeatedly called for a planned and rational programme of industrialization. Stalin undertook the industrialization of the country with a plan that mocked the very purpose of planning and a precipitateness that became a race against reason itself. Targets were set without reference to the availability or development of appropriate skills; the existence of adequate machinery, raw materials or fuel; the capacity of the transport system. And Stalin set about securing compliance in his own way.

Multitudes of workers were dispatched to concentration camps: for political unreliability; for a suspicious indifference to politics; or sometimes, it seemed, merely to encourage the others. When starvation drove disquieting numbers to seek for sustenance in the countryside, internal passports were introduced to prevent such officially unsanctioned movements of population. Workers were locked by law to their places of work, and any 'unjustified' absence or late arrival was punished. There remained a wilderness of difference between the various targets proclaimed by the regime and the conspicuous reality. And into it countless scapegoats, laden with the responsibility for failure, were duly driven. Some technicians were put on trial. They confessed to having conspired with enemies of the Soviet Union and having committed acts of sabotage. Others were charged and summarily shot. Perhaps they had proved less susceptible to the pressures of the secret police for serviceable confessions.

One trial brought together, amongst others, Nikolai Sukhanov, the chronicler of 1917, and two eminent economists, Groman and Ginsberg who, as members of the Planning Commission, had dared to express their doubts over the course of economic policy and to warn of its consequences. All were accused of having plotted with the Social Democrat Second International to foment war against the Soviet Union. They escaped a formal death sentence, but were dispatched to various destinations from which they never emerged. Few, however highly placed, were safe. Prominent party officials were eliminated in the cellars of the secret police; some for showing too little zeal, some for showing too much. Syrtsov, chairman of the Russian Soviet of People's Commissars, simply disappeared, leaving no trace apart from rumours that he had criticized forced collectivization.

Increasingly, leading members of the Opposition were drawn to make their peace with the regime. Stalin might be careering in the direction of socialism. But at least it was the proper direction. And those who saw how dangerously he drove had a duty to leave off wringing their hands at a distance. Famine and inflation, peasant insurgency and worker discontent threatened the survival of the revolution itself. In May 1929,

Preobrazhensky received permission to visit Moscow and negotiate peace terms. He urged an end to the terror; the rehabilitation of victimized comrades; the withdrawal of Trotsky's banishment order. But it soon became clear that the only available terms were those of unconditional surrender. In the middle of July, Radek, Smilga, Preobrazhensky and 400 other members of the deported Opposition submitted.

When Trotsky read Radek's abject recantation in *Pravda*, he was distressed and alarmed. How far, he wondered, was the moral rot to spread? And from Prinkipo he cried against those who had abandoned the cause, to those who had not yet done so. Stalin's bureaucratic Five Year Plan was the bait on the hook of his continuing ascendancy. He was, for his own purposes, chastising Bukharin and the rest of the right within the party. 'Has it then been our task to make one part of the ruling group chastise the other? Has the approach to fundamental political questions changed?'

But Trotsky could not stop the wind. In October, after more than four months of negotiation, Smirnov and other one-time close associates of Trotsky's also succumbed. Almost to the last they had insisted on publicly calling for Trotsky's return. And even when they had given way on this, they had still refused to denounce Trotsky in their statement of submission. Some dignity they kept, for the while. And that Stalin permitted them to do so was a sign of how serviceable, in his gathering difficulties, he found their surrenders to be. He would deal with them again, in his own good time.

Rakovsky seemed to be made of different metal. Stricken by repeated heart attacks, he yet clung to the entire programme of the Opposition. 'As long as the political part of our programme remains unfulfilled,' he declared, 'the whole work of socialist construction is in danger of being blown sky high.' A party leadership that extracted from its opponents confessions of imaginary errors merely imitated the Catholic Church, which made the atheist recant on his deathbed. Such a leadership 'loses every title to respect; and the Oppositionist who changes his convictions overnight deserves only utter scorn'. But within a few years, he too would capitulate. And subsequently, put on trial, he would confess to imaginary crimes.

There were those who never submitted. But most of them suffered and died, uncounted and with anonymous courage. It was in general only the capitulators who bore numbers and names, for transmission through the megaphones of Stalin's propaganda machine. And meanwhile the same machine was purging the past, to magnify Stalin's role, and to distort Trotsky's, in all the records. Encyclopedias, histories, memoirs, novels, poetry disappeared from the shelves, permanently or to re-emerge in suitably amended versions. Gorky himself was persuaded to correct his

Recollections of Lenin, so as to substitute for Lenin's praise of Trotsky hints that Trotsky had always been regarded by Lenin with distrust. Documents and photographs were doctored to sustain new accounts of party history, the revolution and the civil war. And new accounts were, in their turn, withdrawn for the latest version of the only truth. The popular collective memory was treated like some enormous palimpsest. And swift was the punishment that fell upon anyone from whose mind the original writing seemed not to have been entirely erased. Indeed, the guardians of orthodoxy were not to be satisfied by superficial conversion. 'Unconscious Trotskyism' came to be considered a crime that was scarcely less serious than the conscious kind.

Trotsky cried out against this process, again and again. But who in the Soviet Union could hear him? Increasingly he seemed to be calling into a chasm which swallowed up his voice. At first messages had come, on scraps of paper the size of postage stamps, from camps and prisons in the Soviet Union. By 1931, there were few successful break-outs from the closely guarded silence. Copies of the *Opposition Bulletin* could only seldom be smuggled into the Soviet Union; and once there, were more likely than not to end up in the dossiers of the secret police. In 1932 there was published in Russian from Berlin his detailed reply to the rewriting of history: *Stalinskaya Shkola Falsifikatsii (The Stalin School of Falsification)*. It was a telling indictment. But whom in Russia did it reach?

The real immediate struggle lay in the West, where Trotsky's voice was not so easily to be buried. There, he might speak for the world-wide revolutionary commitment, against that Stalinist doctrine of 'socialism in a single country', which denied the whole logic of Marxism. There, he might denounce the bureaucratic corruption of the established Communist parties and rouse their members to demand that 'democratic centralism' which offered discipline only as the product of a genuinely free dispute and decision. There, he might rally the disheartened, as he had rallied the forces of the revolution so often in the darkest days of the civil war, to fight for the future.

In France and Germany, Italy, Holland and Belgium, prominent revolutionary Marxists, some of them previously, and others still, members of the Communist Party, were in their different ways assailing Stalinism. For most of them, Trotsky's arrival in exile offered a leadership that burned with the original, pure flame of the Russian revolution. In the United States, two members of the party central committee, and in Canada the party chairman, adhered to his cause. In Mexico a group of Communists, influenced by the celebrated painter Diego Rivera, tore off their Stalinist bandages.

But the decisive mass support for which Trotsky laboured was not to materialize. In part this was a consequence of his very eminence. Whatever the reasons which had determined Stalin to deal with Trotsky by dispatching him into exile abroad, they did not apply, it soon became clear, to any other leading opponents of the regime. Trotsky was to remain not only the greatest, but the only great figure of the October revolution allowed to carry his dissidence with him into the West. And he bulked so large above his followers there that they seemed altogether lost in the shadow that he cast. Had those other leading opponents within the Soviet Union at least continued to defy the regime, this might not have mattered so much. But the well-publicized surrender of so many among them made it seem that Trotsky's virtual isolation abroad was more than matched by his isolation at home.

How far Trotsky might yet have succeeded, by an immediate attempt to gather around him a new movement, must remain the merest speculation. For to the establishment of any such movement, as urged by some of his adherents, Trotsky was resolutely opposed. The Communist International might have expelled him. But he continued to give it his allegiance. And he did so because he continued to regard its constituent parties, for all their Stalinist corruptions, as containing the revolutionary vanguard of the workers.

If anyone had shown that he could move those in the vanguard of the workers with his voice it was Trotsky. But to move them, he had to reach them in the first place. And how was he to do this? He was scarcely less isolated on the island of Prinkipo than he had been in the sleepy little town of Alma-Ata. Here, to be sure, he might speak through his books, pamphlets and articles. But how were these to be heard above the constant drumming in the popular press of the party? And those in the rank and file who seemed to be stirring towards him were dealt with at once: by warnings, or, where these did not suffice, by excommunication.

In due course, Trotsky would disown the Communist International and its constituent parties. But by then it would be too late. The very peril which the policies pressed by Trotsky might have prevented, and which the policies pursued by Stalinism had served to promote, made Stalin seem to many, even outside of the party, as the principal hope for the survival of democracy.

Shortly after his arrival in the West, Trotsky had written, for an American paper, on the coming peril.

In an analogy with electricity, democracy may be defined as a system of safety switches and fuses to guard against the violent shocks generated by national or social struggles. No other epoch in the history of man has been so filled with antagonisms as our own. The overloading of the current shows itself more and more at various points in the European system. Under the too-high tension of class and international antagonisms, the safety switches of democracy fuse or break. This is the essence of the short circuit of dictatorship.[32]

Stalin, however, took a different view of the prospects in Europe. The violent lurch to the left within the Soviet Union was accompanied by a similar lurch in the policies imposed on the Communist parties abroad. To the Communist International which he had been selected to lead, Molotov proclaimed the Third Period Theory. The first period, of revolutionary stresses, had lasted from the end of the war to 1923, when it had been succeeded by the 'relative stabilization of capitalism'. This second period had closed in 1928, and the third, now opening, was to be the grave of the capitalist system. There would be no escape for the bourgeoisie from the next inevitable economic crisis; and organized workers, drawing behind them not only their unorganized comrades but inflamed peasant multitudes, would take power.

In the period of 'relative stabilization', the Social Democrats had been appropriate partners, and Communists had been required to urge upon them the obvious advantages of a united front. But in the period of final struggle, Social Democrats were bound to back the counter-revolution, and Communists now needed to treat them as enemies. Indeed, since the Social Democrat camouflaged his function with the colours of democracy and socialism, he must be regarded as an even more dangerous enemy than the open Fascist. And most dangerous of all were the Left Social Democrats, who camouflaged themselves to seem almost indistinguishable from Communists, and who were to be exposed and assailed, therefore, with the utmost vigour.

Trotsky watched with mounting alarm the adoption of these policies by Stalin's obedient Communist parties. And repeatedly he attacked the assumptions on which the Third Period Theory was based. That capitalism had yet once again reeled from boom into slump, and predictably into a deeper slump than ever before, did not mean that it was about to fall into its grave. It would, one way or another, attempt to preserve its dominion. And a Communist leadership that called only for offensive action, as though there was nothing against which the workers needed to defend themselves, was inviting calamity. Even in armed insurrection, at the climax of revolutionary struggle, some defensive disposition was essential. And how much more evidently was this so, when fascism was on the offensive?

The main battlefield, of course, was Germany where, in the elections of September 1930, the Nazis had polled some 6,500,000 votes, to become the second largest party in the Reichstag. The Social Democrats, whose party was still the largest, had lost more than 1,000,000 votes; or around as many as the Communists, with their 4,500,000, had gained. If any proof had been required of how serious the Nazi challenge was becoming, this had now been provided. And in November Trotsky called upon all German workers to make common cause against Hitler. But the German

Communist Party had its eyes closed and its fingers in its ears. It continued to assail the Social Democrats as 'social fascists' and with scarcely less passion than it spent on the fascists themselves.

Indeed, in the summer of 1931, it went so far as to ally itself with the Nazis in a frontal assault on the Social Democrats. Mounting a campaign for a 'People's Revolution' against the party that had 'accepted the slavery and humiliation of the Versailles Peace', the Nazis wrested a referendum in Prussia on the survival of the Social Democratic government there. The Communist Party then presented the Social Democrats with an ultimatum. It would call for a vote against them unless they agreed to a number of demands. The demands were such that no Social Democratic leadership could accept them without sinking to its knees, and they were duly rejected. The Communist Party proceeded to campaign for a vote against the government, in what it now chose to call the 'Red Referendum'.

In the event, the government was upheld at the polls. But the campaign left behind it a working populace more deeply divided than ever. If the Communists attacked Social Democrats as virtual fascists, what were Social Democrats to think of a Communist Party that had effectively formed a united front with the Nazis? It was becoming increasingly difficult to tell the propaganda of the Nazis and that of the Communist Party apart. The Communists, too, spoke of a 'People's Revolution', to achieve Germany's 'social and national liberation' from the bondage of Versailles. Trotsky denounced this 'national communism', which he derived from Stalin's doctrine of socialism in a single country, and warned that the leadership of the German Communist Party was carrying the proletariat to disaster. The working class must unite and oppose Hitler with armed resistance, he declared. 'The strength of Nazism lies in the division of the working class.' The Communist press inveighed against him as the 'henchman of the social fascists'.

In a Reichstag of some thirty different parties, Chancellor Brüning, leader of the Catholic Centre, headed a coalition government whose principal constituent was the Social Democratic Party and whose overall majority was a makeshift shelter that threatened to collapse in every wind. In the presidential elections of March 1932, the vote for Hindenburg, backed by the Social Democrats, fell just short of an absolute majority, while Hitler received just over 30 per cent, and Thaelmann, leader and candidate of the Communist Party, just over 13 per cent. With the fourth candidate, of the right-wing German National People's Party, dismissed, new elections followed in April. Hindenburg succeeded, with 53 per cent. But Hitler increased his vote to almost 13,500,000, or 36.8 per cent of the total, while the vote for Thaelmann dropped below 4,000,000, to 10.2 per cent. In the aftermath, Brüning, no longer able to command an overall majority in the Reichstag, or to secure approval from Hindenburg for emergency reform by presidential decree, resigned as chancellor.

In new Reichstag elections at the end of July, the Nazis won 230 of the 608 seats, to become by far the largest party, while the Communists gained twelve, to come third, with a total of eighty-nine. Between them, therefore, Nazis and Communists held a majority of seats. Together they could paralyse parliamentary government. And together, this is what they proceeded to do. Trotsky had written at the time of the Red Referendum:

> To go out into the street with the slogan 'Down with the government of Brüning and Braun [leader of the Prussian Social Democrats]' is a reckless adventure when the whole balance of strength is such that the government of Brüning and Braun can be replaced only by a 'government of Hitler and Hugenberg [leader of the German National People's Party]'.

The alliteration, it was now to emerge, had caught the glitter of the blade.

The Reichstag was once again dissolved, and in the November elections, the Nazis were reduced to 196 seats, while the Communists gained another eleven, at the expense of the Social Democrats. But Hugenberg's Nationalists had increased their representation as well, to fifty-two seats. The new Reichstag proved to be as unmanageable as its predecessor. In January 1933 Chancellor Kurt von Schleicher resigned, and the president invited Hitler to form a government. With the support of the Nationalists and a few strays, Hitler did so, but only to arrange for further Reichstag elections in March. 'Now it will be easy,' Goebbels wrote in his diary on 3 February, 'to carry on the fight, for we can call on all the resources of the State. Radio and press are at our disposal. We shall stage a masterpiece of propaganda. And this time, naturally, there is no lack of money'.[33]

On 27 February, the Reichstag building was set on fire, and the Nazis at once blamed the Communists. Hitler persuaded President Hindenburg to sign a decree 'for the Protection of the People and the State', suspending those sections of the constitution that guaranteed civil liberties. Prominent Communists, Social Democrats and various liberals were arrested; newspapers, suppressed; and public meetings, banned or disrupted. At the polls on 5 March, the Nazis received 44 per cent of the vote, and their Nationalist allies 8 per cent. Little more than a fortnight later, on the 23rd, the Reichstag passed the 'Enabling Act', which effectively placed the country under Hitler's dictatorship.

Rundschau, official mouthpiece of the Communist International, offered comfort. 'The Fascist dictatorship, in destroying all democratic illusions, is ridding the masses of noxious social democratic influences and hence accelerating Germany's march towards proletarian revolution. . . . Only fools will say that the German Communists have been defeated.' There were, however, few German Communists left in a condition to receive, let alone celebrate the glad tidings of their progress towards victory. The new German regime had lost no time in ensuring that they should be otherwise engaged.

To the anguish of having to watch the Communist International help Hitler to power was added for Trotsky an anguish of a more private kind, which had begun, two years before, in so much joy. In the middle of January 1931, his surviving daughter Zina arrived at Prinkipo with her five-year-old son Seva. She was broken in health, from tuberculosis and long mental stress. Her husband had been deported, and she herself had twice been detained. She had been allowed to go abroad, after appeals from influential friends of Trotsky's in the West, only at the price of leaving her daughter as a hostage behind.

At first came only the wonder and delight of the reunion. Trotsky himself was tenderly, perhaps guiltily, giving towards a child of his whose life had been so distant and who resembled him so closely, from the brilliance of her eyes among the sharp dark features of her face, to the fervour of her political commitment and her penetrating sense of irony. And to Zina, Trotsky was more than her father. He was the hero of the revolution whom she had heard holding a multitude with his words, and who had lost power only to gain in stature by his struggle. She longed to be of some help to him and to be shown that he needed her. And the very intensity of her devotion blew, like some blinding blizzard, between them.

Her brother Lyova, whose reserve seemed a reproach to her own tumultuous temperament, enjoyed her father's confidence and shared the secrets of Opposition activity. She saw their tight attachment to each other but not the related tensions, which came from the enormous demands which Trotsky made on his son as on himself, without regard to their different abilities. It had, indeed, already been decided that Lyova should go as Trotsky's representative to Berlin, where the *Opposition Bulletin* was now published and an International Secretariat in the process of being established. In February he at last received his German visa.

But his departure relieved none of the new strains developing in the family. Soon after Zina's arrival, a mysterious fire raged through part of the house. Trotsky rescued his archives and the manuscript of his *History*. His library was lost; along with the preliminary material for a projected book on Marx and Engels.[34] The household removed to a nearby hotel and then, for a year, while the home on Prinkipo was being made habitable again, to a house in an eastern suburb of Constantinople. Investigation revealed no evidence of GPU responsibility for the fire, but suspicions of such involvement remained and served to emphasize the threat of Stalin's reprisals. Zina must have brooded the more anxiously over the fate of the husband and child she had left behind.

Her tuberculosis flared up, so that she had to have several operations on her lungs. And her mind seemed increasingly disturbed. She had been lavishly attentive and affectionate to Natalia but now her resentment and her jealousy broke cover, to provoke in her father the very reaction that she feared. 'Don't shout at me, Papa, don't – ' she would write to him, in recollection, a year later. 'Your shouting is the one thing I cannot endure; in this I am like my mother.'[35] She craved all the more for his reassurance; to be taken into his confidence and given work of responsibility to do. Yet her very condition argued the more tellingly against his opening the files of Opposition secrets to her. She might decide to return to Russia at any time; driven back by her anxiety over her husband and daughter. And how was her stricken mind to withstand Stalin's relentless inquisitors? The files remained closed to her, and she believed herself to be neither trusted nor loved. 'To Papa,' she repeatedly complained, 'I am a good-for-nothing.'

Trotsky was unable to cope. Reason was the light by which he lived. He felt helpless and lost among the shadows of her mind. And he felt, too, their rebuke. In all her resemblances to him, she seemed like some living copy appallingly flawed. And he could not escape the thought that the flaw had been of his making, in his early abandonment and subsequent neglect of her. He pressed her to go to Berlin, for psychoanalytical treatment. She refused. She would have to leave her son Seva behind, for it would be difficult to care for him there on her own. And she would be separated again from a father she had made such sacrifices to join. Besides, she did not want to submerge herself in what she called the 'filth' of her subconscious. But she had begun to have fits of delirium. And, at last persuaded, she left for Berlin in the autumn of 1931. In her last talk with her father, she reported to Lyova, he had said to her, in a severe voice: 'You are an astonishing person, I have never met anyone like you.'

Her doctors seemed to think that she was responding to their treatment. Her own comment was that they only confused her; 'but I have confused them, poor creatures, much more. . . .' She brooded over her parting from her father and looked forward to his letters. But however expressive of his concern for her, they did not satisfy her need of his love. She avoided Lyova, whose work for her father made her jealous and despise herself as 'Zina the idler'. Her loneliness and self-reproach promoted a deterioration which she could not disguise from her doctors. They advised that she return to her family in Russia. It was too late. In February 1932, Stalin struck with a decree that deprived of Soviet nationality not only Trotsky himself but such of his relatives as shared his exile; and prohibited them from ever returning. The doctors suggested that Seva be sent to Berlin, so that his mother might occupy her mind with him. But Seva, too, was now stateless. He could get to Berlin, his grandparents were informed, only if they or his mother took him there.

Lyova began having trouble with the police. He urged Zina to leave and continue her treatment in Vienna. She refused, and wrote to complain that Lyova was bullying her. Trotsky, too, urged her to leave. But she would not listen. She had her father's own word for it that the fate of mankind for many years to come was being decided in Germany. He expected Lyova to stay. Again she felt belittled and rejected. She blamed herself for being a financial burden on her father and moved to a cheap boarding house, where the rowdy residents were often in fights that she could stop only by flinging herself in between. She resented all attempts to get her away and demanded to be left in peace.

Trotsky would praise Lyova, on whom he had come so much to depend, and then storm at him, for incompetence, or for showing too little patience and affection in dealing with Zina. But this was the raging of his own remorse, at the plight of his daughter and at the insistent, excessive demands that he continued to make on his son. And it was the raging, too, of his frustration. He, who had been for so long at the centre of events and thought how he might affect them by being at their centre again, was now forced to stand so far away and watch them, with only the feel of the field-glasses in his hands. Natalia understood and tried to explain: entreating Lyova and Zina to believe in the deep love he bore them. 'The trouble with father, as you know, is never over the great issues, but over the tiny ones.' And in truth, the same man who confronted, without flinching, the hostility of a world, would fret at the lateness of a letter. Sometimes even Natalia allowed her shoulders to slump. 'What is to be done – nothing can be done,' she wrote to her son.

Then suddenly the shutters opened, a little way, for a little while. Trotsky was invited by Danish Social Democratic students to deliver a lecture in Copenhagen. And much to his surprise, the Danish government agreed to provide visas for Natalia and himself. They had hoped to take Seva along, and to send him on from Copenhagen to Berlin. But the necessary papers for this were refused, and he had to be left behind, in the care of a secretary. At last, on 14 November, Trotsky, together with Natalia and three of his assistants, took ship from Constantinople. He was travelling under the name of Sedov, but this did not deceive the press. Once apprised of his trip, various newspapers proceeded to disclose confidently, if inconsistently, the concealed purpose.

At Athens, he was greeted with quayside cheers, but his welcome stopped there. The authorities refused him permission to visit the city. At Naples he was allowed to disembark, for a visit to the ruins of Pompeii, but only under police escort throughout. At Marseilles, a motor launch removed him and his party from the ship, to decant them a little way further down the coast. And from there, they were rushed, by car and train, to the docks at Dunkirk. The Danish authorities took similar precautions and made them disembark at Esbjerg, to enter Copenhagen from behind. This did not prevent groups of Stalinists from gathering at stations along the route. But, as Natalia would recall, 'they only managed a few shouts and cat-calls'.

Trotsky's lecture, given in German to some 2500 gathered at the Copenhagen Stadium, was a restatement of faith in the October revolution and a memorable exercise in impassioned restraint; for the authorities had insisted that he avoid controversy. The organizers had sought to have it broadcast over the radio, but pressure from the Danish court had made this impossible. The royal family was sufficiently distressed that Trotsky was in Denmark at all. The mother of Nicholas II had been a Danish princess. And meanwhile the Soviet embassy was expressing its government's displeasure at the hospitality being shown to its principal opponent.

Trotsky once again explored the possibility of some asylum away from the isolation of Prinkipo. In an interview with American journalists, he asked whether it was merely a dream that he should be permitted to work in one of the great American libraries for two or three months. And silence gave him his answer. He applied for a Swedish visa. But he was told that the Soviet ambassador in Stockholm had raised insurmountable objections. He must have smiled wryly at the news. The Soviet ambassador in Stockholm was Alexandra Kollontai, who had once led the Workers' Opposition. He appealed for an extension of his eight-day visa, so that he and Natalia might have medical treatment in Copenhagen. The Danish government refused. It would not even give Lyova a visa to visit his parents.

At least once a day, they spoke by telephone to Berlin. And much of the talk was about Zina, whose behaviour, Lyova reported, was increasingly deranged. She had begun to believe that Germany was rapidly moving towards a Communist revolution and had even made some contact with the party. Lyova feared that she would attract the attention of the police and pressed his parents to do what they could to get her away to Austria. But what could they do? Natalia appealed urgently to the French premier that her son be permitted to meet her in France on her return journey. Before she received a reply, the Danish government insisted that Trotsky's time was up and that he must leave immediately. No boat was available to take him and his companions that day. But the government was not to be denied. It arranged for them to be rushed about the country by car until they could embark.

Trotsky poured scorn on professing democracies so apparently fearful of a single unarmed man that they could not rid themselves of his presence fast enough. And, indeed, they seemed determined to behave with as little reason as dignity. At Antwerp, where the harbour was so thick with police that an insurrection of the very sea might have been expected, frontier guards boarded the ship and threatened Trotsky with arrest when he refused to answer their questions. He was not even disembarking in Belgium but continuing to a port in France. At the Gare du Nord in Paris, where the party arrived on 6 December, police again surrounded them. But here at least there was occasion for joy. Lyova was at the station.

They had been told that they would have to wait more than a week for a boat to Constantinople, and they had made delighted plans to stay outside of Marseilles. But the moment that they arrived there, police ordered Trotsky to board an Italian cargo boat leaving that night. When he found that there was no accommodation for passengers and that the boat was due to be at sea for fifteen days, he suspected a trap, disembarked, and physically resisted attempts by the police to put him on board again. Protests were dispatched to Paris, and an urgent telegram was sent to Rome for a transit visa. Mussolini's government agreed at once to provide a visa, and the French police sped the party to the first departing train. Trotsky and Natalia, having taken leave of Lyova across a police cordon, after so short and turbulent a time together with him, sat in their dark compartment and cried.

Less than a month after the return to Prinkipo, a cable came from Lyova in Berlin, to tell them that Zina had committed suicide. A week before, Seva had at last joined her. She could not cope with him. And the police had just ordered her to leave Germany. 'I feel the approach of my terrible disease,' she wrote. 'In this condition I do not trust myself, not even with the handling of my child.' She placed him with a German woman she knew, barricaded herself in her room, and turned on the gas.

Trotsky shut himself away for several days. He would see only Natalia. And when he emerged, his secretaries noticed how much greyer his hair had become. In an open letter to the Soviet leadership, he blamed the decree that had deprived her of her nationality and her right to return, for having broken her spirit. 'There was not even a shadow of any political sense in the persecution of my daughter – there was nothing in it but purposeless, naked vengeance.' Alexandra Lvovna Bronstein wrote from Leningrad, to blame Trotsky himself. His daughter had so adored him and so yearned for that warmth which he had withheld; had been so like him in needing scope for her political commitment, and had been denied. 'You, her father, you could have saved her.' But then, as though seeking to bandage the wound she had made, she added that Zina would have died of consumption all the same, had she remained in Russia. 'Our children were doomed,' she wailed. And she feared now for her grand-children. 'I do not believe in life any longer.'

It was a terrible cry that Trotsky, not even in the most secret place of his pain, would utter. For whatever else he kept there, locked away, so that only Natalia was with him when he stumbled down the steps and turned the key, it was not this last despair. He continued fervently to believe in life, and to fight back at those who would deny it. Meanwhile, there was something to celebrate in the midst of all this anguish. He had come increasingly to fear that the Nazis would seize Lyova and kill him. But Lyova, having gone into hiding, succeeded in slipping across the frontier, into France.

To rally the living, it was necessary first to recognize and to bury the dead. In the middle of March, Trotsky did so for the German Communist Party.

Just as a doctor does not leave a patient who still has a breath of life, we had for our task the reform of the party as long as there was the least hope. But it would be criminal to tie oneself to a corpse. The KDP today represents a corpse.[36]

This did not mean, however, that the Third International was yet to be abandoned. The German 'catastrophe itself could provoke a healthy reaction in some of the sections. We must be ready to help this process.'

By the middle of July, this hope, too, was buried. 'The Moscow leadership has not only proclaimed as infallible the policy which guaranteed victory to Hitler,' Trotsky wrote,

but has also prohibited all discussion of what has occurred. And this shameful interdiction was not violated nor overthrown. . . . An organization which was not roused by the thunder of fascism and which submits docilely to such outrageous acts of the bureaucracy demonstrates thereby that it is dead and that nothing can ever revive it. . . . In all our subsequent work it is necessary to take as our point of departure the historical collapse of the official Communist International.[37]

But Trotsky clung, for a few months more, to the party of the revolution. He insisted that the schism must stop at the borders of the Soviet Union. And then, in October, he tore down this last barrier, too. It was a recognition that all hope of reforming the Soviet regime from within was now gone, and that the Opposition had no recourse but to engage in revolutionary struggle against Stalin, with a party of its own.

For some time, his French admirers had been pressing their government to revoke the order of 1916, expelling Trotsky forever from France. And Trotsky himself, in his eagerness, gave assurances that he would, if granted asylum there, behave with the utmost discretion. At last, in early July 1933, he was granted a visa, on stringent conditions. He would have to live incognito, under the closest police surveillance; would be restricted to one of the southern departments; and was not to visit Paris. He did not hesitate. It was an acceptable price to pay for asylum in France, whose language and art were so dear to him, and where he would once again be close to momentous events.

Yet, in his diary, four days before his departure, his comments were already more suggestive of nostalgia than of exultation. He wrote of the 'peace and forgetfulness' that Prinkipo brought, and of the insistent sea, where he had so often fished with his tutor, the old man Charolambos.

This morning the fishing was poor. The season is over, the fish have gone to deep water. Toward the end of August they will return, but then Charolambos will be fishing without me. He is now downstairs nailing up cases of books, of the utility of which he is obviously not entirely convinced. Through the open window can be seen the small steamer which brings the functionaries from Stamboul to their summer homes. Empty shelves yawn in the library. Only in the upper corner over the arch of the window does the old life go on as usual. Swallows have built a nest there, and directly above the British 'blue books' have hatched a brood which has no interest in French visas. For better or worse, the chapter called 'Prinkipo' is ended.[38]

His health deteriorated, Natalia had long ago noticed, whenever he was deeply troubled. And on board the boat to France, he suffered so severe an attack of lumbago that he was confined to bed. The right-wing press in France was already protesting furiously at the decision to admit him, while the French Communist leadership accused the Daladier government of revealing, in its hospitality to Trotsky, its desire for war with the Soviet Union. Some way outside of Marseilles, the boat was stopped by French police, and Trotsky, in great pain, disembarked with Natalia into a tug, where Lyova and an old friend, Raymond Molinier, were waiting. At Marseilles, Trotsky's secretaries sent on his luggage to Paris and then followed it themselves. The manoeuvre was successful. Trotsky's enemies and the press came to believe that he had gone into hiding somewhere in Paris, and they would not discover his whereabouts for nearly six months.

From Cassis, where the tug brought them ashore, Trotsky and his companions made their way, slowly because of his pain, to Saint-Palais, north of Bordeaux. There, by the side of the Atlantic, Molinier had rented a villa, 'Les Embruns' ('Sea Spray'). Trotsky went to bed with a high fever and, within an hour of his arrival, was driven from his new home by a fire. The exceptionally hot summer seems to have started it, without any more sinister help. But it was an ominous beginning. And for the nine weeks or so of his stay at Saint-Palais, Trotsky spent most of the time in bed. He had difficulty in sleeping, suffered from repeated headaches, and could not shake off his fever. Visitors noticed how easily he tired and would stay on so as to have several short talks with him. To Natalia, away in Paris that September to consult doctors, he wrote that he felt very old among the young men who visited him, and that at night he awoke to call, 'like an abandoned child', for her.

At the beginning of October, they went together to Bagnères de Bigorre in the Pyrenees, for a few weeks of rest. And the change seems to have done Trotsky good. He felt ready to take up his work again and wrote to his British publisher, Victor Gollancz, that he would apply himself to his promised book on the life of Lenin. The Sûreté, now satisfied of his discretion, raised no objections to his resettlement closer to Paris, provided that he continued to live incognito. He shaved off his grey goatee 'so as to look', Natalia would recall, 'like a middle-class French intellectual'. And on 1 November, he moved to a house just outside of Barbizon. Sentries and guard-dogs protected his privacy, and he was soon back at his industrious routine: rising at six in the morning and starting work while the household slept around him; stopping only for breakfast, lunch and an hour's rest, a brief afternoon tea, and supper; then presiding over discussions in the evening.

He had much, apart from his book on Lenin, to occupy his mind. In January 1934, the financial manipulator Stavisky, finding that his influential friends were no longer able to protect him from the consequences of his frauds, committed suicide. The far right claimed that he had been murdered to prevent him from revealing the rampant corruption in the government of the Third Republic. And on 6 February, demonstrators converged on the Chamber of Deputies, in what looked like an attempt to overthrow the parliamentary regime. If such had, indeed, been its purpose, the attack was a signal failure. Armed police dispersed the demonstrators with gun-fire, and a general strike, in response to the challenge of Fascism, united the mass of French workers for the first time in years. At last, if rather late, Stalinism was awake to the mistakes it had made in Germany, and the lurch to the politics of the Popular Front had begun.

Trotsky had not been slow to recognize the failure of his own attempt to lay the foundations of a Fourth International with the scant and incohesive material of his immediate following. A mass movement against Fascism was clearly developing; and by joining it, his followers could provide the yeast for a revolutionary resurgence. They would not, of course, be permitted to enter the movement through the Communist turnstile, except by paying the admission fee of an abject surrender to Stalinism. And so Trotsky advised them to join the SFIO, the Social Democratic party to which the majority of French workers still adhered. There they might use the loose structure of the party, with its competing factions, to press their own ideas and 'carry their revolutionary programme to the masses'.

But this was a suspension bridge that ended in the air. The leadership of the SFIO was willing enough to accommodate Trotskyists in the party, while they used the platform of reformist Social Democracy to inveigh against Stalinism. In this way, it might continue its ideological struggle against the Communists, while blaming on the intruders all infractions of solidarity in the developing popular front. But when the Trotskyists began inveighing against reformist Social Democracy too, the leadership quickly lost patience and expelled them from the party. Meanwhile, Stalinist propaganda had pounced on Trotskyist adherence to the SFIO as revealing the lengths to which the arch-renegade would go, in betraying the sacred cause of the revolution. And what was the end of one length but the beginning of another? A Trotsky who could be made to seem an agent of Social Democracy would in due course be translated by the Kremlin into an agent of Adolf Hitler and the Mikado.

In April 1934, the sanctuary at Barbizon was suddenly invaded. Rudolf Klement, Trotsky's German assistant, was travelling along the Paris road one evening when the headlight on his motor-bike failed, and he was stopped by a policeman. When he refused to give his address, he was taken to a local police station, and there, under vigorous questioning, revealed his connection with Trotsky. The police, who had been kept in ignorance of Trotsky's whereabouts by the authorities in Paris, were elated at their discovery. And they hastened to seek public congratulation for it. The *procureur* of the district, with attendant examining magistrate and a small army of detectives and police, came to interrogate Trotsky, while a crowd collected at the gates, and the two guard-dogs of the household barked an incessant protest. From the newspapers of the extreme right and of the Communist Party broke a fresh storm of invective against the government, for harbouring an enemy of France.

Ordered by the police to leave Barbizon, Trotsky went to stay with Lyova in Paris. Then, leaving Natalia behind, he set off with friends to find some place to settle. Moving from hotel to hotel, southwards and into the mountains, he at last reached Chamonix, where Natalia joined him. But the local press got wind of his presence and published the description and even the registration number of the 'small, rather antique' car that he was using. The car was hurriedly exchanged for another, and Trotsky went to ground with Natalia in a suburban *pension*. To avoid provoking suspicion at the dining table, Trotsky proposed that they take all meals in their rooms and wear mourning clothes as their excuse. Natalia at first refused to engage in such a pretence but eventually submitted to the logic of necessity. Their young French colleague was introduced as their nephew, and he was assigned to the observation post of the common table.

Trotsky noticed with some surprise the engravings that hung in the hall, prominent amongst which was one on 'The Parting of Marie-Antoinette with Her Children'. The explanation was provided by the 'nephew' after his first session in the dining-room. The *pension* was a nest of squawking royalists. But attention was soon enough diverted from the mysterious couple in mourning by the arrival of an agent from the Sûreté as another paying guest, whose professional loyalty to the republic involved him in meal-time differences of opinion. The ensuing conversations, recited by the 'nephew', provided Trotsky and Natalia with much merriment; though precluding any audible laughter which might cast doubt on the depth of their bereavement.

At last they found a suitable small house to rent, in a village some twenty miles away. The prefect of the department objected that they had chosen a 'hotbed of clericalism', whose mayor was a personal enemy of his. Tired of moving and drained of funds, they refused to leave. But the prefect was not to be denied. The local weekly published news of Trotsky's latest refuge, and he was forced to move on once again. At last, early in July, he and Natalia found a home with a teacher at a primary school, in a village some twenty miles from Grenoble. And there, for ten months, in two rooms given over to them, they lived in secrecy.

At the beginning of December 1934, Sergei Kirov, a member of the Politburo, secretary of the central committee and head of the Leningrad party organization, was assassinated outside his office in the Smolny. He was a brilliant orator: the greatest, it was whispered, that Russia had produced since Trotsky. And his popularity, as an exponent of reform, was breaking the bounds of prudence. At the party congress in February, his address had been greeted with such acclaim that there was talk in the corridors of its having exceeded the usual tribute to Stalin. There were signs of Stalin's displeasure. And Kirov was not invited to certain meetings of the Politburo.

Indeed, evidence has subsequently accumulated to suggest that Stalin himself had arranged for the success of the assassination attempt.[39] But whatever the actual extent of his responsibility, he certainly seized the occasion for a campaign of terror that was eventually to claim millions of victims.

From the start, guilt by the most remote association became a principle of action. The assassin had belonged to a Young Communist Club in Leningrad, disbanded a decade or so before. A woman who had worked as a librarian at the club was arrested, along with her sister, her sister's husband, the secretary of her party cell, and anyone who had ever recommended her for a job. It was only the beginning. From Leningrad alone, more than 50,000 people were dispatched to the prison camps of the Baltic, the Volga or Siberia. For weeks, the railway stations were crammed with these human consignments.[40]

In the middle of December, Kamenev and Zinoviev were arrested; and one month later, put on trial with seventeen other accused. They were reported as admitting to at least moral responsibility for the assassination, and were, for the while, treated with relative indulgence. Zinoviev was sentenced to ten years' imprisonment, and Kamenev to five.

Trotsky, listening to the radio transmissions from Moscow, and convinced that the assassination was intended to provide a pretext for terror, feared for members of his family in Russia, and with reason. His two sons-in-law had their terms of internment extended without the bother of a trial. Alexandra Lvovna Bronstein, now in her sixties, was deported to Siberia: leaving the care of her own and Trotsky's three grandchildren to her sister. A letter from Sergei, Trotsky's younger son, written to Natalia on 12 December, ended with the ominous sentence: 'My general situation is very grave, graver than one could imagine.' It was the last letter that his parents were to receive from him.

To the diary which he kept for seven months, from 7 February 1935, Trotsky confided the dreariness as well as the agony of those days. From the grating of his refuge, he stares at the pinched preoccupations of French provincial life. 'There is no creature more disgusting than a petty bourgeois engaged in primary accumulation,' he sighs to himself. 'I have never had the opportunity to observe this type as closely as I do now.'[41] Indeed, he feels the confinement of his surroundings like a cell. 'We are shut up in our house and yard and meet people no more often than we would at visiting hours in a prison. . . .'[42] And faced by the blank walls of his cell, he paces the passages of his memory.

Again and again, in the pages of the diary, he recalls the various warnings given him of Stalin's slow and watchful malice. And as though turning a corner in his mind, he comes upon the shape of that Stalin whose shadow he has so long misjudged.

His craving for revenge on me is completely unsatisfied: there have been, so to speak, physical blows, but morally nothing has been achieved. There is no refusal to work, no 'repentance', no isolation; on the contrary, a new historical momentum has been acquired which it is already impossible to halt. This is the source of gravest apprehensions for Stalin: that savage fears ideas, since he knows their explosive power and knows his own weakness in the face of them. At the same time he is clever enough to realize that even today I would not change places with him: hence the psychology of a man stung. But if revenge on a higher plane has not succeeded – and clearly it will not succeed – it is still possible to reward oneself with police blows against people close to me. . . .[43]

The thought of his son's imperilled innocence nudges the memory of the Tsar's children, summarily shot along with their parents. On two successive days, he deals with the subject: recalling his proposal for a public trial of the Tsar; his absence at the front when the Politburo ordered the executions; and his subsequent 'touch of surprise' on learning the fate of the family. But he proceeds to protest the necessity of those killings. And then, as though uneasy at reasons that might be crouching in Stalin's mind also, he seeks some comfort in the final difference between the children of a Tsar and his own son. 'The Tsar's family fell victim to that principle which constitutes the axis of monarchy: dynastic succession.'[44]

It is not only for his son that he suffers, but for Natalia too, 'who feels all this immeasurably more deeply than I do'.[45] He cannot protect her; and she, as always, does what she can to protect him. He is frequently ill; running a fever and sometimes with an 'extraordinary humming' in his ears. He cannot work, and wonders whether sickness or Stalin will soon put an end to him. On 8 May, at the start of a new notebook, he reports that there is no news yet from his son, and then comments: 'Old age is the most unexpected of all things that happen to a man.'[46] Eight days later, Natalia, too, is ailing, and he writes:

Every time N. is ill, I feel anew the place she fills in my life. She bears all suffering, physical as well as moral, silently, quietly inside herself. Right now she is more upset about my health than her own. 'If only you would get well,' she said to me today, lying in bed, 'that's the only thing I want.' She rarely says such things. And she said this so simply, evenly, and quietly, and at the same time from such a depth, that my whole soul was stirred. . . .[47]

Before the end of the month, they learn that Sergei was arrested at the turn of the year and is still in prison. 'Poor boy. . . . And my poor, poor Natasha . . . ,' Trotsky writes.[48]

On 8 June, he mentions having reminded Natalia of Arvakum: the seventeenth-century archpriest who attacked the prevailing corruption in the church and defended the peasantry: to suffer imprisonment, torture, exile, and eventually burning at the stake. From a cheap edition of the priest's autobiography, Trotsky has cut a passage and pasted it into the diary; it follows a reference to how the priest went to help his wife, as they stumbled through the snow of his Siberian banishment, and she, in her exhaustion, kept falling behind. 'And I came up, and she, poor soul, began to reproach me, saying: "How long, archpriest, is this suffering to be?" And I said, "Markovna, unto our very death." And she, with a sigh, answered: "So be it, Petrovich, let us be getting on our way." ' Trotsky has heavily underlined the passage from the words, 'How long', in pencil. And then he has added: 'I can say one thing; never did Natasha "reproach" me, never – even in the most difficult hours; nor does she reproach me now, in the most sorrowful days of our life, when everything has conspired against us. . . .'[49]

In March 1935, the Labour Party came to power in Norway: a party that had once adhered to the Communist or Third International, then broken away from it, but never to join the Second International instead. Trotsky, all too aware that the hospitality of the French government was growing cold, applied for Norwegian asylum. Influential friends in Oslo supported the request. But the decision on so momentous a matter was not to be hurried. It was 8 June when Trotsky heard at last that he was to be granted a visa. Frantically the household packed and left for Paris, to find that the visa had not been issued. The Norwegian government was apparently disturbed at the implications of its own generosity. And the French security authorities, maintaining that Trotsky had manufactured the whole affair as a pretext for visiting Paris, ordered him to leave the country within forty-eight hours. Urgent appeals to Oslo at last extracted the visa, but with permission to reside for only six months. Trotsky and Natalia left at once for Antwerp, where the Belgian government refused them the grace of even a single day to do the rounds of the main museums, and boarded the boat for Oslo.

Their arrival was greeted by Norwegian Fascists with the protest: 'What does the leader of the world revolution want in Oslo?' And the local Stalinists furiously denounced a grant of asylum to the leader of the world counter-revolution. But the Labour Party newspaper, *Arbeiderbladet*, expressed the delight of all 'right-thinking and unprejudiced people' at the government's decision and declared that Norwegians felt honoured at the presence of Trotsky in their country. The government was less sensible of the delight or more suspicious of the honour. It did not lift the time limit on Trotsky's stay; extracted a pledge from him that he would refrain from any involvement in Norway's domestic affairs; and reserved the right to fix his place of residence at a reassuring distance from the capital. Konrad Knudsen, a socialist editor, was officially approached to assist in settling Trotsky and, encountering much difficulty in finding a suitable house, invited him to share his own, at Vexhall, a village near Honnefoss, some thirty miles to the north of Oslo.

Natalia at once set to work, making a new home for them. 'How many times she has done this!' Trotsky recorded in his diary.

There are no wardrobes here, and many other things are lacking. She is hammering nails in by herself, stringing cords, hanging things up and changing them around; the cords break; she sighs to herself and begins all over again.... I easily 'let down' under difficult conditions; that is, become reconciled to the dirt and disorder around me, but N. – *never*. She raises every environment to a certain level of cleanliness and orderliness, and does not allow it to fall below that level. But how much energy, inventiveness, and vital forces it requires![50]

And his own vital forces were much depleted. When he felt well, he would get up shortly after five o'clock in the morning; moving very quietly so as not to disturb anyone; take a little food from the pantry, and begin work. But he was now so often ill. And the book that he had begun on the development of Soviet society, *The Revolution Betrayed*, was interrupted time and again, as he found himself incapable of any exertion.

On 19 September he entered the Oslo Municipal Hospital for examination and treatment. He remembered how he had, almost twenty years before, found himself lying on a bunk in the cell of a prison in Madrid and had wondered at the turn of events that had brought him there. He had burst into laughter then. And now he wondered again, at what had brought him to a bed in an Oslo hospital. But there was no laughter this time. After a series of exhaustive tests, he left, with the source of his persistent illness undiscovered, and his financial resources reduced to a hundred crowns, so that he was driven to asking for help from some of his friends. Back at home, he mended only slowly, with relapses that kept him in bed much of the time: raging at his helplessness and at the quarrels by which his followers in various countries, particularly France, seemed determined to demonstrate their vigour. Standing one day with Natalia in the snow, he turned to her and said: 'I am tired of it all – all of it – do you understand?'[51]

Then, just before Christmas, he went with Knudsen and a group of young Norwegians on a trip to the north of Honnefoss. He was nowhere near their equal on skis and on one occasion needed rescuing. But the break apparently did him good. For, soon after his return, he felt well enough to continue with his book. And for the next six months, he worked at it steadily, till he had completed it.

The Revolution Betrayed is both Trotsky's defence of the revolution and a reaffirmation of its necessity for backward countries.

Having themselves arrived in a blind alley, the highly civilized nations block the road to those in process of civilization. Russia took the road of proletarian revolution, not because her economy was the first to become ripe for socialist change, but because she could not develop further on a capitalist basis. Socialization of the means of production had become a necessary condition for bringing the country out of barbarism.[52]

The record of the Soviet regime, for all the distortions of Stalinism, had demonstrated a capacity for economic growth which only the conquests of the revolution had made possible. But this accelerated pace of development only emphasized the gap that stretched between the advanced capitalist states and Soviet society: a gap that, even in the unlikely event of a continuing capitalist stagnation, it would take 'a whole historic period' to close.[53] For it was a gap not only in the quantity of output per worker, but in the quality as well: and 'to characterize industrial progress by quantitative indices alone, without considering quality, is almost like describing a man's physique by his height and disregarding his chest measurements'.[54]

Yet the Soviet regime, while admitting that it was still far from the attainment of communism, had taken to claiming the attainment of socialism, or the lowest stage of communism, at least. And it based this claim on the dominance of state trusts in industry; of the collective farms in agriculture; of state and co-operative enterprises in commerce. Socialism, however, was something more than the socialization of productive property. It was, for Marx himself, who had expected it to arrive first in the countries of advanced industrialization, a higher stage of development than capitalism had ever achieved. And since, far from having reached such a stage, the Soviet Union was still in the process of 'importing, borrowing and appropriating the technical and cultural conquests' of the capitalist countries, its regime had accordingly to be considered not as socialist, but rather as 'a *preparatory* regime, *transitional* from capitalism to socialism'.[55]

Nor was socialism merely a stage of more advanced productive means. The very attainment of such means would provide adequate resources to reduce those material inequalities by which wealth had otherwise to be wrested; and, correspondingly, those two forces, money and the state, by which material inequalities were secured. 'In a communist society, the state and money will disappear. Their gradual dying away ought consequently to begin under socialism.'[56] But in the Soviet Union, the state was not dying away, or even beginning to do so. On the contrary: it had grown into an unprecedented apparatus of compulsion. And attempts by the Soviet regime, in its transitional stage, to do without the traditional disciplines of money, had only produced a massive inflation, that had entailed 'a substitution of fictitious for real magnitudes', and that had corroded the planned economy from within.[57] The disciplines of money had had to be restored.

Trotsky was concerned to establish the historical character of Soviet society not only to explode the socialist pretensions of Stalinism. By determining what the regime could not be, he was the more convincingly able to demonstrate what it was. And what it was, in contrast to what it had once promised to be, was not merely a transitional regime, but one which, within this transition, had become a retreat rather than any advance; a betrayal rather than a reinforcement of the revolution.

Then, facing the challenge of how and of why this should have occurred, Trotsky maintained that a reaction had been inevitable in the circumstances of the time. There had been no subsequent revolutions in the West to provide help, but rather military intervention from alarmed regimes. Instead of the prosperity that the revolution had been expected to bring, there had been a protracted and ominous destitution. The outstanding representatives of the working class had either died in battle or, in mounting to power, broken from the masses. Exhaustion and disillusionment had made room for the mean-spirited and the careerist.

Yet reaction could not have conquered without conquering the Bolshevik Party. And here Trotsky placed the start of the degenerative process in the days of Lenin's leadership and his own. The dedication to Soviet democracy had, under the pressures of civil war, given way to the banning of one opposition party after the other. And this had been followed by a ban on factions within the party, to secure for the leadership the same dominion that the party enjoyed in the state. Each had been regarded as an exceptional measure, to be abandoned as soon as circumstances allowed. Each was a step in the descent to Stalinism.

The prohibition of oppositional parties brought after it the prohibition of factions. The prohibition of factions ended in a prohibition to think otherwise than the infallible leaders. The police-manufactured monolithism of the party resulted in a bureaucratic impunity which has become the source of all kinds of wantonness and corruption.[58]

All this remained a matter of 'how' rather than 'why'. And the answer to 'why' was one which raised the essential issue of the conflict between original Marxism and the very phenomenon of proletarian revolution in Russia before anywhere else. Forced to climb out of the depths of poverty without help from a revolutionary West, the Soviet regime had come increasingly to rely on that dynamic of material inequality by which bourgeois society had achieved its superior productive means. To reach the productive level of bourgeois society, in short, Soviet society had proceeded to assume bourgeois features itself. And to protect these features, without abandoning the very basis of a workers' state and returning to bourgeois property relations, the dominion of the bureaucracy had developed. It was the bureaucracy that decided how the inadequate supply of goods was to be distributed and that kept order in the shuffling lines of hopeful purchasers. It was the bureaucracy that gave privileges to a relative few, so as to make of inequality a whip for the encouragement of the many.

But in handing out privileges, the bureaucracy had not neglected its own claims. 'Nobody who has wealth to distribute ever omits himself.' The distributors had taken the cream; and with their appetite growing as it fed, they had become a factor independent of the social function they had risen to serve. The more that, in the process, the bureaucracy moved away from the social and moral disposition of the masses, the less it was prepared to 'permit any control over either its activities or its income'.[59]

No wonder the study of Marxism in the Soviet Union had become a peddling of old ideas, or at least such of them as enjoyed endorsement in advance; while literature itself had been confined in a kind of artistic concentration camp.

Gifted writers who cannot do sufficient violence to themselves are pursued by a pack of instructors armed with shamelessness and dozens of quotations. The most eminent artists either commit suicide, or find their material in the remote past, or become silent. Honest and talented books appear as though accidentally, bursting out from somewhere under the counter, and have the character of artistic contraband.[60]

Predictably, since foreign policy reflects the domestic preoccupations of a regime, the Soviet bureaucracy had effectively turned its back upon the original and essential Soviet commitment to international revolution. It had made of the Communist International itself, by a series of purges, a subservient apparatus, in pursuit of the *status quo*, through a non-aggression pact with capitalism. But war could not be avoided by wishing it away. And how could the Soviet Union hope to escape defeat in the coming great war? 'A defeat of Germany in a war against the Soviet Union would inevitably result in the crushing, not only of Hitler, but of the capitalist system.'[61] And that was an eventuality to which the capitalist regimes were not blind. To be sure, theirs was a system torn by contradictions. Were it not, indeed, for just such contradictions, the Soviet Union would long since have vanished from the scene. But before the immediate threat of proletarian revolution, these contradictions were bound to subside. 'If it is not paralysed by revolution in the West, imperialism will sweep away the regime which issued from the October revolution.'[62]

Yet if the danger of war and the defeat of the Soviet Union was a reality, the revolution was a reality also. 'If the revolution does not prevent war, then war will help the revolution. Second births are commonly easier than the first.'[63] And this time the revolution would not stop half-way. 'The toilers have not the slightest interest in defending existing boundaries, especially in Europe – either under the command of their bourgeoisies, or, still less, in a revolutionary insurrection against them.'[64]

War and the revolution it must bring were not, however, the only source of change within the Soviet Union. The bureaucracy was, in its promotion of its own privileges, promoting the challenge to its survival.

If a ship is declared collective property, but the passengers continue to be divided into first, second and third class, it is clear that, for the third-class passengers, differences in the conditions of life will have infinitely more importance than that juridical change in proprietorship. The first-class passengers, on the other hand, will propound, together with their coffee and cigars, the thought that collective ownership is everything and a comfortable cabin nothing at all. Antagonisms growing out of this may well explode the unstable collective.[65]

There were two main hypotheses for the future of the Soviet Union. The first was that the Soviet bureaucracy would be overthrown by a revolutionary party, with all the attributes of the old Bolshevism enriched by recent experiences. 'Such a party would begin with the restoration of democracy in the trade unions and the Soviets. It would be able to, and would have to, restore freedom of Soviet parties.' It would conduct a ruthless purge of the state apparatus. It would abolish ranks and decorations, all kinds of privilege, and would limit inequality in the payment of labour to the minimum demanded by the sustenance of the economy. It would provide the youth with 'free opportunity to think independently, learn, criticize, and grow'. But it would not need to alter the basis of property relations. Its political revolution, accordingly, would require reforms, but not another social revolution.

In the second hypothesis, a bourgeois party would overthrow the bureaucracy. It would have to conduct some purge of the state apparatus, but probably less of a one than a revolutionary party would need. It would, however, step by step, restore private property in the means of production, and thus essentially undertake a social revolution. There remained a third hypothesis: that neither a revolutionary nor a counter-revolutionary party seized power, and the bureaucracy continued to command the state. But then the bureaucracy itself would inevitably set out to restore bourgeois property relations.

Privileges have only half their worth, if they cannot be transmitted to one's children. But the right of testament is inseparable from the right of property. It is not enough to be the director of a trust; it is necessary to be a stockholder. Were the bureaucracy to succeed in this, it would become a new possessing class, and the second hypothesis would effectively apply. Were it to fail, the responsible success of the proletariat would secure a revival of the socialist revolution and the first hypothesis. The third way, therefore, merely divides into the other two.[66]

It is not difficult to find passages in *The Revolution Betrayed* at which time has pointed a disparaging finger. The great war was to break out soon enough, but only after the Soviet Union had concluded a non-aggression pact with Germany. And when, in due course, Germany attacked the Soviet Union, the alliance of Germany's enemies persisted until Germany's defeat. The crushing of Hitler did not lead to the crushing of the capitalist system, and it was with the help of the Red Army rather than of revolutionary insurrection that the Soviet Union spread its power across eastern Europe, to encompass half of Germany itself. Least of all did the war provoke within the West a proletarian resistance to the defence of existing boundaries; and when, subsequently, some established nationalisms sought association in the European Economic Community, it was their bourgeoisies rather than the toilers that took the lead.

Within the Soviet Union itself, neither a revolutionary nor a bourgeois party overthrew the regime. And on Trotsky's third hypothesis, the bureaucracy did not set out to restore bourgeois property relations. Privilege proved, in general, easy enough to transmit from parent to child, without testamentary dispositions. The advantages of background; the appropriation of places at suitable schools and universities; the effect of sponsorship in the pursuit of political or military office: all went a considerable way towards counteracting the handicaps of natural selection. A stagnant economy would, of course, have made this procreation of privilege more difficult. But the rapid development of the economy, after the ravages of the war, sustained a sufficient increase in the bureaucracy to accommodate within its ranks recruits from the population at large as well as from the progeny of the bureaucrats. And with economic development, there came, too, a popular material advance which reduced the provocations of privilege. Indeed, if privilege itself descried new heights of consumption to scale, the actual extent of material inequality diminished.

How far Trotsky was correct in defining the Stalinist era as a bureaucratic one is elsewhere considered (see pp. 383–6). It is less doubtful a definition of the party regime before and afterwards. And to this extent the intervention of Stalin's personal and paranoiac absolutism distorted the calendar. By contrast with his rule, the years following his death, and especially the revelations of the twentieth congress, constituted a period of relative, if still closely restricted, release. And this makes the succeeding bureaucracy scarcely more than a generation old. In short, for many Soviet citizens, this is still an era of reform. And it is only when reform will have become, for the vast majority, a stable repression, that the instabilities, in which Trotsky placed his hope, may finally emerge.

But in any event, most of Trotsky's analysis is as relevant today as it was when it was written. The Soviet Union has, indeed, grown so greatly in material power that it is overshadowed only by the United States. Yet in productivity it lags far behind the developed capitalist countries: so that even in factories purchased whole from the West, it takes up to eight times the labour force to reach the same output. The Soviet worker may not have turned in revolt to a revolutionary party with all the attributes of the old Bolshevism. But he reveals in alcoholism, absenteeism, and frequent shifts of job a widespread discontent with the command of the economy. The result is that the lines outside the store are still long, and it is the bureaucracy that decides who is to be served and who is to be kept waiting or supplied only with the most shoddy of merchandise. At the head of the line are the military, whose demand for ever more advanced and expensive equipment has to be met first. At the back is that multitude for whom Trotsky's 'unique law of Soviet industry' continues to apply:

'commodities are as a general rule worse the nearer they stand to the mass consumer'.[67]

Securing order in the line remains the ultimate function of the bureaucracy. And the compulsions of the state, by which this function is performed, are no less finally formidable for the retreat from arbitrary violence that has followed the burial of Stalin. Indeed, such compulsions have enabled the Soviet regime to contain the process of inflation far more successfully than its capitalist counterparts have done; so that it has, paradoxically, sustained more successfully, too, the essentially bourgeois meaning and mystique of money. In sum, therefore, however the Soviet regime may be defined, it is no more socialist today than it was when Trotsky denied it the description. And the arguments by which he then denied it are as vital as ever, in rescuing socialism, its nature and values, from the disrepute of those regimes which have usurped its name.

Certainly, there is a new devotion to the indispensable virtue of Soviet democracy in *The Revolution Betrayed*, and a resonance of regret in Trotsky's retreading of the steps by which he and his colleagues had initiated the descent into Stalinism. He had never imagined where those first steps would lead. He could never have imagined what was now to emerge from the depths.

On 15 August 1936, Moscow announced to the world that Kamenev, Zinoviev and fourteen other accused were to stand immediate trial for treason and terrorism; that Trotsky, with his son Leon Sedov as his chief assistant, were at the centre of the conspiracy; and that the Gestapo, with which one of the accused had confessed to having had direct contact, was involved. Trotsky at once publicly refuted the charges, as 'the greatest forgery in the world's political history'. The accusation that he had fomented terrorism from his refuge in Norway was, he declared, designed to rob him of this refuge and of any opportunity to defend himself. He proposed that the Norwegian government investigate the charges itself, and he appealed for an impartial and international commission of inquiry.

If Stalin read reports of Trotsky's denunciation, he was scarcely disturbed. He had ordered the secret police to obtain confessions, and the secret police had done so. Where torture had been ineffective, threats to their families had swayed the accused. In the end, all sixteen had accepted Stalin's terms, which had guaranteed them their lives and the liberty of their families in return.[68]

On 19 August, the trial opened in the small October Hall of the Trade Union House, before an audience of some 150 selected Soviet citizens, mainly members of the secret police, and some thirty foreign journalists and diplomats. The accused, looking tired and worn, waived their right to defending counsel and, with only two exceptions, proceeded to plead guilty on all counts. Smirnov, who had been so close a colleague of Trotsky's, now confessed to having received terrorist instructions from him; Holtzman, a former follower, that he had conveyed such instructions. But both denied having themselves participated in the preparation or execution of terrorist acts. The rest seemed only in haste to accomplish their self-abasement. They arraigned themselves, one another, and some who had escaped the indictment. Tomsky, one of those cited in the course of the trial as involved in the conspiracy, committed suicide on learning from Vyshinsky, the prosecutor, that all charges by the accused were to be investigated.

Zinoviev confessed to having been second only to Trotsky in the bloc that had secured the assassination of Kirov and had planned to assassinate Stalin himself. 'My defective Bolshevism became transformed into anti-Bolshevism and through Trotskyism I arrived at fascism. Trotskyism is a variety of fascism, and Zinovievism is a variety of Trotskyism.' Kamenev agreed that his various expressions of loyalty to the party had been deceit and treason. 'We have served fascism, we have organized counter-revolution against socialism. Such has been the path we took, and such is the pit of contemptible treachery into which we have fallen.'

From the moment that the indictment had been published, there had been calls in the Soviet press for a sentence of death on the traitors. And in the middle of the trial, *Pravda* published three grotesque statements from former eminent members of the Trotskyist Opposition. Piatakov demanded that the accused should be destroyed like carrion. 'Many of us, including myself, by our heedlessness, our complacency and lack of vigilance, towards those around us, unconsciously helped these bandits to commit their black deeds.' Rykov inveighed in similar vein. And Rakovsky, even Rakovsky, who had shown so much courage for so long, now proclaimed: 'No pity for the Trotskyist Gestapo agents!' On 24 August, the accused were all found guilty on all counts and sentenced to death. If they petitioned, as the law allowed, for pardon, they were left with little time to wonder whether Stalin would now honour his guarantees. Only twenty-four hours after the court verdicts, it was officially announced that the sixteen had been executed. Zinoviev, rumour had it, screamed, when the guards came to fetch him, for Stalin to keep his word. Kamenev went without complaint. Smirnov commented: 'We deserve this for our unworthy attitude at the trial.'[69]

Many years later, the defection of Alexander Orlov, a senior officer in the secret police, would bring to the outside world the report of a grisly postscript. On 20 December 1936, Stalin presided over a small banquet for the heads of the secret police; and when everyone had drunk abundantly, one of the officers, supported by two others in the role of warders, played the part of Zinoviev being dragged to execution. Moaning and mouthing, the officer fell to his knees and, holding one of the supposed warders by the boots, cried: 'Please, for God's sake, Comrade, call up Yosif Vissarionovich.' Stalin roared with laughter, and the performance was repeated. Then the officer, improvising, raised his hands and cried: 'Hear, Israel, our God is the only God!' And Stalin, choking with laughter, signalled that he could take no more.[70]

When the record of the trial was published, a discrepancy emerged. Holtzman had claimed to have stayed at the Hotel Bristol in Copenhagen and there, in the lounge, to have received Trotsky's instructions from Leon Sedov in person. Danish Social Democrats quickly pointed out that the Hotel Bristol had been demolished in 1917. The Soviet secret police had apparently been careless in finding the name of a serviceable hotel. It was not the only discrepancy. Lyova was able to demonstrate that he had never been in Copenhagen with his father at the time of the alleged meeting. Zinoviev and Kamenev had been in prison or in exile for most of the period during which the plotting was supposed to have taken place. Smirnov had been in prison since the start of 1933. Nor was there any credible proportion between the proclaimed extent of the conspiracy, with its numerous intended victims, and the results allegedly achieved.

Yet it was not only those who were blinded by their allegiance to the homeland of socialism who accepted the justice of the verdicts. Others, uneasy at the methods by which the confessions might have been obtained, still assumed that the confessions were proof of a sufficient guilt. And many of those who had doubts suppressed them in pursuit of what they saw as the overriding objective. Hitler had just marched into the Rhineland, and the Popular Front had formed a government in France. This was no moment, surely, to disrupt, by antagonizing the Soviet government and its obedient Communist parties, the developing alliance in the struggle against Fascism.

With all his old energy flooding back into him, Trotsky set out to defend himself and his son, as well as those who had been driven to deny the whole meaning of their lives. To the press he gave interviews and statements, refuting the accusations and pointing to the weaknesses in the reported evidence. Then suddenly, on 26 August, he was presented with a demand from the Norwegian Minister of Justice: that he sign an undertaking to refrain from interfering, 'directly or indirectly, orally and in writing, in political questions current in other countries'. He refused. The two police officers who had brought the demand immediately placed him under house arrest and ordered him to make no further statements for publication. The Soviet ambassador had, it subsequently emerged, warned the Norwegian government that the continued grant of asylum to Trotsky would impair friendly relations with the Soviet Union and provoke economic reprisals.

The Norwegian government saw no way of deporting Trotsky, in the absence of some other asylum. To be sure, the Soviet Union might now be willing to have him back. But this was an alternative that not even the distressed ministers could bring themselves to consider. They were reduced, therefore, to imposing a form of moral internment which they hoped might sufficiently appease the Soviet government. On 28 August, Trotsky was taken before the Minister of Justice and presented with a pledge that he, his wife and his secretaries would not engage 'in any political activity directed against any state friendly to Norway', or involve themselves 'in political questions current either in Norway or abroad'. Even his 'writings of a theoretical nature' were not to be 'directed against any government of any foreign state'. He was to reside wherever the government chose to put him and 'further agree that all mail, telegrams, telephone calls, sent or received by myself, my wife, and my secretaries be censored'.

Trotsky dismissed the document with contempt. Had he ever been willing to accept such terms, he would not be in exile now. And he was not about to give the minister what Stalin had never been able to obtain. Had he ever interfered in Norwegian affairs? The minister said no. Did the Norwegian government believe that he was using its territory as a base for terrorist activities? The minister said no. The Norwegian government only maintained that in particular writings and in his contacts abroad, with the various formations of his followers, Trotsky had broken his original undertaking to refrain from all political activity. Trotsky replied that he had never given such an undertaking, and that no true socialist ever would. Then, seeing no purpose in further argument, he raised his voice in warning. 'You think yourselves secure and free to deal with a political exile as you please. But the day is near – remember this! – the day is near when the Nazis will drive you from your country, all of you. . . .' The minister, Trygve Lie, and his colleagues were, in 1940, to remember that warning as they prepared to seek refuge in England from the Nazi invasion.

Since Trotsky was not prepared to shackle himself, Trygve Lie proceeded to do the shackling for him. Trotsky's two secretaries were deported, and Trotsky was placed under guard within Knudsen's house, so that he could not even communicate with his host. Since such treatment, outside the due process of the courts, was in breach of the Norwegian constitution, Trygve Lie procured a Provisional Royal Decree to permit it. Then, at the beginning of September, Trotsky and Natalia were taken under escort and deposited in a house, at the edge of a fjord, some twenty miles south of Oslo. They had their quarters on the first floor; while on the floor below, a force of fifteen police maintained a bored and often noisy guard. They were forbidden to move beyond the grounds of the house; were required to submit all their correspondence to censorship; and were allowed visits only from Trotsky's Norwegian lawyer.

At first, Trotsky found a certain release in his isolation from news, letters and telephone calls. But soon, when the censor allowed him to receive Russian newspapers, the restrictions of his internment became a torture to him. His articles for the press and his letters to followers, he submitted, under protest, to the censor. Impatiently he waited for some sign that his words had made their way to the outside world. There was only silence. The censor confiscated everything that Trotsky wrote. Trygve Lie either did not care who was doing his work for him or had a curious sense of humour. The censor, as well as one of the two officers in charge of Trotsky's guard, belonged to Quisling's pro-Nazi party. And meanwhile, in the pages of *Bolshevik*, Vyshinsky proclaimed that Trotsky could have nothing to say in his own defence, or surely he would be saying it.

Wrenching at his gag, Trotsky instructed his lawyer to institute proceedings for defamation against the editors of two Norwegian newspapers, one of them pro-Nazi and one Stalinist, which were agreed at least in echoing the Soviet charges. But no sooner had the court summons been issued than Trygve Lie stopped the case. And since the constitution provided him with no powers to do so, he procured another Provisional Royal Decree, which declared that an interned alien could appear as plaintiff in a Norwegian court only with the Ministry of Justice's concurrence. Such concurrence, the Ministry of Justice announced, was, in this instance, withheld. Trotsky turned to the possibility of suing for defamation in other countries. But Trygve Lie was not to be bypassed. He announced that the Ministry of Justice would oppose any attempt by Trotsky to take legal action before a foreign tribunal, and he placed an immediate ban on all communication between Trotsky and lawyers abroad.

One small chance still hovered for Trotsky to make himself heard. Some followers of Quisling had raided Knudsen's house in early August and carried off a few of Trotsky's papers. They were being prosecuted, and Trotsky was called to give evidence at the trial. But once again Trygve Lie intervened. When Trotsky entered the witness box, the courtroom was cleared of all press reporters and members of the public. His long, precise and passionate refutation of all the Stalinist charges against him reached out only to the rows of empty seats.

The nightmare would have been complete, had it not been for Lyova, who published in Paris his own book on the trial, *Livre Rouge sur le procès de Moscou*. It exposed the fabricated facts and it demonstrated how the whole Soviet case rested not on any real evidence but on confessions that were self-denying in their very extravagance. When Trotsky received a copy and started to read it, he found the opening pages, with their familiar political formulations, disappointingly pallid. But its original analysis of the trial excited him. And joyfully he discussed with Natalia the achievement of their son.

But there came a warning from Paris as well. Concerned for the safety of his archives there, Trotsky had asked Lyova to place some of the papers with the local office of the Dutch Institute for Social History. And no more than a few days after this had been done, the office was burgled and some of Trotsky's papers were removed. Since cash, valuables, and various more precious historical documents were left behind, it seemed all too likely that agents of the Soviet secret police were responsible. Yet only two close associates of Lyova's, along with a single employee of the institute, had known of the transfer. Trotsky must have known, with new alarm, how vulnerable was his son and defender to the prowling and sudden pounce of Stalin's revenge.

It was to his own and Natalia's vulnerability, however, that his mind was soon directed. Mexican admirers of his, led by the painter Diego Rivera, had approached Lázaro Cárdenas, the reformist president of Mexico, to grant Trotsky asylum there. And on 18 December, Trygve Lie visited Trotsky to convey in person the news that Mexican asylum had been granted and to inform him of the arrangements already made for his departure. The Norwegian government had chartered a petrol tanker which would leave the following day. Trotsky and his wife would be taken under escort to board it and be accompanied on the voyage by a commanding officer of the guard at the house.

Trotsky suspected a trap in the haste and surreptitiousness of the arrangements. He argued that he should not be smuggled out of the country but released from internment and allowed to communicate with his friends and with the Mexican government, so as to choose his own route and take the necessary precautions. He would rather go by way of France. And why should the French authorities refuse him a transit visa, now that he had Mexican asylum? But Trygve Lie waved away all objections and demands with impatient reassurances. And the more impatient he seemed, the more suspicious Trotsky became. 'Of course,' Trotsky warned, revealing the drift of his doubts, 'you are in a position to destroy us physically, but morally you will break your necks just as the German Social Democrats broke theirs on Karl Liebknecht and Rosa Luxemburg.' Trygve Lie, taking his leave, held out his hand. Trotsky turned away in disgust.

While Natalia packed their belongings, Trotsky wrote a letter to Lyova, to tell him of their imminent departure. 'If something happens to us *en route* or elsewhere, you and Sergei are my heirs. . . . As you know, I have in mind future royalties on my books – apart from these I possess nothing.' He had made his will, and was now ready.

On 19 December, they set out, with their police guard as the only other passenger, on the tanker *Ruth*. In the rough winter seas, they stayed in their cabin and read books about Mexico. In his diary, Trotsky wrote, on 31 December, 'This was Cain's year.' The next morning, the tanker welcomed the New Year with sirens. But the only reply was the restless silence of the sea.

12

Auto-da-Fé

On 9 January 1937 the tanker docked at the port of Tampico. Trotsky remained distrustful and warned the Norwegian officer that he would not disembark unless there were friends to meet him. The friends were there; along with a special train provided by the Mexican government. At last the couple arrived at their destination: the home of Diego Rivera and Frida Kahlo, in a suburb of Mexico City. It was a low house, painted blue, with pre-Columbian objects and numerous pictures in the rooms.

Frida, a beautiful woman who wore long, embroidered dresses of the richest colours, and Diego Rivera, with his Rabelaisian shape and vitality, were as welcome as the Mexican sunshine. But the shadows seemed all the darker by contrast. The Communist Party and the Confederation of Mexican Workers, under Stalinist leadership, protested at Trotsky's admission and proclaimed that they would not rest until he was expelled. More dangerous were the threats of a summary retribution. And President Cárdenas was sufficiently persuaded of their seriousness to order the stationing of police guards outside the Blue House in Coyoacan.

These were no defence against the horror streaming out of Moscow. On 23 January 1937 there opened a new show trial in the October Hall, with Trotsky once again arraigned as the all-purpose Lucifer. He had, the prosecution alleged, been conspiring with both the German and the Japanese governments; in the belief that war was now inevitable and that the Soviet Union would be defeated. In return for their agreement to make him master of Russia, he had promised Germany an 'independent' Ukraine and Japan outright possession of the maritime provinces; as well as various economic concessions, which would further his own purpose of creating a powerful capitalist class to sustain him. Meanwhile, he had undertaken to promote disorder and demoralization in the Soviet Union by acts of terrorism and a widespread campaign of sabotage. Indeed, the prosecution contended, this campaign had already been responsible for various mining disasters, railway accidents and factory explosions: to produce serious delays in major industrial projects.

Soviet expansion after 1945

Once again, the defendants were made to provide their own moral firing squad. Rataichak, former head of the chemical industry, confessed that his Trotskyist colleagues had arranged for various accidents, which had caused the death of many workers; Livshitz, former Deputy People's Commissar for Transport, that numerous railway derailments had been organized on 'Trotskyist orders'. Radek confessed to having received over the years several letters from Trotsky, all of them destroyed, which had outlined his plans and conveyed his directives. And Piatakov, former Deputy People's Commissar for Heavy Industry, confessed that he had flown in the middle of December 1935 from Berlin to Oslo, where Trotsky had told him of his secret understanding with Rudolf Hess, and ordered him to set the campaign of sabotage in motion.

As Trotsky and Natalia listened to the radio and read the newspapers, they felt that 'insanity, absurdity, outrage, fraud and blood were flooding us from all sides'.[1] Trotsky knew how confidently the charges would be chorused, by Stalin's captive Communist parties and press, around the world; and how their very extravagance might recommend them to belief. For surely, it would be said, the Soviet regime would never have made such seemingly incredible allegations, without the assurance of sufficient evidence to establish their truth. But it was easier to fabricate evidence inside the Soviet Union than abroad. Piatakov's story of his secret flight to meet Trotsky in Oslo was immediately contradicted by the Norwegian paper *Aftenposten*, which reported that no civil aircraft had landed at Oslo's airport throughout the month of December 1935. And a few days later, after further investigation, the Norwegian Social Democratic *Arbeiderbladet* reported that no aircraft at all had used the airport between September 1935 and May 1936.[2]

Trotsky now publicly demanded that Piatakov be asked in court the full details of his flight, including the name used on his false passport, for further checking. And he challenged the Soviet government to seek his own extradition in a Norwegian court, where the facts could be established. But Trotsky might have been trying to make himself heard through the glass walls of a nightmare. The defendants were all found guilty and, with four exceptions that included Radek, sentenced to death. The death sentences were carried out immediately. Radek, who received his ten-year sentence with manifest relief, was subsequently dispatched to a labour camp in the Arctic, where he would be murdered by another prisoner in 1939.

In England, the Webbs reasserted their admiration of Soviet justice; while the Left Book Club published a report on the trial, by a barrister, Dudley Collard, that might have been written by Vyshinsky, the prosecutor, himself.[3] Leon Feuchtwanger, the celebrated German novelist, reported that on setting foot in the courtroom, 'my doubts melted away as naturally as salt dissolves in water. If that was lying or prearranged then I don't know what truth is.'[4]

Nor were the more worldly and the less sympathetic to the socialist pretensions of Russia any sounder in judgement. Joseph E. Davies, newly arrived United States ambassador and a faithful capitalist, dutifully attended the trial and found nothing suspicious in the eagerness of the defendants to 'heap accusation upon accusation upon themselves'. And he informed Washington that his opinion was generally shared. 'I have talked to many, if not all, of the members of the Diplomatic Corps here, and, with possibly one exception, they are all of the opinion that the proceedings established clearly the existence of a political plot and conspiracy to overthrow the government.'[5]

In a speech, delivered on his behalf at a meeting in New York, Trotsky announced his readiness to appear before a public and impartial commission of inquiry. And he undertook in advance, should such a commission find him guilty in the slightest degree, to place himself voluntarily in the hands of Stalin's executioners. Friedrich Adler, the son of his old friend and now secretary of the Second International, did what he could to associate the western Social Democratic parties and trade unions with the establishment of the commission. Léon Blum, the head of a Popular Front government in France, which relied on Stalinist support, used his considerable influence to prevent any such involvement in the provocations of a counter-trial. And the Western intelligentsia proved scarcely more solicitous of demonstrating its devotion to the cause of justice and truth, which it otherwise so passionately proclaimed.

Eighty-eight American intellectuals, including such literary eminences as Theodore Dreiser, Dorothy Parker and Nathanael West, urged a boycott of the commission.

Should not a country recognized as engaged in improving conditions for all its people, whether or not one agrees with all the means whereby this is brought about, be permitted to decide for itself what measures of protection are necessary against treasonable plots to assassinate and overthrow its leadership and involve it in war with foreign powers?[6]

But even those less determined to travel in the special observation coach of the Stalinist express were unsympathetic. Some were persuaded, by the confrontation of the times, that criticism of the Soviet regime could only give comfort to Fascism and, in particular, weaken the struggle against it in Spain. Others seemed concerned to stay as far away as possible from any excavations that might uncover something disagreeable. Sections of the Jewish press in the United States were disturbed by Trotsky's claims of an anti-Semitic undercurrent in the show trials. The editor of the New York *Tag* declared that the Jewish press had become accustomed to regarding the Soviet Union as 'our only consolation', in a period of insurgent anti-Semitism. 'It is unforgivable that Trotsky should raise such groundless charges against Stalin.'

Still others were simply unwilling to risk the personal consequences of involvement in the counter-trial. They were left in no doubt that their participation would produce orchestrated attacks on their motives and integrity, till they came to be cast in the public mind as Trotsky's co-defendants rather than as his impartial judges. At all events, even some, like André Gide and H. G. Wells, who were initially prepared to involve themselves, decided to keep a discreet distance instead. It was the seventy-nine-year-old John Dewey, the great American philosopher and educationalist, who came to the moral rescue of his own liberal tradition; and who, by agreeing to chair the commission of inquiry, gave it much of its authority. He was not to be dissuaded by the outcry from self-avowed progressives, who were driven to accuse him of senility; or by the pressure from members of his family, who begged him not to interrupt his work and risk his reputation by involvement in so squalid an affair. Since Trotsky could not get permission to enter the United States, the counter-trial was to take place in Mexico. Dewey was warned that the Mexican trade union movement might set out to prevent the proceedings by violent demonstrations. He was unmoved. Every attempt to discourage him only had the opposite effect. As he was to explain in his inaugural statement to the commission, he could have acted otherwise only by being false to his life's work.

The commission sat for a week, from 10 April, at the Blue House. The Soviet embassy in Washington, the Communist parties of the United States and Mexico, and the leading Mexican labour organizations had been invited to send representatives who might cross-examine Trotsky themselves, but had either ignored or abusively refused the invitation. The cross-examination was accordingly left to the commission, and its members showed from the first that they were not disposed to let Trotsky dictate his own verdict. Dewey was convinced only that the Moscow trials had failed to establish Trotsky's guilt, and made it clear that the establishment of his innocence was an altogether different matter. Several members, most notably Otto Ruhle – a long-distinguished German socialist who, along with Karl Liebknecht, had voted in the Reichstag against war credits in 1914 – were hostile to Bolshevism itself. They believed Stalinism to have been its inevitable development and while ready enough to condemn the Moscow trials for what these were, would need persuading that Trotsky should be acquitted of all moral responsibility for them. One member, Carlton Beals, on the other hand, seemed concerned to establish that Stalin had led Bolshevism away from the Trotskyist frenzy for world revolution into the responsibilities of nationalism.

Trotsky placed all his archives, his accounts of income and expenditure, his voluminous writings at the disposal of the commission. He evaded no questions and sought to clarify rather than cloud every issue. He denied that Bolshevism could be blamed for a Stalinist degeneracy, which had been promoted by the failure of the revolution to spread beyond the borders of Russia. The one ugly exchange was provoked by Beals, who asked Trotsky whether he had not sent a certain Borodin, in 1919 or 1920, to establish the Communist Party in Mexico. When Trotsky denied this, Beals asserted that Borodin himself had admitted it. This assertion not only implied that Trotsky had been lying to the commission; it seemed directed at embarrassing Trotsky's Mexican protectors and endangering his asylum. Trotsky demanded to know the source of the information. Beals refused to disclose it; was censured in private session by his colleagues; and resigned from the commission.

After days of cross-examination, Trotsky, by now so exhausted that he asked permission to remain seated, read his final statement. And one by one he tore away the rickety supports of the Stalinist case. What could the Opposition have hoped to gain from acts of sabotage in coal mines and factories, or from an alliance with Hitler and the Mikado? It was Stalin who had gained an excuse, for the consequences of his impetuous industrialization and for the extermination of his opponents. That was why there was no real evidence for the alleged conspiracy. It was essential to show that the connections went abroad and led there to Trotsky or his son. Yet precisely because they went abroad, they could not be manufactured with the immunity to examination that they enjoyed in the Soviet Union. And it had been easy to demonstrate that the very contacts which were crucial to the credibility of the plot could not have taken place. The whole case accordingly rested on confessions. And how had such confessions been extracted? The relevant victims could not be questioned, since they had been shot or imprisoned. But the commission had affidavits from Russian and European Communists which testified sufficiently to the techniques of Stalin's political police.

The commission had as well the immense documentation which Trotsky had supplied and which provided the psychological and historical authenticity so absent from the version in the Moscow trials. Surely, if he were guilty, one among that multitude of papers which he had supplied to the commission would have betrayed him. It was inconceivable that all his letters, his articles, his books, had been directed at concealing his real designs; as though he had 'built a skyscraper to camouflage a dead rat'. He remained convinced that Soviet society, for all the horror of Stalin's purges, still represented the greatest progress in social organization that man had so far achieved. If Soviet workers were apathetic in the face of Stalinist monstrosities, it was because they saw themselves confronted by a choice between Stalin and Hitler. They preferred Stalin, and in this they were right. But they would shed their apathy as soon as they saw some prospect abroad of new victories for socialism.

That is why I do not despair . . . I have patience. . . . The experience of my life, in which there has been no lack either of success or of failures, has not only not destroyed my faith in the clear, bright future of mankind, but, on the contrary, has given it an indestructible temper.

It was a masterly defence spoken, as the cross-examination had been conducted, by his own choice, in English: though he would have had so much more eloquence at his command in German or French, let alone Russian. But he wanted the most immediate, personal contact with his listeners. And this he had cumulatively achieved. At the end of his final remarks, the members of the commission were long silent. Dewey himself had intended to provide some summing-up, in formal conclusion. He changed his mind. 'Anything I can say', he stated, 'will be an anti-climax.' The commission left for New York where it was to continue its work and write its report.

Relentlessly the horror grew. Even before the commission's arrival in Mexico, Trotsky and Natalia may have given up hope that their younger son Sergei was still alive.[7] He had been deported to Krasnoyarsk in central Siberia; and been given work as an engineer at a factory there. The Moscow papers had then reported an accident at the factory, with the accusation that Sergei had 'organized the mass gassing of workers'. He had never been interested in politics and had, at school, refused to join the Komsomol, or Young Communist League. Trotsky and Natalia had once hoped that he might come in time to share their priorities. But the only passions he had developed had been for mathematics and engineering. They were no protection. It was enough that he was Trotsky's son. There was no trial. And despite the pressures to which he must have been subjected, there was no confession. 'The executioners,' Natalia wrote, 'were silent.' She composed for the press an appeal, *To the Conscience of the World*, protesting Sergei's innocence and integrity. The world had too much on its conscience already. Trotsky felt that his own death might have saved his son. And it seemed to Natalia that he was sorry to be alive.

At the January show trial, Radek had warned 'Trotskyists in Spain, France and other countries that they will pay with their heads unless they learn from our example'. In the coming months, while the Spanish Communist Party expended scarcely less passion on its campaign to eliminate the Trotskyist POUM (Partido Obrero de Unificacíon Marxista) than on waging the war against Fascism, Soviet agents in Spain disposed personally of various socialists who were considered dangerous to the

Stalinist cause. Erwin Wolf, who had so devotedly served as Trotsky's secretary in Norway, set out for Spain. 'You are going to certain murder,' Victor Serge warned him.[8] But Wolf was determined. He could not live in peace while a revolution was struggling for its life. He was kidnapped in the streets of Barcelona and never seen again. Supervising the Stalinist purge in Catalonia as Soviet consul-general was Antonov-Ovseenko, Trotsky's old colleague who had led the storming of the Winter Palace in October 1917. His obeisance to Stalin did not save him. He would be recalled home, to take up an appointment as People's Commissar of Justice in the Russian Soviet Republic, and be liquidated on his arrival.

In May 1937, Marshal Tukhachevsky, with five of the Soviet Union's most distinguished generals and Yan Gamarnik, chief political commissar of the Red Army, were charged with treason. Gamarnik committed suicide. All the others were executed. They had received the reward of their talents and revolutionary devotion under Trotsky as Commissar of War. Now they were accused of complicity with him and with Hitler in designing the military defeat of the Soviet Union. General Yakir wrote a letter to Stalin protesting his innocence. Stalin wrote on it: 'Scoundrel and prostitute'. Perhaps it was their very innocence that he feared. Perhaps, in the miasma of his mind, innocence itself appeared as a rebuke and as a threat. But it was, too, a time for the paying off of old scores. Stalin had never forgotten or forgiven Tukhachevsky's criticism of his role in the war with Poland. And shortly after Tukhachevsky's execution, Stalin dealt with those Georgian Bolsheviks who had resisted his policies during Lenin's last days. Trotsky and Natalia were haunted by the faces of those whom they had known. 'We wandered about in our little tropical garden in Coyoacan, surrounded by distant ghosts, each with a hole in his forehead.'[9]

The strain was telling on Trotsky. He suffered from headaches, dizziness and high blood pressure. But if he was, in consequence, sometimes impatient or rude, he was immediately contrite. On one occasion, he lost his temper with a secretary and stalked out of her room. A few minutes later, there was a knock on the door, which then opened to a tentative Trotsky. He held a bunch of flowers, picked from the plants on the patio, behind his back. And seeing enough to be satisfied that his offering would be accepted, he placed it on her desk and silently withdrew.[10]

Natalia herself was under additional strain. That Trotsky was attractive to other women she had always known. And that he had often responded with an easy flirtatiousness had never disturbed her. But now she suspected, with reason, that he was not merely flirting with Frida Kahlo. She was deeply jealous and showed it.

In July, Trotsky left with his bodyguard for a stay in the mountains, to ride and hunt. At least once a day he wrote to Natalia; begging her to stop competing with a woman who meant so little to him and expressing, again and again, his love for her. 'How I love you, Nata, my only one, my eternal one, my faithful one, my love, my *victim*. . . .' Only in such letters are there glimpses of the Trotsky that he never permitted the world to see: his self-reproach at her sufferings; his sadness over an 'old age that has caught us by surprise'; his desire; and his need of her own strength. 'You will still carry me on your shoulders, Nata, as you have carried me throughout our life.'[11]

An occasional flash cut through the dark. In July, Ignaz Reiss, chief of a secret Soviet network in Europe, resigned in protest at the purges; returned the Order of the Red Banner, awarded to him in 1928; and announced his adherence to the cause which Trotsky represented. He revealed not only the techniques, the torture and blackmail, which had been used to extract the show trial confessions, but the stubborn courage of young Communists who had resisted to the end and gone to their deaths with the cry of 'Long live Trotsky'. In early September, he was visited at his Swiss hideout by Gertrud Schildbach, a Soviet agent who had known him for fifteen years and had come ostensibly to ask his advice. She brought chocolates, subsequently found to have been poisoned, for his wife and child. He left the house with her, and his bullet-ridden body was found shortly afterwards on a road near Lausanne.

The Swiss and French police identified the assassins, and their connection with the Society for the Repatriation of Russian Émigrés, which was sponsored by the Soviet embassy in Paris. And in the course of their investigations, the police discovered that the same gang had been closely shadowing Lyova and planning his elimination. Lyova himself was astonished at the accuracy with which the GPU agents had known of his movements. It was clear to the Trotskyists that there was a Soviet spy among them; and some suspicion fell on a certain Mark Zborowski, or Étienne as he was known, who had not so long ago been working at the Society for the Repatriation of Russian Émigrés. But Lyova would hear nothing against a man so deeply in his confidence that he had given him the key to his letter-box and the most precious of the files in Trotsky's archives to keep.

The French police were sufficiently convinced of the danger to Lyova's life that they assigned a guard to protect him. One of Lyova's colleagues wrote to Trotsky and Natalia, warning them that their son was ill and exhausted, and in serious danger, but regarded himself as irreplaceable in Paris. They suggested that they get him to Mexico, if only for a while, to rest and recover his strength. But Trotsky was far from convinced that Mexico would be any safer than France. GPU agents were gathering in Mexico too, and promoting the clamour against Trotsky and his followers. Trotsky wrote to his son advising him to remain where he was.

That August, he wrote an article, *In the Face of a New World War*, that was rich in insights soon to be confirmed by events. Germany, he warned, would pursue its ambitions by seeking an accommodation either with Britain and France against the Soviet Union, or with the Soviet Union against Britain and France. The United States wanted to stay aloof, but this was impossible for the most powerful nation of all; and the main threat to it would come from the Far East. Totalitarian states were the better equipped for total war, and the democracies would be compelled to copy their methods. Germany needed at least another two years to prepare, so that the first possible date for the outbreak of war would be August 1939. But no sweeping victory was to be expected; there was not sufficient strategic air power for that. Those capitalist countries that had not resolved the agrarian problem, such as Poland, Hungary and Romania, would be the first to succumb. Germany and Italy might achieve brilliant successes at first, but they would be subjected to social convulsions long before their enemies. France would emerge a second-rate power with an unstable social structure. The British empire was bound to be weakened and decline. 'The collapse of imperialism will usher in an epoch of social upheaval. . . . The face of the world will change.'

What he did not, or would not, allow himself to admit, was the coercive strength of the regime in the Soviet Union. He expected its overthrow to be hastened by the war; and seemed never to have thought that it would, without any essential change, actually expand its dominion across half of Europe. He believed that its command of technology would enable the United States to dominate the world; if only a world so devastated, and 'reduced to barbarism', that this 'might spell the twilight of American civilization'. That the capitalist system was still to experience its most productive period, and with reforms which only promoted the allegiance of organized labour, he did not foresee. He never expected the working class to prevent the outbreak of war. But he did propose the possibility that it might act rather more promptly than it had done in the First World War. In the event, of course, it would act throughout for democracy and for the nation state rather than for the revolution.

In December 1937 the Dewey Commission finally released its report. It found the Moscow show trials of August 1936 and January 1937 to have been 'frame-ups'; and Leon Trotsky, with his son Leon Sedov, 'not guilty'.[12] The news delighted Trotsky and Natalia. But within a few days, their delight was plunged in still more blood. From Moscow came the report that seven prominent figures in the Commissariat of Foreign Affairs had been shot, along with the Georgian, Avelii Yenukidze, who had been for fifteen years Secretary of the Central Soviet Executive and, once, a neighbour of the Trotskys in the Kremlin. He had known Stalin from his youth, and the two had seemed like brothers. But Yenukidze had revealed his qualms over Stalin's persecutions. And Stalin did not countenance qualms, from anyone. 'That Cain!' Trotsky commented, again and again.

Lyova did not bring out a copy of the *Bulletin*, reporting the verdict of the Dewey Commission, as speedily as his father had expected. From Mexico came complaints of his 'political blindness' and a threat to transfer the *Bulletin* to New York. Lyova was sick with fever and sleeplessness. He had recurrent attacks of appendicitis but kept putting off an operation that would interrupt his work. Early in February 1938, he sent off the proofs of the *Bulletin* to Mexico, without any mention of his ill health. On the eighth, he had the worst of his attacks and decided to delay his operation no longer. It was to Étienne that he entrusted the arrangements; and in accordance with these, he entered, as a French engineer, a small private clinic run by some Russian émigré doctors. His operation that evening was a success, and in the following few days he seemed to be recovering rapidly.

Then, suddenly, there was a serious relapse. On the night of 13 February, half-naked and raving in Russian, he wandered through corridors and wards that were unaccountably devoid of all attendants and guards. In the morning, the surgeon who had operated on him was so startled by his condition that he wondered whether Lyova had not attempted suicide. An emergency operation was carried out; followed by blood transfusions. On the 16th, after suffering much agony, Lyova died. An inquest accepted the evidence of doctors that death had been due to post-operative complications, heart failure, and low resistance. The surgeon who had suspected a suicide attempt now retreated into a frightened silence. The possibility of poisoning by agents of the GPU was never to be proved. But many years later, Étienne himself would reveal his role as a Soviet spy, and confess that he had informed GPU agents immediately after summoning the ambulance that took Lyova to the clinic.

Diego Rivera, alarmed by suspicious movements near the Blue House, had persuaded Trotsky to stay for a few days at the home of an old Mexican revolutionary. It was there that he burst in on Trotsky with a message that he had received from some journalists. 'Leon Sedov is dead!' 'What? What did you say?' asked Trotsky. Rivera showed him the message. 'Get out of here!' Trotsky shouted: needing to be alone before he lost control of himself.

Natalia was at the Blue House, sorting out old photographs of the children. When Trotsky arrived, she was surprised to see him and then noticed that he was more bent than he had ever been before. His face was grey, and he seemed to have turned into an old man suddenly. 'What is it?' she asked in alarm. 'Are you ill?' And he answered in a low voice. 'Lyova is ill, our little Lyova. . . .' And she began to understand. By her own account, she had been so afraid for Trotsky himself that the thought of anything happening to Lyova had never occurred to her.[13]

They were overwhelmed with grief and stayed in their room, refusing to see secretaries or friends. When, after eight days, Trotsky emerged, his eyes were swollen and he could not speak. He wrote a lamentation, which was to be published in the March issue of the *Bulletin* and as a separate pamphlet in English. He recalled how Lyova had given his youth to his ideals; had followed his parents into banishment and into exile; had been so invaluable a colleague as well as so loving and so devoted a son. Trotsky did not spare himself. He had demanded so much from Lyova. But then he had always demanded the most from those who were closest to him. And who had been closer than Lyova? Now he was no more. And the bell that Trotsky tolled was also for Natalia and himself. 'He was part of us, our young part. . . . Together with our boy has died everything that still remained young in us. . . .'

On 2 March there opened in Moscow the third and most fantastic of the show trials. Among the twenty-one arraigned for having constituted 'an anti-Soviet bloc of Trotskyists and Rightists' were three former members of Lenin's Politburo – Bukharin, Rykov, and Krestinsky. No charge was too bizarre for the prosecution to level. Bukharin was accused of having planned, with Trotsky's blessing, the murder of Lenin in 1918. Yagoda, former head of the secret police and stage manager of the first show trial, had supervised the imprisonment, torture and extermination of numberless Trotskyists: now he was on trial as Trotsky's tool. Several distinguished doctors, including one who had been first Lenin's and then Stalin's personal physician, were charged with having poisoned, on Yagoda's orders, Maxim Gorky: a revelation, indeed, to Russians previously encouraged to believe that their leading writer had merely succumbed to long ill health and old age.

Again there were extravagant confessions. Chernov, former People's Commissar for Agriculture, declared that his interest in animal diseases had involved a secret determination to spread them; Zelensky, former chairman of the Consumer Co-operatives, that he had arranged for the insertion of glass and nails in butter. Chief Prosecutor Vyshinsky would find in this an easy explanation for the economic difficulties which the homeland of socialism, basking in the sunshine of Stalin's rule, should otherwise not have experienced. 'It is now clear why there are interruptions of supplies here and there; why, with our riches and abundance of products, there is a shortage first of one thing, then of another. It is these traitors who are responsible for it.'

Rosengoltz, until recently Commissar for Foreign Trade, confessed to having directed large sums of foreign currency, from state funds held abroad, into Trotsky's hands. And Rakovsky, whose self-abasement must have given Trotsky the most pain, confessed that as early as 1926, Trotsky had told him that he was working for the British intelligence service. But this time, there were embarrassing divergences from the script. Krestinsky, at the very outset, refused to plead guilty and retracted the testimony that he had given at the preliminary investigation. When Vyshinsky accused him of having misled the prosecution, Krestinsky replied: 'I simply considered that if I were to say what I am saying today – that it was not in accordance with the facts – my declaration would not reach the leaders of the Party and the Government.' What happened that night in the Lubyanka cannot be known. On the following day, in a flat and hopeless voice, Krestinsky retracted his retraction.

There were, however, significant gestures of resistance from others as well, who denied particular charges under cross-examination. And Bukharin himself, under cross-examination and in his final statement, so effectively disposed of the specific accusations against him that his acceptance of a general guilt merely mocked itself. He denied enlistment by any intelligence service and pointed out that at the time when he was supposed to have plotted with Left Social Revolutionaries against Lenin's life, he had himself been injured by a bomb from the hand of a Left Social Revolutionary. How, he asked, could those in the dock have constituted a group, when several of them were unknown to him, and he had never spoken of counter-revolutionary matters with others? How, if the bloc had been formed, as alleged, in 1928, long before Hitler, could it have been organized on the instructions of Fascist intelligence services? And he remarked scathingly: 'The confession of the accused is a medieval principle of jurisprudence.'

The court sentenced eighteen of the accused, including all the major figures, to death, and the sentences were carried out almost at once. Rakovsky and the sixty-six-year-old Dr Pletnev, Russia's most celebrated heart specialist, were sentenced to long terms of imprisonment. There were the usual orchestrations of support from foreign Communist parties and from their progressive comrades in arms. But many neutral observers found their intelligence more than usually insulted, especially by the alleged medical plot. The mystery of Gorky's death remains. In 1963, his widow, Ekaterina Peshkova, meeting an old American acquaintance of her husband's in Moscow, grew exceedingly agitated when told that people now supposed Gorky's death to have been natural. 'It's not quite so, but don't ask me to tell you about it!' Perhaps Gorky, increasingly disturbed by the course of Stalinist rule, was threatening to become troublesome; and if this were so, Stalin himself had most to gain from his elimination. Of all the confessions, Yagoda's, of having arranged for Gorky's poisoning, was the least incredible. And the mixture of fact and fantasy, with his own guilt concealed in the accusations against innocent doctors, might well have appealed to Stalin's sinister sense of humour.

But the show trials were only the steel and glass outer office of Stalin's slaughter house. The carnage was conducted in the sheds behind. From the spring of 1938, groups of still loyal Trotskyists were taken from the camps to be summarily shot. And they were a tiny proportion of those who fell to Stalin's frenzy. Estimates that in the three years, 1936–8, one million people were executed, while double that number were killed by conditions in the camps, seem, on the available evidence, all too probable.[14] But there were few who could bring themselves to suspect this at the time. In the months that followed the execution of Marshal Tukhachevsky and his colleagues, most of the marshals, generals and admirals who had signed the relevant communiqué were sent to join them. Eminent German, Polish and other foreign Communists who had sought asylum in the Soviet Union disappeared. And the fate of these was easily assumed. But that, by the end of 1938, some twelve million people should have been behind barbed wire, and that literally thousands were being shot day after day: there was no place for such horror in the civilized mind of the time.

It is evident, from his various writings, that Trotsky himself never suspected the extent of Stalin's holocaust and, in consequence, the effectively total loss of a leadership able to mount any challenge to the regime for many years to come. There was nothing in his experience of Tsarist or any other repressions which might have prepared him for so systematic and relentless an extermination. And, furthermore, he continued to see Stalin through the distorting mirror of his own contempt. Arguing on one occasion against the value of a terrorist response in the Soviet Union, he asked:

What political and moral satisfaction indeed could the working class derive from the assassination of Cain-Djugashvili, whom any new bureaucratic 'genius' would replace without difficulty? In so far as Stalin's personal fortunes can be of any interest to us at all, we should only wish that he should survive the crumbling of his own system; and that is not very far off.[15]

But Stalin was not simply a bureaucratic 'genius', whose qualities of leadership corresponded to the degeneracy of the revolution. The methods and magnitude of Stalin's violence could as properly be attributed to the nature of a bureaucratic regime as the extermination of the Jews in Hitler's gas chambers to no more than the nature of Fascism. The truth was that Trotsky's particular imagination could grasp personal character only as the feature of a system. It was this which constituted, in art as in politics, the source of both his strength and his weakness. It was this which made him so great a historian and so poor a biographer.

His reasons for choosing to write a biography of Stalin were obvious enough. It was a project that promised a unique opportunity to rescue the historical record from the distortions of the Kremlin hagiographers. And, not least, Trotsky must have been drawn by the prospect of portraying the man who was so likely to be his own ultimate murderer. From the first of the Moscow show trials, he and Natalia had been 'expecting the assassins with absolute certainty'.[16] If he could only write enough of the book in time, the victim would yet be striking the last blow.

Biography no less than history must be dramatic to become art. And Trotsky's *Stalin*, or the substantial portion that he wrote, is as empty of drama as his *History of the Russian Revolution* is full. The explicit argument, with official Soviet histories and individual hagiographers, over Stalin's record, is more a manifestation of this than it is a cause. In inviting the audience to leave its seats and examine the scenery, Trotsky does not disrupt the action on the stage, but offers, rather, a substitute for it. And there is no action on the stage, because the action of biography is the development of character, and there is no development of character in *Stalin*.

The delineation of personality by epigram served a dramatic purpose in the *History of the Russian Revolution*, precisely because the development there was one of event and not of character. Indeed, the very contrast between the dynamic narrative and the static quality of this epigrammatic delineation illuminated the major theme of irony. In *Stalin*, however, the portrayal of the central character had itself to be dynamic, and this could not be achieved by any number of static delineations. Sometimes Stalin's vulgarity is more marked than his slyness; sometimes his malevolence dominates his laziness and his stupidity. All that results from these is a series of different patterns made from the movement of the same coloured glass fragments among the mirrors of Trotsky's own mind.

Stalin fails, then, totally as art. But it fails, too, as 'scientific' biography. For it presents, inevitably, two crucial problems, and resolves neither of them. How could a man of such mean abilities and motives have come to enjoy absolute command of the revolution? And how should such a man then have committed crimes of so uncharacteristic a magnitude? Trotsky's answer to the first question, that Stalin's peculiar qualities fitted him to become the leader of the bureaucratic reaction, would serve if Stalin had risen only as the revolution declined. But Stalin did not leap from obscurity at Lenin's graveside, or while Trotsky's back was turned. He was a full member of the small and effectively supreme Politburo from its very beginning in 1919, and became general secretary of the central committee, with control of the party organization, in 1922. Either, therefore, his qualities were of a kind to support his assumption of these responsibilities; or Lenin was culpably obtuse in sponsoring it, and Trotsky himself culpably negligent in his acquiescence. In admitting neither possibility, Trotsky consigns not only Stalin but, along with him, Lenin and even himself, to a blurring twilight.

The second question is no more successfully answered. For Trotsky, far from denying the magnitude of Stalin's crimes, augments them, by proceeding to accuse him of having poisoned Lenin. Yet he continues to insist on Stalin's mediocrity, and denies him comparison not only with Lenin, or with Cromwell, Robespierre and Napoleon, but even with Mussolini and Hitler.[17]

However meagre the 'ideas' of Fascism, both of the victorious leaders of reaction, the Italian and the German, from the very beginning of their respective movements displayed initiative, roused the masses to action, pioneered new paths through the political jungle. Nothing of the kind can be said about Stalin. The Bolshevik Party was created by Lenin. Stalin grew out of its political machine and remained inseparable from it. He has never had any other approach to the masses or to the events of history than through this machine.[18]

Surely, however, to deny Stalin's originality on the grounds that he mastered a machine created by another is as untenable as to maintain that Napoleon lacked originality because he was not the only true begetter of a citizens' army. Lenin himself produced Bolshevism not out of a void, but from the Russian Social Democratic Labour Party. And Stalin did far more than transform the party of Lenin so as to leave it with little more than its socialist pretensions. He succeeded in preserving the widespread acceptance of these pretensions, to pioneer his own new path through the political jungle.

Furthermore, this was achieved not in the Soviet Union alone, but in the different conditions of the democracies, where party discipline lay in general beyond the reach of Stalin's secret police, and where party propaganda was confronted on public platforms, in books and the press.

His success was in large measure due to his doctrine of socialism in a single country, which enabled him to support his system at home with the appeal of nationalism, and subordinate the parties abroad to Soviet national interests. For Trotsky, this was the supreme socialist heresy. Yet he refuses Stalin the distinction of originality that the founder of so momentous a heresy would deserve. Instead he declares:

The bureaucracy feared more and more that it was jeopardizing its position by the risk of involvement implicit in an international revolutionary policy. The campaign against the theory of permanent revolution, devoid in itself of any theoretical value whatsoever, served as an expression of a conservative nationalistic deviation from Bolshevism. Out of this struggle emerged the theory of socialism in a separate country.[19]

But it was not, of course, some mysterious bureaucratic marsh that exhaled the doctrine like a mist. It was Stalin himself. And Trotsky's resort to the impersonal emanation is an attempt, conscious or unconscious, to bury the personal magnitude of Stalin in bureaucratic myth.

In the end, Trotsky seems driven to maintain that a man as essentially mediocre as the Stalin he describes must have muddled his way into becoming a monster.

> If Stalin could have foreseen at the very beginning where his fight against Trotskyism would lead, he undoubtedly would have stopped short, in spite of the prospect of victory over all his opponents. But he did not foresee anything. . . . The absence of a creative imagination, the inability to generalize and to foresee killed the revolutionist in Stalin when he took the helm alone.[20]

Yet the very Stalin drawn by Trotsky would never have been deflected by any foresight of the costs from the prospect of victory over his opponents.

Much earlier in the book, when dealing with Stalin's initial adherence to Bolshevism, Trotsky presents someone for whom 'well-organized violence' was, from the beginning, 'the shortest distance between two points', and revolution, a matter of method rather than a commitment of mind.

> The Russian terrorists were in essence petty bourgeois democrats, yet they were extremely resolute and audacious. Marxists were wont to refer to them as 'liberals with a bomb'. Stalin has always been what he remains to this day – a politician of the golden mean who does not hesitate to resort to the most extreme measures. Strategically he is an opportunist; tactically he is a 'revolutionist'. He is a kind of opportunist with a bomb.[21]

The pieces do not fit into each other, or with the historical record. So many of Stalin's victims represented no rationally conceivable challenge to his rule. Some would seem to have been selected by sheer vindictiveness rather than by opportunism in any political sense; and others, perhaps most, were simply swept up by the blind whirlwind that blew from within his mind. Stalin was shrewd. He was patient and cunning, and a master of intrigue. But he was also mistrustful, with a fear that reached into madness. The very loyalty of his minions struck him as suspicious, so that they paid for their loyalty with their lives. And he was malignant beyond the impulses of mistrust. The many well-attested instances of the sheer delight that he took in the suffering and the humiliation of others reflect a malevolent vanity which may be considered the essence of evil.

There is much more, however, to that description of Stalin as 'a kind of opportunist with a bomb' than the apparent inability to appreciate and re-create the complexities of Stalin's character. There is in it the underlying theme of Stalin as ultimately no more than the representation of a bureaucratic system, itself a form of institutionalized opportunism, dependent for survival on violence. And if *Stalin* fails as art because it treats the personality of the subject as merely the feature of a system, its failure as 'scientific' biography, too, may in large measure be ascribed to the same reason. For the system, which Stalin's personality is projected to reflect, may properly be called bureaucratic only if the meaning of the word is stretched so far as to crack. It is not the mirror but the image which is flawed.

And it is the flawed image not of *Stalin* alone, but of all Trotsky's writings on the Stalinist state. For he simply refused to recognize that the Soviet regime had become an autocracy more absolute and more arbitrary than that which the revolution had removed. The law of Tsarist Russia might, in theory, be whatever the Tsar himself chose to make it. But in practice he was seriously constrained both by the structure of government and by the nature of the society that supported it. Those ministers whom he appointed or dismissed at his pleasure remained political intermediaries in the adjustment of policy. But below this summit, on the other side of the rolling clouds in between, the state continued to be administered, as before, by a multitude of professional officials. 'Russia is not ruled by me,' a predecessor, Nicholas I, had said with an element of truth as well as modesty, 'but by my forty thousand clerks.'

The power of which many such officials, particularly those in immediate contact with the public, were able to dispose, was considerable. But it was a power derived from their formal functions; and a power both sustained and circumscribed by the rule of law. Nicholas II might have resented the corresponding restrictions on his autocracy. He was often enough outraged by the conduct of the courts. But a variety of factors, from the reliance of his regime on foreign loans to the fear of driving the middle class beyond mere contemplation of reform, effectively prevented him from making the law what he pleased, and secured his ultimate subjection to the law as it was.

This does not mean, to be sure, that the rule of law was inviolable; any more than the courts themselves were impervious to pressure. The numerous organized pogroms, with the protected activities of hooligan squads like the Black Hundreds, were manifestations of Tsarism's resort to lawless terror. But this terror, like the substitution of special tribunals for the courts, in a state of emergency, existed at the edges of the system, while the rule of law occupied the centre. Indeed, it was essentially this occupation of the centre by the rule of law to which many of the most important revolutionaries, once arrested, owed their lives.

Under Stalinism, terror itself became the law. Adjustments to the criminal code extended culpability for political offences to children down to the age of twelve; provided for the punishment of all adult members in the family of a political offender, whether or not they had been aware that the offence was intended or committed; and defined these offences so widely and so vaguely that charge and judgment were alike reduced to arbitrary acts. But no less significant than what Stalinism did with the law was what Stalinism did without it. Even such prominent victims as Marshal Tukhachevsky were disposed of so surreptitiously that doubt still remains whether they were ever given any sort of trial; and certainly countless others, seized by the secret police, were executed or deported to labour camps, without troubling the courts. The chief prosecutor, Vyshinsky, is on record as having several times proclaimed, 'When it is a question of annihilating the enemy, we can do it just as well without a trial.'

By the time that the rage of mass purges receded in late 1938, with the fall of Nikolai Yezhov as head of the secret police, it seems that at least one in twenty of the total population had been arrested. Indeed, the rage might well have receded precisely because it had reached the limits of the system's capabilities. Prisons and concentration camps were so packed; the political administration and the economy so battered; that some immediate relaxation had become imperative. But if the terror did recede, and was not to recur on anything like such a scale, it continued unceasingly, now flowing again, now ebbing, and with the threat of another flood ever present in the source of Stalin's total domination.

The system, of course, required an enormous number of functionaries to sustain it. The state was not just responsible for public services such as education and health. It controlled directly the factories and farms, banks and shops, railways and radio, books and ballet. And alongside the functionaries of the state were the functionaries of the party. If bureaucracy is to be defined simply by the proportion of officials in a society, then the bureaucratic character of the Stalinist system was plain. The multitude of judges and magistrates, prosecutors and interrogators, prison and concentration camp administrators, might itself have been enough for the purpose. But a bureaucracy is more than that. It depends upon the source and security of power. By this determinant, the government of Russia under the last of the Tsars was in substance a bureaucracy with the appearance of a personal despotism. By the same determinant, the government of the Soviet Union under Stalin was in substance a personal despotism with the appearance of bureaucracy. No formal function informed the power of the official. And no official was safe. The terror disposed equally of the high and the low; and even its principal instruments, the commanders of the secret police, fell at a nod from Stalin.

If Trotsky refused to recognize this despotism for what it was, he had the deepest of reasons. Mere bureaucratic degeneracy would not deny the surviving achievement of the revolution, in the existence of a workers' state. Indeed, if degeneracy came to the workers' state, in consequence of the revolution's failure to extend beyond the boundaries of Russia, bureaucratization was, surely, the logical form for it to take. But to argue that a workers' state could sustain a personal despotism was impossible. For if a workers' state could degenerate to the point where it was no more than the clay of a single will, what meaning did it have? And how should it still represent the greatest progress in social organization that mankind had so far achieved?

A part of Trotsky's mind, in the writing of *Stalin*, saw and recognized the truth. The very extent of the despotism emerges, from the encompassing confusion, in the lurid flash of an epigram.

'*L'état, c'est moi*' (I am the State) is almost a liberal formula by comparison with the actualities of Stalin's totalitarian regime. Louis XIV identified himself only with the State. The Popes of Rome identified themselves with both the State and the Church – but only during the epoch of temporal power. The totalitarian state goes far beyond Caesar-Papism, for it has encompassed the entire economy of the country as well. Stalin can justly say, unlike the Sun King, '*La Société, c'est moi*' (I am Society).[22]

But this was a truth too terrible for acceptance. Trotsky continued to distinguish between the regime and the society. He insisted that while Stalinism must everywhere be fought, the Soviet Union itself was to be unconditionally defended.

Already at the end of 1937, some of his friends and followers began rebelling against his formulations. They were not satisfied to accept the innocence of Bolshevism, as though the rise of Stalin to dominion had been an organic break. And they rejected Trotsky's claim that the failure of the revolution to spread beyond the borders of Russia had itself made that rise inevitable, in a resurgence of Russian backwardness. They looked for a moment of revolutionary sin. And they found it in 1921, with the crushing of the Kronstadt revolt. For had this revolt not been the first true proletarian protest at the retreat of the revolution from its ideals? And had the repressive response of the Bolsheviks not been the proper precursor of Stalinist terror?

Trotsky had no patience with this mythology. He dismissed the idealization of the Kronstadt revolt and declared that the failure to act would have opened the gates to counter-revolution. It was possible that there had been innocent victims. Civil war was scarcely a school for humane behaviour. Revolution was always blamed, by idealists and pacifists, for 'excesses'. But 'excesses' sprang from the very nature of revolution, which was itself an 'excess' of history. Let those who wished to do so reject revolution on this ground. He did not. He admitted his full political responsibility for the decision of the Politburo to crush the Kronstadt rising. He had supported the decision at the time.

His critics denounced him for the 'Jesuitic' immorality of justifying the means by the end. He replied in an essay, *Their Morals and Ours*, whose first draft he was finishing when he learned of Lyova's death and which he then dedicated to Lyova's memory. He poured scorn on those democrats and those anarchists of the left who were moved by the victories of reaction, to 'exude double their usual amount of moral effluvia, just as other people perspire double in fear'. In fact the Jesuits had merely expounded the truism that acts might be morally neutral in themselves, and to be justified or condemned by reference to the ends which they served. There was nothing right or wrong about firing a gun. What made it right or wrong was the purpose for which it was fired.

And who denied this? Did not all governments, even the most 'humanitarian', send their armies to exterminate the greatest possible number of the enemy, and so accept the principle that the end justified the means? But the end had also to be justified. And for Marxists, 'the end is justified if it leads to an increase of man's power over nature and to the abolition of man's power over man'. It was an end that conditioned its own means, in socialism, which was itself a prerequisite end to be reached by revolutionary class struggle. Thus, such means as united revolutionary workers in hostility to their oppression, consciousness of their historic tasks and readiness for self-sacrifice, must be considered permissible and even obligatory. And it followed that certain means had to be rejected, as incompatible with the chosen end. Socialism could not be reached by fraud; by a worship of leaders which humiliated the masses; by being imposed on workers against their will. In the dialectic of ends and means, a choice of the wrong means brought a different end into being.

It was a brilliant defence of Marxist morality. Yet its very brilliance lit a challenge to the means that Bolshevism had chosen. For had not the Bolshevik exercise of power been precisely a form of political fraud; the desertion of Soviet democracy for a dictatorship by the party, and increasingly by the leadership of the party, over the proletariat? And was it not this choice of the wrong means which had brought, soon enough, a different end into being? If Marxist morality was not to be mocked, the character of the end in itself proved the mistake of the means.

What, then, was the source of the mistake? It lay in the very assumption that politics was merely the shadow of economics, and that to take the appropriate economic measures was sufficient to ensure that the appropriate political shape would follow. But, in the event, economics and politics proved to be a duality of means: with the first of them, the vehicle; and the second, the road. To reach the point at which a single man might be able justly to claim, 'I am Society', both the total domination of the economy by the state and the total domination of the state by the party were essential. The extent of the dictatorship exercised by the party leadership was then correspondingly total. But it did not follow that the dictatorship should become a Stalinist one. For the peculiar horrors of that, a further mistake was necessary: the promotion of Stalin himself to an undivided dominion. And here it was a coincidence of particular characters, Lenin's and Trotsky's as well as Stalin's own, which was responsible.

Trotsky's rebellious friends and followers did not see the failure of the revolution in these terms. Having begun with an arbitrary moment of supposed revolutionary sin, they proceeded to reject socialism also, as guilty by association. Max Eastman denounced Marxism as an 'antique religion', which had begotten not only Stalinism but Fascism. Both Mussolini and Stalin, as well as many of Hitler's followers, had been socialists. It was time to declare that the 'dream of socialism' had finally collapsed.

Even the occasional victory seemed to issue only as a whisper. *Partisan Review*, an influential magazine of the intellectual left in the United States, announced its abandonment of Stalinism, but in an almost apologetic way. Trotsky was unimpressed. 'Weak, weak, too weak! They declare their independence, good! They will think for themselves, fine! They will be free, yes, but not too long. They speak too much on their knees, they speak with excuses as if they are half ashamed.'

The young American visitor to whom these remarks were addressed asked whether the world had not had enough of ringing manifestos and rhetoric. Was not this moderation also an effective way? 'Do we have to denounce the lies in creation before we set out to live life as we think we should?' And the answer came back at once: 'In politics, yes. Absolutely. If lies speak loudly, then truth must speak twice as loud.'[23]

How few of the faithful were left was indicated by the foundation congress of the Trotskyist Fourth International, at the home of Alfred Rosmer, near Paris, on 3 September 1938. Twenty-one delegates, from organizations in eleven countries, attended. But the membership of these organizations in general stretched from a few dozen to a few hundred; and even the strongest of them, the Socialist Workers' Party in the United States, formed after various splits and mergers in the preceding January, had less than 1000.[24] The two Polish delegates, while agreeing that the Second and Third Internationals were now 'morally dead', argued against attempting to establish a new International in 'a period of intense reaction', on the grounds that it would be 'an empty gesture'. They were defeated by nineteen votes to three.

President of the congress was Max Shachtman, of the United States Socialist Workers' Party. Along with James Burnham, professor of philosophy at New York University, he was foremost among Trotsky's remaining disciples in castigating those who had deserted: accusing them of 'treason to the working class and Marxism'. With the conclusion of the

Stalin–Hitler Pact and the outbreak of the Second World War, they too deserted. Burnham insisted that it had become 'impossible to regard the Soviet Union as a workers' state in any sense whatever'. And Shachtman, defining the Soviet seizure of eastern Poland as 'imperialist', pressed that the Socialist Workers' Party abandon its pledge to defend the Soviet Union.

The pact, like the outbreak of war, came as no surprise to Trotsky. He had been warning since 1933 that Stalin would seek an understanding with Hitler. And he did not now accept the Stalinist apologies for military conquest as the triumphant march of socialism. 'It is true', he wrote in the *New York Times* of 4 October 1939,

that in the occupied regions the Kremlin is proceeding to expropriate the large proprietors. But this is not a revolution accomplished by the masses, but an administrative reform, designed to extend the regime of the USSR into the new territories. Tomorrow, in the 'liberated' regions, the Kremlin will pitilessly crush the workers and peasants in order to bring them into subjection to the totalitarian bureaucracy. Hitler does not fear this type of 'revolution' on his borders – and, in his own way, he is absolutely right.[25]

But he saw in this no reason to change his view of Soviet society. And, on his own terms, he was right. If the Soviet Union had been a workers' state before the pact and the invasion of Poland, it did not cease to be so in consequence of either.

The dispute raged the more furiously with the Red Army's invasion of Finland. Trotsky called it a 'shameful war' and a 'tragic adventure', launched 'without moral and material preparation'. He derided the recently proclaimed 'super-Napoleon' who had not even thought to visit the front, and had 'remained cautiously in the Kremlin surrounded by telephones and secretaries'.[26] But rejecting the call for armed intervention by the Allies to help Finland, he again insisted that the defence of the Soviet Union must be every revolutionary socialist's overriding resolve. He recited the declaration that he had made to a central committee meeting in August 1927. 'For the socialist fatherland? Yes. For Stalin's course? No!'[27]

His critics within the Socialist Workers' Party would have none of this. Burnham refused to 'fight alongside the GPU for the salvation of the counter-revolution in the Kremlin'. He and Shachtman, finding themselves in a minority, withdrew to form a new party, which soon disintegrated in an abandonment of revolutionary socialism altogether. Other Trotskyist groups, especially in France, lost some of their leading members. Trotsky turned to whip such apostasy. But he could not disguise his sorrow at the end of his association with so close and long-devoted a colleague as Shachtman. There were so few left who had shared the struggle of his exile and whose qualities had earned his respect. And even these were now abandoning him.

In late 1938, Diego Rivera publicly attacked President Cárdenas as 'an accomplice of the Stalinists' and backed, for the forthcoming elections, a general who promised to deal severely with the trade unions. Trotsky announced that he continued to hold Rivera's artistic genius in the highest regard, and to believe in his personal integrity; but that he would not support Rivera's 'political blunderings' and, therefore, felt himself unable to continue accepting his hospitality. He rented, and then bought, a large house on the outskirts of Coyoacan, which had a wide stream, generally dry, on one side, and a dusty road, with some adobe hovels, on the other. Around the grounds a wall was built, with a solid iron gate which opened to a visitor only after he had been examined through a spyhole, and the guards had been given explicit instructions to admit him. Now more than ever, Trotsky expected some agent of Stalin's to strike at him.

All this had involved considerable expense, at the same time as his earnings were much reduced. His American publisher, impatient at the rate at which portions of the *Stalin* manuscript were arriving, refused further advances, and literary agents were finding it difficult to place his articles. In order both to raise money and to lodge them beyond the reach of Stalin's agents, Trotsky offered his archives for sale to the New York Public Library, to Stanford and to Harvard. The institutions seem to have been strangely unexcited by the prospect of acquiring the most valuable collection of Russian revolutionary material outside the Soviet Union. The negotiations dragged on for over a year. At last, Harvard, having refused to consider paying more than 6000 dollars, acquired the archives for 15,000 dollars. In purely financial terms, it proved to be a bargain of which Harvard's Puritan founders might well have been proud.

Meanwhile, he was forced to borrow from friends, and must have felt all too keenly the shame of having to do so. His enemies in Mexico never rested for long in their campaign against him. When General Cedillo organized a revolt against President Cárdenas, Trotsky was accused in the press of complicity in the attempt. When President Cárdenas ordered the nationalization of the Mexican oil industry, Trotsky was accused of having master-minded the move. Each denial seemed only to provoke another charge. Never far from his mind was the thought of those who had been so close and had fallen to Stalin's ferocity; and never far, too, the thought that he might be next to fall. He knew how much of a prison his own home had become, and how useless all his precautions were likely to prove. Beyond the iron gate, some thirty paces away, a few Mexican police stood guard against the emissaries of Stalin. No one needed to tell Trotsky that when the emissaries came, they would not so easily be stopped. He suffered from violent headaches. Natalia sometimes heard him, alone in his study, sighing deeply and saying to himself: 'I am tired, so tired. I can't take any more.'[28]

But he would not have been Trotsky if he had given way to despair. Each morning early, before the Mexican sky caught fire, he dressed and relaxed, by feeding his chickens and rabbits, and examining the cactus plants that he had brought back from the lava desert of Pedregal. Perhaps in these plants, which seemed so to delight him, he found a symbol of the very will to win against all the odds. Then, emerging only for meals, he would shut himself the whole day in his study: dictating to his Russian secretary; reading and researching; receiving visitors at his desk. On occasions, he would leave the fortified house in Coyoacan: to go fishing in the gulf or driving far in search of new cactus varieties for his collection. He carried part of his prison with him; for he was always accompanied by his bodyguards. But he tried to forget, for the while, the cold at the edge of the sunlight. And sometimes he would laugh, and his companions would notice that the troubled look had gone from his blue eyes, and he would return to his work with replenished energy.

In October 1939, his old friends, the Rosmers, visited him from France and brought with them his grandson Seva. It was the end of an ugly struggle for possession of the child. Lyova's wife Jeanne had taken care of him since his mother's suicide and, childless herself, had clung to him all the more fervently after Lyova's death. Trotsky invited her to come with the child and live at the house in Coyoacan, but she refused. And since she belonged to a Trotskyist sect at odds with Trotsky himself, she was publicly supported by her political colleagues in her decision to keep the child. Persuaded that there was no alternative, Trotsky resorted to the law. And twice he received judgment in his favour. But Jeanne would not comply and removed the child from Paris, to place him in hiding. He was traced at last by Marguerite Rosmer, who seized possession of him.

The long struggle was the more distressing for Trotsky because he recognized that Jeanne had earned, by her love and care of the child, a moral claim. Indeed, he had declared this in a letter to the court; and even, despite the bitterness of the quarrel, had repeated his proposal that she come to Mexico herself. But he would not surrender his own right to the child. As he wrote to the boy, he wished personally to explain 'the high value of these ideas and purposes, for the sake of which our family has suffered and is suffering so much'. And most urgently, he must have longed to see Seva: the only one of his grandchildren outside of Russia and, for all he knew, the last of them left alive. If he paused to ask himself how safe Seva might be in the house at Coyoacan, he would have remembered remorsefully how he had discouraged Lyova from leaving France. But then, what place was safe from Stalin's fury? And, indeed, in that same October that Trotsky was at last able to hug and kiss his grandson, his own murderer arrived in Mexico.

Ramon Mercador was the son of a Spanish Communist, Caridad, who had become the mistress of a senior official in the GPU.[29] Sent by the official to a school for secret agents in Spain, he graduated to an institution of higher learning in Moscow, and by 1938 seems to have been considered ready to assume his role. Calling himself Jacques Mornard, he was in Paris for the arrival of Sylvia Agelof, an American Trotskyist who was to act as an interpreter at the foundation congress of the Fourth International. Kindness would have called her plain. And he was conventionally handsome. She became his mistress. He took her to expensive restaurants and night clubs. He had an abundance of money. It came, he told her, from his rich father in Brussels and from his own writings on sport for various newspapers. He promised to follow her, as soon as possible, to New York.

When he arrived there in September 1939, the two lived together, for a short while, in Greenwich Village. He was travelling on a Canadian passport, in the name of Frank Jacson. He claimed never to have been in New York before, but seemed to know his way around the city. Such particulars puzzled her. But he was always ready with an explanation. And he appeared only bored by her attempts to interest him in Trotskyism. In October he left for Mexico City, where he was to work, he told her, for an export–import firm. He asked her to join him there, and she agreed to do so when she could get leave from her own job with the City Home Relief Bureau.

In January 1940, she arrived in Mexico and was soon, with her command of Russian, proving useful to Trotsky. Frank Jacson drove her to the house in Coyoacan each morning, and collected her in the evening. But he indicated no desire to be invited inside. He contented himself with getting to know the guards and making himself amiable to the Rosmers, whom he met one day at the gates and subsequently took out to meals in Mexico City or on sightseeing trips. Only once did he seriously arouse Sylvia's suspicions. He gave her the address of his office, and she found that he had lied to her. When she confronted him, he explained that he had made a mistake and gave her another address. Remembering a similar mistake of his in Paris, she asked Marguerite Rosmer to investigate. The second address appeared to be genuine, and the Rosmers expressed themselves satisfied. But Sylvia might have had some nagging doubt. At all events, before returning in March to New York, she extracted a promise from him that he would not enter the house at Coyoacan in her absence.

It was a promise that he soon broke, but with an excuse that Sylvia was bound to accept. Rosmer fell ill, and Jacson, that 'obliging young man' of Sylvia's, was called to help. He drove Rosmer to the hospital, brought him back, and ran various related errands. He still made no effort to meet Trotsky. But he was now familiar with the inside of the fortified house, and with its guards. One of these, a young American with red hair, called Robert Sheldon Harte, became a friend, and the two of them often went out together. On the night of 23/24 May, some men visited Jacson at the holiday camp where he was living, and took away with them a trunk and two suitcases which he had deposited in the office.

At around four o'clock on the morning of the 24th, Trotsky was woken by the sound of gun-fire. His head was still heavy with the effect of the sedative he had taken, and at first he thought that some Mexicans must be celebrating with fireworks one of those numerous national or religious holidays. But Natalia whispered to him: 'They're shooting! They're shooting into the room!' Covering his body with her own, she pushed him on to the floor, between the bed and the wall. And there they lay, while flashes pierced the darkness, and bullets spattered the room. Suddenly, they heard Seva scream, 'Grandfather!' in a cry that seemed at the same time a warning and a call. 'They've taken him,' Trotsky whispered. The firing continued, and then stopped. In the long silence that followed, Natalia was sure that all the others had been killed and that someone must come soon to kill Trotsky as well. What could she do? Where could she hide him? And at last there came Seva's voice, ringing out, 'Al-fred! Mar-gue-rite!'

They tried to open the door that led from the bedroom into the study, but it had been locked by the assailants. Natalia was to remember noting, through the bullet holes in the door, 'the papers and books looking immaculate in the calm glow of the shaded lamp on the desk'. Fire from an incendiary bomb was eating at the floor and a wardrobe in Seva's room, to which the door stood open. Natalia, seizing some rugs and blankets, smothered the flames; burning her arms and legs. Then they pounded on the study door, and one of the secretaries came to open it. Seva had been wounded slightly in the foot, and a trail of blood led into the garden. There he was playing quietly, as the grass smouldered from another incendiary bomb. Nearby was a third bomb, which was packed with enough dynamite to have destroyed the whole house, but which had failed to explode. Seva, too, had saved himself by rolling to the floor at the sound of firing.

When the members of the household assembled, Sheldon Harte, whose turn it had been to do sentry duty at the gate, was found to be missing. The great iron gate itself was standing open. The two cars, kept in readiness with their keys in the ignition, were gone. And the police guards in the hut outside were tied and helpless. They reported that Harte had been led out by two of the raiders, who had held him by his arms, and that he had offered no resistance. Colonel Sanchez Salazar, chief of the presidential police, was at the house within half an hour. His suspicion stirred at the 'perfect self-control' which Trotsky and his wife displayed, and was fortified by the signs of how extensive the raid had been: so many attackers, he thought, so many fire-arms, even bombs, and only a slight injury to the grandchild's foot. When Trotsky led him away to the rabbit hutches and told him in a low voice that the author of the attack was Stalin, acting through the GPU, Salazar finally assumed that it had all been a put-up job. The motive was obvious to him: Trotsky would gain widespread sympathy and discredit his opponents in the Mexican Communist Party. Salazar ordered the immediate arrest of three servants, and then of two secretaries.

What Salazar assumed, the local Stalinist press was trumpeting; and the accusation was repeated by the New York *Nation* in an article entitled 'Mexico's Phantom Conspiracy'. Trotsky was enraged at this campaign and at the course that the investigation appeared to be taking. He protested at the arrest of his secretaries to President Cárdenas, who ordered their instant release. The police arrested some of the raiders and discovered, as Trotsky himself had suggested, that the trail led to David Alfaro Siqueiros, a celebrated painter, who had been among the founders of the Mexican Communist Party and was editor of the Communist paper, *El Machete*. It was he, it emerged, who had obtained the police uniforms in which the raiders had been dressed, the arms and the transport; he who had, in the uniform of a major, personally directed the raid. He went into hiding; and from there, far from denying the part that he had played, proudly proclaimed it. Indeed, he warned that 'all the enemies of the Communist Party can expect similar treatment. . . .' He was subsequently arrested; and, released on bail, escaped from Mexico.

One of the minor figures in the affair, an out-of-work electrician, told the police of a dilapidated farmhouse some thirteen miles from Mexico City in the desert, where he had spent several days in solitary charge of a tall young American with red hair. On 25 June, police visited the house and found the earth of the basement floor disturbed. Digging with pick-axes, they uncovered the body of Sheldon Harte. A bullet had been fired, at close range, through the head. The following morning, Trotsky arrived at the police station to identify the body. He stood for some moments looking down at it, and his eyes filled with tears.

Salazar himself was convinced that Sheldon Harte had been an accomplice in the assassination attempt. Witnesses reported that the young man had wandered freely and alone around the area of the farmhouse. His own father, arriving from New York while the search was still proceeding, expressed surprise that Sheldon had been working for Trotsky. In his bedroom at home, the boy had had a photograph of Stalin. That the GPU had first used and then killed him, in fear of what he might say if he fell into the hands of the police, seemed to Salazar the only explanation that fitted the facts.[30] But Trotsky would not be persuaded that one whom he and Natalia had so trusted might have betrayed him. Upon a wall of the garden in Coyoacan, he had a stone plaque placed: 'In Memory of Robert Sheldon Harte, 1915–1940. Murdered by Stalin.' Years later, Natalia herself would recall the 'fair-haired young man with fine features, an idealist who had lost his heart to Mexico. He had loved watching the brilliantly coloured birds in the aviary. . . .'[31]

On 28 May, only four days after the raid, Jacson met Trotsky for the first time. The Rosmers were to leave by ship for the United States; and, explaining that he had business of his own in the port city of Vera Cruz, he had offered to drive them there. Arriving to collect them just before eight in the morning, he encountered Trotsky, who was busy feeding his rabbits. The two men shook hands; talked briefly about rabbits; and then Jacson went off to give Seva a toy glider. At Trotsky's suggestion, Natalia invited the visitor to breakfast. And from then on, the guards would open the gate whenever he called. A fortnight later, he came to Coyoacan again; but only for a few minutes, to say that he was going to New York and would leave his car behind, for the use of the household. He returned a month later but did not call at the Trotsky house and disappeared for a week or two. Then he telephoned Sylvia, who was still in New York; told her that he had been ill; and pressed her to join him. On 29 July, he visited the house to collect his car. And he came again on several occasions in August, bringing chocolates or flowers for Natalia and toys for Seva.

But there had been a change in him since his visit to New York. And Sylvia, who had come to Mexico City, noticed it at once. He had always been so alert and taken so much trouble with his clothes. Now he loitered about in pyjamas for much of the day and carried an old raincoat over his arm when he left the hotel. He had been an easy talker. Now he jumped from subject to subject or lapsed into sudden silence. On one occasion, when driving along a mountain road, he swerved the car and it stopped only at the very edge of the drop. Sylvia began to suspect that he was involved in some secret service work. But he now expressed open admiration of Trotsky; and would say, again and again, 'He has the greatest intellect in the world!' Indeed, at the house in Coyoacan, it was she who defended the view of Trotskyist dissidents such as Shachtman, while he made it clear that he sided with Trotsky himself.

Natalia noticed how pale his complexion had become, and she asked him whether he was ill. One of the guards described him as sweating and almost green: 'as if some poison were working its way through to the skin'. He was sometimes morose and then all at once ebullient. He boasted about his 'boss', a 'brilliant businessman' who had made a fortune from speculation. Both Trotsky and Natalia found this talk distasteful; and Trotsky, wondering whether that 'fabulously rich boss' was 'some profiteer with Fascist tendencies', suggested that 'it might be best to stop seeing Sylvia's husband altogether'. But it was a suggestion made in a moment and left there.

On 17 August, Jacson arrived at the house, with the draft of an article attacking the Shachtman dissidents. He asked Trotsky to read and, where necessary, correct it. After ten minutes alone with him in the study, Trotsky emerged obviously troubled. The draft was without interest; confused and full of banal phrases. And instead of taking a chair, Jacson had sat on the edge of the table, without removing his hat, and still carrying his raincoat over his arm. It had seemed more than mere discourtesy. 'I don't like him,' Trotsky said to Natalia. 'What sort of fellow is he? We ought to make a few inquiries. . . .' But beyond confiding, two days later, his disquiet to one of his secretaries, Trotsky said nothing to prevent another visit. Indeed, he had already invited one: by recommending a few amendments to the draft and telling Jacson to return when he had made them.

It was subsequently to emerge that Jacson had come, on the 17th, with an ice-pick such as mountain climbers use, a dagger and an automatic pistol, all concealed in the raincoat that he carried over his arm. He had succeeded in getting Trotsky alone with him in the study and had perched himself on the table in a position to make his attack. Why, then, had he failed to act at once? His behaviour risked the arousal of Trotsky's suspicions and a closer surveillance next time, if not a refusal to receive him altogether. If this was a dress rehearsal, then that in itself was curious: since assassins have not commonly gone to such lengths in preparing for the actual performance. His state of mind must remain a mystery. But it is likely enough that he had been given his final instructions during his visit to New York, and that the agitation which he displayed on his return reflected his distress at the assignment. Since the GPU would scarcely have chosen someone of untested metal, it must be supposed that this distress was a response to the nature not of the act but of the victim.

He might well have found it difficult to resist altogether the spell of Trotsky's personality. And he doubtless found it difficult to reconcile the man he had met with the monster of the Stalinist script. Above all, perhaps, the sheer magnitude of the part he was now required to play dismayed him. For this was no minor political figure he would stab, in some dark alley, so that he might hope to escape unseen. He was to strike down a giant of the times, and on an open stage before the footlights of history. His strange conduct, his various moods and talk of suicide, his loose lies, suggest a virtual invitation to premature exposure. Rather than a dress rehearsal, his visit on the 17th might well have been the intended performance for which, at the last moment, his nerve failed him. But it is at least conceivable as well that he was engaged, consciously or not, in a challenge to his fate; presenting his victim with a decisive opportunity to suspect him and so to save them both.

Trotsky, however, was not to be saved. And he was not to be saved because the conditions of his safety were not such as his very view of life would allow. Some American friends, visiting him in June after the raid, entreated him to 'go underground' and allow himself to be smuggled into the United States, where they assured him of a secure refuge. He refused. He would not spend the rest of his life hiding from death. One well-wisher sent him a bullet-proof vest. He 'piously admired' it and consigned it to the use of the sentry on the watchtower. Grudgingly he agreed, under pressure from the Mexican authorities, to the further fortification of the house, with armoured doors and with steel shutters on the windows. Inspecting the changes, he remarked in revulsion to Joseph Hansen, one of his secretaries: 'This reminds me of the first jail I was in. The doors make the same sound. . . . This is not a home; it is a medieval prison.' Repeatedly his secretaries urged that a bodyguard should be present when he received strangers in his study and that visitors should be searched for hidden weapons. He objected that those who came to see him might wish to discuss personal matters and feel inhibited by the presence of a guard. And he would not consider having those who expected his trust searched in suspicion. Indeed, even after his disquieting interview of the 17th, he curtly dismissed a suggestion, from one of the Americans in the household, that Jacson should be searched.

'Come, come!' he cried. 'What are you thinking of?' He refused to believe that anyone who had been for two years the companion of a friend 'so unaffected and agreeable' as Sylvia, and who had, moreover, been received with such courtesy and kindness in his home, might be planning his murder. And this reaches to the deepest truth of his tragedy. For Trotsky, despite all that he had seen and all that he had endured, retained to the end his trust and his essential innocence. But then, perhaps only because of this trust and this innocence, had he been able to continue in defiance of so much; so faithful to his faith in man and to his love of life.

And, paradoxically, it was just this love of life that made him so ready to accept the necessity of death. On 27 February, he wrote his testament. His blood pressure was high and rising; and he declared 'the outcome' to be 'evidently near'. He refused to defend his revolutionary honour against the lies of Stalinism. New revolutionary generations would rehabilitate it, along with that of all others who had fallen victim to similar slander. He warmly thanked the friends who had remained loyal to him through the most difficult hours of his life, but named none of them because he could not name them all. He paid particular tribute only to Natalia Ivanovna Sedova, who had, for almost forty years of their life together, been 'an inexhaustible source of love, magnanimity and tenderness'. She had undergone great sufferings, especially in the last period of their lives together, but he found some comfort in the fact that she had also known days of happiness.

He followed this with a short credo.

For forty-three years of my conscious life I have remained a revolutionist; for forty-two of them I have fought under the banner of Marxism. If I had to begin all over again I would of course try to avoid this or that mistake, but the main course of my life would remain unchanged. I shall die a proletarian revolutionist, a Marxist, a dialectical materialist, and, consequently, an irreconcilable atheist. My faith in the communist future of mankind is not less ardent, indeed it is firmer today, than it was in the days of my youth.

But these were the words and not the music of his mind. And as he watched the movements of Natalia, he found the music also.

Natasha has just come up to the window from the courtyard and opened it wider so that the air may enter more freely into my room. I can see the bright green strip of grass beneath the wall, and the clear blue sky above the wall, and sunlight everywhere. Life is beautiful. Let the future generations cleanse it of all evil, oppression and violence, and enjoy it to the full.

He signed and dated the document. Suddenly, realizing that he had still in due form to dispose of his property, he added a grant of all his possessions and literary rights to 'my wife, Natalia Ivanovna Sedova'. Again he signed and dated the document. And then he was struck by a thought. 'In case we both die. . . .' But he left the rest of the page blank. Perhaps it was the one possibility that he could not bring himself to face. For when, a few days later, on 3 March, he returned to the document, he did not complete the sentence. Instead, he provided a postscript on the possibility of his suicide. The nature of his illness, he wrote, suggested that his end would come suddenly and, 'most likely', through a brain haemorrhage. He could not wish for a better end. But if he was to prove mistaken, and should be 'threatened with a long-drawn-out invalidism', then he reserved the right to determine for himself the time of his death.

The 'suicide' (if such a term is appropriate in this connection) will not in any respect be an expression of an outburst of despair or hopelessness. Natasha and I said more than once that one may arrive at such a physical condition that it would be better to cut short one's own life or, more correctly, the too slow process of dying. . . . But whatever may be the circumstances of my death, I shall die with unshaken faith in the communist future. This faith in man and in his future gives me even now such power of resistance as cannot be given by any religion.[32]

It is in this context that those occasional sighs of tiredness and distress, which Natalia would hear coming from him as he worked in his study alone, must be understood. They were cries of protest not against life itself, but against so much that conspired to make it ugly. And if he did not look to death as to a refuge, nor did he look away from it, in revolt. He was ready: to receive it when it came, or run to meet it, if the very dignity of life required that he should not wait. It was this, more than his customary courage, that explains the calm, indeed, the serenity, of his reaction to the raid in May.

He had taken a double dose of sleeping pills on the night of 19 August, and woke to the following day with a now all too rare feeling of vigour. He did not make his usual comment to Natalia: 'There you are. We've slept through a whole night and nobody has killed us. And you're still not satisfied.' Instead, rising almost at once, he told her how well he felt. 'I'll do a good day's work.' By quarter past seven, he was busy in the garden, seeing to his rabbits and plants. At nine he went into breakfast and then to his study, where he dealt with his post. He wrote light-hearted letters to two American Trotskyists who were serving prison sentences for strike activity and were about to be released. He thanked an American friend for having sent him a *Dictionary of American Slang*.

At meal times I must permanently keep this book in my hands in order to be able to understand the conversation. . . . I had hoped to find some abbreviations for the various sciences, philosophical theories, etc.; but instead I found about 25 expressions for an attractive girl.

Then he took up the article he had begun on his attitude to military service in the war. He was clearly moving away from his outlook of a Leninist revolutionary defeatism, towards alignment with the majority of American workers, who had recently declared themselves, in a public opinion poll, in favour of conscription. He continued to hold that the Second World War was a continuation of the First. But he saw it also as a 'development', a 'deepening', in which it was proper to defend democracy against fascism, as part of the larger revolutionary struggle.

At lunch-time, he discussed with his Mexican lawyer some of the attacks made on him in the local Stalinist press and agreed to take the offensive with proceedings for defamation. After his usual siesta, he returned to his work; and Natalia, opening the door of the study from time to time, noted with gladness how well he looked. At five o'clock, they had tea together. And then, some twenty minutes later, she saw him at the bottom of the garden, near the rabbit hutches, with another man. She did not recognize the visitor until he came up to her and took off his hat. It was Jacson, and she caught herself wondering why he had taken to visiting them so often. 'I am terribly thirsty,' he said. 'Could I have a glass of water?' She asked him whether he wanted a cup of tea. But he replied, 'No, I had a late lunch, and I'm full up to here,' pointing to his throat. His face looked green, and he was more nervous than she had ever seen him before. 'Why are you wearing your hat and raincoat in such fine weather?' she asked. 'Because it might rain,' he replied. But the question had clearly disturbed him, for he did not at first reply when she asked him how Sylvia was. Then, recovering himself, he muttered, 'Sylvia? Sylvia? She is always well.' He drank a glass of water and told her that he had brought his article, typewritten this time, for Trotsky to see.

She accompanied him to the rabbit hutches, where Trotsky told her that Sylvia was coming and that the two would be leaving for New York the following day. She mentioned that she had offered their visitor tea, but that he was not feeling well and had only taken a glass of water. Trotsky looked at him closely and commented: 'You don't look well. That's not good.' Then, he said, 'Oh, well, are you going to show me your article?' Reluctantly, he took off his gardening gloves. Natalia went along as far as the study door and then into the next room. Three or four minutes later, she heard 'a terrible piercing cry'.[33]

In the study, Trotsky had sat at his table to read the article. And Jacson, taking the ice-pick from his raincoat pocket, had brought it down on Trotsky's head, with such great force that it penetrated several centimetres deep. Trotsky had leapt to his feet, with that scream which to Jacson himself seemed 'infinitely long'; snatched objects from the table and hurled them at Jacson; then seized and struggled with him; wrested the ice-pick from his hand; and grabbing a finger, bit it. Jacson backed away, knocking over a bookcase and chairs; then pushed Trotsky, who staggered through the door to the dining-room.

He leant against the door-frame: his face covered with blood; his blue eyes, without his glasses, glittering; his arms hanging limply by his side. 'What has happened? What has happened?' Natalia cried; putting her arms around him. 'Jacson,' he answered calmly; as though to say, she felt, 'Now it is done.' He slumped down on the floor. 'Natasha,' he said, 'I love you. . . .' She wiped the blood from his face and put ice on the wound in his head. He spoke with increasing effort. 'Get Seva away. . . . You know . . . in there,' and he signalled towards the study. 'I thought . . . I understood . . . what he wanted to do . . . he wanted . . . once more . . . I didn't let him.' And Natalia caught a note of satisfaction in that murmur, of how he had stopped his assassin from striking a second blow.

In the study, members of the household were hitting Jacson with their fists and pistol butts. He cried: 'They made me!' And then: 'They've got my mother!' Trotsky, whether aware of what was happening or only suspecting the reaction of his followers, murmured to Natalia: 'He must not . . . be . . . killed . . . he must talk.' But Jacson said little more, beyond repeating, 'Sylvia had nothing to do with this. . . . The GPU had nothing to do with this. . . .' When the guards stopped beating him, he asked, 'Why don't you kill me?' Natalia and Joseph Hansen knelt beside Trotsky. He thought that Jacson had shot him. Hansen told him that he had been struck with an ice-pick and that his wound was not serious. But Trotsky, pointing to his heart, murmured: 'I feel . . . here . . . that this is the end. . . . This time . . . they've . . . succeeded.' Again and again he pressed Natalia's hand to his lips. And he asked Hansen to take care of Natalia. 'She has been with me many years.' Natalia bent over him; crying and kissing his wound.

The police on duty outside had already rung for an ambulance, and one of the guards had run for a doctor. When the stretcher-bearers arrived, Natalia, thinking of Lyova's death in hospital, did not want Trotsky taken away: and he, too, refused. But when Hansen promised that the guards would accompany him, he gave his consent. The city was already lit for the night when the ambulance raced through the streets, its siren wailing. Trotsky's left arm lay paralysed, while his right made helpless circles in the air, till it found Natalia. At the hospital, the stretcher-bearers had to thrust their way through a crowd of the curious, and Natalia shivered in fear that someone might strike at him there, yet again. A nurse started to cut his grey hair. And he smiled at Natalia: whispering, 'You see, here's the barber.' They had spoken earlier that very day of sending for one. Then, turning to Hansen, he asked him to take out his notebook and he dictated a few, scarcely audible, disconnected sentences.

I am close to death from the blow of a political assassin . . . struck me down in my room. I struggled with him . . . we . . . entered . . . talk about French statistics . . . he struck me . . . please say to our friends . . . I am sure . . . of victory . . . of Fourth International . . . go forward.

The nurse began to cut away his clothes, for his operation. Suddenly he spoke with grave distinctness, to Natalia: 'I don't want them to undress me . . . I want you to do it. . . .' She undressed him and pressed her lips to his. He returned the kiss three times. And then he lost consciousness. Five surgeons operated on him. But the damage to the brain was too serious. All night, Natalia sat at his bedside; waiting for him to recover and thinking of how often he had come safely through dangers that had seemed so certain to overwhelm him. Throughout the night and the next day, he remained in a coma. Natalia at last fell asleep in an armchair, and then suddenly awoke to find two doctors in white looking down at her.

She understood at once. Trotsky had died a few moments before, at 7.25 on the evening of 21 August.

Jacson had been taken to the same hospital. In the ambulance, on the way, the police read the letter which he had been carrying on him. It declared that his real name was Jacques Mornard; and that he had come to Mexico as one of Trotsky's fervent followers, with help from the Fourth International. But he had then discovered the existence of Trotsky's 'close ties . . . with certain leaders of capitalist countries', and he had come to realize that Trotsky himself was using the struggles of the workers only to satisfy his own petty desire for revenge. Ordered by Trotsky to see no more of the woman whom he loved with all his heart, and to visit Russia for the purpose of arranging Stalin's assassination, he had rebelled and decided to assassinate Trotsky instead.

Salazar, in charge of the investigation and suspicious of Sylvia's complicity with Jacson, had her brought to the hospital as well. And there he arranged for the two to confront each other. When Jacson saw her, he struggled to free himself from his guards and cried: 'Why have you brought me here? What have you done? Take me out.' Sylvia, lifting her head and looking at him, screamed: 'Kill him! He has murdered Trotsky. Kill him! Kill him!' Salazar told her of the statement by Jacson that he had killed Trotsky out of love for her. 'All lies,' she screamed. 'What have you to reply?' Salazar asked him. 'Nothing! Nothing!' Jacson shouted: 'Take me away!' Salazar asked Sylvia: 'What do you think of him?' Sylvia, looking at Jacson, tried to spit in his face.

Jacques Mornard, alias Jacson, was brought to trial in the spring of 1942 and sentenced, a year later, to twenty years in jail. His mother Caridad received from Stalin the Order of Lenin for herself; and, to keep for her son, the order making him a Hero of the Soviet Union. In 1950, his identity as Ramon Mercador was established by a Mexican psychiatrist, who visited Spain and matched the fingerprints of Mornard with those of Mercador in the police files there. He proved to be a model prisoner and studied electrical engineering to such effect that he was put in charge of his prison's electrical system. In 1960 he was released; spent some time in the Soviet Union; and then settled in Prague, where he worked as a radio and television mechanic.

For five days, Trotsky's body lay in state, and some 300,000 people filed past it. In the streets of the city, a popular ballad lamented how destiny had conquered him in his own home, with the hand of a cowardly assassin. A short note in *Pravda* informed the people of the Soviet Union that Trotsky had been murdered by 'a disillusioned follower'. On 27 August, the body was cremated, and the ashes were buried in the garden of the house at Coyoacan. On the white rectangular stone raised over the grave, there are only the two words, LEON TROTSKY, with a hammer and sickle below.

In early March 1953, Stalin had a haemorrhage in the brain which slowly but relentlessly affected his breathing, till he was choking to death. In his final hours, his face grew dark and his lips black. Then, just before the end, his daughter would recall, he

opened his eyes and cast a glance over everyone in the room. It was a terrible glance, insane or perhaps angry and full of fear of death. . . . He suddenly lifted his left hand as though he were pointing to something up above and bringing down a curse on us all. The gesture was incomprehensible and full of menace, and no one could say to whom or what it might be directed.[34]

Khrushchev would, not long afterwards, come to command the state. He had been among the main minions of Stalin's terror and had known how to cringe before the narrowing eyes of Stalin's mistrust. He would take his safe revenge, for all those years of self-abasement, in his selective disclosure of Stalinist crimes to the twentieth congress of the Party in February 1956.

It was the start of that process, which Trosky had predicted so confidently would occur, to rehabilitate the 'revolutionary honour' of Stalin's more prominent victims. Towards Trotsky himself, however, the new regime remained relentless; paying him, by refusing to reconsider his historical role, the tribute of its fear.

The relentlessness remains, through every announcement or rumour of a new rehabilitation. Yet on the surface, there is little to feed so much fear. Within the Soviet Union itself, the various brave trickles of dissent have other sources. Jews demanding the right of emigration to Israel; those such as Solzhenitsyn, whose devotions burn with all the smoking oil of Holy Russia; campaigners for the civil liberties allowed in Western democracies: these are not Trotsky's particular disciples.

In the protectorates of eastern Europe, no movement of revolt has spoken in Trotsky's name. Even in the Czechoslovakia of 1968, where the reform of a Marxist regime rather than the assertion of nationalism was the dynamic, no photograph of Trotsky led a procession through the streets. And elsewhere in the world of institutional Marxism, Trotsky represents no more immediate or conspicuous a threat. In the development of its conflict with the Soviet Union, Maoist China chose to define its ideological differences not by honouring Trotsky, but by continuing to honour Stalin.

In the advanced capitalist world, which is the ultimate prize, Trotskyism is a factional disorder. There is no danger to the domain of the Communist parties from those who wave the banners of Trotsky in the air only to send them crashing down on one another's heads. It is, rather, the Communist parties themselves, with their search for a national character and some accommodation to the values of liberal democracy, which alarm the Soviet leadership. And this is a search that not even the Soviet leadership would associate with Trotsky.

But then the fear of Trotsky is not a fear of his followers. It is a fear of himself.

It is a fear, first, of his explicit challenge to the authority of the regime. Before his death, he had denied the dogma of party infallibility; the claim of the party to represent the revolution; the right of the party to the government of the Soviet Union. From anyone else, securely dead, such denials might be merely dismissed. From Trotsky they come with all the authority of his historical life.

The fear of Trotsky is, indeed, the fear of history. For the regime can maintain its authority only as long as much of the past remains buried. That is why its undertaking to rehabilitate the victims of Stalinism has stopped at clearing away some of the soil. For to dig any deeper may uncover too many traces of Trotsky's revolutionary role and, with them, too many traces of the revolution itself.

In the end, the fear of Trotsky is the fear of that very revolution which the rulers of the Soviet Union have abandoned in all but name. And Trotsky speaks to them in its threatening voice. He speaks for the power of people against those who speak for the power of the state. He speaks against privilege to those who speak for the subservience of others. He speaks for the liberation of ideas, to those who speak only for the confinements of their own. He speaks for the will to resist, regardless of cost, to those who know only how to speak for the intimidation of dissent.

It is in the voice of this revolution, too, rejecting and offering, that Trotsky speaks still for humanity. As he spoke when millions of men marched, for the conflict of their countries, to the resolution of the bayonet and the machine-gun, he speaks now to a world of multiplied nationalisms and nuclear weapons. He speaks to a world where within particular states, storehouses contain such hoards of surplus food that terms are borrowed from geography to describe them; while a few jet hours away, famine crosses the frontiers of sovereignty without recognizing the requirement of a passport. And he will speak for as long as wealth is no more than the obverse of want, in the coinage of a system that proclaims itself the source of personal freedom and that provides instead the imprisonments of property.

It is a voice that does not recite the doctrines of the past. Trotsky himself qualified the perceptions of Marx, and history has qualified the perceptions of Trotsky. Capitalism was not, as Trotsky maintained to the end of his life, in its death throes. It was not even, as Fascism believed, hopelessly bed-ridden. In the years since it got to its feet to fight the

Second World War, it has produced, and wasted, more material wealth than in all the many decades of its previous development. It has discovered remedies for some of its ailments. And it has, as an essential part of the process, so transformed the labour force of industrial advancement that this bears scarcely any resemblance to the proletariat of the revolutionary texts. In place of one united by destitution and despair, is one, at least in the main, divided by distinctions of prosperity and addicted to hire-purchase hope. In place of a leadership driven to confront the state as the directorate of private capital is one that belongs to the board of the mixed economy.

What rebellion there has been within the rich world has most notably come from among the very children of enrichment. They are heirs who have rejected their inheritance: the subservience of poverty and the violence required to preserve it; the incorporated greed that fouls and even poisons the very environment on which it feeds; the neon-lit merchandizing of personality, along the pavements of so many lives. In their rejection, they have been far closer to Trotsky than have those militant workers whose militancy is directed to the terms of a new wage contract and whose concern with the workers of the world is less one of affinity than of fear. It is not a closeness that extends to the cult of the drug or the drop-out. It is not a closeness that permits the confusion of the revolutionary with the mystic or the terrorist. But it may be that these rebels, like their predecessors in the Russia of Tsarism, are a symptom of the system's senility; a sign that it is the bars, rather than the spaces between, which are now increasingly seen.

Trotsky believed that men had only to recognize the cage around them to find the means of making their escape. And he struck, above all else, at the cage that is within the mind: of an original sin that consigns redemption to the safe-deposit of another world; or of a permanent primal savagery that informs a past of repeated warning and a future of corresponding restraint. He speaks still, as he spoke in the commitment of his life, for the promise of man's imagination and reason; for the limitlessness of man's reach.

He speaks with the voice of his own achievements: as an intellectual who raised and led to victory the armies of the revolutionary republic; as a politician who made history before, as an artist, re-creating it. In an era of so much separate futility: when so many intellectuals sit whining on the sidelines of events, and so many artists turn their backs to play patience with their sensibilities; when politics is a specialized form of white collar employment, and soldiering asks for all the moral investment of warrior ants: Trotsky bears witness to the creative force of that essential revolutionary, the integral man.

And if he is as well a tragic witness, to the limits imposed by his times and to his own fallibility, he offers, in being tragic, the ultimate in human affirmation. For the protagonist of tragedy transcends as he fulfils his fate. In the long aftermath of his fall, Trotsky remained true to himself: answering so much death around him with his ardour for life; so much despair with his faith. And in this, he speaks for that joy and that defiance in humanity which no defeat can contain.

Notes and references

1 Beginnings (pages 9–21)

1 Thus, though they constituted only 11.6 per cent of the population in the Pale, some 72.8 per cent of all those engaged in commerce there, and 31.4 per cent of those engaged in crafts, were Jewish. See *Encyclopaedia Judaica* (Jerusalem, 1971), vol. 13, *Pale of Settlement*, and vol. 14, *Russia*.
2 Quoted in Joseph Nedava, *Trotsky and the Jews* (Jewish Publication Society of America, Philadelphia, 1971), pp. 22–3.
3 The old Russian calendar was thirteen days behind the Western one. In January 1918, the government of Soviet Russia decreed the adoption of the Western calendar from 1 February, which accordingly became 14 February. Rather than scatter the text throughout with two sets of dates, I have chosen to use the old calender when events in Russia before February 1918 are involved; the Western calendar where otherwise appropriate; and the dates in both calendars when some purpose advises it.
4 Leon Trotsky, *My Life* (Butterworth, London, 1930), p. 9.
5 *Ibid.*, p. 9.
6 *Ibid.*, p. 25.
7 Max Eastman, *Leon Trotsky: The Portrait of a Youth* (Faber & Gwyer, London, 1926), p. 11.
8 Trotsky, p. 38.
9 *Ibid.*, pp. 67–8.
10 *Ibid.*, p. 74.
11 *Ibid.*, pp. 81–2.

2 Commitments pages (22–36)

1 In the decade 1883–92, the population increased by 16 per cent; taxation, by 29 per cent.
2 She was six years older than he, and her father had been a Populist himself.
3 G. A. Ziv, *Trotsky* (New York, 1921), p. 15.
4 *Ibid.*, p. 28.
5 Leon Trotsky, *My Life* (Butterworth, London, 1930), p. 110.
6 Ziv, p. 36.

7 *Ibid.*, pp. 45–6; 41.
8 Isaac Deutscher, *The Prophet Armed* (Oxford University Press, London, 1954), p. 56.

3 Congress and Conflicts (pages 37–53)

1 David Shub, *Lenin* (Penguin, Harmondsworth, 1966), p. 48.
2 The text is in James Maxton, *Lenin* (Peter Davies, London, 1932), pp. 49–52.
3 Quoted in Shub, p. 74.
4 Nadezhda Krupskaya, *Memories of Lenin* (Panther, London, 1970), p. 62.
5 Shub, p. 76.
6 A. V. Shotman, *Reminiscences of an Old Bolshevik* (Moscow, 1932), quoted in Shub, p. 78.
7 V. I. Lenin, *Sobranie Sochineniia*, 4th ed. (Moscow, 1946), vol. 4, p. 311.
8 Leon Trotsky, *Lenin* (Harrap, London, 1925).
9 Leon Trotsky, *Trotsky's Diary in Exile* (Faber, London, 1958), pp. 56–7.
10 Joseph Nedava, *Trotsky and the Jews* (Jewish Publication Society of America, Philadelphia, 1971), p. 95.
11 Krupskaya, p. 86.
12 E. H. Carr, *The Bolshevik Revolution, 1917–23* (3 vols, Penguin, Harmondsworth), vol. 1, p. 43.
13 *Ibid.*
14 As Carr points out, the Russian word *raskol*, which Lenin used, was commonly associated with religious dissent, so that 'schism' seems an appropriate English translation. Carr, vol. 1, p. 48.
15 Leon Trotsky, *My Life* (Butterworth, London, 1930), p. 147.

4 Insurrection (pages 54–84)

1 Quoted in Bertram D. Wolfe, *Three Who Made a Revolution* (Dial Press, New York, 1948), p. 293.
2 David Floyd, *Russia in Revolt* (Macdonald, London, 1969), p. 64.
3 Father Gapon, *The Story of My Life*, quoted in Roger Pethybridge (ed.), *Witnesses to the Russian Revolution* (Allen & Unwin, London, 1964), p. 30.
4 Pethybridge, p. 45.
5 Bernard Pares, *The Fall of the Russian Monarchy* (Cape, London, 1939), pp. 503–4.
6 Leon Trotsky, *1905* (Allen Lane, The Penguin Press, London, 1971), pp. 116–17.
7 *Ibid.*, p. 123.
8 There was not now, and never would be, any question of his obtaining a divorce from Sokolovskaya. For all three this would have involved a surrender to mere convention.
9 Trotsky, *1905*, p. 172.
10 *Ibid.*, p. 176.
11 Just before the fall of the St Petersburg Soviet, Bolsheviks and Mensheviks

were so far in accord as to produce three issues of a joint newspaper, *Severnyi Golos*, to rally support.

12 Nadezhda Krupskaya, *Memories of Lenin* (Panther, London, 1970), p. 126.
13 Leon Trotsky, *My Life* (Butterworth, London, 1930), p. 160.
14 Bernard Pares, *The Fall of the Russian Monarchy* (Cape, London, 1939), p. 91.
15 David Floyd, *Russia in Revolt* (Macdonald, London, 1969), p. 102.
16 *Kadets* in Russian, from the initial letters of their name: *Ka – Dey*.
17 Trotsky, *My Life*, p. 163.
18 Leon Trotsky, *Permanent Revolution* and *Results and Prospects* (New Park Publications, London, 1962), p. 209.
19 Trotsky, *My Life*, p. 164.
20 *Ibid.*, p. 166.
21 The full text of the speech may be found in Trotsky, *1905*, pp. 384–400.
22 The Black Hundreds were an organization, dedicated to 'the unlimited Russian autocracy' and to 'the dominating position' of the Orthodox church in the state, whose gangs were prominent in the conduct of pogroms.
23 Two others received short terms of imprisonment. The remaining thirty-four were acquitted.
24 Trotsky, *1905*, p. 406.
25 *Ibid.*, p. 416.
26 *Ibid.*, p. 413.
27 Trotsky, *My Life*, p. 173.

5 Recession (pages 85–106)

1 Bernard Pares, *The Fall of the Russian Monarchy* (Cape, London, 1939), p. 124.
2 C. E. Vuilliamy (ed.), *The Red Archives* (Geoffrey Bles, London, 1929), p. 40.
3 Alan Moorehead, *The Russian Revolution* (Collins with Hamish Hamilton, London, 1958), p. 83.
4 The Mensheviks refused to recognize it as a party congress; but the Bolsheviks came, in the end, to command the arithmetic.
5 A. Lunacharsky, *Vospominaniya o Lenine* (Moscow, 1933), p. 21.
6 Paul Frölich, *Rosa Luxemburg*, trans. Edward Fitzgerald (Gollancz, London, 1940), p. 105.
7 *Ibid.*, p. 106.
8 Leon Trotsky, *My Life* (Butterworth, London, 1930), p. 176.
9 Maxim Gorky, *Fragments from My Diary* (1924), quoted in Roger Pethybridge (ed.), *Witnesses to the Russian Revolution* (Allen & Unwin, 1964), pp. 54–5.
10 Leon Trotsky, *Collected Works* (1926–9), vol. 10, p. 88.
11 Mark Twain, for instance, was so hostile to Tsarism that he wrote: 'If such a government cannot be overthrown otherwise than by dynamite, then thank God for dynamite.'
12 Trotsky, *My Life*, p. 178.
13 *Ibid.*, p. 183.

14 He thought that it had probably been the appearance of his first book in German that had finally reconciled his parents to his 'fate'. And he recorded this, in his memoirs, before dealing with his mother's illness and death.
15 *Materialism and Empirio-Criticism: Critical Notes on a Reactionary Philosophy.*
16 Quoted in Louis Fischer (*Lenin* (Weidenfeld & Nicolson, London, 1965), p. 69.
17 David Shub, in *Lenin* (Penguin, Harmondsworth, 1966), p. 143, maintains that there were three spies among thirteen voting delegates: but most authorities admit two, among fourteen.
18 Trotsky, *My Life*, p. 195.
19 Joseph Nedava, *Trotsky and the Jews* (The Jewish Publication Society of America, Philadelphia, 1971), pp. 43–5.
20 Trotsky, *My Life*, p. 199.
21 Quoted by Nedava, p. 79. Trotsky's three articles on 'Evreskii Vopros', or 'The Jewish Problem', were published in *Kievan Thought*, nos. 226, 229, 230; and are included in his writings, *Sochinenya*, vol. 4: *1925–7*.
22 Maurice Samuel, *Blood Accusation* (Weidenfeld & Nicolson, London, 1967), gives a detailed account of the affair.
23 Reprinted in Trotsky, *Sochinenya*, vol. 4, pp. 462–76.
24 E. H. Carr, *The Bolshevik Revolution, 1917–23* (3 vols, Penguin, Harmondsworth), vol. 1, p. 74.
25 Leon Trotsky, *Stalin* (Hollis & Carter, London, 1947), p. 244.

6 War and Revolution (107–35)

1 Leonard Schapiro, *The Communist Party of the Soviet Union* (Eyre & Spottiswoode, London, 1970), pp. 141–2.
2 David Shub, *Lenin* (Penguin, Harmondsworth, 1966), p. 156.
3 Sir George Buchanan, *My Mission to Russia* (2 vols, Cassell, London, 1923), vol. 1, p. 215.
4 Leon Trotsky, *My Life* (Butterworth, London, 1930), pp. 203–4.
5 Nadezhda Krupskaya, *Memories of Lenin* (Panther, London, 1970), p. 249.
6 A. V. Lunacharsky, *Revolutionary Silhouettes* (Allen Lane The Penguin Press, London, 1967), p. 63.
7 *Ibid.*, p. 64.
8 Trotsky, *My Life*, p. 213.
9 The International Working Men's Association founded by Marx in 1864.
10 *Nashe Slovo*, 19 October 1915.
11 *Ibid.*, 14 February 1915.
12 Trotsky, *My Life*, p. 232.
13 *Ibid.*, p. 236.
14 Bernard Pares, *The Fall of the Russian Monarchy* (Cape, London, 1939), p. 237.
15 Buchanan, vol. 1, p. 219.
16 E. H. Carr, *The Bolshevik Revolution, 1917–23* (3 vols, Penguin, Harmondsworth), vol. 2, p. 144.
17 Buchanan, vol. 2, pp. 38–9.
18 *Ibid.*, p. 46.

19 N. N. Sukhanov, *The Russian Revolution*, Joel Carmichael (trans. and ed.) (Oxford University Press, London, 1955), p. 3.

20 *Ibid.*, p. 5.

21 The new name given to St Petersburg, which was considered too German for patriotic taste.

22 W. H. Chamberlin, *The Russian Revolution, 1917–21* (2 vols, Macmillan, London, 1935), vol. 1, p. 82.

23 Louis de Robien, *Diary of a Diplomat in Russia* (Michael Joseph, London, 1969), p. 16.

24 Sukhanov, p. 61.

25 Alexander Kerensky, *The Crucifixion of Liberty* (Barker, London, 1934), p. 259.

26 Sukhanov, pp. 229–30.

27 Leon Trotsky, *The History of the Russian Revolution* (3 vols, Gollancz, London, 1932–3), vol. 1 (1932), p. 341.

28 Krupskaya, p. 286.

29 Sukhanov, p. 272.

30 *Ibid.*, p. 273.

31 Carr, vol. 1, pp. 90–1.

32 De Robien, p. 59.

33 Quoted by Carr, vol. 1, p. 98.

34 *Novy Mir*, quoted in Isaac Deutscher, *The Prophet Armed* (Oxford University Press, London, 1954), pp. 245–6.

35 Trotsky, *My Life*, p. 241.

36 Buchanan, vol. 2, pp. 120–1.

37 Sukhanov, p. 340.

7 The Thrust to Power (pages 136–71)

1 A. V. Lunacharsky, *Revolutionary Silhouettes* (Allen Lane The Penguin Press, London, 1967), p. 64.

2 Leonard Schapiro, *The Communist Party of the Soviet Union* (Eyre & Spottiswoode, 1970), pp. 172–3.

3 Angelica Balabanoff, *My Life as a Rebel* (Hamish Hamilton, London, 1938), pp. 175–6.

4 Lunacharsky, p. 67.

5 Leon Trotsky, *The History of the Russian Revolution* (3 vols, Gollancz, London, 1932–3), vol. 1, p. 487.

6 N. N. Sukhanov, *The Russian Revolution*, trans. and ed. Joel Carmichael (Oxford University Press, London, 1955), pp. 376–7.

7 W. H. Chamberlin, *The Russian Revolution, 1917–21* (2 vols, Macmillan, London, 1969), vol. 1, p. 155.

8 *Ibid.*, p. 152.

9 E. H. Carr, *The Bolshevik Revolution, 1917–23* (3 vols, Penguin, Harmondsworth), vol. 1, p. 100. Most of those from other groups aligned themselves with the majority, and the total opposition vote was no more than between 120 and 125 (Sukhanov, p. 379).

10 Sukhanov, p. 395.
11 Lunacharsky, p. 65.
12 Leon Trotsky, *My Life* (Butterworth, London, 1930), p. 254.
13 The All-Russian Central Executive Committee of the Soviets, instituted by the First Soviet Congress as its concluding act.
14 Sukhanov, p. 471.
15 Trotsky, *The History of the Russian Revolution*, vol. 2, p. 105.
16 R. H. Bruce Lockhart, *Memoirs of a British Agent* (Putnam, London, 1934), p. 188.
17 Trotsky, *The History of the Russian Revolution*, vol. 2, pp. 333–9; and Chamberlin, pp. 280–2.
18 Sukhanov, pp. 528–9.
19 V. I. Lenin, *Selected Works* (English ed.), vol. 5, pp. 215–17.
20 Trotsky, *The History of the Russian Revolution*, vol. 3, p. 134.
21 V. I. Lenin, *Collected Works* (1928), vol. 21, p. 241.
22 Louis de Robien, *Diary of a Diplomat in Russia* (Michael Joseph, London, 1969), p. 121.
23 Sukhanov, *op. cit.*, pp. 539–40.
24 *Ibid.*, p. 540; and Trotsky, *The History of the Russian Revolution*, vol. 3, p. 69. Trotsky's own record gives his speech as ending with the cry, 'All power to the Soviets!' and not, interestingly in the light of subsequent events, with that of 'long live the Constitutent Assembly!'.
25 Sukhanov, p. 556.
26 Trotsky, *The History of the Russian Revolution*, vol. 3, p. 149.
27 *Ibid.*, pp. 156–7.
28 Sukhanov, pp. 561–2.
29 Gorky's newspaper had published Lenin's reply to the attack by Kamenev and Zinoviev on the policy of insurrection.
30 *The Bolsheviks and the October Revolution* (Pluto Press, London, 1974), p. 112.
31 Sir George Buchanan, *My Mission to Russia* (2 vols, Cassell, London, 1923), vol. 2, pp. 196, 201.
32 *Ibid.*, p. 202.
33 Sukhanov, pp. 583–5.
34 Trotsky, *My Life*, p. 275.
35 Chamberlin, vol. 1, p. 309.
36 John Reed, *Ten Days that Shook the World* (Lawrence, London, 1932), pp. 57–60; Sukhanov, pp. 616–17; Trotsky, *The History of the Russian Revolution*, vol. 3, pp. 224–6.
37 Trotsky, *My Life*, p. 278.
38 Reed, p. 62.
39 Leon Trotsky, *Lenin* (Harrap, London, 1925), pp. 122–4.
40 Trotsky, *The History of the Russian Revolution*, vol. 3, p. 366.
41 Trotsky, *My Life*, p. 280.
42 Sukhanov, p. 629.
43 Reed, p. 69.
44 P. N. Miliukov, *History of the Second Russian Revolution*, vol. 1, pt 3, p. 232, quoted in Chamberlin, vol. 1, p. 318.

45 P. Maliantovich, *In the Winter Palace* (1918), quoted in Roger Pethybridge (ed.), *Witnesses to the Russian Revolution* (Allen & Unwin, London, 1964), pp. 232–4).

46 M. Philips Price, *My Reminiscences of the Russian Revolution* (Allen & Unwin, London, 1921), pp. 145 ff.

47 Sukhanov, p. 646.

8 The Revolution Transformed (pages 172–221)

1 Leon Trotsky, *My Life* (Butterworth, London, 1930), pp. 289–90.

2 N. N. Sukhanov, *The Russian Revolution*, trans. and ed. Joel Carmichael (Oxford University Press, London, 1955), pp. 665–6.

3 Trotsky, *My Life*, p. 292.

4 *Ibid.*, pp. 291–2.

5 John Reed, *Ten Days that Shook the World* (Lawrence, London, 1932), pp. 104–5.

6 *Ibid.*, p. 108.

7 Sukhanov, pp. 661–2.

8 Reed, pp. 115–18; Sukhanov, pp. 663–4; Leon Trotsky, *The History of the Russian Revolution* (3 vols, Gollancz, London, 1932–3), vol. 3, pp. 332–4.

9 Louis de Robien, *Diary of a Diplomat in Russia* (Michael Joseph, London, 1969), p. 134.

10 Muralov, one of the insurrectionary leaders, was subsequently to estimate the enemy at 10,000, only one-fifth of the armed numbers on the Bolshevik side. W. H. Chamberlin, *The Russian Revolution, 1917–21* (2 vols, Macmillan, London, 1935), vol. 1, p. 337.

11 Leon Trotsky, *Lenin* (Harrap, London, 1925), pp. 145–6.

12 Russian Social Revolutionaries had polled some 16,500,000 votes; Ukrainian and other non-Russian Social Revolutionaries, 4,400,000; the Bolsheviks, 9,000,000; the Cadets, 1,850,000; other middle-class and conservative parties, 2,750,000; and minor socialist parties, mainly the Mensheviks, a total of 1,700,000.

13 This was further enlarged by 100 representatives of the armed forces and 50 representatives drawn from the leadership of the trade unions.

14 P. Sorokin, *Leaves from a Russian Diary* (1924), quoted in Roger Pethybridge, (ed.), *Witnesses to the Russian Revolution* (Allen & Unwin, London, 1964), p. 272.

15 E. H. Carr, *The Bolshevik Revolution, 1917–23* (3 vols, Penguin, Harmondsworth, vol. 1, p. 125.

16 Trotsky, *Lenin*, p. 149.

17 De Robien, pp. 145–6.

18 R. H. Bruce Lockhart, *Memoirs of a British Agent* (Putnam, London, 1934), p. 204.

19 Isaac Deutscher, *The Prophet Armed* (Oxford University Press, London, 1954), pp. 357–9.

20 Count Otto Czernin, *In the World War* (Cassell, London, 1919), p. 259.

21 *Ibid.*, p. 232.

22 The *Tägliche Rundschau*, quoted in Trotsky, *My Life*, p. 317.

23 De Robien, pp. 203–4.
24 Published in England as *The History of the Russian Revolution to Brest-Litovsk* (Allen & Unwin, London, 1919).
25 Carr, vol. 1, pp. 126–7.
26 E. Sisson, *One Hundred Red Days* (Yale University Press, 1931), quoted in Pethybridge, pp. 273–80.
27 David Shub, *Lenin* (Penguin, Harmondsworth, 1966), p. 325.
28 M. Gorky, *Untimely Thoughts*, trans. Herman Ermolaev (Paul S. Eriksson, New York, 1968), pp. 123–6.
29 Rosa Luxemburg, *Die Russische Revolution* (Berlin, 1922), p. 113.
30 J. Wheeler-Bennett, *The Forgotten Peace: Brest-Litovsk* (Morrow, New York, 1939), p. 188.
31 *Ibid.*, p. 197.
32 On 1 February, the Russian calendar was brought into line with that of the West, by making that day the 14th.
33 Trotsky, *My Life*, pp. 331–2.
34 Lockhart, p. 228.
35 *Ibid.*, p. 229.
36 Louis Aragon, *A History of the USSR* (Weidenfeld & Nicolson, London, 1962), p. 94.
37 Leonard Schapiro, *The Communist Party of the Soviet Union* (Eyre & Spottiswoode, London, 1970), p. 185.
38 *Ibid.*, p. 188; Chamberlin, vol. 1, p. 407.
39 Wheeler-Bennett, p. 263.
40 Trotsky, *My Life*, p. 337.
41 E. Ludendorff, *Meine Kriegserinnerungen 1914–18* (Berlin, 1919), p. 447.
42 *Chicago Daily News*, 13 March 1919.
43 David Lloyd George, *War Memoirs* (6 vols, Nicholson & Watson, London, 1936), vol. 6, p. 3163.
44 Carr, vol. 2, p. 151.
45 Lockhart, pp. 297–9.
46 Chamberlin, vol. 2, p. 55.
47 C. Vellay (ed.), *Discours et Rapports de Robespierre* (1908), p. 332.
48 P. L. Ford (ed.), *The Writings of Thomas Jefferson* (New York, 1895), vol. 6, pp. 153–4.
49 Quoted by Carr, vol. 1, p. 163.
50 *Izvestia*, 6 December 1917.
51 Leon Trotsky, *The Defence of Terrorism* (Labour Publishing Co., London, 1921), pp. 51–2.
52 De Robien, p. 206.
53 Entry for 22 July 1918, De Robien, p. 281.

9 The Heel of Achilles (pages 222–71)

1 Victor Serge and Natalia Sedova Trotsky, *The Life and Death of Leon Trotsky* (Wildwood House, London, 1975), pp. 83–4; Max Eastman, *Leon Trotsky: The Portrait of a Youth* (Faber & Gwyer, London, 1926), p. 16.

2 D. Fedotoff White, *The Growth of the Red Army* (Princeton University Press, Princeton, NJ, 1944), pp. 37–8.

3 *Ibid.*, pp. 90, 98–9.

4 Alexander Barmine, *One Who Survived* (Putnam, New York, 1945), pp. 70–1.

5 Leon Trotsky, *Stalin* (Hollis & Carter, London, 1947), p. 289.

6 Not to be confused with Boris Kamenev, the member of the Politburo.

7 Years later, when official historians were required to adjust the record, Kamenev's strategy became Trotsky's; and Trotsky's, Stalin's own. See, for instance, *History of the Communist Party of the Soviet Union* (Short Course authorized by the Central Committee; Foreign Languages Publishing House, Moscow, 1939), pp. 238–9.

8 Leon Trotsky, *My Life* (Butterworth, London, 1930), p. 364.

9 Victor Serge, *Memoirs of a Revolutionary, 1901–1941* (Oxford University Press, London, 1975), pp. 93–4.

10 Trotsky, *My Life*, p. 369.

11 The pretext for the award was Stalin's work on the southern front, in the successes against Denikin's army. It both explicitly exaggerated his military role and implicitly diminished Trotsky's responsibility for the plan of the campaign.

12 Alfred Rosmer, *Lenin's Moscow* (Pluto Press, London, 1971), p. 39.

13 *Ibid.*, p. 43.

14 Arthur Ransome, *Six Weeks in Russia in 1919* (Allen & Unwin, London, 1919), p. 152.

15 Maurice H. Dobb, 'Russia: economic and financial conditions', in *Encyclopaedia Britannica*, vol. 19 (1937), p. 707.

16 E. H. Carr, *The Bolshevik Revolution, 1917–23* (3 vols, Penguin, Harmondsworth), vol. 2, pp. 197–8.

17 Serge, pp. 115–16.

18 Carr, vol. 2, pp. 214–15.

19 *Ibid.*, pp. 224–5*n*.

20 Leonard Schapiro, *The Communist Party of the Soviet Union* (Eyre & Spottiswoode, London, 1970), p. 204.

21 Quoted in White, pp. 148–9.

22 It would be the middle of 1921 before this challenge was crushed.

23 To the eleventh party congress, in March 1922, he would declare: 'Since the war it is not at all working-class people but malingerers that have gone to the factories. And are our social and economic conditions at present such that genuine proletarians go to the factories? No. They should go, according to Marx. But Marx wrote not about Russia – he wrote about capitalism in general, capitalism as it has developed since the fifteenth century. All this has been correct for 600 years, but is incorrect in present-day Russia.' And Shliapnikov would tauntingly reply, by remarking to the assembled representatives of the party: 'Permit me to congratulate you on being the vanguard of a non-existing class.'

24 Control commissions had been established in November 1920 as independent tribunals to consider appeals against the bureaucracy. And, as an assurance of their independence, they were to be elected, not appointed: the

local commissions by the local party conferences; the Central Control Commission by the party congress. In the event, however, those who commanded the bureaucracy lost no time in ensuring that their own candidates were elected to command the commissions.

25 Gosudarstvennoe Politicheskoe Upravlenie, or State Political Administration.

26 Carr, vol. 1, p. 219.

27 From Gosudarstvennaya Obshcheplanovaya Komissiya, or State General Planning Commission.

28 Having reached only 6 per cent of 1912 output in 1920, it recovered to 9 per cent in 1921, and then fell in the following year to 7 per cent. Carr, *op. cit.*, vol. 2, p. 310.

29 Schapiro, p. 242.

30 David Shub, *Lenin* (Penguin, Harmondsworth, 1966), p. 426.

31 Trotsky, *My Life*, pp. 402–3.

32 Trotsky himself would, in his memoirs, assume this. See *My Life*, p. 403. Deutscher places the formation some months later, in December 1922 or January 1923. See *The Prophet Unarmed* (Oxford University Press, London, 1959), p. 76. The two accounts are not necessarily incompatible. The delay in informing Trotsky of Lenin's stroke does suggest that the first step had been taken. But Lenin's gradual recovery might well have produced an interval of cautious inactivity until, with Lenin's later and more serious stroke, the triumvirate was decisively established.

33 Moshe Lewin, *Lenin's Last Struggle* (Pantheon, New York, 1968), pp. 151–2.

34 The letter is undated, but was probably dictated and sent on 10 December. The text of this, as of subsequent letters from Lenin on the issue, may be found in Leon Trotsky, *The Stalin School of Falsification* (Pioneer Publishers, New York, 1937), pp. 59–63.

35 Trotsky, *My Life*, pp. 408–9.

36 Lewin, p. 48.

37 Trotsky, *The Stalin School of Falsification*, p. 69. The closing phrase was an unusually warm one for Lenin to use in correspondence with his colleagues; and when Stalin, under pressure, eventually came to disclose the contents of the letter to the central committee, in July 1926, he altered it to the more formal 'with communist greetings'.

38 Trotsky, *My Life*, p. 413.

39 Lenin had ordered copies for Kamenev and Zinoviev. And Kamenev might already have been given one. But at all events, he must have been informed of the contents; for he seems, from Trotsky's account, to have informed Trotsky in turn.

40 Trotsky, *My Life*, p. 414.

41 Shub, p. 438.

42 Trotsky, *Stalin*, p. 366.

43 Schapiro, pp. 277–8; Trotsky, *Stalin*, pp. 366–7.

44 Trotsky, *My Life*, pp. 410–11.

45 *Ibid.*, p. 414.

46 Deutsche, *The Prophet Unarmed*, p. 91.

10 The Fall (pages 272–318)

1 Victor Serge, *Memoirs of a Revolutionary, 1901–1941* (Oxford University Press, London, 1975), pp. 168–9.
2 He had, in fact, been asked by Heinrich Brandler, leader of the German party, to come incognito and take charge of the planned uprising.
3 It had been 25 October only in the old Russian calendar, of course, and never in the German one, where it had been 7 November.
4 Serge, p. 170.
5 Leon Trotsky, *Literature and Revolution* (Allen & Unwin, London, 1925), p. 60.
6 *Ibid.,* pp. 24, 28.
7 *Ibid.,* p. 41.
8 *Ibid.,* p. 50.
9 *Ibid.,* p. 64.
10 *Ibid.,* p. 68.
11 *Ibid.,* p. 81.
12 *Ibid.,* p. 128.
13 *Ibid.,* pp. 149–51.
14 *Ibid.,* p. 152.
15 *Ibid.,* p. 190.
16 *Ibid.,* p. 170.
17 *Ibid.,* p. 218.
18 *Ibid.,* pp. 220–1.
19 *Ibid.,* p. 239.
20 Indeed, the description is itself so much of a melodic piece that fragments are essentially meaningless, and the reader is referred to the whole: *Ibid.,* pp. 240–56.
21 *Ibid.,* p. 115.
22 Along with the articles, this was to be subsequently published as a special pamphlet, entitled 'The New Course'.
23 Leon Trotsky, *My Life* (Butterworth, London, 1930), p. 421.
24 Anton Ciliga, *The Russian Enigma* (Routledge, London, 1940), pp. 85–6.
25 From Natalia's memoirs, quoted in Trotsky, *My Life*, p. 426.
26 *Ibid.,* p. 434.
27 Victor Serge and Natalia Sedova Trotsky, *The Life and Death of Leon Trotsky* (Wildwood House, London, 1975), p. 128.
28 Leon Trotsky, *The Suppressed Testament of Lenin* (New York, 1935), p. 17.
29 Alfred Rosmer, *Lenin's Moscow* (Pluto Press, London, 1971), p. 220.
30 Leonard Schapiro, *The Communist Party of the Soviet Union* (Eyre & Spottiswoode, London, 1970), pp. 288–9.
31 Rykov had taken Lenin's nominal place, as chairman of the People's Commissars, and Kalinin was a candidate member of the Politburo.
32 Alexander Barmine, *One Who Survived* (Putnam, New York, 1945), p. 161.
33 Serge, *Memoirs of a Revolutionary*, p. 191.
34 Leon Trotsky, *Where is Britain Going?* (Allen & Unwin, London, 1926), p. 53.

35 *Ibid.*, p. 69.
36 *Ibid.*, p. 67.
37 *Ibid.*, p. 87.
38 *Ibid.*, p. 119.
39 The new name given to Petrograd in tribute to Lenin soon after his death.
40 *Pravda*, 14 April 1925.
41 The month in the calendar of the French Revolution when the Jacobin era effectively ended, with the overthrow of Robespierre.
42 To the Dewey Commission, thirteen years later.
43 Leon Trotsky, *Stalin* (Hollis & Carter, London, 1947), p. 417.
44 Trotsky, *My Life*, p. 445.
45 Serge, pp. 213–14.
46 Eastman, who had received the text from Paris and given it to *The Times*, believed that the decision to make it known had come from the leaders of the Joint Opposition; and that by consigning it to him, they had soothed their variously troubled consciences. See Isaac Deutscher, *The Prophet Unarmed* (Oxford University Press, London, 1959), p. 295. Schapiro, on different evidence, believes the source to have been Krupskaya herself (p. 306).
47 Serge and Natalia Sedova Trotsky, p. 165.
48 Inessa, the daughter of a Russian actor-musician, had married the son of a French textile manufacturer and had borne him five children. In 1910, she met Lenin in Paris, and he grew deeply attached to his brilliant admirer, as beautiful and elegant as Krupskaya was dowdy. For a time, all three lived together, and together travelled back to Russia in the 'sealed' train. When Inessa died of cholera in October 1920, Lenin seemed, one observer remarked, to have shrunk with sorrow. And Alexandra Kollontai would later maintain that Inessa's death had hastened his own.
49 Stuart Schram, *Mao Tse-tung* (Penguin, Harmondsworth, 1966), p. 96.
50 A police raid on the offices of the Soviet trade mission in London had allegedly uncovered evidence of subversive activities.
51 Austen Chamberlain, the British Foreign Secretary at the time.
52 Trotsky had declared that if war did, indeed, break out, the present leadership would be incapable of defending the Soviet Union, and the Opposition would need to persist in its challenge, so as to assume command of defence.
53 And a massive deception it would, indeed, prove to be, until the outbreak of the Second World War, when pretence would at last be brought into line with practice.
54 Serge, p. 219.
55 *Ibid.*, p. 220.
56 Those who knew how ill and in how much pain he had been recognized that this was no facile excuse.
57 Serge, pp. 233–4.
58 Formerly Pishpek, it had been renamed in honour of Trotsky's successor as Commissar of War.
59 Ciliga, p. 85.

11   The Freezing Sea (pages 319–66)

1 Leon Trotsky, *My Life* (Butterworth, London, 1930), p. 494.
2 Victor Serge and Natalia Sedova Trotsky, *The Life and Death of Leon Trotsky* (Wildwood House, London, 1975), p. 165.
3 Trotsky, *My Life*, p. 19.
4 *Ibid.*, p. 30.
5 *Ibid.*, p. 32.
6 *Ibid.*, p. 33.
7 *Ibid.*, p. 171.
8 *Ibid.*, pp. 253–4.
9 *Ibid.*, pp. 234–5.
10 Serge and Natalia Sedova Trotsky, p. 165.
11 Leon Trotsky, *The History of the Russian Revolution* (3 vols, Gollancz, London, 1932–3), vol. 1, p. 23: the first page of the actual text.
12 *Ibid.*, p. 25.
13 *Ibid.*, p. 31.
14 *Ibid.*, pp. 38–9.
15 *Ibid.*, p. 79.
16 Leon Trotsky, *1905* (Allen Lane, The Penguin Press, London, 1972), p. 135.
17 Trotsky, *The History of the Russian Revolution*, vol. 1, p. 71.
18 *Ibid.*, pp. 74–5.
19 *Ibid.*, p. 112.
20 *Ibid.*, pp. 126–7.
21 *Ibid.*, p. 207.
22 *Ibid.*, p. 202.
23 *Ibid.*, p. 243.
24 *Ibid.*, pp. 237–8.
25 *Ibid.*, vol. 2, p. 163.
26 *Ibid.*, vol. 1, p. 393.
27 *Ibid.*, vol. 2, p. 150.
28 *Ibid.*, vol. 3, p. 240.
29 *Ibid.*, vol. 3, pp. 21–2.
30 *Ibid.*, vol. 2, p. 9: Introduction to vols 2 and 3.
31 Leonard Schapiro, *The Communist Party of the Soviet Union* (Eyre & Spottiswoode, London, 1970), p. 390.
32 *The New Republic*, 22 May 1929.
33 Quoted in William L. Shirer, *The Rise and Fall of the Third Reich* (Secker & Warburg, London, 1962), p. 189.
34 Leon Trotsky, *Trotsky's Diary in Exile* (Faber, London, 1958), p. 27.
35 Deutscher was able to draw on family correspondence in the closed section of the Trotsky archives, and his account of Zina's illness and suicide remains invaluable. It may be found in *The Prophet Outcast* (Oxford University Press, London, 1963), pp. 146–51, 176–81, 188–90 and 195–8.
36 Written on 12 March 1933 and published in Communist League of America, *International Bulletin*, no. 2/3 (April 1933). *Writings of Leon Trotsky, 1932–3* (Pathfinder Press, New York, 1972), pp. 137–9.

37 Written on 15 July 1933 and published in Communist League of America, *Internal Bulletin*, no. 13 (1933). *Writings of Leon Trotsky, 1932–3*, pp. 304–11.

38 Extracts were published as an article, 'Farewell to Prinkipo', *Modern Monthly*, March 1934. *Writings of Leon Trotsky, 1932–3*, pp. 312–18.

39 For a presentation of the evidence, see Robert Conquest, *The Great Terror* (Macmillan, London, 1968), ch. on 'The Kirov Murder', pp. 43–61. At the twenty-second party congress in October 1961, Khrushchev himself, in referring to the Kirov case, declared: 'Great efforts are still needed to find out who was really to blame for his death. The more deeply we study the materials connected with Kirov's death, the more questions arise. . . .' The 'thorough inquiry', whose institution he went on to announce, apparently reached only such conclusions as the Soviet leadership considered it injudicious to reveal. But in the summer of 1963, Stalin's daughter Svetlana was moved to complain of the 'transparent hints' linking her father's name with the killing of Kirov. Svetlana Alliluyeva, *Letters to a Friend* (Hutchinson, London, 1967), p. 150.

40 Alexander Barmine, *One Who Survived* (Putnam, New York, 1945), p. 250.

41 *Trotsky's Diary in Exile*, p. 27.

42 *Ibid.*, p. 37.

43 *Ibid.*, pp. 66–7.

44 *Ibid.*, pp. 79–81.

45 *Ibid.*, p. 66.

46 *Ibid.*, p. 99.

47 *Ibid.*, p. 109.

48 *Ibid.*, p. 116.

49 *Ibid.*, pp. 121–2.

50 *Ibid.*, p. 131.

51 Serge and Natalia Sedova Trotsky, p. 206.

52 Leon Trotsky, *The Revolution Betrayed* (Doubleday, Garden City, NY, 1937), p. 5.

53 *Ibid.*, p. 20.

54 *Ibid.*, pp. 13–14.

55 *Ibid.*, pp. 20 and 47.

56 *Ibid.*, p. 65.

57 *Ibid.*, p. 71.

58 *Ibid.*, p. 105.

59 See especially *ibid.*, pp. 112–13.

60 *Ibid.*, p. 184.

61 *Ibid.*, p. 227.

62 *Ibid.*

63 *Ibid.*, p. 231.

64 *Ibid.*, p. 233.

65 *Ibid.*, p. 239.

66 *Ibid.*, pp. 252–4.

67 *Ibid.*, p. 13.

68 For evidence of the pressures exercised, see Conquest, pp. 100–4.

69 Victor Serge, *From Lenin to Stalin* (London, 1937), pp. 145–7.

70 Alexander Orlov, *The Secret History of Stalin's Crimes* (London, 1954), p. 350. Quoted in Conquest, p. 163. Orlov had not been present himself at the banquet and was only recalling the subsequent recital that became gossip within the secret police. But there is an authentic resonance in the story. Stalin's combination of cruelty, crude humour and anti-Semitism would have encouraged and enjoyed just such a performance.

12 *Auto-da-Fé* (pages 367–406)

1 Victor Serge and Natalia Sedova Trotsky, *The Life and Death of Leon Trotsky* (Wildwood House, London, 1975), p. 212.
2 Robert Conquest, *The Great Terror* (Macmillan, London, 1968), p. 169.
3 Dudley Collard, *Soviet Justice and the Trial of Radek and Others* (Gollancz, London, 1937).
4 David Caute, *The Fellow Travellers* (Weidenfeld & Nicolson, London, 1973). Quoted in his chapter, 'Conducted Tours', which gives many other examples of such gullibility.
5 Joseph E. Davies, *Mission to Moscow* (Gollancz, London, 1942), p. 39.
6 A letter in *Soviet Russia Today*, March 1937.
7 In the memoirs that Natalia wrote with Victor Serge, the passage on Sergei's murder immediately precedes the section on the counter-trial: Serge and Natalia Sedova Trotsky, pp. 218–19. Isaac Deutscher, in *The Prophet Outcast* (Oxford University Press, London, 1963), pp. 401–2, deals with Sergei's death as 'almost certain' by February 1938.
8 Victor Serge, *Memoirs of a Revolutionary, 1901–41* (Oxford University Press, London, 1975), p. 337.
9 Serge and Natalia Sedova Trotsky, p. 225.
10 Peter Berlinrut, 'A Talk with Trotsky', *Harper's* (NY), February 1977.
11 Deutscher, *The Prophet Outcast*, pp. 385–6.
12 After well over 100,000 words of cited testimony and of analysis, the commission returned the verdict:
'In the light of all this evidence the conclusion appears inevitable that the indictments and confessions in the widely publicized series of trials of alleged plotters against the Soviet régime were determined in each case – including the trials of August, 1936, and January, 1937 – by the current internal difficulties, economic and political, and by the current situation in the foreign relations, of the Soviet régime. In other words, we find that the trials have served not juridical but political ends.
'On the basis of all the evidence herein examined and all the conclusions stated, we find that the trials of August, 1936, and January, 1937, were frame-ups.
'On the basis of all the evidence herein examined and all the conclusions stated, we find Leon Trotsky and Leon Sedov not guilty.' Dewey Commission, *Not Guilty* (Secker & Warburg, London, 1938), p. 394.
13 Serge and Natalia Sedova Trotsky, p. 225.
14 Conquest, pp. 527–9.
15 *Bulletin*, no. 65 (1938).

16 Serge and Natalia Sedova Trotsky, p. 251.

17 Leon Trotsky, *Stalin* (Hollis & Carter, London, 1947), p. 456.

18 *Ibid.*, pp. 336–7.

19 *Ibid.*, p. 396.

20 *Ibid.*, p. 393.

21 *Ibid.*, p. 51.

22 *Ibid.*, p. 421.

23 Berlinrut.

24 Dwight Macdonald, one of its leading intellectuals, recorded in his memoirs that it had 'about eight hundred members'.

25 The article was entitled 'The U.S. Will Participate in the War'.

26 'Stalin After the Finnish Experience', first published, in a garbled form, by the *Sunday Express* of Scotland, on 17 March 1940. The full text appears in *Writings of Leon Trotsky, 1939–40* (Pathfinder Press, New York, 1973), pp. 160–4.

27 *Ibid.*

28 Serge and Natalia Sedova Trotsky, p. 255.

29 Nicholas Mosley, *The Assassination of Trotsky* (Michael Joseph, London, 1972), provides, from various sources, what is known of Mercador's early career.

30 The case for Sheldon Harte's complicity is presented at length by General Leandro A. Sanchez Salazar (in collaboration with Julian Gorkin), in his *Murder in Mexico: The Assassination of Leon Trotsky* (Secker & Warburg, London, 1950).

31 Serge and Natalia Sedova Trotsky, p. 257.

32 Leon Trotsky, *Trotsky's Diary in Exile* (Faber, London, 1958), pp. 139–41.

33 Serge and Natalia Sedova Trotsky, p. 267.

34 Svetlana Alliluyeva, *Letters to a Friend*, Priscilla Johnson (trans.), (Hutchinson, London, 1967), p. 18.

Select bibliography

Works by Leon Trotsky

Results and Prospects (1906) and *The Permanent Revolution* (1930). Published together by New Park Publications, London, 1962

1905. London: Allen Lane The Penguin Press, 1972

The Bolsheviki and World Peace. New York: Boni & Liveright, 1918

The History of the Russian Revolution to Brest-Litovsk. London: Allen & Unwin, 1919

The Defence of Terrorism: A Reply to Karl Kautsky. London: Labour Publishing Co., 1921

Between Red and White. London: Communist Party of Great Britain, 1922

Literature and Revolution. London: Allen & Unwin, 1925

Lenin. London: Harrap, 1925

Where is Britain Going? London: Allen & Unwin, 1926

The Real Situation in Russia. London: Allen & Unwin, n.d.

My Life. London: Butterworth, 1930

What Next? Vital Questions for the German Proletariat. New York: Pioneer Publishers, 1932

The History of the Russian Revolution. 3 vols. London: Gollancz, 1932–3

The Young Lenin. First published in Paris, 1936. Harmondsworth: Penguin, 1974

The Revolution Betrayed. Garden City, NY: Doubleday, 1937

The Stalin School of Falsification. New York: Pioneer Publishers, 1937

Stalin. London: Hollis & Carter, 1947

Trotsky's Diary in Exile. London: Faber, 1958

Writings of Leon Trotsky, 1929–1940. 12 vols. New York: Pathfinder Press

Other works

This list of further material excludes the encyclopedias and general histories, as well as the classic texts of Marxism, consulted. It is headed, in defiance of alphabetical order, by Isaac Deutscher's trilogy, as some indication of my indebtedness to this pioneering work.

DEUTSCHER, ISAAC. *The Prophet Armed: Trotsky 1879–1921*. London: Oxford University Press, 1954

DEUTSCHER, ISAAC. *The Prophet Unarmed: Trotsky 1921–1929*. London: Oxford University Press, 1959

DEUTSCHER, ISAAC. *The Prophet Outcast: Trotsky 1929–1940*. London: Oxford University Press, 1963

ALLILUYEVA, SVETLANA. *Letters to a Friend*. Trans. Priscilla Johnson. London: Hutchinson, 1967

ARAGON, LOUIS. *A History of the USSR*. London: Weidenfeld & Nicolson, 1962

BALABANOFF, ANGELICA. *My Life as a Rebel*. London: Hamish Hamilton, 1938

BARMINE, ALEXANDER. *One Who Survived*. New York: Putnam, 1945
The Bolsheviks and the October Revolution: Minutes of the Central Committee of the Russian Social-Democratic Labour Party (bolsheviks) August 1917–February 1918. London: Pluto Press, 1974

BONAVIA, DAVID. *Fat Sasha and the Urban Guerilla*. London: Hamish Hamilton, 1973

BUCHANAN, SIR GEORGE. *My Mission to Russia and Other Diplomatic Memories*. 2 vols. London: Cassell, 1923

CARR, EDWARD HALLETT. *The Bolshevik Revolution 1917–1923*. 3 vols. Harmondsworth: Penguin, 1966

CAUTE, DAVID. *The Fellow Travellers*. London: Weidenfeld & Nicolson, 1972

CHAMBERLIN, W. H. *The Russian Revolution 1917–1921*. 2 vols. London: Macmillan, 1935

CHURCHILL, WINSTON S. *Great Contemporaries*. London, 1937

CILIGA, ANTON. *The Russian Enigma*. London: Routledge, 1940

COLLARD, DUDLEY. *Soviet Justice and the Trial of Radek and Others*. London: Gollancz, 1937

CONQUEST, ROBERT. *The Great Terror*. London: Macmillan, 1968

CZERNIN, COUNT OTTOKAR. *In the World War*. London: Cassell, 1919

DAVIES, JOSEPH E. *Mission to Moscow*. London: Gollancz, 1942

DEUTSCHER, ISAAC. *Stalin*. London: Oxford University Press, 1949

DEWEY COMMISSION. *Not Guilty: Report of the Commission of Inquiry into the Charges made against Leon Trotsky in the Moscow Trials*. London: Secker & Warburg, 1938

EASTMAN, MAX. *Leon Trotsky: The Portrait of a Youth*. London: Faber & Gwyer, 1926

FISCHER, LOUIS, *Lenin*. London: Weidenfeld & Nicolson, 1965

FLOYD, DAVID. *Russia in Revolt. 1905: The First Crack in Tsarist Power*. London: Macdonald, 1969

FRANKLAND, MARK. *Khrushchev*. Harmondsworth: Penguin, 1966

FRÖLICH, PAUL. *Rosa Luxemburg*. Trans. Edward Fitzgerald. London: Gollancz, 1940

GORKY, MAXIM. *Untimely Thoughts: Essays on Revolution, Culture and the Bol-*

sheviks, 1917–1918. Trans. Herman Ermolaev. New York: Paul S. Eriksson, 1968.

KERENSKY, ALEXANDER. *The Crucifixion of Liberty*. London: Barker, 1934

KHRUSHCHEV, N. S. *Khrushchev Remembers*. Trans. and ed. by Strobe Talbott. London: Deutsch, 1971

KROPOTKIN, P. *The Conquest of Bread*. London: Chapman & Hall, 1913

KROPOTKIN, P. *Fields, Factories and Workshops*. London: Nelson, n.d.

KRUPSKAYA, NADEZHDA. *Memories of Lenin*. London: Panther, 1970

LEWIN, MOSHE. *Lenin's Last Struggle*. New York: Pantheon, 1968

LLOYD GEORGE, DAVID. *War Memoirs*. 6 vols. London: Nicholson & Watson, 1936

LOCKHART, R. H. BRUCE. *Memoirs of a British Agent*. London: Putnam, 1934

LUNACHARSKY, ANATOLY VASILIEVICH. *Revolutionary Silhouettes*. London: Allen Lane The Penguin Press, 1967

MANDELSTAM, NADEZHDA. *Hope Against Hope*. London: Collins & Harvill, 1971

MAXTON, JAMES. *Lenin*. London: Peter Davies, 1932

MOOREHEAD, ALAN. *The Russian Revolution*. London: Collins with Hamish Hamilton, 1958

MOSELEY, NICHOLAS. *The Assassination of Trotsky*. London: Sphere, 1972

NEDAVA, JOSEPH. *Trotsky and the Jews*. Philadelphia, Pa: The Jewish Publication Society of America, 1971

NICOLAIEVSKY, BORIS, and MAENCHEN-HELFEN. *Karl Marx: Man and Fighter*. London: Allen Lane The Penguin Press, 1973

PARES, BERNARD. *The Fall of the Russian Monarchy*. London: Cape, 1939

PETHYBRIDGE, ROGER, ed. *Witnesses to the Russian Revolution*. London: Allen & Unwin, 1964

PRICE, M. PHILIPS. *My Reminiscences of the Russian Revolution*. London: Allen & Unwin, 1921

RANSOME, ARTHUR. *Six Weeks in Russia in 1919*. London: Allen & Unwin, 1919

REED, JOHN. *Ten Days that Shook the World*. London: Lawrence, 1932

ROBIEN, LOUIS DE. *The Diary of a Diplomat in Russia 1917–1918*. London: Michael Joseph, 1969

ROSMER, ALFRED. *Lenin's Moscow*. London: Pluto Press, 1971

SALAZAR, GENERAL LEADRO A. SANCHEZ (with the collaboration of Julian Gorkin). *Murder in Mexico: The Assassination of Leon Trotsky*. London: Secker & Warburg, 1950

SALISBURY, HARRISON E., ed. *Anatomy of the Soviet Union*. London: Nelson, 1967

SAMUEL, MAURICE. *Blood Accusation: The Strange History of the Beiliss Case*. London: Weidenfeld & Nicolson, 1967

SCHAPIRO, LEONARD. *The Communist Party of the Soviet Union*. London: Eyre & Spottiswoode, 1970

SCHRAM, STUART. *Mao Tse-tung*. Harmondsworth: Penguin, 1966

SERGE, VICTOR. *Memoirs of a Revolutionary 1901–1941*. London: Oxford University Press, 1975

SERGE, VICTOR, and TROTSKY, NATALIA SEDOVA. *The Life and Death of Leon Trotsky*. London: Wildwood House, 1975

SHIRER, WILLIAM L. *The Rise and Fall of the Third Reich*. London: Secker & Warburg, 1962

SHUB, DAVID. *Lenin*. Harmondsworth: Penguin, 1966

SHUKMAN, HAROLD. *Lenin and the Russian Revolution*. London: Batsford, 1966

SMITH, DAVID. *Russia of the Tsars 1796–1917*. London: Ernest Benn, 1971

SOLZHENITSYN, ALEXANDER. *The Gulag Archipelago*. London: Collins & Harvill, 1974

STEWART, GEORGE. *The White Armies of Russia*. New York: Macmillan, 1933

SUKHANOV, N. N. *The Russian Revolution* and Trans. ed. Joel Carmichael. London: Oxford University Press, 1955

TOLSTOY, LEO. *The Slavery of Our Times*. Maldon, Essex: Free Age Press, 1900

TROYAT, HENRI. *Tolstoy*. Harmondsworth: Penguin, 1970

VULLIAMY, C. E., ed. *The Red Archives: Russian State Papers and Other Documents relating to the Years 1915–1918*. London: Geoffrey Bles, 1929

WEI, HENRY. *China and Soviet Russia*. Princeton, NJ: Van Nostrand, 1956

WHEELER-BENNETT, JOHN. *The Forgotten Peace: Brest-Litovsk*. New York: Morrow, 1939

WHITE, D. FEDOTOFF. *The Growth of the Red Army*. Princeton, NJ: Princeton University Press, 1944

WOLFE, BERTRAM D. *Three Who Made a Revolution*. New York: Dial Press, 1948

WOLFE, BERTRAM D. *Strange Communists I Have Known*. New York: Stein & Day, 1965

WYNDHAM, FRANCIS, and KING, DAVID. *Trotsky: A Documentary*. New York: Praeger, 1972

Index

About the Author

Ronald Segal was born in South Africa. As publisher of the journal *Africa South,* he had to seek exile in England. He has studied in both Britain and America and has published more than half-a-dozen books, including *The Struggle Against History, The Race War, The Americans,* and *The Decline and Fall of the American Dollar.*